This book is about the conceptual foundations of an intermediate way between liberalism and socialism. From a standpoint of economic theory, this middle way is conceived of as a synthesis of classical (Ricardian) and Keynesian political economy. While the former deals with proportions between individuals or collectives and society in tackling the problems of distribution and value on the basis of the surplus principle, the latter is concerned with the scale of economic activity as explained by the principle of effective demand. Political economy pictures the economic aspects of the functioning of the institutional system within which the behaviour of individuals is embedded. The economy considered is, primarily, neither a market nor a planned economy, but, rather, a monetary production economy. To establish an alternative to liberalism and socialism requires setting up a system of the social sciences. In this work suggestions are made for linking political economy with other social sciences, i.e. sociology, law and politics in the traditional sense, thus establishing the unity of the social sciences. In a Keynesian vein, the social sciences are conceived of as moral sciences, a view which gives rise to a specific philosophy of history. To complete the picture, issues of method associated with the theory of knowledge in the social sciences and the problem of linking theory with historical reality are also covered.

Institutions, behaviour and economic theory

Institutions, behaviour and economic theory

A contribution to classical-Keynesian
political economy

HEINRICH BORTIS
University of Fribourg

CAMBRIDGE
UNIVERSITY PRESS

CAMBRIDGE UNIVERSITY PRESS
Cambridge, New York, Melbourne, Madrid, Cape Town, Singapore, São Paulo

Cambridge University Press
The Edinburgh Building, Cambridge CB2 2RU, UK

Published in the United States of America by Cambridge University Press, New York

www.cambridge.org
Information on this title: www.cambridge.org/9780521570558

First published 1997
This digitally printed first paperback version, with corrections, 2006

A catalogue record for this publication is available from the British Library

Library of Congress Cataloguing in Publication data
Bortis, Heinrich.
    Institutions, behaviour and economic theory: a contribution to
classical-Keynesian political economy / Heinrich Bortis.
        p.   cm.
    Includes bibliographical references.
    ISBN 0 521 57055 7 (hc)
        1. Classical school of economics.   2. Keynesian economics.
    3. Institutional economics.   4. Economic policy.   5. Social
    sciences – Philosophy.   I. Title.
    HB94.B67   1997
    330.15′3–dc20   96-10444   CIP

ISBN-13   978-0-521-57055-8 hardback
ISBN-10   0-521-57055-7 hardback

ISBN-13   978-0-521-02899-8 paperback
ISBN-10   0-521-02899-X paperback

To the Memory of my Father

'But look', the Rabbi's wife remonstrated, 'when one party to the dispute presented their case to you you said "you are quite right" and then when the other party presented their case you again said "you are quite right", surely they cannot both be right?' To which the Rabbi answered, 'My dear, you are quite right!'

A. P. Lerner, The burden of debt, *Review of Economics and Statistics*, 43 (1961), pp. 139–41. Reprinted in R. W. Houghton (ed.), *Public Finance*. Harmondsworth: Penguin (1970), pp. 312–17.

The outstanding faults of the economic society in which we live are its failure to provide for full employment and its arbitrary and inequitable distribution of wealth and incomes.

Maynard Keynes, *The General Theory of Employment, Interest and Money*. Collected Writings, vol. VII. London: Macmillan (1973), 1st edition 1936, p. 372.

Keynes evidently did not make much of [Sraffa's 1928 draft of *Production of Commodities by Means of Commodities*] and Sraffa, in turn, never made much of the *General Theory*. It is the task of the post-Keynesians to reconcile the two . . . Post-Keynesian theory has plenty of problems to work on. We now have a general framework of long- and short-period analysis which will enable us to bring the insights of Marx, Keynes, and Kalecki into coherent form and to apply them to the contemporary scene, but there is still a long way to go.

Joan Robinson, Keynes and Ricardo, *Journal of Post Keynesian Economics*, 1, no. 1 (Fall 1978), pp. 14, 18.

Contents

Preface

The history of economic theory is also the history of its increasing fragmentation. The remarkable unity of the subject to be found in Ricardo's *Principles*, the masterpiece of classical political economy, has vanished in the course of time. The classical system, built upon François Quesnay's physiocratic foundations, already contained the seeds of divergence and gave birth to alternative grand systems. Adam Smith's emphasis on behaviour and exchange favoured the development of neoclassical economics, as first comprehensively systematized by William Stanley Jevons, Léon Walras, Alfred Marshall and Carl Menger. David Ricardo started from the social process of production to tackle the fundamental problems of value and distribution. His labour theory of value and his surplus principle of distribution became parts of a fundamental critique of capitalism within the wider framework of the economic theory of socialism, sketched by the early French socialists and by Karl Marx and Friedrich Engels, and elaborated by a variety of economists, prominent examples being Maurice Dobb, Oscar Lange and Paul Sweezy. Large parts of liberal (neoclassical) and socialist economics are strongly normative in character in that the functioning of markets and of the planning mechanism are studied under conditions which are ideal in certain respects, and where real-world imperfections are interpreted as deviations from the norm. However, the occurrence of periodic crises maintained the doubts over Say's law on the impossibility of *general* overproduction, even among the classical economists, as the example of Thomas Malthus shows. Subsequently these doubts gave rise to the elaboration of comprehensive positive systems aimed at explaining the functioning of free and mixed market economies. Here, the work done by Karl Marx and by Maynard Keynes towers above other attempts to understand the way in which capitalist societies work.

Out of these comprehensive designs variations have developed, and specialization has increased. As a consequence the grand systems have been divided into compartments. The doors linking these are getting narrower and narrower. Economics, then, is today a divided science, as a quick glance at the wide spectrum of post-World War II economic theories clearly shows. The area to the right of the centre is largely occupied by different variants of the presently dominant liberal or neoclassical economic theory: moving from right to left, one might distinguish between Austrian economics, supply side economics, the rational expectations system, monetarism *à la* Friedman, general equilibrium theory, disequilibrium economics (a Walrasian interpretation of Keynes) and, last but not least, Marshallian partial equilibrium economics which dominates the standard textbooks. Critiques of socialist theory and reality are also mainly located on the right; however, some of these critiques also appear in the centre or, based on Marx's early writings, even on the left. Here, various shades of the economic theory of socialism emerge, complemented by fundamental critiques of capitalist theory and reality from a socialist point of view, i.e. differing strands of Marxism and of Radical Economics which partly overlap. Moving towards the centre, the Neoclassical Synthesis appears, combining Marshall and Keynes. The centre itself is dominated by various types of positive economics, for instance Keynesianism, which is theoretically based, and institutional economics, which is largely pragmatic; located around the centre, there are also various normative systems of the 'third-way type', Christian Social Doctrine being an example. On the left of the centre other positive theories emerge, most importantly various strands of post Keynesian economics: Keynesian Fundamentalist, Robinsonian (or Kaleckian) and neo-Ricardian approaches. Finally, Pasinetti (1981) and Lowe (1976) represent normative models of the classical-Keynesian type.

To describe the spectrum of economic theories in these terms is bound to remain crude and incomplete. Many additions and refinements could be made and intricate overlappings would have to be taken into account. The purpose here is merely to indicate the great variety of economic theories.

Diversification and specialization are certainly required when an attempt is made to explain unique historical events or the behaviour of individuals and collectives in various situations. However, problems arise if the number of explanations of the central socioeconomic phenomena, i.e. production, value, distribution, employment and money, grows excessive, if crucial problems are lost sight of, or if important approaches are unduly neglected. The latter implies that specialization and diversification take place exclusively on the basis of one specific approach.

The consequences of such a state of affairs are manifold. Four related points seem to be particularly important for the theoretical economist. First, it is extremely difficult to offer students of economics a fair and balanced survey of existing theories. An attempt to describe the various theories one by one by bringing out the characteristic features of each theory confuses students. For them, it is indeed impossible to master the tremendous amount of information arising from lectures and from secondary and tertiary literature. The flood of information is by no means confined to the academic sphere: it is, partly as a consequence of the scale of scientific knowledge, also a serious problem for practical economists, including politicians, seeking conceptual tools in order to interpret economic phenomena or to prepare decisions.

On the other hand, to master the swelling flood of information, the teacher may try to get down to fundamentals by identifying groups of theories characterized by a common approach to economic problems. This implies examining the premises underlying the various approaches so as to bring out the crucial differences between them and to put them into perspective. Such a procedure involves a time-consuming study of primary or first-class secondary literature and requires a solid knowledge in other social sciences: sociology, law, political science, history, philosophy, and, above all, philosophy of the social sciences. From this a balanced survey of existing theory and of its historical development might result. There is, however, little time to develop such themes in economics faculties with heavily loaded teaching programmes.

In this context a second issue arises. In spite of the diversity in economic theory, the teaching of economics seems to be remarkably uniform in most universities. For various reasons, ideological or other, neoclassical equilibrium economics utterly dominates teaching in most countries, possibly to be joined by some of the formerly socialist countries in the near future. The basic premises of the approach are taken for granted. Introductory courses usually deal with Marshallian partial equilibrium economics. Advanced students are confronted with more sophisticated material: general equilibrium theory, disequilibrium theory and the 'rational expectations' system. Naturally a syllabus structured in this way attracts the mathematicians and puts off the social scientists, especially those who see economics as political economy. This is particularly so if mathematization leads on to the purely formal games which are all too evident in the content of many books and journals. Would-be students of political economy, who cannot see the relation between models and reality, frequently abandon economics proper and turn to managerial economics, including commercial sciences and portfolio management, i.e. to subjects with immediate practical applications. This is not to deny the great importance of managerial economics, nor, of course, of mathematical economics and of econometrics, if applied in appropriate ways, but it is sad to see a traditional subject like political economy gradually losing ground in many universities.

The great practical importance of such developments is linked with a third point: the isolation of pure economic theory within an 'ivory tower' leads to other professionals taking over important tasks that ought to be performed by economists. Historians, philosophers, lawyers and experienced managers are, in many instances, successfully explaining what is going on in the real world with respect to economic phenomena. In some countries, the most respected advisers to governments on economic affairs are not economists proper but social scientists in a wider sense of the word. The pure economist who develops highly sophisticated mathematical models during the day is simply not mentally prepared to give sound policy advice on real-world problems in the evening. It may be objected here that policy-making is not the domain of the theorist. However, theory, if it is not to remain sterile, must prepare the terrain for policy action, which may include systems policy aimed at shaping the socioeconomic system by the creation of new institutions or the modifications of existing ones.

Finally, the dominance of neoclassical equilibrium economics has grave consequences for socioeconomic policy-making in many countries. Some policy-makers think almost exclusively along microeconomic lines as is illustrated by supply side economics. The only macroeconomic problem of major importance seems to be the quantity of money and its regulation. This very simple policy approach stands in strange contrast to complex neoclassical theorizing. To the Keynesian observer it seems evident that the neoclassical approach to economic policy-making involves much unnecessary hardship, mainly in terms of severe unemployment and growing inequality accompanied by increasing poverty. As is well known, the situation is particularly striking in many underdeveloped and heavily indebted countries (which will perhaps be joined by some of the formerly socialist countries), most of which are desperately short of foreign exchange while being asked by international monetary institutions to perform so-called structural adjustments which, from a socioeconomic and political point of view, are not rational policies. But even in some of the rich and very rich countries ruthless competition on world markets involves increasing pressure on workers, employees and managers, for the struggle is not about relative positions in a full employment situation linked with sound competition but is about avoiding the precipice of involuntary unemployment which usually means social as well as economic deprivation. Nor is the pressure confined to adults; schoolchildren and students preparing for the struggle for survival are equally concerned. All this is not to blame policy-makers facing these pressures. Rather, dominant economic theory simply cannot provide a sound basis for long-term policies. In some instances, the latter are based on stubborn fundamentalism in which the main problems of unemployment, distribution and poverty are largely ignored; instead, attempts are made to regulate the 'quantity of money' and to manage the foreign exchange rate and the foreign balance position by means of variations of the rate of interest and of austerity policies respectively – an approach Keynes called 'foolish and highly dangerous', because it encourages short-run economic policies which frequently resemble financial tightrope-walking and leaves governments helpless in the face of high unemployment levels.

These are some of the problems that arise from the neglect of important theoretical approaches and from the excessive diversification of economic theory within one approach. Yet, any attempt to unify economics would be foolish and unnecessary. Today's world is profoundly pluralistic. This should advance the progress of science in general and of economics in particular if scientists are sufficiently open-minded to respect the merits of alternative and, even, rival points of view. What can be done, however, is to bring out the nature of the basic approaches which characterize broad groups of theories, for example socialist, neoclassical and classical-Keynesian theories. In fact, the approaches in question are based upon differing visions of society and man which, in turn, largely depend upon social philosophies and their associated value systems. These and the respective conceptual approaches are too complex to be readily discriminated by empirical and/or theoretical means. Consequently each economist will, consciously or unconsciously, choose the approach which, in his view, seems most appropriate to tackling real-world problems. The choice will be influenced not only by basic values but also by theoretical and practical experience. The latter involves the continuous comparison of some theory with reality, while the former involves constantly confronting one's own theory with rival theories. Such a 'testing' of theories should be comprehensive in that it should take into account the wider implications that arise from the premises of the various theories. To organize complex ways of reasoning social scientists may again have to ask metaphysical questions; for example: What is the vision of society and man implied in some theory? What is society? What is the position of the economy within society? How is economics related to ethics? This may sound archaic. Yet true progress in the social sciences will be possible only if the relationship between metaphysics and science is redefined. Some outstanding recent books, Brown (1986), Eccles (1984), Fitzgibbons (1988), Hodgson (1988), Lloyd (1986), and O'Donnell (1989), illustrate the need to give up, partly at least, the familiar positivistic way of looking at things.

Constructive mutual criticism should result from comprehensive and open-minded testing of economic theories. This process may facilitate a broad classification of economic theories reflecting the basic positions held by economists. Teaching, decision-taking and policy-making should be clarified when the flow of empirical and theoretical information is broadly systematized.

Thus the answer to the present diversification of economic theory does not lie in an attempt to restore unity but rather in seeking to broadly classify theories so that eventually a loosely structured body of economic science might obtain. The present study tries to contribute to this undertaking. However, no attempt will be made to tackle the problem of classification of economic theories in general terms since the argument would probably remain vacuous. Instead, a concrete problem will be examined, namely describing the broad meaning of classical-Keynesian political economy and its approximate position within the spectrum of economic theories. It will be argued that this type of political economy seems to be a superior alternative to neoclassical equilibrium theory and that to ground socioeconomic policies on alternative assumptions would entail less hardship than is caused by today's economic policies. By and large, this is tantamount to saying that the economics of Walras and Marshall should, to a considerable extent, be replaced by the political economy of Ricardo and Keynes.

This formulation of the problem inevitably involves a critique of neoclassical equilibrium theory (and, implicitly, of the economic theory of socialism). However, the general tone of the study is conciliatory in the sense that the considerable degree of complementarity existing between the various economic theories is recognized: we do not want to exclude but to combine and to bring ideas together. This implies recognizing the merits of rival points of view and should, it is hoped, allow economists adhering to differing schools to co-operate more closely, which is badly needed in view of the immense socioeconomic and ecological problems facing us on a world scale. In fact, much harm has been done by excessively emphasizing certain aspects of socioeconomic life, frequently with the help of quite sophisticated models which neglect important features of the real world, thus losing sight of society as a whole. Liberal economists praise the virtues of the market and of private initiative while socialist economists have insisted on the necessity of planning and on forging a new, socially minded human being. Historical experience, however, shows that man is a *social* individual in the sense that individuals act within social structures, that is a system of institutions encompassing all the spheres of social and individual life. In this view, the market and the plan (on various levels) are but specific institutions both of which are required to organize socioeconomic life in and between countries or regions, the problem being to blend plan and market in a way properly adapted to a particular historical situation. The main question, then, is not to falsify theories in order to establish the supremacy of one 'correct' theory. This is beyond the reach of the capabilities of the human mind anyway. Rather, it should be recognized that each theory may be useful in explaining some aspect of reality. The crucial issue is to find out which theory is more fundamental. This requires creating broad and comprehensive theoretical frameworks in which partial theories can be put into perspective, the purpose of such frameworks being to explain in principle how economies and societies *as a whole* function. In what follows an attempt will be made to argue that classical political economy in a broad sense, i.e. complemented by Keynesian elements, constitutes such a framework, alongside liberal and socialist economics.

The necessity to elaborate comprehensive theoretical frameworks implies that classical-Keynesian political economy cannot consist of just one tidy and universally applicable model. Rather, in order to take account of widely varying socioeconomic, political and cultural differences, modern political economy ought to represent a conceptual framework for historical investigations allowing us to draw policy conclusions adapted to specific circumstances. The integration of economic theory and economic history is, indeed, the main methodological point taken up in this study. In this, we may rely on Karl Marx and on Carl Menger. Both masterfully combined theory and history in the spirit of the founder of the social sciences, Aristotle, whom both admired. Marx tackled the evolution of social systems; Menger attempted to ground the social sciences upon the behaviour of individuals.

Accordingly, modern political economy should allow for broadly based co-operation between social scientists. This book attempts to argue that, as a first step, it should be possible to synthesize the various post Keynesian strands of thought actually existing. Subsequently, a properly adapted system of political economy should facilitate the integration of parts of neoclassical microeconomics and of the economic theory of socialism. The two are largely complementary: the former deals with the behaviour of individuals in the economic sphere, the latter with the social structures within which individuals act. Consequently, neoclassical and socialist economists who might find classical-Keynesian political economy attractive would not have to give up all their presumptions. Quite the contrary, by bringing in their analytical powers they could greatly contribute to the construction of a comprehensive system of political economy. 'The truth', Hegel once said, 'is the whole' – '*Die Wahrheit ist das Ganze*'. In a way, this profound insight certainly holds in particular for the various strands of post Keynesianism and in general for economics and for the social sciences taken together. A comprehensive view of social matters is presently more needed than ever.

However, Hegel, in the tradition of Plato, wrote from the point of view of the absolute, an unthinkable undertaking today. In the course of the twentieth century, scientists of all kinds have become more modest than their nineteenth-century counterparts and awareness of the limits of human knowledge has increased. It is more and more recognized that knowledge is scrappy and imperfect, above all in the social sciences. Among the great social scientists of the twentieth century, Keynes has perhaps been most conscious of this fact. Indeed, in a fundamental philosophical work, the *Treatise on Probability*, Keynes strongly stresses the probabilistic and qualitative nature of thinking in the social sciences (see on this Fitzgibbons 1988, and O'Donnell 1989): absolute truth is inaccessible; all that can be done is to attempt to get some clarity about principles to move on in the right direction. To be able to choose the supposedly right way, the social scientist has to make use of *all* the information available: metaphysical, accessible through introspection based on pure reason and intuition, empirical and theoretical, relying on applied reason, and, last but not least, historical, i.e. the history of facts and of ideas. Indeed, insight into socioeconomic affairs can be greatly enhanced by taking due account of the immense intellectual heritage, based on Greek and Roman social and political thought.

This is not a fancy. Some of the founders of political economy, James Steuart, François Quesnay and Adam Smith for example, incorporated historical heritage – in a very broad sense – in their work. The historical development of facts and ideas played a crucial role with German social scientists: Karl Marx, Gustav Schmoller, Max Weber, Werner Sombart and August Oncken, to name but a few. Marshall was very keen on the historical continuity of economic thought: he was anxious to show that there was no marginal revolution, but an evolution of classical political economy; his work on Hegel (Groenewegen 1990) suggests that he took pains to put his economic system into a wider context. Maynard Keynes, too, is deeply rooted in pre-modern thought, as is brought out by Carabelli (1985), Fitzgibbons (1988) and O'Donnell (1989) in particular. In view of the considerable intellectual confusion currently prevailing, there is, it seems, a real need to go back to the great socioeconomic and political thinkers of the past which means that the history of economic, social and political thought will have to occupy a much larger place in future syllabi than is now the case.

The above implies that the social sciences cannot be 'value-free' as is still frequently claimed. (Indeed, on deeper reflection, a value-free science would only be possible if absolute knowledge were already held or could be reached in principle.) Values – material, intellectual, moral, aesthetical, individual and social – are related to all spheres of individual and social life and are embodied in various institutions; specific value structures define the way of life in different countries and regions and in various epochs. As such, value systems not only are closely linked with the organization of societies and with the aims of human actions but also enter the premises of theories set forth to explain real-world phenomena, the latter reflecting the tentative and probabilistic – in Keynes's sense – nature of thinking. Even today many social scientists see themselves as moral scientists because of the crucial role of values played in social life. This goes along with a growing preoccupation with ethics and politics in the sense of political philosophy (examples are Utz 1964–94, Schack 1978, Brown 1986 and Barrère 1991). In this context, it should be remembered that one of the founders of political economy, Adam Smith, first worked out an ethical system – *The Theory of Moral Sentiments* – before tackling economic issues in the *Wealth of Nations*. Both works are parts of a greater whole, based on the idea that an orderly social life must rest on solid ethical foundations. Similarly, François Quesnay built an elaborate system of political philosophy around his *tableau économique*. Finally, Keynes always understood economics and the social sciences as moral sciences, a fact emphasized by Fitzgibbons (1988) and O'Donnell (1989). In this book, then, some consideration is given to the role of ethics in the social sphere in order to contribute to the elaboration of a complete system of the social sciences of which political economy is a part.

Clearly, however, it is too soon to aim at producing a logically watertight treatise on classical-Keynesian political economy. For, as will become evident from the opening pages of this book, there are different strands of thought in this domain which, at first sight, are not mutually compatible. Thus, before treatises or even textbooks on political economy can be written, a considerable amount of preparatory work has still to be done to clarify the main issues. The following is meant to be a contribution to this preliminary work. The chain of argument forms a loosely connected set of ideas which are not fully explored. Problems may be merely mentioned and connections just hinted at. As such, the present study is only an essay, intended to initiate and to stimulate further work and discussion, and is perhaps best understood as an inventory of some of the problems which arise in attempting to work out a comprehensive system of political economy and its underpinnings, as well as its implications for other social sciences – politics, law and sociology, in particular.

The present study is based on the presumption that to bring some order into the system of social sciences a social philosophy is needed. This springs from the simple fact that each society is an immensely complex entity, the broad functioning of which cannot be captured by partial models based on specific hypotheses. Whenever socioeconomic macroissues – employment, value and distribution – are considered there are no realistic hypotheses to start with (Keynes). Therefore, the analysis of such issues must necessarily start from a 'pre-analytic vision' (Schumpeter) which governs, to an important extent, the way of reasoning, whether this is made explicit or not.

Visions rest on social philosophies. The latter constitute the unifying frameworks for *all* systems of social sciences.

Two great social philosophies have, in various versions, dominated the intellectual scene since the French Political Revolution and the English Industrial Revolution: liberalism and socialism. The neoclassical system of economics grew out of the former, the economic theory of socialism out of the latter. It is precisely the solid social philosophical foundation which has given both neoclassical economics and the economic theory of socialism their tremendous intellectual and political strength. If, now, classical-Keynesian political economy is to succeed in at least partly supplanting neoclassical economics and the economic theory of socialism, then it will have to be put on equally solid social philosophical foundations. This amounts to elaborating an appropriate third-way social philosophy which is, obviously, an immense task that can only be undertaken by experienced social scientists; this is the main reason why social philosophical issues will be merely touched upon in the following pages. Nevertheless, it is felt that in developing a third-way social and political philosophy, it will be possible to rely upon a rich intellectual heritage, ranging from Aristotle to Keynes, as is implied by Brown (1986), de Laubier (1987), Fitzgibbons (1988) and O'Donnell (1989), among others. (The term 'third-way' is auxiliary and provisional and is used interchangeably with 'intermediate' and 'middle-way'; a more informative notion, i.e. 'humanist', is provided in chapter 2, where the fundamental approaches in social philosophy are broadly defined.)

If a comprehensive and solidly based system of political economy could be established as a rival to liberal and socialist economic theory, political implications would also emerge. For, given that, broadly speaking, liberal (neoclassical) economics may be seen as the economics of the political right (based upon an élitist liberalism) and the economic theory of socialism as the political economy of the left, classical-Keynesian political economy could be interpreted as the socioeconomic theory of the progressive centre, that is of social democracy, and of similar and associated movements, including, for example, conservatives who care about people and do not bother too much about abstract doctrines. Incidentally, this was Keynes's and Kaldor's political position, too. Most importantly, 'Keynes's system was consciously cast as a third alternative to both [socialism and liberalism]' (Fitzgibbons 1988, pp. 1–2). So there is no need to invent the third-way alternative (which, incidentally, attracts growing attention in recent post Keynesian literature; see for example Dutt and Amadeo 1990).

There is some hope that many politicians and social scientists, not necessarily economists, will sympathize with the attempt to establish a classical-Keynesian system of political economy of the centre. In fact, in the course of recent history, social and political action of the centre has, time and again, been hampered by the weakness of its conceptual foundations. Consequently, there has been, in accordance with the currently prevailing *Zeitgeist*, a strong and persistent tendency for the universalist and clear-cut liberal and socialist arguments, frequently in a fundamentalist dress, to win through, a fact at present confirmed by the events taking place in many of the formerly socialist countries who want to convert, by a stroke of magic so to speak, centrally planned systems into free market economies.

Modern liberal and socialist fundamentalisms are both essentially materialistic – society and nature are, in fact, subordinate to the economy. The race for ever higher levels of material well-being has resulted in immense inequalities and is one of the main reasons for the currently disastrous socioeconomic and ecological situation worldwide. The few islands of material well-being, embellished at times by cyclical upswings, should not deceive us when assessing this statement. Moreover, those living in these islands of affluence should bear in mind that markets and private initiative are but necessary, not sufficient, conditions for economic success. Human actions may indeed not bring about the effects desired if objective historical conditions are not favourable.

It is quite evident that we are today living in a neo-mercantilist world where foreign trade, associated with a strong position in key industrial and service sectors, is crucial for economic development, and, in some instances, for exercising political influence. Since, in open economies, everything has to be done to remain competitive on world markets, far-reaching economic, social and ecological policy actions are rendered very difficult in the presence of severe unemployment. Hence full employment, or near-full employment, seems indispensable if more social justice is to be brought about worldwide and if our environment is to be preserved, since aggressive trade policies would then no longer be required. In the course of the argument set forth in this book it will be seen that this typically Keynesian assertion gains its full force only if Keynesian employment theory is combined with a theory of value and distribution based upon the classical (Ricardian) surplus approach.

Acknowledgements

In any scientific undertaking, even as tentative and preparatory as the present study, intellectual debts are heavy since writing is essentially a social process although, on the surface, it is seemingly an individual task. The reader will soon remark that, as regards content, the work done by two great political economists, David Ricardo and Maynard Keynes, underpins the arguments used. Methodological suggestions largely build on Karl Marx's unique combination of theory and history. And, behind the scenes, there is François Quesnay, perhaps the true founder of political economy, whose famous *tableau économique* was rightly denoted as a stroke of genius by Karl Marx in his *Theorien über den Mehrwert*.

The influence of many contemporary post Keynesian economists will also be immediately apparent. Furthermore, I am heavily indebted to my teachers in economics in the University of Fribourg (Switzerland): Pietro Balestra, Ernst Billeter, Basilio Biucchi, Willy Büchi, Florian Fleck, Josef Schwarzfischer and Jean Valarché have provided their students with a solid and broadly based introduction to the social sciences.

I am also greatly in debt to my Cambridge supervisors, David Champernowne, Phyllis Deane, Nicholas Kaldor and Richard Stone, who initiated me into the great Cambridge tradition of political economy. The present study stands entirely in this non-technical and humanist tradition of looking at socioeconomic phenomena. According to Keynes, economics in its being a branch of ethics is, in fact, part of the arts, not of the sciences; the meaning of this and the consequences ensuing for the economist have, perhaps, been stated most clearly by Keynes in his obituary on Marshall (Keynes 1972a, pp. 161–231). Phyllis Deane has considerably influenced the spirit of this study, especially my assessment of the present state of economic theory. Incidentally, she has recently insisted on the distinction between *economic science* and the *art of political economy*. The late Lord Kaldor, my thesis supervisor, decisively shaped my views on fundamentals in economic theory and policy. His capacity to blend, in a unique way, theory and historical reality has always been admired by students and readers. Inevitably, then, the present study bears heavily the marks of Nicholas Kaldor.

In the early seventies, Cambridge research students had the privilege to benefit from a unique intellectual atmosphere, with Francis Cripps, Gérard Debreu, Maurice Dobb, John Eatwell, Pierangelo Garegnani, Wynne Godley, Frank Hahn, Geoffrey Harcourt, Richard Kahn, Nicholas Kaldor, Donald Moggridge, Luigi Pasinetti, Joan Robinson, Robert Rowthorn and Ajit Singh lecturing on a very broad spectrum of economic theories: neoclassical, Marxian, neo-Ricardian, Keynesian and post Keynesian. With Piero Sraffa in the background, capital theory was perhaps the favourite topic of discussion among research students. The present study is a direct outgrowth of that particular intellectual climate.

In writing the book, I have benefited greatly from the unsurpassable clarity of exposition of Luigi Pasinetti, whose work represents the natural analytical starting point for bringing together, at a fundamental level, Ricardo and Keynes. On the one hand, Pasinetti's (1977, 1981, 1993) books are a prerequisite to reading the present study, while, on the other, the following intends to shed some light on the wider significance of Pasinetti's work (on the latter, see also Bortis 1993a). I also express my deep gratitude to Phyllis Deane, Mauro Baranzini, Geoffrey Harcourt, Luigi Pasinetti, Alessandro Roncaglia, Roberto Scazzieri and Sidney Weintraub. They have shown understanding for my work, in spite of its numerous imperfections, made useful comments and have encouraged me to continue. For very useful discussions on general theoretical issues I am indebted to Krishna Bharadwaj, Izumi Hishiyama and Josef Steindl. In the mid eighties Krishna suggested to me that I should set out a comprehensive and broadly systematic overview of classical-Keynesian political economy. Some of my Fribourg students, particularly Christoph Minnig, Patrick Vuille and Urs Weber, made helpful remarks on the final draft. My special thanks go to Phyllis Deane, Marcello Corti, Geoffrey Harcourt, Luigi Pasinetti, Alessandro Roncaglia and Roberto Scazzieri who have, several times in some instances, fought their way through the thicket of arguments set forth in various drafts of this book, eliminating a very great number of small mistakes, discovering major blunders and improving the literary style as far as this has been possible. Specifically, Geoffrey Harcourt made very .useful suggestions on fundamentals in post Keynesianism and on Marshall's notion of equilibrium. His lectures and seminars on 'Cambridge economics and Cambridge economists' delivered in May 1995 at the University of Fribourg (Switzerland) provided a final sharpening-up of essentials. In the very last stages, several referees of Cambridge University Press made very helpful comments. Nevertheless, it goes without saying that the author remains fully responsible for content and presentation.

This is also the place to express my gratitude to several institutions: first, and foremost, to my Alma Mater, the University of Fribourg, whose great philosophical tradition shapes the way of thinking of her students perhaps more than is commonly thought. The splendid facilities of Churchill College, among them a set of beautiful lawn tennis courts, rendered life and work at Cambridge very easy and pleasant. Geoff Harcourt secured superb accommodation at Jesus, his college, during my many visits to Cambridge in recent years. Several participations in international workshops organized by members of the research project 'The wealth of nations and economic theory' of the universities of Bologna, Milan, Padua and Verona, and at the Trieste Post Keynesian Summer School provided the opportunity for very fruitful exchanges on crucial issues in economic theory. There is also the Swiss Science Foundation which requires research students to go abroad in order to enhance their acquaintance with new ideas. Finally, Cambridge University Press treated the manuscript with much goodwill.

I am particularly grateful to Paul Inderbinen who compiled the index and read the proofs. I should also like to thank Mrs Suzanne Delessert, Mrs Gabrielle Grivel and Mr Christoph Minnig for excellent secretarial assistance. Mr Minnig, in his capacity as a personal computer expert, has greatly facilitated typing and editing work. Last, but not least, my thanks go to my wife Nicole and to my sons Pierre-Alain and Richard who have created the environment needed for sustained work.

H.B.
Fribourg (Switzerland), December 1995

Symbols

A	labour productivity
B	gross inflow of foreign finance p.a. (gross of interest payments and of repayment of debt)
C	output of consumption goods
C_C	consumption goods consumed in the consumption goods sector
D	public and private foreign debt
G	government expenditures in real terms
I_t	gross investment in time-period t
I^*	$I_e + I_r$ = trend gross investment
I_e	'expansion' investment
I_r	'replacement' investment
K_t	capital stock in time-period t
K^*	trend (equilibrium) capital stock
M	import quantities
N	volume of employment (number of productive workers and employees, producing a surplus over wages)
N^*	normal (trend) employment linked with standard utilization of K^*
N_f	full employment level
N_C	employment in the consumption goods sector
N_I	employment in the investment goods sector
P	gross profits in real terms
Q	gross national product
Q^*	trend output linked with standard utilization of K^*
Q_c	(standard) capacity output linked with standard utilization of K_t
Q_f	full employment output
Q_e^*	trend output governed by the external employment mechanism
Q_i^*	trend output governed by the internal employment mechanism
R	rents in real terms
W_I	real wages in the investment goods sector

X	exports in real terms
Y	expenditures (effective demand) in real terms
a	rate of growth of labour productivity (rate of technical progress)
b	import coefficient
c	$c_p+(c_w-c_p)(1/k)=1-z=$average propensity to consume
c_p	fraction of property income consumed
c_w	fraction of wage income consumed
d	drop-out ratio of fixed capital (K)
e	exchange rate; length of 'experience' period relevant for entrepreneurial investment decisions
g	growth rate of Q
g^*	trend growth rate of Q^*
g_G	trend growth rate of G
g_X	trend growth rate of X
h	rate of growth of population
i	rate of interest
k	realized mark-up on wages determining property income, i.e. profits and rents
k_e	average realized mark-up over e time periods (from $t-e$ to t)
k^*	normal (desired, satisfactory) mark-up at normal capacity utilization
k_f	full-cost mark-up
$1/k$	wage share in gross domestic income
$1-(1/k)$	property share in gross domestic income
m	$z-(g^*+d)v^*=$leakage minus gross investment–output ratio
$1/m$	internal or government expenditures multiplier
n	natural rate of growth$=a+h$
p	domestic price level$=$money price of a bundle of (necessary) consumption goods
p^*	long-run normal price level$=$normal prices linked with k^* and with standard capacity utilization
p_c	estimated normal prices based on normal utilization of Q_c
p_f	the full-cost price level, which implies a mark-up k_f such that the target rate of profits is achieved at any rate of capacity utilization
p_M	import price level
q	reaction parameter linking deviations of realized profits from target profits to actually undertaken gross investment
r	realized profit rate
r^*	normal (desired, satisfactory) profit rate
s	marginal and average saving ratio

s_C	propensity of the capitalists to save
s_P	fraction of property income saved
s_W	fraction of wage income saved
t_P	fraction of property income paid on taxes
t_W	fraction of wage income paid on taxes
u	involuntary unemployment as a fraction of total labour force
$1-u$	employment scalar
v	capital coefficient at standard capacity utilization
w	real wage rate
w_n	money wage rate
z	average leakage coefficient $=z_W+(z_P-z_W)(1-(1/k))$
z_P	$1-c_P=$leakage coefficient of property incomes
z_W	$1-c_W=$leakage coefficient of wage incomes
∂	fraction of foreign debt D to be repaid p.a.
π	terms of trade$=ep_M/p$
$1/\pi b$	export multiplier

Abbreviation

a.tr.	author's translation

1 Introduction

Observations on the state of alternative economic theory

In the fifties and sixties the evolution of the Keynesian message resulted in an alternative approach in economic theory which was first labelled neo-Keynesian economics and subsequently post Keynesian economics or political economy. Some of the founders of the new school clearly sought to reconcile the classical (Ricardian) theory of production, value and distribution based upon the surplus principle with the Keynesian theory of employment and output determination through effective demand; others mainly tried to preserve and to elaborate Keynes's heritage which was considered anticlassical because of its rejection of Say's law. In general, the post Keynesians wanted to overcome the neoclassical orthodoxy and consequently considered their approach to be progressive.

The notion 'post Keynesian' immediately gives rise to a definitional problem related to the title of the present book which is about 'classical-Keynesian political economy'. At this stage, it is sufficient to note that the latter is a historically based elaboration of the former, in which Quesnay, Ricardo, Marx and Keynes are of particular importance. The term 'post Keynesian' is defined in this section. At the end of the next section a working definition of 'classical-Keynesian' is provided. This notion is examined more fully in chapter 3 (pp. 76–81).

The return to classical economics starting from Keynesian ground is, indeed, the common theme in much post Keynesian work, for example some of Michal Kalecki's essays written as early as the thirties and forties (Kalecki 1971), Joan Robinson's *Accumulation of Capital* (Robinson 1965; 1st edn 1956), Nicholas Kaldor's articles on growth and distribution (for example Kaldor 1955/56) and, most importantly, Piero Sraffa's *Production of Commodities by Means of Commodities* (Sraffa 1960). More recently, Luigi Pasinetti presented a fundamental framework of analysis (Pasinetti 1977, 1981, 1993), in which Ricardian and Keynesian theoretical elements are combined and elaborated. Kregel also sees the 'reconstruction of political economy' as a synthesis of Keynesian and classical elements of analysis (Kregel 1975). The same is true of Garegnani (Garegnani 1970, 1978/79, 1983, 1984, 1987). Geoffrey Harcourt greatly contributed to the spread of post Keynesian ideas (Harcourt 1977, 1982, 1986, 1992, 1993, 1995). The effort made by the late Krishna Bharadwaj to reappraise classical political economy deserves a special mention here (Bharadwaj 1986, 1989).

Since large parts of neoclassical equilibrium economics have moved quite far away from reality, as, for instance, the 'rational expectations' system clearly shows, one would have expected post Keynesian economics to gain ground with the change in the economic situation in the mid seventies when the post-war era of growth and optimism had come to an end. After all, Ricardo, Keynes and the post Keynesians have always endeavoured to explain aspects of the real world and to propose appropriate policy measures.

The contrary has happened, however. Explanation of reality has been widely replaced by a dogmatic belief in the blessings of an unrestricted free market system. In the field of economic policy, deregulation has become one of the key notions. This return to liberal fundamentalism, accelerated by the recent downfall of the centrally planned systems, has, quite naturally, been accompanied by sweeping successes of the traditional neoclassical school, that is of the neoclassical synthesis, general equilibrium theory, neo-Walrasian disequilibrium theory, monetarism, rational expectations, supply side economics and neo-Austrian economics. The neoclassical tide has not only swept away large parts of what has remained of Keynesianism proper but has also seriously hampered the rise of post Keynesianism. As a consequence, the post Keynesian alternative is not widely appreciated today. Only a tiny minority of economists adhere to it, and the movement even seems to have lost some ground in recent years.

In fact, it is normal that there should have been a neoclassical reaction against post Keynesianism. After all, post Keynesian economic theory is, in some respects, in direct opposition to neoclassical mainstream economics. What is worrying, however, is that there are deep cleavages within post Keynesianism. These have prevented the emergence of a coherent post Keynesian system until now. Presumably, this is the main reason why the new approach to economic problems has not yet found the recognition it deserves: 'few professors of economics seem aware of [the post Keynesian] alternative – and fewer still seem willing to expose their students to it' (Eichner 1978, p. vii).

This state of affairs has not changed in the recent past. In a recent German textbook (Felderer and Homburg 1989) post Keynesian economics and some leading authors are barely mentioned and post Keynesian theory is not dealt with at all. The authors argue that this is impossible because a coherent post Keynesian system simply does not exist (Felderer and Homburg 1989, pp. 100–1). This important proposition is complemented, quite ironically, with a quotation from R. M. Solow who asserts that post Keynesianism is more of an ideology (*Weltanschauung*) than a science (p. 101n).

Certainly, there are, besides a possible lack of coherence, other reasons why post Keynesianism is widely ignored. One of these might be the difficulty of 'escaping from habitual modes of thought and expression' (Keynes 1973a, p. xxiii). There is also the Marxian point of view stating that theories find acceptance only if they serve the vested interests of some social group. Finally, one could argue with Thomas Kuhn that those who adhere to an old paradigm have to retire in order that a new paradigm may be established.

The problem of coherence seems particularly important because post Keynesian economists disagree, in a fundamental way, on the nature of their system. There are rather acrimonious discussions between post Keynesian subgroups going on. Harcourt distinguishes three different strands of post Keynesianism (Harcourt 1981). In the first place, there are the Keynesian Fundamentalists: Paul Davidson, Hyman Minsky and Sidney Weintraub, for example. A second group are the Robinsonians: Joan Robinson, Richard Kahn, Michal Kalecki, A. Asimakopulos, Jan Kregel and a group of Australian economists (Harcourt 1981, p. 5). Finally, there are the neo-Ricardians: Krishna Bharadwaj, John Eatwell, Pierangelo Garegnani, Heinz Kurz, Murray Milgate, Alessandro Roncaglia, Bertram Schefold and Piero Sraffa.

These lists are far from being exhaustive, nor is the classification set forth here something definite, since it could presumably be refined and rearranged in various ways. The point is simply to illustrate the variety of the post Keynesian movement. Well-known authors, like Phyllis Deane, Alfred Eichner, Donald Harris, Kenneth Galbraith, Nicholas Kaldor, Edward Nell, Luigi Pasinetti, Josef Steindl and Paolo Sylos Labini for instance, have not been included simply because of the difficulty in classifying them. The same is true of the German group of political economists around Adolph Lowe, for example Harald Hagemann and Peter Kalmbach.

A brief look at the basic tenets of each of these post Keynesian groups may help to bring the main divergencies into the open. The Keynesian Fundamentalists aim at preserving and developing the legacy of Keynes, that is the *Treatise on Money* and *The General Theory of Employment, Interest and Money*. Paul Davidson formulates their motto as follows: '[Our] analysis will be developed on the basic assumptions that in the real

world (1) the future is uncertain . . . (2) production takes time and therefore
. . . someone must make a contractual commitment in the present involving performance and payment in the uncertain future, and (3) economic decisions are made in the light of an unalterable past, while moving towards a perfidious future. It is only under these three basic assumptions that the role of money in the real world can be analysed' (1978, pp. 7–8).

The Robinsonians see the essence of the Keynesian revolution in the fact 'that Keynes's *General Theory* smashed up the glasshouse of static theory [i.e. equilibrium economics]' (Robinson 1965, p. v). Equilibrium analysis ought, in their view, to be replaced by historical analysis where history is seen as a sequence of short-term events. This implies that 'the long period has no independent existence' (Harcourt 1981, p. 5). 'The long-run trend is but a slowly changing component of a chain of short-period situations' (Kalecki 1971, p. 165). The essential analytical tool of the Robinsonians is a two-sector model linking investment and profits or the rate of growth of capital and output and the rate of profit. This relationship between profits and growth is a familiar theme in classical economic theory. It is also present in the Marxian reproduction schemes of volume two of *Das Kapital* (Marx 1973/74a [1867–94], vol. II, pp. 391ff.) and in Keynes's Fundamental Equations set forth in the *Treatise on Money* (Keynes 1971b, vol. I, pp. 111ff.).

The neo-Ricardians strongly emphasize the classical origins of their theoretical views. Their starting point is the capital theory debate, the outcome of which has put to the fore the fundamental differences between neoclassical and neo-Ricardian theory in the fields of long-period value, distribution and employment (Garegnani 1970). The analytical core of neo-Ricardianism is the classical surplus approach to distribution (Garegnani 1984). The division of a given social product into real wages and the surplus (profits and rents) is essentially a social, not an economic or market phenomenon. Once distribution is determined normal prices are also fixed. These depend on the technical conditions of production and on distribution, i.e. equal profit rates everywhere or a hierarchy of desired rates. The given output need not equal full employment output, owing to a lack of effective demand. The neo-Ricardians also stress the importance of long-period analysis. Normal prices are supposed to be stable in the long run and are consequently seen as centres of gravity, around which short-period or temporary market prices fluctuate.

There are crucial differences between the three strands of post Keynesian thought. The Keynesian Fundamentalists emphasize uncertainty and the role of money in an uncertain world. They reject the importance of the capital theory debate and the various problems related to it, e.g. reswitching and measuring capital independently of distribution, which Davidson, quoting F. H. Knight, sees as 'theoretical conundrums which are often debated with great joy and zest by economists who [according to F. H. Knight] essentially "are to make their living by providing pure entertainment" for other economists' (Davidson 1978, p. 7). Moreover, American Keynesian Fundamentalists 'do not want to know about the Classical-Marxian roots' (Harcourt 1981, p. 2) of both the neo-Ricardian and the Robinsonian variants of post Keynesian economics.

On these points the neo-Ricardians would strongly disagree. In particular, they emphasize the crucial importance of the capital theory debate. The neoclassical theory of value and distribution (supply and demand determine prices in both the short and the long runs) is shown to be wrong for the long run; moreover, even under ideal conditions, i.e. perfectly functioning markets, there may be no tendency towards full employment in any neoclassical world. Hence in the neo-Ricardian view, the capital-theoretic critique eliminates neoclassical theory as a long-period approach to economic problems and is a necessary prerequisite for the setting forth of a neo-Ricardian long-period economic theory. Consequently, the neo-Ricardians want to get rid of the neoclassical vestiges in Keynes's *General Theory*, that is the theory of investment contained in chapter 17 and the first (neo)classical postulate (the real wage equals the marginal product of labour). Both might provide starting points for reintroducing neoclassical methods to analyse long-period problems.

Uncertainty and money are, in the neo-Ricardian view, not very important in the long run, where the normal prices are determined by technology and institutions. Uncertainty, indeed, plays a minor role if the normal functioning of institutions is expected to continue with a high degree of confidence.

However, the Robinsonians would tell the neo-Ricardians that uncertainty is very important and that, therefore, long-period analysis associated with normal prices and quantities does not make much sense: '[Uncertainty] destroys the basis of [neo]classical economic theory which, in Keynes's words, is "one of these pretty, polite techniques which tries to deal with the present by abstracting from the fact that we know very little about the future". [Thus,] long-period movements are obtained by linking up a sequence of short-period results – they have no independent existence' (Asimakopulos 1983, p. 31), a statement which also applies to neo-Ricardian long-period theory. To this the neo-Ricardians would reply that it is not sufficient to develop a theory of fluctuations. A theory of the long-term trend is also required since it matters whether fluctuations are around trends implying lower or, in contrast, higher levels of persistent unemployment (Garegnani 1983).

This brief review illustrates that there are deep cleavages within the post

Keynesian movement. This largely explains why neoclassical economists, even those who are conscious about the weaknesses of their approach, are reluctant to take post Keynesianism seriously. They simply do not find a coherent system which is ripe for textbook presentation and, thus, for teaching. As a consequence, post Keynesian economics remains, in a way, sectarian.

At the end of her life Joan Robinson clearly perceived the issue at stake. On the one hand, she recognized the need for synthesis within post Keynesianism: 'Keynes evidently did not make much of [Sraffa's neo-Ricardian work] and Sraffa, in turn, never made much of the *General Theory*. It is the task of post-Keynesians to reconcile the two' (Robinson 1978, p. 14). On the other hand, she felt that the undertaking would not be easy: 'Post-Keynesian theory has plenty of problems to work on. We now have a general framework of long- and short-period analysis which will enable us to bring the insights of [Ricardo,] Marx, Keynes, and Kalecki into a coherent form and apply them to the contemporary scene, but there is still a long way to go' (p. 18). Some of it we attempt to cover in the subsequent chapters.

Problems and plan

The aims pursued in this study follow from the above-mentioned lack of coherence of alternative economic theory. First, an attempt is made to argue that there is room for a synthesis of classical and Keynesian elements of analysis on the basis of their respective historical heritages (chapter 4). Consequently, it should be possible in a further step, not to be undertaken here, to set up a coherent classical-Keynesian system by elaborating the present study; this could mean writing treatises on classical-Keynesian political economy. Second, in order to bring out the significance of this approach within economic theory, it seems important to identify the fundamental differences between classical-Keynesian political economy and neoclassical equilibrium economics (chapter 5). Third, and most importantly, it is attempted to argue that the classical-Keynesian system may be considered the political economy of the intermediate or middle way between liberalism and socialism. This argument requires a look at some fundamentals in the social sciences (chapter 2) and in classical and Keynesian political economy itself (chapter 3). In the final chapters, 6 and 7, a wider view is taken of a few crucial problems of economic theory and policy, of the social sciences and of social philosophy.

These aims are related to an extremely complex subject matter comprising various issues of content and method in the social sciences in general, and in political economy and in economics more particularly. As a consequence, the problem posed here cannot, in our view, be dealt with by a series of neatly defined piecemeal studies since this would only aggravate the current confusion in economic theory. A global approach therefore seems indispensable because, in a Keynesian vein, 'society and thinking about society make up an immensely complex organic whole'. Some preliminary explanations with respect to content and method are thus required. From these a more detailed plan of the study will broadly emerge. The study's limitations, mainly its tentative and preparatory character, will also become apparent. In fact, the present contribution merely intends to explore the subject matter in order to point to the direction to move in. This exploration necessarily comprises a historical dimension since the present theories rest on the basic ideas of the great authors of the past.

In this book we conceive of classical-Keynesian political economy as a synthesis of Ricardo and Keynes. This simplifying definition poses two problems. The first is about the relationship between Adam Smith and David Ricardo and is associated with the meaning of 'economics' and of 'political economy' respectively; this problem will be discussed in chapter 3 (pp. 75–89). The second issue concerns Keynes and Ricardo whose theoretical systems are, at first sight, sharply opposed. For example, Keynes mentions that the neglect of 'the aggregate demand function is fundamental to the Ricardian economics' (1973a, p. 32) and conceives his *General Theory* as an attempt to repair this defect of the Ricardian system. Or, the neo-Ricardian equilibrium system pictured in Sraffa (1960) stands in sharp contrast to the *General Theory* where uncertainty about the future figures prominently. Some issues related to Keynes and Ricardo are discussed in chapter 3 and a possible synthesis is suggested in chapter 4. There it emerges that classical and Keynesian theories are complementary rather than mutually exclusive: classical political economy deals with objective and historically grown structural factors – the institutional and technological system – while Keynesian theory focuses on the behaviour of individuals and their co-ordination by the socioeconomic system within given structures. The former deals with normal magnitudes (prices, profit rates and employment levels) associated with stock equilibria and determined by the functioning of the socioeconomic system; the objects of the latter are actually realized magnitudes resulting from the decisions taken by individuals in the past and in the present on the basis of expectations about the future.

The fundamental importance of Ricardo's system and its modern neo-Ricardian elaboration by Sraffa (1960) and Pasinetti (1977, 1981, 1993), on the one hand, and of Keynes's theory and its development, on the other, gives rise to a definitional question. Why not simply call modern political economy either *neo-Ricardian* or *post Keynesian* rather than *classical* or *classical-Keynesian?* The main reason is that the neo-Ricardian theory of value and distribution as developed by Sraffa and his followers has been widely used for critical (negative) purposes. It should be remembered that Sraffa's (1960) book carries the subtitle 'Prelude to a critique of economic theory'. Subsequently, the ideas set forth there have indeed become the conceptual starting point for a fundamental critique of neoclassical equilibrium economics in the course of the capital theory debate. The theoretical discussions on fundamentals have, since the late sixties, turned into a bitter ideological struggle, the significance of which can be understood best by recalling that the subtitle of Marx's *Kapital*, i.e. *Kritik der politischen Ökonomie*, strongly resembles the subtitle of Sraffa's (1960) work. Subsequently, Ricardo and neo-Ricardianism were associated with Marx and Marxism. The sinister atmosphere of the Cold War led to further associations. Marx's work was largely equated with Soviet communism or even with Stalinism. Associations like these are clearly due to sheer ignorance or to fundamental misunderstandings but are, consciously or unconsciously, present in the mind of many social scientists. Therefore, even in the context of generalized *détente*, some care is still required when speaking of Ricardo. Similarly, post Keynesianism was, and still is, associated with criticism and, as suggested in the previous section, does not form a comprehensive and consistent theoretical system.

In the subsequent chapters of this book it will become evident why modern political economy should be termed *classical* or *classical-Keynesian*. Classical political economy in the Ricardian sense implies a vision of society that is entirely different from the conventional liberal vision which is ultimately based upon Adam Smith's system (chapters 2 and 3). In the former the question of proportions, i.e. part–whole relations, is fundamental, and this implies that society is primary and is more than the sum of its parts. This is not the case for the latter where the individual stands in the forefront and society is derived from individual behaviour.

However, the term 'classical' must be complemented by the attribute 'Keynesian', either implicitly or explicitly. Consequently we shall use the notions 'classical' and 'classical-Keynesian' interchangeably in the following, but with a preference for the latter. The point is that classical political economy is intimately associated with Say's law; in fact, Thomas Malthus was not able to convince the political economists of his time that effective demand might limit the accumulation of capital. Consequently, Ricardo and his modern followers have, starting from the circular process of production, worked out a long-period theory of value and distribution (Ricardo 1951 [1821]; Sraffa 1960; Pasinetti 1977, 1981). This means dealing with proportions, *given* the scale of economic activity. Yet, to work out a long-period theory of employment and output along Keynesian lines, i.e. a theory of the scale of economic activity, is indispensable in establishing a synthesis of classical and Keynesian elements of analysis. Such a theory is, in fact, required to replace the classical and neoclassical long-period full employment theories based on different versions of Say's law. A combination of the classical approach to value and distribution and Keynesian employment theory based on the principle of effective demand will then emerge. Given the overwhelming importance of this principle, which allows one to catch the influence of the *whole* socioeconomic and political system on the scale of economic activity (chapter 4, pp. 142–204), the attribute *Keynesian* to complement the term *classical* is fully justified to denote non-orthodox efforts made to explain what is going on in the real world.

This point is reinforced by the fact that Keynes was not just a conventional economist, but a social scientist in the broader sense of the word who sought to establish a middle-way alternative to both *laissez-faire* and central planning (see Fitzgibbons 1988, pp. 1–2). Keynes's work is based on a clear-cut social and political philosophy and on a fundamental theory of knowledge (Keynes 1971c). The latter adapts traditional metaphysical thinking, based on deductive logic associated with certainty, to modern scientific requirements, taking due account of the tentative and imperfect nature of human intellectual activities. These essential points have been extensively argued by Fitzgibbons (1988) and O'Donnell (1989). Keynes's all-embracing vision of things constitutes a crucial element in laying the foundations for a comprehensive classical-Keynesian system (chapters 2 and 7).

The principal aim of this study is precisely to suggest that classical-Keynesian political economy may be considered the economic theory of the *third-way* alternative to both liberalism and socialism. This requires a wider view of the social sciences that would allow for a search for principles which, on the one hand, could serve as a basis to enhance the coherence within the classical-Keynesian system and, on the other, could establish the position of this system as the political economy of the *middle way*. To prepare the ground, a few fundamentals are examined in the next two chapters. Some basic issues in the social sciences are discussed in chapter 2. Starting from a specific definition of the 'social' and from the concept of 'institution', observations are made on the relationship between social philosophies and the social sciences, on ethics and economics and on determinism and causality. Subsequently, some issues of knowledge about social affairs are sketched. Fundamentals related specifically to classical-Keynesian political economy are set forth in chapter 3 which begins with some definitional issues and continues with a sketch of the classical-Keynesian vision of society and the role institutions play therein.

Institutions are particularly important with the old classicals. Therefore, in the subsequent section, the theoretical heritage of classical, and physiocratic, political economy is briefly examined; there it is suggested that the classical system of thought needs to be complemented by Keynesian economic theory. The final two sections of this chapter are methodological. The former outlines a very general framework to broadly systematize theoretical work; the latter provides some hints as to how a classical-Keynesian synthesis might supply a framework to help organize historical investigations. This important methodological point will be taken up at several places, e.g. in chapter 4 (pp. 241–51).

Subsequently, an attempt is made to clear the way to develop a classical-Keynesian synthesis (chapter 4). Since a large body of classical-Keynesian theories already exists, the emphasis is laid on filling gaps and on suggesting how existing pieces of classical and Keynesian theory might be combined. The latter are not presented explicitly. Only comments will be made and implications brought out.

The most obvious gap is the lack of a comprehensive long-period theory of employment, and this is sketched in the third section of chapter 4. Starting from the basis laid by Pasinetti (1981) it will become evident that, presumably, no major difficulties exist in combining long-period theories of employment and output along Keynesian lines with neo-Ricardian views on value and distribution. This long-period (neo-Ricardian and Keynesian) basis may be combined with Robinsonian or Kaleckian cycle-cum-growth theory. Finally, some suggestions are given as to how uncertainty and money might be integrated into a classical framework.

Chapter 5 deals with some fundamental differences between classical-Keynesian political economy and neoclassical economics. Initially a few divergences with respect to content and method are discussed. Later, some implications hidden behind the premises underlying the two approaches are examined, and the crucial importance of the capital theory debate for discriminating between the classical-Keynesian and the neoclassical approaches on the theoretical level is set forth.

The final chapters, 6 and 7, attempt to uncover the practical relevance and the deeper social and philosophical meaning of classical-Keynesian political economy.

On the methodological level the present study represents an extension and application of Ricardo's *essentialist method* (Pribram 1986, p. 597) put to use in his *Principles of Political Economy and Taxation*. Observable reality, i.e. empirical facts, appearances or phenomena, merely provide the starting point to consider *principles* in various domains of the social sciences, mainly political economy and economics, and, if necessary, in social philosophy, politics, law and sociology. To deal with principles means looking for essentials and enables the theorist to set up and to combine simple causal models, for example Keynesian multiplier models and production models of the Sraffa–Pasinetti type.

Principles and the associated essentials are perfectly general and hold at all times and places. For example, Keynes's multiplier principle – a short-period specification of the principle of effective demand – aims to explain the determination of the short-period level of employment in general, not for some specific country or region. The 'general' is the domain of pure theory. If the level of abstraction were lowered to consider particular cases, clarity would be lost and exposition would become exceedingly complex because specific applied models which reflect the different institutional set-ups prevailing in various countries and regions would have to be developed. This is the task of practical and specialized social scientists who are familiar with particular situations, not of the theoretical economist. Hence to identify fundamentals and to discuss principles allows us to keep the size of the present study manageable.

In the social sciences, perhaps even more than in the natural sciences, the complexity of the object of inquiry, i.e. society, requires dealing with principles. Society is an interrelated whole which, as will be suggested, is something more than the sum of its elements. Individuals act within social structures, i.e. systems of (complementary) institutions, having laws of their own whereby actions and structures mutually influence each other. Aspects of the social structure and of the behaviour of individuals may be analysed separately, but links between these different aspects of reality have to be established continuously in the light of the broad functioning of society as a whole, whereby account has to be taken of how the latter is perceived. Moreover, since each historical situation is unique, analysis and synthesis on the theoretical level have to be complemented by an understanding of unique socioeconomic phenomena if specific historical investigations are undertaken. Given the complexity of the object, the premises underlying social theories cannot be found empirically. These are derived from the vision held by the theorist; however, empirical facts, i.e. real world phenomena, initiate, as a rule, systematic reasoning.

The highly complex subject matter considered, combined with the fact that the study of principles is primary, has various implications. First, it will be seen in chapter 4 that classical-Keynesian political economy cannot consist of a single all-purpose basic model – such as the general equilibrium model – to be put to use mechanically to explain *all* economic events on the basis of a single principle, e.g. supply and demand. Purely theoretical and fundamental models (e.g. Pasinetti 1981), which picture *essential* features of some sphere of reality, are merely *part* of a comprehensive classical-Keynesian framework, which consists of pure *and* applied theory; the structure of Keynes's *Treatise on Money* provides a good example of this classification: volume I is denoted 'The pure theory of money', volume II 'The applied theory of money'. The body of pure theory is perhaps best seen as a combination of a set of causal models, each of which is designed to explain on a fundamental or essential level – that is, in principle – some important socioeconomic phenomenon, for example value, distribution or employment (chapter 3, pp. 103–18, and chapter 4, pp. 142–204). Since social phenomena are organically interrelated, classical-Keynesian economics will have to be, essentially, political economy and must, as such, be closely linked to other social sciences (sociology, politics, law, history). To ensure coherence between the various social sciences these must be based on a vision of man and society, which, in turn, requires a social philosophy (chapter 2).

If classical-Keynesian theory were not put into a wider philosophical framework, there would be the danger of its becoming an auxiliary theory to be used to repair certain defects of liberal or, eventually, socialist economics; for example, Keynesian economics was absorbed by Samuelson's neoclassical synthesis. The reason is that the rival approaches, neoclassical economics and the economic theory of socialism, are themselves based on social philosophies, i.e. liberalism and socialism; this partly accounts for the powerful impact on policy-making of neoclassical economics and of the economic theory of socialism. Hence the social philosophy underlying classical-Keynesian political economy and the way in which it is linked with other social sciences must be sketched broadly if the attempt to establish an alternative to neoclassical and to socialist economic theory is ultimately to succeed (chapters 2, 3, 5 and 7).

Second, given the great number of problems arising, it is inevitable that most of them can only be outlined. For example, at various points, suggestions are made on how to integrate uncertainty into the classical-Keynesian framework (specifically in chapter 3, pp. 103–18, and chapter 4, pp. 220–9). The precise way in which this is to be done on the basis of existing work (by Keynes, Davidson, Minsky and Shackle, for instance) is left to the specialized reader. Thus, whenever issues are simply raised, presentation is necessarily very sketchy, leaving to the reader the task of completing the picture. However, when it seemed clear that gaps had to be filled, a more specific and textbook-like way of presentation was adopted. This especially holds for chapter 4 (pp. 142–204) where a long-period theory of output and employment determination is outlined.

Third, the complexity of the object of investigation renders some repetitions unavoidable in spite of the fact that the analysis is confined to a few fundamentals only. The same point has to be taken up in different contexts, which, it is hoped, will make reading easier. However, since the vision of society underlying the present study is not mechanical and individualistic, but organic and social in an essential way, the reader must not expect a linear and logically impeccable presentation of the main issues, i.e. an exposition starting from given premises. Rather, the following analysis is circular in the sense that an attempt is made to grasp the main problems by looking at the object – economy and society – from different points of view, while always having an eye on the functioning of society as a whole; given this, there are no realistic premises to start with. This implies that the study is a composition which should be seen as an integrated whole; it would thus not be legitimate to consider sentences and passages in isolation. Moreover, many passages, taken for themselves, may be only partly true or even wrong, although the argument as a whole may be broadly sound. Given all this, 'much goodwill . . . and a large measure of co-operation [will be required from the reader]. [For it is] of the essential nature of economic exposition that it gives, not a complete statement, which, even if it were possible, would be prolix and complicated to the point of obscurity but a sample statement, so to speak, out of all the things which could be said, intended to suggest to the reader the whole bundle of associated ideas' (Keynes 1973b, p. 470).

Fourth, since in this study we deal exclusively with general and abstract principles and pure theories derived therefrom, presentation is bound to be rigid and mechanistic and a dogmatic flavour may be attached to it. This is not to enounce 'absolute truths', however. The subsequent propositions are meant to be tentative and probable in the sense of Keynes's theory of knowledge which will be sketched in chapter 2 (pp. 57–64). Hence the following is not about real world phenomena, but about the principles that might govern these. Statements about the former are merely used to illustrate the latter.

Finally, no attempt has been made to integrate systematically the very extensive secondary and tertiary literature. This would have obscured the argument and swelled the book to encyclopaedic proportions. A few basic works form, then, the background of subsequent argument: Quesnay's *Tableau économique*, Adam Smith's *Wealth of Nations*, Ricardo's *Principles* and Marx's *Kapital*, Marshall's *Principles*, Walras's *Elements* and Keynes's *General Theory*, complemented by modern presentations and variations of classical and Keynesian theories, for example Sraffa (1960), Pasinetti (1977, 1981, 1993), Robinson (1962a, 1965), some of Kaldor's articles on growth, distribution and economic development, and Kalecki (1971). It is hoped that this way of proceeding will facilitate reading, though it must be admitted that many issues dealt with below have been treated more fully, and hence in a more satisfactory way, somewhere else in the secondary literature.

In some instances, we have even refrained from taking account of primary literature and presented very sketchy personal views only. This particularly holds true of chapters 2, 3 and 7 where some fundamental concepts and issues in the social sciences are discussed; for example, the concept of *institution* which enables us to establish links between political economy and other social sciences (sociology, political sciences, law), and *social philosophies* which underlie the various approaches in economics and in other social sciences thus providing a unifying framework for all the social sciences. To discuss systematically the immense amount of literature available on institutions and social philosophies would, on the one hand, exceed by far the capacities of a single author; on the other hand, any attempt to discuss at length some fundamental work of sociology or social philosophy would have been arbitrary and would have diverted too much from the main line of argument. However, the chapters on fundamentals could not have been written without the continuous support provided by Johannes Hirschberger's great history of philosophy (Hirschberger 1984, 1988).

In the present work, the social sciences – politics, law, political economy and sociology – are considered a unity. Each social science deals with a specific aspect of the socioeconomic system; however, the various domains complement each other to make up an entity. This study is, therefore, addressed to all social scientists, including social philosophers and historians. To be sure, there is a considerable danger that specialized social scientists may be disappointed by the following. However, on deeper reflection, specialists should be aware that the significance of their work is greatly enhanced if put into a larger context. Consequently, the present study is essentially constructive. An attempt is made to set up a comprehensive framework that should enable us to broadly classify and to mutually recognize work done in the social sciences. It is our conviction that each serious and well-intentioned theoretical or empirical piece of work is useful and thereby contributes to the increase of knowledge on social matters in the broadest sense.

Nevertheless, in what follows, some critical remarks on neoclassical economics will be made, mainly in chapter 5. To avoid misunderstandings, however, it should be mentioned that the term *neoclassical economics* is used here in the sense of *equilibrium economics* of the Walras–Arrow–Debreu type and the Marshallian textbook simplifications derived therefrom. What will be criticized is *not* the description and analysis of equilibrium situations, but the fact that the question of tendencies towards possible equilibria has been unduly neglected by equilibrium economists. Consequently, equilibrium economics appears to a classical-Keynesian political economist as essentially normative or, eventually, hypothetical:

equilibria picture states of the world which are desirable in certain respects because they imply allocative efficiency and, most importantly, full employment. It is very likely that Walras also conceived of the competitive equilibrium as a normative guiding star (see Jaffé 1983b). The concepts used in equilibrium models provide the glasses through which reality is examined. Marshall in particular identified the law of supply and demand as the fundamental principle regulating economic life. Subsequently, neoclassical economists interpret reality in terms of deviations from these ideal (or hypothetical) states of the world, whereby various obstructions may prevent economies from getting into equilibrium, such as rigid money wages, monopolies, and excessive state and trade union activity.

In many instances, however, neoclassical economists, when trying to explain reality in terms of deviations from equilibrium, became involved in explaining reality to such an extent as to forget about the equilibrium model which had served as a starting point. Schumpeter is an important example. His *History of Economic Analysis* focuses on the Walrasian equilibrium system. In large passages of *Capitalism, Socialism and Democracy*, however, Schumpeter gives, among other topics, a brilliant account of capitalist reality which is thoroughly classical-Keynesian in spirit and is, as such, completely independent of equilibrium economics. This dichotomy between pure normative theory and theoretical attempts to explain reality also appears in the work of other neoclassical, or originally neoclassical, authors, Marshall, Wicksell and Keynes being perhaps the most prominent figures in point. Even Walras felt the need to go beyond pure normative theory and to deal with the real world. Some of his writings in this field are gathered in *Etudes d'économie appliquée (Théorie de la production de la richesse sociale)* and in *Etudes d'économie sociale (Théorie de la répartition de la richesse sociale)*. In Jaffé (1983a, pp. 36–52) and Walker (1987) some surprising statements on Walras as an 'applied social scientist' can be found. For example, he proposed that taxes be abolished, and land be nationalized 'and rented by the state to private users, providing it with revenue . . . Arguing that his advocation of nationalization of land and natural monopolies was based upon a scientific analysis, Walras called himself a "scientific socialist"[!]' (Walker 1987, p. 860).

The case of Keynes is particularly interesting. On the one hand, regarding the long run, he remained a neoclassical equilibrium economist: he accepted the first neoclassical postulate (the real wage equals the marginal product of labour) and used the concept of the marginal efficiency of capital. But Keynes considered long-period equilibria as irrelevant. What is the point of discussing such equilibria if, starting from a heavy disequilibrium situation, it takes twenty, thirty or even fifty years to reach a long-period equilibrium even when the given situation works out without being disturbed – which is never the case anyway? Keynes's answer is well known: since 'in the long run we are all dead', let us concentrate upon the short run where the action takes place. This pragmatic way of looking at things led Keynes to analyse real world problems, e.g. involuntary unemployment. In the process of working out a short-period theory of employment he rediscovered the old principle of *effective demand*, implicitly held by some mercantilists, and formulated it in a theoretically satisfactory way (see especially chapter 23 of the *General Theory*). In doing so Keynes provided one cornerstone of middle-way economic theory – the other was provided by Piero Sraffa who initiated the definitive revival of classical (Ricardian) economics.

Incidentally, Keynes was clearly aware of the double nature of neoclassical economics, i.e. 'normative equilibrium economics' and 'analysis of reality':

So long as economists are concerned with what is called the [neoclassical!] theory of value, they have been accustomed to teach that prices are governed by the conditions of supply and demand; and, in particular, changes in marginal costs and the elasticity of short-period supply have played a prominent part. But when they pass in volume II, or more often in a separate treatise, to the theory of money and prices, we hear no more of these homely but intelligible concepts and move into a world where prices are governed by the quantity of money, by its income-velocity . . . by hoarding, by forced saving, by inflation and deflation *et hoc genus omne* . . . We have all of us become used to finding ourselves sometimes on the one side of the moon and sometimes on the other, without knowing what route or journey connects them, related, apparently, after the fashion of our waking or dreaming lives (Keynes 1973a, p. 292).

It seems evident that the understanding of real world phenomena has been furthered by using the framework of monetary theory, i.e. 'volume II-type work'. Again, Keynes is the best example one can find. Starting from *The Economic Consequences of the Peace* and *A Tract on Monetary Reform*, passing through the *Treatise on Money*, he ended up with the *General Theory*. Many neoclassical economists (Marshall, Wicksell and others), in doing 'volume II-type work', paved the way for Keynes's performance. As such, this type of neoclassical writing has been preparatory to classical-Keynesian theory, too, and is obviously not the target of the critical remarks on neoclassical theory to be found in the following lines. Whenever neoclassical economics is criticized below, we have in mind neoclassical equilibrium theory linked with claims that, in the real world, there should be an inherent tendency towards a state of full-employment equilibrium if markets were functioning satisfactorily.

In criticizing neoclassical equilibrium theory, we do not mean that Walrasian and Marshallian equilibrium economics and its developments are wrong or even useless. Neoclassical equilibrium economics is a great system which had to be worked out in order to clarify the basic issues associated with the economic theory of liberalism. Walrasian economics deals with a very important question: can a social optimum implying full employment, i.e. allocative efficiency, be derived from actions based upon the pursuit of individual aims, that is utility and profit maximization, if the institutional set-up allows for a sufficient degree of competition? This question can be put in other ways. For example, Adam Smith dealt with the implications of the invisible hand. Or, Max Weber and Carl Menger attempted to find out whether methodological individualism could provide a conceptual basis for the social sciences.

This question is of crucial importance and answers had to be attempted, almost of historical necessity. To this end, neoclassical economists of the Walrasian strand worked out equilibrium systems, the logical beauty of which was widely admired. Quite soon, however, it became evident that the possible existence of an equilibrium or of a set of equilibria was one thing, but the tendency towards an equilibrium was another. The terrain became very slippery once disequilibrium situations were faced and dynamic processes investigated. This implies that the Marshallian textbook simplifications aimed at analysing real world problems with the help of 'partial equilibrium models' stand on shaky foundations, especially if macroeconomic problems, like the determination of the scale of output and employment or the distribution of national income are tackled.

All this does not mean that no more work ought to be done in equilibrium economics, but simply that other approaches, like classical-Keynesian-cum-Marxian political economy for example, should get more attention and thus a fairer treatment. What is criticized here is the 'excessive generalization of the principle of exchange' linked up with an equally excessive formalization and mathematization. It is certainly justified to formalize aspects of reality in order to clarify concepts and to delimit the scope for generalization. However, we should not lose sight of the link between a selected aspect of social life and society as a whole. Specifically, the influence of institutions on the outcome of economic and social events should again be given increased attention by economists. It is not sufficient to study only the actions of individuals in the market-place and to take the social structures within which individuals act as given, nor to consider problems of social structure as being the concern of the politician, the sociologist, the lawyer and the historian.

To avoid misunderstandings it ought to be mentioned that, when considering institutions, we do not primarily adopt here the point of view of modern 'institutional economics', or 'new institutionalism', which, in fact, represents the pragmatic application of simplified neoclassical economics to economic, social and political institutions (see, for example, Pies 1993, who deals with the work of Max Weber, Hayek, Becker, Buchanan, Olson and Williamson). While this approach is very useful in explaining the coming into being, the functioning and the desirability of single institutions, it cannot deal with the institutional set-up, i.e. society as a whole, which is something more than the sum of all institutions. In the present book, specifically in chapters 2 and 3, we shall mainly be concerned with the functioning of the social system which is broadly in line with 'old-fashioned' institutionalism. This implies considering single institutions as parts of the entire institutional system.

A broad definition of classical-Keynesian political economy can now be provided, although this definition will be discussed more fully in the next chapter. Negatively, all economists who are neither neoclassical equilibrium economists nor adherents to the economic theory of centrally planned socialism may be considered classical-Keynesians. Positively, this holds for all political economists who, when attempting to explain aspects of socioeconomic reality, recognize explicitly or implicitly the following three principles: first, long-period normal prices are set by adding a mark-up on primary or variable costs at normal capacity utilization so as to cover fixed costs and to achieve some target rate of profit. There may be variations of this general rule: for example, the mark-up may be on total costs at normal capacity utilization. In the short- and medium-term market prices may vary with demand conditions; or, if technical full-capacity utilization is approached prices may increase with 'marginal costs'. Second, functional income distribution is, in the long run, not regulated on factor markets but is governed by institutions, e.g. trade unions, entrepreneurial associations and the state, which may intervene to fix wage minima: distribution is a social, not an economic problem. In the medium and short terms, profits are determined according to the Kaldorian mechanism, i.e. by investment activity. Again, in the short run, market wage rates and realized profits may deviate from their respective long-period normal levels. Third, output and employment are, in a monetary production economy, governed by effective demand. The supply of resources governs economic activity in full-employment situations only when, or if, on account of structural imbalances, bottlenecks occur.

Two broad groups of classical-Keynesian economists may be distinguished. First, there are the empirically and historically minded political economists who primarily describe historical developments and the functioning of institutions in the tradition of the German Historical School and of American Institutionalism. Within this pragmatic strand, theory is pushed into the background which means that the above principles are assumed implicitly. A second group of classical-Keynesian political economists is theoretically minded. Their precursors are Quesnay, Ricardo, Marx, Keynes and Kalecki. This group includes Joan Robinson, Geoffrey Harcourt, Nicholas Kaldor, Luigi Pasinetti and Piero Sraffa and their followers. This book is devoted to both groups, although the theoretical strand is emphasized.

2 Some basic concepts and issues in the social sciences

The present chapter deals with a few essentials related to society and to knowledge about society. These will enable us to broadly sketch the wider significance of classical-Keynesian political economy. The fact that essentials are dealt with is crucial. The starting point is not provided by real existing societies about which generalizations are made. Instead we start with sets of principles which are supposed to reflect different visions of the essence of man and of society. For example, the liberal social scientist will consider the individual as primary and social phenomena as derived and secondary, and vice versa for the social scientist adhering to the socialist vision.

Starting from the definition of the social state of affairs, or the *social*, the problem of institutions and behaviour is sketched. Subsequently, some implications of specific social philosophies for the respective systems of social science are set forth. The relationship between ethics and economics is dealt with briefly. Here, the notion of alienation, which links the positive to the normative, is of particular importance. Finally in this section a few suggestions are made on the issues of determinism, free choice and causality.

The second section starts with some remarks on the nature of knowledge in the social sciences, broadly based on Keynes's *Treatise on Probability* (1971c). Subsequently, the importance of the vision for theoretical approaches is stressed. The section closes with some remarks on the relationship between ethics and knowledge.

Society and individuals

Defining 'the social'

Whether made explicit or not, all systems of social science, and indeed all social theories, rest on a social philosophy. The latter could be defined as the analytical articulation – the formulation of constitutive principles – of a social scientist's vision of the broad functioning of societies. In this sense we may speak of the social philosophy of liberalism or of socialism. The notion of 'the social state of affairs' or, to simplify, 'the social' is fundamental to characterizing social philosophies. It would seem that two basically different meanings of the social are conceived of and used in a great number of varieties and combinations in systematic. thinking on social matters. With the first meaning, the social denotes relationships and interactions between formally equal, autonomous and self-contained individuals and collectives striving at individual aims; specialization, competition and substitution characterize these relations. Social phenomena come into being through explicit and implicit contracts between individuals and collectives. The relationship between sellers and buyers would be a social phenomenon in this sense.

The second meaning of the social stands for the relationship between unequal, incomplete and therefore mutually dependent individuals who require each other to be able to reach common aims, on the one hand, and social groups or entities, including society as a whole, on the other. Such part–whole relationships are characterized by complementarity between various functions, which in turn requires co-operation and co-ordination. The concept of social status is one way of summarizing complex qualitative part–whole relationships. Examples for this meaning of the social are the position and the function of individuals or groups in some enterprise within which a sophisticated division of labour prevails, the determination of shares in a given national income, the structure of wages in a monetary production economy, or the status of dignitaries in a feudal society. This second, more fundamental meaning of the social is used in the following if not otherwise indicated.

Each type of the social is associated with specific kinds of institutions. The first is linked with individualistic institutions which include regulated behaviour of individuals (regulated by habits, for example) and permanent and standardized interactions between individuals and collectives (e.g. permanent relationships between buyers and sellers). In this kind of institution the regulated actions of individuals directed at individual aims are primary and the social – the interaction between individuals – is secondary. The second meaning of the social is associated with social institutions: here the social entity – the enterprise, the production system or the state – is primary and the social behaviour of individuals secondary.

Institutions and behaviour: the social system and the behaviour of individuals

The notion of *institution* plays a crucial role in the social sciences. Socioeconomic and political institutions make up the social structure within which individuals and collectives behave in specific ways. Hence society may be conceived of as an arrangement of institutions which constitutes the social groundwork within which individuals and collectives act. In this subsection, institutions are broadly defined and a few problems related to institutions raised; some of these problems will be taken up later on, for example in chapter 3 (pp. 75–89) where the classical-Keynesian vision of society is set out. Here, issues are merely touched upon. Only passing account will be taken of the immense literature in sociology and political science where institutions are dealt with extensively. This leaves the widest possible scope for elaborating on the theme of 'political economy and institutions'.

What, then, is an institution? According to Veblen's definition, recalled by Eric Roll, '[i]nstitutions are principles of action about the stability and finality of which men entertain practically no doubt' (Roll 1973, p. 445). This definition reflects Veblen's psychological and behavioural approach (p. 445): institutions are habits that have developed historically and represent regulated behaviour directed towards individual aims. Gustav Schmoller, however, sees institutions as *social* phenomena (social in the proper sense); social aims shape definite areas of social life and determine the associated social behaviour: 'By a political, legal or economic institution we understand a largely independent partial order of social life directed towards a definite aim which provides a durable framework for persistent action' (Schmoller 1920, vol. I, p. 61; a.tr.). Property, slavery, markets and money are, according to Schmoller, examples of institutions. The social and the system aspects are clearly emphasized by him: 'Each sphere of action directed at common purposes encompasses a system of agencies which form a whole and develop in intimate connection and partly simultaneously with agencies of other domains of life' (p. 63; a.tr.). Social institutions are interrelated and complement each other to form part–whole relationships with society as a whole; economic institutions, particularly production, provide the material basis for social, political and cultural life; legal institutions set up and enforce rules that are required for the proper functioning of all spheres of life; political institutions ought to deal with the socially appropriate arrangement of all institutions such that the scope for freedom is as large as possible.

This suggests that there are basically two different ways of looking at institutions. Traditional institutionalism, as is implied in the work of Marx, specifically in his *Kapital*, and of the German Historical School (for example, Schmoller 1920), does not consider the individual institution *per se* but as part of the institutional structure; institutions are complementary and interrelated; society forms a system and is, therefore, something more than the sum of the individual institutions. There must be macroprinciples, for example the principle of effective demand or the value system prevailing in a society, that govern the shape of social structures or the arrangement of institutions. This is in striking contrast to the procedure adopted by the neoclassical new institutionalism which investigates how individual institutions work, whereby it is implicitly postulated that the co-ordination between individuals and institutions and between institutions themselves is performed by some anonymous mechanism of the invisible-hand type, for example voting procedures and markets. The new institutionalism is very useful if a partial understanding of social life is sought. However, to enable social scientists to develop an approximate knowledge of the functioning of society as a whole this type of institutionalism has to be complemented by traditional institutionalism, which is put to the fore in this study.

These preliminary remarks lead on to distinguishing two broad types of institution. First, there are institutions which come into being if one, several or all individuals of a society persistently behave or are forced to act in the same (or in a strongly similar) way in order to reach individual aims. Such types of regulated behaviour or of determined action we call *individualistic institutions*. These are brought about by custom and habits, having developed historically, or by legal rules which may be enforced if necessary. For example, specific types of 'conspicuous consumption' (Veblen) may become an institution brought about by custom; the same is true of certain ways to achieve short-period utility maximization. In contrast, the obligation to drive on the left-hand side (in certain countries) is a legally enforced institution which makes it possible to achieve an individual aim in an orderly way. Persistent actions of outstanding individuals, such as artists or political leaders, having a significant impact on other individuals are also individualistic institutions.

A second type of institution, the *social institution*, obtains if several or all members of a society persistently pursue common or social aims that isolated individuals could not achieve. In doing so, individuals or groups of individuals exercise differing complementary functions (planning or executive, physical or intellectual) within a social institution; co-operation and co-ordination are essential if such institutions are to function properly. In this sense, football teams, choral societies and enterprises are social institutions. But the most striking example of a social institution is the process of production, made up of the relations and the forces of production (technology). This reflects the classical-Marxian view of production as a social process: in a monetary production economy based upon extensive division of labour, production of commodities goes on by means of commodities and labour; each sector of production and each enterprise (themselves social institutions), and each individual performs a specific function within the process of production, and thus contributes to reaching a common (social) aim, that is the production of the social or national product. The social nature of production is discussed very extensively in Marx's *Grundrisse* (Marx 1974 [1857/58]).

Social institutions make up the bulk of what we call civil society and the state: football teams pertain to the social sphere; the parliament and the civil service are political institutions; choral societies belong to the cultural sphere; finally, the production system, enterprises, trade unions and entrepreneurial associations (institutions in the sphere of distribution), the system of property rights prevailing in a society and the monetary and financial system (the central bank, commercial banks and insurance companies) are socioeconomic institutions.

For the social scientist in general and the political economist in particular it might be convenient to distinguish between individualistic and social macro-, meso- and microinstitutions respectively, which distinction exhibits an analogy with a well-known classification in economics. An individualistic macroinstitution would relate to the regulation of behaviour of all individuals making up a society, enforced by legal rules for instance; the obligation to drive on the left-hand side would be a case in point. Individualistic mesoinstitutions would refer to the specific individual behaviour of large groups or social classes, obvious examples being provided by group-specific patterns of consumption. Individualistic microinstitutions are associated with persistent types of action by individuals belonging to small groups or by outstanding individuals. For example, Churchill and de Gaulle evidently were institutions in Britain and in France respectively. The most obvious social macroinstitution is the process of production; money and the financial system also constitute social macroinstitutions: they fulfil specific roles within the entire socioeconomic system. A sector of production is a social mesoinstitution. Finally, enterprises or households constitute social microinstitutions.

Another classification of considerable significance should be mentioned here. Some institutions are purposefully created and, as such, result from acts of convention or from acts of legislation; other institutions, however, have developed spontaneously, like money, markets, towns, the division of labour (Menger 1969, pp. 153ff., 171ff.) and the social process of production. The latter could be called natural institutions since they come into being by necessity, because the circumstances or the nature of things enforces them. The distinction between natural and purposefully created institutions is a logical one which relates to principles only. In concrete historical situations, a single institution, money for example, may have come into being spontaneously or by acts of legislation.

In any country or region, institutions have developed historically through purposeful or spontaneous individual and social action and normally change but slowly. Permanence is a very important characteristic of institutions. This property enables institutions to stabilize social and individual life and renders rational action possible. Together with technology, institutions constitute the permanent, but not invariable, long-term forces the neo-Ricardian economists speak about (see, for instance, Bharadwaj 1983, pp. 18–22). Broadly speaking, individualistic and social institutions and their interplay represent the social structure. In any society, institutions are arranged hierarchically: there are more dominant and less dominant institutions; this shapes the qualitative character of social structures.

Societies and the corresponding ways of life are characterized by particular institutional set-ups which rest upon value systems embracing all spheres of individual and social life. Values are intimately related to the aims pursued within institutions and to the means set up to reach these aims and are, as such, of an essentially ethical character. This theme will be taken up later on. Here, another issue should be mentioned. Each society is characterized by a specific hierarchy of values. Actually, economic values, specifically profit-making, dominate in most societies to various extents. Values related to military and economic power always featured prominently. This is not to deny that at times cultural and religious values dominated in specific societies. The point now is that each value system, i.e. a specific hierarchical order of values, is unique. The same is true of the institutional set-up of any society and of its evolution. The unique character of each society has a very important consequence for single institutions. Since each institution performs a specific function in a particular society, the institutional set-up, i.e. society, is a very complex interrelated entity. This renders the transfer of institutions very difficult (Montaner 1948, p. 7), which has important implications for the theory of socioeconomic development, a point briefly taken up in chapter 7 (pp. 393–410).

Owing to the complementarity existing within and between institutions, society is a more or less structured entity which is more than the sum of its parts and which possesses laws of its own. Therefore, 'in regard to practically every economic problem, scientific study must concern the entire social system . . . The reason why this is a methodological imperative is the fact that, among all conditions in that system, there is circular causation. This implies interdependence' (Myrdal 1976b, p. 82). Basically, society may be considered an entity because of the values that are permanently pursued within institutions; values are in turn hierarchically ordered; this specific value system constitutes the essence of any society. Consequently, each institution has a particular significance within some society since there are unique and complex relationships between the parts (institutions) and the whole (society). All this is intuitively evident if one attempts to compare, even broadly and superficially, British, French, German and Italian society, for example.

There is an interplay between institutions – the socioeconomic and political system – and the behaviour of individuals. The system, e.g. legal prescriptions and customs, shapes behaviour in important respects. On the other hand, behaviour gradually modifies the system; for instance, new gross investment resulting from entrepreneurial behaviour slowly changes the composition of the real capital stock. In the opening pages of *Die deutsche Ideologie* Karl Marx and Friedrich Engels remark on this: 'In each period of time there is a material historical result, a collection of productive forces, equipments and circumstances, which, on the one hand, is modified by the new generation, and which, on the other hand, prescribes specific conditions of life to precisely this generation and shapes its development in a definite way – *hence the circumstances shape man, and man gradually forges the circumstances*' (Marx and Engels 1978 [1845], p. 38; a.tr.; our emphasis). The interaction between the circumstances (the institutional system) and human action (behaviour) is a central theme of the present study.

Hence behaviour is partly determined by institutions, but partly there is freedom of choice. Determined behaviour corresponds to the German *Verhalten*; freedom of choice is associated with actions or goal-oriented behaviour (*zielgerichtetes Handeln* or simply *Handeln*). This issue will be taken up in various instances, specifically later in this chapter (pp. 53–7). Here, three concluding remarks on the relationship between institutions and behaviour can be made. First, as is implied in the above, social behaviour takes place within social institutions, e.g. firms; permanent actions aimed at reaching individual aims are regulated by individualistic institutions, e.g. habits. In a way, regulated social and individualisic behaviour always implies participating in already given institutions. This leads to a second point: social and individualistic institutions are interrelated and complementary. Individual aims, writing books for example, can only be reached on the basis of social preconditions, e.g. the scientific work done by other individuals in the course of time, that is the body of scientific knowledge in a particular field. Or, individual acts of consumption can only take place once the social process of production has taken place. Third, behaviour may be permanent – and repetitive – or more or less quickly changing. To permanently obey a legal prescription belongs to the former type of behaviour, the adjustment of prices or of the marketing mix to rapidly evolving market situations to the second. In the present study two different kinds of behaviour are distinguished. Institutionalized or regulated social and individualistic behaviour is associated with institutions, i.e. the socioeconomic and politico-legal system. The more or less quickly changing short- and medium-term behaviour of individuals and collectives in the political, legal, social and economic sphere takes place within the institutional system.

The way in which social scientists perceive the broad functioning of the institutional system and its evolution is of paramount importance to the approach they will choose in order to explain economic phenomena (e.g. value, distribution, employment). Neoclassical and classical-Keynesian economists have entirely different views on this. In the neoclassical view, non-economic institutions influence economic events only indirectly through a natural institution, e.g. the market: institutions govern the position of the various demand and supply curves. In classical-Keynesian political economy direct links between institutions (the entire socioeconomic and political system) and economic phenomena are postulated; this issue will be dealt with in chapter 3 (pp. 89–95) below.

The significance of the institutional system and of changing behaviour is perceived very differently by different social scientists. The social philosophy explicitly or implicitly held by each social scientist is crucial in this respect. The connection between social philosophy and the social sciences is the theme of the next subsection.

Social philosophy and the social sciences

At the level of principles three different social philosophies may be distinguished, each of which has many variants: *liberalism*, *socialism* and *humanism*. Liberalism and socialism are familiar notions. Liberalism puts the individual to the fore, socialism emphasizes society. These systems are primarily normative in character since both represent projects of society. The notion of 'humanism' however is far less familiar. Before defining this term more fully below suffice it to state here that humanism implies a comprehensive vision of man and of society. The individual and the social natures of man are taken account of, as well as positive and normative elements: what is and what ought to be are both grounded in the nature or the essence of man and society. Hence the term humanism is grounded on the Aristotelian system of social and political thought (for an excellent exposition of neo-Aristotelian political philosophy see Brown 1986, chapter 6). In this section we attempt to argue that humanism constitutes a middle-way social philosophy between liberalism and socialism.

The significance allotted to social and to individualistic institutions respectively characterizes social philosophies and implies a specific conception of the social sciences, i.e. politics, economics and political economy, sociology, and private and public law. Put in a nutshell, the meaning and the significance of the term *social* referred to above determines the property of social philosophies and the system of social sciences ensuing therefrom.

The social in the proper sense comprises three elements. First, the common aim, e.g. the production of a good in an enterprise. Second, to reach the common aim in a rational (for example, cost-minimizing) way, division of labour is required; each type of activity defines functions to be exercised by the individuals participating in a social activity. These functions are complementary which presupposes inequality of the individuals participating in some social activity; this is particularly evident in the social process of production based upon division of labour. Third, division of labour requires co-ordination of activities and co-operation between the actors.

Social activities take place in all spheres of life, e.g. in the economic, cultural and political domain. However, in modern industrial societies the social, in the proper sense, features most prominently in the sphere of production. This fact will be stressed in chapters 3 and 4 on classical-Keynesian political economy. Individual actions directed towards individual aims usually take place on the basis of a social foundation. An obvious example is individual consumption activities which necessarily follow the social process of production.

In this subsection we first provide very general working definitions of the social sciences (politics, law, sociology and economics) from two fundamental points of view, i.e. from the perspective of the social system as a whole (implying the social in the proper sense) and from the viewpoint of the behaviour of individuals and collectives (here the social consists of relationships between individuals). This will enable us to sketch the fundamental characteristics of the three above-mentioned social philosophies and to hint at some consequences ensuing for the associated systems of social science.

The object of *politics* in the traditional – Aristotelian – sense is the organization of the social system, i.e. society and the state. Normative politics deals with attempts to approach a harmonious or balanced arrangement of all of society's institutions as closely as possible; the complementarity of socioeconomic, legal and political institutions is emphasized; social facts are rendered possible by the inequality of individuals with respect to dispositions and abilities; inequality enables individuals to fulfil distinct functions when common aims are pursued. An associated problem of traditional politics concerns the form of government and of political institutions both in general and when adapted to particular political communities. Politics in the traditional sense is based on ethics and is therefore teleological; for example, a fundamental question is about the nature of the public interest or the common weal (on this, see the following subsection, pp. 39–53) and how the government should proceed in order to realize this basic political aim as closely as possible. The main problem of traditional politics is therefore about the ethically appropriate organization of society, that is of the social system.

Politics in the modern – Machiavellian – sense deals with the behaviour of politicians and political collectives, political parties for example. The central question is how to get into power and how to preserve power. The New Economic Theory of Politics deals with precisely this question by applying optimizing methods borrowed from neoclassical economics. The question of how to govern is taken for granted and pushed into the background. The main problem here is to create a legal and political framework such that the optimizing behaviour of individuals and collectives may result in a social optimum characterized by a maximum welfare subject to resource constraints. Within this framework, automatic mechanisms are supposed to solve specific problems. The prime example is markets in the economic sphere.

Legal arrangements also relate both to the behaviour of individuals and collectives and to their relationship to society as a whole. The behavioural aspects pertain to the sphere of *private law*, the social or system aspect to the domain of *public law*. Private law orders relationships between individuals or collectives which presupposes equality of individuals with respect to the legal arrangements in question; for example, contracts between – legally equal – sellers and buyers are partly regulated by private law. The corresponding legislation aims at securing certain rights of the individuals concerned.

Public law (in the widest sense of the word) lays down the relations between unequal individuals and some public or social entity. For example, the regulation of income distribution, most importantly functional income distribution and the wage structure, is a social problem and the corresponding legal prescriptions are social arrangements. The problem is to distribute the result of a common – social – effort, the national or social product, according to the performance and the social status of each type of labour. Again, the distribution of power between central and local government is also a matter of public law.

Sociology in the traditional sense deals with the social properties of large groups and with the relationships between them, e.g. the characteristics of the working and propertied classes and their relationship, or with similarities and differences between the population living in towns and in rural areas. The links between such groups and society as a whole and the study of general social phenomena – e.g. the relationship between unemployment and political extremism and crime – are also part of the subject matter of traditional sociology. This kind of sociology deals with the social system as a whole and could be called macrosociology; this is sociology in the sense of Marx and others. Another type of sociology, initiated by Max Weber, deals with the social behaviour of individuals within collectives, families and firms for instance. This is microsociology.

Finally, *political economy* deals with the functioning of the socioeconomic system as a whole in order to explain specific socioeconomic phenomena. For example, Ricardo and Marx brought in the relationship between classes (workers, capitalists and landlords) to explain distribution; or Keynes used the macroeconomic principle of effective demand to show how the scale of employment is determined. *Economics*, however, analyses the behaviour of agents – individuals and collectives – in the economic sphere and the co-ordination of behaviour by the market, which is a natural mechanism.

Given these broad definitions of the social sciences from the point of view of the system and from the perspective of behaviour, the characteristic features of the three fundamental social philosophies may now be sketched.

Liberalism is based on the principle of individualism. The behaviour of the autonomous individual is primary, social phenomena are derived and come into being through explicit or implicit contracts between individuals. This holds for social groupings such as the family and the various economic, political and cultural associations to be found in a society. Some liberal philosophers claim that even the state has come into existence through a contract (*Staatsvertrag*) between individuals.

In the liberal view, the individual, even if socially active, remains autonomous and self-sufficient which means that a liberal society is an atomistic society. Social phenomena do not influence in an essential way the nature or the identity of individuals. Social entities, the family, the enterprise or pressure groups, are merely vehicles which enable individuals to reach individual aims more completely. This implies that liberal institutions essentially reflect regulated behaviour linked with persistent efforts to reach individual aims. Institutions are located, so to speak, in different spheres of life (economic, political, social, legal) where individuals become active as workers, employees, economists, lawyers or politicians. In some spheres individual actions are co-ordinated in a socially meaningful way by 'natural', i.e. not man-made, institutions, or mechanisms: in the economic field, for example, the profit and utility-maximizing actions of economic agents are supposed to be co-ordinated by the market mechanism such that a social optimum obtains, provided there is a sufficiently high degree of competition. Alternatively, in the realm of politics, voting procedures are, in a popular view at least, supposed to bring about socially meaningful solutions to specific political problems.

Hence certain types of regulated behaviour, e.g. investment behaviour of firms or consumption behaviour of households, are the dominating institutions in liberal social philosophy. This automatically implies that social institutions, above all macroinstitutions related to society as a whole, have no meaning of their own; social institutions are explained in terms of the social behaviour of individuals. This involves neglecting in principle the historically grown social structure which, in the real world, may determine individual actions.

Consequently, liberal social philosophy implies a behavioural view of the nature of the social sciences, i.e. politics, law, sociology, political economy and economics. The government and the civil service, which are both social institutions, are there to facilitate the proper functioning of man-made and natural institutions, the market for instance, and to guarantee certain human rights and are, as such, of an auxiliary nature. Politics is essentially power politics: how to get into power and how to preserve it. Specialized experts may provide advice on how to exercise power in specific domains; for example, economists advise governments on economic issues, sociologists provide advice on social problems, lawyers deal with the questions of passing and applying laws; the central problem is to create frameworks for natural mechanisms, e.g. markets and voting procedures, which co-ordinate the optimizing behaviour of individuals. Co-ordination between the various spheres of individual activity has been largely neglected. Presently, consciousness about this lack of co-ordination seems to be growing among liberals. This increasingly results in interdisciplinary activities uniting specialists coming from various fields. Interdisciplinary work in this sense is certainly useful as far as the co-ordination of behaviour is concerned. The limits are set by the fact that the system is more than a co-existence of spheres regulated by automatic mechanisms; the system has laws of its own.

In the light of liberal social philosophy, the social sciences appear as essentially individualistic. The basic problem of the political sciences consists in analysing the behaviour of politically active individuals and parties with the view of getting into power and maintaining power. The liberal legal system primarily aims at partly regulating relations between individuals and collectives in the various spheres where individuals are active, for example in the economic, social and cultural spheres. Private law dominates public and social law: for example, in the sphere of distribution, market forces – relations between individuals, i.e. entrepreneurs and workers – are supposed to govern wage levels and relative wages; distribution is, in a liberal view, not an issue associated with the social system but with the interactions between individuals, whereby these interactions are supposed to be regulated by market forces. Public law may modify private law; for example, the state may fix minimum wage levels and partly regulate working conditions. Sociology deals, in the liberal view, with social behaviour, e.g. with the formation and the behaviour of collectives; as such, sociology is essentially microsociology. This does not exclude the possibility that social goals on the level of society as a whole are pursued; the provision of certain collective goods, e.g. defence and education, are prominent examples. Finally, economics deals with the optimizing behaviour of individuals in the economic sphere and its co-ordination in the market-place. Economics entirely dominates political economy, the object of which is the entire socioeconomic system.

Extreme forms of *socialism*, associated with collective property and with comprehensive central planning of economic activities, are based on the principle of holism; the principle of individualism is of negligible importance, which implies a severely restricted possibility of freedom for individuals. Society is considered an organized whole, a tightly structured entity directed towards some social goal, which might be seen as a complex organism or as a huge machine. Individuals are solely parts of society and are defined by the functions which they exercise within society. Their actions are, therefore, almost uniquely determined by social requirements. For example, in a centrally planned economy, managers of enterprises have limited scope for taking decisions on pricing and on the quantity and the quality of production; socialist factories stand in the service of the central planners and thus of the state. Taken in isolation, the individual is, if socialism takes on extreme forms, as largely devoid of significance as are the individual parts of an engine. The latter are intrinsically useless; put together they form a powerful entity. Socialism, if pushed to the extreme, thus ends up in totalitarianism. Only society counts and the individual is neglected. As recent history shows this is valid for socialist societies of the right or of the left type.

In such a society, a single social institution, e.g. the government or the state or party bureaucracy, pursues social goals such as strengthening the power and the international position of a country and dominates all other institutions. Duties towards the community become all important and dominate the rights of individuals. This means that public law which regulates the relationships between individuals and society dominates; private law, ordering relations between individuals, is of secondary importance. Natural institutions like the market or voting procedures are not allowed to function or are largely meaningless in a totalitarian society. Sociology is essentially macrosociology which deals with the role of institutions within the social structure and with the relationship between large social groups, for example workers, the bureaucracy, and the rural and urban populations. Politics is about how to govern: Soviet governments had to follow strict rules established by the party; for example, in the thirties an important social aim was to maximize investment and government expenditures and to minimize consumption. Individualistic aspects of politics are of secondary importance. How to get into power may raise temporary problems, e.g. the election of a new party leader; however, to stay in power is, in principle, devoid of difficulties, given the extreme concentration of power which may make use of sheer force. Finally, political economy essentially means planning of prices and quantities, at least in the sectors producing essential goods. The economic theory of socialism essentially aims at perfecting the planning mechanism and is, as such, pure political economy. Economics is not required in a centrally planned system because behaviour in the economic sphere is largely determined by the system, i.e. the planning mechanism. The market system merely enters the picture in the form of shadow or black markets.

There are other forms of socialism besides the totalitarian type. Karl Marx, for instance, clearly thought of society as being an integrated whole which has, however, to serve individuals: society ought to constitute a framework within which individuals may prosper. This not only emerges from some of Marx's early writings, the *Paris Manuscripts* for instance, but is also illustrated by a famous passage in *Das Kapital* (Marx 1973–74a [1867–94], vol. III, p. 828) where Marx speaks about the realm of necessity (*Reich der Notwendigkeit*) and the realm of liberty (*Reich der Freiheit*). The former relates to the social process of production where determinism prevails, the latter to leisure time and to the use of the surplus which is associated with freedom. These non-totalitarian forms of socialism are in fact variants of middle-way social philosophies.

The various forms of liberalism and socialism are essentially normative. Both are projects of society which ought to be brought into being or to which concretely existing liberal or socialist societies ought to correspond as closely as possible. The idea of progress is fundamental to liberalism and socialism. In the liberal view, material and institutional progress is conceived to be continuous with the ideal being gradually approached. For most socialists the normative element was unimportant since socialism, characterized by the abolition of private property and of class differences, was self-evident and was considered the inevitable goal of an objective and deterministic historical process.

Finally, *humanism* represents a middle way between liberalism and socialism. This not very familiar notion may perhaps be characterized most appropriately by two historical reference points provided by Aristotle and Marx. Aristotle's conception of society and of man is set forth in his *Politics* and *Nicomachean Ethics:* 'Man is a social being' (Aristotle, *Politics*, 1253a1) and, it could be added, an individual. In his *Grundrisse* Marx speaks of the *social individual* (Marx 1974 [1857/58]). This double dimension of man makes each individual a unique person who has duties towards society and simultaneously possesses personal dignity and individual rights. In his early writings, particularly in his *Paris Manuscripts* (Marx 1973 [1844]), Marx sketches his vision of a harmonious society within which individuals could prosper. Marx equates humanism and naturalism to designate a vision of a society which is free from the internal contradictions and the alienation which characterize unrestricted capitalism (Marx 1973 [1844], p. 577). In this context Marx mentions that 'naturalism or humanism is distinct from idealism and materialism and encompasses both notions' (p. 577; a.tr.). Hence humanism also encompasses, besides the social and the individual, positive and normative elements of the real world and provides as such a comprehensive vision of man and of society.

To be sure, there are problems with the term humanism, mainly because it is already associated with specific meanings; for example, individualistic humanism is associated with the resurgence of ancient literature and philosophy in the fifteenth and sixteenth centuries and with the Enlightenment in the eighteenth century. Nevertheless, humanism in a broader sense, encompassing the social dimension of man, seems most appropriate for denoting a specific middle-way social philosophy of the Aristotelian type which may provide solid conceptual foundations for the social sciences associated with classical-Keynesian political economy. One of the main links between humanist social philosophy and political economy is provided by Karl Marx who, after having partly abandoned Hegel, started off as a humanist social philosopher along Aristotelian lines (for example, Marx 1973 [1844], and Marx 1978 [1845]) subsequently to become an important political economist in the classical tradition (Marx 1973/74a [1867–94], 1973/74b [1862–63]).

Social philosophy on Aristotelian lines has a long and distinguished tradition. Great social and political scientists as diverse as Aquinas, Adam Smith, Karl Marx, Carl Menger and Maynard Keynes all admired Aristotle. Moreover, modern writers, such as Brown (1986, chapter 6), de Laubier (1987) and Schack (1978), all present social philosophies elaborated on Aristotelian lines. On the actual significance of Aristotle Brown and de Laubier are particularly explicit. Having considered the utilitarian system, the theory of John Rawls, the approach of Robert Nozick and Marx's position, Brown states: 'The distinctive features of [these approaches] are presented as leading on to [a] more adequate theory, that of neo-Aristotelianism. This, the last of the methods considered, is argued to be the correct approach to political philosophy both on the basis of the failures of its rivals and on its own merits' (Brown 1986, p. 10). Similarly, de Laubier states: 'Aristotle's astonishing genius decisively contributes to the understanding of human and social issues even if one cannot agree with some of his conclusions. Better than anybody else he enables us to come to grips with a very complex debate by setting forth the great possible options' (de Laubier 1987, p. 8; a.tr.).

Aristotle starts from the indestructible human nature which encompasses the individual and the social or co-operative dispositions: man is a social being or a social individual. In modern terms, these dispositions are expressed by individualistic and social institutions in each society. The existence of the latter implies that, in a logical sense, society is primary and individuals secondary. This does not imply that man is solely part of the social machine as is the case with totalitarian socialism. On the one hand, social institutions – production, the legal system, the organization of political life – are preconditions for the actions of individuals; on the other hand, to participate in social activities, e.g. production or social and cultural associations, is essential for individuals to prosper, i.e. to more fully realize their potentials. Within the institutional framework individual and social aims are pursued. Technology and social institutions thus represent the historically grown social structure within which individuals act. The most striking feature of the social structure is perhaps the natural arrangement of institutions: the process of production, a social macroinstitution, provides the material basis of social and individual life; the use of the social surplus emerging from production shapes the institutional superstructure which comprises political, legal and cultural institutions. This aspect of society was emphasized by the classical political economists and by François Quesnay and Karl Marx and will be considered more closely in chapter 3 (pp. 89–95).

Three features of the social philosophy of humanism require some consideration. There is first its essentially ethical character which follows from Aristotle's teleological approach: actions of individuals or collectives are always directed towards some individual or social aim. The hierarchically ordered set of aims pursued on the basis of the corresponding value system within a given society determines the character, the specific feature of that society which may be broadly summarized by the concept of *way of life*. The interrelated value system and the associated organization of individual and social life, reflected in institutions, makes any society a structured entity. The values held are part of the real world and may be ethically good or bad in varying degrees: there will always be a smaller or larger gap between the value system actually prevailing in some society and an objectively given but imperfectly known ideal value system which simultaneously represents the essential features of society and man; this gap represents a form of alienation, which, as will be suggested in the next subsection, constitutes the link between the positive and the normative. Hence the social sciences – politics, law, political economy and sociology – are moral sciences because each human action contains an ethical dimension. However, the social sciences are also positive sciences if values, and hence alienation, are considered to be given. The social sciences become normative once they aim at proposing measures to reduce alienation, i.e. to improve a given situation.

These suggestions give rise to a definitional issue. If humanist social philosophy and the associated social sciences refer to a positive state of affairs, with values given, it might be called *social realism, historical realism* or, simply, *realism*. The causal forces pictured by the social and the behavioural sciences appear in many different shapes in the real world, which gives rise to specific historical investigations in various fields. This terminology is broadly in line with Christopher Lloyd's (1986). If normative issues are dealt with, the humanist social philosophy along Aristotelian lines and the associated social sciences may be termed *natural* systems. The notion 'natural' here stands for the essence of the ethically good, i.e. for a set of ethical principles. Examples of such principles are the *public interest* and *distributive justice*. The content given to these ethical principles depends upon the social philosophy adopted: the liberal, the socialist and the humanist social philosopher will attach entirely different contents to the notion of distributive justice, for example. Finally, it must be emphasized that ethical principles are related with ideals incapable of perfect realization in the real world. For instance, with respect to the public interest, perfection can never be achieved, the degree of perfection depending upon human capabilities and possibilities. This implies that the basic problems, for example employment and distribution, are always there and must be solved afresh in changing circumstances.

A second feature of neo-Aristotelian social philosophy is that the *social* as is reflected in social institutions like the state is *essential*, not secondary as is the case with liberalism. This requires rules which regulate the relationships between the social – society and the state – and individuals. Two widely discussed normative principles of neo-Aristotelian Christian Social Doctrine are fundamental here: *solidarity* and *subsidiarity*. Solidarity implies that society and the state ought to exercise ancillary functions: they ought to provide the social groundwork within which individuals may act according to their dispositions and abilities. In modern societies full employment and a fair distribution of incomes are perhaps the most important of these social preconditions. However, to prevent the state from dominating too strongly, i.e. to check possible tendencies towards totalitarianism, the principle of solidarity must be complemented by the principle of subsidiarity: the state ought to intervene only if individuals and collectives are not in a position to solve an essential problem. Hence state activities ought to promote the public interest or the common weal, which might be conceived as the perfect realization of the principles of solidarity and subsidiarity. This implies in turn that the policies pursued ought to be governed by political ethics based on social theories like political economy. This neo-Aristotelian – and Keynesian – view of the state will be taken up briefly in this section and in chapter 7 (pp. 393–410).

Third, the concepts of equality and inequality are related to the individual and social nature of man respectively and hence to the two notions of the social mentioned at the outset of the present part. The concept of equality is connected with basic human rights (equality before the law, the right to work, the right to possess property) which have been abundantly discussed since the French Revolution. Moreover, interactions between equal individuals represent manifestations of the 'social' in the liberal sense. What has been emphasized much less, however, is that the genuine social dispositions of man are necessarily linked with inequality: 'for a city does not only consist of a large number of inhabitants, but [they] must be of different sorts [which implies that inequality is based upon the inequality of dispositions and abilities]; for were they all alike, there could be no city' (Aristotle, *Politics*, 1261a). Genuine social organizations like states are structured entities which imply part–whole relationships, and the essential shortcomings of single individuals require such organizations: 'That a city then precedes an individual is plain, for if an individual is not in himself sufficient to compose a perfect government, he is to a city as other parts are to a whole' (1253a). These sentences are of the utmost importance in the social sciences since they provide the starting point for arguing that society is something more than a collection of individuals, i.e. a structured entity in which division of labour prevails *and* which requires co-operation and co-ordination. The social nature of man manifests itself most vigorously within social institutions. Here, individuals attempt to realize common aims through common action, implying co-operation, whereby individuals exercise different complementary functions. The latter is inevitably associated with inequality. It should be emphasized, however, that social inequality does not measure intrinsic importance. In a social entity, be it an enterprise, a football team or society as a whole, *each* member makes a significant contribution to achieving the common aim and is, as such, important: a social institution as a whole cannot function properly if some part is not fulfilling its task adequately. In modern societies with extensive division of labour, the social nature of man manifests itself most vigorously in the process of production as was perceived by the classical economists including Quesnay and Marx.

The existence of inequality of dispositions and of ability is also of the highest importance on ethical grounds since the social activities based on inequality may procure far more satisfaction to many individuals than does the pursuit of individual aims. Moreover, social activities implying inequality allow individuals, having widely varying dispositions, propensities and abilities to find appropriate occupations. To bring about even an approximate correspondence between activities and abilities (the right person at the right place) is obviously an exceedingly complex socioeconomic and political problem, which can be tackled adequately only if there is social mobility based upon a fair access to education, and full employment.

The social philosophy of humanism is associated with a specific conception of the social sciences and their interrelationship. The nature of the state offers the clue for coming to grips with this issue. In the Aristotelian view, the state is a moral entity: the state ought to aim at securing the public interest or the common weal which, essentially, means creating the social preconditions to render possible a 'good and decent' life for the citizens. According to Aristotle (*Nicomachean Ethics*), the latter consists in the permanent pursuit of fundamental values in the various spheres of life: 'physical and mental health, material affluence (within limits), the development of (some of) one's potential, useful or "meaningful" work, a set of personal relationships [e.g. friendship], and to regulate these, a rational plan of life to be lived in a rationally organized society' (Brown 1986, p. 136). The latter would imply a harmonious arrangement of the various institutions. However, a rationally organized society is an objectively given but unattainable ideal. Contrary to Plato – the idealist – this was clearly perceived by Aristotle – the realist. In his *Politics*, therefore, Aristotle's concern was about a realistic second or third best institutional set-up adapted to the mentality of the population (see also Brown 1986, chapter 6, and Schack 1978, chapter 5). In a modern society, encompassing a monetary production economy, full employment and a fair distribution of income and wealth are certainly the most important social components of the common weal since, as will be argued subsequently, there is no automatic tendency towards full employment in such an economy and an unequal income distribution is associated with more involuntary unemployment.

Thus, the role of the state is to co-ordinate, to co-operate with social institutions – trade unions and entrepreneurial associations, for example – and to create as much harmony between the various institutions as is possible, which implies minimizing social antagonisms. In terms of alienation (pp. 39–53 below) this means reducing system-caused alienation, for example eliminating involuntary unemployment. The rules and guidelines for policy actions have to be provided by the *science of politics* by co-ordinating the results obtained by other social sciences on the basis of a specific social philosophy. The object of politics is society as a whole. Therefore, this science is the queen of the social sciences, not political economy, economics, law or sociology which deal with specific aspects of social and individual life.

A science of politics of its own is required because society – in the widest sense of the word – is something more than the sum of its individuals: society is a structured moral entity, the supreme aim being the common weal. To achieve this aim as closely as is humanly possible the science of politics must rely upon and co-ordinate the knowledge provided by the subordinate social sciences, that is political economy, law and sociology, on the respective social phenomena to be explained; for example, political economy ought mainly to deal with the scale of economic activity (which includes the employment problem), the social process of production, the formation of prices and the regulation of distribution. The object of this third-way conception of politics is to lay social foundations such as will *enable* individuals to prosper. Politics in this sense differs radically from modern neoclassical political economy (new political economy) which applies economic principles to power politics. The new political economy renders possible the analysis of behavioural outcomes resulting from party politics, for example, and is as such extremely useful. It has, however, to be complemented by traditional political science dealing with society as a whole and with the public interest.

Thus, political economy, sociology and law are, in a humanist view, ancillary sciences to politics. Political economy deals with the material basis of a polity; we shall return to this very extensively in subsequent chapters. Sociology is macrosociology which investigates the relationship between large social groups, i.e. workers and capitalists, rural and urban populations, and the role played by these groups within society as a whole. Private law regulates part of the relationships between individuals and collectives, e.g. between buyers and sellers. Public law deals with the relationship between individuals or collectives and society as a whole. For example, the political weight to be given to regions or local government is a matter of public law; this is also true in part of income distribution: the determination of the wage and profit share in national income represents a social relation, i.e. the relationship between large groups of individuals and society.

The middle-way social philosophy of the Aristotelian type suggested here provides a broad framework to order the results obtained by the social and the behavioural sciences, i.e. to put scientific results or knowledge and intuitive insights or understanding into perspective. The social sciences – politics, political economy, macrosociology and public law – deal with the social foundations of a polity or of a social system. The behaviour of individuals within social institutions and the – partial – regulation of behaviour is the subject matter of what could be called the behavioural sciences: economics, microsociology, private law and modern political sciences.

Ethics and the social sciences

The previous subsection dealt with basic ontological principles underlying social philosophies; these are related to 'what is'. In this subsection some remarks are made on 'what ought to be' regarding individuals and society.

Moreover, we define the crucial concept of *alienation*, which links the positive and the normative states of affairs.

Individual and political ethics

Each human action is directed towards an individual or social aim which is, in turn, associated with a corresponding subjectively perceived value. In the Aristotelian view, values are objectively given and present in every sphere of life: material values related to goods and services in the economic domain, truth in science, beauty in the cultural sphere, justice in law; social values are embodied in political institutions and in very diverse associations between individuals. These specific values form a hierarchical structure or a system, because the supreme ethical aims – happiness for individuals and the common weal or public interest for societies – are complex entities: both consist of an interrelated set of values. This is so because individuals and societies are themselves structured, and hence multidimensional, entities possessing specific identities. Institutions represent the vehicles which enable individuals to pursue social and individual aims and the associated values persistently. Legal institutions render possible the implementation of laws; economic institutions ought to provide each member of a society with the necessities of life. The social structure or the entire institutional system therefore reflects the way of life of a given society, which is governed by the value system prevailing in that society. As emerges from Priddat (1995) this point was strongly emphasized by Gustav Schmoller, the head of the German Historical School, at the end of the nineteenth century.

The essentially ethical character of institutions has an important consequence: the social sciences – social philosophy, politics, law, political economy, sociology and history – which deal with the functioning of different parts of the institutional system and its evolution from the point of view of society as a whole are moral sciences. This view of things was systematically established by the founder of the social sciences, Aristotle: 'Every art and every technique, just as every action and every decision aims at an apparent good' (Aristoteles, *Nikomachische Ethik*, 1094a1; a.tr.); the concept of the apparent good corresponds to the notion of the subjectively perceived hierarchy of values governing the institutional set-up of a society. In the opening passage of his *Politics* Aristotle says: 'As we see that every city is a society, and every society is established for some good purpose; for an apparent good is the spring of all human actions; it is evident that this is the principle upon which they are every one founded, and this is more especially true of that which has for its object the best possible, and is itself the most excellent, and comprehends all the rest. Now this is called a city, and the society thereof a political society' (Aristotle, *Politics*, 1252a).

The willingness of citizens to co-operate under the guidance of the government in order to attempt to realize a good society, i.e. to aim at the common weal, is constitutive of the polity:

The gift of speech also evidently proves that man is [primarily a social being]: for nature . . . does nothing in vain, and man is the only [being] who enjoys it. Voice indeed, as being the token of pleasure and pain, is imparted to others also, and thus much their nature is capable of, to perceive pleasure and pain, and to impart these sensations to others; but it is by speech that we are enabled to express what is useful for us, and what is hurtful, and of course what is just and what is unjust: for in this particular man differs from other [creatures], that he alone has a perception of good and evil, of just and unjust, and it is a participation of these common sentiments which forms a family or a city (Aristotle, *Politics*, 1253a).

Hence justice ought to provide the foundation of any polity. In modern terms justice might encompass a socially fair distribution of income and wealth, full employment, a stable value of money, an appropriate distribution of power between local and central government, and the fair treatment of ethnic, linguistic and religious minorities.

The attempt to realize the good (justice) in some society on the basis of a specific constitution is extremely complex since the interrelated value system associated with a set-up of complementary institutions makes of society an entity, even an organic whole – a notion used by Keynes (see O'Donnell 1989, pp. 127–30) and by various nineteenth-century social scientists, especially the members of the German Historical School (see Priddat 1995), to characterize social entities, including society and the state. It is very important to note that

the notion of a city *naturally precedes* [author's emphasis] that of a family or an individual, for the whole must necessarily be prior to the parts; for if you take away the whole man, you cannot say a foot or a hand remains, unless by equivocation . . . That a city then precedes the individual is plain, [the individual] is to a city as other parts are to a whole (Aristotle, *Politics*, 1253a).

Individuals may act rationally, i.e. strive for individual and social aims, only if there is an institutional framework: the social system is logically and in time prior to the behaviour of individuals.

Hence a crucial implication of the Aristotelian approach is that both man and society are considered structured entities. This specific property gives rise to part–whole relationships in the individual and social spheres.

To conceive of the social sciences as moral sciences has a long tradition. For Aristotle and Aquinas it went without saying. Adam Smith, before writing the *Wealth of Nations*, had, in his *Theory of Moral Sentiments*, elaborated the moral preconditions required to guarantee justice in socioeconomic life; the basic notion is 'propriety' (of behaviour), a morally correct combination of 'fellow feeling' and 'self-interest'. For Adam Smith moral philosophy thus relates to the regulation of behaviour, not to the organization of society, which is typically liberal. Brown (1986, chapter 6) revisits the issue of teleology in the political sciences. Schack (1978, chapter V, section 4) speaks of a normative socioeconomic way of life (*normative sozialökonomische Lebensordnung*). Keynes '[wanted] to emphasize strongly the point about economics being a moral science' (Keynes 1973c, letter to Harrod, p. 300). Recent writings on Keynes's views elaborate on this point (Fitzgibbons 1988, especially chapter 3 and part III; O'Donnell 1989, chapters 6 and 8); for instance:

economics and ethics are close companions in Keynes's intellectual framework . . . the role of economics was that of service to the higher discipline of ethics. Along with other moral sciences, its task was to contribute towards bringing into existence as much intrinsic goodness as possible, this being 'the ultimate end of human action and the sole criterion of social progress' [Moore, *Principia Ethica*]. Ultimately, Keynes's goal was the development of an ethically rational society consciously tending towards higher levels of goodness; and economics, like all moral sciences, was an instrument in its attainment (O'Donnell 1989, p. 164).

The importance of ethics in humanist social philosophy and in the associated social sciences does not imply that these are of an essentially normative nature in the sense that they cannot deal with concretely existing positive situations. From an ethical point of view the individual and social aims actually pursued by the individuals and groups making up a society may be good or bad in varying degrees; for example, earning an income by well-done and socially useful work is obviously good, making money by cheating people is evidently bad: each human action and each institution embodies an ethical dimension. On a different level, a lawyer would argue that actually existing positive law need not correspond, partly or entirely, to the right or natural law. Correspondingly, positive social philosophies of the humanist type take values, and thus the ethically more or less good or bad aims that are pursued in some actually existing society, as given; on this basis positive social sciences attempt to explain the functioning of socioeconomic systems.

It is not sufficient, however, to consider the ethical status of an action or an institution *per se*. More importantly, an attempt must be made to evaluate the impact of certain types of actions and of institutions on, respectively, the ethical quality of lifestyles and the socioeconomic system as a whole: ideally, each action and each institution ought to be evaluated in overall terms, i.e. in terms of the good for individuals which is included in the common weal or the public interest. In the social and, above all, the political spheres some institutions evidently promote the public interest, for example a well-functioning social security system. These are constructive institutions of which the monetary system, the process of production and the legal system are other examples. On the other hand, there are destructive institutions which are obviously damaging to the public interest to a greater or less degree. Some of these are purposefully created, like criminal organizations; however, destructive institutions may also result deterministically from the functioning of the socioeconomic system. An important example is involuntary unemployment, which, together with other factors, may give rise to other destructive institutions, for example slums. Finally, there are institutions the impact of which is ambiguous: to save more may be rational and good for each individual and damaging to the system because involuntary unemployment may rise. This is Keynes's paradox of saving to which we shall refer at several instances in subsequent chapters. Therefore, each existing institution embodies an ethical dimension: each institution is intrinsically good or bad to various degrees or promotes or hampers the proper functioning of society as a whole.

To clarify the discussion on ethical problems a distinction ought to be made between

ethics (or moral philosophy) and politics (more accurately political philosophy [or political ethics which is partly equivalent to the German *Sozialethik*, H.B.]). Ethics is concerned with the individual: how ought he to live his life; what values and ideals ought he to adopt, what rules ought he to observe? Political philosophy is concerned with the social side of this question or . . . with the problem of how society ought to be organized (Brown 1986, p. 11).

Political philosophy deals with the ethically correct arrangement of the social structure. The concepts of harmony in the social sphere – the right proportions between institutions – complementarity and co-operation, the postulates of full employment and a fair distribution of incomes and wealth are all important constituents of the humanist political philosophy in the tradition of Aristotle's *Politics*. The corresponding ethical system is set forth in his *Nicomachean Ethics*.

To avoid misunderstanding it is appropriate to point out what seems to be the crucial difference between Aristotelian-type humanist ethics associated with classical-Keynesian political economy and liberal ethics implied in neoclassical economics. The hallmark of Aristotelian ethics is 'moral objectivity' (Brown 1986, p. 134). The faculty to perceive the objectively given *good* is rooted in human nature. In different cultures and epochs very diverse material means have been used to realize the good in a coherent way in the various spheres of life. However, '[proper] attention to the historical and anthropological data shows that the basic forms of human good . . . are recognized, by human beings, both in thought and action, with virtual universality, in all times and places' (p. 136); the same point is made by Schack (1978, pp. 16–18). This implies that ethics in the Aristotelian sense consists in the realization of material or concrete values, for instance ever more perfection embodied in an artisan's work.

Ethics (*Individualethik*) deals with the essence of the good and decent life for individuals which, if realized, would result in happiness. From this, prescriptions for ethically good actions may be derived which, if permanently effected, produce individualistic institutions compatible with human nature. The good is a complex entity and made up of a set of values related to physical and mental health, to a reasonable level of material affluence, to the satisfaction obtained by exercising a profession and to social activities, for example pursuing a common aim within a team, to the search for truth in scientific work, to justice in relations between individuals – the fair or just price is associated with justice in exchange between producer and consumer – and to the creation and the enjoyment of the beautiful in the arts. Since each person is unique, the value system corresponding to his individual nature will equally be unique. Moreover, Aristotle insists on the fact that the good life does not naturally come about. This objectively given potential can only be imperfectly perceived and its approximate realization requires continuing efforts.

The fundamental value of political philosophy is *the public interest* or *the common weal*. This notion is also most complex because it relates to the adequate organization of society as a whole. The public interest would be entirely realized if social organization were such that each individual of a society were in a position to realize his specific natural potential, i.e. to live a good and decent life. The Keynesian values of full employment and fair distribution are most important constituents of the public interest. Distribution is a major problem of political philosophy (*Sozialethik*) because the concepts of 'normal profits' or the 'socially appropriate wage structure' are related to the notion of distributive justice which deals with the relationship of individuals or social groups on the one hand to society on the other – more generally, with the relationship between parts and wholes. The notion of public interest thus comprises the natural value system – an interrelated set of invariable ethical principles – which is governed by objective reason (*ratio recta*). At this stage we should mention that the realization of these principles is at once imperfect and historically variable regarding accidental factors. Most importantly, the way in which ethical principles are realized depends upon the state of technological knowledge; for example, the presence of computers requires legislation to protect the private sphere of individuals; or the modern mass media give rise to entirely new problems in education. These issues are also connected with the Marxian problem of the relation between the material basis of a society, i.e. its socioeconomic institutions, and the institutional super-structure, to which we shall return in chapter 3.

In the liberal view, and hence in neoclassical economics, ethics is outside the sphere of economics and belongs to the framework. To deal with ethical problems, individuals have to leave the realm of economics to become moralists: if 'an economist wants to talk [about a patently inequitable income distribution], he must divest himself of any pretence of being an economist and say explicitly that he is speaking in some other capacity (as a politician, a philanthropist, etc.)' (Pasinetti 1981, p. 20). Similarly, the content of the utility function is not discussed by neoclassical economics. The goods, or eventually values, that enter the utility function do not matter: the economist takes these as given. Given the shape and the general content of the utility function, i.e. the goods entering the utility function, the economic problem becomes a purely formal one: to give the content a specific form – to select specific quantities of goods – such that utility is maximized. Hence utilitarian ethics is, in a Kantian vein, subjective and formal, contrary to Aristotelian ethics which is objective and concrete (material).

'Political' ethics is, in the liberal view, confined to the relationship between individuals. This is in line with the individualistic neoclassical approach. A political philosophy proper is not required since society is no more than the sum of its individuals. The optimizing behaviour of individuals is co-ordinated by anonymous natural mechanisms, the market or voting procedures. In the economic domain the general problem is to reconcile ethical postulates with market outcomes. As a rule, satisfactorily working markets are supposed to produce ethically acceptable results *if* the framework surrounding the market is appropriate: the market price is the 'just price'. However, if contradictions between the market outcome and ethical postulates occur, the question of an eventual market regulation arises; this amounts to a change in the framework, i.e. 'the rules of the game' (Joan Robinson).

If competitive markets produced a strong tendency towards equilibrium it would be very difficult to set up a rival ethical theory to the various forms of utilitarianism (on the latter, see Brown 1986, pp. 24–33). In chapter 5 it will be argued that such a tendency does not – and cannot – exist, however. Hence the optimizing behaviour postulated by utilitarianism in general and neoclassical economics in particular cannot result in a social optimum. This clears the way for establishing a middle-way ethical theory along Aristotelian lines which is hinted at above.

Moreover, Brown argues that 'the human good cannot be conceived in [the utilitarian] manner' (Brown 1986, p. 51). 'The main problem facing utilitarianism . . . is that it does not seem to take seriously the ideal of a person framing a plan of life, something which gives meaning to his life as a whole' (p. 52). The goods entering the utility function, whether having a price or not, are not independent of each other. The good life, in the Aristotelian sense alluded to above, requires an ordering of complementary values, for example such that material values – the necessities of life – are a means to aim at non-material values in the widest sense of the word, e.g. the satisfaction derived from well-done work or the enjoyment derived from contemplating works of art; utility is only one and certainly not the most important of the values which make for the happiness of individuals. The human good is thus a complex organic entity because values are inter-dependent and hierarchically ordered. It is a *qualitative* notion, not a quan-titative one as is the case in utilitarianism.

However, '[if] the human good is [qualitative] then it may be better to say that the good life is something we can be closer to or further from rather than something we can have more and more of' (Brown 1986, p. 52). To strive at more and more utility – whether measurable or not – implies that there is no upper limit to the acquisition of material things: the quantita-tive notions of income and/or material wealth which govern the amount of utility that can be achieved are undetermined. In a humanist perspective this must lead to social conflicts: resources are limited and there is no ten-dency towards a harmonious – equilibrium – state of affairs brought about by market forces (chapter 5). Aristotle (*Politics*, 1257b) insists on the fact that the material means required for a good life must be limited, while there is no limit in the efforts to be made to realize approximately some non-material end – for example, aesthetical perfection in the arts or striving for the good in the moral domain. These continuing efforts being made in order to approximately achieve non-material values – which have no price! – cannot be explained on the basis of income-constrained utility maximiza-tion. In this vein, Schumpeter gives an admirable critique of utilitarianism:

if we go very far beyond the grossest gratifications of the simplest appetites, we come dangerously near to identifying expectation of 'pleasure' with all the possible motives whatsoever, even with the unintentional suffering of pain, and then . . . the doctrine becomes an empty tautology. Worse still, if we allow too much scope to such 'pleasures' as may be afforded by exertion, victory, cruelty, and the like, we may get a picture of human behavior . . . that differs totally from what [utilitarians] actu-ally envisaged (Schumpeter 1954, pp. 130–1).

Utilitarianism may be useful for dealing with scarce goods that have a price, i.e. with quantities. However, if qualitative values come into the picture – kinds of knowledge, aesthetic principles – and if the values included in the utility function are complementary rather than substitutive, this social philosophy does not seem to be adequate. The purely formal character of the theory and its entire neglect of material values reinforce this proposition.

However, the most important defect of utilitarianism and of neoclassical economics is that they largely ignore the consequences of the social nature of man (on this, see also Brown, 1986, pp. 491ff.) which is associated with the fact that man and society are structured entities. For example, the elements entering the utility function of others may be part of our utility function; this happens with Veblen's 'conspicuous consumption' or with Duesenberry's 'demonstration effects'. Again, neoclassical economics cannot deal adequately with the social process of production where the production of the national or the social product results from a common effort. Most importantly, however, utilitarianism and neoclassical economics completely neglect the deterministic influence of the institutional system *as a whole* on the behaviour of individuals. (This is not to say that liberal theory does not deal with institutions: the new institutionalism investigates the behavioural aspects of single institutions and effects of actions undertaken.) In particular, if markets, even under ideal conditions, i.e. perfect competition, do not produce a tendency towards full employment, effective demand may, across the socioeconomic system, govern the level of economic activity (chapter 4). The result will be involuntary unemployment. The disastrous effects on society and its individuals are only too well known: there is psychological distress, which hits the unemployed and all those who fear for their jobs (and this may be the majority of the working population), families break apart, poverty grows, intolerance spreads, violence becomes normal. Marx and Keynes perceived with unsurpassable clarity that economies organized along liberal lines, i.e. capitalist economies, may produce unemployment, even mass unemployment. Keynes looked for the *causes* of this phenomenon in terms of the principle of effective demand (Keynes's views on this issue and its long-period elaboration will be set out in chapters 4 and 6). Marx primarily examined the social *effects* of what he called the industrial reserve army in terms of the gap between the natural and the positive state of affairs, taking the cause for granted. In doing so he used an important social-philosophical notion, which we now briefly consider.

Links between positive and normative states of affairs

In his *Paris Manuscripts*, Marx coined a specific term to designate the harmful impact of capitalism as a *system* on the situation of the working class, i.e. *alienation* (Marx 1973 [1844], pp. 510ff.): workers are separated – alienated – from the means of production and from their produce; an alien power – the capitalists – fixes work conditions and the distribution of income. Alienation culminates in the fact that the workers' own produce determines their fate: capital accumulation determines employment, and fluctuations in the pace of accumulation lead to variations in the industrial reserve army. All these phenomena denote alienation in the economic sphere. According to Marx, economic alienation is basic and leads to alienation in other spheres of life: for example, political alienation shows up in the fact that the state and state bureaucracy do not act in the public interest, but defend the interest of the economically dominant capitalist class; religion as the 'opium of the people' reflects religious alienation: religion is a tool in the hands of the ruling class.

System-caused alienation arises because society is not in its natural state which would enable individuals to flourish, whereas in his *Paris Manuscripts* Marx equates the natural state with humanism and communism (Marx 1973 [1844], p. 536). It is impossible here to discuss fully this complex term. An excellent discussion of alienation in Marx's sense is provided by Meszaros (1973), and its wider meaning is set forth in Kolakowski's work on Marx and Marxism (1977, vol. I, specifically chapters 1 and 12). In the following we merely provide a few hints on the meaning of system-caused alienation in terms of Aristotelian ethics and of Keynes's principle of effective demand. This implies accepting Marx's formal definition of alienation while giving it a different content.

Marx takes for granted that alienation is basically caused by the institution of private ownership of the means of production since capitalists act in their own interest and not in the public interest (in fact, capitalists cannot act according to the latter since the public interest is nothing but the aggregate of private interests). They appropriate the social surplus and decide upon its use, i.e. consumption or accumulation of capital in the widest sense. Marx's obvious policy conclusion is to abolish private property, i.e. to socialize and to nationalize the means of production. However, it will be suggested in chapter 4 (pp. 154–90) that private property is an important *social* institution and that the main cause of capitalist alienation is involuntary unemployment caused by a lack of effective demand. Alienation is brought about by misfunctioning of the *entire* socioeconomic system expressed through the principle of effective demand (chapter 4, pp. 142–204). This indicates the crucial importance of this principle and implies that the main cause of system-caused alienation is essentially a Keynesian one.

Hence in Marx's and, partly, in Keynes's view the individual capitalists are not responsible for alienation, which is caused by the capitalist *system*. System-caused alienation could be defined as the degree of irrationality in social organization. A rationally organized society would provide the preconditions for the development of the natural social and individual dispositions and abilities of its individuals. For example, there would be no involuntary unemployment, everybody would have an adequate social position, and income distribution would be mutually accepted. Consequently, an irrational organization of society may show up in a socially unacceptable distribution of income and wealth, in socially inappropriate state expenditures and, most importantly, in permanent involuntary unemployment. The latter is likely to reinforce the misfunctioning of the social system: poverty and crime may increase; or defence expenditures have to be kept at a high level, or the export of weapons has to be promoted in order to secure jobs.

The disparity between the common weal and an actually existing situation could be called alienation: it is the gap existing between the Platonian ideal, the perfect society, and the real world. In this view alienation is a measure of the tension existing between the real, or the positive, and the normative. (In an Aristotelian spirit, however, the positive and the normative coincide on the level of principles or essences; it is the historical realizations of essences, i.e. various forms of existence, that give rise to various kinds of alienation.)

This conception of alienation raises two points: first, the common weal implies an ideal state of affairs never capable even of approximate realization. It is in fact frightening to think of some requirements that ought to be fulfilled to accomplish this supreme social value, e.g. absolute knowledge on the nature of the individuals and on the functioning of society. Each individual ought therefore to be capable of becoming aware of his natural dispositions so as to be able to organize his life rationally. Simultaneously, the task of politics would be to create institutions and to favour the coming into being of institutions such that each individual may prosper, which implies his occupying an adequate social position. These tasks are compounded if technical change takes place. Each major technical change in fact requires a reorganization of society in line with the public interest; for example, to make use of the computer and of the mass media in the public interest raises immensely complex psychological and social problems. Given the complexity of the social ideal, the common weal can never be realized, simply because detailed knowledge will always be lacking; the public interest is but a guiding star that enables us to walk in the right direction. This was also the standpoint taken by Aristotle. In spite of the relatively simple political problems of the small Greek city states he refused in his *Politics* to follow Plato and engage in speculation upon the ideal and utopian society. Aristotle's concern was with the *real* man with all his strengths and weaknesses. This justifies the term *historical realism* proposed above for positive humanist social philosophy and the associated social sciences. Here, the art of politics consists in setting up institutions that are adapted to the mentality of the people making up a state and that promote the common weal, thus reducing alienation.

A second point relates to the nature of alienation. The impossibility of realizing an ideal society implies that some alienation will always be present in any society even if well organized in the sense that income distribution is socially acceptable and that near-full employment prevails. In such a society, alienation is the result of human weaknesses of some kind: for example, the excessive egoism of some individuals results in an exaggerated pursuit of economic, social and political power. This type of alienation is at the level of individuals, i.e. at the psychological level. However, this was not the kind of alienation Marx was dealing with in his *Paris Manuscripts* (Marx 1973 [1844]) and in *Das Kapital* (Marx 1973/74a [1867–94]). Marx's problem was alienation caused by an inappropriate organization of society which results in a misfunctioning of the socioeconomic system: 'The landlord and the capitalist are persons only in so far as they personify economic categories and carry specific class relations and interests . . . The evolution of socioeconomic formations is a process of natural history; therefore an individual is not responsible for given circumstances [which *determine* his actions]' (Marx 1973/74a [1867–94], vol. I, p. 16; a.tr.). This is also the kind of alienation put to the fore here: a misspecified organization of the socioeconomic system results, through the functioning of the system, captured by the principle of effective demand, in permanent involuntary unemployment (chapter 4), which is the major source of alienation caused by the socioeconomic part of the system. This view of things implies more a Keynesian than a Marxian view of system-caused alienation. Private property is not, as Marx thought, at the root of systemic alienation, resulting in a very unequal distribution of income and in an industrial reserve army of unemployed, but is an essential socioeconomic institution that contributes to the appropriate functioning of societies (the role of private property will be alluded to in chapter 4 under the heading of long-period distribution theory (pp. 158–75)). In a Keynesian view alienation is associated with the way in which monetary production economies function, in which effective demand problems are of particular importance (pp. 142–204).

Marx clearly perceived that economic alienation distorts or perverts to a greater or lesser extent other domains of social and individual life and hence leads to new types of alienation (Marx 1973 [1844]). To take a modern example, in both socialism and capitalism, system-caused alienation may pervert or destroy ethical values. In the socialist system the individual is largely sacrificed in favour of the system; under capitalist rules the fear of involuntary unemployment and slackening profits may justify the export of weapons, ruthless behaviour on world markets to promote exports of manufactures, riotous living of the rich, or vice in so far as this is associated with the spending of money that would otherwise be hoarded. This is a variant of the argument advanced by de Mandeville in his *Fable of the Bees.* Incidentally, de Mandeville got high praise from Marx and from Keynes for his insights into the functioning of a capitalist system (see, for example, Keynes 1973a, pp. 359ff.). A similar perversion may take place in the sphere of the social sciences. Certain principles which underlie the explanation and organization of parts of social life are given too much weight and are generalized too much. In socialism the planning principle is overemphasized, in capitalism too much weight is given to the market, i.e. the principle of supply and demand. The latter is also reflected in a distorted social science in which the theory of value founded upon the forces of supply and demand – general equilibrium theory – is considered to be fundamental and the prices of production resulting from the social process of production are pushed into the background or not considered at all. Consequently, liberal economists are, in many instances, prevented from understanding what is going on in the real world. Again the point is made with great clarity by both Marx and Keynes. In the *Paris Manuscripts* Marx argues that the liberal economists 'put economic reality [the market system] into general and abstract formulae which subsequently get the status of laws; however, [the liberal economists] do not understand these laws' (Marx 1973 [1844], p. 510; a.tr.). A modern example of the liberal failure to understand the functioning of the socioeconomic system is provided by the neoclassical claim that, apart from structural problems, unemployment is voluntary and can be eliminated by lowering real wages. This may be true for the individual entrepreneur but not for all entrepreneurs taken together. The reason is that in a monetary production economy, wages are the most important source of effective demand (chapter 4). Or, in the *General Theory*, Keynes mentions at several points that the [neo-]classical economists picture ideal worlds and are not able to come to grips with essential parts of the real world, for example involuntary unemployment and its consequences (see for instance Keynes 1973a, pp. 33–4).

Hence socialism and liberalism are both associated with specific types of alienation. Under centrally planned socialism the determinism exercised by the system is very strong. Consequently, on the behavioural level, socialism enormously reduces the scope of individual liberty, with all the corollaries that follow from this, e.g. reduced possibilities for creative action; for example, since prices, quantities and product quality are all planned, the socialist manager's scope for independent action is heavily reduced, which implies that he is more of a bureaucrat than an entrepreneur. Centrally planned socialism results in a very low labour productivity; moreover, natural resources are squandered which is, in turn, associated with environmental problems on a huge scale. On the other hand, capitalism, i.e. the implementation of liberalism, provides considerable liberty for a greater or lesser part of the members of society. The capitalist system produces, however, a tendency towards a more unequal distribution of incomes and wealth and, above all, permanent unemployment; the latter is, as a rule, associated with growing poverty or even the formation of a two-class society consisting of those who are included in the system and those who are excluded. For those who are excluded from the system or earn very low incomes, individual liberties are purely formal: the material basis for enjoying liberties is largely or entirely lacking.

The above provides some hints at how humanist social philosophy might deal with the problem of alienation. The starting point is that man and society are entities which would be in their rational or natural state if the different parts of human activity and of society – i.e. the individualistic and the social institutions to be found in the material, cultural, social and political spheres – were intrinsically good and in the socially appropriate proportions. The concept of individual and of social harmony in the widest sense of the word is associated with the common weal. However, owing to the ignorance, fallibility and weakness of man the common weal can never be realized – the best of all possible worlds will ever remain utopia. This means that alienation will always be there. Even if a perfect socioeconomic and political system could be created, alienation would occur on account of the imperfection of individuals and their weakness, and this would, in turn, reduce the perfection of the system. More importantly, a lack of effective demand may lead to permanently high unemployment levels. Involuntary unemployment represents system-caused economic alienation, which will as a rule produce derived, system-caused alienation in other domains, for example growth of poverty and political extremism in the social and political spheres respectively. All that can be done in a humanist view is to eliminate *system-caused* alienation as far as is humanly possible. This does not require increased regulation of behaviour – as is frequently done now – but an improved organization of society. The latter cannot be achieved by abolishing private property as Marx proposed, which is strongly confirmed by the experience of the centrally planned socialist economies. Keynes's propositions are much sounder: in each society one must attempt to bring about a socially acceptable distribution of income and to eliminate involuntary unemployment to the largest possible extent. This provides the cornerstone of a sound social framework within which individuals may prosper. The latter implies the right to own private property to a socially appropriate extent. In this view, alienation can be reduced by institutional reform: the problem is to create constructive institutions that are adapted to the mentality of the population, i.e. institutions that promote the public interest. Given the continuous changes in technology and the evolution of the value system, institutional reform aimed at the reduction of alienation is a continuing task.

Two issues related to ethics remain to be dealt with: the problem of the scientific character of the social sciences, given their ethical nature, and the problem of ideology, which is intimately linked with the value system prevailing in a society. Both will be sketched in the next section. In the remainder of the present section two problems associated with the functioning of society as a whole are dealt with briefly: determinism and choice, and the meaning of causation.

Definitional remarks on determinism, freedom of choice and causality

Determinism and free choice

Determinism, as is exercised by the institutional system upon the behaviour of individuals, and freedom of choice are not contradictory but are two different facets of human existence. This is not the place to consider in depth this immensely complex issue. We shall merely sketch the relations between determinism and freedom of choice on the one hand and the concepts of system and behaviour on the other. Some observations on this issue will be made in subsequent chapters.

Large parts of behaviour are determined by institutions, i.e. the social structure. Determinism is mainly exercised by social institutions within which individuals perform certain functions in order that common (social) aims may eventually be achieved. Determinism appears here in the form of duties. For example, the education system is a social macroinstitution established in order to reach a social aim, i.e. to secure a socially appropriate education for all individuals making up a society. This means institutionalizing curricula and specific tasks for teachers. To perform these tasks properly represents a duty for each individual teacher. However, duties do not entirely determine the actions of teachers. Each teacher will develop, as a rule, her or his personal style to reach the educational aims prescribed: teachers are, to a large extent, free to choose the means to reach a broadly specified aim.

Determinism associated with individualistic institutions shows up in the regulation of behaviour by customs, habits and legal prescriptions. Restricted freedom of choice enters the picture if institutions are changed by deliberate action, e.g. the legislator who changes a law under given social and political constraints.

There is also considerable determinism in the economic sphere, mainly within the social and circular process of production. The behaviour of producers is largely determined by the pattern of past accumulation. With technology, patterns of expenditure and growth rates given at any moment of time, certain interindustry flows of intermediate goods and services and intersectoral flows of final goods *must* take place if production is to go on in an orderly way, that is, if the economic system is to reproduce itself and if a surplus is to be produced. This is clearly evident from the 'input–output' view of the social process of production. However, there are possibilities of choice within the sphere of production. For example, the degree of capacity utilization is open to choice in the short run, or the possibility of selecting alternative or new techniques of production represents some scope for freedom in the long run.

Determinism is also associated with the principle of effective demand. Global levels of employment and unemployment are determined by the socioeconomic system (institutions and their interplay): aggregate demand sets a constraint to economic activity and determines at any moment of time a certain percentage amount of involuntary unemployment; this specific issue will be dealt with extensively in chapter 4. Involuntary unemployment appears to the individuals concerned as the working of blind fate. But even with heavy involuntary unemployment, there is some scope for individuals to choose between different jobs.

Finally, temporary deviations from institutionally determined economic variables are to some extent open to choice. For instance, according to classical [Ricardian] theory prices are, in a long-run view, governed by the conditions of production and by functional income distribution (the rate of profits). In addition, capacities are supposed to be utilized normally. In the short run, however, entrepreneurs may fix prices and/or degrees of capacity utilization that deviate from their respective long-run normal levels in order to adapt them to specific market conditions (Bortis 1990, pp. 90–1).

Social and individualistic institutions are thus associated with determinism. Actions of individuals take place within given institutions – a given social structure – which thus form a set of more or less rigid constraints. In the short run, freedom of choice consists of the possibility of participating in some of these institutions, i.e. to select the aims to be pursued and to choose the corresponding means. Individuals can act fully rationally from their point of view only if the institutional groundwork is appropriate. For example, full employment is required for the individuals' search activities for jobs to be rational. In the long run, however, the scope for freedom is far larger: new institutions may deliberately be set up. This leads to changes in the institutional system.

These brief remarks on determinism and freedom point to the basic aim of institutional reform. If carried out in the public interest, institutional reforms ought to narrow the gap between an actually existing situation and the ideal represented by the common weal, i.e. to diminish alienation. This means reducing determinism and augmenting the scope for freedom. The former would imply, for example, the elimination of involuntary unemployment, the latter the creation of new institutions that open up new possibilities of action for individuals.

Forms of causality

In the present study, Aristotle not only plays a fundamental role in the domains of ethics and politics, but also regarding the method to be used in the social sciences. Here, we merely sketch and extend somewhat Aristotle's views on causality. Some additional methodological suggestions along Aristotelian lines will be made in subsequent passages, e.g. in the final section of chapter 3 (pp. 118–30). Some implications of Aristotle's views on causation for Keynes's theory of knowledge are explained in the next section.

Aristotle distinguishes four types of causes that structure the whole of reality, i.e. nature, individual actions and society: the material cause, the efficient cause, the final cause and the formal cause (Aristote, *Métaphysique*, vol. I, pp. 21ff., 41ff.; de Laubier 1987, pp. 88–94; Hirschberger 1984, 1988, vol. I, pp. 199–208; a.tr.). The *formal cause* states how an act of causation goes on in principle and in general. In the real world the formal cause is always complemented by the *material cause*, which designates the application of some formal cause to a specific situation. Both types of causes act simultaneously. For example, the principle of the multiplier, the formal cause, states how a dependent variable, the national product, is always governed by the autonomous independent variables and by the multiplier. This principle is embodied in any concrete multiplier process which might be going on in the real world, linking, for instance, the investment sector with the consumption sector, i.e. the producers acting in both sectors, using specific means of production. The latter represent the material, so to speak, which is shaped by the formal cause (thus the notion 'material cause'): given autonomous expenditures, the multiplier determines the scale of economic activity, hence the number of producers and the quantities of means of production put to use. Two additional types of causation specify how the formal cause works. The *efficient cause* captures determinism: a given cause produces a specific effect; for example, effective demand determines employment. Hence the deterministic impact of the socioeconomic system upon the behaviour of individuals represents a very complex process involving the efficient cause. Dynamic processes can also be captured by the efficient cause: heavy unemployment may set into motion changes in the structure of society, e.g. reduce the importance of the middle class. The *final cause* is related with teleology: an aim to be realized is the cause of the corresponding actions, which represent the means used to achieve that aim. The final cause manifests itself in the purposeful actions of man in the individual and social spheres, for example in the domain of economic policy-making.

The way in which the formal cause acts may change in the course of time. This is the driving force behind evolutionary processes which may be linked with objective factors bringing about structural change (the efficient cause) or with finality, i.e. the endeavour of individuals and groups to reach individual and social aims (the final cause). Again, the efficient cause and/or the final cause concur with the material cause to result in real world evolutionary processes, for example export-led economic development in some country or region during a specific period of time.

The two conceptions of the social suggested at the outset of the present section and the social philosophies set forth above (pp. 20–1) give rise to a further classification of causal forces. The notion of causation in liberalism and in socialism is essentially *mechanical*, that is the relations between quantities are primary. Liberalism is associated with mechanical individualism: causal acts go on between individuals and things as is exemplified by the profit- and utility-maximizing behaviour of producers and consumers, and between individuals, for example the interactions between individuals on markets. This type of causation is on the behavioural level. The Walrasian general equilibrium model implies mechanical relations between individuals, on the one hand, and prices and quantities, on the other, and mechanical interactions of individuals on the various markets. The notion of the marginal product exemplifies the basic endeavour of mechanical individualism which is to neatly separate causal forces (the productive force of an additional quantity of factors of production) that bring about an effect (incremental output).

Socialism is linked up with mechanical holism, which is perhaps best exemplified by the input–output model. Here quantitative part–whole relationships are set forth. Each sector exercises a specific function regarding the production of the social product. Central planning activities relate precisely to the regulation of prices and quantities based upon the functional part–whole relationship between complementary sectors. This implies a social regulation of distribution since part–whole relationships between sectors and 'factors' of production do not allow the isolation of the contribution of an individual sector or 'factor'.

Mechanical causation, whether individualistic or holistic, plays a secondary role in humanist social philosophy. Here man and society are considered organic entities which implies that *organic causation* plays a fundamental role. The various causes mix up and merge with the effect that a neat separation of causes becomes impossible; in a way, the mixture of causes is of a chemical, not a physical nature. For example, interrelated sets of values cause individuals to strive for specific aims (Aristotle's final cause). Or the entire institutional system concurs to governing the scale of economic activity (Aristotle's efficient cause). The presence of organic causation in the real world certainly requires analysis to set up explanatory frameworks to come tentatively to grips with specific phenomena; however, insight based on intuition is necessarily put to the fore, which means that understanding becomes much more important than explanation when causes are linked up organically.

Finally, a sharp distinction must be drawn between the objectively given causes present in the real world and the subjective perception of these in schemes or models of thought. The former are true, but largely unknown, the latter are approximations to truth. This leads to the second issue to be dealt with in this chapter: knowledge about social phenomena.

Knowledge about society

Remarks on the nature of knowledge in the social sciences

In his fundamental work on the theory of knowledge, the *Treatise on Probability*, Keynes deals with the nature of knowledge:

Part of our knowledge we obtain direct; and part by argument. The Theory of Probability is concerned with that part which we obtain by argument, and it treats of the different degrees in which the results so obtained are conclusive or inconclusive. In most branches of academic logic, such as the theory of the syllogism or the geometry of ideal space, all the arguments aim at demonstrative certainty. They claim to be *conclusive*. But many other arguments are rational and claim some weight without pretending to be certain. In metaphysics, in science, and in conduct, most of the arguments, upon which we habitually base our rational beliefs, are admitted to be inconclusive in a greater or less degree. Thus for a philosophical treatment of these branches of knowledge, the study of probability is required (Keynes 1971c, p. 3).

Keynes's theory of knowledge is dealt with in depth by Carabelli (1985), Fitzgibbons (1988, chapter 2) and O'Donnell (1989, chapters 2, 3 and 4). Here we merely sketch some links with the theory of knowledge in the Aristotelian tradition which underlies the present study (a more extensive treatment of Aristotle's theory of knowledge is in Hirschberger (1984, 1988, vol. I, especially pp. 175–82)). We shall return to this theme in the final chapter where a wider view on some fundamental issues will be outlined.

A philosophy along Aristotelian lines implies that each distinct class of elements in nature and in society possesses a definite natural property, identity or essence. This is valid for man, for society and parts of society, for the economy, and for legal and political institutions. The social philosophies set forth above (pp. 27–39) represent attempts to come to grips with the essence of society and man. To give further examples: a neoclassical economist would claim that the law of diminishing returns is an essential characteristic of the process of production, and the Keynesian political economist would refer to the principle of effective demand as an essential causal force governing the level of employment. Essences are associated with the four types of causality mentioned above (pp. 55–7): every existing phenomenon must have a cause. This implies that the empirical world which is accessible through the senses is structured by invisible causal forces which are objectively given.

The hallmark of a theory of knowledge along Aristotelian lines is that the approximate knowledge of principles, i.e. the *essence* of things, is fundamental, *not* the knowledge about empirical facts; the latter is only a starting point for research and, moreover, complements the reasoning about the essence of things. Empirical facts are to be explained on the basis of principles which illuminate, so to speak, the facts from inside. Based upon a coherent set of principles a system of pure theory may be erected. In the domains of economics and political economy such systems are, for example, the models worked out by Ricardo, Walras, Sraffa and Pasinetti. Empirical research is only possible on the basis of pure theory. The latter directs the former: it tells the researcher which variables to take account of and which relations between variables to establish in order to attempt to explain a given phenomenon, i.e. to attempt to discover causal relations that are active in the real world.

Essences represent objectively given ideas which structure the real world. The degree of correspondence between propositions on specific phenomena – which are also ideas – and the objectively given essences of those phenomena depicts the degree of truth contained in the propositions in question. Perfect correspondence represents truth. Pure theorizing aims at reducing the gap between subjectively held explanation in principle of a specific phenomenon, e.g. prices, and the objectively given essence of that phenomenon. Material logic or the theory of knowledge aims at laying down guidelines for the systematic search for truth; if complex states of affairs are considered, e.g. the determination of employment in a capitalist economy, no realistic premises are available to start with. Formal logic deals with deduction, i.e. conclusions that follow from given premises.

Traditional metaphysics applied formal logic mechanically to the theory of knowledge to reach definite conclusions within the framework of syllogism, for instance: 'all humans are mortal, Aristotle is a human being, thus Aristotle is mortal'. Here the conclusions are implied in the premises. If complex situations were considered the conclusions simply represented dogmatic statements since no theoretical frameworks existed to allow inferences in cases where no clear-cut premises could be formulated; for example in the Middle Ages, for theological and empirical reasons [!], the earth was considered the centre of the universe and the sun was supposed to rotate around the earth. However, the explanation of complex facts may not be unequivocal since competing theories may exist between which the scientist has to choose. Hence arguments get non-syllogistic.

[Besides dogmatism a] major shortcoming of classical logic was its restriction to the syllogism with the consequent exclusion of non-syllogistic forms of deduction. [Bertrand] Russell's definition of logic as the study of all types of deduction thus required new foundations, the outcome being a highly formalised axiomatic system. Just as Russell surmounted these limitations of classical logic with a more general theory of deduction, so Keynes proposed the further step of a non-demonstrative inference which would overcome the limitations of deductive logic. The syllogism was absorbed by Russell, and deduction was embraced as a special case by Keynes. But in achieving his goal, Keynes had to prise apart the links Russell had forged between logic and deduction, and between inference and implication. It is 'a matter of very great importance [that we] reach a definition of *inference* distinct from *implication*, as defined by Mr Russell' [Keynes 1971c, p. 127]. It is thus inference which is the foundation of Keynes's logic . . . The laws of thought or inference then become 'the laws of probability' [Keynes 1971c, p. 142]. What Russell . . . said of his own programme could have been penned by Keynes with equal conviction: 'The old logic puts thought in fetters, while the new logic gives it wings' (O'Donnell 1989, p. 33).

In his *Treatise on Probability* Keynes developed a *general* system of formal logic capable of being applied to *all* domains of the real world, aiming thus at setting up the foundations for a complete material logic or theory of knowledge. '[Keynes's] theory of rational inference . . . takes the whole of human thought as its domain, ranging across areas as diverse as actuarial studies, legal disputation, moral reasoning, metaphysical speculation, psychical research and mathematical argument, not to mention daily life and all branches of the natural and social sciences' (O'Donnell 1989, p. 38). We shall return to aspects of Keynes's vision in the last chapter of this book; here we link up some of Keynes's basic concepts to the argument developed so far in this subsection.

The starting point is the concept of *probability* which, 'for Keynes, is essentially about logical relations between sets of propositions [particularly to those pairs of sets] that constitute the premises and conclusions of arguments. Keynes labels these logical relations "probability relations". In general, they are relations of partial entailment or support . . . Keynes also claims that the probability relation expresses the degree of rational belief that may be placed in the conclusion of an argument' (O'Donnell 1989, p. 34). The degrees of certainty vary between certainty and impossibility (p. 35). Probability is relative to evidence and is concerned with *rational* belief and not with mere, or psychological, belief: 'Probabilities are [therefore] always *objective* and never subjective. This is so because they are essentially connected to logic and not to psychology. Logical relations are viewed as objective because they are grounded in an *external immutable realm* [our emphasis] which timelessly transcends mere individual opinion' (pp. 37–8). This is crucial as to the meaning of truth which is 'a property of a proposition . . . a certain conclusion becomes a true conclusion when the premises are true' (p. 36). Material logic deals, in Keynes's view, with the correspondence of thought and the objectively given real world comprising, on the one hand, essences of things and of relations between things, i.e. the 'external immutable realm' just mentioned, and the appearances that are accessible through the senses, on the other. This definitely links Keynes to the great metaphysical tradition of Plato and Aristotle.

In all epochs, metaphysics was temporarily superseded by positivism of some kind: the Greek sophists, the nominalists in the Middle Ages and modern empiricists, subjective rationalists and Kantian idealists all attempted assaults against the metaphysical fortress. The assault on traditional metaphysics was particularly systematic and all-embracing from the sixteenth century onwards (Hirschberger 1984, 1988, vol. II). This onslaught was presumably necessary because the open-minded metaphysical way of thinking in the tradition of Aristotle and Aquinas had been gradually transformed into sterile games of formal logic and into equally sterile dogmatism. The anti-metaphysical movement culminated in English empiricism:

[Empiricism represents] a radical rupture with the metaphysical tradition of Plato and Aristotle, which dominated occidental thought up to Leibniz. Now there is no metaphysics any more, no transcendence and, most importantly, no eternal truths . . . Empiricism is content with sensual experience of the external world . . . Sensual experience leads on the way to truth, values, ideals, justice and religion . . . Everything gets relative with respect to space, time and individual behaviour . . . The British Isles were to become the stronghold of empiricism which reached perfection in the systems of Hobbes, Locke and Hume (Hirschberger 1984, 1988, vol. II, p. 188; a.tr.).

Keynes is definitely *not* within the tradition of English empiricism: '[According to Russell] Keynes's theory of knowledge depends on "a kind of knowledge which empiricism holds to be impossible"' (O'Donnell 1989, p. 93; see also Fitzgibbons 1988, p. 28). This type of knowledge is metaphysical in the tradition of the great Greek philosophers: '[Regarding philosophical influences on Keynes exercised by] the Ancients, Plato is clearly foremost, with Aristotle also significant' (O'Donnell 1989, p. 47).

This leads to an important proposition: in our view, Keynes, in his *Treatise on Probability*, attempted to *reconcile* traditional metaphysical reasoning and modern natural and social science. General metaphysics deals, first, with fundamental properties of the immaterial and material world

(Hirschberger): the meaning of 'being' (*Sein*) in general, realizations and development potentials of all things, and their essence and forms of existence; secondly, the specific properties of each thing – unity and identity, multitude, truth, goodness and beauty – are another part of metaphysics; a third domain is concerned with the categories of the existing: what is essential to a thing, what is accidental? How is the existing characterized by quantity, quality and relations to other things. Fourthly, there are the general causes that may transform potentialities into existence (Hirschberger 1984, 1988, vol. I, p. 183): the formal and material cause as well as the efficient and final cause mentioned above (pp. 55–7). If specific domains are considered, metaphysical reasoning is basically about grasping the probable essence of things, i.e. of fundamentals or principles. While the objectively given principles are universal and timeless, knowledge about these principles is historically variable in accordance with the degree of insight achieved in each epoch. The systems of Ricardo, Walras, Sraffa and Pasinetti deal with principles in the socioeconomic domain and represent, as such, pieces of pure theory. The social philosophies presented at the beginning of this chapter are also typically pieces of metaphysics, i.e. pure theory. Each social philosophy attempts to come to grips with the essence of society and man and the fundamental roles played by the economic, social, legal and political institutions within society. Attempts to establish principles in a particular domain require that the process of abstraction be comprehensive: the procedure of eliminating accidentals to get down to supposed essentials requires a global vision of things; for example, in the attempt to find out about the essence of 'price' the whole of society must be the starting point because of the complementarities existing between the various parts of society.

Modern science – mainly based upon French subjective rationalism, initiated by René Descartes, and English empiricism, founded by Francis Bacon – claims to be anti-metaphysical. Formal logical thinking and experience through the senses are the means to obtain scientific knowledge. Starting from hypotheses, observations are made, experiments carried out and tests performed; the original hypotheses are either confirmed or new ones are established. The continual establishment and revision of theories is the vehicle of scientific progress. In this view no permanent objectively given truths exist. Everything is relative. In the extreme case the observing and thinking subject – the individual – determines what truth is. The atomistic real world, dominated by chance, is illuminated and shaped by the scientific activities of individuals: the subject determines the object. This was the main tenet of Kant's Copernican revolution.

Nobody would deny the immense achievements of the natural sciences and, to a certain extent, the social sciences since the sixteenth century.

Several problems arise, however, in this context. First, metaphysics can never be eliminated if science tackles complex problems. Materialism, empiricism and scepticism all rest on metaphysical propositions on the essence of nature, man and society which may be entirely or partly true or false. Hence the premises of a theory always imply value judgements. Second, scientific activities always involve complex ethical issues. For example, it is evident that science should not be misused to enhance the power of particular individuals but rather should promote the public interest; or what can be done technically should, on ethical grounds, not always be done, in order to protect man, society and nature. Third, it would seem that the progress of the natural sciences has been faster than that of the social sciences. Keynes indeed wanted to forge a new political economy that would enable society and man to benefit more extensively from progress in the natural sciences. The problem of poverty existing side by side with an immense productive potential always preoccupied him intensely. These and related questions will be briefly taken up in the final chapters.

The above implies that there are two broad approaches in the theory of knowledge, one is metaphysically based, the other rests on empiricism and subjective rationalism. Karl Pribram suggests that both can be found in the history of economic thought, too (Pribram 1986). Some economists and social scientists believe in the power of reason to grasp approximately the essence and the profound significance of things; these 'essentialists' (Pribram) adhere as a rule to an organic conception of man and society, whereby both are considered complex entities. Other social scientists, however, limit the faculties of reason to formulating hypothetical conditions in which the existence of causal relations could be supposed; these 'hypotheticians', as Pribram calls them, adopt as a rule an atomistic and mechanistic view of the real world (Pribram 1986, p. 616). According to Pribram, many economists mix up, presumably unconsciously, the essentialist and the hypothetical methods: 'One may easily . . . show the extent to which hypothetical reasoning predominates in the Ricardian approach – in which, however, important elements of scholastic thinking remain, [e.g.] the belief in the concept of the substance of things' (p. 597; a.tr.).

In his *Treatise on Probability* Keynes contributes to reviving the metaphysical approach and thereby to reversing Kant's Copernican revolution. He rejects the view that the senses and subjective reason alone determine what reality is and that metaphysical knowledge about the essence of things is impossible. Keynes proposes a synthesis of the two methods. His theory of rational inference attempts to incorporate metaphysical speculation *and* all branches of the modern natural and social sciences (O'Donnell 1989, p. 38). Metaphysical reasoning associated with intuition aims at understanding society and man in their entirety on a fundamental level; the crucial role of intuition is emphasized throughout Keynes's *Treatise*. On the other hand, scientific work consists in formulating and testing hypotheses using statistical and econometric techniques in the social sciences; these techniques are complemented by experiments in the natural sciences. Scientific work confirms and complements metaphysical reasoning and intuitive insights. Keynes's endeavour for a synthesis of metaphysics and science shows up, for example, in the proposition that 'the probability of the same statement varies with the evidence presented [which may be of all kinds: empirical, based upon *a prori* theoretical reasoning or on intuition]' (Keynes 1971c, p. 7).

This synthesis in the theory of knowledge is related to another synthesis which refers to a metaphysical view on the basic constitution of the universe:

[As early as 1905] Keynes produced [a] classification, embracing both the moral and the natural sciences, [which] integrated his ideas on quality and quantity with thoughts on part–whole relations. By way of explanation he wrote as follows: 'Most but not all of the qualities dealt with in pure and applied mathematics and capable of exact measurement [imply that the degree of the whole equals the sum of degrees of the parts, e.g. weight or extension]. [The principle of organic unities appears if the whole is independent of the parts as is the case with beauty, utility and the public interest.]' (O'Donnell 1989, pp. 61–2).

In terms of the social philosophies considered above, the first type of quality just mentioned – the degree of the whole equals the sum of the degrees of the parts – relates to liberal social philosophy: here individuals are autonomous and self-contained and society is atomistic and its functioning mechanical; the behaviour of the individuals is all important, and the co-ordination of behaviour is performed by automatic mechanisms; the corresponding theory of knowledge is based upon empiricism and subjective rationalism. The principle of organic unity however is associated with both socialist and humanist social philosophies, though in different ways: in the former the whole dominates the parts, i.e. the individuals and social classes; in the latter the whole – the system – stands in the service of individuals; in humanist social philosophy the functioning of the system and the behaviour of individuals are both important: the system partly determines behaviour while institutionalized social and individual behaviour shapes the system. The theory of knowledge is associated with the essentialist method in so far as an understanding of the functioning of society *in principle* is required to tackle social problems, e.g. the determination of the level of employment, on a fundamental level, i.e. on the level of principles or of pure theory (chapter 4, pp. 142–58). Modern scientific methods may be applied to deal with the behaviour of individuals within a given system.

Complex questions, like the determination of the employment level, and fundamentals, such as the essence of the price, cannot be dealt with by standard scientific methods, i.e. by testing theories, since at each step of the argument the hypothetical premises would have to be tested in turn. This would entail an infinite regression resulting in agnosticism, because there are no realistic hypotheses to start with. Metaphysical reasoning is therefore indispensable to the provision of the foundations for scientific activities. The foundations, however, will never be secure. Metaphysics can provide a broad and more or less tentative overall view, on social issues for example, so as to enable the social scientist to reason within an orderly framework. Metaphysics, as Aristotle remarks, is the architectonic science, suggesting what is fundamental and what is secondary; this allows us to order scattered pieces of knowledge. What is considered to be essential and primary and what is looked at as accidental and secondary will depend upon the value system prevailing in a society.

Value judgements and theoretical approaches

Some *a priori* understanding of reality is required before building a model or, more modestly, developing a theory to explain some economic phenomenon, e.g. unemployment, functional distribution or pricing: 'in order to be able to posit to ourselves any problems at all, we should first have to visualize a distinct set of coherent phenomena as a worth-while object of our analytic efforts. In other words, analytic effort is of necessity preceded by a preanalytic cognitive act that supplies the raw material for the analytic effort . . . this preanalytic cognitive act will be called Vision' (Schumpeter 1954, p. 41). 'Now it should be perfectly clear that there is a wide gate for ideology to enter into this process. In fact, it enters on the very ground floor, into the preanalytic cognitive act of which we have been speaking. Analytic work begins with material provided by our vision of things, and this vision is ideological almost by definition' (p. 42). This very important methodological statement leads right into the heart of a hotly discussed problem in the social sciences, i.e. the theorist's problem of giving shape to his vision which inevitably requires value judgements (pp. 804–7). At this stage, however, Schumpeter seems to minimize the importance of the vision, as he does throughout his work: 'if an economist is inspired by the typically historical sense for environment, he may be able to proffer – from a knowledge of which value judgements are associated with a given environment – historically relative advice without leaving the precincts of his professional competence. This goes some way . . . toward justifying economists' value judgements. It also explains, in part at least, why the controversy on value judgements did not produce any very important results'

(p. 807). This statement may mean, for instance, that values may be important in determining the nature of the problems posed for economists in a given society, or the objectives of the decision-takers, but irrelevent to the tools of economic analysis. In postulating this, Schumpeter makes, however, far-reaching value judgements. For example, he gives priority to exchange, thus relegating production to a secondary role. His enthusiasm for the Walrasian system (see pp. 912–13, 998–9, for instance) probably accounts for this. Indeed, the neoclassical, basically Walrasian way of theorizing is the only possible one for Schumpeter, as his devastating verdict on Ricardo shows: 'Ricardo was completely blind to the nature, and the logical place in economic theory, of the supply-and-demand apparatus and . . . he took it to represent a theory of value distinct from and opposed to his own. This reflects little credit on him as a theorist' (p. 601). This categorical rejection of Ricardo and his production-based approach to economic problems is another value judgement.

The postulate that values should not enter the domain of economic – and social – science (*Wertfreiheit*) was introduced by Max Weber and is explicitly or implicitly accepted by most liberal (neoclassical) economists. This doctrine implies that the neoclassical approach is taken for granted, or the the basic neoclassical hypothesis related to the invisible hand is considered a realistic starting point which does not imply a value judgement. On this basis, specific theories required to explain economic phenomena – the functional distribution of incomes, for example – are, in principle, supposed to obtain by theoretical and empirical means (testing). In this view theories are explanatory techniques independent of a specific historical and social environment (Dobb 1973, introduction). From these theories, means may be derived to reach given aims as determined by the politicians. The normative enters the scene in relation to the choice of aims. The neoclassical view of things may be useful if clearly defined partial problems are investigated; once complex issues related to the functioning of society as a whole are considered – employment and distribution for instance – problems may arise. For example, the invisible hand may not work properly because of the essentially social nature of the process of production (chapter 5, pp. 281–93).

Since there are no realistic hypotheses to start with whenever complex problems are considered (this chapter, pp. 57–64 above and chapter 5, pp. 293–304), the approach, associated with the kind of the tools used to analyse economic problems, is necessarily value-loaded. The neoclassical economist will choose different tools to explain unemployment than the Keynesian political economist. Similarly, the classical-Keynesian political economist will hold an entirely different view as to the nature of the price system than the neoclassical economist (Pasinetti 1986, pp. 419, 423–4).

Hence values are inevitably present in positive and normative economic analysis because human knowledge is always limited: it is impossible to find a secure starting point. Therefore, we might argue – as does Myrdal (1976a) – that the theoretical economist ought to identify the values which are necessarily implied by the premises he starts from. This would indeed greatly clarify the current disputes between the various economic schools of thought mentioned in the preface to this book. Luigi Pasinetti makes a similar point. He states that both the pure preference model and the pure labour model 'spring from a particular social philosophy' (Pasinetti 1986, pp. 419, 424), and then goes on to

suggest the image of the theorizing process as a sort of telescope, which is used in both directions: to magnify, in one direction, those aspects on which the theorist has chosen to concentrate; and to shrink, in the opposite direction, or reduce to irrelevance, those aspects that are to play secondary roles.

But who is going to choose those aspects that are to be magnified and those aspects that are to be reduced? This is a worrying question. The obvious answer – 'the intuition of the theorist' – begins to sound less satisfactory on this point. It has been pointed out already, with specific reference to the theory of value, that one may identify, at a pre-theoretical stage, so to speak, the choice of a particular conception, or 'vision', of the world. This, in the social sciences, may well be a device to achieve consistency among the type of simplifications made (Pasinetti, 1986, p. 428).

In this study, Pasinetti's view on the problem of value judgements is broadly adopted and elaborated.

The *vision* of the nature of man and of society is, perhaps, the most important preanalytic element which enters economic theory through its premises. It is crucial for analysing an economic problem, for example whether a neoclassical or Keynesian model is used to explain unemployment. The choice of model is based on a value judgement and reflects the economist's conscious or unconscious values underpinning his social philosophy. Value systems or moral institutions are, in general, important for society as a whole and for economic theory in particular. Given this, the relationship between vision, social philosophy and values held has to be defined and each of their roles in theorizing briefly sketched. This, and the broad classification of social philosophies presented above, leads to an equally broad classification of economic theories, which will be compared in chapter 5.

A vision of a complex social state of affairs, for example the broad functioning of society, or of a complex social phenomenon, the persistence of involuntary unemployment, say, is explicitly or implicitly based upon a *social philosophy*. A wide spectrum of social philosophies exists: various forms of liberalism, of socialism and of humanist social philosophies, the underlying principles of which were set out above (pp. 27–39). The social scientist's choice is based on *values* (is a liberal society to be preferred, in principle, to a socialist one or vice versa?), which determine indirectly, i.e. through the social philosophy chosen and the vision derived therefrom, his explanations for economic phenomena. For example, when attempting to explain the phenomenon of unemployment a neoclassical economist primarily looks at the labour market and the forces operating there while the classical-Keynesian political economist tries to find out why effective demand is deficient. The reasons why and how an economist or a large group of economists comes to choose a specific approach are summarized by Schumpeter's statement that value judgements enter the hypotheses underlying positive models, aimed at explaining existing or past situations. In this sense, the values held by social scientists are part of a given historical reality which influences their reasoning on socioeconomic phenomena. This partly explains the historical relativity of theories, e.g. the fact that neoclassical theory was largely replaced by Keynesian conceptions after the Second World War and until the late sixties, and vice versa since the early seventies.

Why social scientists adopt broad approaches and specific theories to explain social phenomena is only partly covered by what is called the sociology of knowledge. The scientists' social group or milieu certainly plays an important role. But his choice of theoretical conceptions is also heavily influenced by the general socioeconomic situation (on this, see Screpanti and Zamagni 1993, introduction). There can be little doubt that the severe unemployment prevailing during the thirties and its social consequences greatly favoured the (temporary) success of Keynes's *General Theory*. The prevailing climate of ideas, or the *Zeitgeist*, is also a crucial factor governing the choice of theories. The political philosophy of absolutism (Hobbes) favoured mercantilist ideas while the Enlightenment, linked with the social philosophy of liberalism (Locke, Hume, Montesquieu and Voltaire), was basic to the rise and the long-lasting success of neoclassical economics. Furthermore, the fundamental values associated with various spheres of individual and social life in the form of evolving customs and habits (Schmoller 1920, vol. I, pp. 60–4) also influence social scientists' visions of society; an example might be the changing significance of the family in modern societies.

Finally, these objective factors mentioned so far may be complemented by individual (psychological) factors, also important in the choice of the theoretical approach. An economist may, initially, hold certain values linked up with a given social philosophy and a specific vision of things which lead him to choose a certain conceptual framework to explain economic phenomena. Subsequently, he may become dissatisfied with the approach chosen, e.g. the neoclassical one, and this may lead him to examine more closely the premises underlying it and eventually to explore other possible approaches (Keynesian, classical or Marxian). This process might be called theoretical experience. The capital theory debate (chapter 5, pp. 281–93) typically is a piece of theoretical experience in that it consists of an examination of the premises underlying the neoclassical theory of production and distribution. The process of continuously comparing the content of one's theory with objectively given reality, so becoming more and more familiar with specific aspects of the real world, including its historical developments, might be called practical experience.

Both theoretical and practical experience are explicitly or implicitly based on metaphysical foundations relating to the nature of things. These basics result from intuition and pure reason. It is here that values, social philosophies and visions enter the picture. In the last instance, it is reason which enables us to put together scattered pieces of knowledge so as to obtain a system of thought, which is associated with the specific vision held by an individual. All these processes may lead to a gradual change in an economist's hierarchy of values, his social philosophy and his vision of socioeconomic reality. A new vision of things may result in an alternative theoretical conception. The role of values, social philosophies and visions in positive economics is, evidently, of tremendous complexity and gives rise (and has given rise) to a host of exciting historical studies. In this field, a highly interesting subject of research was proposed by Schumpeter who argues that the theoretical model contained in Keynes's *General Theory* is the analytical formulation of a vision already present in the *Economic Consequences of the Peace* (Schumpeter 1954, pp. 41–2). Certainly, it would now be of some interest to compare Schumpeter's proposition with the findings on Keynes's vision obtained by Carabelli (1985), Fitzgibbons (1988) and O'Donnell (1989).

Hence values enter analytical work through the premises underlying positive theories. However, they also determine, together with objectively given factors, the objects of investigation. Is the study of the process of economic growth to be emphasized, or should priority be given to the study of the causes of unemployment, to the factors regulating distribution, or to some other research area? Moreover, values are also related to systematic descriptions of desirable states of the world, i.e. normative economic theory. Here, the role of values is much more evident than is the case in positive theory.

Presumably, an economist's system of values determines simultaneously his way of looking at the real world and his way of conceiving of desirable situations. In socioeconomic matters, the liberal, the socialist and the classical-Keynesian economists see what *is* and what *should be* through their respective glasses. However, a social philosophy and its associated vision may have a positive or a normative bias and, accordingly, economic theory may be essentially positive in character, as is the case with classical-Keynesian political economy, or essentially normative, as in the case of liberal and socialist economic theory.

The values held by social scientists are part of the evolving cultural environment in the widest sense of the phrase and have to be taken as given. Therefore, the crucial concept required in defining the nature of the vision is that of social philosophy which has been dealt with in the preceding chapter. Some of the concepts used subsequently to characterize the different types of visions are borrowed from Lloyd (1986), whose work provides an excellent survey of explanatory approaches in social history and will certainly play an important methodological role in the construction of a coherent system of the social sciences.

The social philosophies of liberalism and socialism and the associated social sciences are essentially of a normative nature. Real world situations are interpreted as deviations from the norm. For example, in the economic theory of liberalism, i.e. neoclassical economics, market imperfections give rise to various problems; monopoly profits are just one issue. However, the humanist social philosophy sketched above (pp. 27–39) underlies both positive and normative visions. A positive (realist) vision broadly corresponds to the preanalytic view on how actually existing societies function in principle, whereby 'functioning' essentially means the interplay of institutions. Visions of this kind interact with theoretical and practical experience and provide starting points for systematic theorizing. Keynes's monetary theory of production is an example of a positive or realist vision in the socioeconomic sphere. Pure normative systems – like Pasinetti's *natural system* – constitute a set of principles underlying ideal societies organized along humanist lines. The normative and the positive are linked up through the notion of alienation (pp. 47–53 above). This concept conceives of the normative as the ethically appropriate form of the positive.

The various types of social philosophy may be broadly ordered with the help of the constitutive principles underlying them (pp. 27–39 above). Liberalism is based on the principle of individualism, socialism on holism. Humanism, encompassing (positive) social realism and (normative) natural systems, might be grounded on the principle of *structurism* (Lloyd 1986, pp. 15ff.): the network of institutions forms the *social structure* (Lloyd 1986, ch. 8, pp. 148ff.) within which individuals act. The different kinds of social philosophy may be conceived of as a spectrum of views lying between the extremes of pure individualism and pure holism. The former would correspond to anarchy and the latter to a tightly organized totalitarian society.

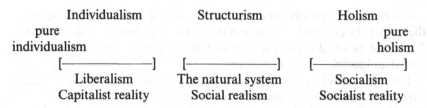

Neoclassical equilibrium economics is based upon the liberal vision of society while the economic theory of centrally planned socialism is built upon the socialist vision. The economic theory associated with social or historical realism corresponds to classical-Keynesian political economy. This proposition will be substantiated in the subsequent chapters.

The essentially normative nature of neoclassical equilibrium theory and of the economic theory of centrally planned socialism shapes the methodological procedures adopted by liberal and socialist economists: first, the respective normative system is worked out with great logical care. In a second step, capitalist and socialist reality is explained as a deviation from the liberal or the socialist norm, i.e. the respective ideal situation. This is the hallmark of imperfectionism. Consequently, in neoclassical equilibrium theory, reality appears as a deviation from the (Pareto-optimal) state of perfect competition which is linked with allocative efficiency, implying full employment. Unemployment is accounted for by market imperfections. In the socialist view, economic problems, e.g. supply deficiencies or inappropriate product quality, occur because of deficiencies of the (central) planning mechanism. This procedure implies introducing a heavy speculative element into the analysis of facts which as a rule implies a neglect of historical experience. The normative element is given too much weight which leads to a biased interpretation of reality: reality is not perceived as it is but as some liberal or socialist economists would like to see it. This may imply ideology or false consciousness in the sense of Marx, which is in turn associated with alienated science (pp. 47–53). This issue will be taken up in chapters 5 and 7.

Classical-Keynesian political economy contains both positive and normative strands of thought. The former is sketched in chapter 4, the latter in chapter 6. The social philosophy underlying positive classical-Keynesian theory (social or historical realism) essentially consists of views related to the interplay of institutions, i.e. the social structure of actually existing societies. Pure positive theory deals with principles, i.e. abstract causal forces; for example, with the principles of price or employment determination; applied theory leads to historical observation, i.e. to the interpretation of facts on the basis of pure theories (chapter 3, pp. 81–9). Pure normative classical-Keynesian models picture how ideal societies ought to look in

Social philosophy	Positive theory	Normative theory
Liberalism	Explanation of capitalist reality as a deviation from the liberal norm (I)	Neoclassical (equilibrium) economics (II)
	Explanation of socialist reality as a deviation from the liberal norm (III)	Criticism of socialism in terms of the liberal norm (IV)
Socialism	Explanation of socialist reality as a deviation from the socialist norm (V)	Socialist political economy (central planning theory) (VI)
	Explanation of capitalist reality as a deviation from the socialist norm (VII)	Criticism of liberalism in terms of the socialist norm (VIII)
Humanism: social or historical realism; natural systems	Explanation of aspects of the real world based on classical-Keynesian political economy (IX)	Natural systems of the classical-Keynesian type (Quesnay–Pasinetti) (X)

principle from a humanist viewpoint; Quesnay's *tableau économique* (see, for example, Kuczynski and Meek 1972) and Pasinetti's *natural system* (Pasinetti 1981, 1993) constitute such models. Applied normative models of the classical-Keynesian type would refer to specific societies.

The accompanying table relates the basic approaches in economic theory to the visions and social philosophies underlying them. This scheme could be refined and extended in various ways. It allows for a broad classification of economic theories and provides an approximate survey of the content of this study. In this chapter we have examined selected aspects of the conceptual or social philosophical underpinning of all the theories contained in the scheme. Chapters 3 and 4 are devoted to positive classical-Keynesian political economy (IX in the above scheme). In chapter 6 a normative classical-Keynesian system (X) is sketched, i.e. Pasinetti's natural system (Pasinetti 1981, 1993). Chapter 5 is devoted to a comparison between positive classical-Keynesian political economy (IX), on the one hand, and normative neoclassical equilibrium economics (II) and the associated explanation of capitalist reality in terms of deviations from the liberal norm (I), on the other.

Ethics and knowledge

The ethical character of the social sciences seems to deprive them of their scientific status since, allegedly, one cannot argue scientifically about moral values: 'According to Hume, neither probabilistic arguments nor ethical arguments conform to the demonstrable rules of inferential logic, and so both sorts of reasoning are subject to the imagination and are subrational' (Fitzgibbons 1988, p. 35). Moral statements seem to be linked with more or less strong feelings on socioeconomic hardship – such as unemployment, lack of distributional equity and so on – frequently coupled with claims for urgent solutions, and are, as such, devoid of rational scientific arguments. For example, referring to the social reforms carried out in France and Germany from 1870 onwards, Schumpeter states:

I do not hesitate to say that this achievement was one of the most important in the records of the economic *profession* . . . That achievement . . . evidently did not belong to the sphere of scientific analysis . . . What does concern us is . . . its influences on teaching and research . . . The efficiency of teaching indubitably suffered . . . The German 'socialists of the chair' certainly fulfilled the ideal of progressive politicians and laymen – the ideal of the professor who preaches reforms and denounces obstructing interests. Lujo Brentano addressed his classes as he would have political meetings, and they responded with cheers and countercheers. Adolf Wagner shouted and stamped and shook his fists at imaginary opponents . . . such lectures need not necessarily be weak in the technical instruction they impart, but as a rule they are. He who thinks this a cheap price to pay for ethics and ardor will please consider for a moment where, say, internal medicine would be if its teachers, instead of developing the analytic powers of their pupils, indulged in rhetoric about the glories of healing (Schumpeter 1954, p. 802).

Some 'socialists of the chair' seemed to suggest that the aims to be reached and, much more importantly, the ways to reach specific aims were self-evident and did not require a scientific foundation. This voluntarist view was similar to the position taken by many members of the historical school, including institutionalists, who claimed that only historical investigations were needed to understand the real world, theory being of little or no use.

To establish the scientific character of the social (moral) sciences, it seems convenient to start from the fact that ethical postulates, associated with desirable states of affairs, form a hierarchical system of immense complexity: '[For Keynes,] goodness is not atomic, but complex and organic, meaning that we do not want particular arrangements of atoms to occur, but *evaluate each set of circumstances in overall terms* [*i.e. in terms of the socioeconomic system*; our emphasis]' (Fitzgibbons 1988, p. 19). This implies considering society an entity: the institutional system, i.e. economic, social, legal and political institutions, represents a system of means aiming at realizing a hierarchy of values. The degree to which the specific values are realized makes up the level of public welfare or common weal, which represents the fundamental and all-embracing value in political philosophy. Various imperfections, e.g. ignorance or the exaggerated pursuit of particular interests, will persistently result in a larger or smaller gap between some actually existing level of welfare and the common weal or the public interest. If this gap is caused by a misfunctioning of the socioeconomic and political system we speak, following Marx, of alienation, of which involuntary unemployment is the prime example. The point now is that some understanding of the functioning of society as a *whole* is required if some specific policy action is to be undertaken. For example a change in taxation may influence distribution which, in turn, may affect the longperiod employment level, which, as will be suggested in chapter 4 (pp. 158–75), is directly or indirectly governed by *all* socioeconomic and political institutions.

Moreover, a system of values implies, as a rule, conflicts between aims to be achieved. For example, if the aims of full employment *and* job security are both to be realized, then an entirely planned economy must be set up. The latter, however, implies that other values may not be realized: personal liberties will have to be drastically reduced; other consequences might be an excessively low labour productivity associated with a deficient supply of necessary goods. On the other hand, if personal liberties in the economic sphere are not restricted at all and if the solution of the important economic problems is left exclusively to the market mechanism, a very unequal distribution of incomes accompanied by mass unemployment may result. This renders it impossible to achieve generally the values associated with personal liberties, which, for example, have no meaning for the involuntarily unemployed person who is crushed by his fate. This example gives rise to a scientific problem: what is the nature of unemployment or what are the forces governing the level (the scale) of employment? The classical-Keynesian political economist will reject the socialist solution to achieving full employment by fully planning the economy and analyse subsequently the liberal (neoclassical) theory of employment: can markets produce a tendency towards full employment *in principle*? In chapter 5 (pp. 281–93) it will be suggested that this is not likely to be the case. Starting from the principle of effective demand, the classical-Keynesian political economist may now elaborate a theory of normal output, of business cycles and of short-run fluctuations (chapter 4). Having isolated the forces determining involuntary unemployment, he may look for the causes bringing about structural unemployment (Pasinetti 1981). All these positive theories prepare the way for full employment policies in line with other values (personal liberties, for example) which are part of a complete ethical system along humanist lines. However, the permanently existing conflict of values is a major reason why it will never be possible to eliminate alienation – the gap between the positive and the normative – completely.

The social sciences attempt to explain phenomena of social interest. Subsequently, means may be proposed to reach aims, a higher employment level for instance, such that an established and broadly recognized hierarchy of desirable values is not upset: to reach a coherent system of ends, a coherent system of means has to be established. Hence the benevolent intention to reach socially desirable aims is not sufficient, as the 'socialists of the chair' believed: *ethics requires a scientific underpinning to be provided by the social sciences*. This is 'the kernel of Keynes's philosophy, his vision, [according to which] truth is likewise a prerequisite for *correct action*' (Fitzgibbons 1988, p. 51).

In this view, ethics and the social sciences are not opposed and contradictory, but represent two complementary dimensions of scientific activity. On the basis of given values the social scientist selects problems to be dealt with and looks for theoretical approaches from which pure and applied theories are derived in order to grasp the essence of specific aspects of the real world or to explain unique historical situations. While given values are associated with positive theory, ethically desirable values are linked up with normative theories. Positive and normative theories are both required to set up socioeconomic policies.

3 Some basic issues in political economy

This chapter, like the preceding one, deals with fundamentals, but at a lower degree of abstraction and on a more specific level: instead of considering the whole of society, some basic issues relating to classical-Keynesian political economy are dealt with briefly. The first section is devoted to definitional issues concerning the content and the method of political economy. In the subsequent section the classical-Marxian vision of the institutional set-up is sketched. The third section deals with the classical heritage and the Keynesian problem, to be combined in classical-Keynesian political economy. The classical element in political economy will be examined quite closely and will be taken for granted subsequently. The object of section four is the seemingly abstract question of space and time, which has to be dealt with to be able to tackle some methodological difficulties and to prepare the ground for a broad classification of existing classical-Keynesian economic theories. The main concern of the methodological final section is with the relationship between theory and history. It is necessary to deal with this issue in order to attempt to bridge the gap existing between the institutionally and historically minded political economists on the one hand and the theorists on the other.

Definitional issues in political economy and economics

This section links up the preceding and the subsequent chapters. Some connections are established between the fundamentals in the social sciences and some aspects of the content and the method of political economy. The first subsection aims at broadly defining the notions of political economy and economics. Subsequently the meaning of classical-Keynesian political economy is elucidated somewhat. In the methodological final subsection an attempt is made to provide a broad classification of the various types of models and of equilibria.

Political economy and economics

Ricardo wrote on the principles of *political economy* (Ricardo 1951 [1821]), Marshall on the principles of *economics* (Marshall 1920). This is a highly significant distinction in the development of socioeconomic theory since the notions of political economy and of economics imply two entirely different theoretical approaches to dealing with social and economic phenomena. In this subsection both notions are broadly sketched. They will be treated more fully subsequently.

The two definitions of the social (chapter 2, pp. 20–1) perhaps provide the clue to bringing into the open the differences between economics and political economy. Economics is associated with the social in the liberal sense, i.e. as an interaction between individuals. This interaction takes place in the various markets between the individuals representing the supply and the demand sides respectively. Markets co-ordinate the utility-maximizing behaviour of consumers and workers and the profit-maximizing or cost-minimizing behaviour of producers. Hence economics is on the behavioural level. The starting point is the individual and exchange; production is secondary and is a field of application of exchange which shows up in the notion of factor markets. In principle, markets co-ordinate the behaviour of the individuals in a socially meaningful way. Ideally, the Walrasian general equilibrium implies a Pareto optimum. All the great economic problems – value, distribution and employment – are market problems.

Political economy embodies the social in the Aristotelian sense which comprises the common aim, complementary functions and co-ordination and co-operation. The social in this sense manifests itself most forcefully in the circular process of production as is pictured by Leontief–Sraffa models. The process of production forms the material basis of society: the social surplus produced within production enables society to set up an institutional superstructure made up of political, legal, social and cultural institutions. Hence the natural starting point in political economy is society in general and production in particular, which implies that all the great socioeconomic problems are genuinely social problems. This is particularly true of distribution which is the basic problem in political economy (Ricardo 1951 [1821], p. 5). In Ricardo's view distribution is not about the behaviour of individuals in the market-place, as is the case with Adam Smith, but about proportions, or part–whole relationships, between social classes and society independent of behaviour. In Ricardo's view, wages, profits and rents perform specific social functions; for example, profits enable the accumulation of capital. The problem of value can only be tackled once distribution is determined. This emerges from Sraffa price systems: the normal prices or the prices of production depend upon the conditions of production pictured by the various production coefficients and upon the money wage level and the rate of profits. In the real world both money wages and profit rates are governed by a complex set of institutions, of which customs and habits and trade unions are perhaps the most important. The scale of activity is undetermined in Sraffa models. This leaves room for bringing in Keynes's principle of effective demand.

The founder of economics is Adam Smith. To be sure, Adam Smith begins by discussing socioeconomic issues like production, division of labour, the size of markets and money in the first four chapters of his *Wealth of Nations*. However, production is treated individualistically; the emphasis is laid on the increased skills that result from the division of labour, which is illustrated by the production of pins (Smith 1976b [1776], pp. 14–15). However, Adam Smith switches to exchange and to the behaviour of individuals to tackle the issues of value and distribution from chapter 5 onwards, whereby behaviour ought to be grounded on the ethical principles of *self-interest* and *fellow feeling* set forth in the *Theory of Moral Sentiments*. Simultaneously, the problem of the scale of activity which preoccupied the mercantilists so intensely entirely disappears from the agenda. Smith's individualistic exchange approach was taken up by J. B. Say, who together with other Smithians like Longfield and Senior prepared the way for the neoclassical revolution in the 1870s brought about by Jevons, Walras, Marshall and Menger, a development recounted in a masterful way by Maurice Dobb (1973, specifically chapters 2, 3, 4 and 7). From then on the development of (neoclassical) economics is straightforward: the Walrasian, Marshallian and Austrian variants progressed steadily, although with varying strength, to form the body of modern neoclassical economics, which is essentially Adam Smith without the ethical foundations provided in the *Theory of Moral Sentiments*.

The modern line of development of political economy starts off with the mercantilists and cameralists and culminates with James Steuart who provides excellent definitions of economics and political economy (Steuart 1966 [1767], pp. 15–17). The founder of modern political economy is, however, François Quesnay. His *tableau économique* (see, for example, the presentation by Oncken 1902, pp. 386ff.) pictures the circular and social process of production and exhibits the surplus principle of distribution. Both production and distribution are about the proportions that must exist if the process of production is to go on undisturbed. But the scale aspect is also taken account of. The spending of rents by the landlords sets production into motion, and Quesnay worries time and again about eventual leakages that might reduce the scale of activity and hence bring about unemployment (see, for example, Oncken 1902, p. 396). Ricardo definitely established political economy as a coherent system of thought. In his

Principles, he mainly deals with the problems of value and distribution with the tacit understanding that the process of production is circular and social in the sense of Quesnay. The result was the surplus principle of distribution and the labour theory of value which constitute the theory of distribution and value in line with the political economy approach. This approach was taken up by Karl Marx who put the Quesnay–Ricardo system into a wider social, historical and philosophical framework; for example, he systematically made use of the classical 'material basis cum social superstructure' scheme to tackle socioeconomic problems. This device allows the merging of the institutional system and its evolution in political economy. The neat integration of theory and history in Marx's system is of great methodological importance in modern political economy. Partly as a reaction against Ricardo and Marx, the political economy approach became predominantly historical and institutional, and devoid of theory, in the hands of the American Institutionalists and the German Historical School. Keynes brought back theory in the form of the principle of effective demand which enabled him to deal with the scale of activity, thus complementing Ricardo's emphasis on proportions. In doing so Keynes clarified theoretically a strand of thought initiated by the mercantilists, particularly James Steuart, and carried on by writers as diverse as Malthus, Sismondi, Marx, Hobson and others (on this, see Keynes 1973a, chapter 23; surprisingly James Steuart is not quoted here in spite of the fact that he was an obvious forerunner of Keynes as is evident from Andrew Skinner's introduction to Steuart 1966 [1767], p. lviii, n.1). The classical-Marxian preoccupations with value and distribution and Keynes's concern with the scale of activity and with the role of money were taken up by the post Keynesians (chapter 1, pp. 1–6) and by most Marxists. Both groups are associated with important features of modern political economy.

The meaning of classical-Keynesian political economy

The attribute 'classical-Keynesian' raises two problems. The first is about the meaning of 'classical', the second about the relationship between classical and Keynesian elements of analysis.

The significance of 'classical' broadly emerges from the preceding subsection. Conventionally Adam Smith and David Ricardo are both considered classical political economists. There are, however, fundamental differences between the most eminent representatives of the so-called 'classical school' (which are accounted for most accurately by Dobb (1973, chapters 2, 3 and 4)): Ricardo's starting point is society, particularly the circular and social process of production. Adam Smith's emphasis, however, is on the individual and exchange. Consequently, Ricardo is a political economist, and Adam Smith an economist, although the latter attempted to ground his economic work upon an ethical system. Smith's ethics (Smith 1976a [1759]) is, however, about regulating the behaviour of individuals, not about the organization of society. Since the present study is about political economy, the notion 'classical' is used here in the Ricardian sense. Classical political economy thus encompasses Ricardo's system, but also large parts of Quesnay and Marx. Its meaning will become broadly evident in this and the subsequent chapters.

The relationship between Ricardo and Keynes is even more complex. At first sight the Ricardian and Keynesian systems seem to be sharply opposed. Ricardo mainly deals with natural long-period situations where employment is governed by capital accumulation, Say's law prevails, uncertainty plays no role and money is neutral. Keynes's *General Theory*, however, rests on a short-period approach with the capital stock given; time and uncertainty about the future, combined with non-neutral money, are used to demolish the classical and, to some extent, the neoclassical versions of Say's law, which implies disproving the claim that *general* overproduction is impossible. This cleared the way for Keynes to establish his own theory of employment based upon the principle of effective demand expressed by the investment multiplier (Keynes 1973c, pp. 109–23, reveals this two-stage way of proceeding). However, Keynes never attacked the classical approach to value and distribution, but showed profound sympathy for it, e.g. on pp. 41ff., 213–14 and 394ff. of the *General Theory* (Keynes 1973a). This also emerges from Keynes's favourable attitude towards Sraffa's criticism of Marshall's treatment of the laws of return (Sraffa 1926) and of Hayek's theory of interest (Sraffa 1932). Moreover, he laid the foundations for Kaldorian (or Robinsonian) distribution theory in the *Treatise on Money*, symbolized by the famous widow's cruse parable, which has classical origins too (Keynes 1971b, vol. I, p. 125). Finally, in the same work, he used extensively the concepts of normal profits and normal prices, the latter being based upon the costs of production (vol. I, pp. 111, 121–4).

Nevertheless, Keynes was prepared to accept those *neo*classical principles which he believed would do no harm to his theory of output and employment as a whole; perhaps he did so for tactical reasons: the author of the *Essays on Persuasion* was possibly aware that, in order to convince the academic public, he could not reject outright the entire body of orthodox theory. Consequently, he accepted the first *neo*classical postulate that '*[t]he wage is equal to the marginal product of labour*' (Keynes 1973a, p. 5) without much ado, complementing it by his concept of the marginal efficiency of capital. In this Keynes was misguided. The objections against neoclassical theory derived from the presence of uncertainty associated with money as a store of value have, indeed, not proved strong enough to prevent the subsequent re-establishment of neoclassical equilibrium economics. The crucial point is that the neoclassical equilibrium mechanism, i.e. the supply and demand apparatus, is based upon real factors with money playing no role. The marginal principle, embodied in the law of supply and demand in various shapes, ultimately solves the central problems of economic theory, i.e. value, production, distribution and employment, if markets are working perfectly – as in the general equilibrium model – or satisfactorily, if the real world is considered. Hence, if the long run is considered, the neoclassical theory of value and distribution implies full employment, or, as liberal practitioners would argue, a strong tendency towards full employment would come into being if an institutional environment favouring competition were created. It is only the capital theory debate which brought about the necessary clarification (chapter 5, pp. 281–93). From this debate it emerged that, if the process of production is conceived of as a social and circular process, there are no regular long-period associations between factor quantities and factor prices in the neoclassical sense. Factor markets thus do not work in an appropriate way, which implies that, in the long run, the marginal principle cannot solve any of the problems just mentioned. Hence, from a political economy viewpoint, a long-period theory of employment (and unemployment) based upon the principle of effective demand and implying quantity adjustments must be combined with the classical approach to value and distribution since in the latter, contrary to the neoclassical approach, the theory of value and distribution is separated from the theory of employment. Moreover, the classical (Ricardian) theory of employment (employment is governed by capital accumulation), in spite of its being based upon Say's law, does *not* postulate full employment. The classical version of this law only states that saving governs investment; however, the volume of investment may not be sufficient to create full employment; hence classical or Marxian unemployment, due to a lack of capital accumulation, may arise. In this vein W. A. Lewis very aptly christened the classical theory of development and employment as 'economic development with unlimited supplies of labour [provided by the agricultural sector]' (Lewis 1971). This point is emphasized by Milgate (1982), and confirmed by Pasinetti, who states that classical production models govern only *relative* prices and quantities, i.e. proportions, and leave the *scale* of activity undetermined (Pasinetti 1981, p. 23, n. 30). Consequently, there is no logical objection to linking the classical approach to value and distribution with a theory of employment along Keynesian lines while, at the same time, abandoning classical employment theory based on Say's law. Attempts systematically to explain value and distribution on the one hand and employment on the other along classical-Keynesian lines thus naturally result in separate theories which may be combined subsequently. This viewpoint is also adopted by Pasinetti (1981, 1993), Garegnani (1978/79, 1983), Milgate (1982), Eatwell (1983) and Eatwell and Milgate (1983). As suggested above, Keynes would presumably not have objected to this way of proceeding which, obviously, is contrary to the neoclassical position where value, distribution and employment are explained by a single model, i.e. by supply and demand theory. Defining, then, classical-Keynesian political economy as the synthesis of the Ricardian theory of value and distribution and the Keynesian theory of employment determination through effective demand appears as a logical necessity.

Different kinds of models and the nature of equilibria

The notions of 'positive' and 'normative' provide a convenient starting point for classifying socioeconomic models. Two types of positive model may be distinguished. *Pure* models deal with the principles or causes governing, in general, specific phenomena and their evolution: for example, Ricardo looked for the principles regulating value and distribution and the movement towards a stationary state; Sraffa and Pasinetti elaborated the Ricardian principles to produce pure theories of the social process of production, value and distribution; in *Das Kapital* Marx sought for the principles governing the evolution of the capitalist mode of production. Walras dealt with the principles regulating perfectly competitive economies. Pure models differ in their complexity: if the causal relation sequentially relates a few variables we speak of simple causal models; Keynes multiplier is an example. If variables are determined simultaneously we speak of equilibrium models; obvious cases in point are Walras's general equilibrium model picturing market equilibria and Sraffa's production of commodities by means of commodities and labour which exhibits how the social process of production functions in principle. Pure models are perfectly general in that the causal relations in question hold in all cases where a specific cause is at work; for instance, the causal relation pictured by the multiplier is embodied in all specific multiplier processes. Pure causal models are probable reflections of the essence or the nature of objectively given causal relations.

The application of principles (pure theories) to some real-world situation gives rise to explanatory frameworks to explain real-world phenomena, for instance to explain how distribution is regulated or employment is determined in some specific country or region in a specific period of time. Explanatory frameworks represent a second type of positive model, i.e. *applied* models. These are specific because historical situations are unique.

To contribute to the integration of theory and history it seems fruitful to link up the conceptions of pure and applied models with two notions that are widely used in the German literature, that is ideal type (*Idealtypus*) and real type (*Realtypus*). Both concepts are dealt with in Machlup's (1960/61) work *Idealtypus, Wirklichkeit und Konstruktion* which establishes various links with the literature, above all in the highly important work by Carl Menger *Untersuchungen über die Methode der Socialwissenschaften, und der Politischen Oekonomie insbesondere* (Menger 1969), which constitutes Menger's main contribution to the *Methodenstreit*. In an Aristotelian vein Menger associates coherent sets of pure causal models with pure theory which is timeless and perfectly general. Realizations of principles in time and space result in concrete situations which may be determined by a very great number of causes. To find out the most important of the causes governing a specific historical situation is the object of the historical sciences of which applied political economy and empirical economics are part.

In this view, ideal-type models are equivalent to pure models which are tools of thought to acquire probable knowledge on how objectively given causal forces work in principle. The amount of truth embodied in knowledge is determined by the probable degree of correspondence between the contents of thought and the objectively existing causal relations (Keynes 1971c). The pure models of production, value and distribution of Sraffa (1960) and Pasinetti (1977, 1981, 1993), Kalecki's cycle theories, the *logical* theory of the multiplier (Keynes, 1973a, p. 122) and the supermultiplier (chapter 4, pp. 142–204) are all ideal-type models in that they aim at bringing out the essence of the causal forces or determining principles that are probably at work in specific spheres of the socioeconomic world. The variables and parameters (employment levels and investment volumes for example) embodied in pure models and the relations between them, the multiplier for instance, also represent ideal types. In a wider view, sociological, political, legal and historical notions like capitalism, the working class, parliamentary democracy, the right wing, contract, the joint stock company, the medieval city and the Middle Ages are all ideal types. Real-type models, on the other hand, are explanatory frameworks dealing with concrete real-world situations governed by a great many causal forces. Frameworks to explain distributive outcomes or employment levels on the basis of some set of principles, e.g. classical-Keynesian or neoclassical theory, in specific countries or regions would represent real-type models. Correspondingly, the notion, say, involuntary unemployment in France, is a real type.

Handling pure or ideal-type models, i.e. dealing with principles, is, as a rule, mechanical and relatively simple; the explanation of real-world phenomena with the help of real-type models is, however, extremely complex because of the organic nature of the real world. Keynes held the view that socioeconomic phenomena were organically linked because of the ethical nature of the social sciences. So did Marshall who, incidentally, clearly perceived that dealing with principles with the help of pure models was mechanical while the realization of numerous principles in a concrete – real-world – state of affairs leads to situations of organic complexity: 'The Mecca of the [applied] economist lies in economic biology rather than in economic dynamics. But biological conceptions [to explain organic real-world phenomena] are more complex than those of mechanics; a volume on Foundations [i.e. principles] must therefore give a relatively large place to mechanical analogies' (Marshall 1920, p.xiv). Marx also dealt with this specific point which will be taken up in the final section of this chapter (pp. 118–30).

This study deals almost exclusively with principles, that is, pure or ideal-type models. Complications arising with real types are alluded to only in some instances: hints at real-world situations are made to illustrate the principles. Given the heavy 'ideal-type' bias of the following, the manner of arguing is largely mechanical: arguing on the basis of pure models always means arguing in a vacuum, i.e. by strictly applying the *ceteris paribus* principle. For example, on the basis of Sraffa's model the effect of a change in distribution – the profit rate – upon relative prices may be analysed in a pure form (see Pasinetti 1977, pp. 74ff.).

Normative models, in contradistinction to positive models, picture states of the world that are desirable in some respects. Such models depict harmonious orders of real-world elements. For example, in a humanist view, the notion of the common weal mentioned previously is normative in nature: the entire socioeconomic, legal and political system ought to be organized in a way such that individuals may achieve the fundamental values that make up a good and decent life. In this view, a model implying full employment and a fair distribution of incomes would be a normative model because these elements represent essential socioeconomic components of the common weal. An example is Pasinetti's natural economic system (Pasinetti 1981, 1993). Similarly, competitive neoclassical equilibrium models are normative because they imply a Pareto optimum and full employment. The crucial issue is which of these normative models is more fundamental. This question will be discussed in chapter 5 below on the basis of the first section of chapter 2 (pp. 20–57).

The distinction between pure models dealing with principles and applications of the principles to some real-world situation also applies to normative models. Pasinetti's (1981) natural system depicts the principles characterizing an ideal economy. Full-employment policies along classical-Keynesian lines, adapted to specific circumstances, would require normative real-type models, telling us what the desired state of affairs ought to look like in some specific country or region and what policy measures ought to be taken on the basis of specific conditions.

The second point to be dealt with here relates to the nature of equilibria. Two types of equilibria are distinguished: system equilibria and behavioural equilibria. The former are associated with the functioning of the socioeconomic system: the interplay of social and individualistic institutions produces certain equilibrium outcomes; the variables governed by the entire institutional system are normal variables. For example, Sraffa's model of production, value and distribution shows how the (normal) prices of production are governed by the conditions of production and the social regulation of distribution; or the supermultiplier relation set out in chapter 4 implies that the whole socioeconomic system (all institutions) comes in to determine the normal level of employment. There it will become evident that the system equilibrium is determined once income distribution is regulated. By definition, normal magnitudes – prices or employment levels, for example – are persistent because institutions represent steady social and individual behaviour associated with the pursuit of social and individual aims. Regarding system equilibria, the functioning of the system is primary and fundamental and the behaviour of individuals is secondary. The contrary holds for behavioural equilibria, of which market equilibria are the prime example. Here behaviour is fundamental and the system – the market system, for instance – is merely an automatic natural mechanism of secondary importance which costlessly co-ordinates the actions of individuals. This stands in striking contrast to the classical-Keynesian system equilibria. Here no automatic tendency towards an equilibrium exists, which means that ethically grounded policy efforts are required to improve existing situations.

Long-period variables (normal employment or normal prices for instance), which represent outcomes of the socioeconomic system, cannot be observed directly since the persistently acting causal forces act simultaneously with medium- and short-period forces to fully determine specific phenomena. At any moment, long-period magnitudes governed by the system are superseded by medium- and short-term behavioural outcomes. This point can be illustrated with the help of figure 1.

What can be directly observed is the whole of output Q (ad at t_1) which results from short-period entrepreneurial behaviour based upon short-period expectations: expected effective demand leads entrepreneurs to produce corresponding output quantities, hence to use existing capacities to a certain degree; the system governs a short-period equilibrium position determined by autonomous expenditures and the Keynesian multiplier. Abstracting from varying degrees of capacity utilization, capacity output Q_c (ac at t_1) obtains, i.e. the normal output that could be produced with existing capacities. Capacity output is governed by the past investment (accumulation) behaviour of entrepreneurs; this we denote medium-term

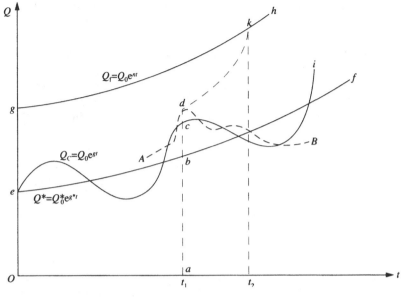

Figure 1.

behaviour because of the gradual revision of investment plans that takes place on the basis of comparisons between expected and realized results. Opposed to the behavioural outcomes is the outcome of the functioning of the institutional system, i.e. normal output Q^* (ab at t_1) to which correspond normal prices (see chapter 4, pp. 175–80) both of which cannot be observed directly. If now total output is above (long-period) normal output, as is the case at period t_1, then the short-period deviation cd and the medium-period deviation bc have to be subtracted, in order that the long-period trend output ab may be obtained. Contrariwise, if total output is below the long-period trend the short- and medium-period deviations have to be added to output actually observed so as to get trend output. Hence the 'trend' line ef is an *invisible* demarcation line telling us that ab is that part of output governed by long-period forces and that bd is determined by medium- and short-period factors. Similarly, long-run normal prices never appear in a pure form. These are always accompanied, so to speak, by deviations from normal prices as brought about by cyclical movements of an economy or by short-term vagaries of the market. The same reasoning also applies to independent (predetermined) variables and parameters: exports, government expenditures, leakages out of income, the capital–output ratio, the import coefficient, the coefficients of production and profit rates may deviate temporarily from their respective (institutionally governed) long-period values which are constant or change but slowly. The fact that, owing to institutional change, normal magnitudes evolve is of some importance here: the institutionally governed normal variables are not equivalent to statistical trends. The former result from the functioning of the socioeconomic and political system at any moment of time; the latter are an average of past and present realized variables representing short- and medium-term behavioural outcomes. Normal magnitudes would coincide with the statistical trends in stationary conditions only, implying the absence of institutional changes.

Hence the term 'normal' is not employed here in the sense in which Marshall conventionally used it: for him 'the normal, or "natural", value of a commodity is that which economic forces tend to bring about *in the long run*. It is the average value [related to a fully adjusted situation, H.B.] which economic forces tend to bring about if the general conditions of life were *stationary* [our emphasis] for a run of time long enough to enable them all to work out their full effect' (Marshall 1920, p. 347).

In this study normal magnitudes are also associated with a fully adjusted situation which, however, is not located in the future but in the present. Hence there is no need to postulate a stationary state. The fully adjusted situation is that part of economic reality which is governed by the socioeconomic system, i.e. actually prevailing institutions and technology which have evolved historically. Such a situation would be realized if behavioural outcomes coincided with the outcomes of the (institutional) system, which is impossible since entrepreneurs, when taking investment decisions in the past, had only a sketchy knowledge about the presently prevailing fully adjusted situation. It is equally impossible for entrepreneurs to get into a – future – steady state which would obtain if long-term expectations and investment remained invariant for a sufficiently long period of time.

However, it is interesting to note that 'Marshall used the term "the long period" in two quite distinct senses, one in which there is time for *substantial* alterations to be made in the size of the plant, and one in which it stands conceptionally for the Never-never land of unrealized tendency' (Robertson 1956, p. 16). Obviously, the former relates to Marshall's conventional use of the term with the fully adjusted situation in the future, while the latter implies that the fully adjusted situation is in the present, which is the way the notion of 'long period' is used in this study.

A further point is worth noting. Contrary to Marshall, we shall distinguish between the *natural* and the *normal* in this study. The former notion has normative implications and is as such associated with ethically desirable states of affairs, while the latter refers to positive situations to reflect outcomes of given institutional set-ups. Hence natural and normal magnitudes diverge with respect to their material content. However, on the level of principles and regarding formal aspects the natural and the normal coincide. For example, in Pasinetti's natural system (Pasinetti 1981, 1993) the principle of effective demand governs the scale of activity which equals, however, the natural or ethically desirable – full employment – level. However, it will be argued in chapter 4 (pp. 142–204) that the formally identical principle of effective demand determines a normal employment level that may be persistently below full employment. Hence regarding the material content of theories the natural is the ethically appropriate form of the normal: full employment – the natural employment level – is the ethically desirable scale of normal activity.

The fully adjusted situation consists of the normal prices p^* (governed by the conditions of production and by the institutions regulating distribution, specifically target profit rates) and of the normal quantities, that is the normal output and employment levels Q^* and N^* (determined by the supermultiplier relation set out in chapter 4) and the technically associated normal capital stock K^*. At the sectoral level, normal prices and quantities are associated with normal sector sizes. Hence fully adjusted situations are stock equilibria which guarantee the normal going on of production and reproduction in a technical sense within a given institutional framework, and bear as such a formal resemblance to steady states. Institutional change implies a change in the fully adjusted situation.

To conceive of a fully adjusted situation we have to start from the actually existing sector sizes, i.e. the capital stock K, the result of past accumulation behaviour, and the corresponding capacity output Q_c that could be produced if existing capacities were normally utilized. A fully adjusted situation would obtain if each sectoral capital stock and the corresponding capacity output existing in some short period were multiplied by a certain coefficient, greater or smaller than unity, to yield the normal capital stock K^* and normal output Q^*, e.g. the quantities that could be sold at the normal prices p^*. In Marshallian terms this would amount to augmenting, or reducing, the number of representative firms in each sector of production, each representative firm being associated with the normal price and the normal output governed by the average technology and the prevailing institutional set-up. If the period of time considered is situated in a period of prosperity, most coefficients would have to be smaller than unity since capacities are larger than those making up the fully adjusted situation, and vice versa. This procedure bears some similarity to the construction of Sraffa's 'standard commodity', which also starts from some given real-world situation. The fully adjusted situation in our sense is pictured by the multi-sector model set forth by Pasinetti (1981, part I), complemented by the trend levels of employment and output (chapter 4, pp. 154–75), whereby the normal or desired capital stock embodies the average technology in use.

It has been suggested already that a fully adjusted situation would obtain if invisible lines of demarcation were drawn through selected parts of the real world: productive capacities, employment and output levels and prices. Fully adjusted situations thus cannot be directly observed. This institutionally governed part of the real world has to be brought into the open by reasoning and selected observation. Probable knowledge about fully adjusted situations increases with the degree of understanding of the functioning of some specific society.

The classical-Keynesian equilibrium conceptions set out above lead to a definition of the notion of change of socioeconomic variables, e.g. the level of employment and the volume of investment. If long-period (trend) values of variables are considered, a change in the level of a variable simply denotes a shift in its normal level brought about by a permanent change in some institutionally governed predetermined variable. For example, if there were a permanent increase in government expenditures, i.e. an institutional change, the normal output line *ef* in figure 1 would, in principle, shift upwards; this will become evident from the supermultiplier relation to be dealt with in chapter 4 (pp. 142–204). In the short and medium term, variations of a variable signify changes in behaviourally determined variables, e.g. investment volumes in the course of the cycle, which modify the deviations from the corresponding normal variables.

A final point is related to the notion of 'equilibrium' which is used in various ways in the following. 'Equilibrium' in positive classical-Keynesian analysis relates to a presently existing state of affairs and is linked up with the degree of persistency of some determined variable which has no tendency to change as long as the predetermined variables and parameters stay firm. The degree of persistency is relatively small for short-term dependent variables but increases for medium- and long-term dependent variables. A long-period equilibrium (a fully adjusted situation governed by the socioeconomic system) is a slowly evolving reference situation which may attract short- and medium-term behavioural outcomes. It should be noted, however, that long-period equilibria, for example normal output levels or normal prices, do *not* represent centres of gravity since system outcomes reflected in normal magnitudes are *not independent* of behavioural outcomes; for example, current investment gradually modifies the normal capital stock, or if market prices deviate from normal prices for a lapse of a considerable time, the former may modify the latter. In chapter 4 it will be seen that classical-Keynesian long-period 'equilibria' usually imply persistent involuntary unemployment which means that these are not normative in so far as employment is concerned. This is contrary to the neoclassical notion of 'equilibrium' which implies allocative efficiency and full employment and is therefore essentially normative.

Three different types of classical-Keynesian equilibria are dealt with below. In terms of figure 1, the long-period or normal output associated with a fully adjusted situation is governed by the socioeconomic system. The cyclical-cum-growth evolution of capacity output (*eci* in figure 1) defines medium-term equilibria associated with the normal utilization of the capacities existing at any moment of time. Lastly, the curve *AB* in this figure describes a succession of short-period flow equilibria implying varying degrees of capacity utilization of equipment existing in some short period.

Other economic variables also have several equilibrium values simultaneously. For instance, the long-period normal prices are governed by the conditions of production and by the institutions regulating distribution, e.g. entrepreneurial associations and trade unions or individual bargaining. In the medium term, i.e. in the course of the cycle, and in the short term, market prices will deviate from their respective normal levels.

Institutions and the classical view of society

To simplify, classical-Keynesian political economy may be conceived of as a synthesis of Quesnay, Ricardo, Marx and Keynes. Like the Keynesian strand of thought, the classical contribution to political economy goes beyond the scope of socioeconomic theory since it extends to the vision of society underlying classical theory. This can be made more precise by sketching the classical-Marxian view on the arrangement of and the interactions between the institutions which make up society.

The starting point in political economy is the circular and social process of production. Circularity means that 'commodities are produced by means of commodities' (Sraffa 1960) and of labour and land. In this view, each basic sector of production delivers part of its output to other basic sectors in order to enable production there. This implies that each sector receives goods and services from other sectors which allow the sector considered to produce one, or, if there is joint production, several goods.

It is appropriate to distinguish between two kinds of circularity, one relating to intermediate, the other to final products; both are contained in Quesnay's 'expanded' *tableau économique*, the overwhelming importance of which will become evident subsequently. The standard model exhibiting in principle the circulation of intermediate products in an economy is the Leontief–Sraffa model; this pictures the importance of land in the process of production: the primary products transformed in the process of production are all extracted from the soil. In this vein the Leontief–Sraffa model exhibits the links between man and society on the one hand and nature on the other. The most famous model of circulation on the level of final goods is Marx's two-sector model set out in the second volume of *Das Kapital* where the relationships between the consumption and investment goods sectors are recorded by means of schemes of production and reproduction (Marx 1973/74a [1867–94], vol. II, pp. 391ff.). This model plays an important role in modern classical-Keynesian political economy, for example in Robinson (1962a, 1965); in the simplest case – wages are consumed and profits saved and invested – intersectoral equilibrium requires that profits in the consumption goods sector be equal to the wage sum in the investment goods sector (see, for example, Kregel 1975, p. 55). The Marxian schemes exhibit the fundamental role of labour and the means of production (past labour) in the process of production and reproduction; as such these schemes imply specific relations between social classes participating in the production, the distribution and the use of the social surplus. Necessary consumption goods are required to maintain the labour force, and capital goods are needed to replace (reproduce) means of production used up in the process of production. The distribution and use of the social surplus is an intricate social problem which will be briefly dealt with below and in the next section.

The two types of circularity are linked up with two kinds of basic goods in the Sraffian sense, i.e. goods that are required in the production of all goods (Pasinetti 1977, pp. 104ff.). A first type of basic is the intermediate goods which appear in Leontief–Sraffa models. A second type of basic is final products, i.e. the necessary consumption goods required to maintain the labour force and the capital goods used in the production of both kinds of basic.

A quick glance at the intermediate and the final goods model reveals that, in both, circulation, taking place on markets, largely stands in the service of production: intermediate and final goods (investment goods and necessary consumption goods) circulate in order to maintain or eventually to expand the productive powers of an economy. The final goods remaining are devoted to non-necessary consumption and to maintain and to extend the institutional superstructure (scheme 1). This is the essence of the surplus principle.

Besides being circular, the process of production is also a social process. Three dimensions of this process are of some importance. First, there is division of labour to a considerable degree between sectors of production and within these sectors: simplified work processes allow for specialization, mechanization and computer-integrated production; workers may be equipped with more and more fixed capital goods which leads to a higher labour productivity. Second, the division of labour requires co-ordination of activities and co-operation between producers to enable a society to reach, third, a common (social) aim, i.e. the production of the gross social product. This broadly reflects Friedrich List's and Luigi Pasinetti's views on the organization and the improvement of the productive forces of an economy (List 1920 [1841], pp. 204ff.; Pasinetti 1981, 1993). With the capital stock given, co-operation between producers largely goes on spontaneously. Historically evolving structures of production and the level of effective demand *determine*, in fact, the actions of producers. The former result in technically required flows of goods between sectors; the latter governs the scale of activity (chapter 4). Given this, an important task of the government would consist in creating the institutional conditions conducive to maximizing the *social* surplus, given the amounts of original factors of production (land and labour), technology, and social and natural constraints (the way of life and the natural environment). In the course of time, the social surplus may be enhanced by organizational progress (learning by doing) and by new technologies, which are diffused through gross investment. In the real world many factors may obstruct this, for instance, an initially low labour productivity, conflicts about distribution and a lack of effective demand.

The process of production is a social macroinstitution: productive activity is directed towards a social aim on the level of society as a whole, with the various sectors performing specific functions. Following Marx it may be useful to distinguish between two aspects of the process of production: the forces and the relations of production. The former relate to the technical aspect of production, i.e. the relationship of man and society to nature (presently, environmental problems are crucial ingredients of this relationship); the latter comprise the social relations occurring in the process of production: the organization of work, industrial relations, property rights, all of which are closely linked with the distribution of the surplus resulting from the productive activities of a society; it is the social relations of production which make the social process of production a social macroinstitution.

In the classical (and Marxian) and in the classical-Keynesian view, the process of production has a deeper social significance, however. This macroinstitution provides the material basis for all the other institutions making up the permanent features of any society: the existence of a social surplus enables a society to build up a social, political and cultural superstructure. This very important insight was first systematically developed by François Quesnay in his extended *tableau économique* and may now be pictured by input–output schemes: the directly productive workers and employees produce gross output, which includes intermediate products. Not all the goods and services produced are at society's disposal, however. Two broad categories of goods have to be deducted: intermediate products (including worn-out fixed capital) used up in the process of production and physiologically necessary consumption goods which are required to maintain the productive capacity of the labour force. Hence the *social surplus* is made up of those goods and services which leave the various sectors of an economy and are at the free disposal of society. The surplus contains physiologically non-necessary consumption and provides the material basis for accumulation and for maintaining the various institutions making up the civil society and the state.

In present-day statistics the concept of the social surplus cannot be found; perhaps this is due to the difficulty of separating necessary from non-necessary consumption; the central concept is 'gross social product' – gross national and gross domestic product – which, as a rule, will be used in the following; however, the concept of the social surplus remains important for analytical purposes. This emerges for example from Paul Baran's *Political Economy of Growth* in which a whole chapter is devoted to the notion of the economic surplus (Baran 1973, chapter 2).

The workers and employees who produce the social surplus are 'productive' in the classical sense. Those members of the population who are maintained by the surplus – teachers and civil servants, for example – are 'unproductive'. Friedrich List rightly argued that these notions are not strictly valid (List 1920 [1841], ch. 12, pp. 220ff.): productive workers in the classical sense produce goods and render services on the basis of given productive forces and of a given institutional set-up of society. Those who are unproductive in the classical sense (researchers, teachers, artists, lawyers, politicians) enhance the productive forces and contribute to the adequate functioning of a society in so far as their work is socially useful. Hence the latter may contribute to maintaining and improving the institutional set-up of society.

Three related aspects of the social process of production are particularly important: the relations of production, the distribution or appropriation of the social surplus, and the use of the social surplus. The relations of production (broadly Marx's *Produktionsverhältnisse*) correspond to the social and legal set-up of the productive process: the ownership of the means of production – i.e. property rights – social relations showing up in a specific hierarchy of workers and employees and the work conditions are perhaps most important. The relations of production are closely linked with the overall institutional set-up of a society. Production will be organized differently in a feudal and in an unrestricted capitalist economy, or in a mixed and a socialist economy. These Marxian conceptions may prove useful for political economy. There is, however, no need to set up rigid chains of succession of the different modes of production as Marx did. This is in fact impossible since there are no strictly determined relations between the material basis and the institutional superstructure. They interact in very complex ways: determination and free choice are there simultaneously.

The distribution of the surplus is closely associated with the relations of production. The classical economists, particularly Ricardo, attempted to describe the laws which govern the distribution of the surplus among the different social classes (Ricardo 1951 [1821], p. 5). The general problem is to determine those parts of the surplus which accrue to workers and employees in the form of 'surplus wages' in excess of necessary wages, to entrepreneurs as profits, to capitalists as interest and to landowners in the form of rents. The regulation of distribution will differ with the institutional set-up within the sphere of production and within society in general. In Ricardo's view distribution does not result from a relation between individuals, that is between individual workers and capitalists. Distribution is, for him, a social phenomenon: it expresses the relation of social classes – landlords, capitalists and workers – to society as a whole. This view of distribution will be taken up in chapter 4 (pp. 158–75) where the classical-Keynesian theory of distribution is sketched.

The use of the surplus, which is closely linked with distribution, is also a social phenomenon. There are five broad uses to which the surplus may be put: gross investment (replacement and accumulation of real capital), state consumption (education, defence, administration), contributions to social security, non-necessary and luxury consumption, and expenditures for cultural purposes. Some of these categories may overlap, especially the last two.

In any society, the permanent features of the relations of production, of distribution and of the use of the social surplus are regulated by a complex set of individualistic and social institutions. This is perhaps the main reason why the classicals, particularly Ricardo and Marx, used the notion 'political economy'. The classical view of production and its relationship to other institutions can be made more precise, as illustrated in scheme 1.

In the classical view, production, comprising the relations and the forces of production, is the basic macroinstitution in any society. This does not mean that production rigidly determines the shape and the functioning of the other institutions (as Marx argued in some instances). The classical political economists simply wanted to say that production provides the material basis for a higher social and individual life. The existence of a social surplus renders possible non-necessary consumption and permits the accumulation of capital and the erection of an institutional superstructure which regulates the permanent features of legal, social, political and cultural life in a society.

There are very complex interrelationships between the various types of

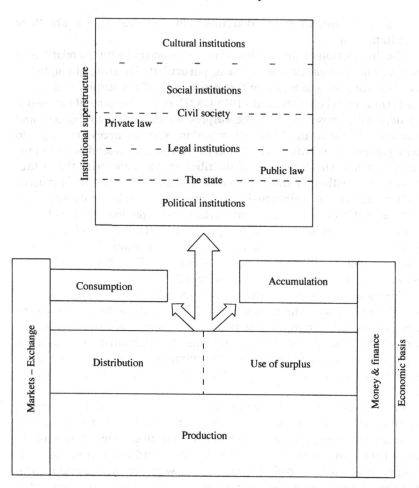

Scheme 1.

institution shown in scheme 1. The economic basis in general and production in particular partly determine the shape and the functioning of the institutional superstructure. There are, however, also causal relations from the superstructure to the basis. The complexity of the institutional set-up is basically due to the complementarity between the political, economic, legal, social and cultural institutions. This gives rise to intricate part–whole relationships. For example, the economy has to provide the material basis for all social and individual activities across the production of the social surplus; the legal sphere partly regulates social and individual behaviour in all domains of society.

Here is not the place to go on to a description of possible interactions between institutions. This is an economist's task only to a certain extent. To explain how institutions actually do work and to prescribe how institutions should work are also the tasks of the lawyer, the sociologist and the political scientist; the historian deals with past institutional change in order to explain the present.

The importance of institutions for the social sciences was perceived with great clarity by Friedrich List who is perhaps the true founder of modern institutional economics (List 1920 [1841]). Schmoller says that 'List intuitively grasped the idea that it is not isolated individuals but social formations who are the actors in economic history; he understood that institutions, which regulate socioeconomic life under the guidance of social and public interests, constitute the true object of political economy' (Schmoller, in List 1920 [1841], introduction, p. VIII; a.tr.). In this book it will be argued that institutions play a fundamental role in positive classical-Keynesian political economy. The system equilibrium referred to in chapter 4 (pp. 142–204) is governed by the institutional system shown in scheme 1. This implies that, in the long run, all the great socioeconomic problems – most importantly value, distribution and employment – are *directly* associated with institutions.

Many classical-Keynesian political economists, for example Garegnani (1984, 1987), have stressed the fundamental importance for political economy of the social process of production and of the associated surplus principle. Geoffrey Harcourt has taken up these issues and put them in a wider context, pointing thereby to the normative dimension of classical-Keynesian political economy: '[The purpose of economics is] to make the world a better place . . . to produce a more just and equitable society. In order to do that, [we must] understand how particular societies work . . . Economics . . . is very much a moral as well as a social science and [as such] a handmaiden to progressive thought. It is really the study of the processes whereby surpluses are created in economies, how they are extracted, who gets them and what they do with them' (Harcourt 1986, p. 5). This statement is particularly important since production, distribution and use of the social surplus are, in a classical-Keynesian system's view, all governed by institutions if the long run is considered. To improve a given situation in these respects requires ethically appropriate institutional change – hence the essentially moral character of the social sciences.

The classical heritage and the Keynesian problem

The main methodological feature of the political economy approach is that institutions and technology shape the permanent features of economic reality. Classical-Keynesian long-period theory is made up of a set of simple models which provide probable pictures of causal relations which link up institutionally regulated predetermined (exogenous) variables and parameters, and determined (endogenous) variables. This proposition will be substantiated in chapters 3 and 4.

The purpose of this section is to provide an introduction to the classical-Keynesian approach to long-period economic problems, which may conveniently be conceived of as a synthesis of Ricardian and Keynesian elements of thought. First, we shall have a quick look at the classical heritage embodied in modern political economy, i.e. the classical theories of distribution, of value and of proportions between sectors of production. Second, we shall consider in a preliminary way how Keynes's contribution,. a theory of output and employment determination and of interest and money, complements classical theory; this issue will be taken up extensively in chapter 4. Finally, the problem of the choice of techniques in a classical-Keynesian framework is briefly discussed.

The starting point in classical political economy is the circular and social process of production. Here the productive forces of an economy (fixed and circulating capital goods, land and labour) are produced and reproduced, and maintained. Moreover, a surplus is produced which enables a society to build up and to maintain an institutional superstructure (scheme 1) and, eventually, to accumulate capital in the widest sense of the word. This view of production is embodied in Quesnay's *tableau économique*, in Ricardo's *Principles* and in Marx's *Kapital*. Modern versions of the classical view on production have been expounded by Leontief, von Neumann and Sraffa. Examples of treatises and textbook presentations are Pasinetti (1977, 1981, 1993) and Walsh and Gram (1980).

The essential features of the classical production process may be represented best by the so-called transaction table (scheme 2) (for a simple numerical presentation, see Pasinetti 1977, p. 38, table II.3). The square matrix 'intermediate products' records the quantities of intermediate goods used up in the circular process of production. Rows contain outputs delivered to the various sectors, columns record inputs received. Value added in the various sectors appears as a row vector, final output as a column vector. The same holds for gross output which is the sum of intermediate production and final output, made up of consumption goods and gross investment. Final output is thus produced by intermediate products and by the services of labour, land and fixed capital goods; those inputs which are required in the production of all goods and services contained in final output are basic goods in the sense used by Sraffa. Basic goods are price-determining, the prices of non-basics are determined (on this issue, see Pasinetti 1977, pp. 104ff.). From the rules of national accounting it is

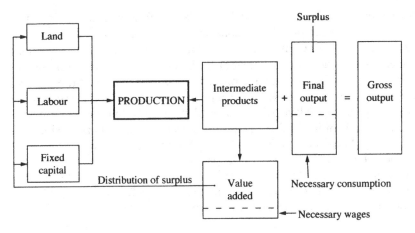

Scheme 2.

evident that value added must always equal final output. If necessary wages are deducted from value added or necessary consumption from final output, we get two different expressions of the social surplus. One relates to the distribution, the other to the use of the surplus. In scheme 2 only primary distribution is pictured; in a second stage, the state comes in to appropriate part of the surplus through taxation and putting it to particular uses through government expenditures.

Starting from this view of the process of production the first problem which has to be tackled is distribution. How is value added divided into wages, profits (including interests) and rents? In the Ricardian view, this is, essentially, a social problem: distribution is a relation between parts and a whole, i.e. between social classes and society. This is sharply opposed to the modern neoclassical view which conceives of distribution as a relationship between individuals, i.e. entrepreneurs and workers, whereby the behaviour of individuals is co-ordinated by an automatic mechanism, that is factor markets, which is supposed to regulate the functional distribution in the long run. In the classical long-period view, factor markets do not exist; however, these may influence distribution in the short run in that they bring about deviations from the long-run, institutionally governed distributional outcomes. Hence, given the labour force, land, the stock of fixed capital goods and, consequently, gross and final output, distribution must be determined by a non-economic, i.e. a social, mechanism. Different solutions have been proposed. In Ricardo 1951 [1821], rents are determined by a specifically classical version of the marginal principle: additional labour in the agricultural sector is associated with decreasing rents on land, and marginal land gets no rent. The natural wage of labour is a social phenomenon (variable in time and space) and is fixed near the subsistence level such as to keep population constant. Profits appear as a residual and govern the pace of accumulation. Karl Marx, in volume I of *Das Kapital*, argued that social relations inherent in the process of production govern distribution. In the long run, the propertied classes, owing to the existence of a permanent reserve army, are in a position to drive wages towards their (necessary) existence level which means that, given technology, the surplus accruing to them in the form of profits, interests and rents is maximized. Modern political economists like Joan Robinson, Kaldor, Kalecki and Pasinetti have made distribution dependent on the composition of final output at a given employment level (full employment is assumed by Kaldor (1955/56) and by Pasinetti (1962), but not by Joan Robinson and Michal Kalecki): given the propensities to save, the profit share increases with the share of investment in output, or the rate of profit is proportional to the rate of growth (the Cambridge equation).

In chapter 4 it is suggested that the positive long-period classical-Keynesian theory of distribution ought to be based on a variant of the classical, i.e. Ricardian-Marxian, mechanism, not on the Cambridge equation (in Bortis 1993b, pp. 115ff. it is implied that the Cambridge equation is a long-period equilibrium relation which must always hold at a *given* employment level and hence leaves open how the *scale* of employment is determined). In the long run, distribution is the outcome of a social process, i.e. the interplay of specific institutions: the government, trade unions and employers associations, and habits and customs concur to determine money wages and normal prices embodying target profit rates. Distributional outcomes may be based on mutual agreement reflecting a social consensus; such is likely to be the case in some economically advanced countries. This institutional process may consist, for example, in the determination of a hierarchy of profit rates. However, in economically backward countries and in countries with heavy involuntary unemployment the Marxian conflict theory may be appropriate to explain distribution in the long run. Since the classical-Keynesian long-period theory of income distribution rests on the functioning of socio-economic systems, generalizations are hardly possible. Empirical and historical investigations related to individual countries and regions will be required.

The role of the Cambridge equation in regulating distribution will become evident in chapter 4. A variant of this relation explains how (medium-term) distribution is regulated in the course of the business cycle (Bortis 1993b, pp. 123–4). Changing proportions between the investment and the consumption goods sectors during the cycle lead to deviations from long-period distributional outcomes.

A second economic problem to be touched upon here is the classical and classical-Keynesian long-period theory of value, i.e. the determination of prices of production or normal prices. Normal value and distribution are closely linked in political economy. They are determined simultaneously although the institutional determination of distribution is logically prior to the determination of value. The essence of the classical relationship between value and distribution is set out by Pasinetti (1977, pp. 72–3). In an economy $n-1$ basic commodities are produced by $n-1$ commodities and labour. There are $n-1$ cost or price equations (system V.3.1 in Pasinetti 1977, p. 73) and $n+1$ unknowns: $n-1$ money prices, the money wage rate w_n and the uniform rate of profits. An appropriate numéraire good may be selected, good 1 for instance. This implies dividing by p_1 on each side of all equations. The number of unknowns is thus reduced by one: $n-2$ relative prices of the type p/p_1 the *real* wage rate w_n/p_1 and the rate of profits r, that is n unknowns. With only $n-1$ price equations given, the necessity to fix one of the unknowns arises. Since there is no economic sense in fixing one of the relative prices, the real wage rate or the rate of profits must be determined *exogenously*. Ricardo and Marx have opted for determining the real wage rate which implies that the real profits, or the rate of profits, appear as a residual. In the modern classical-Keynesian view, long-run distribution is the outcome of an institutional process which fixes the rate of profits or the hierarchy of profit rates, and real wages are a residual (see the normal price equations in chapter 4, pp. 175–80).

Once distribution is determined, classical-Keynesian long-period normal prices are fixed, too: in principle, absolute prices depend upon the coefficients of production, the rate of profits and the money wage rate (see the price equation V.5.18 in Pasinetti 1977,.p. 80; or, in the case of vertically integrated sectors, system II.7.3 in Pasinetti 1981, p. 44). Relative prices are governed by the technical conditions of production and by income distribution, i.e. the profit rates (see again Pasinetti 1977, p. 82, or Pasinetti 1981, p. 44). In the medium and short term, market prices deviate from long-run normal prices.

Joint production could be brought into the picture, too. Normal prices may now also depend upon the composition of demand governed by individual preferences which are, in turn, shaped by complex social processes: individual preferences may depend upon the consumption behaviour of other individuals. In this study we do not deal with joint production and socially determined demand structures because, in our view, the social processes taking place in production are far more important than those occurring on the demand side; moreover, the treatment of the great issues – value, distribution and employment – may be altered, but is not essentially changed, by the presence of joint production. However, joint production can be brought in at any time to capture the influence of demand on normal prices or to deal with environmental issues (Schefold 1985a, b).

A third important problem dealt with in classical and classical-Keynesian long-period theory is that of appropriate sector proportions at a *given* level of activity. This was one of the main themes in Quesnay's *tableau économique*, in Adam Smith's industry-agriculture model in book III of the *Wealth of Nations* and in the Marxian schemes of circulation and reproduction in the second volume of *Das Kapital*. The problem of sector sizes also appears in Keynes's *Fundamental Equations* as developed in the *Treatise on Money*, in Robinson (1965) and in Kregel (1975). Input–output models, elaborated by Leontief, Sraffa and von Neumann on the basis of Quesnay's *tableau*, also deal with sector proportions; a more general treatment is Pasinetti (1981).

The problem of the appropriate proportions between sectors can be understood best by looking again at scheme 2: the fraction of value added (incomes) spent on consumption (governed by income elasticities and by income distribution) and the size of investment and government expenditures govern the composition of final output, which, in turn, determines the size and composition of intermediate goods industries. If there are only consumption and investment goods sectors, equilibrium between sectors obtains once expenditures of the consumption sector on gross investment equal the demand for consumption goods arising in the investment sector. In macroeconomic terms: investment must equal saving, or leakages have to match injections. This condition is implied in the classical and Marxian schemes of production and reproduction and in the modern classical-Keynesian versions of these schemes; it also holds if more than two sectors are considered.

The profound economic meaning of this equilibrium condition between sectors was perhaps expressed most clearly by Marx. There is, in fact, a continuous circulation of money and goods between the consumption and investment goods sectors; this is to realize a social aim related to the economy as a whole, i.e. the maintenance and eventual extension of the productive forces of an economy which are the labour force and the stock of fixed capital: the consumption goods sector receives investment goods in order to maintain and, eventually, to expand its stock of fixed capital goods; in exchange for the investment goods received the consumption goods sector delivers consumption goods to the investment goods sector enabling the latter to maintain the workers employed here and, eventually, to render possible an expansion of the labour force employed. Similarly, in input–output models industries mutually depend on each other; certain deliveries (to which receipts always correspond) must go on in accordance with existing technology which is the heritage of past accumulation. There is a fundamental complementarity between sectors and industries which requires that the proportions between sectors and industries must be appropriate if the process of production is to proceed in an orderly way.

The problems of the composition of final demand and of proportion between sectors emphasize the circular and social character of production. The consumption goods sector and the other final goods sectors of an economy, on the one hand, and the input–output system, on the other, must be interlocked appropriately so as to enable the productive system of an economy not only to reproduce (and eventually to expand) its productive capacity but also to provide for the material basis of the social, political and cultural life of a country (schemes 1 and 2).

The question of proportions relates not only to interindustry and final product flows but also to stocks. The latter allows the classical theory of sector proportions to be adapted to modern issues as is shown by a quick glance at scheme 2. The composition of the stocks of capital goods and of labour ought to be appropriate if the production is to continue in an orderly way: the right types of capital goods must have been accumulated in the past and the various kinds of labour ought to have had an appropriate vocational training. Land, comprising agricultural land, stocks of raw materials, some of which are wholly or partly non-reproducible, and the natural environment, play a particularly important role: ideally production ought, in individual countries and worldwide, to be organized in such a way as to ensure production and reproduction indefinitely, i.e. the process of production ought to be in harmony with nature. While the difficulties of approaching capital and labour stock equilibria seem tractable, the issues arising in attempting to establish a harmonious relationship with land and nature, even approximately, are evidently of immense complexity. The latter, however, largely pertain to the domain of the natural sciences and give rise to interdisciplinary work between social and natural scientists.

The classical heritage regarding the problems of value, distribution and sector proportions has been taken up by many classical-Keynesian economists and will be taken for granted in the following. However, in chapter 4 (pp. 142–204) we shall deal with a fourth fundamental socioeconomic problem, i.e. the Keynesian theory of output and employment determination through effective demand. This is required because classical political economy postulated that employment was governed by the pace of capital accumulation. Saving determines investment if incomes (value added) are always entirely spent to buy final products (scheme 2): production (supply) always generates the demand required to buy it (Say's law). Given this, there is no reason why, in principle, an economy should not permanently operate at the full employment level if capital accumulation were sufficient; and unemployment would not be due to permanent general overproduction.

Indeed, the classical political economists always argued that unemployment arises on account of inappropriate proportions between sectors, mainly brought about by structural change.

However, on empirical and theoretical grounds, it is highly probable that effective demand governs the level or the scale of output and employment in the short as well as in the long run. Therefore, in chapter 4 (pp. 142–204), we attempt to complement the classical heritage by a long-period theory of employment and output determination through effective demand. It will be seen that Pasinetti (1981) provides a convenient conceptual starting point for doing so.

There remains the problem of the choice of techniques which, in the classical-Keynesian view, is closely linked with distribution, prices, sector proportions and the level of employment. Entrepreneurs will choose that technique of production, which, given the rate of profits and the money wage rate, minimizes the cost of production (see Pasinetti 1977, chapter 6, and Pasinetti 1981, sections IX.8–13): the costs of production are, in principle, proportional to the amount of direct and indirect labour used to produce a unit of output (indirect labour is embodied in the means of production, including used-up fixed capital); in the real world this principle is modified because the ratios of indirect to direct labour differ in the various industries. The rate of profits may be interpreted as a uniform rate or as a weighted average of different desired or satisfactory rates. To minimize the costs of production implies minimizing the prices of production (long-period normal prices) and maximizing the real wage rate (see figures VI.2 and VI.3 in Pasinetti 1977, pp. 157, 161): the best (cost-minimizing) techniques form the 'technological frontier of income distribution possibilities' (pp. 156–60) which constitutes the north-eastern boundary of technical possibilities in a real wage against rate of profits diagram. To each rate of profits corresponds a maximum real wage rate and vice versa. Thus, to choose the best technique implies maximizing the social surplus once necessary consumption is defined. In classical-Keynesian political economy the choice of techniques is, therefore, a *social* process: the social surplus is to be maximized, *not* the profitability of individual investment projects.

Some remarks on this criterion of technical choice are required here. First, the technological frontier is, like the prices of production and trend output and employment, part of the permanent or slowly changing features of economic reality. Again, permanent does not mean invariable, rather, slowly changing, which shows up in shifts of the technological frontier. Second, the concept of the technological frontier, from which a specific technique of production is selected, does not imply constant returns to scale: a given technological frontier is dependent upon a given scale of production (gross domestic product) governed by trend effective demand. However, if the latter evolves, the technological frontier may shift to the right due to increasing returns to scale. New technological possibilities arise and firms are in a position to select better techniques associated with lower unit costs. The technical possibilities of introducing improved methods of production are linked up with the division of labour and are limited by the extent of the market as had already been observed by Adam Smith and as was brought to the fore in this century by Allyn Young and Nicholas Kaldor (Kaldor 1978, p. 181). Third, technological change in general and increasing returns in particular lead to rightward and upward shifts of the technological frontier of income distribution. Given the desired profit rates, real wages will increase with rising labour productivity, accompanied, as a rule, by an increasing capital–labour ratio. The latter is sometimes interpreted as substitution of labour by capital in neoclassical theory; this substitution process occurs because 'labour' gets more expensive relative to 'capital'. This and other points are convincingly refuted by Pasinetti (1977, pp. 167–79; 1981, pp. 201–5). In fact, according to classical and modern classical-Keynesian long-period theory of production, there can be no substitution in the neoclassical sense since changes in the real wage – rate of profits ratio lead to unpredictable changes in the capital–labour ratio. Fourth, not all the firms are in a position to choose the best possible techniques lying on the technical frontier of income distribution. In each sector there are firms which, for some reason, are forced to choose inferior techniques of production (see on this concept figures VI.2 and VI.3 of Pasinetti 1977, pp. 157, 161). This is particularly true of smaller firms which may not have sufficient access to skilled workers, engineers and managers or to bank credits necessary to finance the introduction of the most advanced equipment. The structure of markets (the number of small and large firms present in a market) is thus an important determinant of the choice of techniques (Bortis 1979, pp. 95–6). Firms using inferior techniques of production will pay lower money wages than firms using advanced techniques, and realized and satisfactory profit rates will, as a rule, be lower in the former than in the latter.

The technique of production in use in an economy is an *average technology* which represents some combination of best possible and inferior techniques. This notion of technology underlies the analysis in chapter 4 (pp. 154–80).

Layers of reality and the treatment of time: system equilibrium versus uncertainty and expectations

In the present study we conceive of modern political economy as a synthesis of Ricardo and Keynes. David Ricardo was the first economist to have developed a logically consistent theory of value and distribution based upon the surplus principle. Maynard Keynes, on the other hand, was the first to show convincingly that in a monetary production economy an unemployment equilibrium may come into existence, the volume or the scale of employment being governed by effective demand.

In chapter 4 we shall suggest that classical-Keynesian political economy is able to deal with all the great economic problems (value, distribution, employment, structures or sector proportions, money, international trade) in a coherent way and is, as such, an alternative to neoclassical economics. But can this proposition stand up given the opposing strands of thought in post Keynesian economics mentioned in chapter 1 (pp. 1–6)? What is the organizing principle which allows us to combine and to develop these strands within a consistent framework of classical-Keynesian political economy?

The methodological difficulties commence with Ricardo and Keynes. There are similarities in their respective systems, for example both use causal models instead of equilibrium models (see chapter 5, pp. 259–72). However, divergences predominate. Ricardo deals with abstract principles and concentrates on selected permanent or slowly evolving features of the real world which are associated with a specific notion of equilibrium. To examine the functioning of socioeconomic systems, Ricardo starts with production and distribution, i.e. the institutional determination of the natural wage rate; value and growth are analysed on the basis of production and distribution. The employment problem is eliminated by Say's law and money is neutral. Behavioural aspects, exchange and markets are neglected. The latter implies abstracting from transient features of the real world considered to be of secondary importance.

Keynes, however, is concrete in that he tackles the real world in its full organic complexity; he deals mainly with the short run where individuals act on the basis of the heritage of the past and are faced with an uncertain future. Behaviour is thus important; the functioning of the system comes in through the principle of effective demand which governs the scale of economic activity. Keynes dislikes abstract and mechanistic models, above all if the notions of equilibrium and of long period are involved.

The differences between Ricardo and Keynes are largely reflected in the contrasting views of neo-Ricardians, on the one hand, and of Robinsonians and Keynesian Fundamentalists, on the other (referred to in chapter 1). The issues involved are complex and interrelated and can be disentangled only to a certain extent. To do so it is appropriate to start with a very simple way of treating time and space (scheme 3). There, we shall suggest that the notions of *behaviour* and *institutions* – dealt with in chapter 2 (pp. 20–57) – might provide the starting point for synthesizing and elaborating the various classical-Keynesian strands. Two kinds of outcome will be distinguished: behavioural and institutional. The former represent the aggregate results of the actions initiated by the various decision centres (individuals and collectives) within a *given* institutional framework; these are associated with (constrained) freedom of choice but also with uncertainty. The latter result from the functioning of the socioeconomic system (the interaction of institutions) and are linked up with determinism and near-certainty. The behavioural and the institutional systems interact: on the one hand, individual actions are co-ordinated and to some extent determined by the system and, on the other hand, certain types of behaviour, e.g. investment behaviour or legislative activities, result in an evolution of the socioeconomic and political system; in a way, aggregate behaviour represents a flow, and the institutional system a stock. These interaction and co-ordination processes are perceived differently by Ricardo and the neo-Ricardians, by Keynes and the Keynesian Fundamentalists, by the Robinsonians, and by liberal and socialist economists. From this the organizing principle to synthesize the various classical-Keynesian strands emerges: the problem is to sketch the corresponding behavioural and institutional systems and to fit together these complementary parts to obtain a comprehensive system. This will be attempted in chapter 4. In chapter 5, we shall see that the way in which the interaction between the behaviour of decision-makers and the socioeconomic system is perceived rests on a specific vision of man and society. The differing social philosophies implied in the corresponding visions will enable us broadly to compare classical-Keynesian political economy and neoclassical economics.

To prepare the ground for the subsequent analysis it is appropriate to order relevant elements of reality according to their stability over time. This involves forming *layers of reality* arranged vertically to the time axis. The rapidly changing temporary factors constitute the top layer. Moving downwards, stability gradually increases. Consequently, the lowest layer contains elements which are invariable as time goes by. This very simple idea is illustrated by scheme 3.

The elements of reality pictured in this scheme are largely illustrative and are associated with the overall argument of this book. It expresses Aristotle's (and Keynes's) view that objectively given and subjectively held ideas, principles or causal laws ultimately govern socioeconomic reality; the way in which ideas or principles are realized depends upon the institutional circumstances prevailing at any period of time – this is a Marxian element. Thus, given objective laws – the principle of effective demand, for instance – there is an interaction between institutions and behaviour. The two top layers are dominated by the behaviour in the spheres of exchange and of accumulation, and the socioeconomic system enters the picture only in a secondary way. The central layers (III, IV and V) are primarily associated

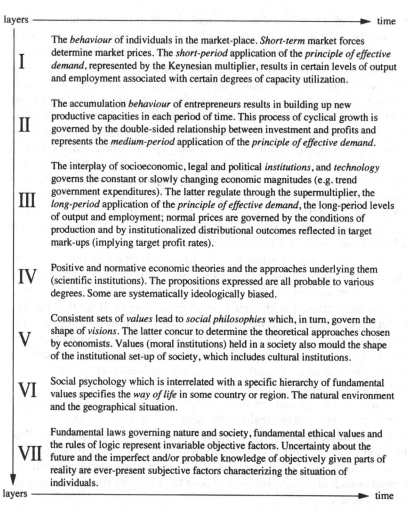

layers ——➤ time

I   The *behaviour* of individuals in the market-place. *Short-term* market forces determine market prices. The *short-period* application of the *principle of effective demand*, represented by the Keynesian multiplier, results in certain levels of output and employment associated with certain degrees of capacity utilization.

II   The accumulation *behaviour* of entrepreneurs results in building up new productive capacities in each period of time. This process of cyclical growth is governed by the double-sided relationship between investment and profits and represents the *medium-period* application of the *principle of effective demand*.

III The interplay of socioeconomic, legal and political *institutions*, and *technology* governs the constant or slowly changing economic magnitudes (e.g. trend government expenditures). The latter regulate through the supermultiplier, the *long-period* application of the *principle of effective demand*, the long-period levels of output and employment; normal prices are governed by the conditions of production and by institutionalized distributional outcomes reflected in target mark-ups (implying target profit rates).

IV   Positive and normative economic theories and the approaches underlying them (scientific institutions). The propositions expressed are all probable to various degrees. Some are systematically ideologically biased.

V   Consistent sets of *values* lead to *social philosophies* which, in turn, govern the shape of *visions*. The latter concur to determine the theoretical approaches chosen by economists. Values (moral institutions) held in a society also mould the shape of the institutional set-up of society, which includes cultural institutions.

VI   Social psychology which is interrelated with a specific hierarchy of fundamental values specifies the *way of life* in some country or region. The natural environment and the geographical situation.

VII Fundamental laws governing nature and society, fundamental ethical values and the rules of logic represent invariable objective factors. Uncertainty about the future and the imperfect and/or probable knowledge of objectively given parts of reality are ever-present subjective factors characterizing the situation of individuals.

layers ——➤ time

Scheme 3.

with the social process of production and with social institutions; here, the system is primary and behaviour secondary. The lowest layers contain objectively given elements of reality shaping the institutional set-up of a society.

Some of the vertically arranged elements of reality are contained in space and are, as such, accessible to the senses, while others, ideas and principles for instance, are invisible; the horizontal axis represents historical time. The whole of reality moves on along the time axis. In doing so, some elements (those contained in *layer I*) change rapidly. In the economic sphere, some quickly evolving behavioural outcomes are linked with market prices and quantities. These vagaries of the market may be linked with rapid changes in the marketing mix of enterprises, the changing behaviour of consumers and with speculative activity. With productive capacities given, the Keynesian multiplier principle results in certain output and employment levels linked with specific degrees of capacity utilization; this represents the outcome of the socioeconomic system. A non-economic example of a first-layer element would be the rapidly changing mood of undecided voters during an election campaign. This political element may be economically relevant, however, in that it influences investment decisions; this is a short-run causal relation. Short-period expectations related to economic and political events also belong to the first layer of reality.

The *second layer* contains causes and effects of (medium-term) movements of cyclical growth (chapter 4, pp. 142–204): on the basis of the income effect of investment the system links higher volumes of investment with higher profits and incomes which, on the behavioural side, induces entrepreneurs to invest more; this upward movement is reversed as soon as the capacity effect of investment works out and entrepreneurs invest less to avoid underutilization of productive capacities. This layer also contains structural adjustments to fully adjusted (long-period) situations or system equilibria (pp. 82–9 above) made up of long-period normal levels of output and employment associated with normal prices (chapter 4, pp. 175–80). The fully adjusted situation, governed by the interplay of socioeconomic and political institutions (the socioeconomic system), is contained in the *third layer*. This layer is largely dominated by the system, which sets restrictions to the changeable behaviour which takes place in layers I and II; behaviour plays only a secondary role since institutions imply fixed or slowly evolving individual and social behaviour.

In the *fourth layer* of reality persistent economic ideas appear, i.e. economic theories and the approaches underlying them. These may shape economic institutions. For example, in the fifties and sixties, Keynesian economic theory influenced economic policy-making; neoclassical theory did the same in the seventies and eighties. There may also be feedbacks from the working of institutions to ideas; in this context, Marx argued that economic institutions exercise a decisive impact on dominant economic ideas; this may be true partly and at times, but we do not consider this to be a general rule.

Layer V contains moral institutions. A given system of values associated with habits and customs leads to the persistent pursuit of social and individual aims within institutions. These partly regulate social and individual life in the most diverse spheres: socioeconomic, political, legal, scientific and cultural. The values held in a given society at some epoch may be ethically good or bad to varying degrees. Knowledge about the extent of alienation – the distance between an existing situation and an ideal situation in which the common weal would be realized – can be merely probable and sketchy (chapter 2, pp. 47–53 and 57–64). More specifically, systems of values provide the foundations for social philosophies which lead to pre-analytic visions (in the sense of Schumpeter 1954, p. 41) on the way societies basically work. Visions are, in turn, associated with broad approaches (neoclassical, classical-Keynesian and socialist) on the basis of which specific theories of value, distribution and employment, for example, are worked out.

Hence the *central layers* of reality all contain institutions, i.e. socio-economic and political institutions (layer III), scientific institutions (layer IV) and moral, legal and cultural institutions (layer V); all of which are closely linked across a system of means and ends. This reflects the fundamentally ethical character of the social sciences (chapter 2, pp. 39–40).

Layer VI is made up of the basic features characterizing the people and the land of a region or of a nation. A specific social psychology, interrelated with a system of fundamental values, shapes the *way of life* prevailing in some country or region, which is expressed by a specific arrangement of institutions contained in the central layers. This makes each society a structured entity, which is *unique* in every respect. The way of life, although it may, on account of varying material circumstances, take on various forms, usually remains remarkably constant in the course of time. The same is obviously true of the geographical situation, the significance of which may change, however, if new means of communication come into being. For instance, the newly built Channel Tunnel may bring about an essential change in Britain's geographical situation.

Finally, *layer VII* contains invariable elements of reality; the rules of logic and the ideal of beauty are prominent examples. Many social scientists would maintain that there are fundamental ethical values which do not change as time goes by: the classical virtues, the ideals of justice, of truth and of the common weal (for this, see Schack 1978, chapters 1 and 5 or Brown 1986, chapter 6; according to Fitzgibbons 1988 and O'Donnell 1989, Keynes held a similar position). If related to complex situations, it is out of the reach of the human mind to know precisely how fundamental values should be realized; for example, it will never be possible to say exactly what a 'just distribution of incomes' means in a given society at some epoch. Therefore, the various institutions contained in the central layers of reality are but probable (Keynes 1971c) and imperfect realizations of the natural, fundamental (and true) principles of socioeconomic and political organization of layer VII. Hence alienation arises which measures the gap between the positive and the ideal (chapter 2, pp. 47–53).

This is in line with the view held by many scientists that there are objectively given invariable laws governing nature, man and society. Numerous neoclassical economists would maintain that the law of diminishing returns is an unchanging natural law of production which governs, together with marginal utility, natural prices and quantities. In the classical-Keynesian view, examples of invariable laws in the realm of society would be the principle of effective demand or 'production of commodities by means of commodities'. Both of these social laws are always there in the form of an unvarying principle, although they may appear in widely different forms in various places and at different periods of historical time in the upper layers of reality.

Finally, it is important to note that uncertainty about the future and imperfect or probable knowledge of objectively given present factors, e.g. of the causes which bring about unemployment in some country, are invariable ingredients of human existence (on this, see Fitzgibbons 1988, chapter 1, and O'Donnell 1989, part I). The various elements of reality set out in the above scheme are linked by a complex network of causal relations. This network forms a structured system because both man and society represent an entity directed towards a fundamental aim, ideally the common weal in case of society. A very simple formal notion of causality is adopted here: predetermined variables and/or parameters govern determined variables (see Pasinetti 1964/65; Corti 1989 provides a survey of the problem of causation). A classification of material types of causality on Aristotelian lines is provided in chapter 2 (pp. 55–7); these are linked up with two broad types of causality to be presented in the next section. Here, we merely make a few remarks on how causality is implied in scheme 3.

Acts of causation go on in historical time and usually link up different spheres in space. For example, past realized profits govern actual investment decisions; in terms of space this means that the market-place (the sphere of circulation) where profits are realized is linked with the sphere of production where investment goods are produced. Similarly, the Keynesian multiplier captures the causal link existing between the investment goods sector on the one hand and the consumption goods sector and the level of economic activity on the other.

Causal relations may occur between elements pertaining to a given layer. For instance, the short-period Keynesian multiplier links current investment with current output and employment (layer I). Or, in the third layer, institutions govern certain normal independent variables and long-period magnitudes of parameters, both of which determine, in turn, a dependent variable, e.g. the long-period level of employment; these causal links are represented by the supermultiplier relation set forth in chapter 4 (pp. 142–204).

However, there are also causal relations relating variables located in different layers. For example, it is likely that a kind of double-sided relationship exists between the various socioeconomic and political institutions (layer III) and economic ideas, i.e. scientific institutions, contained in layer IV. The way in which the former influence the latter is not dealt with here; this is the subject matter of the sociology of knowledge. On the other hand, economic ideas shape institutions located in layer III; for instance, the General Theory had an important influence on the nature of state activity after the Second World War. Speculative activities, located in layer I, may have a damaging influence on production (layer III). Or the basic ethical, ontological and aesthetic principles located in layer VII shape – partly through human action and partly through the functioning of the socioeconomic system – visible reality, contained in the upper layers of reality.

Economists will concentrate on explaining economic phenomena occurring in the first three layers of the above scheme: this implies selecting and combining appropriate causal relations, i.e. to construct economic theories aimed at explaining the behaviour of individuals and collectives and at grasping the way in which the socioeconomic system functions. The body of plausible theories put forward by economists then becomes itself a part of reality (layer IV).

The way of looking at reality proposed in scheme 3 implies that, *analytically*, different components of the *same variable*, be it predetermined or determined, or of the *same parameter* pertain to *different layers* of reality. The stable or slowly changing long-period parts would be included in layer III while the rapidly changing parts would appear in layer I. In between, i.e. in the second layer, we would have medium-term components of variables. This principle holds for both simple and composite magnitudes; the former consist of just one, the latter of several elements. A price set by some firm is a simple variable which may be split up (analytically) into two parts: a long-run normal price which covers the cost of production at standard capacity utilization and includes a satisfactory rate of profit *and* a short-run deviation from the normal price which is brought about by market conditions. The level of employment, on the other hand, is a composite variable made up of a great number of elements (workers, employees and managers). Again, this variable may be split up in components. In figure 1 (p. 85), the level of output at a certain point – a short period – of time (t_1) is *ad*. Its long-period component *ab* is to be explained by the long-period supermultiplier relation (chapter 4, equation 7). Medium-term (business cycle) theory has to explain *bc*. Finally, *cd* is due to the effect of short-run factors.

This procedure does not imply that the real world consists of separate layers that are artificially fitted together. There is only one socioeconomic reality which is the result of past and present human actions. To conceive of layers of parts of the real world is merely an analytical device to assess the influence of various objectively given factors on some phenomenon. To split up employment and output levels into three components enables us to study the influence of the principle of effective demand, which co-ordinates the functioning of a monetary economy, in the long, medium and short runs. Employment and output are examined from *two* points of view: the two – visible – top layers result from aggregate entrepreneurial behaviour; 'trend' or normal output and employment are, however, governed by the socioeconomic and political system. For example, past decisions of entrepreneurs (accumulation behaviour) result in a certain capital stock (K), which, if normally utilized, would enable an economy to produce a certain capacity output Q_c in the present (*ac* in figure 1). Now, given the present investment volume and the marginal propensity to consume which are determined by the individual decisions to invest and to consume (investment and consumption behaviour), the Keynesian short-run multiplier will determine how much entrepreneurs as a group will be able to sell in the present (*ad* in figure 1); this is the short-run application of the principle of effective demand, which pictures how the economic system as a whole determines output and employment in the short term. Short-run effective demand is associated with certain degrees of capacity utilization and with realized profit rates in the various sectors of production which will, as a rule, differ from the institutionally determined target (desired or satisfactory) rates.

Hence, capacity output and actual output (*ac* and *ad* in figure 1) represent *behavioural* outcomes. *Current* normal output (*ab*), however, is the outcome of the socioeconomic system, i.e. the interplay of *presently* existing institutions. Since the hierarchy of desired profit rates is part of the institutional set-up, the latter implies a *fully adjusted situation*: normal sector sizes are associated with normal prices and trend output levels. This notion, defined above (pp. 81–9), represents a modification of the 'multisector model of economic growth' set out in part I of Pasinetti (1981), which pictures the evolution of natural prices and quantities in time.

The difference from Pasinetti is twofold. First, the fully adjusted situation is associated with normal magnitudes which are positive; Pasinetti's natural system, however, has normative implications. Second, Pasinetti postulates full employment which is his natural employment level. In the present study, the fully adjusted situation implies a normal level of output and employment which is compatible with persistent long-period involuntary unemployment. The normal employment level is institutionally determined through the supermultiplier relation (equation 7 in chapter 4). Since, as a rule, institutions evolve slowly, this relation is a long-period causal relation: the nature of causality, i.e. the act of bringing about an effect, remains essentially the same over a long period of time. It is this relation which, in figure 1, explains the evolution of *normal* output *ef*.

The short- and medium-term deviations from the 'trend' can be represented in terms of a modified supermultiplier relation: the variables and parameters in this relation would now deviate from their respective long-period values. However, the business cycle movement and the short-run evolution of output (*ei* and *AB* in figure 1) can also be described by appropriate medium- and short-period causal relationships: a business cycle theory and the short-run (Keynesian) multiplier relation linking investment and output. Correspondingly, these theories are medium- and short-term because the way in which causality works remains essentially unchanged for medium and short periods respectively.

The example just given points to the specific relationship existing between socioeconomic reality – set in space – and time in classical-Keynesian theory. The independent short-run, medium- and long-term causal factors (predetermined variables and parameters) exercise their influence upon the determined variables at *any* moment of time. Hence a long-period situation (an unemployment 'equilibrium' governed by the institutional system) is *not* something which is to be brought about *in the future* if a given situation is allowed to work out without disturbances. *The long run is always there.* In terms of scheme 3, it is the effect caused by those parts of independent variables and parameters which are institutionally determined, i.e. by the socioeconomic and political system, upon the corresponding components of dependent variables, i.e. normal employment and output and normal prices.

This implies that the dependent variables which may be observed in the real world, the level of employment for instance, are governed by a great many long-, medium- and short-period factors. The analysis need by no means remain confined to the economic sphere, partly represented by short-run movements of employment, cyclical variations of economic activity and the position of the employment trend. One may go a step further and inquire into non-economic factors influencing these independent economic variables, for instance into the institutions governing the position of the employment trend through the supermultiplier relation (chapter 4, pp. 142–204). This procedure is similar to Marx's method of analysing socioeconomic phenomena which is summarized in the *Einleitung zur Kritik der Politischen Ökonomie* (Marx 1975 [1857]), which will be briefly considered in the next section.

The treatment of time and space suggested here has a long tradition. Krishna Bharadwaj remarks that an important analytical distinction was made [in classical, Marxian and neo-Ricardian economics] between 'permanent' and persistent forces that act upon the system and the transient influences that are accidental, sometimes unforeseen or possessing a random impact. It was maintained that the persistent tendencies (designated 'long run' or 'natural' [the classicals equated *natural* and *normal* which we do not; they are separated by alienation!]) were the subject of theoretical analysis (Bharadwaj 1983, p. 18).

The permanent forces in question, institutions and technology, determine 'equilibrium' values of economic variables, e.g. normal output and employment levels and normal prices associated with a fully adjusted situation. In a capitalist economy, these 'equilibrium' magnitudes are not normative, but represent outcomes of the system as it exists at a certain moment of time; these equilibria *may* attract medium- and short-term behavioural outcomes. This vision of things allows us to deal with disequilibrium situations linked with dynamic processes without major difficulties (see chapter 4).

The neo-Ricardian way of treating space and time seems to be partly acceptable to many Robinsonians and Keynesian Fundamentalists although different uses are made of it: 'Like many others Joan Robinson reserves the concepts of long period and short period to classify variables according to the degrees of permanence of their effects. In Robinson's works, however, this criterion is used to classify variables in their *actual* existence, not in aprioristically established equilibrium relations' (Carvalho 1984/85, p. 229). In Joan Robinson's view, actually existing short- and long-period factors seem to govern the corresponding expectations. This point is also taken up by Keynesian Fundamentalists who emphasize the Keynesian distinction 'between long run and short run *expectations*: they are distinguished by the action each one induces, e.g., investment decisions result from long run expectations and output decisions from short run expectations' (Carvalho 1984/85, pp. 225–6). This is true only for each individual investment project and hence for the volume of investment undertaken in some period of time as a result of aggregate investment *behaviour*. However, the volume of long-period (normal) investment is not governed by *subjective* factors (expectations) but by *objective* ones, i.e. institutionally governed effective demand resulting from the functioning of the socio-economic and political *system* (pictured by the supermultiplier to be derived in chapter 4, pp. 142–204). This crucial point also holds for capacity output and employment and market prices, on the one hand, and for normal output and employment and for normal prices, on the other. The former are governed by behaviour, the latter are outcomes of the system.

The classical-Keynesian treatment of space and time is sharply opposed to that adopted in *modern* neoclassical equilibrium economics. Here, the starting point is a *short-period* equilibrium situation with market prices and quantities exchanged determined by endowments, consumers' tastes and technology. If present stocks of capital goods are not compatible with the *long-period* equilibrium position, then these have to be changed. However, changes in stocks require time. The neoclassical long-period equilibrium will be reached if a given situation can work out without further disturbances; this is Marshall's *stationary state* (Marshall 1920, pp. 366ff.). The time span required to reach the long-period equilibrium is the long run itself. Hence, according to *neoclassical* theory, the long-period equilibrium is in the *future*, not in the present as in classical-Keynesian theory. This may be illustrated with the help of figure 1 (p. 85). At t_1 the level of output *ad* is below the full employment path *gh*. If all the markets worked in a satisfactory way, then the ordinary neoclassical economist (not the sophisticated general equilibrium economist) would postulate a tendency towards full employment equilibrium output (point *k* for instance) which might be reached at t_2. The time-span lying between the *present* (t_1) and the *future* time-period t_2 at which equilibrium will eventually be reached is the neoclassical long run. More will be said on classical-Keynesian and neoclassical equilibria in chapter 5 below.

However, different views on the equilibrium concept are also held by post Keynesian economists belonging to the three broad groups mentioned in chapter 1. Related to the problem of conceiving equilibria is the question of the compatibility of *uncertainty and expectations* on the one hand with the notion of *system equilibrium* on the other. These issues will be discussed more fully in the subsequent chapters; however, to avoid misunderstandings, some preliminary remarks on the question of 'uncertainty and expectations versus system equilibrium' are required at this stage.

In scheme 3, the realm of the neo-Ricardians (who are a subset of the classical-Keynesians) is layer III containing the institutional and technological structure (the system) which, through the long-period application of the principle of effective demand (the supermultiplier relation discussed in chapter 4), governs the normal levels of output and employment. Given these, technology, operating across the laws of production (Pasinetti 1977, 1981), and institutions determine normal prices and quantities and normal sector proportions, i.e. a fully adjusted situation. This neo-Ricardian, perhaps more appropriately classical-Keynesian, 'equilibrium' does *not* refer to a hypothetical or to a normative state of affairs which might lie somewhere in the future and towards which there might eventually be a tendency. A classical-Keynesian equilibrium is that part of reality which is governed by *presently existing* objective factors, i.e. institutions and technology or the socioeconomic system.

What about uncertainty and expectations in the long run? If the state of confidence concerning the proper functioning of institutions is very strong, uncertainty will be almost entirely absent with respect to global normal magnitudes, i.e. the *volumes* of trend employment, output and investment, though not to the *composition* of these composite variables. For example, the *volume* of *trend* investment may be governed by objective factors – the institutional *system* – devoid of uncertainty, while considerable uncertainty may be attached to the *individual* investment projects which make up the investment volume resulting from aggregate investment *behaviour*: it is highly uncertain which projects will be successful in the long run and which will fail. This illustrates quite well the neo-Ricardian position adopted here. Objective (certain) factors and uncertainty co-exist. Both are different aspects of reality. The former relate to the institutional system, the latter to behaviour. A similar argument holds for single variables, prices for instance. There is little uncertainty about the objectively determined long-run normal prices, while uncertainty about the evolution of market prices may be considerable.

Hence the neo-Ricardians deal with the impact of objectively given institutional factors, resulting from past behaviour, and with social processes which cannot be readily changed in the present. The importance of historically evolving structures means that there is an undeniable element of *determinism* implied in neo-Ricardian analysis: structures, to a large extent, determine behaviour through the laws of production and the principle of effective demand.

While neo-Ricardians look at socioeconomic events almost uniquely from the point of view of the socioeconomic system as a whole, Keynesian Fundamentalists and Robinsonians emphasize behavioural aspects. In the short run (layer I in scheme 3) the stock of capital goods is assumed to be given. Present aggregate investment (determined by entrepreneurial investment behaviour) and the Keynesian multiplier (representing the impact of the system) determine output and employment, and a certain degree of capacity utilization. In the medium term (layer II) the stock of capital goods and the associated output and employment levels vary cyclically as a result of the volume of investment undertaken in each short period of time. Entrepreneurial investment behaviour interacts with the system: given investment volumes govern certain profit levels, according to the mechanism set forth in Kaldor (1955/56), through the economic system; realized profits influence, in turn, the amount of investment undertaken by entrepreneurs. Because of the uncertainty attached to the fate of each individual investment project and to the changing expectations of entrepreneurs the volumes of investment, output and employment may be highly unstable. Hence, to postulate that the volume of investment is governed by *subjective* factors only implies that little can be said on the evolution of economic systems and that theorizing becomes impossible. Indeed, if everything is subordinate to uncertainty, agnosticism is the final result.

Given this, it is understandable why Robinsonians and Keynesian Fundamentalists argue that uncertainty and the possibility of disappointed expectations destroy the possibility for equilibrium analysis. A long-period equilibrium could only get established if long-term expectations (governing investment) remained unchanged for a sufficiently long time-period. This would correspond to some type of golden age (Robinson 1962a, pp. 52ff.). However, in the Robinsonian and the Keynesian Fundamentalist view, it is impossible for an economy ever to get into a steady state equilibrium. There are always disturbing factors preventing this. Short-run expectations may be disappointed which, in turn, leads to changes in long-term expectations and thus in the level of investment (see, e.g., Kregel 1975). The steady state or the golden age thus represents, in Joan Robinson's own words, 'a mythical state of affairs' without real significance.

The impossibility of equilibrium analysis would be denied, for different reasons though, by both the neoclassical economist and the neo-Ricardian or, more appropriately, the classical-Keynesian political economist. Both would accept that there may be considerable uncertainty if an *individual* investment project or if an *individual* 'economic agent' is considered: will a certain investment project be a success or will it fail? Will a specific worker be employed or unemployed? However, the classical-Keynesian political economist would maintain that normal investment and employment volumes and normal prices and quantities are governed by the socio-economic system. The neoclassical economist would invoke objectively given market forces which, if functioning satisfactorily, are supposed to bring about a persistent tendency towards an equilibrium, implying allocative efficiency. But the classical-Keynesian political economist would deny that a tendency towards a *future full employment* equilibrium situation exists (chapter 5, pp. 281–93) and would argue that the equilibrium of the system is located in the *present* and governed by presently existing constant or slowly changing factors (chapter 4, pp. 142–204). Fluctuations may occur but are, in normal circumstances, attracted by the evolving equilibrium magnitude which may be the 'trend' level of employment and output, a normal price or a normal productive capacity in a sector of production.

However, classical-Keynesian political economists would agree with Robinsonians and Keynesian Fundamentalists about the important link existing between uncertainty and money: the speculative demand for money due to uncertainty is an indispensable prerequisite for establishing the principle of effective demand at any moment of time. Given this, it will be possible to include the Keynesian theory of money and interest almost *tel quel* in the classical-Keynesian framework proposed here (chapter 4, pp. 220–35).

To summarize: neo-Ricardians mainly examine the determining impact of the socioeconomic system on behaviour. Robinsonians and Keynesian Fundamentalists combine behavioural aspects with the impact of parts of the system. In chapter 4, it will be suggested that behavioural outcomes are complementary to those produced by the system; moreover, both outcomes interact. Therefore, a classical-Keynesian synthesis seems possible.

Finally, a remark on some of the different uses of the notions of certainty and uncertainty is required here. The neo-Ricardian political economist considers the institutionally determined part of the real world as it exists in the present and in its historical evolution (the central layers of scheme 3) as objectively given and devoid of uncertainty in so far as the existence of institutions and the associated system outcomes, in the near future at least, are concerned. For example, from the seventies onwards Japan was obviously a strong exporter; in 1980, say, it was quite certain that this proposition would also be true in 1985, and beyond, *if* no major institutional changes occurred in Japan or elsewhere in the world. This is inextricably linked up with the nature of an institution which, by definition, is persistent. A Keynesian Fundamentalist might deny this and assert that individuals may be very uncertain about many objectively given parts of reality. However, this kind of uncertainty is more appropriately called 'ignorance' or 'imperfect knowledge'. Because of imperfect knowledge, different theories aimed at explaining a given fact, e.g. unemployment, co-exist which is another way of saying that economists are, to some extent at least, ignorant about the nature of the causes of unemployment. Imperfect knowledge about given objective factors as an essential and ever-present ingredient of human existence has been included among the invariable features of reality in layer VII of scheme 3: Keynes strongly emphasized the fact that all knowledge is *probable* to varying degrees (chapter 2, pp. 57–64). Moreover, Keynes frequently related *uncertainty* not to present situations but to the future. Neo-Ricardian and classical-Keynesian political economists would agree that there is, for each individual, a considerable amount of uncertainty about the future with respect to large parts of reality. The future evolution of rapidly changing elements of reality, market prices for instance, may be highly uncertain. However, very little uncertainty may be attached to institutionally determined factors, such as trend employment or trend investment for instance, if institutions are working properly and if this situation is strongly expected to continue in the future.

Remarks on integrating theory and history

Time plays a crucial role in classical-Keynesian political economy which is, therefore, not only theoretical and timeless but also *essentially* historical. Objectively given causal forces pictured by applied or real-type causal models are historical by nature since the process of causation – predetermined variables governing determined variables – goes on in historical time. For example, effective demand governs long-period output and employment levels across the entire institutional system in a specific way which may evolve as time goes by. Pure theory however is timeless and consists of a coherent set of ideal-type causal models which exhibit how causal forces work in principle. Some of the classical-Keynesian models are set out in chapter 4, particularly the supermultiplier relation which pictures the probable relationship between the institutional system and the level of economic activity.

The contradistinction between pure and applied theory raises the problem of integrating theory and history. In this section it will be suggested that the solution to this problem is associated with the Aristotelian classification of causes defined in chapter 2 (pp. 55–7) and the various types of models explained earlier in this chapter (pp. 81–9). The Aristotelian approach to integrating theory and historical reality was taken up and elaborated, in different but complementary ways, by Karl Marx and by Carl Menger.

In an Aristotelian vein the efficient cause, expressing determinism, and the final cause, associated with aiming at individual and social ends, are always associated with the material cause. The former may be pictured by pure or ideal-type models which consequently exhibit how the process of causation goes on in principle and in general. If the material cause is combined with the efficient or the final cause applied causal models emerge which may be used to explain concrete and unique historical facts.

Hence, on the basis of pure or ideal-type models, applied or real-type models may be developed to attempt to explain real-world situations. Historical economists will take a further step: they will try to explain how a certain situation has come into being and will, subsequently, try to sketch future institutional developments. Thus, historical economists are not content with attempts to explain given situations, they are also concerned with their coming into being and with possible tendencies for change.

The full application of the historical method is, however, possible in the central, i.e. institutional, layers of reality only, that is layers III, IV and V of scheme 3. There is, in fact, not much sense in going very far into the past in order to explain a short-term situation which is temporary anyway. Moreover, prediction is very difficult because of the high degree of uncertainty which is attached to rapidly changing events, e.g. the evolution of market prices. Hence, in layer I, a given short-period situation may, as a rule, be explained by factors occurring in the same time-period. However, in layer II, the recent past may become a determinant of what is going on in the present. Regarding business cycles, for instance, a past upswing may be the cause of the present downswing as will be suggested in chapter 4 (pp. 204–20) where the cycle is presented as an interaction between the income and the capacity effect of investment. Once the probable nature of the cyclical mechanism is established, predictions of possible future developments may be attempted.

The historical method is also of lesser importance regarding layers VI and VII in scheme 3. The factors located here *always* play an important role, which may vary in the course of time, but will not essentially change. For instance, a French historian used to open his lectures on British history by saying that Great Britain is an island. He simply wanted to argue that this geographical fact has always been of great importance in shaping British economic, political, social and cultural life. Geographical facts, invariable objective laws governing the real world, fundamental ethical and aesthetic values, the rules of logic, uncertainty about the future and imperfect knowledge (layers VI and VII in scheme 3) are thus important at all times, but to explain their coming into being may be quite difficult if not impossible and also unnecessary.

However, the historical method becomes very important in the realm of institutions which are located in the central layers of scheme 3. Many institutions which today govern large parts of our behaviour have a very long history. Socioeconomic and political institutions emerged spontaneously or as the result of deliberate past actions which, in turn, were based upon socioeconomic theories, however crude, and values held in the corresponding time-periods. Moreover, the significance of theories and values actually held can be understood best by studying their evolution in the course of time. To explain present institutions, their interaction and the effects they produce in terms of past developments is the main task of the historian, more specifically of the economic historian if the economic aspect of reality is being investigated.

To explain given situations and tendencies for change, conceptual frameworks made up of causal models are needed. These have to be worked out by theoretical economists. Modern classical-Keynesians have, in the main, proposed models aimed at explaining given situations. Multiplier models and input–output frameworks are prominent examples. The classical precursors of modern political economists, however, were primarily concerned with tendencies for change; the explanation of given situations was merely a first step in their theoretical undertakings. The most striking illustrations

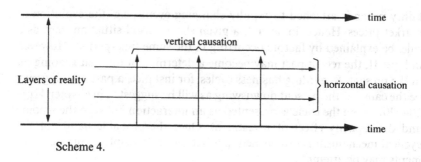

Scheme 4.

of what has been called the 'magnificent dynamics' of classical political economy are Adam Smith's model of economic growth and development (books II and III of the *Wealth of Nations*) and Ricardo's laws on the tendencies of distributional shares. There can be little doubt, however, that Marx's *Kapital* towers above all other attempts to capture the laws of motion of socioeconomic systems. Therefore, many historically minded social scientists think that Marx's method is much more important than the material content of his work.

The classical-Marxian tradition for dealing with tendencies for change is somewhat neglected by modern political economists. Nevertheless, a few models aimed at explaining tendencies for change exist. Obvious examples are Pasinetti (1981), in which a formal model of structural change is set out, and the Kaldor–Myrdal model of cumulative causation designed to explain growing differences of wealth between regions and nations (Kaldor 1970).

The theoretical *and* historical character of classical-Keynesian political economy emerges from two types of causal models which are, in turn, based on two types of causality, i.e. *vertical* or static causality and *horizontal* or dynamic causality. These concepts rest on the idea that the causal effects exercised by the predetermined magnitudes on the determined ones take place at any moment of time, although the ways in which causalities are exercised may change as time goes by; this holds, in principle, for all the causal relations at work in the real world. Scheme 4, which is closely related to scheme 3, helps to explain this.

A few examples taken from classical and classical-Keynesian theory may illustrate the concept of vertical causation. In the classical social and circular process of production and reproduction (scheme 2, p. 97) gross and (net) final output is produced by putting to use non-produced means of production (labour and land) and produced means of production (circulating and fixed capital goods) in any period of time (one day, a month, a year, five years). Starting from Quesnay's *tableau*, Leontief, Sraffa and Pasinetti developed an enlarged input–output model to capture how the process of production goes on *in principle*. This model embodies causal links between predetermined variables (the means of production) and determined variables (gross and net final output). To give other examples: in principle, long-period distribution is governed at any moment of time by a complex interplay of institutions, implying an intricate combination of causal relations. The same is true of absolute and relative normal – long-period – prices which depend upon the level of money wages, the conditions of production and on distribution. Market prices indicate deviations from the normal prices and are influenced by the short-run vagaries of the market, i.e. governed by the principle of supply and demand. According to the supermultiplier relation – to be discussed in chapter 4 – the long-period trend level of employment depends at any instant of time on the autonomous – normal – components of demand multiplied by the supermultiplier, i.e. on long-period effective demand. Short-period levels of output and employment depend on short-period effective demand. The cyclical movement is governed by a double-sided relationship between investment and profits (chapter 4, pp. 204–20).

These examples help to explain the notion of *vertical causality*. The causal forces just mentioned depart from the underlying principles located in layer VII (scheme 3) to structure the various layers of reality at any moment of time through behavioural or system outcomes: causality is thus vertical to the time axis. This is why vertical causality may conveniently be called static causality: the *material content* of the causal processes just mentioned does not change as time goes by.

Pure models reflect objectively given causal forces or principles shaping specific spheres of reality. In the economic domain, Quesnay's *tableau économique*, Adam Smith's *natural system*, Ricardo's *Principles*, Marx's theory of value and of surplus value, Walras's *Principes d'économie politique pure*, Keynes's *logical* theory of the multiplier (Keynes 1973a, p. 122), and, above all, Sraffa (1960) and Pasinetti (1977, 1981, 1993) are all outstanding examples of *pure theory* trying to capture the essence of objectively given causal forces. These and other pure models are logically true in a formal sense, i.e. they are free of internal contradictions. However, pure models represent *probable* material truth only: it can never be unequivocally proved that the models in question are logically true in the material sense that they adequately picture the objectively given causal forces. Complex effects, such as prices, distributional outcomes and employment levels are due to a great number of causal forces which unite organically. Since it is extremely difficult to disentangle the bundles of causal forces at work, effects can be explained in different ways. For example, neoclassical economists and classical-Keynesian political economists fundamentally diverge on the explanation of unemployment in terms of fundamental causal forces. Hence all that can be done to give scientific status to some pure model is to advance arguments based on observation, theoretical reasoning and introspection associated with a vision of things; the weight of a comprehensive argument so constructed and the degree of probability associated with the available evidence establish the extent to which a pure model might correspond to the objectively given but invisible causal forces. In this view, knowledge is approximate comprehension of the essence of things, not about some empirical fact: it is probable correspondence between the contents of thought and objectively existing ideas. This antipositivist stance is broadly in line with the theory of knowledge set forth in Keynes's *Treatise on Probability* (Keynes 1971c) and sketched in chapter 2 (pp. 57–75). We shall return to some issues related to the theory of knowledge in chapters 5 and 7.

The *form* (the *way*) in which causality is exercised by the predetermined on the determined variables changes in the course of time because the predetermined variables evolve; changes may be caused by the functioning of the system or by purposeful action. This leads to changes in the quality of causation. Variations in the form of causality will be more frequent and possibly more pronounced in the upper than in the lower layers of reality (schemes 3 and 4). For example, market prices located in layer I may fluctuate considerably in spite of the fact that the law of supply and demand remains invariant in principle, while the long-period prices of production to be found in layer III are relatively stable in the course of time.

To explain changes in the form of causation, variables and parameters related to different dates have to be taken account of. For instance, according to business cycle theory, past realized profits may govern present investment levels. A past invention leads to variations of coefficients of production in a Leontief–Sraffa–Pasinetti system now. Reforms of the educational system in the present may link up with an improved quality of output in the future; this, in turn, may stimulate future exports, reduce future import dependence and, as such, change the way in which the supermultiplier works (chapter 4, pp. 142–204). These examples show why the second type of causality may be termed 'horizontal' or 'dynamic' causality: the dynamic causal effect is exercised *along* the time axis; the determined and predetermined magnitudes belong to different periods of time. Objectively given dynamic causal forces can be pictured by *probable* 'pure dynamic models', i.e. pure models of the business cycle, growth models or models of structural change (for the latter, see Pasinetti 1981).

The concepts of vertical and horizontal causality can easily be linked up with the familiar concepts of statics and dynamics. Vertical causality is connected with statics since time-lags play no role here: predetermined and determined variables refer to the same time-period which may be short, medium, long or very long. Horizontal causality is, in contrast, clearly connected with dynamics and change; time-lags are essential here. In chapter 4 (pp. 142–204), it will be suggested in successive sections how both types of causality can be combined: the first section is about vertical causality, i.e. the determination of long-period economic activity by institutions at any moment of time, the second about horizontal causality, i.e. business cycles going on in the course of time. At this stage, we may mention that regarding production, value and distribution, vertical and horizontal causalities are combined on a fundamental and general level in Pasinetti (1977) and in Pasinetti (1981). In Pasinetti (1977) pure models exhibiting vertical causality are set out, i.e. classical production models of the Leontief–Sraffa type. Pasinetti (1981), however, examines horizontal causality, i.e. pure models of structural change going on in time. The way in which the two types of causal model are integrated is set out in chapter VI of Pasinetti (1981, pp. 109–17).

The auxiliary notions of vertical and horizontal causality may be combined with the four Aristotelian causalities mentioned in chapter 2 (pp. 55–7). This yields a wide spectrum of types of causality that can merely be hinted at here. Vertical causality is equivalent to the formal cause: how are causes related to effects *in principle*, e.g. changes in investment to changes in output in the pure theory of the multiplier; this is the question about the probable essence of causal relations. In the social sciences it might be appropriate to consider the final cause and the efficient cause as two variants of the formal cause. The final cause is related to the goal-oriented behaviour of individuals and collectives within given institutions, e.g. certain ways of organizing production, of consuming or of spending leisure time; or behaviour may aim at institutional change, e.g. a reform of the government or of the legal system. The efficient cause, which implies determination of the effect by the cause, may be most appropriately put to use to capture the *impact of the institutional system upon behaviour*: for example, long-period effective demand, which depends upon the entire socioeconomic system, determines the level of economic activity and the extent of permanent involuntary unemployment (chapter 4, pp. 142–204). Horizontal causality may also be associated with the formal cause to mean fundamental and accidental changes in the way in which a causal force acts in pure form or in principle. For example, pure models of the business cycle capture accidental changes in the principle of effective demand: the sizes of investment and of the multiplier may change in the course of the cycle owing to varying realized profit volumes, but the principle of effective demand remains. Fundamental changes in the way in which a causal force acts may arise if profound institutional changes occur: for example, Marx argued that the relation of surplus labour to necessary labour governs the degree of exploitation; this (pure) causal relation underwent a fundamental qualitative change with the transition from feudalism to capitalism.

All the causal relations just mentioned represent pure or ideal-type models which exhibit principles or pure theory. If any of these types of causal relations is combined with the material cause (chapter 2, pp. 55–7), applied or real-type models obtain. These models apply principles to specific situations; for example the supermultiplier principle may be applied to different countries or regions to attempt to explain involuntary unemployment. Or, evolutionary processes involving determinism may, in specific cases, be partly captured by applying the pure model of accumulation set forth in Marx's *Kapital*.

Two related issues linked with the concept of a causal model and its relation to the real world remain to be briefly examined here: first, the unidirectional character of causality and the question of feedbacks and, second, the integration of theory and history. Both points will be taken up in greater detail later on.

It is a hallmark of a causal model, e.g. the multiplier relation, that only unidirectional causal links are considered. Predetermined variables and parameters govern determined variables in the course of time (on this, see Pasinetti 1974, p. 44, and Bortis 1978, pp. 57–60), linking different spheres of space: in the process pictured by the multiplier relation, events happening in the investment goods sector produce effects in the consumption goods sector by means of the spending of incomes by households. Classical-Keynesian causal models – like the multiplier model – seem to stand in striking contrast to neoclassical equilibrium models in that feedbacks apparently are not taken account of. There are several points to be mentioned here.

Pure models dealing with principles are always unidirectional in some sense. This is even true for the Walrasian general equilibrium model: there is in fact a one-way causal relation between the equilibrium values of the variables and the parameters determining them.

There are also classical-Keynesian pure models which take account of feedbacks and of equilibrium elements. An obvious example is the Leontief–Sraffa model. The crucial point is, however, that the notion of 'general equilibrium' is entirely different in neoclassical and classical-Keynesian models. In neoclassical economic theory the 'general equilibrium' is an essential component of the theory and hence inherent to it. The Walrasian general equilibrium model is in fact the basic and the only 'true' neoclassical model. This model is confined to the economic sphere only. In classical-Keynesian theory, however, the 'general equilibrium' is not to be found in the economic sphere, but on a higher and all-embracing social and political level: the general equilibrium is a *system* equilibrium. This implies that classical-Keynesian causal models containing equilibrium and feedback elements are always partial equilibrium models; there is no classical-Keynesian general equilibrium model in the economic domain.

In real-type causal models, feedbacks cannot be ignored since, in the real world, acts of causation usually lead to a feedback of some kind. The feedback may be weak or strong; it may occur immediately or after some time. A few examples may illustrate some of the issues at stake.

Consider a country of which the manufactured exports are growing rapidly and steadily, which may be leading to export surpluses and to high output and employment levels. Given effective demand worldwide, the export successes of one country may lead to a reduction of economic activity in other countries. After some time, this might influence negatively the exports of the country in question: a feedback occurs which may be captured by a separate causal relation. Hence, feedbacks may be taken account of by combining causal models, a typical example being the multiplier-accelerator model.

However, the feedback in response to a country's exports may be negligible, so that there is no need to set up a new causal relation. Two reasons might account for this. The country considered may be a small one so that no significant reduction of world economic activity occurs. Or, the forces behind the export success (technical dynamism, work discipline, aggressive sales methods, etc.) are so strong that eventual feedbacks due to diminished world economic activity or to rising prices of export goods are reduced to insignificance – which is another way of saying that the forces at work are not symmetrical.

Finally, the feedback engendered by some effect may be almost immediate: the causal relations are at work simultaneously. From this the necessity to set up an interdependent equation system arises. An illustration is the Leontief–Sraffa model picturing the circular process of production: the production of some good i requires inputs of other goods, the production of which requires, in turn, inputs of several other goods including possibly good i. The Leontief–Sraffa system thus captures causal forces operating simultaneously in space. Indeed, causal models of the classical-Keynesian type can only be set up because reality is set in space and time (scheme 3). Initial effects and feedbacks can be separated because they take place at different points in time. Conversely, simultaneous and mutually dependent causal forces can be disentangled because they occur at different places in space.

The preceding methodological remarks are in the classical-Marxian line and lead to the second point to be considered here, i.e. a brief discussion of Marx's views on the integration of theory and history. Some of Marx's remarks on method are set forth in his *Einleitung zur Kritik der Politischen*

Ökonomie (Marx 1975 [1857]), and the structure of *Das Kapital* reflects the application of Marx's methodological principles. In the *Einleitung* Marx states that 'the concrete is concrete because it is the result of many determining forces and thus unites the manifold: Das Konkrete ist konkret, weil es die Zusammenfassung vieler Bestimmungen ist, also Einheit des Mannigfaltigen' (Marx 1975 [1857], p. 632). This sentence clearly illustrates the important Aristotelian roots of Marx's thought, and he did not hesitate to state clearly the metaphysical underpinnings of his work. Marx's statement implies that a great variety of causal forces unite to determine concrete things to be found in the real world; how the causal forces determine a specific object – man, society or a commodity – is governed by the formal cause, i.e. the form-giving principle. Incidentally, *Das Kapital* builds upon an analysis of the commodity which unites physical, social, economic, legal and political aspects; for example, to say that a commodity is owned by a capitalist implies the institution of 'private property'.

Marx's proposition directly links up with the concept of vertical causality in pure and applied form or the four Aristotelian causalities mentioned before. The example of price formation will illustrate this. *In principle*, the price of a commodity is, according to Marx, proportional to its value which, in turn, depends upon the quantity of direct and indirect labour time embodied in a commodity: value is the essence of price. This basic and invariant causal relation would be located in layer VII in scheme 3. However, various circumstances modify the principle of the pure labour theory of value. The conditions of production and the way in which distribution is regulated (this being reflected in the rate of profits) govern the prices of production which, on account of varying technical conditions and social relations of production, differ from values; the corresponding causal relations would be found in the third layer of scheme 3 where persistent or slowly evolving elements of the real world are pictured, i.e. institutions and technology. Cyclical movements and the vagaries of the market bring about medium- and short-run deviations from the prices of production. Limited effective demand may even prevent the commodity from being sold at all. The sale of a commodity may be a most perilous undertaking: Marx sees it as a *salto mortale* to be performed by any commodity (Marx 1973/74a [1867–94], vol. I, p. 120).

The causal forces just mentioned all represent vertical causalities and unite in *each* price that can be observed in the real world. This holds for any economic phenomenon; for example, distributive outcomes and employment levels represent the effect caused by a multitude of causal forces operating in the real world in different layers of reality across the behaviour of individuals (layers I and II) and the functioning of the institutional system (layer III). Each phenomenon is, in fact, governed by a most diverse set of 'vertically acting' causal forces.

Horizontal causality in the form of the efficient cause – expressing determination – may now be brought in easily. In *Das Kapital* Marx (1973/74 [1867–94], vol. I, chapter 8) mentions that, given technology, the amount of surplus labour extracted from the labour force is governed by the length of the labour day. This principle, while remaining invariant in time, may take on widely differing forms according to the mode of production prevailing at a given place in a specific period of time, for example in a feudal or in a capitalist society. Any principle expressing the material content of some theory may appear in varying forms in the real world. Hence, horizontal causality underlies historical processes.

Vertical causality relates to the material content of a theory and horizontal causality to the changing ways (or forms) in which a principle materializes in the real world. In this context, Marx would speak of *Inhalt und Form*, two concepts which are put to widely differing uses in his work. The whole of his *Kapital* is in fact a combination of vertical and horizontal causality, i.e. of pure theory and of history.

Marx's method perhaps comes out most clearly in the structure of *Das Kapital*. The starting point is the commodity, which summarizes the various effects brought about by the causal forces at work in the socioeconomic and political domain. *Das Kapital* is, in fact, a synthesis which presents in an orderly way the analysis of the commodity, the cell of the capitalist mode of production. Starting with the discussion of use value and of exchange value and the nature of money, the main theme of volume I is the process of production: here commodities are produced and value and distribution determined; effective demand (the *salto mortale* of the commodity) may prevent any commodity from being sold. Volume I ends up with capital accumulation. Volume II considers the circulation of capital and culminates in the famous consideration of the appropriate proportions between consumption and investment goods sectors which must hold if production is to go on in an orderly way. The methodologically relevant point is that volume III, *Der Gesamtprozess der kapitalistischen Produktion*, takes up the processes of production and of circulation *again*. In this volume, however, socioeconomic phenomena pertaining to the upper layers of reality are being considered: prices of production and market prices, rents, profits and wages; some of these, like market prices, are part of the surface and are, according to Marx, appearances. Volumes I and II, however, deal with principles or fundamentals, that is, with values, surplus value and rates of exploitation for instance. The upper layer phenomena (e.g. profits, interest and rents) can only be understood properly if the fundamentals (e.g. surplus value) have been grasped, a fact that emerges clearly from part 7 of the third volume of *Das Kapital*. Therefore, appearances must not be the primary object of science; in fact, science would not be needed at all if the fundamental causal principles at work could be perceived immediately by looking at the appearances: '[alle] Wissenschaft wäre überflüssig, wenn die Erscheinungsform und das Wesen der Dinge unmittelbar zusammenfielen . . .' (Marx 1973/74a [1867–94], vol. III, p. 825). This is why the quickly changing behavioural outcomes of the upper layers must be left aside to direct attention to the more stable lower layers where institutions are located, which give rise to system outcomes in the socioeconomic sphere – prices of production and trend employment levels, for example (scheme 3).

These considerations regarding the structure of *Das Kapital* relate to vertical causality. In the real world, however, static causal forces always appear together with horizontal causalities. Consequently, 'it is the fundamental purpose of this work [*Das Kapital*] to uncover the economic law of motion of modern society' (Marx 1973/74a [1867–94], vol. I, pp. 15–16; a.tr.). Part 7 of the first volume of *Das Kapital* on the accumulation of capital represents perhaps the finest piece of horizontal causality elaborated by Marx; here Aristotle's efficient cause exhibiting determinism is put to the fore in the social sphere.

In Marx's vision, the properties of the capitalist mode of production unite in its basic and characteristic element: the commodity. The various causal forces unite *organically* in each commodity so that it is extremely difficult to disentangle separate causal forces. In the preface to the first edition of *Das Kapital* Marx mentions that the causal forces at work in the real world can only be discovered through abstraction (Marx 1973/74a [1867–94], vol. I, p. 12): in the section on *commodity fetishism* (vol. I, pp. 85–98) he explains how difficult it is to uncover the socioeconomic properties of commodities; these can, in fact, not be seen when looking at a commodity and have, therefore, to be thought out; this is associated with analysis and abstraction. In modern terms, Marx's 'analysis' is equivalent to theorizing, i.e. to working out pure causal models to capture how the objectively given causal forces work *in principle*. Conversely, to explain some aspect of reality, e.g. the level of employment in some country at a certain point of time, several pure causal models have to be combined appropriately. Finally, the synthesis represents the orderly presentation of the results of abstraction. In this sense *Das Kapital* represents the synthesis of Marx's analytical work.

A very simple example might illustrate the difficulty linked with analysing organic facts. A specific composite colour obtained by mixing up pure colours in certain proportions would constitute an organic fact. To analyse it, the scientist would have to separate the causal forces, i.e. the pure colours and the corresponding proportions, which have brought about the composite colour. The immense difficulties the social scientist is faced with become evident if appropriate account is taken of the fact that societies are themselves tremendously complex organic wholes, structured by an equally complex hierarchy of values and by natural propensities of the individuals composing it. Marx and Keynes were conscious of this. However, in the spirit of the nineteenth century and mainly under the influence of Hegel, Marx aimed at establishing absolute truths regarding the functioning and the laws of motion of societies. In contradistinction to Marx, Keynes tried to work out merely *probable* propositions (chapter 2, pp. 57–64) on the working mechanism of monetary economies, thus putting the capacity to acquire knowledge on a level which properly reflects human possibilities. This is evident from his *Treatise on Probability* and from Fitzgibbons (1988) and O'Donnell (1989).

Nevertheless, Marx's historical method provides a signpost which may guide future methodological developments in political economy. Roman Rosdolsky's work *Zur Entstehungsgeschichte des Marxschen 'Kapital'* (Rosdolsky 1974) provides an authoritative introduction to Marx's method; Morf (1951) and Sweezy (1942) remain important on this issue. At first sight, it might seem rather strange to go back to Marx in these days. However, we should remember that Max Weber, though vigorously opposed to the material content of Marx's work, had high praise for his historical method which he denoted as 'uncomparably fruitful'.

The methodological sketch of this section would be incomplete without a reference to the *Methodenstreit*. The members of the German Historical School under the leadership of Gustav Schmoller rejected classical, mainly Ricardian, theory, and neoclassical theory, as had come into being around 1870, as too abstract and therefore as irrelevant. They sought to come to grips with socioeconomic and political reality with the help of historical studies. In this way they attempted to discover historical regularities which might lead to 'theories'. This is pure inductionism: theory was to be derived from the observation of historical reality. In this the Historical School failed; this is also true of American Institutionalism. Theories are needed in order to organize historical research because reality is so complex that it cannot be grasped in its entirety and at one stroke, so to speak. Around the beginning of the twentieth century the lack of theory became obvious and led on to a feeling of frustration: 'We are tired of collecting materials, we want to come to grips with the available stuff; we want to penetrate the details conceptually in order to approach the great aim of science: a general and comprehensive *Weltanschauung*' (H. Diels in 1900, quoted in Oncken 1902, p. V; a.tr.).

In his reply to the 'historians' and specifically to Schmoller, Carl Menger showed that theory and history were not opposed but complementary (Menger 1969). Pure theory deals with principles, i.e. with the fundamental causes operating in individual and social life. These ideal-type models help to organize historical research through real-type models (on this, see also the definitional section above, pp. 81–9). Menger's methodological approach is thus Aristotelian and bears as such a close similarity to what has been said on methodological issues in this and in the preceding sections. There is, however, an important difference. Menger attempts to reduce social phenomena to the behaviour of individuals, and he can be considered as one of the founders of methodological individualism. Therefore, his method enables him to deal with behavioural outcomes but not with outcomes of the entire socioeconomic and political system. In this Menger needs to be complemented by the classical-Keynesian methodology sketched in the above and to be applied in chapter 4, which also includes Marxian elements. Social phenomena have laws of their own. This is due to the common aims pursued within social institutions and the complementarities existing here. Hence, social phenomena are essentially organic (chapter 2, pp. 20–57), which implies in turn that attempts to come to grips with the functioning of societies and with social phenomena require an overall or global view of society. This is the specific element inherent in the methods employed by Ricardo, Marx and Keynes, and of the German Historical School and American Institutionalism. It has been suggested that the two latter failed because of a lack of a socioeconomic macrotheory. Keynes attempted to remedy this with his *General Theory*. In the preface to the German edition he expresses his desire to provide a conceptual underpinning for the historical research undertaken by the German school of political economy (Keynes 1973a, pp. xv–xvii).

The above suggests that theory and history must be combined on the behavioural level and on the level of the institutional system to lay the basis for studying interactions between the behaviour of individuals and the system. This methodological thread will be taken up in chapters 4 and 5.

4 Towards a coherent system of political economy

The classical economists dealt with all the great problems of economic theory – i.e. value, distribution, growth, proportions between sectors – except the determination of the employment level. Based upon Say's law they postulated that saving governs capital accumulation to determine employment in the long run. In the classical view persistent unemployment could only arise because of insufficient capital accumulation relative to population growth. A lack of overall demand for goods that would result in a *general* glut in the markets was excluded by Say's law. The classicals entirely neglected the mercantilist heritage that was taken up again by Keynes (chapter 23 of the *General Theory*).

At the outset of the final chapter of the *General Theory*, Keynes states that the persistence of involuntary unemployment represents the major problem of our times. In his early writings, especially in his *Paris Manuscripts* (Marx 1973 [1844], pp. 510–22), and in *Das Kapital* Karl Marx considers involuntary unemployment – the existence of an industrial reserve army – a crucial ingredient of alienation, which has been defined as the gap existing between some prevailing social situation and an ideal state of affairs in which the common weal would be realized (chapter 2, pp. 39–53).

Both Marx and Keynes held the opinion that involuntary unemployment was not due to some ethical shortcoming of entrepreneurs or workers, nor to a market failure, but was due to a basic defect of the socioeconomic system which Keynes denoted a monetary production economy. Because of the social importance of persistent involuntary unemployment, the present chapter is essentially devoted to this and to associated problems.

The employment problem was rediscovered in the crisis of the thirties. Keynes worked out a short-period theory of employment. Kalecki and others dealt with cyclical movements of economic activity. Some excursions into the long run were undertaken within the framework of growth theory. On the whole, however, *long-period employment*, governed by long-period effective demand, was rather neglected; notable exceptions are Eatwell (1983), Garegnani (1978/79, 1983), Milgate (1982) and Pasinetti (1981, 1993). In the present chapter, an attempt is made to contribute to the understanding of this issue, mainly in the central section where a theory of the institutional output and employment 'trend' is set out. To do so, Keynes's short-term *General Theory of Employment* appears to be the natural starting point. The relationship between the institutional 'trend' and the cycle is dealt with in the second section. Following the central section already referred to, the object of the fourth section is the Robinsonian or Kaleckian cycle-cum-growth theory which complements long-period 'trend' employment theory. The subsequent section deals with Keynesian Fundamentalism: some issues related to uncertainty and money are raised and a classical-Keynesian short-period framework is exhibited. The concluding remarks contain some complementary observations regarding the content of the present chapter and a few methodological implications of the classical-Keynesian approach.

Extending Keynes to the long run

Without exaggeration one may assert that Keynes was the first economist to have shown in an intellectually convincing way that an unemployment equilibrium may exist. Many social scientists before him had a strong feeling that there might not be an automatic tendency towards full employment in a monetary economy: William Petty, James Steuart, Thomas Malthus, Karl Marx, John Hobson, Rosa Luxemburg, and others. But none of them managed to convince the economists' profession. Keynes's main task consisted of showing that, somewhere, there was a failure in the market mechanism. He concluded that the capital market did not function in the neoclassical way: an act of saving does not lead to a reduction in the rate of interest and thus to a higher volume of investment. Keynes argued that more saving meant less demand for consumption goods. The volume of saving passively adjusts to investment through a change in the level of output. Compared with neoclassical economics, this implies a fundamental change: equilibria are established through quantity adjustments, not through price variations. This is captured by the multiplier relation

$$Q=(1/s)I \tag{1}$$

which summarizes Keynes's *short-period* theory of employment. Given this, his main problem consisted in finding a new explanation for the rate of interest. The money market linked with uncertainty and expectations provided the solution. In some instances Keynes crossed the boundaries of his short-run framework to make incursions into the long run. For example, he was aware of the long-run 'capacity effect' of investment:

the problem of providing that new capital-investment shall always outrun capital-disinvestment sufficiently to fill the gap between net income and consumption, presents a problem which is increasingly difficult as capital increases. New capital-investment can only take place in excess of current capital-disinvestment if *future* expenditure on consumption is expected to increase. Each time we secure to-day's equilibrium by increased investment we are aggravating the difficulty of securing equilibrium to-morrow. A diminished propensity to consume to-day can only be accommodated to the public advantage if an increased propensity to consume is expected to exist some day (Keynes 1973a, p. 105).

This is, incidentally, one of the themes taken up by Garegnani (1978/79) and Milgate (1982).

This very important passage from the *General Theory* raises the question as to the nature of the long-period theory of employment to be erected upon the short-period foundations laid by Keynes. At least four possibilities seem open: the neoclassical solution, Keynes's own theory, growth theory and Kalecki's theory of cyclical growth.

The neoclassical way of extending Keynes to the long run starts from the fact that Keynes accepted the first (neo)classical postulate: 'the wage is equal to the marginal product of labour'. This amounts to implicitly assuming the existence of factor markets, at least with respect to the long term where 'substitution' is said to be possible. If these are functioning satisfactorily there will be a tendency towards full employment in the long run. Here, effective demand does not play any role: economies are supposed to be resource-constrained. The neoclassical argument crucially depends on the existence of long-period factor markets. In chapter 5 (pp. 281–93) it will be suggested that such markets do not exist if production is conceived of as a social process.

Keynes suggests a long-period theory of employment in chapter 17 of the *General Theory*. On the one hand, a high level of the own-rate of interest of money, i.e. the liquidity premium, may prevent the additional production of reproducible goods before full employment is reached. On the other hand, 'beyond a certain point money's yield from liquidity does not fall in response to an increase in its quantity to anything approaching the extent to which the yield from other types of assets falls when their quantity is comparably increased' (Keynes 1973a, p. 233). Once the own-rates of reproducible goods, valued in terms of money, equal this (minimum) own-rate of money, additional production stops; specifically, 'no further increase in the rate of investment is possible' (p. 236). The maximum level of investment may not be high enough to bring about full employment. Hence '[u]nemployment develops, that is to say, because people want the moon; – men cannot be employed when the object of desire (i.e. money) is something which cannot be produced and the demand for which cannot be readily choked off' (p. 235). This is the long-period counterpart to the short-period 'liquidity trap' in Hicks's IS–LM framework.

However, we cannot be content to say that, in the long run, an unemployment equilibrium is possible because there is a monetary economy. It has to be explained how this equilibrium is determined by basic economic and non-economic factors. This requires a long-period theory of output and employment (Garegnani 1983, p. 78). What determines, for instance, the own-rates of interest of capital goods? Income distribution might play a role here: a more equal distribution of income might be linked up with a higher volume of purchasing power and increased demand for consumption goods, which, in turn, may raise the own-rates of interest of the capital goods employed in the consumption goods sector. Or, what is the interpretation of the own-rates of interest of capital goods? Is it the marginal productivity interpretation along neoclassical lines or something else?

Hence, Keynes's long-period theory of employment (taken up by some post Keynesian economists) is somewhat question-begging. If for some reason the IS curve cannot be shifted sufficiently to the right to bring about full employment, the problem would consist of diminishing the own-rate of interest of money or of money substitutes (see Keynes's remarks on Silvio Gesell: Keynes 1973a, pp. 353–8). Full employment would eventually be reached by reducing the importance of money as a store of value which is equivalent to removing a 'market imperfection'. This inevitably implies a return to neoclassical long-period theory, as the history of economic theory since the publication of the *General Theory* clearly shows.

A third way of extending Keynes into the long run obtains by working out a theory of the trend, that is a theory of economic growth. For different reasons *all* conventional growth models are left aside here: neoclassical models starting from Solow (1956), because a perfect functioning of factor markets is assumed, an assumption to be criticized in chapter 5 (pp. 281–93); Keynesian growth models of the Harrod type (Harrod 1939) imply too high a degree of instability; and post Keynesian models of the Kaldorian variety (Kaldor 1955/56) postulate an inherent tendency towards full employment. All these implications do not seem to square with reality. A fourth class of trend theories is composed of Joan Robinson's golden age models (Robinson 1962a, 1965) which, however, are purely hypothetical constructions. Their main purpose is to show that golden ages may never come into existence: an economy can, due to uncertainty and expectations, never get into an equilibrium. In fact, Robinson herself spoke of the 'mythical nature' of the golden age (1962a, p. 52).

Given this, the Robinsonians – and Kaleckians – argue that the only valid extension of Keynes to the long run is provided by a trade cycle-cum-growth theory based upon a classical-Marxian two-sector model. Presumably, Keynesian Fundamentalists would broadly subscribe to this position which is neatly summarized by Kalecki:

> The contemporary theory of growth of capitalist economies tends to consider this problem in terms of a moving equilibrium rather than adopting an approach similar to that applied in the theory of business cycles. The latter consists of establishing two relations: one based on the impact of the effective demand generated by investment upon profits and the national income; and the other showing the determination of investment decisions by, broadly speaking, the level and the rate of change of economic activity . . . I do not see why this approach should be abolished in the face of the problem of long-run growth. In fact, *the long-run trend is but a slowly changing component of a chain of short-period situations; it has no independent entity*, and the two basic relations mentioned above should be formulated in such a way as to yield the trend cum business-cycle phenomenon [our emphasis] (Kalecki, 1971, p. 165).

Hence for the Robinsonians and the Keynesian Fundamentalists, there is no need for a separate theory of the trend, which is but a statistical average, calculated *ex post* on the basis of the movement of the business cycle.

Some of the Keynesian-minded neo-Ricardians, however, emphasize the need for a theory of the 'trend': 'We must *explain* why an economy may gravitate around [a trend line implying 5 percent unemployment] rather than a [trend line implying 20 percent unemployment], i.e. we must aim at a long period theory of the level of aggregate output' (Garegnani 1983, p. 78). In the present study this thread of thought is taken up; however, 'trend' or normal output levels and normal prices are *not* conceived of as centres of gravity but as long-period system equilibria which are *not* independent of aggregate behaviour.

These statements require some remarks on the relationship between 'trend' and cycle. To avoid confusion with the 'statistical trend' we shall speak of 'normal output and employment' or of 'trend' in the following. This is in line with the definitions set forth in chapter 3 (pp. 81–9).

The trend and the cycle

There is a peculiar difficulty related to combining the trend (normal output) and the cycle: 'the trouble is that [the] *trend* cannot be explained by the same theory [as the trade cycle] and, therefore, has to be introduced *ad hoc*' (Pasinetti 1960, pp. 69–70). This also holds for Robinsonian-Kaleckian cycle-cum-growth theory. However, 'from a theoretical point of view, the situation would not be so unsatisfactory if the two phenomena [trend and cycle] – which . . . are so obviously interconnected in their real manifestations – could be explained by two different theoretical models to be combined and integrated' (p. 69).

But this is precisely what has to be done. The long-period classical-Keynesian model which explains the position of the trend or normal output, and *trend* growth, is different from the Robinsonian-Kaleckian model which describes the cyclical (*actual*) growth of the capital stock (which, in ordinary circumstances, is attracted by the normal capital stock defined in chapter 3, pp. 81–9). The former model pictures *uniquely* the functioning of the *system*, i.e. the interplay of institutions, and is associated with fully adjusted situations; the latter deals with aggregate *behavioural* outcomes, e.g. aggregate investment and consumption behaviour, co-ordinated by parts of the system, i.e. the law of effective demand. The two models thus deal with different spheres of socioeconomic reality; they are complementary and can thus be combined and integrated. There are, however, interactions between the trend and the cycle: on the one hand, the actually existing normal variables (capital stock, output, employment and normal prices) and the various institutions both result from *past* social and individual behaviour and are gradually modified by *present* behaviour – gross investment and institutional change lead to a gradual modification of the normal variables; on the other hand, the normal variables, which reflect the functioning of the system, *determine* present individual actions across the laws proper to the system: the principle of effective demand and the social process of production.

Cycle-cum-growth and trend models are remarkably similar. Both are macroeconomic by nature: the functioning of the economy as a whole must be considered to explain trends and cycles. Thus, having derived the Cambridge equation within a macroeconomic framework, Pasinetti states: 'the foregoing investigation . . . is macroeconomic because it could not be otherwise. Only problems have been discussed which are of a macroeconomic nature . . . They would remain the same . . . even if we were to break down the model into a disaggregated analysis' (Pasinetti 1962, p. 118). The same is true of Keynesian models aimed at explaining the scale of employment.

Yet there is an important difference between trend and cycle models. The latter represent *classical macroeconomics* dealing with the determination of proportions between final product sectors (e.g. the consumption and the investment sectors), *given* the scale of employment. The former typify *Keynesian macroeconomics* in that they aim at explaining the level of employment, *given* the sectoral set-up of an economy.

The Robinsonian (and Kaleckian) cycle model is a two-sector model essentially dealing with proportions: 'The ratio of employment in the investment sector to employment in the consumption sector is equal to . . . the ratio of quasi-rent per man employed in the consumption sector to the wage, quite irrespective of quasi-rent in the investment sector' (Robinson, 1965, p. 75). This ratio varies in the course of the cycle, but is compatible with *any* level of employment and output. The latter means that actual output may fluctuate at a smaller or a greater distance from the full employment level (figure 1, p. 85).

However, a trend model, aiming at explaining the long-period level of employment, must be a long-period macroeconomic model of the Keynesian type implying that the various sectors of an economy are in the appropriate proportions. This is a fully adjusted situation representing that part of socioeconomic reality which is governed by the institutional set-up prevailing at any moment of time, comprising a desired (satisfactory) rate of profits or a hierarchy of desired profit rates. The fully adjusted situation cannot be observed directly and constitutes a 'hidden' part of reality, superseded by actually existing magnitudes which represent behavioural outcomes, i.e. output and employment levels, prices and quantities, realized profit rates and sector sizes; the latter all deviate from the corresponding trend magnitudes contained in the fully adjusted situation (chapter 3, pp. 81–9).

The determination of the level (the scale) of overall output and employment in the short, medium *and* long term is a fundamental problem which is logically prior to other economic problems, i.e. structures, cycles, value and distribution. When working out his famous equation for the warranted rate of growth to establish a theory of the trend, Harrod states:

It may be well to emphasize at this point that no distinction is drawn in this theory between capital goods and consumption goods . . . Some trade-cycle theorists concern themselves with a possible lack of balance between these two categories; no doubt that has its importance. The theory here considered is more fundamental or simple; it is logically prior to the considerations regarding lack of balance, and grasp of it is required as a preliminary study of them (Harrod 1939, pp. 48–9).

Keynes became aware of the essential difference between macroeconomic models aiming at explaining the relationships between the consumption and the investment sectors and those dealing with the scale of employment when he abandoned the *Treatise on Money* to work out the *General Theory*:

[In the former] I failed to deal thoroughly with the effects of *changes* in the level of output. My so-called 'fundamental equations' were an instantaneous picture taken on the assumption of a *given* [our emphasis] output . . . This book [*The General Theory*], on the other hand, has evolved into what is primarily a study of the forces which determine changes in the scale of output and employment as a whole . . . we shall find [that, in a monetary production economy,] changing views about the future are capable of influencing the quantity of employment and not merely its direction (Keynes 1973a, p. xxii).

Harrod's and Keynes's statements apply exactly to our problem of long-period employment and output determination. The corresponding model must be macroeconomic in the Keynesian sense in that forces are considered which affect *all* sectors in the same way. Its variables and parameters must be interpreted as weighted averages depending on the institutional and technological structure of an economy. This is the case of the super-multiplier relation (pp. 142–204 below) which represents a theory of the trend (normal output). Problems of structural change or deviations from existing structures – in the course of a cycle for example – can, subsequently, always be dealt with if the necessity arises.

To characterize the classical-Keynesian long-period theory of output and employment, or theory of the trend, to be presented in this chapter it is appropriate to start from a system of quantity equations proposed by Pasinetti. This equation system pictures an economy in structural equilibrium, i.e. a fully adjusted situation implying a *stock* equilibrium (Pasinetti 1981, equations II.5.2, p. 38): a matrix comprising production and demand coefficients multiplied by a quantity vector, made up of the long-period equilibrium quantities of consumer and capital goods and the full employment labour force, *equals zero*. This implies that the equation system is *independent of the scale of output and employment*: 'the existing quantity of labour does not constrain or limit anything . . . the systems of [price and quantity] equations which will be considered yield solutions for *relative* prices and *relative* quantities, which are *independent* [our emphasis] of the total quantity of labour available' (Pasinetti 1981, p. 23, n. 30): if the quantity vector, containing the full employment labour force and the corresponding full employment quantities of consumer and capital goods, were multiplied by a scalar (called appropriately *employment scalar*) smaller than unity, 0.8 say, then a *trend* or *normal* unemployment ratio of 20 percent would prevail in the economy considered, leaving proportions unchanged. (Full employment would be achieved only if appropriate measures were taken in order to set the employment scalar equal to unity.) Hence in terms of Pasinetti's basic model, a classical-Keynesian theory of the trend must explain the size of the employment scalar implicitly contained in the quantity system just referred to.

In a macroeconomic theory of the trend, the long-run levels of output and employment are the dependent variables. These are determined by institutionally governed normal demand components: autonomous or exogenous variables (government expenditures and exports) and derived or endogenous variables (consumption, imports *and* investment). The former are, in contrast to the latter, independent of the scale of activity. The relationship between exogenous and endogenous variables is given by the *supermultiplier* (Hicks 1950).

Some Keynesians might possibly not agree with the project of setting up
a theory of the trend since, in their view, uncertainty and disappointed
expectations would render such an undertaking impossible: 'the fact that
our knowledge of the future is fluctuating, vague and uncertain, renders
[the accumulation of] wealth a peculiarly unsuitable subject for the methods
of the classical [and neoclassical long-period] equilibrium theory' (Keynes
1973c, p. 113).

My next difference from the traditional theory concerns its apparent conviction that
there is no necessity to work out a theory of the demand and supply of output *as a
whole*. [Indeed] the theory of effective demand, that is the demand for output as a
whole, [has] been entirely neglected for more than a hundred years. [My] theory can
be summed up by saying that, given the psychology of the public [the marginal propensity to consume is strictly linked to the multiplier], the level of output and
employment as a whole depends on the amount of investment (pp. 119, 121).

Uncertainty is, on the one hand, incompatible with equilibrium theory
and is, on the other, a prerequisite for the theory of effective demand; therefore, it would seem impossible to set up a theory of *trend* or *normal* output
and employment based on the principle of effective demand. This requires
some explanatory remarks which link up the propositions on uncertainty
set forth in chapter 3 (pp. 103–18) with those in this chapter (pp. 220–35).
Effective demand, i.e. intended outlays on goods and services, is an objective factor, related to the functioning of an economy as a whole, which
determines the supply behaviour of producers in *all* sectors of production.
There is no major problem with this proposition in the short run, although
investment is governed by subjective (behavioural) factors, i.e. long-run
expectations. The latter are supposed to be provisionally fixed which
implies that the volume of investment is also a given objective factor. Given
this, realized results dominate expected results in the short run and the
difference between the two is of secondary importance,

[f]or the theory of effective demand is substantially the same if we assume that
short-period expectations are always fulfilled . . . I now feel that if I were writing the
book [*The General Theory*] again I should begin by setting forth my theory on the
assumption that short-period expectations were always fulfilled; and then have a
subsequent chapter showing what difference it makes when short-period expectations are disappointed . . . a mistake in the short-period expectation . . . will be one
of the relevant factors in determining subsequent effective demand (Keynes 1973c,
p. 181).

Hence the volume of investment is given in the short run and constitutes,
together with other parts of effective demand, an objective factor determining the behaviour of producers. However, when Keynes comes to
discuss the long-run determinants of investment he almost exclusively

relies on subjective factors. He considers individual investment *projects* which, taken together, make up the *volume* of investment: 'When a man buys an investment or capital-asset, he purchases the right to the series of prospective returns, which he expects to obtain from selling its output, after deducting the running expenses of obtaining that output, during the life of the asset' (Keynes 1973a, p. 135). 'This involves the whole question of the place of expectation in economic theory' (p. 138). 'The considerations upon which expectations of prospective yields are based are partly existing facts which we can assume to be known more or less for certain, and partly future events which can only be forecasted with more or less confidence . . . We may sum up the state of psychological expectation which covers the latter as being the *state of long-term expectation*' (pp. 147–8). Now,

the state of long-term expectation . . . does not solely depend . . . on the most probable forecast we can make. It also depends on the *confidence* with which we make this forecast . . . There is, however, not much to be said about the state of confidence *a priori*. Our conclusions must mainly depend upon the actual observation of markets and business psychology. This is the reason why the ensuing digression is on a different level of abstraction from most of this book [*The General Theory*] (pp. 148–9).

This is the crucial point: to explain an important component of effective demand (an objective factor), i.e. the volume of investment, Keynes does not rely on objective factors related to the functioning of the *system*; instead he relies heavily on subjective factors, dealt with in chapter 12 of the *General Theory* where the *behaviour* of the speculator and of the entrepreneur are described. How, then, does the individual investor behave, given 'the extreme precariousness of the basis of knowledge on which our estimates of prospective yield have to be made' (p. 149)? Keynes answers that

[e]ven apart from the instability due to speculation, there is the instability due to the characteristic of human nature that a large proportion of our positive activities depend on spontaneous optimism rather than on a mathematical expectation, whether moral or hedonistic or economic. Most, probably, of our decisions to do something positive, the full consequences of which will be drawn out over many days to come, can only be taken as a result of animal spirits – of a spontaneous urge to action rather than inaction (p. 161).

It is difficult to see how a long-period *theory* of investment and, therefore, of total output and employment could be built on such fragile subjective foundations. Indeed, if consequently pursued, the behavioural point of view leads to agnosticism: 'expectations do not rest on anything solid, determinable, demonstrable. We simply do not know' (Shackle, quoted in Carvalho 1984/85, p. 227).

To be sure, uncertainty and expectations, i.e. *subjective* factors, are very important if the fates of *individual* investment projects are considered. These subjective factors are also associated with the aggregate of individual investment projects, i.e. the volume of investment undertaken in each time-period, and with capital stocks and capacity output levels as exist at any moment of time. However, the explanation of the *volume* of *normal* or *trend* variables (output, employment and investment), which in ordinary circumstances attract realized magnitudes, must rest on *objective* factors, i.e. institutions and technology related to the functioning of the *socioeconomic and political system*. These factors are located in the *present* and pertain to the constant and slowly changing factors to be found in the third layer of reality (scheme 3, p. 106). Institutions govern 'trend' effective demand which, in turn, determines 'trend' output, employment *and* investment (the supermultiplier relation to be derived in the next section). This is crucial: in long-period theory the volume of *trend* or *normal* investment is *not* an autonomous demand component determined by long-term expectations but constitutes *derived* demand and is ultimately governed by institutions and technology, i.e. the socioeconomic and political system. This proposition will be discussed more fully in the next section.

Long-term expectations enter only *indirectly* into the determination of trend investment, namely through the state of confidence about the proper (future) functioning of institutions. Keynes, in fact, himself lays the basis for this point of view. Referring to the fragility of long-term expectations he states: 'We should not conclude from this that everything depends on waves of irrational psychology. On the contrary, the state of long-term expectation is often steady' (Keynes 1973a, p. 162). The reason for this can be found at the beginning of chapter 12: '[t]he considerations upon which expectations of prospective yields are based are partly *existing facts which we can assume to be known more or less for certain* [our emphasis], and partly future events which can only be forecasted with more or less confidence' (p. 147). There is no problem with including *institutions* among 'the facts of the existing situation [which] enter, in a sense disproportionately, into the formation of our long-term expectations; our usual practice being to take the existing situation and to project it into the future' (p. 148). This even emerges as a necessity and corresponds to the basic position taken up in this study: institutions can be considered as stable or slowly changing objective factors only if their proper functioning is expected to go on indefinitely.

With regard to Keynes's emphasis on expectations (subjective factors) and his relative neglect of institutions (objective factors), in relation to investment in the main, we are in broad agreement with Hodgson who suggests 'that Keynes had a psychologistic and rationalist conception of human action which is defective and leads to a mistaken view of government and the state' (Hodgson 1988, p. 217). 'Keynes sets out his theory of expectations in ahistorical terms and without reference to institutions. To be fair, this latter defect is typical of mainstream economics as a whole, and is not confined to Keynes' (p. 238). '. . . [A] number of modifications are necessary to the Keynesian theory of expectations and investment. These are related, in the main, to giving greater weight to the role of institutions in the economic system' (p. 239). 'The challenge for modern Post-Keynesians is to rebuild Keynes' theory on more adequate, and non-individualistic, theoretical foundations' (p. 241).

A theory of long-period output and employment

The classical-Keynesian long-period theory of output and employment is summarized by the supermultiplier relation. This relation is a piece of pure theory, i.e. an 'ideal-type' model. It pictures how *trend* effective demand governs, *in principle*, *trend* or *normal* output and employment through the functioning of the socioeconomic system as a whole, i.e. the interaction of *all* institutions making up a society (the notion of *normal* – normal employment or normal prices – is associated with positive states of affairs *with values given* and differs as such from *natural* which has ethical implications as will become evident in chapter 6, pp. 314–19). Hence the supermultiplier relation deals in a Keynesian vein with the *scale* of economic activity. However the Ricardian theory of value and distribution which reflects the classical preoccupation with *proportions* is closely associated with this relation as will become evident below (pp. 189–90). Subsequently, problems of content and method associated with the supermultiplier relation will be considered. The initial subsection is devoted to definitional and formal aspects of this relation.

The supermultiplier relation: some general aspects

The long-period theory of effective demand examined here represents an aspect of the Keynesian-Marxian *monetary theory of production*. This notion is symbolized by the sequence $M - C \ldots P \ldots C' - M'$ (Marx 1973/74a [1867–94], vol. II, p. xxx): across the banking system entrepreneurs dispose of finance M which enables them to buy means of production C; within the social process of production P these are transformed into final goods C' which are sold against money M'; like Ricardo, Marx argues that the social surplus $M' - M$ arises in the social process of production. This sequence perfectly characterizes the system of classical-Keynesian political economy conceived of as a synthesis of Ricardo, Quesnay, Marx and Keynes: Ricardo, Quesnay and Marx are associated with *production*, Keynes with *money*.

The supermultiplier can be derived from a macroeconomic equilibrium condition which expresses the principle of effective demand: in a monetary production economy economic activity is governed by the size of various demand components:

$$Q^* = c_w wN + c_p(P+R) + I + G + X - \pi bQ \tag{2}$$

On the left, there is trend output or aggregate supply Q^* (real GDP) which is the determined variable. The various components of normal demand, i.e. the determining variables, make up the right-hand side: consumption out of wages (c_w = fraction of wage income consumed, w = real wage level w_n/p, w_n = money wage level, p = price of a bundle of necessary consumption goods, N = productive employment, i.e. the workers and employees in the consumption goods sector and in the investment goods sector producing the surplus over ordinary wages), consumption out of property income (c_p = fraction of property income consumed, P = profits and R = rents), gross investment I, government expenditures G and exports X; imports πbQ represent a leakage of demand abroad (π = terms of trade and b = import coefficient). All the variables are in real terms, i.e. measured in terms of a bundle of *necessary* consumption goods, the value of which in money terms is p. Hence nominal values are divided by the price level p so as to obtain real magnitudes. Government expenditures include wages for 'unproductive' workers and employees (civil servants and teachers, for instance) who do not produce a surplus but are paid out of the surplus. Problems associated with saving and tax payments by these workers and employees are ignored; these issues leave the main argument unaffected.

In a later subsection (pp. 190–9) it will be argued that equation (2) is associated with two types of employment determination, i.e. the internal and the external mechanisms. The latter is connected with the last two elements in this equation ($X - \pi bQ$), the former with all the other components. The internal employment mechanism embodies the *surplus principle* sketched in chapter 3 (pp. 95–103): consumption out of wages is related to the process of production since this type of consumption broadly contains the necessaries required to maintain the capacity to work of the labour force. Consumption out of property income, government expenditure and investment all relate to the use of the surplus.

Equation (2) also implies that saving and tax coefficients are added up to yield leakages, which are stable elements while saving coefficients are pure residuals in the long run (definition 8). This implies that in a monetary production economy long-period 'equilibria' are established through quantity adjustments: in principle, trend output Q^* varies inversely with the saving ratio. This important issue will be dealt with below (pp. 154–90) in relation to long-period distribution.

Equation (2) contains trend, normal or long-period normal variables and parameters only, all of which are supposed to be governed by institutions and technology, i.e. the social system. For example, normal government expenditures G are regulated by legal prescriptions which are in turn the outcome of complex social and political processes; or the normal mark-up k^* is partly determined by trade unions, entrepreneurial associations, and by habits and customs in the domain of wage and price setting (pp. 199–204 below). To denote the long-period character of this equation, the *dependent* variable in this and other long-period equations is marked with a star, which is omitted for the *dependent* variable of medium- and short-term behavioural-cum-system relations; isolated trend variables and parameters are also marked with a star.

The 'equilibrium' condition (2) implies that saving equals investment, the former having passively adjusted to the latter through variations of output and employment. The principle of effective demand holds at any moment of time. The long-period implications of this principle emerge more clearly if account is taken of the definition

$$Q^*=AN=wN+P+R, \tag{3}$$

(A=average labour productivity) and if equation (2) is rewritten as

$$AN^*=c_wwN+c_p(AN-wN)+I+G+X-\pi bAN. \tag{4}$$

Because of the *capacity effect* of investment, trend gross investment must, in the long run, be proportional to normal output and employment (Q^* and N^*) and to the trend capital stock K^* since the fully adjusted situation – the long-period equilibrium – represents a *stock* equilibrium (chapter 3, pp. 81–9):

$$I^*=(g+d)vQ, \tag{5}$$

where v^*=normal capital–output ratio K^*/Q^* at standard capacity utilization, Q^*=trend output and d^*=normal drop-out ratio of fixed capital. Hence, in the long run, investment represents derived demand because of the capacity effect.

If account is taken of equation (5) and of definition (3) we are left with only two autonomous variables in equation (4), that is G and X. We now provisionally postulate that exports grow at the trend rate g^* and that government expenditures grow at the same rate (other possibilities will be considered below, pp. 190–9). Moreover, technical progress (which need not be neutral, i.e. uniform in all sectors of an economy) raises normal labour productivity by a rate a and the normal real wage rate also grows by this rate. Equilibrium will be maintained if normal employment grows at a rate g^*-a. Hence the trend rate of growth of the autonomous variable g^*

governs the trend growth rates of derived demand and of derived output in the long run, and trend employment *passively adjusts*.

To derive the supermultiplier relation, we still need a theory of value and distribution. The Kalecki–Weintraub normal pricing equation seems best suited to represent the classical-Keynesian views on value and distribution on the macroeconomic level in the long run (Weintraub 1978, pp. 44–53):

$$p^* = \frac{w_n}{A} k^*, \tag{6}$$

where A is labour productivity, w_n the money wage rate, k^* the normal mark-up at normal (standard) capacity utilization, which implies a normal or a hierarchy of normal (satisfactory, desired or target) profit rates (to avoid confusion the normal mark-up is always written as k^*) and p^* is the long-period (normal) price level. The case $k = k^*$ implies that, in the long run, firms aim at building up a capital stock such that, given money wages and demand conditions, normal output could be sold at normal prices. The normal price equation (6) implies a vertically integrated economic system and has exactly the same structure as the mesoeconomic or sectoral price equations (II.7.3) set forth by Pasinetti (1981, p. 44) which are explicitly based on vertically integrated analysis. Moreover, it should be recalled here that, in his *Treatise on Money*, Keynes extensively used the notions of 'normal remuneration of entrepreneurs' (Keynes 1971b, vol I, p. 111) and of normal price (Keynes 1971b, vol. I, pp. 121–4).

In the above price equation only labour productivity A^* and the normal mark-up k^* are really important, while the *levels* of money wages and of normal prices are arbitrary in the long run. Given this, we ought to divide by the level of money wages on both sides of the equation. This would yield the 'labour commanded' measure of value (chosen by Adam Smith and by Keynes) which is, presumably, the best long-period measure of value we dispose of, whether we deal with microeconomic or with macroeconomic issues. Particularly, the theoretical significance of the mark-up coefficient k^* for distribution emerges clearly. From $p^*/w_n = k^*/A$ follows $k^* = [(p^* Q^*)/w_n]/N$: in principle, the relationship of labour *commanded by* output in relation to labour *embodied in* output equals the institutionally determined average mark-up which regulates the division of national income into wage and property income.

For convenience, we do not divide by w_n in the following, which implies postulating a constant money wage level. Since we are not interested in the evolution of money wages and deal with principles, that is ideal-type models, this simplifying assumption is justified. It may be relaxed whenever real-world problems are considered with the help of real-type models.

The supermultiplier relation 'which can be applied to any given level of [autonomous demand components] to discover the equilibrium level of output which corresponds to it' (Hicks 1950, p. 62) can now be derived. The autonomous (exogenous) variables in equation (2) above are exports X and government expenditures G. The induced (endogenous) variables are consumption, imports *and* investment (equation 5). Combining equations 2–6 above we obtain:

$$Q^* = Y^* = \frac{G+X}{z_w + (z_p - z_w)[1-(1/k^*)] + \pi b - (g+d)v} \tag{7}$$

or

$$Q^* = Y^* = \frac{G+X}{z^* + \pi b - (g+d)v} \tag{7}$$

$z^* = z_w + (z_p - z_w)[1-(1/k^*)]$ is the leakage out of gross domestic income (Q^*); $1-(1/k^*)$ represents the property share in income – the wage share is $1/k^*$. Trend effective demand Y^* *determines* trend or normal output Q^* which is directly linked up with trend or normal employment across the relation $Q^* = AN^*$. Similarly to the other parameters in this equation, the leakages

$$z_w^* = 1 - c_w = s_w + t_w$$

and $\tag{8}$

$$z_p^* = 1 - c_p = s_p + t_p, \text{ with } z_p > z_w,$$

are supposed to be constants or vary but slowly. The average consumption coefficients are governed by specific institutions – habits and customs – regulating the behaviour of consumers; therefore, these coefficients remain stable over time or change only gradually. This proposition is empirically confirmed and appears to be a 'stylized fact' (Gordon 1984, p. 437, figure 13–7). The tax coefficients t_w and t_p are also institutionally given; therefore, the saving coefficients s_w and s_p appear as *pure residuals* which means that saving is *entirely passive* in the long run. The consequences of this proposition will be discussed in the next subsection in relation to the Cambridge equation.

The economically relevant tax rates are not the rates that are legally fixed but those which obtain if effectively paid taxes are accounted for. The splitting up of the leakage coefficients z into 'effective' tax rates and saving coefficients is therefore intimately linked with the question of tax evasion. It is well known that the scope for tax evasion is far greater in relation to property income than is the case for wage income, which implies that the difference between s_p and s_w will, in some instances, be larger than the disparity between z_p and z_w. This in turn favours greater long-period inequalities regarding the distribution of wealth between those who already own property and wage earners. On precisely this issue Inhaber and Carroll's (1992) work on income and wealth in America is highly relevant.

The level of trend output can also be obtained by combining a long-period macroeconomic 'demand curve', to be derived from the effective demand equation (2), with a long-period 'supply curve', i.e. the normal price equation (6) (see also Bortis 1984, pp. 598–9). Replacing the real wage w by w_n/p in equation (2), taking account of equation (5) and solving for the price level p yields the macroeconomic demand curve:

$$p^* = \frac{(z_P - z_W)(w_n/A)}{[z_P + \pi b - (g+d)v] - [(G+X)/Q^*]} \tag{9}$$

This ideal-type expression shows how the normal price level p^* and trend output Q^* are related in principle. To a higher Q^* corresponds a lower p^* and vice versa. This expresses a basic post Keynesian tenet. Given the money wage level w_n, a lower price level of consumption goods implies a higher real wage (and a lower mark-up k^*): with $z_P > z_W$, the demand for consumption goods is correspondingly larger. Effective demand increases, which, in turn, is reflected in higher trend levels of output and employment. $z_P > z_W$ is equivalent to the Kaldor–Pasinetti macroeconomic stability condition $s_P > s_W$: given the money wage level, higher prices are related to smaller output levels and vice versa. If this condition were not fulfilled, effective demand and output would, given money wages, rise together with prices and profits and vice versa; the economic system would either produce a tendency towards full employment with inflation or an ever lower level of activity and deflation, i.e. the system would be completely unstable.

Out of the hypothetically possible points on a macroeconomic 'demand curve' only *one* has a *real* meaning, i.e. the point of intersection between the 'supply price equation' (6) and the 'demand price equation' (9). The trend output so determined is, in fact, equivalent to Q^* as determined by the supermultiplier relation (figure 2). The 'equilibrium' position (p^*, Q^*) mapped out in figure 2 pictures a fully adjusted situation with involuntary long-period unemployment – since Q^* may be below full employment output Q_f – and implies that, in the long run, all producers aim at establishing sector sizes such that outputs could be sold at normal prices. The objectively given fully adjusted situation can never be realized since it cannot be observed directly and is largely unknown to individual producers. As such it constitutes the hidden, continuously evolving and system-governed equilibrium which, as a rule, attracts actual magnitudes representing behavioural outcomes. Hence market prices continuously deviate from normal prices. Correspondingly, capacity output levels may be

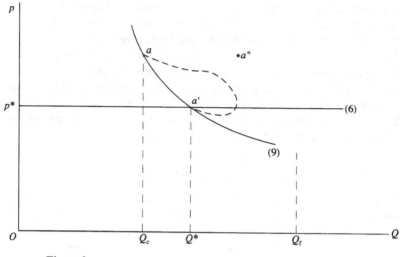

Figure 2.

above or below normal; given this, some sectors tend to shrink, others to expand (pp. 204–20 below).

The interpretation of the 'equilibrium' position (p^*, Q^*) is entirely different from that of similar diagrams of the neoclassical type. This equilibrium position is not a state of affairs to be reached at some future time-period but represents the system-governed part of socioeconomic reality at any moment of time: normal output *and* normal prices (of production) both result from social processes going on currently. There is nothing desirable about the long-run equilibrium output Q^*, which may be considerably below full employment output Q_f.

Like the supermultiplier relation, the 'long-run demand curve' (9) exhibits how effective demand governs normal output and employment *in principle*: this curve is an ideal type which must be handled with great caution if applied to real-world problems. In a real-type model movements 'along' the macro demand curve are strictly speaking not possible because each point on such a curve exhibits a *hypothetical* long-run equilibrium position embodying a specific desired mark-up k^* and a specific normal price level p^*. A *real* movement along this curve can take place only if a (medium-term) deviation from it occurs: if past accumulation has resulted in a capacity output Q_c in figure 2, prices and profits are above the normal levels in the present, and entrepreneurs will wish to expand capacities. Starting from Q_c the economy will now move towards the 'equilibrium' trend output Q^* possibly following the broken line aa' in figure 2: if output is to reach a higher level, the rate of growth of investment, capital, output and employment must temporarily exceed the 'trend' growth rate g^*; workers unemployed hitherto have to be equipped with capital goods, i.e. the size of the investment goods sector must increase temporarily relative to the other sectors of an economy.

This example illustrates Joan Robinson's famous dictum about *time coming out at a right angle* in 'real-type' figures representing *real*, i.e. historical events. Due to various causal forces, the curves mapped out in such figures may change their shape as time goes by. Therefore, different points on a curve, e.g. the demand curve (9) in figure 2, cannot be directly compared because they picture the results of alternative past evolutions. Movements along a given curve are not possible because the curve in question may change its position; or, as has been suggested above, movements along a curve may imply shifts of the curve; in a growing economy, the demand curve moves rightwards regularly; conversely, the supply curve will shift upwards if wages grow faster than labour productivity and vice versa. Moreover, cycles and traversing movements imply medium-term deviations from the corresponding long-run demand curve (9). Hence tendencies towards equilibrium positions have primarily a qualitative rather than a quantitative character: if, in terms of figure 2, an economy is at the disequilibrium point a in period t_1, it will eventually approach the 'equilibrium' point a' at t_2 provided the position of the supply and demand curves (equations 6 and 9) does not vary. If, however, one or both curves shift, the economy considered might approach an equilibrium position a'' at t_3, for instance. Real-type diagrams (and algebraic relations) picturing historical events make, therefore, all the more sense, the greater the stability of the underlying parameters and independent variables: long- and medium-term relations are more meaningful than short-term relations where the determining magnitudes may change very quickly and the corresponding resting point shifts considerably *within* the short time-period considered.

The economic meaning of the supermultiplier relation – seen as an ideal-type model embodying principles – emerges from a simple diagram (figure 3). Full employment output Q_f grows along a path aa' at the natural rate of growth (n), defined as $a+h$ where a is the trend rate of growth of labour productivity and h is the trend rate of growth of population (Harrod 1939). As a rule, long-period equilibrium output Q^* will move along a path below Q_f (aa'), i.e. bb', cc' or dd': the supermultiplier determines the *level* of the path along which long-run output and employment move along in time in different but *given* institutional set-ups. These trends represent ideal-type evolutions. The path ee' pictures changes in the institutional set-up at a given trend level. Institutional (or permanent) change may also be associated with shifts in trend paths; a traverse is a movement from one path to another. Partial breakdowns of institutions are associated with significant

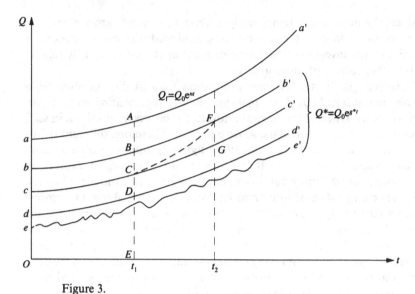

Figure 3.

downward shifts of trends, particularly if the autonomous variables, i.e. trend government expenditures or trend exports, are affected (which, incidentally, happened in the early thirties). A total breakdown of the institutional set-up would mean social chaos with individuals struggling for survival by all means in a Hobbesian *homo homini lupus* world. No employment or output trend would exist and behavioural outcomes would completely dominate the picture.

If the growth path is bb' the normal or trend levels of output are Ob at $t=t_0$ and EB at $t=t_1$. This implies that the fraction of trend or normal involuntary unemployment

$$u=(N_f-N^*)/N_f \tag{10a}$$

is determined in any period of time (N_f is the full employment labour force and N^* represents trend or normal employment). Consequently the employment scalar of a – fully adjusted – system equilibrium is

$$1-u=N^*/N_f. \tag{10b}$$

Hence the supermultiplier determines the employment scalar. The economic meaning of this coefficient emerges very clearly from Pasinetti (1981), once we consider the variables and parameters used there not as *natural* but as *normal* magnitudes (this procedure is legitimate since the *natural* is the ethically appropriate form of the *normal*). The sectoral normal prices depend on the money wage level, production and depreciation coefficients and *target* profit rates (Pasinetti 1981, price equations II.7.3, p. 44) and are synthesized by the macroeconomic normal price equation (6). The corresponding normal quantities are governed by the sectoral demand coefficients for consumption and capital goods and by the *full employment* level of output and income (Pasinetti 1981, quantity equations II.7.2, p. 44). Long-period unemployment may now be brought in easily. If both sides of the quantity system are multiplied by the employment scalar $1-u=(N^*/N_f)$, 0.8 for instance, long-run economic activity will be reduced by 20 per cent with respect to the full employment level; the price system will remain unaffected.

This result emerges with even greater clarity if the quantity system is written in matrix form. The most simple and at the same time the most fundamental quantity system (Pasinetti 1981, equation system II.2.5, p. 31; 1986, equation system 15, p. 422) pictures production by labour alone; the model can easily be reinterpreted to include capital, i.e. indirect labour:

$$
\begin{bmatrix}
1 & 0 & . & 0 & -c_1 \\
0 & 1 & . & 0 & -c_2 \\
. & . & . & . & . \\
0 & 0 & . & 1 & -c_m \\
-n_1 & -n_2 & . & -n_m & 1
\end{bmatrix}
\begin{bmatrix}
Q_{1f} \\
Q_{2f} \\
. \\
Q_{mf} \\
N_f
\end{bmatrix}
=
\begin{bmatrix}
0 \\
0 \\
. \\
0 \\
0
\end{bmatrix}
\tag{10c}
$$

N_f represents the full employment labour force, and the Q_{if} stand for the full employment quantities. The n_i represent the production coefficients which stand for the amount of labour directly and indirectly – to produce intermediate and capital goods – required to produce a unit of the corresponding output, and c_i are the respective consumption or demand coefficients. This linear and homogeneous equation system is a piece of classical macroeconomics which determines *proportions* between sectors and is independent of the scale of activity: the quantity vector in (10c) may be multiplied by any employment scalar (10b). The determination of the *scale* of output and employment is a matter of Keynesian macroeconomics. In the long run this task is, as far as principles are concerned, performed by the supermultiplier equation (7) which governs the size of the employment scalar (10b). Classical and Keynesian macroeconomics thus deal with different problems that can be solved independently, and the results can be combined subsequently: if the quantity vector of the equation system (10c) is multiplied by the employment scalar $1-u$ (10b), proportions remain unaffected while the scale of activity is reduced. *Hence the neo-*

Ricardian price and quantity equations combined with the supermultiplier relation constitute the heart of the synthesis of Ricardo and Keynes. Pasinetti's price and quantity equations (Pasinetti 1981) – seen as *normal,* not as *natural* relations – represent the pure long-period theory of production, distribution and value. The supermultiplier equation exhibits the pure theory of long-period employment determination. This combination of the neo-Ricardian theory of value and distribution and the Keynesian employment theory justifies the notion of classical-Keynesian political economy.

According to the supermultiplier relation, long-period macroeconomic equilibrium (Q^* and N^*) is, in principle, brought about by adjustments in the level of employment which is in perfect symmetry to Keynes's multiplier relation (1). To illustrate this it is assumed that an institutional modification, i.e. a *permanent* change, occurs at time-period t_1, for example an increase in trend government expenditures (figure 3, p. 150); such a change would show up in a higher value of G on the right-hand side of equation (7). This induces a shift in trend output from CE to BE. Since the economy cannot jump from C to B, the increase in G will, in a first stage, lead to a higher mark-up ($k>k^*$) which means that realized profits persistently exceed desired ones. Given this, the (actual) realized growth rate will rise above the warranted (trend) rate g^*; the investment goods sector grows relative to the consumption goods sector: the structure of the economy has to adjust to the higher growth rate. As long as $g>g^*$ prevails, the economy will move along the traverse CF until the new equilibrium path corresponding to the higher level of government expenditures (bb') is reached at point F.

In a specific real-world situation, this dynamic process may be disturbed by many factors; consequently, any real-type adjustment path will be much more complicated than the ideal-type traverse exhibited in figure 3.

The size of permanent change in output (ΔQ^*) brought about by the once-for-all change in government expenditures (ΔG) may be conveniently determined by a familiar relationship which leads straightaway to the supermultiplier formula (7), i.e.

$$\Delta Q^* = \Delta G \{1 + [(1-z) + (g+d)v - \pi b] + [\ldots]^2 + [\ldots]^3 + \ldots\}. \qquad (7a)$$

A permanent change of government expenditures (ΔG) leads to three kinds of derived demand: increased demand for consumption, $(1-z)\,\Delta G$; the amount of additional investment goods required to produce ΔG is $[(g+d)v]\Delta G$; finally, $-\pi b\,\Delta G$ stands for that part of ΔG which is imported from abroad – this leads to a reduction of the multiplier effect. To produce the additional consumption and investment goods (minus imported goods) necessary to produce ΔG, additional goods of the same type are required. These are represented by the term within square brackets in equation (7a). To produce these 'second-order' goods further goods have to be produced, and so on. The sum of the geometrical series in the above relationship yields the supermultiplier which indicates the extent of the permanent change in output due to a permanent change in government expenditures.

The concept of the supermultiplier is not new. Hicks used it in his theory of the trade cycle (Hicks 1950). The first economist, however, who (implicitly) made use of the supermultiplier was François Quesnay. He did so, not in his simplified *tableau économique* usually mentioned in the literature, but in the *complete* (zig-zag) tableau, set forth and commented on by Kuczynski and Meek (1972) and by Oncken (1902). From this construction it emerges beautifully how autonomous expenditures, i.e. the spending of rent by landlords and by government, set economic activity in the agricultural and manufacturing sectors into motion so that the economic system reproduces itself within a year. The same idea is expressed by the supermultiplier relation (7): autonomous expenditures $(G+X)$ here act as an engine which initiates the production of consumption and investment goods which represent derived demand; part of effective demand leaks abroad, giving rise to imports.

The fact that, in the long run, investment demand is derived demand reveals an important property of the supermultiplier relation: only the capacity effect of investment (associated with the stock equilibrium K^*) is relevant; the income effect of investment does not play any role. The capacity effect is represented by equation (5). Here, normal capacity output Q^* is determined by long-period effective demand, i.e. by the supermultiplier relation. The trend rate of growth of effective demand and of output is g^*, which is governed by the evolution of the autonomous variables. In order to provide the capacities required to produce trend output, investment must be of a definite size and has to grow at the (warranted) rate of growth of the economic system (g^*).

To show that, in relation to long-period normal magnitudes, the income effect cannot become effective, we consider a simple example, based on figure 3 (p. 150). Suppose that, hitherto, trend output has been moving along the path cc'. At $t=t_1$, investment is permanently raised above its trend level (defined by equation 5) in order to increase economic activity and to reduce unemployment. In the short run, the income effect of investment will bring about an excess of effective demand over trend output. In the supermultiplier relation, the actual rate of growth (g) now exceeds the trend rate (g^*). In the short and medium terms, the equality between effective demand and output $(Y=Q)$ will be restored by an increase in the realized mark-up k which is now above the desired one (k^*). Once the structure of the economy has adjusted to the higher growth rate g, actual output will, owing to the capacity effect of investment, grow at this rate too (path CF in figure 3). However, normal effective demand still increases at a rate g^*, i.e. the trend rate of growth of autonomous demand, along the path cc'. A widening gap between effective demand and productive capacity will develop, showing up in a gradual tendency for actual output to outpace trend effective demand. Equality ($Q = Y$) is restored by a decline of prices with respect to money wages or by a reduced degree of capacity utilization, and the realized mark-up will gradually fall below k^*. This induces a reduction in the volume of investment and thus in the rate of growth. Actual output will, *ceteris paribus*, gradually approach trend output, i.e. path cc' as determined by the supermultiplier.

Keynes clearly perceived the tension between high levels of investment and output in the present – the income effect of investment – and the capacity effect of investment that gradually works out in the future: 'Each time we secure to-day's equilibrium by increased investment we are aggravating the difficulty of securing equilibrium tomorrow. A diminished propensity to consume to-day can only be accommodated to the public advantage if an increased propensity to consume is expected to exist some day' (Keynes 1973a, p. 105). The same point is made by Garegnani (1978/79): if we reduce the wage share to raise investment and employment in the present, the wage share and consumption will have to be increased in the future to maintain the higher level of output.

This example shows that long-period unemployment cannot be permanently reduced by 'stimulating' investment; a long-period employment policy requires institutional changes, for example an incomes policy to bring about a fairer distribution of incomes, as will be suggested in the policy chapter (chapter 6).

Some theoretical implications of the supermultiplier relation

In this and in the next subsection we examine the implications of the supermultiplier relation regarding those problems that have traditionally been considered the most important by the great authors, i.e. employment and output determination, distribution, value, money, international trade and sector proportions (structures). Only principles associated with pure (ideal-type) models are dealt with (chapter 3, pp. 81–9). To each principle there (probably) corresponds a specific causal force (or a set of causal forces) acting in the real world (chapter 2, pp. 57–64). The supermultiplier pictures how, in principle, various causal forces are co-ordinated by effective demand and persistently act through the socioeconomic system to partly determine individual actions.

Long-period output and employment determination: the scale of activity

The supermultiplier relation is a long-period theory of output and employment determination. The economic meaning of this proposition emerges more clearly if the supermultiplier relation (7) is considered jointly with the foreign balance

$$X^* = \pi b Q^* (= \pi M) \tag{11}$$

and with the government budget

$$G^* = tQ^* = [t_W + (t_P - t_W)(1 - (1/k^*))]Q^*. \tag{12}$$

All the coefficients of the supermultiplier relation are given and 'trend' exports grow at a trend rate g^* to which the rate of growth of government expenditures has adjusted. Hence autonomous demand grows at g^*. This is also the rate of growth of trend effective demand and of normal output. If exports equal imports initially, the foreign balance (11) will remain in equilibrium since output, imports and exports grow at the same rate g^*. The tax coefficients (t_P, t_W) are fixed in a way such as to equate government expenditures and tax receipts. In virtue of assumption (8) this will leave the leakages (z_W, z_P) unchanged; the saving coefficients are pure residuals.

Complications arise at once if exports do not grow at the same trend rate as government expenditures. Suppose, for instance, that exports increase at a rate (g_X) which is larger than the rate of growth of government expenditures (g_G). Effective demand will now grow at a rate g^* which corresponds to a weighted average of g_X and g_G. This state of affairs will be linked with chronic export surpluses. Moreover, with tax coefficients given, tax receipts will be growing at a rate g^*, thus exceeding the rate of growth of government expenditures; as a result, there is a tendency towards government budget surpluses. The situation just sketched is characterized by export-led growth and represents a most comfortable state of affairs for the countries enjoying it or having enjoyed it. Germany, Japan and Switzerland are, perhaps, the most obvious cases in point. The picture radically changes if government expenditures grow faster than exports ($g_G > g^* > g_X$). Chronic import surpluses and government deficits will arise as a consequence. Many industrialized as well as economically underdeveloped countries suffer from these problems.

Hence the institutionally governed trend rates of growth of autonomous normal demand (G^* and X^*) are crucial for the evolution in time of trend effective demand and of normal output and employment. However, the latter also depend upon the size and eventual tendencies to change of the parameters of the supermultiplier relation. These are constants or change slowly if the institutional environment evolves. We now consider how, in principle, variations of the supermultiplier coefficients influence the level of trend output and employment. Smaller leakages (z_w and z_p) are linked up with higher Q^* and N^*. Given the tax coefficients (t_w, t_p), saving coefficients (s_w, s_p) are lower and propensities to consume correspondingly higher. To a relatively higher demand for consumption goods corresponds a larger consumption goods sector. The investment goods sector correspondingly adjusts as certain proportions between the two sectors must hold (see, for example, Robinson 1965 and Kregel 1975).

A lower import coefficient (b^*) and more favourable terms of trade (a lower π^*) are, given exports, linked up with higher levels of trend output and employment: out of a given income less is spent on foreign goods and more on domestic goods; domestic effective demand, output and employment are thus correspondingly higher. Favourable terms of trade also imply a higher standard of living in the country enjoying these: more goods can be imported for a given quantity of exports.

The trend investment coefficient ($g^* + d^*$) v^* is an important determinant of normal output Q^*: the larger are the normal growth rate g^*, the drop-out ratio d^* and the capital–output ratio v^*, the higher will be the trend levels of employment and output. The capital–output ratio v^* is determined by the average technology in use. The trend rate of growth of autonomous demand, and thus of effective demand, g^*, governs an important component of derived demand, i.e. 'expansion investment':

$$I_e^* = gvQ \tag{5a}$$

Given Q^* and its evolution – pictured by the supermultiplier relation – I_e^* has to be undertaken in order to create the additional capacities required to expand output in line with increasing trend effective demand. If I_e^* were below the required level, capacity utilization would be more than standard which would, in principle, induce entrepreneurs to increase investment.

The drop-out ratio d^* determines another component of derived investment demand which could be called 'replacement investment':

$$I_r^* = dvQ \tag{5b}$$

The size of the drop-out ratio d^* and thus of replacement investment mainly depends upon the technical dynamism of entrepreneurs: d^* governs the pace at which existing – old – capital goods are replaced by technically superior – new – capital goods. I_r^* and I_e^*, i.e. gross investment I^*, determine the extent of technical progress, i.e. the rate of growth of labour productivity (a). Obviously both equations (5a) and (5b) are in line with Schumpeter's view of the role of entrepreneurs in economic development.

Finally, and most importantly, a larger wage share ($1/k^*$) is, in the pure theory of output and employment, linked up with higher trend levels of employment and output: in the long run, wages, net of taxes, are almost entirely spent on consumption goods. Contrariwise, large parts of property income, $s_p(P+R)$, are not devoted to consumption, but to increasing private wealth: saving may be used to finance (partly or entirely) investment projects through investing own funds consisting of retained profits or through lending to firms, which includes the buying of new shares; moreover, saving may be 'invested' in goods which cannot be produced or reproduced or the production of which is limited. Land is the most important of these non-producible goods; antiquities, old masters, historically unique buildings, bonds and shares, gold and hard currencies are other cases in point. Finally, saving may be invested in shares and bonds already existing or may simply be hoarded: additional wealth is held in near-money or in money form.

There are physical and psychological limits to consumption. The desire to accumulate wealth, in the form of real and finance capital, of non-reproducible goods and of money seems to be boundless, however. This implies that s_p is bound to be quite large. Moreover, the percentage of property income paid in taxes is, in normal circumstances, larger than that of wage income. Therefore, the leakage coefficient (z_p) will be much larger than (z_w). A redistribution of incomes in favour of wages thus leads to an increased demand for consumption goods and to additional derived demand for investment goods since new productive capacities have to be built up to produce the extra investment goods.

An important point linked up with the influence of depreciation allowances (included in gross profits) on employment should be noted here. Excessive depreciation allowances (exceeding the replacement of existing capital goods) lead to a high desired mark-up and correspondingly diminish the wage share. The latter results in a drop of demand for consumer goods which, in turn, reduces output and employment. This issue is given extensive coverage in Keynes's *General Theory* and is illustrated with the situation which prevailed in the United States in the thirties (Keynes 1973a, pp. 98–106).

The pure theory of the supermultiplier pictures how effective demand governs *probably* and *in principle* output and employment in the long run. The latter allows us to argue on the basis of the *ceteris paribus* clause: for instance we may, on the basis of equation (7), claim that a higher wage share $1/k^*$ is associated with higher levels of trend output and employment. However, principles are modified in various ways in the real world because socioeconomic phenomena, e.g. employment levels, are governed by many causal forces which interact in particular ways. In a specific historical situation the autonomous variables and the coefficients on the right-hand side of the supermultiplier relation will not be independent of each other, but will depend on the way in which institutions interact. For example, a rising wage share may be accompanied by a corresponding increase in the import coefficient b: additional effective demand leaks abroad and does not lead to an increase of trend output and employment at home (pp. 190–9 below). Or, excessively large government expenditures and correspondingly high tax rates may be negatively associated with labour productivity and with the technical dynamism of an economy.

In the above, the terms *trend*, *normal* and *equilibrium* output and employment are used interchangeably. This is not wrong since in the classical-Keynesian view long-period output and employment, determined by constant or slowly changing institutional forces, represent system equilibria from which capacity output (and employment) always deviate. Thus, Q^* and N^* are *potential* resting points which will never be reached. However, several disequilibria are hidden behind these 'system equilibria': 'equilibrium' employment need not correspond to full employment (see figure 3). The foreign balance (equation 11) need not be in equilibrium either. Chronic export surpluses will arise if exports grow faster than government expenditures and output, and vice versa; presumably, in the very long run, the foreign balance will, given X, be squeezed into equilibrium through changes in π^*, b^* or Q^*. Similarly, government expenditures G^* will have to equal tax receipts in the very long run (equation 12); nevertheless, a long-period government surplus or a deficit may be compatible with the 'equilibrium' output determined by the supermultiplier relation. Thus, the latter essentially deals with disequilibrium states, not with equilibrium situations and is as such 'economics without equilibrium' (Kaldor 1985a). Persistent disequilibria may however result in destructive evolutions in that they end up in a crisis which enforces institutional changes; for example, a persistent current account deficit may bring about international insolvency and enforce an austerity programme aimed at reducing overall economic activity: Q^* has to be reduced until foreign accounts are balanced. This is in line with Marx's conception of the crisis, which he saw as the violent solution of some internal contradiction of the socioeconomic system.

Long-period distribution theory and the nature of profits

The supermultiplier relation implies that *normal* or *long-period* distribution is regulated by various institutions. This in turn implies that distribution is fundamentally a genuinely social problem in that part–whole relationships, i.e. relations between social classes and society as a whole, enter the picture. Classical-Keynesian long-period distribution theory is based upon the *surplus principle* (chapter 3, pp. 95–103). This classical and Marxian principle encompasses various dimensions. The technical aspect is related to the social process of production where certain goods – necessary wage goods and intermediate products – are used up and where the social surplus consists of the remaining goods which are at the free disposal of society. From a distributional viewpoint, necessary wages are used up in the production process and the surplus is divided into non-necessary wages, and profits and rents. Finally the surplus may be used up in various ways, for luxury consumption, accumulation of wealth and different state activities, for example. Besides classical elements Keynesian aspects also enter the scene, mainly in relation with the realization and the volume of the surplus. In modern classical-Keynesian theory the surplus principle appears in production and distribution models of the Sraffa type which explicitly deal with the distribution of the social surplus. The principle is also implied in the price-level equation (6): with the social product determined by effective demand, the average desired or target mark-up governs property income – profits and rents – and wages, specifically surplus wages, appear as a residual.

In the following sketch of classical-Keynesian long-period distribution theory it seems convenient to include in the wage sum *normal* or *ordinary* wage incomes only. The normal wage broadly corresponds to the usual wage which is paid for work requiring skills that can be acquired by institutionalized training methods offered, for example, by professional and technical schools and universities. Normal wage differences reflect the reduction coefficients of classical and Marxian value theory and are, as such, not only an economic, but also a socioeconomic phenomenon in that they exhibit the social status of individuals and professions. Normal wages differ widely within and between professions and between countries and regions, and the wage structure evolves as time goes by. 'Normal wages' contain a normative dimension in that the share of normal wages in income and the wage structure usually differ from what might be socially and ethically desirable, i.e. natural wages; the same holds for the normal property share and the structure of property income.

The surplus above normal wages, i.e. normal property income, is made up of gross profits and rents, whereby normal rates of profit on invested capital are implied by the target mark-up. The normal profit rate is a benchmark which entrepreneurs use to evaluate the profitability of investment projects: realized profit rates are compared to target rates; if the former exceed the latter persistently, investment is raised, and vice versa. There need be no tendency towards a uniform rate of profits in the long run. Differences in profit rates between industries (e.g. car producers and textile firms) or within industries (large price-leaders and small, just surviving firms) may persist. The structure of normal rates of profits is part of the institutional set-up of a society.

The rate of interest set by the monetary authorities may contribute to determining the *average* target profit level. However, interest rates can, in a Ricardian vein, exist only if there are profit rates.

Rents are incomes accruing from non-reproducible goods or goods which are difficult to reproduce. Cases in point are land, gold and antiquities, but also *special skills and privileges*. Normal land rents depend upon the value of land, in terms of a bundle of consumption goods, and are such as to yield a satisfactory rate of return on investment in land. Land prices and rents thus increase if the importance of land as a store of value increases. Another type of rent income is provided by speculative gains on non-reproducible goods other than land, e.g. shares and old masters. Finally, 'extraordinary' wage incomes are also included in rents. These accrue, first, on account of special skills of, say, lawyers, surgeons, artists, entertainers, athletes, and may, secondly, be due to privileges enjoyed by established managers, lawyers and surgeons for example, who, in some instances, form associations and limit the numbers of practitioners in order to preserve their privileged positions; for instance, some American managers seem to enjoy privileges which their European and Japanese colleagues do not.

The essential feature of the long-period classical-Keynesian theory of distribution is that the surplus (profits and rents, i.e. property income) is, in principle, determined by the average normal mark-up k^* which, in turn, is governed by 'social, political, and economic factors which have evolved historically, such as the power of workers and property owners, government interventions on minimum wages, the intensity of competition . . .' (Bortis 1984, p. 591), central bank policy, the attitude of investors towards risk (the rate of profits usually contains a risk premium), and legal prescriptions. Hence the average mark-up k^* is, in principle, governed by various institutions. Target profit rates and wage-setting practices may be largely institutionalized by custom and law. The precise way in which k^* is determined will greatly vary between countries and regions. In some instances k^* may rest on a social consensus, in others on some balance of power between interest groups; coercion by some dominant social group is also possible. These permanent forces governing k^* may break down if profound social (institutional) changes take place; they may also be dominated by temporary short-term factors. In both cases a price–wage spiral may develop, which reflects a conflict about distribution.

Hence the long-period classical-Keynesian distribution theory is a sociological or institutional theory of income distribution. John Stuart Mill perhaps best expressed the basic idea underlying it: 'The laws and conditions of production of wealth partake of the character of physical truths. There is nothing optional or arbitrary in them' (Mill 1965 [1848],

p. 199). '. . . It is not so with the distribution of wealth. That is a matter of human institution solely . . . The distribution of wealth . . . depends on the laws and customs of society. The rules by which it is determined, are what the opinions and feelings of the ruling portion of the community make them, and are very different in different ages and countries; and might be still more different, if mankind so chose' (J. S. Mill, *Principles*, 3rd edn (1852), pp. 199–200; quoted in Baranzini and Scazzieri 1986, p. 37). In the field of institutional distribution theory a lot of outstanding work has been accomplished. Phelps Brown (1977), Closets (1982) and Inhaber and Carroll (1992) are representative examples.

A sociological or institutional theory of distribution implies that distribution is *not* a relationship between individuals (supply and demand or employer and employee), but is basically a relationship between individuals and groups of individuals, classes for example, and society as a whole. Distribution is a *social* relationship between *parts*, i.e. individuals and social groups, and the whole, i.e. society. Functional distribution, i.e. the determination of the *shares* of wages, profits and rents, relates to the relationship of classes to society or to the social position of classes. Distribution is a social phenomenon because of the essentially social nature of production: there is no mechanical way of determining factor shares on a behavioural basis as is implied by the neoclassical factor markets. In the long run there are no marginal products, again because the process of production is a social process (chapter 5, pp. 281–93).

The first political economist to have perceived clearly the essentially social nature of distribution was undoubtedly Ricardo: 'The produce of the earth . . . is divided among three classes of the community [land owners, capitalists, and labourers] under the names of rents, profits and wages' (Ricardo 1951 [1821], p. 5). The social element in distribution emerges most forcefully in the case of long-period wage determination: 'The natural price of labour is that price which is necessary to enable the labourers . . . to perpetuate their race, without either increase or diminution' (p. 93). 'It is not to be understood that the natural price of labour, even if estimated in food and necessaries, is absolutely fixed and constant. It varies at different times in the same country, and very materially differs in different countries. It essentially depends on the *habits and customs* of the people' (pp. 96–7; our emphasis). Each income category has a specific social function. For example, wages have to ensure the decent existence of the labourers; profits have to provide for capital accumulation with a view to enhancing economic development. For Marx, distribution is the outcome of class struggle, which constitutes an essentially social phenomenon too.

The social theory of functional distribution has to be complemented by a social theory of personal distribution. In a classical-Keynesian perspective the structure of wages, profits and rents expresses not only economic performance, based upon job evaluation for example, but also the status of individual workers and employees, entrepreneurs and land-owners within the respective class and within society; the structure of wages broadly reflects the reduction coefficients of the classical-Marxian labour theory of value. These coefficients are social phenomena in the proper sense.

Two conceptual remarks on the sociological or institutional theory of distribution are required here. First, since distribution is a social phenomenon, normative distribution theory pertains to the domain of social and political ethics (chapter 2, pp. 39–53). The normative dimension of distribution is related to the concept of the common weal. A distributional arrangement which was ethically perfect would correspond to the ideal of *distributive justice* described by Aristotle and Aquinas and taken up by Christian Social Doctrine. Distributive justice would prevail if the distribution of income and wealth between individuals and social groups were proportional to their status in society; the latter should in turn reflect appropriately their professional and social abilities in the widest sense of the word; in classical (Ricardian) terms this would imply fixing socially and ethically appropriate reduction coefficients. Distributive justice is part of the common weal since it implies social harmony in the sphere of distribution.

The gap existing between some actual situation and the common weal has been called alienation (chapter 2, pp. 47–53); this notion applies to all spheres of social and individual life and therefore encompasses distributional issues. The gap between some specific distribution of incomes in some country in a certain period of time and the ideal distribution corresponding to distributive justice represents alienation in the sphere of distribution. This leads to the second point to be made here. Distributive justice and alienation regarding distribution are obviously immensely complex concepts, mainly because they imply relationships between parts and wholes. Knowledge on distributional issues will therefore always remain sketchy and the corresponding propositions more or less probable in Keynes's sense (Keynes 1971c and chapter 2, pp. 57–75). This is all the more true in changing circumstances: technical progress, e.g. computer technology, continuously brings new professions into being and changes the socioeconomic significance of existing professions.

Formally the close link of the classical-Keynesian theory of distribution with the classical surplus principle emerges from the equation

$$(1-c)C = c(Q-C), \tag{13}$$

and from scheme 5.

In this scheme, C represents the output of *necessary* consumption goods (consumption goods or necessaries for short) which are *basics* in the sense of

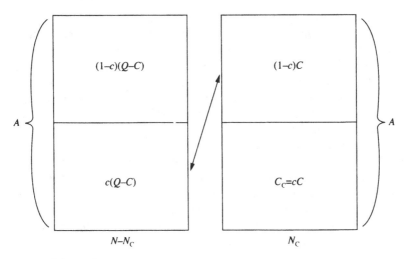

Scheme 5.

Sraffa since they maintain the labour force, an input factor which is essential in all sectors of production. A fraction c of C is consumed in this sector. The surplus in a broad sense – $(1-c)\,C$ – is used to maintain workers and employees in all other sectors of an economy: the investment goods, the luxury consumption goods and the government sectors. Total real incomes generated in the non-consumption sectors equal $Q-C$, of which a fraction c is spent on necessaries, the demand for which arising outside the consumption goods sector equals $c(Q-C)$. Equation (13) thus represents an equilibrium on the market for necessary consumption goods which is equivalent to the $S=I$ equilibrium condition. *Given* the level of output, these conditions would guarantee that the various sectors of an economy were in the appropriate proportions so as to enable the process of production to go on smoothly.

Equation (13) is of general validity; specifically, this relation pictures aspects of the fully adjusted situation and plays a crucial role in long-period classical-Keynesian economic theory. First, equation (13) regulates the proportions between the consumption goods sector and all other sectors of an economy. Bearing in mind that $z=1-c$, equation (13) can be written as:

$$C/Q = AN_C/AN = N_C/N = c. \tag{14}$$

Models embodying variants of this relationship were developed by François Quesnay (the *tableau économique*), by Adam Smith (the two-sector model set out in book III of the *Wealth of Nations*) and by David Ricardo (see the Ricardian two-sector model in Pasinetti, 1974, pp. 6–11). The Marxian schemes of reproduction and circulation and Keynes's

Fundamental Equations in his *Treatise on Money* belong to the same class of models. The same is true of the multi-sectoral model set forth in Pasinetti (1981), of the two-sector models contained in Robinson (1965) and Kregel (1975) and, therefore, of the Cambridge equation (Pasinetti 1962). All these relations regulate proportions and are independent of the scale of economic activity and, therefore, hold for *any* level of output and employment to be determined by the supermultiplier relation. As such they are pieces of classical macroeconomics.

Second, scheme 5 emphasizes the primacy of production over exchange (Pasinetti 1981): the exchanges taking place between the final product sectors stand entirely in the service of production. This emerges clearly if, to simplify, we postulate that the investment goods sector constitutes the only non-consumption goods sector: consumption goods are transferred to the investment goods sector to maintain or, eventually, to expand the work-force active in this sector. Conversely, investment goods flowing into the consumption goods sector are to replace worn-out or technically obsolete capital goods here and, eventually, to expand the productive capacities.

The importance of labour in the process of production explains why distribution must be regulated in the basic goods sector: basic goods enable the labour force to furnish labour which is required in the production of *all* goods. Therefore, the necessary consumption goods sector is of particular importance: the goods produced here are basic to sustaining *all* activities taking place in a society. This vision of things is in line with the classical approach to distribution which emphasizes the intimate connection between production and distribution. The importance of the necessary consumption goods sector in the theory of distribution was most clearly perceived by David Ricardo (1951 [1821]); this emerges from Sraffa (1960), and from Pasinetti (1974, pp. 1–28).

Third, distribution can be linked easily with consumption and saving by rewriting equation (14) and reinterpreting C as including necessary and non-necessary consumption:

$$(C/Q)^* = (N_C/N)^* = c_P + (c_W - c_P)(1/k^*),\tag{15}$$

which is equivalent to

$$(I/Q)^* = s_W + (s_P - s_W)(1 - (1/k^*)).\tag{16}$$

The latter directly leads to a familiar post Keynesian relation (Kaldor 1955/56):

$$(I/Q) = s_W + (s_P - s_W)(1 - (1/k)).\tag{16a}$$

In the long run, the size of the consumption and of the investment sector depends upon the consumption and saving coefficients (with $c_W > c_P$ and

$s_p > s_w$) and upon income distribution, that is the wage or the property share. The property share $1 - (1/k^*)$ and hence the wages share $1/k^*$ are both governed by the institutional factors mentioned above. Given Q^*, as determined by the supermultiplier, and with c_w and c_p also fixed, the size of the consumption goods sector adjusts until equation (15) is satisfied. In equation (16), $(I/Q)^*$ is given in the long run and equals $(g^* + d)v^*$ (equation 5). The property share $1 - (1/k^*)$ is also given and the saving coefficients s_w and s_p must adjust in such a way as to satisfy equation (16). Saving is thus entirely passive in the long run as is the case in the medium and short term too. This typically Keynesian point will be briefly taken up below in relation to the long-period significance of the Cambridge equation.

However, the way in which saving adjusts and distribution is regulated is entirely different in the medium and short run. Here, productive capacities are given (in the short term) or change only slowly (in the medium term), and the investment–output ratio, I/Q, in equation (16a) deviates from its long-period counterpart implied in the fully adjusted situation (($I/Q)^*$ in equation 16). According to standard (Kaldorian) post Keynesian theory, *distribution must now adjust* if macroeconomic equilibrium ($S = I$) is to be preserved. The property share $1 - (1/k)$ rises as I/Q increases and vice versa (equation 16a). Variations in the property share are directly linked with changes in the wage share and the consumption–output ratio. Hence in the medium and short term the proportions between the consumption and investment goods sectors (C/I) and the distributive shares will deviate from their corresponding long-period levels.

The theories of distribution just sketched do not contradict each other but are complementary: in the long run distribution is entirely governed by the institutional system; in the short and medium term, behavioural factors (investment behaviour) determine distribution. Both distribution theories imply an important corollary which is alluded to by Garegnani (1978/79) and by Weber (1993): in the long run, the volumes of investment, output and employment are, according to the supermultiplier principle, inversely related with profits because high investment volumes lead to large employment and output volumes which can only be maintained if additional effective demand is created; the latter can be achieved, for example, if profits decline and wages rise; effective demand will increase because the propensity to consume of wage-earners exceeds the fraction consumed out of property income. In the short and medium term, however, with capacities given or slowly evolving, profits and investment are positively associated according to the familiar Kaldorian mechanism exhibited by equation (16a).

A fourth point relates to the importance of the mark-up k in regulating long-period income distribution in the necessary consumption goods

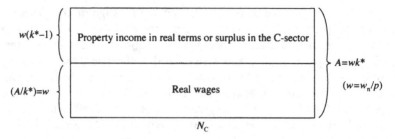

Scheme 6.

sector. The importance of labour in the social process of production requires that real wages be expressed in terms of necessaries: $w=w_n/p=A/k^*$, to be derived from the price equation (6). To render possible the regulation of income distribution through the mark-up k, profits and rents – in real terms – have also to be expressed in terms of consumption goods.

This emerges from scheme 6, which is to be seen jointly with scheme 5. The real wage and real property income in the sector for necessaries is governed by technology (A) and the mark-up (k^*) which is governed institutionally. The mark-up determined in this sector subsequently governs distribution (income shares) in all non-basic sectors of an economy. This important Ricardian property of long-period distribution is set out in Pasinetti's exposition of the Ricardian system (Pasinetti 1974, pp. 1–28). With the distribution among social classes determined, the wage and price structure governs personal distribution.

In the short and medium terms, deviations from long-period distribution ($k<>k^*$) are brought about by variations in the investment–output ratio (equation 16a). In both cases wages appear as a residual. This modern classical-Keynesian way of putting the surplus principle is in line with Pasinetti (1981). It represents a variation of the Ricardian-Marxian version where wages are determined first and profits and rents, the surplus, constitute a residual.

Three issues associated with the long-period classical-Keynesian theory of income distribution remain to be discussed briefly, i.e. the compatibility of this theory with the Cambridge equation, the determination of the surplus volume and the nature of profits.

First, the long-period theory of distribution sketched here is characterized by the absence of a direct link between distribution (k^*) and trend growth (g^*): distribution, represented by the institutionally governed mark-up k^* (which implies a certain target profit rate r^*) is simply one of the factors, although a very important one, governing the trend level of output and employment (equation 7). This seems to contradict a standard classical-Keynesian result, that is the Cambridge equation (derived in Pasinetti 1962):

$$r^* = g^*/s_C \qquad (17)$$

This equation is a macroeconomic equilibrium condition implying that saving equals investment. As such, the Cambridge equation regulates the 'equilibrium' proportions between the consumption and the investment goods sectors for *any* level of employment in steady states or in fully adjusted situations; the latter are implied in the long-period classical-Keynesian theory discussed here. In the conventional view, equilibrium is established through variations in distribution: given g and s_C *and the level of employment*, the rate of profits (r) adjusts passively. However, in the supermultiplier relation the trend growth rate g^* and the desired (satisfactory) rate of profits r^* are both given. The former is governed by the trend rate of growth of the autonomous variables (G^* and X^*), the latter is implied in the desired mark-up k^*. The right-hand side of equation (17) *must* now adjust to r^* across variations in s_C induced by *changes in the level of normal employment*.

Let us illustrate this important point by considering how, in principle, an economy moves from one fully adjusted situation to another. To simplify, it is postulated that there are no taxes out of ordinary wage incomes ($t_W = 0$); the Cambridge equation then states that the fraction of wage income saved (s_W) does not directly enter to determine the profit rate (Pasinetti 1974, pp. 110–12). This result must always hold if fully adjusted situations are considered (Bortis 1993b), but in the present analysis its meaning changes.

Suppose that normal exports and normal government expenditures grow at a rate g^* and that the foreign balance and the government budget are both in equilibrium. Due to a *permanent* change of some trend variable or parameter, (new) normal investment now exceeds (original) normal saving: $r^* < g^*/s_C$ in equation (17). In the short term, equality will be restored by $r > r^*$. Given this, investment increases in the medium term. Because of the capacity effect of investment, output and employment gradually shift above their original normal levels. This implies that tax receipts are growing faster than government expenditures. Budget equilibrium may be preserved by lowering t_p. Due to assumption (8), $z_p = s_p + t_p = \text{constant}$, s_p (and thus s_C) rises, which implies that in the expression $r^* < g^*/s_C$, the right-hand side decreases. This process ends once output and employment have reached their new normal levels. Normal saving now equals (new) normal investment which means that the Cambridge equation (17) is satisfied again in the long run.

The *saving ratios* (s_P, s_C and, if explicitly considered, s_W) are *entirely passive* in the long run and changes in long-period 'equilibria' are brought about by quantity adjustments. This is perfectly symmetrical to Keynes's short-period view on saving and adjustments of saving to investment through variations in the level of employment. In fact, the Cambridge equation is nothing but a classical-Keynesian variant of the Keynesian $S=I$ condition. In the supermultiplier theory suggested here this equation expresses two properties of the long-period macroeconomic equilibrium, that is the fully adjusted situation. First, 'saving equals investment', as is implied in the supermultiplier relation, governs the *level* of trend output and employment (see figure 3, p. 150) and is, as such, a piece of 'Keynesian macroeconomics'. Second, this condition also expresses the fact that the appropriate proportions between the investment sector and the other sectors of an economy are established. This relates to what we have called 'classical macroeconomics' above (pp. 136–7).

However, the 'rate of profit – rate of growth' relationship, of which the Cambridge equation is a fundamental (equilibrium) case, forms the heart of a medium-term theory of income distribution (Bortis 1993b, pp. 123–4). Hence this relationship registers *deviations* from the long-period distributional outcome as is governed by the relevant institutions.

This leads to a second issue associated with classical-Keynesian distribution theory, which is related to the forces governing the *share* of surplus or property income in total income, and the *volume* of property income. To attempt an answer to these questions the supermultiplier equation (7) is solved for the property share in income (to simplify we postulate that ordinary wages are entirely consumed, i.e. that the leakage coefficient z_W is zero):

$$[(P+R)/Q]^* = 1 - (1/k^*) = 1/z_P\{(G/Q) + [(X/Q) - \pi b] + (g+d)v\}. \quad (7b)$$

The gross property share is positively associated with the fraction of property income consumed $(1 - z_P)^*$, the government share $(G/Q)^*$, an eventual surplus on the current account $(X^* > \pi b Q^*)$ and the gross investment–output ratio, i.e. the trend rate of growth (g^*) of autonomous demand $(G^* + X^*)$, the drop-out ratio (d^*) – the size of which reflects the technical dynamism of a society – and the capital coefficient (v^*).

The above equation becomes particularly interesting in case of a zero trend rate of growth $(g^*=0)$ and with the (basic) foreign balance in equilibrium $(X^* = \pi b Q^*)$. The share of net property income, including *net* profits only, now depends upon two factors: the leakage coefficient attached to property income and the government share. Property income equals government expenditures and consumption out of property income. This partly explains why permanent reductions of government expenditures may cause heavy damage to an economy in terms of increased long-period unemployment. Indeed, with exports given, government expenditures are crucial in determining the level of economic activity and of the volume of profitable investment opportunities. This is in line with the macroeconomic model set forth in François Quesnay's extended *tableau économique* where the spending of land rents, including government expenditures, appears as a kind of engine setting into motion economic activity (on this, see Oncken 1902, pp. 394ff.).

From equation (7b) one might conclude that foreign trade is not very important in governing the property share: only an eventual export surplus (linked up with a higher property share) seems relevant here. This may be true if the *property share* is considered. The *volume* of property income and thus the volume of profits depends decisively upon the size of exports and imports, however. This becomes evident if equation (7b) is written in a slightly different way:

$$(P+R)^* = [1-(1/k^*)]Q^* = 1/z_\mathrm{p}[G+(X-\pi bQ)+(g+d)vQ]. \tag{7c}$$

Foreign trade, even in the case of foreign balance equilibrium, is of decisive importance since it governs the level of long-period economic activity, i.e. the level of trend output Q^* which, in turn, governs the volume of property income. Indeed, in equation (7c) trend output Q^* is governed by exports X multiplied by the *foreign trade multiplier* $1/\pi b$. The economic meaning of this typically Kaldorian proposition (set out, for example, in Kaldor 1986) will be discussed below (pp. 190–9). For the time being it may be noted that, given exports, favourable terms of trade, reflected in a low π, and a relatively small import coefficient b are associated with a higher trend output level Q^*. The larger Q^* is, the larger is the volume of property and thus of profit income, given the normal, institutionally determined mark-up on ordinary wages (k^*).

The determination of the share and of the volume of property income is closely linked with the realization problem raised by Marx and by Keynes; in this context the latter spoke of dwindling profitable investment opportunities. Perhaps this issue can be tackled best by first looking at the world economy as a whole. Foreign trade can, in this case, be eliminated as a factor governing the world level of output and employment and thus the volume of profits on a world scale since one country's exports are another country's imports: foreign trade is not relevant for the *scale* of activity in a closed system, although exchange of already produced goods may improve world welfare on the basis of the principle of comparative cost advantages. The crucial importance of government expenditures for the level of world economic activity now emerges from the supermultiplier relation (7) and from the profit equations (7b,c): G is now the only predetermined variable governing, together with the corresponding multiplier, world effective demand and thus world output; the multiplier associated with G is the larger the smaller the property share and the larger the gross investment ratio (pp. 190–9 below). Moreover, government expenditures also largely govern the share and the volume of property and thus of profit income. This explains why generalized cuts in government expenditures might have a devastating influence upon the level of world economic activity.

Hence world economic activity is governed by world effective demand which, according to the internal employment mechanism to be described in the next subsection, depends on government expenditures, income distribution and investment activity. The importance of foreign trade for individual countries can now be put to the fore.

It is beyond dispute that foreign trade, in relation to the principle of comparative advantages, has important welfare effects, summarized here under the heading of 'structural aspects of foreign trade'. In considering these, the scale, the level of trend output and employment is, as a rule, assumed to be *given*. However, as is evident from equation (7c), foreign trade has also a 'scale' or 'employment' effect for individual countries (pp. 190–9 below): if some country manages to export mainly manufactured products at favourable terms of trade while keeping the import coefficient relatively low, its trend level of output and employment will be high, and vice versa. This is the theory of the export multiplier $[Q^*=(1/\pi b)X]$ as is implied in equation (7c). Hence, *given* the volume of *world output and employment*, determined by world effective demand, the scale or employment effect of foreign trade determines the *share* of world economic activity – and employment – allotted to each individual country or region if there is 'free trade'. This share determines, subsequently, the possibilities for realizing profits. Since it is very likely that world effective demand is not sufficient to secure full employment on a world level, the presence of the 'scale effect of international trade' largely explains the growth of creeping protectionism and, most importantly, the ferocious struggle for world market shares actually going on. This fight is, in fact, a struggle for survival in the face of involuntary unemployment and goes along with a search for profitable investment opportunities. Looking at this matter historically, one might say that, in the nineteenth century, protectionism, colonialism and imperialism associated with military force were perhaps the main weapons in securing large parts of the world market for manufactures. In the twentieth century, particularly after the Second World War, technological superiority, international marketing and the creation of dependencies became more important in the struggle for world market shares of manufactures and of high-quality services in order to secure high levels of employment and profitable investment opportunities at home.

Hence, under the capitalist rules of the game, the neo-mercantilist struggle for high levels of economic activity is simultaneously a struggle for securing large profit volumes (equation 7c): trend output and the desired property share determine the volume of property income. This goes along with the determination of the volume of profitable investments which, in the long run, depends upon the evolution of Q^* (equation 5). A relatively low import coefficient and favourable terms of trade are also associated with high employment and profit levels. Favourable terms of trade are particularly important in that these permit a higher level of material well-being in the countries enjoying them: for a given level of exports more can be imported; this is reflected in higher real wages and in larger profit rates. As Nicholas Kaldor strongly emphasized, the scale effect of international trade may be a very important cause of the growing disparities in material well-being worldwide, because it favours the emergence of 'aristocratic' countries or regions while, simultaneously, misery may be growing in other countries or regions. This effect of international trade is due to the functioning of the world socioeconomic system and may be cumulative. Prosperity is, as a rule, associated with democracy and a stable political situation which favour technological progress and strengthen the position on world markets. Contrariwise, deteriorating socioeconomic conditions are usually linked with political instability; both hamper technological progress and the capacity to export, thus weakening the world market position of the underdeveloped countries. These problems are compounded by the fact that growing inequalities between and within countries may hamper world productive activities while at the same time enhancing speculative activities; again these processes may be cumulative as the latter is likely to influence negatively the former.

A third issue related to classical-Keynesian distribution theory is associated with the justification of net profits. The problem arises because, in the long-period classical-Keynesian scheme proposed here, profits are not directly related to the rate of growth, although, as is evident from equations (7b,c), the trend growth rate g^* is *one* of the factors, which, together with an eventual export surplus and government expenditures, govern the share and the volume of net property income. Moreover, when discussing the Cambridge equation, we have mentioned that trend employment and output have to be compatible with a macroeconomic 'saving equals investment' equilibrium: the Cambridge and similar equations must always hold and can, therefore, not explain the *determination* of profits and profit rates in the long run. Finally, if it is postulated that government expenditures and exports do not increase (the trend growth rate and trend net investment are zero) and that the foreign balance is in equilibrium, property income including profits now depends upon $1/z_p$ and upon government expenditures (equations 7b,c).

It is difficult to see now a justification for net profits proper, since there is no growth to be 'financed'. Should therefore, in the zero-growth case or in the stationary state, property income not consist of 'extraordinary' (surplus) wages and of rents on land in the Ricardian sense only?

Considering historical experience broadly it would be wrong to require that profits should be zero in the stationary state. There are three important reasons for allowing some socially acceptable level of desired profits (compatible with full employment), all of which are associated with socio-economic efficiency in a broad sense, i.e. an optimal social surplus. The first is related to the size and the growth of labour productivity. Joseph Schumpeter clearly perceived that the possibility of realizing a profit is a most powerful incentive for economic progress (Schumpeter 1912), since it enhances entrepreneurial activity, i.e. the introduction of new products and more advanced techniques of production. The latter is linked up with rising labour productivity: hence profits and real wages will be relatively higher in innovative firms. Second, competition and the possibility of realizing profits induce continuous efforts to minimize average costs, which, in turn, contribute to economizing on the use of valuable resources which are eventually non-reproducible – some types of energy and of raw materials, for instance. Profit rates imply the existence of interest rates which prevent, in turn, real capital (machinery, for example) from being wasted; the so-called 'overcapitalization' in many socialist countries, due to very low (or even zero) interest rates, is a prominent example. Hence the possibility or even the requirement to realize some socially acceptable target profit rate forces small-scale entrepreneurs and managers of medium and large firms to *care* about human, natural and man-made resources. However, the latter can be implemented only if full employment prevails and if international trade is no longer a struggle for survival and a means to reap profits. For, in order to survive on world markets and to conquer profitable markets, individual producers are, frequently with the consent of the respective authorities, ready to sacrifice everything, most importantly decent work conditions, social security and the natural environment. Third, the rate of profits has an important allocation function. The continuous attempt to equalize profit rates, or to bring about the institutionally determined hierarchy of profit rates, guides investment activities and thus tends to allocate capital in line with the prevailing structure of demand.

In the above, profits appear as a socially useful institution from the point of view of social efficiency. Moreover, to determine the socially appropriate level of the average profit rate, equity issues will enter the picture; these are particularly important because, as is evident from the supermultiplier relation, income distribution affects the employment and output level and hence the size of the social surplus. Finally, profits should be used in a socially useful way, for instance to pay premiums to workers and employees, to finance research and development, to buy new machinery, and, as is frequently done, to finance cultural activities in the widest sense of the word. Hence, the determination of the socially appropriate level of the average profit rate is an intricate problem of political ethics, involving complex part–whole relationships.

Profits are formed in the process of production. This led the classical economists and Marx to distinguish between 'productive' and 'unproductive' labour: productive workers produce the surplus (which includes profits), unproductive workers are maintained by the surplus. In modern terms one could perhaps speak of 'profit' and 'non-profit' sectors of an economy. The former represents the economic basis where production and distribution take place, the latter is linked with activities pertaining to the institutional superstructure (see scheme 1, p. 94). Marx clearly perceived that the distinction between productive and unproductive labour is, in some instances, a matter of institutional arrangement. For example, the education system would belong to the economic basis, i.e. to the 'profit sector', if all schools were private and to the (non-profit) institutional superstructure if they were public. Hence the 'profitability' of investment is not only an economic matter, but also a matter of socioeconomic organization. This implies that the profitability of a *single* investment project is to some extent arbitrary and also not very important. What is important in old classical and in modern classical-Keynesian political economy is the *size of the social surplus* coming out of the social and circular process of production: it is macroeconomic, not microeconomic, 'profitability' that really matters! There is, however, no question of maximizing the social surplus in a classical-Keynesian view by squeezing real wages. The size of the surplus has to be in line with the system of fundamental values prevailing in a society, i.e. with the way of life that is aimed at; in this view, the surplus has to provide the material foundation for a higher social, political and cultural life. This is rendered possible by the institutional superstructure set forth in scheme 1. Moreover, squeezing real wages by attempting to increase the surplus would make no macroeconomic sense: increasing income inequality, reflected in a higher k^*, is likely to lead to a lower economic activity, which, in turn, implies a smaller surplus; this follows from the supermultiplier relation (7) above.

It is appropriate to make a brief remark on the nature of property here. Taking account of historical experience it would seem that small- and medium-scale firms should be privately owned. This is particularly important in agriculture, but also in the service and handicrafts sector. The main reason is that people care about what they own; this is, in fact, the principal argument for private property advanced by Aristotle (*Politics*, 1262b37–1264b25) and taken up by Aquinas and Christian Social Doctrine.

Moreover, quite independently of the possibility of realizing a profit, private property-owners derive a satisfaction from producing goods and rendering services of high quality. Among other factors this may be due to the personal links that usually exist between the producer and the customer. For example, both may enjoy a mutually satisfying price/quality relation, above all if aesthetic elements are involved, as is usually the case with handicraft products. Production is, in this sense, a social process in a wider sense of the word. Hence the institution of private property is not only economically relevant; it also has a social and cultural dimension. The latter shows up most clearly if part of the surplus – profits – is devoted to cultural purposes.

For large enterprises, however, it is not very important whether these are in private hands or publicly owned, by some central or local authority for example, provided management is independent and allowed to realize a profit; a sufficient degree of competition is, however, required to keep profits at socially acceptable levels. Managers of large enterprises are, as a rule, indifferent as to who the shareholders are, provided the latter do not attempt to interfere unduly with running the firms, for example to get high dividends in the short run.

Hence socially appropriate target profit rates are not associated with exploitation but are a social institution which promotes public welfare, i.e. enhances the orderly functioning of society and greatly contributes to a higher material well-being. The latter implies a certain rate of growth of labour productivity. Whether growth takes place or whether stationary conditions continue to prevail ought to be a matter of social choice. Stationary conditions would imply that the rate of growth of labour productivity be compensated by a reduction of working such as to keep the social product constant. If growth goes on at full employment, the economy would grow at the natural rate, i.e. the rate of growth of labour productivity plus the rate of growth of population. In this case, government expenditures may be permitted to grow at the natural rate to permit the continuous realization of desired profits and to preserve full employment: in a long-period classical-Keynesian framework, the rate of profits is an important *determinant* of the natural rate of growth and not the other way round as has been postulated hitherto by most post Keynesians. This does not imply restoring Say's law. Long-period output and employment are, according to the supermultiplier theory, always governed by long-period effective demand which implies that continuous efforts are required to achieve and to preserve full employment.

The preceding remarks do not imply, however, that all economic and social activities ought to be subject to profits and to private property. This leads to a remark on the 'privatization' issue, particularly regarding government activities that are of social importance in that they enhance the orderly functioning of the entire society. Relevant domains are, for example, public transport, communication and mass media, health, education and the social insurance system. Privatization in these domains is likely to be self-defeating. This is associated with the economic relevance of the government sector, which, by its very nature must be 'unproductive' in the sense of the classical economists. Three reasons account for this, all of which are related to the sphere of exchange, not to the sphere of production where the surplus is produced. First, it is socially expedient that government expenditures be financed by parts of the social surplus arising in the social process of production. Government expenditures are associated with the *use*, not with the *production* of the social surplus. Second, and much more importantly, government expenditures are a crucial *determinant* of the surplus (see equations 7b,c). Specifically, in a stationary economy a surplus – including profits! – can only arise if there are government expenditures. The latter are a kind of engine which sets economic activity into motion. This emerges from the supermultiplier relation exhibited above and, as has been alluded to, from Quesnay's extended, or zig-zag, *tableau économique* (Oncken 1902, pp. 394–5). Third, economies of scale and the social nature of the surplus render privatization very problematic. For example, to privatize highly profitable railway lines leads to growing deficits in the remaining public railway sector and implies a transfer of part of the social surplus from the public to the private sector.

From the classical-Keynesian viewpoint privatization of important government activities is self-defeating in three ways. First, a reduction in government expenditures (G) results, in principle, in a lower level of economic activity and consequently the volume of the social surplus which, in turn, diminishes the scope for socially relevant government activity. Second, if all government activities were to be productive, i.e. surplus-producing, no surplus could arise at all in stationary conditions; in a growing economy the surplus, i.e. profits, would be proportional to net investment (equations 7b,c), which would render an economy very unstable since the double-sided relationship between profits and investment could work unfettered (pp. 207–15). Third, the social aims pursued within government institutions in the sectors of transport, education, health, social insurance, etc. could no longer be adequately reached if privatized. Those who cannot afford to pay are simply excluded from benefiting from the institutions in question. This is valid for individuals, social groups and even entire regions.

Normal prices

The price-level equation (6) represents the pure theory of value associated with the supermultiplier relation (7). Long-period normal prices p^* (absolute money prices) ultimately depend upon institutional and technological factors governing income distribution, i.e. the level of money wages and the average target mark-up k^*, and the conditions of production (the various coefficients of production contained in Sraffa–Pasinetti models) synthesized by labour productivity. Here some remarks on the pure theory of normal prices and its relation with real-world issues are made.

Formally, the price equation (6) is a weighted average of the normal sectoral price equations which are associated with a fully adjusted situation (Pasinetti 1981, equation system II. 7.3, p. 44); the only difference is that, in the former, the mark-up also includes rents. Equation (6) may, thus, be easily linked with the analysis of structures and structural change carried out in part I of Pasinetti (1981), which is based upon the concept of vertical integration. From here we may go back to Sraffa (1960) (see Pasinetti 1981, ch. VI, pp. 109–17): normal prices are equivalent to the prices of production which are, in turn, strictly related to labour values (Pasinetti 1977, appendix to ch. V, pp. 122–51). The theory of value connected with the supermultiplier relation is therefore in line with the neo-Ricardian and hence the Ricardian-Marxian views on values and prices. With production conceived of as a social and circular process, long-period or normal prices, i.e. the prices of production, must be based on the labour theory of value since these fundamentally reflect the effort undertaken by society to produce goods (prices are not indicators of scarcity as is the case in the neoclassical demand and supply framework). This emerges with great clarity from Pasinetti (1981, 1993).

Some properties of normal prices are worth noting. First, these prices cannot be directly observed since they are superseded by market prices which result from short-term behaviour of producers and consumers. Normal prices are part of the institutional set-up of an economy, i.e. the socioeconomic system, and are determined by the institutions governing the normal mark-up k^* and by technology. These prices would guarantee the smooth production and reproduction of normal output and ensure that the surplus required to maintain the social and political system regularly accrues. As such normal prices are, like production and distribution, essentially *social* and macroeconomic phenomena since the whole of the social production system comes in to determine each normal price (Pasinetti 1977, 1981).

Second, if the – accidental – conditions of production are abstracted from, the prices of production become labour values. These constitute the essence of the prices of production. Profits and rents appear here as surplus value. This concept need not be associated with exploitation: under the preceding heading it was suggested that profits, which are part of the surplus, play a socially useful role.

Third, the prices of production are closely linked up with functional and personal distribution. The former enters the scene through the normal mark-up k^*, the latter through the structure of wages, profits and rents. In this context the concept of distributive justice plays an important role. This notion is a normative guiding star which can be perceived only dimly (chapter 2, pp. 57–75). The main elements of distributive justice are a just wage structure, reflected in socially appropriate reduction coefficients, and an ethically correct mark-up k^*. If these elements were given, the prices of production would become just or natural prices (as set forth in Pasinetti 1981, 1993), which are associated with justice in exchange (chapter 6, pp. 314–19). In the real world a greater or smaller gap between normal and natural prices will always prevail. This is alienation (chapter 2, pp. 47–53) in the sphere of value and distribution.

The pure theory of normal prices states how long-period price formation goes on in principle and in general. In practice, that is in particular situations, entrepreneurs will never know normal prices exactly since these are objectively given elements of reality governed by immensely complex technological and institutional factors. However, as is evident from any textbook on management, entrepreneurs constantly *estimate* normal costs and normal prices in order to get reference points to guide entrepreneurial behaviour. Estimation goes on the basis of actually existing capacity output Q_c which is associated with the actually existing capital stock K (not on the basis of the normal values Q^* and K^* which are unknown to entrepreneurs): we denote the estimated normal prices by p_c. If realized market prices for intermediate or final products persistently exceed their (estimated) normal prices, or if, with (estimated) normal prices, stocks are persistently run down, investment will rise above its trend level, and vice versa. This procedure presupposes that entrepreneurs, based upon past experience, have acquired an approximate notion of the normal degree of capacity utilization (where average costs are minimized). This enables entrepreneurs to establish normal pricing rules, i.e. to calculate the normal mark-up on the variable (prime) costs arising at normal capacity utilization (Kaldor 1985a, p. 40). A deviation of market prices from estimated normal ones implies a corresponding deviation of the realized mark-up k from k^*: the realized profit rates will not correspond to the target rates. However, k may also deviate from k^*, given the normal price level, through changes in the degree of capacity utilization: with capacity utilization below normal k will fall short of k^*, and vice versa.

Across the average labour productivity (A), the aggregate price-level equation (6) takes account of the average technology in use in an economy. As a rule, money wages and/or profit rates will be higher in firms or sectors of production using advanced technologies because of higher labour productivities, and vice versa. This holds primarily for the industrial and the service sector. In this context the question on the normal prices for primary products (raw materials and agricultural products) arises. Here, institutional factors play perhaps an even more important role than is the case with normal prices for industrial products. For example, normal prices in the primary sector may be fixed by the state. This gives rise to certain land rents which, in turn, govern land values, given target rates of profit for investments in land. Or, with certain investments in land having taken place in the past, target rates of profits in the primary sector and the corresponding normal prices would be determined on marginal land where the conditions of production are most difficult.

Historical experience shows that primary production is exposed to an unbearable strain if the prices of primary products are heavily dependent on the vagaries of the market. For example, rapidly rising raw material prices may, on the one hand, lead to inflation; on the other hand, falling prices of raw materials result in rising unemployment in the primary and secondary sectors because of falling real incomes in the former (Thirlwall 1987, pp. 208–15); a similar argument holds for agricultural products. Hence the endeavour of governments to stabilize prices in the primary sector.

For reasons of distributional equity, primary product prices ought to be fixed in such a way as to ensure a socially appropriate income to the producers of these products. This has several important implications. For example, fixed prices may lead to excess production, which might require production quotas and ecological prescriptions to limit production. Quotas would be particularly important regarding exhaustible natural resources; here intertemporal considerations (preservation of natural resources for future generations) are crucial. In any case it is a great policy mistake to leave price formation of primary products to the vagaries of *laissez-faire*. This not only contributes to destroying the natural environment but also heavily damages the social structure: primary production constitutes the basis on which an industrial sector may be erected; the surplus arising from both the primary and the secondary sector enables a society to build up a social, political and cultural superstructure. Between the various spheres of human activity certain proportions must prevail; for example, production can go on in an orderly way only if the associated distributional outcomes remain stable or evolve but slowly. The latter ensures that sector sizes remain in the required proportions: the producers of primary goods can plan production properly only if their incomes are institutionalized and thus stable. The importance of stable absolute and relative prices and of socially appropriate primary product prices was stressed by the Physiocrats, particularly François Quesnay, and, in this century, by

Nicholas Kaldor (for example, in Kaldor 1983). These principles seem to command a particular importance presently, not only on the national, but also on the world level.

A high degree of price stability for primary *and* industrial goods is essential for long-period entrepreneurial planning in general. Entrepreneurs would never engage in long-term projects, i.e. investments associated with the introduction of new methods of production and of new products, if the market prices persistently and unpredictably deviated from the prices of production as a result of too intensive price competition. Therefore a certain organization of markets by cartels and entrepreneurial associations is socially useful and necessary. These institutions create stability and security for entrepreneurs and enable them to be innovative in the sphere of production. Cartels are socially harmful only if they aim at realizing abnormally high profits. A certain degree of competition is of course required to induce entrepreneurs to introduce new techniques of production and new products. However, this type of competition primarily focuses on maintaining market shares by high quality standards, price competition being of secondary importance. This is another way of saying that the prices of production are fundamental and market prices secondary, a point already made by Ricardo in his *Principles* (Ricardo 1951 [1821], chapters IV, XXX) and taken up by Pasinetti (1981, 1993).

The long-period (Kalecki–Weintraub) theory of pricing sketched here has a long tradition and is not only appealing on *a priori* theoretical grounds; it also has a solid empirical foundation: '[There is] no difficulty in explaining why the mark-up is generally calculated on *normal* capacity utilization (on standard volumes), for any attempt by a single producer to recoup the higher overheads (at low utilization of capacity) by increasing his price strongly tempts his competitors to achieve the same result by *not* following suit and thereby attaining the same end by gaining sales at his expense' (Kaldor 1985a, p. 40). Moreover, since information is imperfect due to the presence of space and time, attempts to adjust prices to rapidly changing market conditions would require a tremendous amount of information and would be very costly if effectively carried out. Hence sticking to (long-period) normal prices seems most efficient in a world of imperfect information and of imperfect foresight where products are *not* homogeneous and each producer is consequently a monopolist to some extent, as was already recognized by Edward Chamberlin, Richard Kahn, Joan Robinson and Piero Sraffa in the thirties. This pricing practice seems to be widespread indeed: 'According to Okun [1981, pp. 175–6], mark-up rigidity seems to be "simply too pervasive across the United States economy to be attributable to oligopoly". Mark-up rigidity is not limited to automobiles, computers, and aluminium, but extends to non-concentrated sectors like retail trades, an "industry which is as atomistic as any trustbuster could wish"' (Kaldor 1985a, p. 40).

The long-period significance of money

In an economy with extensive division of labour, wage, sales and credit contracts are in terms of money. Keynes called such an economy a *monetary production economy*, the essence of which is captured by Marx's famous sequence: $M - C \ldots P \ldots C' - M'$ which has already been alluded to. Finance (M) is required to buy inputs C (including labour power), which, in the social process of production P, are transformed into final goods; the sale of final output C' against money M' implies the problem of effective demand.

Money is essentially a *social* institution because of the social nature of production (Pasinetti 1981, 1993). This gives rise to a first reason for the long-period significance of money, a reason which has two aspects. On the one hand, money permits productive exchange, i.e. flows of intermediate goods, and thus co-ordinates the various productive activities taking place in a widely diversified production system based on the social division of labour. On the other hand, producers are not paid for in terms of the product they produce but in terms of money which enables the producers to act as consumers and investors and to buy specific parts of the social product, i.e. the consumption and investment required. Hence money enables the circulation of goods, by both production and consumption, at any moment of time: deliveries of intermediate goods between industries and the exchanges between the consumption and the investment goods sectors are rendered possible by the help of money. In a long-period system equilibrium – a fully adjusted situation – transactions would take place on the basis of prices of production. Given the employment level, the $S=I$ condition would fix the right proportions between sectors and industries enabling the process of production to go on smoothly. In a monetary production economy labour emerges as the only factor of production and thus as the unique source of value (Pasinetti 1981). This principle is modified by the different conditions of production existing in the various sectors of production and by varying distributional arrangements, mainly concerning rents on land, a fact that directly emerges from the notion of normal prices: labour productivity and the mark-up, including profits and rents, appear as determinants together with money wages. The national or social product emerges as the result of a social effort undertaken by the labour force, and the money wage rate is the monetary expression of a unit of effort undertaken. Therefore, the level of normal money prices, governed by the money wage level, reflects, in principle, the social value of the various goods. As

such, money *represents* value (measured by labour time) which is created by
the labour force in the social process of production. This specific property
enables money to act as an intermediary in the various exchanges going on
in the sphere of production and of consumption.

As a representative of value, money may also function as a store of value,
which constitutes a second reason for the long-period importance of
money. To adequately fulfil its role as a store of value, the value of money
ought to be stable in the course of time: high rates of inflation lead to abandoning money as a store of value; prices of real assets, land for example,
rise which, in turn, enhances inflation. Various distributional conflicts may
upset the stability of the money price level – most importantly, conflicts
relating to the level of real wages, to the wage structure and to relative
incomes of producers of primary products, i.e. agricultural products and
raw materials. In fact, on a microeconomic level, money wages and raw
material prices make up variable costs on which the mark-up is calculated
(Kalecki); moreover, agricultural prices are a crucial determinant of the
real wage.

This leads to a third reason why money is important in the long run.
Money wages and prices are associated with institutionally governed
distributional outcomes: unit labour costs expressed in money and the
institutionally determined mark-up k^* govern normal money prices. These
prices govern the purchasing power of money wages, i.e. the quantity of
goods and services money wages can buy. Hence the real wage rate is a
social or macroeconomic notion because the quantities produced result
from the social process of production which encompasses the entire production system. This point is made by Pasinetti (1981, 1993; specifically
1993, pp. 125–8). The macroeconomic character of the real wage concurs
to reinforce the social nature of money.

If there is a persistent social consensus about income distribution,
money wages will, in the long run, increase with labour productivity (equation 6), and normal prices stay firm. However, if the consensus on distribution temporarily breaks down, a wage–price spiral may develop, which
will reduce the 'real' quantity of money. Once the capacity of the banking
system to create credit money is exhausted, the normal interest rate might
rise if the demand for new credits persists; to prevent this, the Central Bank
would have to expand the monetary base. Hence, in the long term, money
passively adjusts to increases in the price level. These issues are extensively
dealt with by Weintraub (1978).

Fourth, money is important, because production takes time.
Entrepreneurs incur commitments now $(M-C)$ and repay debts out of
incomes $(C'-M')$ accruing in the future. If future incomes are not sufficiently high to repay debts, a financial crisis may result, reflecting the fact

that present effective demand is not sufficient to bring about a normal utilization of productive capacities that have been built up in the past. A long-period view associated with the fully adjusted situation implies that debts must ultimately be repaid: investment must ultimately be financed by saving in the long run.

Fifth, long-period effective demand is expressed in money terms. Once money wages and prices are fixed, output and employment are governed by effective demand. The supermultiplier relation exhibits how the entire institutional system comes in to determine the scale of economic activity through the principle of effective demand; again $S=I$ provides the equilibrium condition. The supermultiplier relation only makes sense because a monetary theory of production in the sense of Keynes and Marx $(M-C...P...C'-M')$ is implied in our analysis. Effective demand comes into the picture with the exchange of final output against money $(C'-M')$. The determination of the level of economic activity by effective demand – a monetary concept – again reflects the social nature of money, since the whole socioeconomic system is relevant here.

A final reason why money is important in the long run is associated with the third point above: the permanent presence of uncertainty leads to a continuous demand for money for precautionary and speculative purposes, which implies that money persistently acts as a store of value: part of wealth is held in money form at any moment of time. This permits the setting-up of a long-period theory of effective demand, which is of crucial importance for classical-Keynesian political economy.

Such a theory rests on the fact that, in the long run, areas of near-certainty co-exist with areas of uncertainty. If the state of confidence with respect to the continuity of institutions is strong, then there will be little uncertainty with respect to global long-period variables (normal output, employment and investment, for instance) as are determined by the supermultiplier: this expresses the deterministic effect of the socioeconomic system. However, there may be considerable uncertainty about eventual institutional changes or about behavioural outcomes leading to deviations from normal magnitudes or about the composition of global magnitudes. For instance, the government may have temporarily to increase expenditures, owing to a natural calamity; there may be uncertainty as to the extent of these expenditures. Or, it may be highly uncertain which individual investment projects will be successful in the long run and which will fail. Finally, the short-run evolution of certain prices may be highly uncertain which renders possible speculative gains. Thus, near-certainty and uncertainty are linked with different aspects of reality: the former reflects the long-run deterministic effect of the socioeconomic system, the latter the short- and medium-term outcomes of individual actions.

Given this, a long-period theory of interest and money might look as follows. The permanent or slowly changing features of monetary policy and of liquidity preference result in a *normal* rate of interest, which is mainly determined by the institutionally governed hierarchy of profit rates as is implied by the normal mark-up k^*, whereby the normal profit rates exceed the normal interest rate: without the possibility of realizing profits in the sphere of production a rate of interest could not exist. This is the Ricardian-Marxian view of interest according to which interests are a claim on the surplus produced by a socioeconomic system. Subjective views on what the normal interest rate is, will, as a rule, differ between individuals, which allows us to conceive of a long-period liquidity preference curve. The demand for speculative money is in real terms, i.e. nominal amounts divided by the price level. The amount of money permanently held as a part of wealth would be associated with a long-period equilibrium on the money market. Given the normal rates of profit of other components of wealth (produced, like real capital, or not reproducible, like old masters), the normal prices of all components of wealth are also determined. Since the long-period liquidity preference, the normal prices, the normal rates of interest on money and the normal profit rates are all institutionally governed, the long-period demand for money is also institutionally determined and is, as such, part of the system equilibrium. Therefore, the long-period demand for money cannot be observed directly; its significance and its socioeconomic effects have to be brought out by an (ideal-type) model, i.e. the supermultiplier relation. The latter permits us to assess the influence of the hoarding of money on economic activity: given the normal interest and profit rates on reproducible and non-reproducible assets, the prices of these assets would rise continuously if holders of wealth were, for some reason, less and less willing to hold money as an asset in the long run. The distribution of wealth would become more unequal and the share of property income would steadily increase with pernicious effects on trend output and employment.

The all-embracing long-period system equilibrium comprising *all* normal prices and quantities – of produced and non-reproducible goods – sketched above bears some analogy to the system set forth in chapter 17 of the *General Theory*. Keynes's own rates of interest formally correspond to our normal interest and profit rates. There is however a crucial difference between the two notions. Keynes's own rates of interest are presumably associated with a marginal productivity adjustment mechanism: a specific own rate declines if the corresponding quantity increases. However, the normal interest and profit rates are institutionally determined, with the quantities of the produced goods governed by long-period effective demand. If goods are not reproducible, prices adjust; this process is governed by decisions related to the composition of wealth. For example, if land gets persistently more attractive as a long-period store of wealth, its price will increase. Given the institutionally governed normal rate of return on land, rents, including flat rents, will also rise.

Hence the classical-Keynesian long-period theory of interest and money is broadly along Keynesian lines, with differing economic implications however. This emerges from the economic significance of the 'quantity of money'. Given the amount of notes and coins in circulation, the level of money wages and the normal rate of interest, the quantity of money, M1 for instance, will, in the short and medium term, adjust to the level of economic activity across variations of the income velocity of money (a purely passive magnitude); this is rendered possible by the capacity of the banking system to create credit money. In the long run the Central Bank will have to adjust the quantity of basic money to prevent interest rates from rising above the institutionally determined normal rate. (If the Central Bank kept the interest rate persistently above the current normal rate, a higher normal interest would come into being and raise the hierarchy of normal profit rates; this broadly corresponds to Sraffa's view of the determination of normal interest and profit rates.) In a monetary economy, the Central Bank is, in principle, not in a position to control the quantity of money (M1 for example): money is endogenous. This broadly corresponds to the views of the early nineteenth-century Banking School mainly represented by Thornton, Tooke and Fullarton (Kaldor 1982, p. 78). Modern classical-Keynesian proponents of an endogenous money supply are, for example, Nicholas Kaldor (1985b) and Basil Moore (1983); see Wray (1994) for a recent survey. An important effort to integrate classical political economy and Keynesian views on money has been made by Bernard Schmitt (1960, 1972, 1984). These views on endogenous money contrast with the neo-classical (monetarist) theory which sees the 'quantity of money' as exogenous.

In long-period classical-Keynesian theory the effect of the normal rate of interest on economic activity is similar to the Keynesian one; the underlying mechanism is different, however. In the Keynesian view, a higher rate of interest combined with a given 'marginal efficiency of capital' and given long-period expectations leads to a lower volume of investment which, in turn, depresses economic activity, i.e. output and employment. In the classical-Keynesian supermultiplier framework, however, a rise in the normal interest rate leads, in principle, to an increase in normal profit rates, to higher mark-ups and to a higher profit share; the latter results in a decline of normal output and employment. As a consequence, normal investment will also diminish. The composition of wealth also influences income distribution: for example, 'investment' in land raises land prices and land rents, *given* the normal rate of return on land; distribution gets more unequal which, across the supermultiplier mechanism, reduces the level of economic activity: in a classical-Keynesian framework, interest and money act upon the scale of economic activity via the distribution of incomes and wealth (on this, see also Panico 1985, pp. 37–60).

International trade

The supermultiplier implies two traditional theories of international trade which are based respectively on two aspects of international trade: the welfare or 'structural' effect of trade based on comparative cost differences and the employment or 'scale' effect due to a favourable composition of exports and imports and to eventual export surpluses.

On the basis of the classical and neoclassical theory of international trade, it can easily be shown – as Ricardo first did – that, *given* the level of employment, international trade has important welfare effects linked up with specific structures of production reflecting the international division of labour. These effects can be realized by exporting goods which can be produced at relatively low cost at home and by importing those with comparatively high domestic costs. The law of comparative costs constitutes the theoretical basis for the free trade doctrine which is unattackable if a long-run tendency towards full employment is postulated, as is done by neoclassical economists. Here, foreign balance equilibria are supposed to be brought about by flexible prices – the terms of trade – and by substitution.

The classical-Keynesian supermultiplier theory, however, implies that there is no automatic tendency towards full employment in a monetary production economy; this proposition, which is strongly confirmed by historical experience, will be examined more closely in chapter 5 (pp. 281–93). In the classical-Keynesian theory institutional rigidities, complementarity between the various spheres of society and quantity adjustments dominate in the long run. With various unemployment levels persisting among trading partners, the employment or scale effect of international trade, i.e. the mercantilist-Keynesian aspect of international trade, is put to the fore. From the supermultiplier relation (7) it follows that a large volume of exports relative to the national product (consisting mainly of labour-intensive manufactured products), combined with favourable terms of trade (a low π) and a relatively small import coefficient b is, in principle, associated with high trend levels of output and employment. A steadily rising social product combined with increasing returns to scale leads to lower unit costs, higher profits and a strengthening of the technical dynamism which, in turn, acts favourably on exports, the terms of trade and the import coefficient. This is the essence of the Kaldorian cumulative process which may be reinforced by export surpluses.

The crucial feature of this process is that not only the volume of exports, but also its structure is an important determinant of the level of employment. Given the volume of exports, the employment effect will be the stronger, the higher is the share of manufactured products in exports (Kaldor 1978, introduction). The latter are labour-intensive; the labour content of final manufactured goods comprises direct and indirect labour, the latter being contained in the intermediate products including parts of fixed capital required to produce the final goods and in research and development activities.

The 'principle of cumulative causation whereby some regions gain at the expense of others, leading to increasing inequalities between relatively prosperous and relatively poor areas' (Kaldor 1985a, pp. 74–5) is of the highest importance in classical-Keynesian trade theory; on the policy level it requires that measures to stabilize employment at a high level must *continuously* accompany trade activities based on the principle of comparative advantage; more will be said on this issue in the policy subsection (chapter 6, p. 326–43). Kaldor sees the mechanism underlying the principle of cumulative causation like this:

If imbalances arise in trade, because one industrial center's exports are larger than its imports, whereas with the other centers imports exceed exports, the export surplus area will tend to expand production because realized receipts will exceed planned receipts causing producers to expand; this will cause imports to rise (since the use of imported commodities will expand in line with [domestically produced ones]), causing the export surplus to diminish, and hence the excess of realized over planned receipts to diminish, until a balance is reached, with exports equaling imports. In the other countries, the reverse process takes place: output and incomes will be reduced in successive steps until imports are reduced to the level of exports . . . However, under the general assumption of increasing returns, this is not the end of the story. If we started with the arbitrary assumption that the various industrial centers expanded at the same rate, we now have a situation in which one of the centers at least grows at a faster rate than the others. Hence its productivity rate will be accelerated and unless its domestic absorption (meaning its domestic consumption and investment) keeps pace with its faster productivity growth, its export surplus will reappear, giving rise to another push, making for faster growth rates for itself and slower growth rates for the others (Kaldor 1985a, pp. 73–4).

In the next subsection it is suggested that the principle of cumulative causation dominates the supermultiplier mechanism: the foreign trade position is crucial for capitalist development.

The terms of trade (π) play an important role in classical-Keynesian trade theory. Their significance emerges from the foreign balance: $X = \pi M$ may be written as $\pi = X/M$; with product qualities given, the terms of trade determine the quantities of goods and services that may be imported for a given quantity of goods and services exported: more favourable terms imply that relatively larger quantities may be imported. As a rule, the terms of trade are the more favourable the higher the share of high-quality manufactured products in total exports. These may be sold at relatively high prices on the world markets because of their specific characteristics: unique features and high quality standards may combine with appropriate advertising and after-sale service. Favourable terms of trade (a low π) are linked with higher levels of output and employment: the fraction of income needed to buy a given quantity of foreign goods is smaller when these are relatively cheap and more effective demand is available to buy domestic goods. This implies that more favourable terms of trade are linked with higher real wages. With $z_w < z_p$, effective demand, output and employment are correspondingly larger.

The principles underlying the long-period formation of the terms of trade ($\pi = ep_M/p$) emerge from the normal price equation (6) ($e=$long-period exchange rate, $p_M=$normal prices of the imported goods in foreign currency and $p=$normal domestic price level). Ideally, i.e. with purchasing power parity, π equals unity; this implies $(ew_n k^*)_M/(w_n k^*)=A_M/A$: with given distributional arrangements (k^*) money wages expressed in the same currency must be proportional to labour productivities. Goods embodying a given amount of domestic labour are exchanged against a certain quantity of goods containing a higher amount of foreign labour if labour productivity abroad (A_M) is smaller than domestic labour productivity (A). This principle rests on the labour theory of value. In the real world, the concept of labour values is modified by various factors, for example different conditions of production which show up in different ratios of direct to indirect labour, i.e. different 'capital'–labour ratios.

At this stage a remark on the nature of the classical-Keynesian theory of the terms of trade is required. It is frequently argued that values and prices of production regulate domestic long-period exchanges but that in international trade the law of supply and demand brings about a tendency towards equilibrium in the foreign balance, i.e. the terms of trade depend upon supply and demand. This may be true in the short and medium terms. In a long-period classical-Keynesian view the determination of the terms of trade and the adjustment mechanism in international trade are entirely different, however. The tendency towards equilibrium in the foreign balance is, in the long run, brought about by quantity adjustments, given the import coefficient (b) and the terms of trade (π). The significance of the latter emerges from the nature of the prices of production which are related to the quantities of labour embodied in the various goods. If relatively large quantities of goods may be imported for a given quantity of exports, domestic labour is valued more highly than foreign labour which, as far as the economic sphere is concerned, implies that the quality standard of domestic production is higher than that of goods produced abroad. The terms of trade are therefore a kind of *international reduction coefficient* that reflects the international status of some country's or region's labour force. However, power relations may also bear on the terms of trade: for example, a country which is heavily dependent on imports necessary to the process of production may be forced to exchange larger and larger quantities of its export goods against a given quantity of imported goods. Finally, cultural factors also influence the terms of trade: certain less developed countries are ready to give up very large quantities of domestic goods in order to obtain Western consumption goods.

The long-period terms of trade are therefore determined by a very complex set of institutions. Looking at the present situation it is evident that the highly industrialized countries are in a very favourable position: they export sophisticated industrial goods and services and import very large quantities of standard industrial products, agricultural products and raw materials. Standards of living, real wages and the motivation of the labour force, profits and research and development expenditures are all relatively high, which, in turn, enhances the international position or status of the labour force.

The prices of manufactured products (and of specific services, e.g. banking) tend to be higher than those of primary products (the terms of trade move in favour of the former). The prices of manufactured goods are also more stable. They are, in principle, cost-determined: the bulk of costs is made up of direct and indirect labour costs; as a rule, wages rise together with labour productivity. Productivity increases thus do not lead to lower prices of manufactures. Primary products prices are, however, dominated by supply and demand conditions; speculation may come in, resulting in erratic fluctuations of prices and, consequently, of the terms of trade.

Moreover, it is likely that successful exporters of manufactured products are less dependent on imports than exporters of primary goods. For the former, the import coefficient b is lower relative to the share of exports in national income. Because of the presence of a machine tool sector – machines that make machines – the industrialized country is also able quite easily to substitute domestic production for large parts of imported manufactures if necessary.

Finally, the above propositions regarding raw materials and agricultural products are also broadly valid for standard industrial products, like certain brands of textiles. We should therefore compare producers and exporters of 'high technology' industrial products and services and countries producing and mainly exporting raw materials, agricultural products, 'low technology' products and standard services, like mass tourism.

In this context, we may mention that an important reason for the break-down of the socialist economies is their gradually becoming 'low technology' countries, with the possible exception of certain sectors such as armaments. The technological gap between the socialist and the advanced capitalist countries widened at a tremendous pace because the planned economies were basically inept at transforming inventions into innovations on a large scale; technological change was an element disturbing the plan. Given this, a major aim of the reformers in Eastern Europe now is certainly to narrow the technological gap in order to enhance the international status of their labour force and thereby improve their export positions on the world markets for 'high technology' products.

Hence, foreign trade taking place on the basis of the actual worldwide division of labour and of the actual world economic order (both being the result of a long historical process) may lead to cumulative discrepancies of wealth and incomes. This is due to the functioning of the system: in the mercantilist-Keynesian game of international trade with the employment or scale effect of international trade dominating, one nation may lose what the other gains, as Montaigne, a precursor of mercantilism, observed in his *Essays* around 1580 (Heckscher 1932, vol. II, p. 16). This is in striking contrast to the happy full employment world where all trading partners benefit from comparative advantages.

Structures: proportions between sectors

The macroeconomic theory of output and employment represented by the supermultiplier relation may be easily linked with structural problems. All the variables and parameters of this relation may be interpreted as weighted averages depending upon sectoral prices and quantities, i.e. the structure of an economy, which is extensively dealt with by Pasinetti (1977, 1981, 1993). The supermultiplier relation thus implies that 'productive equipment . . . be appropriate to the composition of aggregate demand at its (equilibrium) level, so as to abstract from problems of disproportions among industries' (Garegnani 1976, p. 24n). This is a fully adjusted situation or a system equilibrium, i.e. that part of reality which is governed by the permanent forces of a socioeconomic system. The preoccupation with fully adjusted situations is equivalent to looking for the appropriate proportions between the various industries and sectors making up an economy such that, with a given institutional set-up, the process of production and reproduction may go on smoothly. The preoccupation with proportions at a given scale of activity was a central theme of classical macroeconomics (pp. 136–7 above) established by Quesnay's *tableau économique* and carried on and elaborated by Ricardo, Marx, Leontief, Sraffa and Pasinetti.

With technology and institutions evolving, the fully adjusted situation, or the system equilibrium, gradually changes too. Structural changes can be conveniently accounted for in principle by vertically integrated production models (Pasinetti 1981, 1993).

The supermultiplier as a synthesis of the internal and external employment mechanisms

The deeper economic meaning of the supermultiplier relation emerges more clearly if this relation is considered as the synthesis of two different mechanisms governing output and employment: the internal and the external employment mechanisms. Initially in this subsection, each mechanism is dealt with separately so as to bring out its meaning. The two mechanisms are then combined to obtain the supermultiplier relation. Finally, some policy conclusions closely associated with both mechanisms are hinted at; these are supplemented in chapter 6.

The term *internal employment mechanism* suggests that this mechanism describes what is going on inside an economy with respect to the determination of output and employment. The starting point is a familiar macroeconomic equilibrium condition:

$$z^*Q^* = G + I \tag{18}$$

or

$$z^*Q^* - G^* = S = I. \tag{18a}$$

Equation (18) states that leakages equal injections. This is equivalent to saying that private and public saving equals investment (18a).

Normal investment is governed by the evolution of 'trend' output (equation 5). Combining the latter with equation (18) yields:

$$Q_i^* = \frac{G}{z - (g+d)v} = \frac{1}{m}G, \tag{19}$$

where Q_i^* stands for normal gross national product, governed by the internal employment mechanism, i.e. by the institutions governing normal government expenditures, the normal leakage and the normal investment–output ratio, for instance political parties (G), consumption behaviour and income distribution (z), and the technical dynamism of entrepreneurs (d). The expression $1/m$ could be termed the 'internal' or 'government expenditures' multiplier, where m is the difference between the leakage and the gross investment–output ratio; m may differ from the average tax rate t by the ratio of a chronic budget deficit or surplus to gross national income.

The functioning of the *external employment mechanism* can be described by an expression derived from the foreign balance (equation 11):

$$Q_e^* = \frac{1}{\pi b} X, \qquad (20)$$

where Q_e^* is trend gross national product, determined by the external employment mechanism, i.e. by the institutions which govern the volume of trend exports, and the terms of trade and the import coefficient, i.e. the export multiplier $1/\pi b$. The volume of normal exports might depend upon the state of technology, the education system and the degree of aggressiveness on world markets. The export multiplier is the larger, the more favourable the terms of trade (π relatively small) and the less a country depends upon foreign goods and services; this is reflected in a low value of the import coefficient b *relative* to exports. The determination of the terms of trade was sketched in the preceding subsection, the problem of dependence will be taken up below.

The export multiplier has a long history. Presumably, it is implied in Keynes's (1971a) *Economic Consequences of the Peace*. According to Nicholas Kaldor, the concept was set forth explicitly by Roy Harrod as early as 1933 (Kaldor 1978, p. xxiv, n. 1). The present exposition builds on Kaldor's ideas (1978, chapters 4–9; 1986).

Equation (20) pictures the employment or scale effect of international trade for a particular country (pp. 185–9 above): the volume of employment and output (Q_e^*) depends not only on the size, but also on the structure of exports. Given the volume of exports, exporters of labour-intensive industrial goods and services, possibly embodying advanced technologies, enjoy higher levels of employment than countries exporting land-intensive raw materials and agricultural products and low-technology, standard industrial products. Moreover, successful exporters of labour-intensive goods of high quality enjoy more favourable terms of trade (π^* is low as real wages increase with labour productivity) and are, as a rule, less dependent (b^* is low relative to X^*) on the outside world than exporters of land-intensive goods.

There is no reason why Q_i^* should equal Q_e^*. Given this, the employment mechanism which yields the *smaller* value of gross domestic product will, at first, govern economic activity. But there is also a mechanism which combines Q_i^* and Q_e^*. The result is normal output Q^*, governed by the supermultiplier (figure 4). Given normal government expenditures (G_1) and the multiplier $1/m$, the internal employment mechanism determines the 'trend' output level Q_i^*. On the other hand, exports (X_1) and the export multiplier govern the trend output level Q_e^* through the external employment mechanism. In figure 4 Q_i^* falls short of Q_e^*. The internal employment

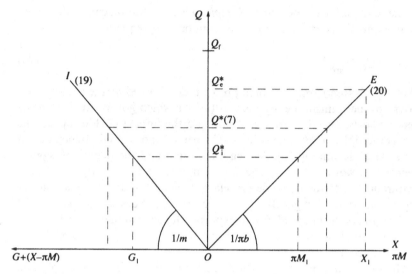

Figure 4.

mechanism therefore governs economic activity. The external mechanism is redundant which implies that an export surplus occurs. Exports (X_1) exceed imports associated with the output level Q_i^*, i.e. πM_1. The export surplus influences the internal equilibrium position, however. Equation (19) must be rewritten as follows:

$$Q_i^* = \frac{1}{m}(G + X - \pi M). \tag{7}$$

Taking account of relations (11) or (20), this expression is equivalent to the supermultiplier relation (7) which thus appears as a synthesis of the internal and external employment mechanisms. The former is based upon the 'equilibrium' condition $S=I$, the latter on $X=\pi M$. The supermultiplier takes account of both conditions: this relation combines the long-period equivalent of the Keynesian saving–investment multiplier (equation 19) and the foreign trade multiplier (equation 20). In the above figure this synthesis is reflected in an institutionally governed 'equilibrium' or normal output Q^* which simultaneously satisfies the internal and the external constraints on output, set by effective demand.

The above does not imply, however, that both multipliers stand on the same footing: 'it may have been unfortunate that the very success of Keynes' [saving–investment multiplier] in explaining unemployment in a depression – essentially a short period analysis – diverted attention from the "foreign trade multiplier", which over longer periods, is a far more

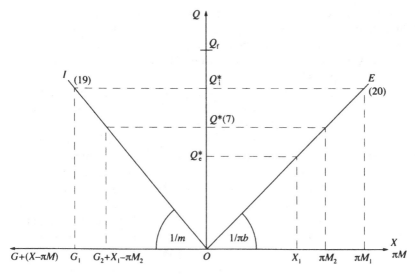

Figure 5.

important principle for explaining the growth and rhythm of industrial development' (Kaldor 1974, p. 210; on this, see also Kaldor 1986). Indeed, from figure 4 it emerges that a country in which the external equilibrium exceeds the overall (supermultiplier) equilibrium ($Q_e^*>Q^*$) is in a most comfortable position. First, the supermultiplier 'equilibrium' is associated with a chronic surplus on the current account which implies that foreign exchange reserves grow steadily. Second, Q^* may adjust to the external equilibrium (Q_e^*) if domestic demand is stimulated. For example, private consumption may be raised through redistributing income; this would be reflected in a lower level of the leakage z and thus of m. The 'internal' multiplier $1/m$ rises and Q^* gets nearer to Q_e^*. The same result obtains if normal government expenditures are raised. Taken together, this implies a permanent increase in private and public consumption which means that prosperity is increasing. It is not very difficult to identify countries which, in practice, enjoy or have enjoyed a dominance of the external employment mechanism. Germany, Japan and Switzerland, as mentioned above, are obvious cases in point.

The picture changes dramatically if the external employment mechanism restricts internally governed normal economic activity. This becomes evident from figure 5 which is exactly analogous to figure 4. Given normal government expenditures (G_1) and the multiplier $1/m$, the internal employment mechanism (equation 19) leads to the output level Q_i^* which is linked up with a deficit ón the current account ($X_1<\pi M_1$). This deficit reduces domestic demand. In principle, national income gradually declines so as to approach the supermultiplier equilibrium Q^* which is compatible with both the internal and the external employment mechanism. However, at Q^*, there is still a chronic deficit on current account: trend imports $(\pi M_2)^*$ exceed trend exports $(X_1)^*$.

Consequently, foreign exchange reserves gradually decline and/or foreign indebtedness steadily increases. Once the debt burden becomes too heavy, long-run equilibrium output Q^* has to be forced down in order to be compatible with the external constraint set by Q_e^*. This adjustment has to be brought about by a permanent reduction of internal demand: government expenditures have to be depressed below their trend level G_2, and private consumption demand has to be diminished. The average propensity to consume (c) declines and the leakage $z = 1 - c$ rises; the latter reduces the multiplier $1/m$ and flattens the line OI in figure 5. A reduction in private consumption demand can be brought about by raising the normal saving coefficients (s_p, s_w) and/or by redistributing income in favour of normal property income. The latter will be reflected in a higher value of the average mark-up k^* and thus of the leakage z. Finally, investment demand may also be reduced. As can be seen from equation (5) above, this might be done by lowering the drop-out ratio of fixed capital (d). This implies that the renewal and hence the modernization of the capital stock is slowed down.

The attempts to adjust the supermultiplier equilibrium to the foreign exchange constraint are equivalent to *austerity policies*. This type of economic policy has to be pursued in many countries all over the world because economic activity is ultimately governed by the external employment mechanism. In most cases, this is linked with very great hardship, mainly because of high levels of unemployment which are reflected in a considerable difference between Q_e^* and Q_f, the full employment level.

The external employment mechanism plays a crucial role because it ultimately governs economic activity under 'free trade' conditions, and the supermultiplier equilibrium Q^* has to adjust sooner or later to the external equilibrium Q_e^*. However, it makes a tremendous difference whether an upward adjustment is possible (initially $Q^* < Q_e^*$ holds – figure 4) or whether a downward adjustment has to be enforced through austerity policies (initially $Q^* > Q_e^*$ prevails – figure 5). Based on this, some policy conclusions will be suggested in chapter 6.

Here, three sets of preliminary remarks regarding these policy conclusions are made. The first is related to the link between import regulation and full employment, the second concerns the relationship existing between foreign debt and employment, and the third the formerly socialist countries.

Under 'free trade' conditions, the level of economic activity is ultimately governed by the external employment mechanism $(Q^*$ has to adjust to $Q_e^*)$.

If Q_e^* is below the full employment level Q_f, it is impossible to reach full employment without incurring a deficit on the current account. This holds for countries which are, initially, in a favourable position with respect to the foreign balance: Q^* is below Q_e^* (figure 4) and for countries where Q^* exceeds Q_e^* (figure 5). Therefore, given normal exports (X^*) and the terms of trade (π^*), governed by world effective demand and by a complex set of domestic and foreign institutions, the import coefficient (b^*) has to adjust if full employment is to be achieved. To show this we distinguish between two kinds of imports:

$$M^* = bQ^* = (b_1 + b_2)Q^*. \tag{21}$$

Here, b_1Q^* are the imports *necessary* to the process of production. To produce a given output Q^*, each country must import certain goods which cannot be domestically produced for institutional reasons linked up with the presently prevailing international division of labour which has developed historically, i.e. certain equipment and spare parts, or for natural reasons: certain raw materials and necessary consumption goods. Without these goods, output could simply not be produced. In Sraffian terms, b_1Q^* could be called imports of basic goods. Hence the import coefficient b_1 is a technical coefficient indicating the fraction of national product that has to be imported in order to render production possible at all.

Besides the necessary imports there are also imports which are related to *non-necessary* consumption (public and private) in the widest sense. To simplify, b_2Q^* could be termed luxury imports. These are related to the use of the surplus (chapter 3, pp. 95–103) accruing from the process of production. Cars, video recorders, television sets, certain types of food and drink are examples. Hence the coefficient b_2 reflects dependence on abroad at the social and cultural level. 'International demonstration effects' which are linked with the desire to imitate Western consumption styles certainly play an important role in determining b_2 in many underdeveloped countries, including the formerly socialist countries.

Taking account of definition (21), the foreign balance (equation 11 or 20) can be written as

$$X^* = \pi(b_1 + b_2)Q^*, \tag{22}$$

If normal output Q^* is to be raised above Q_e^* to approach the full employment level Q_f (figures 4 and 5), the import coefficient $b = b_1 + b_2$ must be reduced to preserve the – fundamental – equilibrium of the foreign balance with exports and the terms of trade given: in the long run, exports have to pay for imports because steadily increasing indebtedness leads into insuperable difficulties (Bortis 1979). However, the coefficient b_1 which indicates necessary imports as a fraction of national product, cannot be reduced:

necessary imports have to stay in line with Q^*. Therefore, b_2 and thus luxury imports have to be reduced correspondingly if a full-employment policy is pursued; in the real world this implies appropriate institutional changes. This conclusion is inevitable if account is taken of the states of affairs mapped out in figures 4 and 5 above.

Hence full employment policies in open economies require a certain 'official' protectionism with respect to luxury imports. It is very important to note that this does not imply a reduction in the volume of international trade (on this, see Cripps and Godley 1978). Quite the contrary: once the major trading partners enjoy positions of near-full employment, the volume of international trade may, based upon the principle of comparative advantage (linked with the 'structure effect' of international trade), expand at will, thus raising welfare everywhere. However, to secure full employment, the 'employment' or 'scale' effect of international trade represented by the external employment mechanism (equation 20) has to be accounted for; this is a necessary social precondition for enjoying the welfare effects of international trade.

The second problem to be touched upon here relates to foreign indebtedness. It is convenient to distinguish between two phases of indebtedness. In the first, debt is gradually built up. Interest payments and repayment of debt are negligible in relation to new capital inflows. The second phase is characterized by high debt levels; the debt service is now high relative to new capital inflows.

The problems arising from growing indebtedness can be considered with the help of equation 22 and figures 4 and 5. In the first phase, creditor countries enjoy export surpluses

$$X > \pi M. \tag{22a}$$

The fact that finance in whatever shape (aid, public credit, private investment) has flowed from creditor to debtor countries (in the case of aid we ought to speak of donor and receiving countries) results in an export surplus and in a favourable impact upon output and employment in the creditor countries (equation 7 and figures 4 and 5). Presumably, these export surpluses were an important reason underlying the sustained upswing of the world economy in the fifties and sixties. The debtor countries, on the other hand, enjoy, in the first phase, the privilege of being able to import more than they export:

$$X < \pi M. \tag{22b}$$

Whether the import surplus which, formally, is equivalent to additional saving, is invested or is used for private and public consumption is another question (Bortis 1979, chapters III, IV).

Hence in the first phase of borrowing and lending the growth of indebtedness is favourable to both creditors and debtors. The situation changes radically in phase two where the debt service, interest payments and repayment of debt due, dominate the picture. If gross capital flows from creditor to debtor countries (ΔB) are not sufficiently high, the debtor countries are forced to achieve an export surplus in order to obtain the foreign exchange required to service the debt, which means that these countries can dispose of fewer goods. As a consequence, the creditor countries now incur a deficit on current account which, according to the theory of the supermultiplier, has persistent negative effects upon employment and output.

The uncomfortable situation of the debtor countries can be understood best if the foreign balance (22) is written as

$$X + B - (i + \partial)D = \pi(b_1 + b_2)Q^*. \tag{23}$$

Here, B is the annual inflow of foreign finance (including aid) gross of interest payments and of debt repayment, D is the foreign debt and $i + \partial$ represents debt service (interest payments and repayments of debt due) as a fraction of foreign debt. The obligation to service the foreign debt reduces the amount of foreign exchange available (export earnings and new capital inflows). Less foreign exchange is now available to buy imports. Now, it is very difficult to reduce import coefficient b_2 (luxury imports as a fraction of national income). This coefficient is governed by a complex set of social and cultural factors and presumably also depends upon the distribution of income. In many underdeveloped countries, most people getting very high property incomes usually practise à Western lifestyle on a grand scale. Institutionalized habits like these cannot be changed easily. The import coefficient b_1 related to necessary imports cannot be changed readily either since it takes time to restructure the real capital stock and the methods of production associated with it. The only variable that can adjust to the reduction of available foreign exchange is national output (Q^*). Hence the scarcity of foreign exchange leads to increasing unemployment in debtor countries because goods required in the process of production cannot be imported.

Several factors may aggravate this situation. First, due to foreign dependence the import coefficients b_1 and b_2 are, as a rule, very high in many underdeveloped debtor countries. Second, it is difficult to export manufactured products to creditor countries because of the heavy unemployment there. As a consequence, the terms of trade are likely to worsen (π in equation 23 rises), mainly because of desperate attempts to export agricultural products, raw materials or standard industrial goods at ever lower prices; this rests on the argument set forth within the context of the Kaldorian cumulative process (pp. 185–6 above). Important side effects may accompany this, e.g. the ruthless destruction of the natural environment in many debtor countries and worsening social conditions, above all work conditions. Moreover, the debt service ratio $i + \partial$ is bound to increase, owing to high interest rates in creditor countries and to increased short-term borrowing. If overall indebtedness is high, new capital inflows (B) will, as a rule, diminish due to a decline of confidence of the creditor countries regarding the capacity to repay of the debtor countries, reducing further foreign exchange availability. Finally, there is capital flight from many heavily indebted countries: B declines. This occurs for a host of political, social and economic reasons, the lack of investment opportunities and heavy inflation being perhaps most important. All these elements result in a heavy decline of normal output (equations 7 and 23). The dramatic consequences for long-period employment are only too visible in many debtor countries: these countries are virtually strangled by the scarcity of foreign exchange.

To complete the picture, one ought to remember that a version of the argument just set forth was advanced by Keynes in relation to the Treaty of Versailles and to German reparation payments (Keynes 1971a). There is a lesson to be learnt from history which we shall briefly come back to in chapter 6 where some policy conclusions are suggested.

Thirdly, and finally, a brief remark on the formerly socialist countries is required here. These countries want to replace, at a stroke so to speak, the socialist system by a liberal one. The market is seen as a kind of magic institution which is expected to bring about a substantial improvement of the economic situation almost immediately (on the assumption that the resistance of the former planning bureaucracy can be overcome). The problem is, however, what the market can do and what it cannot. If there is no automatic tendency towards full employment and if effective demand, as may be working through the external employment mechanism, is crucial in determining long-run economic development in market economies, the formerly socialist countries may suffer most cruel disappointments. How, for example, are they going to conquer the world market for (high quality) manufactured products, given saturated markets, ruthless competition and hidden protection? Hence the formerly socialist countries ought to consider seriously a Keynesian-Kaldorian 'third way' regarding economic development, relying thus on the internal employment mechanism (equation 19), while, at the same time, regulating their foreign trade activities through adjustments of the import coefficient b_2 so as to preserve a foreign balance equilibrium or to achieve a slight surplus to gradually reduce foreign indebtedness (equation 23).

Methodological aspects of the supermultiplier relation: institutions and stability

One of the most important implications of the supermultiplier relation is that equilibrium, normal or 'trend' investment represents derived demand (equations 5 and 7). In long-period analysis, investment is a stable magnitude because the capacity effect links it strictly to long-period equilibrium output, determined by the supermultiplier, which is itself stable. In the foregoing it has been suggested that stability for normal investment obtains because *all* the magnitudes contained in the supermultiplier relation are *directly* determined by institutions and by technology. Since all institutions are interrelated the whole socioeconomic and political system enters the picture; hence the supermultiplier relation captures how, in principle, the socioeconomic and political system governs the level of economic activity and the associated volume of normal investment.

Institutions represent persistent actions of individuals and collectives directed towards individual and social aims (chapter 2, pp. 21–7). Because of their permanent or only slowly changing character, institutions and technology represent the social structure, which is an immensely complex whole; this is due to the interrelatedness of the hierarchy of aims pursued (chapter 2, pp. 27–53). Evolving structures largely *determine* the actions of individuals in the present through the social process of production and the principle of effective demand: this is the impact of the socioeconomic system upon individual actions which becomes more evident when the institutional content of the supermultiplier relation is examined.

Normal exports (X^*) and its rate of growth (g_X)* are determined by the world economic order and by the export strength (or weakness) of a particular country which in turn depends on a complex set of institutions and the interaction between these: the quality of the education system, the intensity of research and development and the social and political climate (all of which must be specified and analysed more precisely if a specific real-world situation is considered, this being the task of applied political economists, sociologists and political scientists). In the preceding sections it has been suggested that the normal terms of trade depend, in principle, upon the international status of a country's workforce, its relative position of power and other institutions. The normal import coefficient b is a reflection of outside dependence in production and consumption, which materializes through various technological, social and cultural institutions. The size and the structure of trend government expenditures G^* are the outcome of a complex process in which socioeconomic and political institutions are involved. The components of trend G^* cannot be changed at will since they

The normal leakages $(z_W, z_P)^*$ depend upon normal – institutionalized – consumption behaviour; the trend rate of growth g^* and the drop-out ratio d^* are partly the outcome of the technical dynamism of a society. Most importantly, the satisfactory or desired mark-up upon wages at standard capacity utilization k^*, is determined by a set of socioeconomic and political institutions that concur in regulating distribution (pp. 154–85 above).

The fact that the two autonomous 'trend' demand variables (G^* and X^*) are institutionally determined is of decisive importance for the classical-Keynesian long-period theory of output and employment. Indeed, economic activity is set into motion by the autonomous demand variables while normal consumption, investment and imports are derived demand variables. Hence the political and socioeconomic institutions governing G^* and X^* (and the associated supermultiplier) ultimately determine long-period economic activity. Through the principle of effective demand these objective factors set restrictions on the actions of producers and consumers.

Institutions render stable the outcomes of the socioeconomic and political system (e.g. normal prices and trend output and employment levels). Institutional stability goes together with the stability of the long-period level of investment (equation 5), which, in a long-run view, is *derived* demand governed by the evolution of long-period output which, in turn, depends upon the autonomous demand components (and their rate of growth) and on the size of the supermultiplier, both determined by institutions and technology; expectations and uncertainty play a secondary role in the long run. Indeed, if the state of confidence regarding the continuity of the institutional set-up of a society is very high, uncertainty is almost entirely absent. This important proposition should not be misunderstood: institutions (the system) determine only composite variables, i.e. trend output and employment or trend investment, or single variables which are determined by composite variables; normal prices, for example, depend upon the structure of production and upon income distribution. Perhaps the highest degree of determination is to be found within the process of production which is a circular and social process and as such constitutes a macroinstitution. On account of the forces of production that have evolved historically, certain flows of goods and services have to go on within an interindustry framework if production is to go on at all; the corresponding actions of the producers are thus determined by the technology in use. However, considerable uncertainty may be associated with individual elements contained in the objectively determined variables: which firms will be successful in the long run in the sense that they are achieving (on average) the target profit rate over a long period of time? Or, who will be unemployed or employed? Aggregate behavioural outcomes, for example current investment and output levels, are also largely uncertain.

Many highly industrialized countries provide good examples of the long-term stability of most institutions. In the last forty years or so, the state of confidence with respect to the continuity of important institutions has been very strong in these countries. People have been confident about the stability of government expenditures. Moreover, the state of confidence regarding their ability to export high-quality goods at favourable terms of trade and to dominate internal markets, which is reflected in a relatively low import coefficient relative to the export share, has been very strong. From the supermultiplier relation (7) and the foreign balance (11) we can immediately see that the favourable foreign trade position must result in relatively high long-period levels of output and employment. Since export orders came in steadily, the rate of growth of 'trend' exports has, in the countries in question, governed g^*, i.e. the long-period (warranted) trend growth rate of the entire economic system. The whole edifice has, finally, been reinforced by a solid social consensus about income distribution, that is about the size of the long-period equilibrium mark-up k^*. Hence, regarding the stability of these basic institutional facts, there was very little uncertainty in the countries in question.

The *normal* output and employment levels, associated with institutional stability, may be considered as evolving system equilibria attracting *actual* levels more or less strongly (pp. 204–20 below). Similarly, normal prices (equation 6) tend to attract market prices once money wages are given. Normal and actual magnitudes exist simultaneously: the former represent outcomes of the system, the latter are due to aggregate behaviour. The two, system and behavioural outcomes, interact, but the determining influence of the former on the latter is much stronger: the system-governed normal variables continuously attract actual variables; however, the influence of the latter on the former is marginal only. For example, gross investment only marginally modifies the actually existing and the trend capital stock.

The long-period stability of the capitalist system reflects a stylized fact which is perhaps best illustrated by the near-constancy of unemployment percentages in various countries over longer periods of time. Keynes himself seems to have adhered to the stability hypothesis: 'it is an outstanding characteristic of the economic system in which we live that, whilst it is subject to severe fluctuations in respect of output and employment, it is not violently unstable. Indeed it seems capable of remaining in a chronic condition of sub-normal activity for a considerable period without any marked tendency either towards recovery or towards complete collapse' (Keynes 1973a, p. 249).

Most of the long-period analysis carried out in the present study is based on the assumption that institutions are functioning normally, which, moreover, is expected to go on indefinitely; this is compatible with regular technological and institutional change going on. Given the latter, the trends of independent and dependent variables are evolving smoothly in the course of time as is shown by the curves bb', cc' and dd' in figure 3 (p. 150). Two important sets of forces at work in the real world may, however, disturb this too bright a picture: first, irregular technological and institutional change resulting from actions undertaken by individuals and collectives and, second, the partial or total breakdown of institutions resulting from contradictions inherent in the system. Both are related to tremendously complex issues which can only be alluded to here.

Institutional change initiated by individual and collective action is going on in every society and is inextricably linked with changes in the value system of a society. Change may relate to a few institutions only or may be linked up with many or all institutions in different spheres of individual and social life. The party system may, in a particular country, undergo substantial variations – this amounts to a change in political institutions. In the economic sphere, trade unions may change regarding their aims and their structure; the behaviour of consumers may profoundly change owing to increased travel abroad, or financial institutions may evolve rapidly on account of information circulating faster on a global level. The most important changes relate, however, to the sphere of production.

Pasinetti (1981) provides a fundamental analytical framework picturing technological (and structural) changes. The latter may lead to irregular changes in the fully adjusted (equilibrium) sectoral set-up of an economy and in important economic trends. Some sectors will shrink while others will expand; new sectors of production may be opened up while others disappear. This implies that, owing to changes in the forces of production, institutional change occurs within the process of production, affecting the relations of production, e.g. work conditions. As Marx clearly perceived, changes in the process of production (the socioeconomic basis) will inevitably require or induce changes in the legal, social, cultural and, eventually, political institutional superstructure. For example, the possibility of setting up data bases requires legal prescriptions regarding the protection of the private sphere of individuals. No strict determination is exercised by the basis upon the superstructure, but strong links between the two spheres inevitably prevail because activities carried out within the superstructure always require an economic basis.

With institutional and technological change going on irregularly at times, the underlying trends of an economy, the output and employment trends for instance, may no longer evolve smoothly. Gradual shifts in trends may be followed by irregular jumps (trend ee' in figure 3). Given this, individuals, when forming expectations about the persistence of institutions, will presumably attempt to figure out the 'trend of the trend' (figure 3) while taking account of relevant information pointing to eventual jumps in the evolution of institutions and thus of trends. The system equilibria then preserve their importance in the same way as if trends moved on smoothly.

In this context, the question as to the pace of technological and institutional change arises, which, as Luigi Pasinetti and others have pointed out, may eventually be too rapid: the institutional set-up within the economic basis, the process of production, may evolve so quickly that the institutional superstructure (legal, social, political and cultural) is unable to adjust. As is evident from figure 3 this may leave trends intact, but may lead to very serious problems, e.g. structural and involuntary unemployment and social and cultural alienation. However, technological change, associated with gross investment, affects the capital stock and the associated institutions only marginally which softens somewhat its impact on the various societies. The bulk of the production system (and some associated institutions) persist while becoming gradually more diversified: in most countries, almost archaic ways of producing goods co-exist with very advanced techniques of production.

The technological and institutional system resulting from past individual and collective action produces, broadly speaking, constructive and destructive outcomes that determine the behaviour of individuals and collectives; the latter are associated with increasing alienation, the former reduce alienation (chapter 2, pp. 39–53), i.e. the gap between an actually existing and the ideal situation where the common weal would be realized. From the socioeconomic point of view the most important elements of a constructive outcome are certainly a socially acceptable income distribution and full employment (in the sense of absence of persistent involuntary unemployment). Such a situation may permit the extension of socially useful (constructive) institutions: the social security system, cultural activities and increased protection of the environment. Hence institutional or system outcomes may be said to be constructive if they contribute to an increase in the public interest (public welfare or the common weal). However, if particular interests dominate and the pursuit of the public interest is neglected, destructive system outcomes may result. For example, increasing inequalities in income distribution may, on account of the super-multiplier mechanism, produce more and more involuntary unemployment which may, in turn, result in increasing poverty, the formation of slums and social unrest, including increasing crime. Destructive system outcomes in particular countries may also come about through the functioning of the international economic system: if a country does not succeed in the neo-mercantilist struggle for high-quality jobs heavy involuntary unemployment may result; such processes are pictured by the external employment mechanism set out in the preceding subsection.

Destructive system outcomes cause increasing strain on the whole institutional system: rising involuntary unemployment leads to physical and mental stress, to an increase of criminal activities which entail higher expenditures for internal security, to exploding budget deficits which in turn force governments to reduce expenditures for social security. All this may ultimately lead to a partial or total breakdown of the institutional system. System equilibria (normal employment levels and normal prices, for instance) will, consequently, cease to exist. This may happen in times of severe political and social unrest or in revolutions. The partial breakdown of international institutions, regulating political, commercial and financial relations between countries, which occurred in the thirties of this century, may also lead to a collapse of institutional trends. Presently, we witness considerable institutional change on the global level which results in important shifts of trends in individual countries. In such circumstances, classical-Keynesian theory associated with institutions becomes an inappropriate tool for analysing economic events, and Robinsonian and Keynesian Fundamentalist theory becomes more relevant: cycles and the vagaries of the market dominate the picture. Uncertainty will increase dramatically since the areas of stability and near-certainty created by institutions will now no longer exist. Such a situation will soon become untenable: chaos may ensue and, inevitably, new institutions will emerge and/or old ones be renewed.

A theory of the medium term: cycles-cum-growth

The analytical basis of cycle-cum-growth theory

An important analytical tool of the Robinsonian strand of classical-Keynesian political economy is the double-sided relationship between the rate of profit and the rate of growth (Robinson 1962a, p. 48): higher growth rates raise rates of profit through the functioning of the system; higher rates of profit induce larger growth rates, because entrepreneurs invest more, which represents a change in an aggregate behavioural outcome. This relationship provides the starting point for classical-Keynesian medium-term analysis.

If the rate of growth – rate of profit relationship is used to develop a theory of the trend, a rather strange construct emerges, namely the 'golden age', or a variety of possible golden ages (Robinson 1962a, pp. 52ff.), the stability of which is secured by 'tranquil conditions' (p. 53). However, these are not brought about by *objective and persistent* factors to determine the normal volume of investment as is the case in the supermultiplier relation. In the golden age, tranquillity is ensured by stable long-term expectations, i.e. subjective factors, linked up with individual investment projects which, taken together, make up the volume of investment. However, with the great number of uncertain factors that may influence the profitability of each investment project (the vagaries of the market, uneven technical progress, the changing behaviour of competitors with respect to pricing, marketing, etc.), the tranquillity assumption becomes very unrealistic: an economy can never get into equilibrium. As a consequence, the concept of stable long-run expectations linked with a golden age becomes largely meaningless (a mythical state according to Joan Robinson) and constitutes an easy target for neoclassical criticism. Therefore, the investment–profit (rate of growth – rate of profit) relationship should not be used to develop a theory of the long-period trend. This relationship seems to be much more fruitful if it is seen as the analytical basis of business cycle-cum-growth theory as has been proposed by Michal Kalecki, an opinion now presumably shared by most Kaleckians and Robinsonians. As such, Robinsonian-Kaleckian theory can be considered as the medium-term complement of the classical-Keynesian long-period theory exhibited in the previous section. The latter represents the application of the principle of effective demand to the long run, the former the application of this principle to the medium term. Classical-Keynesian supermultiplier theory pictures the determining impact of the socioeconomic system as a whole on individual actions. Robinsonian-Kaleckian cycle-cum-growth theory shows how the investment decisions of entrepreneurs are co-ordinated by a two-sector model linking the investment and consumption goods sectors. This results in a medium-term theory of income distribution implying given employment levels (determined by past accumulation) for each short period considered.

Factors causing cyclical movements

Cyclical movements are shaped by both *endogenous* and *exogenous* forces. The former are linked with the ordinary working mechanism of an economy, the latter are associated with external factors.

Two important concepts must be carefully distinguished to picture the influence of the endogenous factors on the cycle, namely *trend* or *normal output* (Q^* in figure 6, p. 209) and *capacity output* which would obtain if the presently existing capital stock K were normally utilized (Q_c in figure 6). Normal output is part of the system equilibrium implying a fully adjusted situation and, as is suggested below, attracts capacity output Q_c, which is associated with the real capital stock K, the result of past accumulation. K and Q_c will always diverge from K^* and Q^* since the system equilibrium is largely unknown to individual entrepreneurs who take investment decisions independently of each other: an economy can, therefore, never be in 'equilibrium', i.e. in the institutionally governed normal situation. Consequently, sector proportions embodied in K and Q_c will not correspond to those implied by the fully adjusted situation; some sectors will be too large while others will be too small; these are structural imbalances related to classical macroeconomics which deals with proportions. Moreover, in the various phases of the cycle *all* sectors will deviate from the sector sizes implied by the system equilibrium, i.e. K and Q_c diverge from K^* and Q^* respectively: the scale of activity occurring in the course of the cycle diverges from the 'equilibrium' scale governed by the institutional system; issues relating to the scale of economic activity pertain to Keynesian macroeconomics.

While K and Q_c can be perceived, K^* and Q^* cannot be directly observed since these institutional third-layer aspects of reality are 'covered' by the behavioural top layers. Trend magnitudes can only be approximately and probably known. These are the outcome of the working mechanism of the socioeconomic system as a whole; considerable analytical and empirical work based upon an understanding of how a specific society works will be required to get probable knowledge of adjusted situations associated with trend variables. In the following we are, therefore, not concerned with explanatory frameworks aimed at explaining how the cycle works in a specific country or region (real-type models defined in chapter 3, pp. 81–9) but with the *principles* governing cyclical movements (ideal-type models).

If Q_c is below Q^* in figure 6 (to the left of Q^* in figure 7), not enough capital has, on the average, been accumulated in the past (and vice versa). However, with Q_c smaller than Q^*, realized profits will exceed desired (target) profits. If this situation persists investment increases because of the income effect of investment, thus causing a further rise of profits. This leads to a cyclical upswing during which actual output Q tends to exceed capacity output Q_c which, in turn, implies that profits and/or prices or degrees of capacity utilization get above their normal levels. If investment goes on rising, the *actual* rate of growth (g) gradually rises above the *trend* growth rate (g^*) which implies that actual output will tend to exceed trend output. (All the movements are reversed if Q_c is above Q^* with investment and profits diminishing.) The meaning of the endogenous mechanism of cyclical movements now begins to emerge: cycles occur because economies are *never* in a long-period equilibrium, that is to say capacity output Q_c never equals trend output Q^*, simply because entrepreneurs do not know what the fully adjusted situation is. Entrepreneurs take investment decisions on the basis of information which they consider to be important (past and present evolution of sales and profits) and expectations about the future. However, the fully adjusted situation is the outcome of the functioning of society (institutions) as a whole. The latter sets restrictions for individual actions, thus determining entrepreneurial investment behaviour in the medium term (equation 24 below). Contrarily, actual magnitudes (gross investment) gradually shape the fully adjusted situation if conditions are not stationary, i.e. with technological and institutional change occurring. Cyclically growing actual variables thus interact with the institutional trend.

Disequilibrium is thus an endogenous factor which underlies the cyclical growth of a capitalist economy (see the following subsection). External or exogenous factors, however, represent outside influences. As emerges from the supermultiplier relation, any deviation of an actual predetermined variable from the corresponding long-period variable is associated with deviations from normal output, employment and profit levels. This reinforces or weakens an already existing cyclical movement: for example, a temporary increase of government expenditures raises effective demand. In the short run, various things may happen. Imports may rise and the foreign balance deteriorate. The deficit may disappear as government expenditures fall back to their original level and the story may be closed then (the only permanent effect will be a reduction of the foreign exchange reserves). The temporary increase in G may also lead to an increase of market prices or to improved degrees of capacity utilization in some sectors of production. In each case, the realized mark-up k will rise in the industries in question. If this persists for some time, entrepreneurs might decide to invest more which implies an increase in the actual rate of growth (g). The latter will result in an additional rise of the realized mark-up k: prices of investment goods go up and/or capacity utilization in investment goods industries improves. An increasing rate of profit, implied by a rising k, may induce entrepreneurs to invest even more. This process of cumulative causation, based upon the investment–profits (or g–r) relationship, thus reinforces (or weakens) an already existing cyclical movement initiated by the endogenous mechanism. The same is true, for example, of exports growing at a rate higher than the trend rate for some time, of non-neutral technical progress leading to a temporary increase of the capital–output ratio or of an innovation linked up with a sudden increase of the drop-out ratio.

The mechanism of the cycle

The double-sided relationship between investment and profits constitutes the heart of classical-Keynesian trade cycle theory. This emerges clearly from the work of Michal Kalecki (1971), who may be considered as the founder of this theory. The investment–profit relationship can, on the basis of the supermultiplier framework, be formulated as follows:

$$I_t = [(g^* + d^*) + q(k_e - k^*)]K_t \qquad (24)$$

(I_t represents gross investment undertaken in period t; k_e is the average realized mark-up over e time periods, starting from $t-e$ (e is a kind of *experience period*; events that have happened during this period influence the decisions taken by entrepreneurs at time period t); q is a reaction parameter which links differences between realized and target profits to actually undertaken gross investment, and K_t represents the capital stock existing in period t). This equation pictures an intricate interaction between (medium-term) aggregate behavioural outcomes (implying possibilities of choice) and the functioning of the system which, in the long run, determines (sets restrictions to) entrepreneurial actions.

Actual investment I_t would fall into line with normal investment (I^* in equation 5) if the (average) realized mark-up k_e had equalled the actually desired mark-up at normal capacity utilization k^* during the time-period $t-e$; this would imply $K_t = K^*$. Such a state of affairs is impossible, however, as it presupposes a perfect knowledge of the fully adjusted situation and its evolution in time by entrepreneurs: economies can never be in 'equilibrium' since individual entrepreneurs do not know the equilibrium outcomes produced by the system. In the real world k_e always differs from k^*; actual investment I_t will deviate from trend investment I^* which implies that the actual growth rate g will not coincide with the trend rate g^* either. From the supermultiplier relation (7) it is evident that, in the short and medium term, $g <> g^*$ ($I <> I^*$) will be linked with $k_e <> k^*$. This is the *income effect* of investment. However, as time goes by, the *capacity effect* of investment starts working out: if $g > g^*$, then the actual capital stock K will gradually tend to exceed its long-period trend level (K^*), which means that productive capacities are getting too large. Q_c gets above Q^* in figures 6 and 7, and the growth rate of trend effective demand (g^*) falls short of the growth rate of productive capacities (g); underutilized capacities will appear and/or prices will fall relative to money wages. The realized mark-up k_e will be gradually depressed below the desired mark-up k^*, which, according to equation (24), initiates a downward movement of all important economic variables. In particular, actual output Q will now fall short of capacity output Q_c.

The principles governing cyclical movements may be represented by a couple of diagrams (figures 6 and 7) of which the first is derived from figure 3 (p. 150), the second from figure 2 (p. 148). In figure 7 aa' represents the long-period macroeconomic demand curve (equation 9) and the horizontal line stands for the long-period supply price level (equation 6). Since capacity output Q_c, rendered possible by past accumulation K, is below trend output Q^*, prices p and/or degrees of capacity utilization are, on the average, above the normal level; given money wages, the realized mark-up k

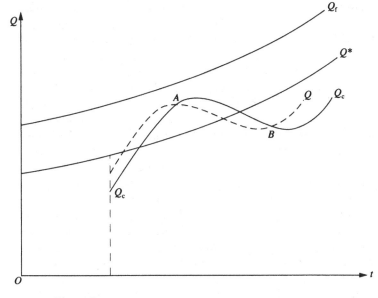

Figure 6.

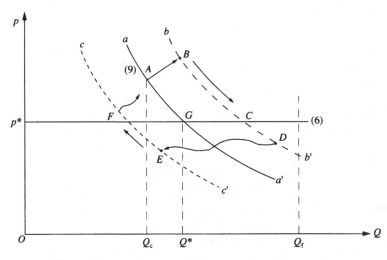

Figure 7.

exceeds the desired one (k^*). As a consequence, the short-period demand curve will be located to the right of the long-period curve aa'. If this situation persists, then, according to equation (24), investment rises above its actual level, resulting in an additional rightward shift of the *short-period* demand curve, which thus moves further away from the *long-period* curve aa'. The final position of the short-period demand curve, determined by the inflation barrier for instance, might be bb'. Given productive capacity Q_c, rising prices and higher degrees of capacity utilization have resulted in a movement of prices and quantities from A to B in figure 7. Hence the *income effect* of investment results in a *shift* of the macroeconomic demand curve.

If the volume of investment implied in the demand curve bb' is maintained, actual investment I_t will exceed 'trend' investment I^* (or $g > g^*$). Productive capacities (K) expand rapidly. As time goes by, the capacity effect will work out. Capacity output Q_c will rise above trend output Q^* which grows at a rate g^*. In terms of figure 7, the capacity effect shows up in a movement *along* the demand curve bb', from B to C, and eventually to D. In figure 6, Q_c would move from a position below Q^* to a position above Q^* as time goes by.

With productive capacities expanding at a rate g and with normal effective demand increasing at g^*, a point will be reached where realized prices fall below normal ones (and/or capacity utilization is less than normal) as aggregate supply outpaces aggregate demand. This will happen beyond point C in figure 7 or beyond point A in figure 6. Given money wages, realized profits will fall below desired ones, entailing a reduction in investment and hence a leftward shift of the macroeconomic demand curve. A complicated dynamic movement of prices and quantities may be set into motion (DE in figure 7). Investment may get stabilized at some low level implying that now the actual rate of growth (g) is smaller than the trend growth rate g^*. Capacity output Q_c will go on diminishing: in figure 7, prices and quantities move from E to F and, in figure 6, quantities from A to B. Capacity output Q_c will now gradually fall below trend output Q^* which implies that realized profits rise above desired levels. Given the latter, the economy will pick up at some point (F in figure 7; B in figure 6) and an upward movement will get started. The description of the pure theory of the business cycle, i.e. the principles underlying cyclical movements, is now complete. In the real world, the 'pure' cyclical movement sketched here is modified in many ways by outside influences, deviations of government expenditures or exports from their respective trend levels, for example. Things may be complicated further by shifts in the system equilibrium (G in figure 7) due to institutional and technological change associated with the cyclical-cum-growth process; in figure 6 this would be reflected in an upward or downward shift of the Q^* trend line; even without shifts in the trend, the system equilibrium changes continuously because the autonomous trend variables, $G^* + X^*$, grow at the trend rate g^*.

The investment equation (24) relates to entrepreneurial investment behaviour, and the supermultiplier equation (7) to the functioning of the system. The two can be combined to yield a theory of the business cycle along Kaleckian (Robinsonian) lines (figures 6 and 7). It appears that the *cyclical movement* is brought about by the *interaction* between the *income effect* of investment (I_t is positively linked with k_e) and the *capacity effect* of investment (the negative link between K, Q_c and N on the one hand and k_e on the other). In the cyclical process, the short- and medium-term income effect of investment is a cause of *instability* while the long-run capacity effect turns out to be a *stabilizing factor* which attracts realized outputs towards the trend level. The crucial point is that the analysis of fluctuations-cum-growth has been carried out with respect to objectively given institutionally governed factors, i.e. Q^*, K^*, k^* and p^*. This confirms the decisive importance of long-period analysis since it matters around which normal level an economy fluctuates.

It should be possible to integrate large parts of Keynes's behavioural theory of investment, interest and money, set forth in book IV of the *General Theory*, into the theory of the business cycle outlined above, the conceptual starting points being provided by the parameters q and e in the investment equation (24). The parameter q is governed by the estimated 'profitability of capital' (depending on the expected impact of the income effect of investment and of the capacity effect of investment upon profit rates) and by the rate of interest; the length of the experience period e reflects other aspects of investment behaviour: a small e means that entrepreneurs are impatient and shortsighted, and vice versa. If, then, q is large and e small, entrepreneurs will react quickly and massively to deviations between realized and desired profits, which will lead to wide deviations of investment, capital stock, output and employment from their respective normal levels, and vice versa. From past experience, summarized by k_e in equation (24), entrepreneurs know that higher levels of investment raise profits in the short and medium terms (the income effect of investment). However, entrepreneurs might also know from past experience that larger volumes of investment are negatively linked with profits (k_e) if the (long-run) capacity effect is taken account of. Given this, it is of decisive importance how entrepreneurial expectations are formed. If entrepreneurs are shortsighted the income effect of investment dominates: investment is increased rapidly if profits rise; this results in a cumulative process in which investments and profits drive each other up mutually. This process may be reinforced by speculative activity: rising share prices attract new financial capital, the volume of which may be augmented by bank credits. Rising share prices imply cheap finance which, in turn, may positively influence investment. However, if entrepreneurs are cautious and, when forming expectations about the future, take account of the capacity effect of investment, then q will be relatively small and e large.

The rate of interest may, eventually, influence entrepreneurial investment behaviour in the way envisaged by Keynes, but the role played by the interest rate is likely to be negligible. Entrepreneurial investment behaviour is presumably influenced heavily by differences between realized and target profits, whereby the latter partly depend upon normal interest rates. However, it goes without saying that the banking system plays an essential role; banks finance part of the investment outlays, mainly in a cyclical upswing, and eventually help firms to overcome short-run liquidity problems in times of depression.

The banking system not only contributes to shaping the cycle; it is also influenced by the interaction between the trend and the cycle set forth above. Banks enter the picture because entrepreneurs incur debts to finance part of the investment outlays. In the cyclical upswing the realized growth rates of real capital (investment), output and employment exceed the corresponding trend variables. In the long run, however, trend effective demand governs economic activity; moreover, long-period or normal investment *must* be financed by trend saving since each debt incurred in the present has to be repaid by future incomes. Now, the fact that investment has exceeded its trend level in the cyclical upswing inevitably means that future (trend) incomes will not be sufficient to allow for full repayment of the debts incurred: profits decline in the downswing and are, therefore, not sufficient to finance the service of the debt incurred in the upswing and in the prosperity phase. The business downswing thus results in bad debts and difficulties for the financial sector: this broadly corresponds to Hyman Minsky's (1975) vision of things. Once again the crucial importance of the trend related to the functioning of the socioeconomic system emerges.

The impression cannot be avoided that before the Second World War the amplitude of cycles was rather large which means entrepreneurs were heavily reliant on the income effect of investment when forming expectations about the future. Since the early fifties, however, cyclical movements have been less violent; perhaps, producers have taken increasing account of the capacity effect of investment when taking investment decisions. This might imply that the significantly worse economic situation in the industrialized countries since the early seventies and the present crisis are, in the main, both due to a downward shift in trends and not exclusively to medium-term business downswings. The persistence of high and steadily increasing unemployment levels is an important indicator of lower trend employment volumes.

Two additional remarks related to the amplitude of cycles remain to be made. The first concerns the *inflation barrier*, the second the problem of complete instability of an economic system. The concept of the inflation barrier (Joan Robinson) implies that, given money wages, prices and profits increase together with investment in cyclical upswings which means that real wages decrease. In figure 7 this is reflected in a rightward shift of the short-term demand curve *bb'*. Since real wages cannot fall below a certain minimum level, an upper limit will be fixed for the cyclical upswing in figure 6 to which would correspond a maximum rightward shift of the short-term demand curve *bb'* in figure 7. This is the inflation barrier. If the inflation barrier does not become effective, even at full employment (Q_f in figure 6) and if entrepreneurial investment behaviour is governed by the income effect of investment (q is large in equation 24), an economic system may become completely unstable. In the business upswing the macroeconomic demand curve *bb'* will shift to the right until full employment is reached. The volume of investment will now have to adjust to the investment level corresponding to the natural rate of growth *n*, the maximum growth rate attainable at full employment. This results in a leftward shift of the macro-economic demand curve *bb'* since, during the upswing, the actual rate of growth exceeds, as a rule, both the trend and the natural growth rate: investment and profits will decline, thus inducing further leftward shifts of *bb'*. The utmost leftward position (the floor) will be reached when gross investment is zero, with a short-period demand curve lying somewhere to the left of *cc'* in figure 7. Hence in a completely unstable economic system the important economic variables (output, employment, investment) fluctuate between the full employment ceiling and the floor implying zero gross investment (Hicks 1950). If an economic system fluctuated between ceiling and floor, the trend as defined by the supermultiplier relation (7) would largely become meaningless and the cycle would completely dominate the picture. This may happen in exceptional situations, if profound structural changes on the economic, social or political level occur or in times of revolution. On empirical grounds it is, however, implausible that the cycle completely dominates the trend evolution of output and employment in normal circumstances. The view that the economic system is relatively stable in a situation with heavy unemployment is shared by a great number of economists, including Keynes (see Milgate 1982).

This is the place to dispel a neoclassical misinterpretation of the double-sided relationship between investment and profits. According to this relationship prices and profits increase relative to money wages in the cyclical upswing and vice versa. Moreover, investment and employment rise in the upswing and decline or grow more slowly in the downswing. Lower real wages are thus associated with higher employment levels and vice versa.

Neoclassical economists now argue that unemployment occurs *because* real wages are too high, and vice versa (see, for example, Krelle 1992, fig. 1, p. 76); this argument is in fact frequently advanced to explain the crises of the thirties. The classical-Keynesian economist has no difficulties in explaining that high real wages cannot be the cause of high unemployment: in the downswing prices and profits are low relative to money wages because of a breakdown of investment activity which, on account of the investment multiplier, also means that short- and medium-term effective demand and employment diminish. In order to establish his argument the neoclassical economist would have to show that in a downswing, with real wages increasing and rates of profit declining, capital is substituted for labour and that, as a result, the capital–output ratio (K/Q_c) increases, which is far from certain. Hence, in the medium term, the share of wages in income and output (and employment) move in opposite directions according to classical-Keynesian (Kaleckian-Robinsonian) cycle theory; in the long run, however, an increasing wage share ($1/k^*$) is, in principle, positively associated with normal employment; this directly follows from the supermultiplier relation. In this case, behavioural and system outcomes are diametrically opposed; this is true in many other instances too, Keynes's paradox of thrift being a prominent example.

A final remark relates to the problem of 'pricing in the business cycle'. In the course of the cycle (or if structural adjustments occur), present values of investment goods calculated on the basis of expected future earnings and of the rate of interest (as governed by monetary factors) differ from the long-period normal prices of investment goods, which are made up of the costs of production and of desired profits. It is not likely, however, that present values play an essential role in the pricing of investment goods in the course of the cycle. Estimated normal prices (p_c) will dominate the picture; this holds even more so for consumption goods. Adjustments to the market conditions prevailing in a certain phase of the cycle occur through stock variations, changing degrees of capacity utilization and flexible terms of delivery. All this is tantamount to saying that production is of a long-period nature, implying that the prices of production (normal prices) play an essential role in the long run too, and thus relegating the vagaries of the market to secondary importance. This is not to deny that market prices are important: they represent an information system (in Hayek's sense) if seen in relation to normal prices. If the former tend to exceed the latter, entrepreneurs will invest more, and vice versa. Moreover, the prices of agricultural products and of raw materials may be largely governed by supply and demand. Finally, market prices may become temporarily important for manufactured goods if 'clearance sales' are being organized, for example.

Structural adjustments

In the two-way relationship between investment and profits the profit–investment side is behavioural: entrepreneurial investment behaviour depends on realized profits. The investment–profit side, however, expresses the functioning of the system: the investment sector and the other sectors of an economy must stand in a definite relationship to each other, which represents a piece of classical macroeconomics dealing with proportions. Consequently, Robinsonian theory also deals with structural changes taking place during cyclical movements. These relate to the sectoral set-up of capacity output Q_c, the proportions existing between the consumption and the investment goods sectors being the most important feature of this set-up. A very simple example may illustrate what this means in principle. If there are, hypothetically, only two sectors in an economy, a consumption and an investment goods sector, and if, in addition, wages are entirely consumed and profits wholly saved, then

$$P_C = W_I \tag{25}$$

is an equilibrium condition which guarantees that both sectors are in the appropriate proportions (P_C=profits accruing in the consumption goods sector, W_I=wages paid in the investment goods sector). This condition also tells us how a certain labour force N is distributed between the consumption and the investment goods sectors, i.e. determines the proportion N_C/N_I, given N. Equation (25) and the more general Cambridge equation are variants of the general condition regulating sector proportions at given employment levels, i.e. equation (13) above.

A change in the volume of investment and, therefore, in the rate of growth implies structural changes: in a cyclical upswing, the actual rate of growth g will be higher than the long-run trend growth rate g^* which appears in the supermultiplier relation (7). The consumption sector will have to be relatively smaller and the investment goods sector relatively larger than the long-period 'equilibrium' sector sizes, i.e. the fully adjusted situation, implied in the supermultiplier. The same is true of the proportion N_C/N_I. The contrary holds in a cyclical downswing.

An important point linked with the size of the investment sector and prices and profits in this sector should be noted here: once the cycle is set into motion through the endogenous and exogenous mechanisms, it is *investment* which is the dynamic element which determines the shape of a specific cyclical movement (see equation 20, particularly the role played by q). This is possible because the volume of investment and thus the size of the investment sector are *undetermined* in the behavioural system governing the actual capital stock and may thus vary within certain boundaries:

the floor is set by the zero gross investment case, the ceiling by the inflation barrier or the full-employment constraint. Similarly, given money wages, actual profits and price levels in the investment goods sector are also undetermined, thus giving rise to deviations from normal prices and profits. This fundamental lack of determination of investment volumes, profits and prices in behavioural-cum-system outcomes emerges from Keynes's Fundamental Equations (Keynes 1971b, vol. I, chapter 10, pp. 120–35, especially pp. 127–31). The same is true of equation (25) which is closely linked with the Fundamental Equations and Marx's Schemes of Circulation (Marx 1973/74a [1867–94], vol. II, chapters 20–1).

The determination of the normal scale of economic activity ($N=N_C^*+N_I^*$) and of the associated normal proportions (the fully adjusted situation in Pasinetti 1981) goes on in the spheres of *production* and *long-period distribution* and is the outcome of the functioning of the whole socioeconomic system. Medium-term (Robinsonian) theory is about the evolution of actual employment N and the variation of the proportion N_C/N_I during the business cycle. Subsequently, deviations of $N=N_C+N_I$ from $N^*=N_C^*+N_I^*$ may be explained. In the different phases of the cycle, capacity output Q_c is not fully adjusted, and the corresponding sector proportions, price and profit levels are determined within the sphere of *circulation*. Here, the aggregate of individual investment decisions is co-ordinated by the above-mentioned two-sector model. Given this, cyclical movements arise because of the tension (or, in Marx's terms, the contradiction) existing between the aggregate of individual investment decisions, resulting in a certain actual capital stock K in each time-period, and the fully adjusted situation governed by the socioeconomic structure.

This leads to another type of medium-term structural adjustment which is linked with competition in the classical sense: the attempts of entrepreneurs to narrow the gap between realized profits and mark-ups and target profits and mark-ups, and between market prices and normal prices, imply adjustments of actual sector sizes to those implied by the fully adjusted situation. To determine the latter, long-period demand factors and normal prices concur.

Cyclical growth and the institutional trend

The complementarity between the phenomena emerges from two issues associated with both Kaleckian cycle-cum-growth and classical-Keynesian trend theory: the first problem is related to the theory of value and distribution, the second to the mutual relationship existing between trend and cycle.

Changes in the size of the investment sector relative to the other sectors in the course of the trade cycle lead to a specific medium-term theory of distribution. With saving propensities given, realized profits are determined by the volume of investment *actually* undertaken (Kaldor 1955/56): entrepreneurial investment decisions, i.e. aggregate behaviour, govern profits across the system, that is the necessary proportions that must exist between the investment and the consumption goods sectors; since the scale of activity is given in each short period, medium-term distribution pertains to classical macroeconomics. This does not contradict the view that, in the long run, distribution, i.e. the hierarchy of target profit rates, and, in fact, all the trend or normal variables appearing in the supermultiplier, including trend investment, are governed by more fundamental and more stable institutional forces linked up with *production*, which reflects the determining influence upon 'economic variables' of the socioeconomic system as a whole.

The medium-term theory of distribution along Kaldorian and Kaleckian lines complements the long-period theory of distribution in two ways: first, the former shows how *realized* profit shares, mark-ups and profit rates are determined by investment volumes actually undertaken – or by realized growth rates; second, deviations of realized mark-ups from the long-period (target) mark-ups which occur during the business cycle are indicated. These deviations occur partly within *production* (the size, the composition and the utilization of the actual capital stock K does not coincide with the fully adjusted one, i.e. K^*) and partly within the sphere of *circulation*: in a business upswing the realized mark-up k is likely to exceed the normal long-run mark-up k^*, because capacity utilization is, given money wages and long-run normal prices, more than normal; or, if capacity utilization remains normal and money wages are given, prices and mark-ups must exceed their long-run normal levels in order to render possible the business upswing, and vice versa in a downswing.

Hence, the link between the fully adjusted situation (the outcome of the system) and actually existing magnitudes, e.g. K, Q_c, p_c, which result from entrepreneurial behaviour, is established by profit rates and mark-ups: entrepreneurs know *both* realized and target profit rates and mark-ups and behave in a specific way in the face of divergences between k and k^*. These variables play a role analogous to that of the natural and market wage in Ricardo's system.

With the links between classical-Keynesian medium-term and long-period theory broadly clarified, there is no need to go further here. There exists a rich medium-term classical-Keynesian theory of output and employment, of value and distribution and of money. The most convenient historical starting point for a classical-Keynesian theory of cyclical growth is given by the Marxian schemes of reproduction (Marx 1973/74a, [1867–94], vol. II, chapters 20 and 21). A next important stage is the Fundamental Equations in Keynes's *Treatise on Money*. Kalecki (1971),

Robinson (1962a, 1965), Kaldor (1955/56) and Kregel (1975) represent modern partial or comprehensive treatments of medium-term classical-Keynesian business cycle analysis.

Some post Keynesian economists argue that, once a cycle theory is developed, there is no need for a separate theory of the trend. This is illustrated by a statement of Kalecki quoted earlier: 'the long-run trend is but a slowly changing component of a chain of short-period situations; it has no independent entity . . .' (Kalecki 1971, p. 165). This would be true if the trend were a statistical notion only, to be calculated *ex post* for actual or capacity output, i.e. the aggregate outcome of past individual investment decisions. But Kalecki's statement is not valid if trend or normal output is governed by an alternative set of forces, i.e. the socioeconomic system: technology and institutions, representing the persistent or slowly changing long-term forces mainly to be found within the process of production. In this view, trend output represents an invisible and imperfectly known system equilibrium which defines *reference* output levels that may attract actual output levels. Garegnani's crucial remark on the problem of the trend should be recalled here: 'most importantly, it remains to be shown that the "natural position" ["normal" would be more appropriate] around which the economy will gravitate ["from which the economy will deviate" (H.B.)] will not be that of full employment as in orthodox theory' (Garegnani 1983, p. 78). The classical-Keynesian supermultiplier relation is a possible long-period theory of output and employment that may complement medium-term Robinsonian (Kaleckian) cycle-cum-growth theory.

This leads to the second problem, i.e. the possible interactions that go on between trend and cycle. The *way* in which the actually existing capital stock K, to which corresponds a certain capacity output Q_c, has been accumulated in the course of *past* cyclical growth movements exercises important influences upon *present* trend output. For example, with capital accumulation going on, technological and organizational learning processes take place and are embodied in *actual* know-how. The latter governs to an important extent the drop-out ratio d^* and the trend rate of growth g^* that are contained in the supermultiplier relation; both parameters represent the main determinants of trend investment (equation 5). The influence of the actually existing capital *stock* upon the trend (the system equilibrium associated with a fully adjusted situation, not the statistical trend!) implies that *present* institutions and technology result from *past* individual actions. The influence of actual *flows*, e.g. gross investment, on the fully adjusted situations is negligible, however: actual gross investment modifies only marginally the actual trend capital *stock*. On the other hand, the institutions governing the trend (the system) determine entrepreneurial accumulation behaviour in an important way: the amplitude of the cycle will be rather small if entrepreneurs take a long-run view of events and, consequently, rely heavily on the capacity effect of investment, as embodied in the trend, rather than on the (short-run) income effect when forming expectations about the future and taking investment decisions. Or, the system, through the supermultiplier mechanism, governs the amount of permanent involuntary unemployment, which, in turn, determines the behaviour of *all* workers. Hence the institutional trend (the system) and cyclical growth (resulting from aggregate behaviour) interact in complex ways.

Since the publication of Schumpeter's (1939) *Business Cycles*, it is a convention to distinguish between long waves (Kondratiev cycles), medium waves (Juglar cycles) and short waves (Kitchin cycles). The macroeconomic framework suggested in the present part may be linked up with this general theory of capitalist business cycles. In the supermultiplier relation (a theory of the institutional trend) the normal growth rate may vary, owing to slow changes in one or several parameters or independent variables. The latter occur because of institutional changes. These processes could give rise to a long-term cyclical movement: for example, in a Kondratiev prosperity phase and in the subsequent downswing, innovative activity of firms may diminish due to a slackening of competition. The replacement coefficient (d^*) in equation (7) may decline, which, in turn, results in a lower trend growth rate. Once the Kondratiev depression is reached, innovational activity may increase since the struggle for survival intensifies. This may, in turn, initiate a Kondratiev upswing where innovations are likely to remain on a high level. The Kondratiev cycle may also be shaped by long-period changes in the relationship between the industrial and the financial sectors: 'Depressions arise, Keynes wrote in his *Treatise on Money* (1931) when money is shifted from the "industrial circulation" into "financial circulation"' (Skidelsky 1992, p. xxiv). In the prosperity phase financial activities are enhanced at the expense of production and innovation; distribution is likely to get more unequal which, according to the supermultiplier theory, results in higher unemployment levels that characterize the long-period downswing. The Kondratiev depression witnesses partial breakdowns in the financial sector, distribution improves and production gets more important which initiates the long-period upswing. To be sure, things are much more complicated as is shown by empirical work that has been done and is at present being done in this field (see, for instance, Tylecote 1992); specifically, deep crises, like the depression of the 1930s, might be explained by the breakdown of long-period structural trends pictured by the supermultiplier relation. In any case the supermultiplier framework might provide the theoretical underpinning for long-period – Kondratiev – cycle theory.

There is not much to say on medium- and short-term cycle theory here: based upon the pioneering work by Kalecki, the Robinsonians have worked out a theory of medium-term waves which relies upon the invest-ment–profits relationship which is, in turn, based upon the interaction between the income effect and the capacity effect of investment (pp. 207–75). This strand of thought might underpin the empirical (real-type) work done on the Juglar waves. Keynesian Fundamentalists have done important theoretical work in the field of short-run cyclical movements linked with changes in price levels, degrees of capacity utilization and inventories (pp. 229–35); studies of Kitchin waves in specific circumstances would represent the corresponding real-type models.

Some remarks on uncertainty and money

Determinism and absence of uncertainty in institutional long-period theory

The long-period supermultiplier analysis pictures part of the deterministic influence of the socioeconomic system upon aggregate behaviour. Institu-tions and technology govern long-period effective demand, which in turn determines trend or normal output and employment and, through the capacity effect of investment, the normal or trend level of investment. This is the long-period content of the principle of effective demand, which is a social law because the scale of economic activity is governed by the entire institutional system. The latter governs the behaviour of workers and entrepreneurs in various respects. For instance, only a limited number of workers and employees will be able to find jobs in the long run while others may remain permanently unemployed. Or, in the circular and social process of production determinism is exemplified by the technological relations embodied in the actually existing capital stock that regulate commodity flows between industries and sectors; on the level of intermediate products, there are interindustry flows of goods that have to go on if production is to take place at all; similarly, on the level of final goods, there are necessary flows of goods going on between the consumption and the investment sectors: on the one hand, consumption goods move from the former to the latter in order to maintain the workforce present here; on the other hand, investment goods must flow to the consumption goods sector in order to replace worn-out capital goods and eventually to render possible an expan-sion of production through net investments.

Technology and institutions, i.e. the technological and social structure or the system, enable individuals to act, i.e. to pursue social and individual aims. But the social structure also sets restrictions on *all* economic agents, though in different ways. For example, well-established firms may be quite unaffected by diminishing effective demand while, simultaneously, weaker firms may be driven out of the market. In a way institutions form a kind of labyrinth within which individuals move around when acting, i.e. when making and implementing decisions; each economic event, an investment decision for instance, is therefore governed by objective factors, institutions and technology, *and* by subjective elements, e.g. the evaluation of past events, the analysis of a given situation and expectations about the future.

Institutions and technology are the heritage of the past; as such they exist independently of the *present* will of individuals and collectives and partly govern their *current* behaviour through the system. Since the influence of the system on behaviour is persistent, the system outcomes will dominate behavioural outcomes in the long run. This emerges from the analysis of business cycles (pp. 204–20): trend or normal output continuously attracts capacity output levels, if the income effect of investment does not dominate entirely entrepreneurial behaviour.

Given the strong deterministic influence of the social system, uncertainty will play a minor role in the areas of production and of long-period employment and output determination if institutions are expected to remain stable. In this context, the strong link between institutions and the concepts of long-period expectations and of the state of confidence emerges:

[T]he facts of the existing situation [institutions] enter, in a sense disproportionately, into the formation of our long-term expectations; our usual practice being to take the existing situation and to project it into the future, modified only to the extent that we have more or less definite reasons for expecting a change. The state of long-term expectation, upon which our decisions are based, does not solely depend, therefore, on the most probable forecast we can make. It also depends on the *confidence* with which we make this forecast (Keynes 1973a, p. 148).

The state of confidence with respect to the continuity of institutions will be very strong if these are functioning normally. As a rule, there is no reason to suppose that institutions should cease to function suddenly or that institutional evolution should change its direction abruptly. This perhaps partly explains why major institutional changes, e.g. the breakdown of the formerly socialist countries, come as a surprise. Nobody could have predicted this breakdown even one year before the event took place.

The institutionally determined variables are complex macroeconomic magnitudes, e.g. normal output, or single variables determined by complex socioeconomic structures: for example, each normal price depends on the structure of production and upon the various institutions governing the normal or target profit rates. Two points should be noted here. First, the institutionally determined complex and single variables represent a particular form of actually existing variables which shows up in the fully adjusted situation (chapter 3, pp. 81–9). Only this particular aspect of the real world is governed by persistent objective factors and is, as such, devoid of uncertainty. Actually existing variables resulting from individual decisions deviate from trends and are linked with uncertainty. Second, in a monetary produc- tion economy, effective demand is perhaps the most important institutional restriction which economic agents are facing. This social law determines overall economic activity (pp. 142–204 above). All the predetermined vari- ables on the right-hand side of the supermultiplier relation (7) – the long- period law of effective demand – are institutionally determined: for example, the size, the structure and the evolution of trend government expenditures (G^*) are legally fixed. The making of the corresponding laws rests on complex socioeconomic and political processes, many of which are institu- tionalized. Once these legal prescriptions become effective, there is nothing uncertain about normal government expenditure which thus becomes an objective factor. The latter is also true of trend exports which depend upon an interrelated set of institutions: for example, the quality of the educational system, the technical dynamism of a society, reflected in the rate of growth of labour productivity and in the ability to introduce new products, and the degree of aggressiveness of export firms on international markets. These institutional factors are just there and there is nothing uncertain about them. Uncertainty is also absent in other institutionally determined parameters entering the supermultiplier relation: leakages, the normal mark-up and thus the normal wage and profit share, the trend rate of growth of long-period effective demand, i.e. of the autonomous trend components of demand, and the normal drop-out ratio. Similarly, the independent variables governing normal prices (trend labour productivity and the normal mark-up) are institutionally determined and devoid of uncertainty.

Uncertainty and money in the long, medium and short term

Uncertainty in the short and medium terms is associated with the behav- iour – actions and reactions – of individuals and collectives within a *given* institutional framework. The aggregate of individual behaviour gives rise to behavioural outcomes (market outcomes or outcomes of election cam- paigns) which are also uncertain. Long-period uncertainty is attached to institutional change. Since uncertainty is ever present, money is perma- nently held as a part of wealth and for speculative purposes.

In the *long run*, uncertainty becomes important if the state of confidence with respect to the continuity of the objective institutional factors is very weak. This will normally occur in times of social and political unrest: per- sistently high levels of involuntary unemployment may lead to growing protectionism which may, in turn, cause a partial breakdown of the international trade system, as happened in the 1930s; economic activity may be negatively affected everywhere and unemployment will rise further. Or, high trend unemployment may lead to a deterioration of the social climate, poverty may increase and income distribution worsen. Society may partly disintegrate and crime may increase. At the end there may be heavy social unrest. Finally, following Minsky's (1982) argument, financial institutions may be threatened by heavy indebtedness of some individuals, collectives and countries: normal incomes are not sufficient to repay the debts incurred; bad debts come into existence; indebtedness (on a more and more short-term basis) continuously increases, resulting eventually in a partial collapse of the financial institutions. This example shows that, while institutions are, as a rule, associated with stability, some institutions are unstable if they are not handled appropriately: if the rate of growth of debts incurred exceeds the trend rate of growth of an economy, indebtedness gets unmanageable in the long run and breakdowns of financial institutions may occur (Bortis 1979, chapter II). Thus, uncertainty becomes very important with respect to long-period factors if, for some reason, one or several institutions cease to function normally or cease to function at all. This affects other institutions and leads to changes in direction or even to the breakdown of long-run trends. The argument set out above (pp. 142–204) suggests that in such a situation there is no upper limit to involuntary unemployment.

There is also uncertainty in the long run regarding permanent changes in the normal level of the autonomous components of effective demand and of the long-period parameter values contained in the supermultiplier. To give some examples: the government may plan to denationalize the health service. This is likely to result in a permanent reduction of normal government expenditures but there may be considerable uncertainty about the precise amount of the change and its repercussions, for example on normal output, for a long period of time. Or, normal exports may permanently decline due to protectionist measures taken abroad. Again, exporters will be uncertain about the effects of the measures taken but, after some time, a new trend may get established. Finally, an educational reform may result in a permanent increase of labour productivity. However, there may be uncertainty about the effects of the reform so long as these have not completely worked themselves out.

To generalize, we may say that part of long-period uncertainty is related to the way in which existing institutions work or the effects of institutional change. Since the functioning and the evolution of a socioeconomic system is extremely complex, knowledge about these phenomena will ever be highly imperfect. Keynes's probable knowledge (Keynes 1971c) enters the picture here (chapter 2, pp. 57–75).

On the behavioural level, there is permanent uncertainty in the long run regarding the structure of the composite trend variables. Most importantly, uncertainty is about the firms which are producing trend output: which firms will drop out after some period of time? Which firms will survive in the long run? How will market shares develop in the long run? Closely linked to this question is the way in which technical progress is introduced. It is likely that technically dynamic firms will succeed in enlarging their market shares and vice versa. On all this, there is considerable long-period uncertainty. Since technical change is uneven, there is uncertainty about the evolution of normal prices in many areas of production. Structural change is bound to lead to permanent uncertainty for individual economic agents, although the global magnitudes of the supermultiplier relation may be quite stable or may change regularly: with a regularly evolving trend volume of employment determined by the supermultiplier mechanism the question as to whom is going to be employed or structurally or involuntarily unemployed is linked with permanent uncertainty for *each* individual acting within a given institutional set-up. Similarly, *given* the volume and the structure of trend output and long-run Engel curves, no firm, even if well established, can be certain about its still being in the market in ten years' time. Finally, the *permanent* presence of uncertainty induces individuals to hold part of wealth in the form of money with far-reaching consequences on the level of economic activity (pp. 154–90 above).

In the *medium term*, there is uncertainty as to the amplitude of the business cycle. The size of the adjustment parameter q (equation 24) plays a crucial role here: if entrepreneurs rely heavily on the income effect of investment, q largely depends upon (subjective) psychological factors, i.e. optimism or pessimism. A large q, implying very optimistic entrepreneurs in the upswing and vice versa, will lead to extreme cycles: behavioural and system outcomes will diverge widely (figures 6 and 7 above). There will be considerable uncertainty about who will be additionally employed in a business cycle upswing and about who will lose his job in a downswing.

In a monetary production economy the amplitude of the cycles is crucially dependent upon the financial sector: part of investment required in the upswing is financed by borrowing. If banks provide too much finance, cycles may get extreme. In the cyclical downswing the financial sector may get into difficulties since incomes may no longer be sufficient to repay debts. Banks may now get over-cautious and restrict lending to enterprises, which will enhance the downswing since bankruptcies then increase.

In the medium term various structural adjustments occur. In the first place, the structure of the economy has to adjust to the growth rate corresponding to the prevailing cyclical situation: in the upswing the realized rate of growth (g) will exceed the trend growth rate (g^*) and vice versa;

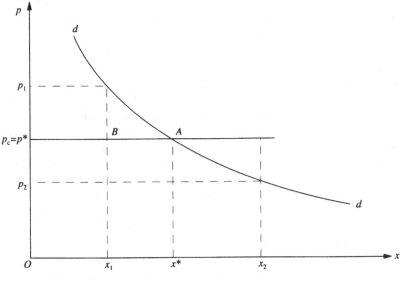

Figure 8.

during the upswing, the output of the investment goods sector tends to be larger than the production of consumption goods, and vice versa in the downturn (equation 25). Moreover, structural adjustments take place in the medium term because realized profits deviate from target rates in the various sectors of an economy: realized mark-ups k differ from desired ones, k^*, or medium-term normal prices do not coincide with estimated long-period normal prices. Sectors with $k>k^*$ will expand, those with $k<k^*$ will shrink: capacities tend to adjust to long-run effective demand at the sectoral level. There is thus a continuing tendency for actually existing capacity output to move towards a fully adjusted situation. This is illustrated in figure 8. Through the supermultiplier mechanism the institutional system determines at any moment of time a long-period equilibrium output, Q^* in figure 2, which is associated with a fully adjusted situation; at the sectoral level this implies that there is in each sector of production a normal capacity output x^* and a normal price p^* (figure 8).

The long-period aspect of reality is, however, a point of reference only, from which various deviations occur at any moment of time. For example, past investment decisions of entrepreneurs result in (socially) inappropriate normal capacities in the present: capacity output brought about by past accumulation does not correspond to a fully adjusted situation. In some sectors of production, normal capacities are below those corresponding to a fully adjusted situation (x_1 in figure 8) and vice versa (x_2 in figure 8). In the former sectors, market prices and realized mark-ups will exceed their corresponding normal levels, or capacity utilization will be more than normal if firms stick to normal prices; the contrary will hold in the latter sectors. Such a situation will produce a medium-term tendency towards the long-period fully adjusted situation.

Structural adjustments raise the question as to which enterprises will produce a given output determined by effective demand. This implies a high degree of uncertainty for many entrepreneurs and workers, as emerges from the situation depicted in figure 8. The long-period equilibrium output (implied by the fully adjusted situation) in a certain sector is x^*. This leaves room for, say, n enterprises each of which could produce an output of x^*/n at the lowest possible costs, i.e. using the best technique of production. Suppose now that there are $n+m$ enterprises in the sector considered and that capacity output equals x_2 for example; this implies that market prices are below long-period normal prices and/or capacity utilization is below the standard level. In the process of structural adjustment m enterprises tend be squeezed out of the market. If all the $n+m$ producers are of approximately equal strength, it will be highly uncertain as to which of them will go bankrupt. (The situation would be quite different if there were some well-established enterprises, having accumulated considerable financial reserves in the past, and which would be in a position to 'knock out' financially weaker firms by selling their output at exceptionally low prices for some time, thus incurring losses.) Hence, given the long-period normal output and the corresponding structure of the output governed by trend sectoral demand, there is a high degree of *subjective* uncertainty as to *who* is going to produce the given output. Uncertainty increases, if fully adjusted sector sizes change in the course of time owing to variations in sectoral demand based on Engel's law.

In the context of structural changes uncertainty also comes into play because of the simple fact that production takes time. While production takes place, there are changes in demand and in technology going on. The expectations of some entrepreneurs will be disappointed. Others will find their expectations overfulfilled. On the macroeconomic level this type of subjective uncertainty relates to the question as to who is going to be unemployed temporarily if rapid structural change is going on in an economy.

In a monetary production economy the structural changes taking place in the medium term are crucially shaped by the financial sector: banks decide to a considerable extent which firms get finance and which do not. For the individual entrepreneur this is an additional source of uncertainty.

Finally, uncertainty may enter the picture in the *short run* through temporary objective and subjective factors which act simultaneously with the objective and subjective medium- and long-term forces mentioned before.

The simultaneity of the various forces is implied in the broad ordering of reality around the time axis (scheme 3, p. 106). More fundamental lower-layer forces act together with upper-layer forces at the same moment of time.

Some examples may illustrate what is meant by temporary objective and subjective factors. For instance, it is well known that, in some economies, rapidly growing exports and favourable terms of trade greatly contributed to securing high levels of output and employment. Switzerland is a case in point. The persistent export strength of the Swiss economy during the last forty years rests on objective (permanent) factors which are not to be analysed here. The state of confidence in Swiss export strength remaining intact was very strong, and uncertainty about this fact was almost entirely absent. However, in 1978, a temporary objective factor which was unforeseeable and thus highly uncertain threatened this happy state of affairs. The value of the dollar on foreign exchange markets declined rapidly. Various dollar-holders wanted to get rid of US money and massively bought Swiss francs. Within a few weeks the value of the Swiss franc had increased sharply with respect to other currencies. The whole of the Swiss export industry seemed threatened by this unforeseeable short-run event. Export orders started to decline. However, the government and the Swiss National Bank stepped in promptly. The 'quantity of money' was permitted to increase quickly (to buy dollars) and, most importantly, a negative interest rate of 40 per cent p.a. was levied on incoming foreign capital exceeding a certain amount. Within a few weeks, the Swiss franc had returned to its (estimated) normal level, and owing to their permanent ability to export, Swiss entrepreneurs continued to enjoy steadily rising export volumes, at least until recently.

This example illustrates how objective long-term factors devoid of uncertainty and a highly uncertain objective short-term factor act simultaneously. Other uncertain objective short-term factors are related to the behaviour of consumers and to the unexpected changes in the techniques of production. A temporary change in the behaviour of consumers will be favourable to some entrepreneurs and damaging to others. Even in times of prosperity, there are enterprises experiencing difficulties in selling their output because consumers' behaviour has changed or has been anticipated wrongly. Similarly, in a boom period, an innovation introduced quickly by large firms may threaten the existence of the weaker producers.

Subjective temporary factors linked with a high degree of uncertainty mainly come in through speculation. As is well known, speculative activities develop because there is uncertainty as to the evolution of market prices. This is particularly true of goods the prices of which are demand-determined (raw materials, agricultural products, old masters, bonds and shares). The purpose of speculation is to get the highest possible return on financial capital, that is to appropriate a certain share of the social surplus of an economy. To this end, money is held for speculative purposes. Keynes was the first to set forth systematically the link between uncertainty and speculative money-holding (Keynes 1973a).

This leads to a consideration of an important connection existing between a short-period behavioural factor (speculation) and the long-period system-governed fully adjusted situation which includes trend levels of output and employment. The fully adjusted situation implies that individuals persistently aim at holding a certain part of wealth in the form of money, the amount of which is associated with normal (target, satisfactory) profit rates or normal own-rates of interest and with normal prices for all goods, produced and not reproducible (pp. 154–90 above). Behavioural outcomes, including short-run speculative waves, always deviate from these reference points which constitute the *fundamentals* financial analysts speak about. For example, if speculators consider that any increase in share prices also represents an increase in wealth, then less than the normal amount of money will be held and shares will be bought. With share prices rising short-run profit rates realized on the stock exchange exceed the normal long-run rate of return. This attracts even more speculative money which is eventually augmented by bank credits. A cumulative upward process may now set in which may be reversed by some external event, a political crisis in an important country for example, or by changing expectations. Given this, the point of time at which the reversal of the upward movement occurs is highly uncertain. If speculative activities have been largely financed by bank credits the whole of the financial system may be threatened in the downswing of share prices.

Keynes clearly perceived (chapter 12 of the *General Theory*) that speculative waves may not only harm the financial system but may also greatly hamper entrepreneurship. Why, in fact, work hard for many years, introduce new techniques, develop new products and do research and development if huge rates of return can be realized by stock exchange activities within very short periods of time? However, it seems rational that firms would rather invest realized profits on the stock exchange instead of buying new machines or intensifying research and development activities if uncertainty about the future is very high. Financial activities linked with speculation located in the first layer of reality may thus negatively influence the process of production situated in the third layer (scheme 3, p. 106).

In the course of capitalist development excessive speculation has, time and again, dominated production, heralding, as a rule, a slump. The latter reflects the fact that the long-period forces or fundamentals associated with the socioeconomic system ultimately determine economic activity (pp.

142–220). In the long run, temporary market prices are attracted by the permanent or slowly changing normal prices, and actual output and employment levels resulting from aggregate behaviour 'fluctuate' around the corresponding normal levels, governed by the socioeconomic system.

Excessive speculation going on in the short run will as a rule not only impair production but also heavily influence income distribution; this will have long-period effects across the supermultiplier mechanism: a higher share of property incomes will reduce the volume of economic activity in the long run (pp. 154–90 above). In 'The end of *laissez-faire*' Keynes mentions this point:

Many of the greatest economic evils of our time are the fruits of risk, uncertainty, and ignorance. It is because particular individuals, fortunate in situation and abilities, are able to take advantage of uncertainty and ignorance, and also because big business is often a lottery, that great inequalities of wealth come about; and these same factors are also the cause of the unemployment of labour, or the disappointment of reasonable business expectations, and of the impairment of efficiency and production (Keynes 1972b, p. 291).

There is no need here to examine further the complex relationship existing between money and uncertainty. This is a domain where Keynes and the Keynesian Fundamentalists (Davidson, Minsky and others) have developed a rich analysis which forms an important part of classical-Keynesian economic theory. In the following subsection, we content ourselves with sketching a short-period classical-Keynesian framework which can be linked to the medium- and long-period analysis set forth above. This short-period framework embodies causal relations which are present in the first layer of reality of scheme 3 (p. 106).

A short-period framework

The objective and subjective temporary factors just mentioned might be summarized under the heading *vagaries of the market* as occur in the sphere of circulation; the corresponding transactions may go on in the financial or in the real sphere. In this section, we deal with the latter only within an (ideal-type) classical-Keynesian demand and supply framework on macroeconomic, sectoral and individual levels. In a monetary production economy, market events result from behavioural (supply and demand) outcomes which are co-ordinated by the system through the principle of (short-run) effective demand, with capital stocks and capacity output levels *given*.

The classical-Keynesian short-period *macroeconomic* framework essentially consists of a demand and supply curve (Bortis 1984, pp. 594–6). The short-period macroeconomic demand curve can be derived from the equilibrium condition (2), bearing in mind the definition of the real wage, $w = w_n/p$. Inserting this definition in equation (2) and solving for the price level yields

$$p = \frac{(z_P - z_W)(w_n/A)}{[z_P + \pi b] - [(I + G + X)/Q]}. \tag{26}$$

This is an inverse relationship between the price level p (the 'demand price') and the level of output Q. All the variables and parameters of this relation are now *short-period* magnitudes (the dependent variable p carries no star) governed by present short-term behaviour, past accumulation and by current effective demand. As such, the behavioural short-period magnitudes deviate from the corresponding long-period reference values determined by institutions.

Like its long-period counterpart (9), this short-period relation expresses a basic classical-Keynesian tenet. Given the money wage level, larger outputs (Q) are associated with lower price levels. This implies higher real wages. Since the fraction of (real) wage income consumed is larger than that of property income, effective demand and thus output both increase as real wages rise. Generally speaking, equation (26) tells us how the variables and parameters on the right-hand side are linked with the price level *in principle* – this relation thus constitutes an 'ideal-type' model (chapter 2, pp. 82–3). If some really existing situation were considered, however, this relation would represent an explanatory framework (a real-type model), and each point on this demand curve would be the result of recent alternative historical developments: only *one* point on the short-period macroeconomic demand curve would have a *real* meaning. The shape of the curve may vary in the course of time. This also holds for the short-period supply curve. Again, *time* would have to be thought of as coming out at a right angle in figure 9.

The short-period supply curve may exhibit various shapes. In the industrial sector, entrepreneurs may stick to the (estimated) normal prices (equation 6) even if capacity utilization is not standard. In agriculture, in small-scale industry, in handicrafts, and in the service sector, output may be at its normal level with prices being governed by demand conditions. Finally, supply prices may vary with changes in the level of output and employment.

Presumably, short-period supply pricing behaviour in an economy may be synthesized best by

$$p = (w_n/A)k \tag{6a}$$

where p is the supply price level. It is very likely that the actual mark-up k will be below the (estimated) target level k_c if capacity utilization is less than

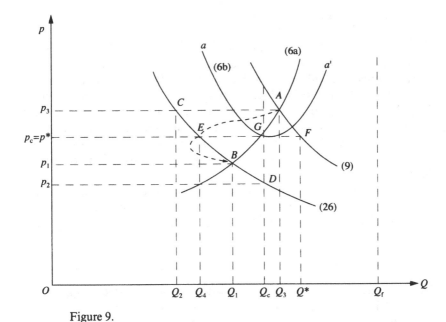

Figure 9.

normal and vice versa. This means that the short-period supply curve is likely to be positively sloped.

The short-period macroeconomic supply and demand curves (equations 6a and 26) can be mapped out in a diagram (figure 9) which provides a convenient framework for analysing the impact of short-term events on the macroeconomic level. In this figure the curve aa' represents the full-cost price level:

$$p_f=(w_n/A)k_f. \tag{6b}$$

Here, the mark-up k_f is such that the target rate of profits is achieved at *any* rate of utilization of the given capacity Q_c. Full-cost prices decline if capacity utilization improves, for two main reasons: overheads per unit of output diminish and labour productivity A increases (Okun's law). However, if capacity utilization becomes greater than standard $(Q>Q_c)$, p_f may increase owing to a declining labour productivity and to rising costs, e.g. overtime pay.

Given the *actually existing* capital stock K determined by past accumulation, capacity utilization is normal (standard) at the output level Q_c (capacity output). At this output level, full-cost prices are minimized and equal (estimated) normal prices

$$p_c = (w_n/A)k^*,\tag{6c}$$

which represent a behavioural outcome. If the estimates are broadly correct p_c tends to correspond to the normal prices (p^*) implied in the system-governed fully adjusted situation since the technology implied in the latter and the technology associated with capacity output Q_c are the same. With $Q_c < Q^*$ in figure 9 capacity utilization would be more than normal *if* the short-period demand curve coincided with the long-period curve (9). Since (6a) reflects the short-run behaviour of producers, the point of effective demand is A (figure 9) and (p_3, Q_3) represents the short-period flow equilibrium.

Finally, there is the system-governed fully adjusted situation which is covered up by short- and medium-term elements of reality and cannot be observed directly. The corresponding normal prices associated with normal output Q^* are

$$p^* = (w_n/A)k^*.\tag{6}$$

The three layers of reality set out in scheme 3 (p. 106) clearly appear in figure 9: there is the institutionally governed long-period aspect, represented by normal output Q^* and normal prices p^*, which implies a stock equilibrium K^*. Aggregate (cycle-cum-growth) accumulation behaviour results in capacity output Q_c and the corresponding estimated normal price level p_c. Finally, short-run behaviour governs the position of the short-run macroeconomic demand and supply curves, (26) and (6a), which, in turn, determine the short-run equilibrium output Q_1 and corresponding price level p_1. Bearing in mind these methodological points, figure 9 provides an ideal-type framework for short-term analysis. (It should be remembered here that Keynes, in his *Treatise on Money*, also distinguished between the long-period normal price determined by costs of production and normal profits and medium and short-term deviations from this price reflected in windfall profits, caused by a divergence between planned saving and planned investment (Keynes 1971b, vol. I, relations (i)–(iii), p. 122).)

We now postulate that, originally, the short-period curve (26) coincides with the long-period macroeconomic demand curve (9) and passes through point A. Suppose now that a sudden shift to the left occurs, i.e. to position *CEBD*. This leftward shift may have been caused by many factors: a sudden drop in exports X, in government expenditures G or in investment I; a rise in the import coefficient b or an unexpected deterioration of the terms of trade (π increases); a sudden rise of prices p with respect to money wages w_n. The parameter z_w may rise because consumers' credit facilities are declining owing to a high degree of indebtedness. What might the movement of prices and quantities, which so far have equalled p_3 and Q_3, look like?

It is likely that, in the very short run, prices p_3 and quantities Q_3 will stay firm as demand diminishes; a gap (AC) between production and effective demand develops. Stocks pile up. If this situation persists for some time, capacity utilization will eventually be lowered. Some firms will reduce prices. If equation (6a) represents the short-period supply behaviour, there may be a tendency of the economy to move towards a new equilibrium at point B (p_1, Q_1), the possible dynamics being represented by the path AB.

Other short-period equilibria are possible: if all the firms maintain the original short-period equilibrium prices when demand diminishes, the new equilibrium level would be given by (p_3, Q_2); if prices were perfectly flexible, capacity utilization might stay normal at (p_2, Q_c). Finally, if all firms were to stick to the (estimated) long-period normal prices (p_c, Q_4) would obtain.

Capacity utilization will be below normal if the new short-period equilibrium is at point B (p_1, Q_1). Since the short-period income elasticity of demand is different for the various types of goods, capacity utilization will deviate in varying degrees from normal utilization in the different sectors of production. But this is not a problem which we have to worry about at a macroeconomic level. The important point is that *all* the sectors of production are hit, in unequal degrees though, by the decline of effective demand represented by the shift of the macroeconomic demand curve from point A to point B in figure 9. The position (p_1, Q_1) implies that, on average, realized profits are below their normal level, though to an unequal degree in the different sectors of production, since the short-run Engel curves vary from one sector of production to another. If this situation persists, the long-period demand curve will shift to the left. Productive capacities Q_c will be reduced gradually. A new (provisional) equilibrium may eventually get established in the region of point E. This means that in all sectors of production, output capacities will be reduced, thus entailing bankruptcies and increasing trend unemployment. These phenomena are linked with high degrees of uncertainty for many individuals: who will go bankrupt, who will become unemployed? If, however, the short-period demand curve (26) returns quickly enough to its original position, i.e. the long-period demand curve (9), then realized profits will exceed desired ones again. In the meantime, the cyclical movement may go on normally: capacity output Q_c will approach and, eventually, go beyond normal output Q^* (pp. 204–20).

To conclude these considerations on the macroeconomic short run, three important points ought to be mentioned. First, in the short run only the income effect of investment is relevant and the capacity effect plays no role by definition: a sudden decline in the level of investment results in a leftward shift of the macroeconomic demand, thereby causing changes in prices and quantities demanded and produced while leaving unchanged capacity output Q_c. Second, in *real-type* models, the dynamic movements leading from one point to another may be very complex. This is illustrated by the path of p and Q leading from A to B (figure 9). Perhaps, the main reason is that the 'independent' variables, i.e. the right-hand sides of relations (26) and (6a), are, in fact, not independent of each other in the real world. Moreover, the way in which prices and quantities change in the short run depends heavily on the patterns of behaviour of entrepreneurs and consumers; the expectations held by individual agents also play a major role. Therefore, in uncertain circumstances eventual predictions on the evolution of the price–quantity path AB mapped out in figure 9 will be based on very shaky foundations. This leads to a third point, which is of a methodological nature: the macroeconomic demand and supply framework mapped out in figure 9 is only a starting point for real-type short-period analysis and is not a tool of empirical analysis: in fact, in a real-type model, each point on the respective curves would have to be interpreted as the result of alternative recent historical developments, which means that only one point has a real meaning. Owing to quickly changing expectations the position of this point may change rapidly. It is precisely in this context that Joan Robinson's famous saying about 'time coming out at a right angle' ought to be taken seriously.

When considering short-term phenomena at the *sectoral* level, we must bear in mind that capacity output Q_c (associated with the capital stock, brought about by past accumulation) never corresponds to trend output Q^*; in terms of figure 8 (p. 225) this means that, in each sector, capacity output levels are below (x_1) or above (x_2) the normal level (x^*) implied by the fully adjusted situation, with the various x^* being determined by long-period Engel curves (Pasinetti 1981). If the short-period demand curve coincides with the long-period curve (dd' in figure 8), output is, in some sectors, sold at prices below normal if *existing* capacities are normally utilized (x_2 and p_2 in figure 8), and vice versa (x_1 and p_1 in figure 8). Or, if the (estimated) normal price ($p_c = p^*$) is set, capacities would be utilized more than normally if capacity output equalled x_1. Conversely, excess capacities would arise with capacity output x_2. The picture may be even more complicated if the short-period demand curve deviates from the long-period demand curve (dd' in figure 8), owing to short-run fluctuations of effective demand (affecting all sectoral demand curves).

The short-period dynamics of prices and quantities of the individual firm is governed by a host of rapidly changing factors: for instance, changing behaviour of competitors in the spheres of marketing and pricing to obtain larger market shares, unpredictable changes in consumers' behaviour, unexpected changes in government expenditures influencing short-period effective demand, and so on. Speculative activity going on in various markets mainly for primary goods and non-reproducible goods complicates short-term situations even more. All these factors contribute to the fact that the evolution of prices and quantities from one short-term period to another, on the sectoral level and on the level of the individual firm, is highly uncertain. Short-term expectations play a major role in shaping short-run behaviour.

Regarding short-term economic events, generalizations leading to the formation of theories hardly seem possible. The economic theorist will be much more inclined to analyse medium- and long-term events. Here the ground is much firmer because the objective (institutional) factors governing economic events are constant or changing but slowly. Or cyclical movements show some regularity. Therefore, the short run and its evolution seem to be the domain of the economic practitioner, the experienced manager for example, not of the economic theorist. But, given the tremendous complexity of short-run situations with all causal forces acting at once, even practitioners would be driven to despair, did they not feel the stabilizing role of the objective (permanent) factors, i.e. institutions. Despair may really set in if long-term trends break down, as is the case in times of political upheaval and of eventual breakdown of the international economic order. The thirties of this century are an obvious case in point.

Concluding remarks

Summary of the chapter

In the preceding sections of this chapter it is suggested that a consensus between the various strands of post Keynesianism (chapter 1, pp. 1–6) should be possible: neo-Ricardians, Robinsonians and Keynesian Fundamentalists investigate different spheres of reality from distinct points of view, each type of investigation being complementary to the two others. A complete classical-Keynesian system would emerge as a synthesis and an elaboration of the three post Keynesian strands. The *neo-Ricardians* consider the socioeconomic and political system *as a whole* and provide the preconditions for elaborating a theory of long-period output and employment determination along Keynesian lines, i.e. a classical-Keynesian theory of the trend represented by the supermultiplier relation (7): effective demand governs, through the functioning of the social system (institutions), output and employment in the long run; this represents an application of Keynesian macroeconomics which deals with the scale of economic activity (pp. 135–42 above). Since a monetary economy is considered, the supermultiplier theory is part of a comprehensive monetary theory of production. Long-period distribution is regulated within the process of production by a variant of the surplus principle (equations 6 and 7): the average mark-up at normal capacity utilization is governed by a complex set of social, political and economic institutions. The price equation (6) states that relative prices depend upon the conditions of production and upon distribution; pricing is a social process in that prices are related to direct and indirect labour embodied in products and thus reflect society's efforts to produce goods (Pasinetti 1977, 1981, 1993). The prices of production enable the process of production and reproduction to go on undisturbed within a fully adjusted situation: here, sectors are in appropriate proportions; this is one of the central issues dealt with by classical macroeconomics (pp. 135–42 above). Pure (ideal-type) classical-Keynesian theory essentially consists of the pure production model set out by Pasinetti (1981, part I), and of the supermultiplier framework set out earlier in this chapter which provides a long-period extension of Keynes's principle of effective demand; the former deals with proportions, i.e. production, value and distribution within the framework of a fully adjusted situation, the latter with the determination of the long-period level (the scale) of economic activity. The target rate of profit (or a hierarchy of profit rates) implied in the mark-up on prime costs plays a particular role in the classical-Keynesian system: once r^* (or k^*) is fixed, the prices of production *and* the employment scalar (pp. 142–54 above), i.e. the fully adjusted situation, are determined too. The role played by r^* (k^*) is analogous to the function of the natural wage rate in Ricardo's system: one of the distributive variables must be known before other problems like value and employment can be tackled. As Ricardo clearly perceived, distribution is the most important and also the most fundamental problem of political economy.

The *Robinsonians* complement classical-Keynesian long-period theory with a (predominantly behavioural) medium-term cycle-cum-growth theory along Kaleckian lines: the aggregate outcome of individual investment decisions is co-ordinated by a two-sector model which implies a relationship between investments and profits (or the rate of growth and the rate of profit); this model pictures an aspect of the functioning of the system and expresses a social law related to classical macroeconomics: the scale of activity is given and the problem is to determine the proportions between the consumption goods and the investment goods sectors. In the course of the cycle, distribution is regulated by a variant of the surplus principle which explains medium-term distribution; distributional outcomes (the investment volume governs profits), prices and quantities always deviate from their long-period normal levels associated with the fully adjusted situation. Capacity output and the associated employment level are the result of past accumulation. Robinsonian analysis also includes structural adjustments to the fully adjusted situation. Adjustment processes are steered by differences between realized and target profit rates: the rate of profits links the behavioural and the institutional system. Again, distribution emerges as the central problem of political economy.

The *Keynesian Fundamentalists* take account of uncertainty and money in the short, medium and long term. Attention is primarily directed towards the short-run behaviour of individuals in the face of uncertainty within a short-run demand and supply framework; goods and financial markets are considered. On the macroeconomic (system) level, it is investigated how the short-run application of the principle of effective demand leads, *given* the capital stock, to a particular degree of capacity utilization.

Robinsonians and Keynesian Fundamentalists examine events occurring within the sphere of circulation. However, Robinsonians are 'nearer' the process of production, since in the schemes of circulation they consider, circulation stands in the service of production. Keynesian Fundamentalists consider production, not from the macroeconomic point of view, but from the viewpoint of the individual entrepreneur (production takes time).

Different ways of looking at reality are thus implied in the three post Keynesian strands and their classical-Keynesian elaboration: the neo-Ricardians deal with the *determinism* exercised by evolving technological and institutional structures, i.e. the socioeconomic system, upon the actions of individuals; if complemented with Keynesian employment theory, neo-Ricardianism results in classical-Keynesian long-period theory. The Robinsonians and the Keynesian Fundamentalists investigate the behaviour of individuals in a given or slowly evolving structural set-up. The former mainly examine the aggregate investment behaviour of entrepreneurs which results in the cyclical growth of the capital stock and the associated capacity output levels. The latter deal, given the capital stock, with the determination of current prices and quantities and with the behaviour of individuals in the face of uncertainty about the future, the speculative demand for money being of particular importance. The behavioural and the institutional systems mutually shape each other. Moreover, long-period, medium- and short-term forces act *simultaneously* at any moment of time (scheme 3, p. 106). Given this, an economist who attempts to explain some economic phenomenon (the level of employment, the share of profits, the level of a price, etc.), will be faced with the problem of assessing the strength or the importance of the causal forces involved. This important point may be illustrated by two examples.

The first example is linked with the explanation of the level of output produced in a certain short period of time. In figure 1 (p. 85) full employment output Q_f moves along gh; 'equilibrium', trend or normal output Q^*, determined by the classical-Keynesian supermultiplier (7), is given by ef. In period t_1, trend output, governed by fundamental long-period institutional forces, i.e. the system as a whole, is ab. Robinsonian-Kaleckian medium-term cycle-cum-growth theory explains the evolution of capacity output Q_c which evolves along ei in the above figure: thus, at t_1, the Robinsonians have to explain ac on the basis of past entrepreneurial investment behaviour. The deviation of capacity output from trend output, bc, can be explained once long-period *and* medium-term employment theory is established. Finally, the Keynesian Fundamentalists deal with the movement in time of actual output Q which evolves along AB: at t_1, ad has to be explained. Since capacity output is given, this amounts to explaining degrees of capacity utilization and the difference between capacity output and actual output, cd.

A second example, the explanation of the level of the price of some consumption good, is directly linked to the example just given. To simplify, the money wage rate is assumed to be fixed. The long-period normal price, governed by technology, the conditions of production, and the institutionally determined mark-up (k^*), is p^* (figure 8, p. 225). The long-period equilibrium output corresponding to a fully adjusted situation is x^*. Now, at t_1 (figure 1) output exceeds the trend level; moreover, it is postulated that the actual rate of growth still exceeds the trend growth rate, as is normal in a cyclical upswing. This implies, in turn, that the investment–consumption ratio I/C is higher than the corresponding long-period ratio that is implied in the fully adjusted situation corresponding to trend output Q^*. If some consumption goods sector is considered, it is likely that capacity output (x_1 in figure 8) is below x^*. According to Robinsonian (Kaleckian) theory, the rate of profit and thus the mark-up will be higher than their long-period counterparts. Hence the market price (p_1 in figure 8) will exceed the (estimated) long-period normal price p_c (or, given p_c, capacity utilization would be more than normal). Finally, if the short-period demand curve were located to the right of the long-period demand curve (dd') due to a temporary change in consumer behaviour, then the market price and/or capacity utilization would be even higher.

Both examples illustrate the fundamental fact that the various forces (long-, medium- and short-term) operate simultaneously. Analysing these forces means looking at different spheres of reality from differing points of view. However, it must be possible to put the various theories together in a logically satisfactory and consistent way (as is the case in a puzzle, for instance). This requires a common approach which in the case of classical-Keynesian political economy is based on a combination of the classical surplus principle and of the principle of effective demand; the economy being considered is necessarily a monetary production economy. The underlying approach must, in turn, be based upon a consistent vision of the functioning of society as a whole, i.e. the humanist social philosophy sketched in chapter 2.

Some remarks on the content of political economy

When one looks at the structure of a standard textbook in economics, a broad division of economic theory into microeconomics and macroeconomics generally appears. The former relates, as a rule, to pure theory, i.e. price formation through supply and demand on goods and 'factor' markets, usually complemented by the pure theory of international trade. Macroeconomics is of a more applied nature: the determination of output and employment, the mechanism of business cycles, the role of money and international economic relations are the main subjects considered. The precise link existing between micro- and macroeconomics is by no means self-evident: there is a dichotomy which has been alluded to in relation to Keynes's distinction between 'volume I and volume II type' work (chapter 1, pp. 6–20). This issue will be dealt with in chapter 5.

When attempting to structure classical-Keynesian theory, it seems convenient not to start from microeconomics, nor from macroeconomics, but from *mesoeconomics*, which, in the present study, has been called *classical macroeconomics*. The economy is divided into sectors and industries in an appropriate way with the aim of studying necessary relations between them, with the scale of economic activity considered to be *given*. There is no need to invent classical-Keynesian mesoeconomics, since a great variety of models dealing with different aspects of mesoeconomic reality is at our disposal: these include Quesnay's *tableau économique*, Adam Smith's industry–agriculture model which has been taken up by Nicholas Kaldor (Thirlwall 1987, pp. 208–22), Marx's schemes of production and reproduction, which describe necessary exchange relations between the consumption and the investment goods sectors standing in the service of production. The Marxian schemes apply to the level of final products and figure prominently in modern Keynesian and classical-Keynesian theory, outstanding applications being the Fundamental Equations in Keynes's *Treatise on Money* and the two-sector model contained in Joan Robinson's *Accumulation of Capital*. On the intermediate product level, there are, building upon Quesnay's *tableau*, the models by Leontief, von Neumann and Sraffa, all of which are described in Pasinetti (1977) and last, but not least, the vertically integrated sector model set forth in Pasinetti (1981) which provides the basis for reconciling mesoeconomic models dealing with intermediate products and mesoeconomic models describing final product flows between sectors. Part I of Pasinetti (1981), can therefore be considered as the analytical starting point for positive classical-Keynesian mesoeconomics. Here, the principles of structural change within fully adjusted situations are developed.

The central problem of classical-post Keynesian mesoeconomics is that of proportions between sectors. Which sector sizes are, on the intermediate and final product level, required to enable the process of production and reproduction of normal output (Q^*) to go on undisturbed? The same question may be asked for capacity output (Q_c) resulting from the process of cyclical growth. Finally, the problem of disproportions between sectors may be tackled. Classical-Keynesian mesoeconomics takes two important aspects of reality as given: first, the scale of output and employment is assumed to be fixed; correct sector proportions are compatible with any level of employment. Second, the microeconomic set-up of each sector is also assumed to be given, most importantly the number of firms, the technology employed and the sizes of target profit rates and mark-ups.

Relaxing these provisional assumptions opens new areas of investigation for classical-Keynesian political economy: we may ask how, in principle, the scale (the level) of overall output and employment is determined in the short, medium and long runs. Attempts to answer this question lead to classical-Keynesian macroeconomics (the three preceding main sections in this chapter). Formally, and if the long run is considered, the problem consists of explaining the employment scalar implied in the quantity equations of part I of Pasinetti (1981); materially, this leads to the theory of the super-multiplier (pp. 142–204 above). Once it is explained how normal employment is determined in principle, employment determination in the medium term may be studied, i.e. cyclical movements of employment; finally, short-run employment determination may be dealt with along Keynesian and Keynesian Fundamentalist lines.

Moreover, the question arises as to how the prices of the goods exchanged between industries and sectors are determined and how value added is going to be distributed. This implies, first, working out a long-period theory of prices and a theory of income distribution, i.e. classical-Keynesian 'microeconomics'; the normal prices (of production) have to be such as to enable the reproduction of the socioeconomic system from year to year. The basic features of a theory of value and distribution along classical-Keynesian lines are set forth in Pasinetti (1981, part I): long-period normal prices correspond to labour equivalents (real costs of production). The normal price equation (6) reflects this view of price formation. Distribution, the determination of profit rates and mark-ups, is, in principle, determined within the sphere of production by a set of socioeconomic and political institutions (pp. 142–204 above). To explain distribution for specific situations through concrete institutional structures, real-type models have to be set up; this is a task requiring historical, sociological, political and economic investigations to be carried out for individual countries or regions; a fine example is Phelps Brown (1977). Starting from a long-period theory of value and distribution, theories explaining pricing and distributional outcomes in the course of the business cycle, the medium term, or in the short run may be set up. In doing so, account will have to be taken of the market structure, mainly exemplified by the size and the number of firms present in a certain sector of production.

A large body of classical-Keynesian microeconomic theory already exists. The main theoretical tools are pricing models based upon the mark-up principle. There is also an important empirical underpinning represented by the work done within the framework of industrial economics. However, classical-Keynesian microeconomics is quite different from conventional neoclassical microtheory. The former emphasizes behaviour, the latter the functioning of the system. In classical-Keynesian microeconomics the social character of the process of production is put to the fore. Extensive division of labour is the most important means to reach more perfectly a common aim, i.e. the production of the social product. The process of production, which is a social macroinstitution (chapter 2, pp. 23–4), *determines*, together with the institutions regulating distribution, the long-term pricing behaviour of entrepreneurs; the level of activity, governed by effective demand (equally a social law), is given in the short, medium and long terms. Hence classical-Keynesian microeconomics carries a heavy 'macro touch', since social (institutional) and technological factors (Marx's forces and relations of production) govern long-period price formation. Normal prices and real wage rates are macrophenomena in the sense that the entire production system enters the picture.

Starting from the broad division of classical-Keynesian theory into mesoeconomics, macroeconomics and microeconomics, one may then go on to investigate relationships existing between these fields of inquiry. What are the influences of changes in the scale of output and employment upon the choice of techniques and upon the pricing behaviour of entrepreneurs? Are there links between the long-period level of unemployment and the pace of technical progress, or more specifically, do innovations mainly occur in times of prosperity or in times of prolonged depression? Questions like these have been asked by empirically and historically minded political economists; the system of classical-Keynesian political economy sketched in the preceding sections should provide the conceptual foundations for such investigations.

Methodological implications

Classical-Keynesian political economy is strongly linked with the *historical method*: ideal-type causal models represent pure theory and picture the (probable) essential properties of socioeconomic phenomena (employment levels, business cycles, distributional outcomes, prices) which are the same in all manifestations of these phenomena; based upon ideal-type models, applied or real-type models may be set up to explain unique historical events and aspects of the real world evolving in historical time. This is Marx's method, but, surprisingly, also Carl Menger's; however, Marx takes the point of view of society as a whole, whereas Menger starts from the individual as is evident from Menger (1969 [1883], book III, chapter 2); on this see chapters 2 (pp. 57–75) and 3 (pp. 118–30). The historical character of classical-Keynesian political economy also emerges from the distinction between the long, medium and short terms which, in fact, involves a classification of causal forces and the corresponding causal relations according to their persistence. This implies that some historically unique event, the crisis of the thirties for example, is brought about by a multitude of causes: each single event is, in a way, an entity which summarizes the effects brought about by many causal relations, i.e. principles governing the real world.

There are a large number of highly interesting investigations that have been carried out along classical-Keynesian lines by empirically minded economists and by historians. More specifically, some representatives of the German Historical School and of American Institutionalism started impressive research programmes. However, the lack of theoretical foundation has led to a gradual abandonment of the historical method in political economy; in fact, in the course of the *Methodenstreit*, the 'struggle' between *theory*, represented by Carl Menger, and *history* (Gustav Schmoller), had turned in favour of theory. Since then empirical investigations of the historical type have been more and more equated with *journalism* by scientifically minded mathematical economists and by many econometricians.

One of the main tasks of *classical-Keynesian political economy* is to provide a *conceptual foundation for historical investigations*. In a first step, relevant causal relations of the vertical type, aimed at explaining in principle specific economic phenomena (unemployment, pricing, distributional outcomes, growth and development), have to be identified; second, tendencies for change have to be captured by models embodying horizontal causality: instances are business cycle models (on both types of causality, see chapter 3, pp. 120–4). The principles so derived provide, subsequently, the basis for applied work. Moreover, classical-Keynesian theory will have to provide a unifying framework allowing us to classify broadly the enormous number of historical and empirical investigations: theory must enable us to bring some order into the immense amount of empirical and historical material while simultaneously providing a starting point for interpreting this material. Keynes, when writing the *General Theory*, clearly had this problem in mind. In the preface to the German edition he wrote:

The orthodox tradition, which ruled in nineteenth century England, never took so firm a hold of German thought. There have always existed important schools of economists in Germany who have strongly disputed the adequacy of the classical [and neoclassical] theory for the analysis of contemporary events ... It can scarcely be claimed, however, that this school of thought has erected a rival theoretical construction ... It has been sceptical, realistic, content with historical and empirical methods and results, which discard formal analysis ... Thus Germany ... has been content for a whole century to do without any formal theory of economics which was predominant and generally accepted. [To be fair, however, it must be recalled, that, in the century in question, Germany produced the greatest of all historically minded social scientists, who had no problems with integrating theory and history, i.e. Karl Marx. H.B.]

Perhaps, therefore, I may expect less resistance from German, than from English, readers in offering a theory of employment and output as a whole, which departs in important respects from the orthodox tradition. But can I hope to overcome Germany's economic agnosticism? Can I persuade German economists that methods of formal analysis have something important to contribute to the interpretation of contemporary events and to the moulding of contemporary policy? (Keynes 1973a, pp. xxv–xxvi).

It is hardly possible to state better the methodological significance of the suggestions regarding a possible classical-Keynesian synthesis as are set forth in the preceding sections of this study.

Three specific problems related to the historical nature of classical-Keynesian political economy have to be discussed briefly. The first is about the significance of two types of causal models defined in chapter 3 (pp. 118–30). The second is connected with the integration of space (historical reality) and time. The third problem is linked up with the relationship between models and reality.

The historical method, i.e. explaining given situations and attempting to discover tendencies for change, requires two sets of causal models which, in turn, embody two kinds of causality, i.e. vertical or static causality and horizontal or dynamic causality. Pure causal or 'ideal-type' models of the vertical or static type tell us how causal forces work *in principle*. For example, in a classical-Keynesian view, effective demand determines output and employment everywhere and at any moment of time. Several types of pure causal models of the static type are then required to explain completely the determination of output levels in principle: the supermultiplier relation has to explain normal or trend output; business cycle theory, the cyclical evolution of capacity output and deviations from the trend; and the short-period multiplier, the short-term fluctuations of output and employment. The enlarged input–output model is also a causal model of the static type. It pictures the circular and social process of production: final products are produced by commodities, i.e.

intermediate products and real capital, and by labour and land at any instant of time.

Pure models cannot be applied directly to explain real-world situations. To do so, explanatory frameworks, corresponding to the 'real-type' models of chapter 3, pp. 81–9, have to be developed. Models attempting to explain persistent unemployment in France or in the United Kingdom on the basis of the supermultiplier principle would constitute such frameworks.

To complete the historical method, causal models of the static type have to be combined with dynamic causal models. Again the distinction between pure ('ideal-type') and applied ('real-type') dynamic models has to be made. Models of this type make up a significant part for classical and Marxian political economy where descriptions of tendencies for change figure prominently. A methodological revival of classical-Marxian economics thus seems crucial for completing a classical-Keynesian system of political economy. A convenient historical starting point regarding methodological issues is provided by Marx's remarks on 'die Methode der politischen Oekonomie' in his introduction to *Kritik der politischen Oekonomie* (Marx 1975 [1857], pp. 631–9). Important methodological implications are contained in Pasinetti (1977) and Pasinetti (1981, specifically in chapter VI, pp. 109–17). Here, pure static and dynamic models are proposed and neatly integrated (on the methodological problems in question, see chapter 3, pp. 118–30).

The combination of traditional classical and modern Keynesian elements of analysis enables classical-Keynesian political economists to deal with questions of considerable practical interest. For instance, with the help of pure and applied supermultiplier models one may quite easily show that exports play a crucial role in determining the overall economic situation in many countries. Subsequently, more complicated questions may be asked, e.g. questions relating to the forces that have brought about the export strength (or weakness!) of some particular country and about possible tendencies in the export strength of some country; are there, for instance, forces undermining it gradually?

The concepts of vertical and horizontal causality, combined with the notions of pure and applied models are not new. In chapter 3 (pp. 120–4) we mentioned that pure models embodying vertical and horizontal causality are put to use in Pasinetti (1977, 1981). In chapter 2 it was suggested that the concepts of vertical and horizontal causality have deep historical roots at the philosophical level (pp. 55–7). Here, it is of considerable interest to note that Keynes made use explicitly of both types of causality when he attempted to come to grips with the essence of his multiplier relation. In the *General Theory*, section IV of chapter 10 (pp. 122–5) is devoted to this subject. Keynes starts from the 'confusion between the logical theory of the multiplier, which holds good continuously, without time-lag, at all moments of time, and the consequences of an expansion in the capital-goods industries which take gradual effect, subject to time-lag and only after an interval' (Keynes 1973a, p. 122).

The association of the logical theory of the multiplier, a piece of pure theory, with static causality and of the 'applied multiplier', i.e. the 'consequences of an expansion in the capital-goods industries', with dynamic causality emerges most clearly from the example provided by Keynes to illustrate this point (pp. 122–3): the logical multiplier represents the multiplier *principle* which acts at all instants and, finally, summarizes the result of a process; the applied and dynamic multiplier, however, tells us in what way or in what form the principle is applied to a concrete real-world situation: the multiplier may change its form, or increase or decrease, in the course of time, owing to variations in the propensity to consume for example. Given an increase in investment, a decline in the propensity to consume may be 'brought about partly by the high prices causing a postponement of consumption, partly by a redistribution of income in favour of the saving classes as an effect of the increased profits resulting from the higher prices . . .' (p. 123). This leads to 'a temporary reduction of the marginal propensity to consume, i.e. the multiplier itself . . . As time goes on, however, the consumption goods industries adjust themselves to the new demand, so that when the deferred consumption is enjoyed, the marginal propensity to consume rises temporarily above its normal level, to compensate for the extent to which it previously fell below it, and eventually returns to its *normal level* [our emphasis]' (p. 124). This example shows that the multiplier principle, i.e. the logical or static multiplier linked with vertical causality, is of striking simplicity; however, its application to a concrete real-world situation set in historical time (the applied dynamic multiplier exhibiting horizontal causality) is very complex.

The possibility of combining static and dynamic causal models is associated with a great methodological advantage. Multiple causality may be taken account of and hierarchies of causal forces may be set up. This can be explained with the help of figure 1 (p. 85). To explain the level of output in time-period t_1, say, three types of causal models embodying vertical causality have to be taken into account: the supermultiplier relation, Robinsonian or Kaleckian business cycle theory and the short-run Keynesian multiplier. Each of these models may, in turn, picture several more basic causal forces acting indirectly upon the level of employment and output. To explain changes in the output level (the shape of the broken line AB in figure 1), dynamic causal models will have to be combined with the static ones on the three layers of reality considered: the evolution of output in time may, in fact, be due to institutional forces associated with the functioning of the system, to a specific investment behaviour resulting in cyclical movements or to changing market situations. The historical economist is now in a position to establish hierarchies of causes: on the behavioural level some of the causal forces at work may be more important than others because of a specific hierarchy of values prevailing in a given situation; some aims may be pursued more intensely and persistently than others; this gives rise to'institutions which remain largely invariant for very long periods of time. Or the deterministic influence of the system may over-rule aggregate behavioural outcomes: individual decisions to save and to invest more may produce the opposite (Keynes's paradox of thrift).

To deal with the second point, i.e. the integration of space and time, it is useful to link up the classification of 'short-, medium- and long-term factors' set out in scheme 3 (p. 106) with 'surface and deeper (more fundamental) phenomena'. An economist looking at economic reality is, at first sight, confronted with an amazing amount of seemingly disorganized surface phenomena: output and employment evolve in an inexplicable fashion (the broken line AB in figure 1), the behaviour of consumers changes in a completely unpredictable way; some producers are faced with diminishing sales, the expectations of others are realized; some prices remain quite stable, others change erratically; government expenditures drop sharply because a new government wants to put state activity on a 'sound' basis again, and so on. No wonder that, when looking at the surface and thereby observing the chaotic movement of short-run (temporary) and mostly subjective factors, economic reality appears to some Keynesian Fundamentalists as a huge kaleidoscope where uncertainty plays a crucial role. These economists are right in saying that it is extremely difficult to make statements of general validity on short-term behavioural phenomena. Therefore, scientific agnosticism may result from dealing with the evolution of economic surface phenomena which are subject to rapid changes.

However, the surface is only the immediately visible part of reality, i.e. its appearance. If the top layer of reality is cleared away, i.e. abstracted from, a second layer appears which is the scientific object of the Robinsonians or Kaleckians; this layer is associated with a certain 'quality' of time, i.e. the 'medium term'. Here regularities begin to emerge: the cyclical movement of capacity output and employment; the positive association between the volume of investment and profits, the negative relationship between profits and expanding productive capacity; the link between money wages and prices, the diminution of output in some sectors and the expansion of production in others.

A further step can be made by abstracting from the (behavioural) cyclical element to bring the institutional trend to the fore. Structures associated with fully adjusted situations now appear. Output is determined by long-term effective demand and moves along a trend which is governed by the entire socioeconomic system. Normal prices depend upon the conditions of production and upon the way distribution is regulated. This implies fully adjusted sector sizes on the intermediate and final product level as are set forth by Pasinetti (1977, 1981). Hence, the supermultiplier equation and the prices of production of Ricardo, Marx and the neo-Ricardians, especially the system of prices set out in part I of Pasinetti (1981) are *not* artificial or purely theoretical concepts. Nor are the prices of production and the quantities governed by normal effective demand – the fully adjusted situation – lying somewhere in the future. Sraffa's system is an attempt conceptually to get hold of the *principles* regulating a fundamental aspect of economic reality to be found in the third layer of scheme 3; the same is true of Marx's prices of production and of his values. Similar to Keynes's logical theory of the multiplier, the prices of production represent a piece of vertical causality. The former operates in the first layer of reality; the principles regulating the prices of production are active in the third layer of reality.

Sraffa's and Pasinetti's purely theoretical models imply that institutions are abstracted from only in order to be able to deal with principles. Hence institutions are implied in their approach but are, so to speak, left in the dark to bring out with more clarity the determinants of the prices of production. It is in this sense that a remark of Sraffa's with respect to method has to be understood. Speaking of his Standard System, he says that this construct 'may give transparency to a system and render visible what was hidden . . .' (Sraffa 1960, p. 23). In this view, 'the main task of the political economist, in particular, and of the social scientist, in general, is to penetrate mentally into the deeper and more stable layers of reality, i.e. to try to discover principles regulating the structure of these layers in order to contribute to explaining, or perhaps more appropriately, to approximately understanding what is happening there in the course of time. The aim is to understand the functioning of socioeconomic and political systems and their evolution, although the understanding will always be sketchy and probable (chapter 2, pp. 57–75).

These remarks explain a rather surprising statement by Roncaglia who has compared the Sraffian system with a 'photograph [taken] at an instant of time' (Roncaglia 1976, p. 21). This system pictures, indeed, some fundamental, i.e. permanent or slowly changing, aspects of economic reality at particular instants of time, i.e. the process of production, value and distribution. In their being part of reality, these long-period forces shaping fundamental spheres of the real world are *always* there and photographs of them may thus be taken at any moment. This is tantamount to coming to grips conceptually with fundamental aspects of socioeconomic reality with the help of pure models. These permit the carrying-out of theoretical experiments. Theorizing means working within the confines of the pure model to explore how given causal forces work in principle. For instance, it may be asked how, given money wages and the production coefficients, the prices of production would change *if* the rate of profits varied. These changes, *if* occurring in the real world, would be equivalent to permanent changes of fundamental (third-layer) aspects of reality.

These remarks shed some light on the classical-Keynesian way of handling *time* (and, we should add, *space*). Social reality is looked at from two different points of view. The first focuses on the behaviour of individuals and collectives, the second on the institutional system. The aim is to attempt to understand the functioning and the evolution of social systems on the basis of principles, i.e. pure models exhibiting vertical and horizontal causality; this implies explaining the actual functioning of systems in terms of past behaviour which is embodied in the presently existing institutions and the modifications of the institutional set-up by actual modes of behaviour. Since each historical situation is unique, specific real-type models have to be worked out. This is the essence of the historical approach. The best example for illustrating this approach is perhaps provided by the work of Karl Marx. Volume III of *Das Kapital* deals with upper layers of capitalist reality, i.e. with the realm of appearances. Volumes I and II, however, deal with (hidden) fundamental layers. Prices of production and profits are, in Marx's approach, located in the upper layers, only superseded by market prices. Values and surplus value, however, are parts of the hidden fundamental reality of capitalism. To be able to deal properly with these fundamental phenomena, Marx abstracts from different organic compositions of capital. The effect of this methodological procedure is the backward transformation of prices of production into values. The fundamental nature of value formation and of the way in which the surplus is appropriated and disposed of, consumed and accumulated within the social and circular process of production can now be set forth; this is the content of volume I of *Das Kapital*. Volume II deals with some characteristics of fully adjusted situations, mainly with the necessary relations between the consumption and the investment goods sectors that must hold if the circulation of capital and thus production is to go on undisturbed. The point is that the appearances, i.e. wages, profits and rents (volume III), can only be understood once the principles are grasped, that is value and surplus value (volume I) and productive circulation (volume II). The way in which principles work changes with the evolution of capitalism, and their realization differs in space.

This brief comparison of the classical-Keynesian and Marxian methods leads to the third problem to be dealt with here which concerns the relationship between models and reality. Both, Marxists and classical-Keynesians, attempt to explain historical reality with the help of simple *causal* models; this can be made somewhat more precise in the light of the preceding chapters.

The concept of causality is used in classical-Keynesian political economy in a simple and straightforward way (Pasinetti 1964/65; Corti 1989): formally, causality is a relationship between a determined and one or more predetermined magnitudes (independent variables and parameters). The latter (the cause) must act upon the former (the effect) in a regular and understandable way. Regarding the content of causation, two types of causes have been mentioned (chapter 2, pp. 55–7): the *efficient* cause which deals with determination; in the social sciences the prime example is the deterministic influence of the socioeconomic system upon the behaviour of individuals; particularly the principle of effective demand governs through the supermultiplier the long-period levels of output and employment. The *final* cause regulates the behaviour of individuals and collectives: the aims pursued determine the actions undertaken.

Pure and applied causal models are means to come to grips in a probable way with the constitutive principles of socioeconomic reality which moves on in historical time. To prepare analytical work, layers of reality have to be formed (scheme 3). Each layer embodies a specific quality of time. In the top layer events change rapidly and are to be explained with the help of short-term models: causal relations between determined and predetermined magnitudes change their form from one short time-period to the next. For example, in the short-period Keynesian multiplier relation the level of investment and the marginal propensity to save (the predetermined magnitudes) may evolve quickly. The causal relationships, the profit–investment relationship for example, explaining events occurring in a second layer of economic reality (cyclical growth, for instance) are stable over a longer period of time which we have called the medium term. Finally, long-period causal models like the supermultiplier aim at explaining stable or slowly changing relationships between magnitudes located in a third layer of economic reality where the socioeconomic and political system is located.

Pure causal models or 'ideal types', exhibiting vertical or horizontal causality, tell us how the predetermined magnitudes govern the determined variables in an abstract way, that is in principle; Keynes's logical theory of the multiplier is an example. However, abstract causal relationships cannot be used *tel quel*, i.e. mechanically, to explain aspects of historic reality. For instance, the supermultiplier may work in a completely different way in country A than in country B. In A, the rate of growth of government expenditures may exceed that of exports. The foreign balance (11) then shows a tendency towards import surpluses. This tendency may be reinforced by a gradually increasing import coefficient (b). The pressure of imports may lead to a low degree of capacity utilization and to profits being depressed below the normal level. The bad economic climate may, in turn, lead to a decline of technical dynamism: the replacement of old machinery by new equipment is thus slow, a fact reflected by a low drop-out ratio d in equation (7). This is likely to influence exports negatively; eventually exports might not suffice to pay for the necessary imports required at the full employment level.

The situation in country B may be exactly opposite and yet, formally, we explain it by the same supermultiplier model. The problem is that the 'independent' magnitudes on the right-hand side of the supermultiplier equation (7) are dependent in a particular way on themselves once we apply the supermultiplier to a particular historical situation or to a specific socioeconomic system. Given this, applied causal models, i.e. explanatory frameworks or 'real-type' models, must be developed to explain particular situations.

While the principles, exhibiting vertical or horizontal causalities, are of striking simplicity, their application to a concrete real-world situation where most diverse vertical and horizontal causalities are active, may be of immense complexity; the Keynesian multiplier or the supermultiplier are telling examples. On this Marx would have said that the basic principles, value and surplus value for instance, are modified by many circumstances when a concrete real-world situation is considered.

Once it is attempted to go beyond temporary behavioural aspects and to investigate interrelated institutional structures (the socioeconomic and political system as a whole), the elaboration of 'real-type' causal models becomes dependent upon *understanding* a specific historical situation. Less important aspects of the real world must be abstracted from in order to enable us to discover those causal relations likely to be relevant for governing some aspect of the real world. In terms of the above example we must try to understand why the functioning of the two societies A and B produces opposite results within the same (supermultiplier) theory. This is an extremely difficult undertaking since societies, broadly defined as the interplay of institutions, are entities of immense complexity. Consequently, applied causality is an equally complex concept in the social sciences because various causal forces interact to produce a certain result: for example, the applied supermultiplier synthesizes a set of causal relations that are associated with the predetermined variables and parameters on the right-hand side of this relation. The way in which the synthesizing of causalities goes on is presumably not mechanical, but organic. This may be due to the fact that individuals act within a social framework, which is of organic complexity: objective factors, institutions and technology, which have historically developed interact among themselves and with individual behaviour, both governed by an interdependent value system embodied in the individual and social aims pursued by individuals within the various institutions. The organic character of causation in the social sciences may have led Marshall to say that '[t]he Mecca of the economist lies in economic biology [and that] biological conceptions are more complex than those of mechanics . . .' (Marshall 1920, p. xiv).

Keynes, too, may be quoted to warn economists against applying pure causal models mechanically: 'The object of our analysis [the General Theory] is, not to provide a machine, or method of blind manipulation, which will furnish an infallible answer, but to provide ourselves with an organised and orderly method of thinking out particular problems; and, after we have reached a provisional conclusion by isolating the complicating factors one by one, we then have to go back on ourselves and allow, as well as we can, for the probable interactions of the factors among themselves. This is the nature of economic thinking' (Keynes 1973a, p. 297).

5 Classical-Keynesian political economy and neoclassical economics

In recent years, the belief in the self-regulating capacity of satisfactorily functioning markets has increased, at least at the level of policy-making. This is expressed by the privatization and deregulation movement and is accompanied by a clear tendency to return to pre-Keynesian neoclassical equilibrium theory. The textbook by Barro (1984) is but one important indication of this. The success of the 'rational expectations school' and the rise of neo-Austrian 'disequilibrium theory' are other indicators of the tendency to take up pre-Keynesian strands of thought; this is reinforced by political factors: the recent breakdown of centrally planned socialism seems to hail the ultimate triumph of liberalism. Finally, it is particularly sad that, in most countries, the parties of the centre and even social democratic parties have abandoned the venerable Keynesian full employment goal and now aim at a 'satisfactory' level of employment.

Some economists might not agree with this bleak view of things. Alan Blinder suggests that, after a period of decline, Keynesian economics is rising again (Blinder 1988). There is also Kuttner's *The End of Laissez-Faire* which praises 'the explanatory power of Keynesian economics' (Kuttner 1991, p. 3) and makes highly interesting proposals for shaping the post Cold War world along Keynesian lines. While such developments must be welcomed, they do not affect the basic line of argument set out in this study. Keynes is too much anchored in the neoclassical world (he accepted the first neoclassical postulate and made use of the marginal efficiency of capital) to be able to provide a complete alternative to neoclassical theory on his own. His all important principle of effective demand can only be definitely established if combined with a theory of value and distribution along Ricardian lines. This is the cornerstone of the classical-Keynesian synthesis suggested here.

A short comparison of neoclassical equilibrium economics and classical-Keynesian political economy is necessary here to bring out the nature and the significance of both approaches. This is to examine some fundamental

252

differences and certain important implications embodied in the premises of the two approaches. Such an analysis is not only required *per se* but is also prerequisite to the policy chapter below (chapter 6). The question whether economic policies ought to be based on – liberal – neoclassical theory or upon – humanist – classical-Keynesian political economy is crucially important. The more robust, the better performing and the more appealing theory will have to be selected.

It should be noted that the present chapter is not a critique of neoclassical economics in general. Neoclassical economists have done great work in analysing the behaviour of individuals and collectives in various spheres of life and in explaining aggregate behavioural outcomes. However, the automatic co-ordination of behaviour by the market – the invisible hand – and the associated market equilibria were perhaps given too much attention. This has led economic policy-makers to take it for granted that competitive economies are self-regulating. The latter is the target of some critical remarks made in the following (on this, see also chapter 1, pp. 6–20).

In this chapter some of the fundamentals alluded to in chapter 2 are taken up and elaborated somewhat. The first section establishes links with chapter 2. The next two sections briefly examine the content and methodological aspects of the approaches underlying classical-Keynesian political economy and neoclassical equilibrium economics. Some implications of the premises underlying classical-Keynesian and neoclassical economics are stressed in the subsequent section. This is followed by a sketch of the crucial importance of the capital theory debate. In the final section, a few remarks are made on the theory of knowledge implied in classical-Keynesian and neoclassical theory.

Two visions of society

Based upon the fundamentals set out in chapter 2, the visions of society underlying neoclassical economics and classical-Keynesian political economy may be sketched. Neoclassical economics is based upon the principle of individualism. Social phenomena arise on the basis of explicit or implicit contracts between individuals; the 'social' consists in interactions between individuals (chapter 2, pp. 20–1). There are automatic mechanisms which co-ordinate the actions of individuals and collectives. The prime example is the market, a natural institution, which co-ordinates the optimizing behaviour of individuals in the economic sphere. The description of competitive equilibria *à la* Walras seems positive and normative at once: on the one hand the attempt is made to capture the essence of a market economy; this, on the other hand, implies a social optimum *à la*

Pareto. In positive neoclassical economics the behaviour of individuals and collectives in the economic sphere is described and explanations of behavioural outcomes are attempted. The co-ordinated interactions between the various agents give rise to a behavioural system which supersedes the institutional system.

The starting point in classical-Keynesian political economy is society. Here social phenomena represent relationships between individuals and society (chapter 2, pp. 20–1); the 'social' is a part–whole relationship. Social institutions are preconditions for the actions of individuals. From a normative viewpoint, social institutions ought to stand in the service of individuals. This humanist vision of society implies that society and man are considered as entities (chapter 2, pp. 20–57). The various spheres of society, i.e. the political, legal, economic and social spheres, are complementary; the same holds for the different domains in which individuals act. Hence humanist social philosophies combine individualism and a moderate form of holism, which has been called structurism in chapter 2. In the classical-Keynesian third-way view there is no automatic co-ordination of individual actions. Social institutions have to be created purposefully to bring about a socially acceptable functioning of society as a whole, mainly to reach the full-employment goal as closely and permanently as possible (chapter 4, pp.142–204). The gap between a perfect society, organized in line with the inherent nature of the individuals composing it, and some actually existing society has been called alienation (chapter 2, pp. 47–53). The most important type of alienation is system-caused permanent and involuntary unemployment. The misuse of political institutions by particular interests leads to alienation in the sphere of distribution: for example, corruption leads to socially inappropriate distributional outcomes. Since the most embracing policy aim must be the reduction of alienation – in order to get nearer to the common weal – humanist or middle-way political economy is *essentially* a moral science.

In neoclassical economics there is no gap between the rationality of the system, i.e. the market mechanism, which co-ordinates the actions of individuals in the economic sphere, and the rationality embodied in precisely these actions. The market co-ordinates the optimizing behaviour of individuals in a neutral way, i.e. the co-ordination function of the market does not alter the quality of the individual optimizing processes. In this respect, a crucial difference between neoclassical economics and classical-Keynesian political economy exists. In the latter, the social structure, i.e. institutions and their interplay, develops a life of its own, largely independent of the will of the individuals making up a society. The latter may be illustrated by Keynes's paradox of thrift. To save more may be perfectly rational from the point of view of each individual in a society, but may be disastrous in a monetary production economy; in this macroinstitution, investment governs saving and not the other way round; a rise in saving will lead to less demand for consumption goods and ultimately to less investment. Social structures develop their proper life because these are entities possessing their own laws: at the outset of his *Politics*, Aristotle states that, on account of the inequality of individuals, the social wholes are more than the sum of their parts; hence there must be a structuring or form-giving principle which co-ordinates the parts if an automatic co-ordination mechanism is lacking. This proposition seems to hold in the social sphere *and* in nature:

[The biologist] Michael Polanyi . . . attacked reductionism of biology to physics and chemistry on the grounds that, in a hierarchy of levels, 'the operations of a higher level can never be derived from the laws governing its isolated particulars, it follows that none of these biotic operations can be accounted for by the laws of physics and chemistry. Yet it is taken for granted today among biologists that all manifestations of life can ultimately be explained by the laws governing inanimate matter. Yet this assumption is patent nonsense.' The reference of Polanyi is of course to a complete explanation of *all* that happens in a living organism (Eccles 1984, pp. 5–6).

This statement also applies to society and its individuals. The complementarities prevailing in the social process of production, in the institutional superstructure and in the system of social and individual values make of each society a structured entity. Hence social phenomena cannot be reduced to the actions of individuals as is postulated by *methodological individualism*. The determinism exercised by historically grown social institutions, having their own laws, and their interplay must be studied as such. This was the position taken on by Aristotle, Marx, historically minded social scientists and the institutionalists; Ricardo's and Keynes's position was implicitly similar, although their penchant for individualism cannot be denied.

In the subsequent sections of this chapter it is suggested that the differing views on the relationship between individuals and society are the essence of the difference between neoclassical economics and classical-Keynesian political economy. This is not to argue that the two approaches are irreconcilable. Classical-Keynesian political economy essentially deals with the functioning of the socioeconomic and political system; here, behaviour is secondary (chapter 4). Positive neoclassical economics, however, essentially deals with the self-interested behaviour of individuals and collectives; the system is secondary: in the economic sphere, the market automatically and costlessly co-ordinates individual behaviour. The work connected with the theory of the firm or with the new political economy which deals with the behaviour of political actors is a prime example of positive neoclassical theory. This type of neoclassicism is complementary

to classical-Keynesian political economy. What is criticized here is neoclassical equilibrium theory which claims that, under ideal conditions, i.e.
perfect competition, markets co-ordinate the individual optimizing behav-
iours in a socially meaningful way.

Neoclassical equilibrium economics and classical-Keynesian political economy

In his *History of Economic Analysis*, Joseph Schumpeter provides a description of the content of neoclassical theory which is so illuminating that a full
quotation of the relevant passages is justified.

[Utility maximizing individuals engage in the exchange of goods already produced
and therefore scarce to varying degrees. Jevons, Menger, Walras and Gossen] all
aimed at the same goal, which was to prove that the principle of marginal utility
suffices to deduce the exchange ratios between commodities that will establish themselves in competitive markets . . . The essential point is that, in the 'new' theory of
exchange, *marginal utility analysis created an analytical tool of general applicability
to economic problems* . . . But Menger went on to say that means of production . . .
come within the concept of economic goods by virtue of the fact that they also yield
consumers' satisfaction, though only indirectly, through helping to produce things
that do satisfy consumers' wants directly. [This analytic device] enables us to treat
such things as iron or cement or fertilizers – and also all services of natural agents
and labor that are not directly consumed – as incomplete consumable goods, and
thereby extends the range of the principle of marginal utility over the whole area of
production and 'distribution'. The requisites or factors or agents of production are
assigned use values: they acquire their indices of economic significance and hence
their exchange values from the same marginal utility principle that provides the
indices of economic significance and hence explains the exchange values of
consumable goods. But those exchange values or relative prices of the factors constitute the costs of production for the producing firms. This means, on the one hand,
that the marginal utility principle now covers the cost phenomenon and in consequence also the logic of the allocation of resources . . . *so far as all this is determined
by economic considerations*. And it means, on the other hand, that in as much as
costs to firms are incomes to households, the same marginal principle . . . automatically covers the phenomena of income formation or of 'distribution', *which really
ceases to be a distinct topic* . . . The whole of the organon of pure economics thus
finds itself unified in the light of a single principle – in a sense in which it never had
before. Most of the problems that arise from this set-up can be discussed only on a
level on which Walras rules supreme (Schumpeter 1954, pp. 911–13).

It is important to note that within this framework the employment problem
is also solved:

Walras's system of the conditions or relations (equations) . . . determine the equilibrium values of all the economic variables, to wit: the prices of all products and

factors and the quantities of these products and factors that would be bought, in perfect equilibrium and pure competition by all households and firms . . . [S]ince the determination of these quantities implies the determination of individual as well as group and social incomes, this theory includes all that is covered by the concept of Income Analysis and that the conditions or relations to be considered, though they are fundamentally microanalytic in nature (they refer fundamentally to the quantities bought and sold by individual households and firms), also include macroanalytic aspects, for example, as regards *total employment in the society* [our emphasis]. It cannot be too strongly impressed upon the reader that it is not correct to contrast income or macroanalysis of, say, the Keynesian type with the Walrasian microanalysis as if the latter were a theory that neglects, and stands in need of being supplemented by, income and macroanalysis (Schumpeter 1954, pp. 998–9).

Hence the *individual and exchange, not society and production* constitute the starting point of neoclassical theorizing. Production appears as a simple application of exchange as is illustrated by the notion of 'factor markets' where the actions of profit-maximizing or cost-minimizing entrepreneurs demanding factors of production are co-ordinated with the actions of utility-maximizing households offering these. The remarkable symmetry existing between goods and factor markets and between the profit-maximizing behaviour of entrepreneurs and the utility-maximizing behaviour of households (consumers) has been noted by many economists.

Money plays a secondary role in neoclassical economics. The most important function of money is to facilitate exchange. More time is then available for production and consumption. The quantity of money determines the absolute level of money prices. Thus, in principle, money is *neutral* in that it does not affect real variables in the long run.

In the *neoclassical theory of international trade* all trading partners benefit from exchange. This is due to the principle of comparative advantages. 'Each country enjoys full employment . . . Equality between the values of imports and exports of each country is quickly established . . . by movements of relative prices brought about through the international monetary mechanism' (Robinson 1966, pp. 3–4).

The content of classical-Keynesian political economy was sketched in chapter 4; here some essentials are taken up. In *classical-Keynesian long-period theory* the starting point is the *circular and social* process of production within which distribution is regulated and the formation of long-period normal prices takes place. Distribution is based upon the surplus principle: the division of the *given* social product between wage and non-wage income (indicated by k^*, the average mark-up at normal capacity utilization) is, in the long run, regulated by a complex set of social, political and economic institutions. Once distribution is regulated, i.e. the rate of profits determined, prices depend upon the conditions of production and upon the level of money wages: it is an objective theory of value; prices thus reflect the efforts undertaken by society to produce goods (Pasinetti). Given long-period normal prices, trend effective demand and long-period Engel curves govern the structural set-up of an economy, i.e. the appropriate proportions between sectors and industries.

Normal prices and quantities represent a fully adjusted situation. The market, supply and demand, tends to enforce fully adjusted situations: differences between market prices and normal prices are registered and corresponding quantity adjustments are set into motion. However, the stabilizing function of markets may be disturbed by cyclical movements which may drag output and employment levels away from their respective system equilibria.

The classical-Keynesian theory of output and employment is based upon a monetary theory of production: long-period output and employment are governed by effective demand through the supermultiplier mechanism. On Keynesian grounds, money is a store of value and is not neutral.

In classical-Keynesian political economy international trade is important because of the welfare effect of trade based upon the classical version of the principle of comparative costs (which affects structures, *given* employment levels), *and* because of the employment effect of trade: export surpluses, high and fast-growing manufacturing exports linked with favourable terms of trade and a small import coefficient (relative to exports) lead, in principle, to higher trend levels of output and employment. This employment and output effect of international trade is based on the mercantilist-Keynesian vision of international trade elaborated by Nicholas Kaldor in his later work.

In the medium and short terms the behaviour of individuals is also co-ordinated by the principle of effective demand. The interaction of the income effect and the capacity effect of investment gives rise to cyclical movements of economic activity. In the short run, effective demand governs the level of capacity utilization.

In classical-Keynesian political economy the fundamental importance of production, associated with the surplus principle and with the principle of effective demand, implies that the *entire* socioeconomic and political structure (the institutional system) comes in to determine the central long-period variables (profit rates and mark-ups, prices and quantities and output and employment levels). Behavioural outcomes will always deviate from system outcomes, but the latter ultimately dominate.

Put in a nutshell: in neoclassical economics behaviour, associated with short-term flexibility, and *price adjustments* dominate; classical-Keynesian political economy is characterized by structural rigidities and *quantity adjustments*.

Methodological issues: positive causal models versus normative equilibrium models

There are also fundamental differences between neoclassical economics and classical-Keynesian political economy at the methodological level. In the present section some of the notions developed in chapters 2 and 3 are put to use in order to compare neoclassical equilibrium methodology with the classical-Keynesian method of combining unidirectional causal models. The first subsection deals with the significance of the normative element in classical-Keynesian and neoclassical theory; in the second the relationship between models and reality in both approaches is alluded to; in the third subsection some properties and implications of equilibrium and of causal models are set out.

Some remarks on the normative element in economic models

Classical-Keynesian causal models attempt to mirror causal forces that shape specific parts of reality. Causal forces may be associated with the determination exercised by the socioeconomic system or with the pursuit of specific aims by individuals and collectives (chapter 2, pp. 53–7). Space and time can be introduced without difficulty through applied or real-type models (chapter 3, pp. 81–9, 118–30). This is true of simple, combined or interdependent causal models, of which the Leontief–Sraffa model is the most prominent example. All these models belong to positive economic theory and are not normative in the sense of implying full employment or a socially acceptable income distribution (chapter 4, pp. 142–204). Nevertheless, the normative element enters positive classical-Keynesian models *indirectly* through the notion of alienation which denotes the gap between an actually existing situation and the ideal one, i.e. the common weal (chapter 2, pp. 47–53). Alienation in this sense encompasses the whole of society, i.e. the entire institutional system; different, though interrelated types of alienation may be distinguished however, for example alienation in the economic, political or cultural sphere (Meszaros 1973). Hence classical-Keynesian political economy takes values, including ethical standards, the extent of alienation, and, consequently, the institutional set-up as given. The object of analysis is some existing situation. It is in this sense that classical-Keynesian causal models are positive. This implies that ethical ideals like the common weal are of a higher order. They are concerned with wholes, i.e. society and man, and not with parts of the real world as governed by specific causal relations, for example the scale of economic activity being governed by effective demand.

Liberalism, however, does not deal in the first place with existing situations; it is a project of society and is as such essentially normative. The same is true of neoclassical equilibrium economics, i.e. the *pure* economic theory of liberalism exhibiting the fundamental principles of a market economy. Here, the starting point is the competitive equilibrium which is ideal (optimal, rational, reasonable or natural) from the *economic* viewpoint in the sense that allocative efficiency is implied: the Walrasian equilibrium is associated with a Pareto optimum. Hence the normative element is *inside* the general equilibrium model which implies that ethics is not of a higher order but stands on the same footing as any other domain of the real world, for example the economic domain.

By definition, equilibrium situations cannot be found in the real world. Equilibria are supposed to lie in the future and picture situations that *would*, in the liberal view, come into being *if* competitive conditions prevailed and *if* a present disequilibrium situation could work out without being disturbed. The equilibrium situation is therefore *outside* historical time and, therefore, out of space, too. This means that historical time and space, both of which play a crucial role in classical-Keynesian 'real-type' theory, cannot be incorporated readily in modern neoclassical equilibrium theory. This is not to say that there are no elements of reality in neoclassical economics. In fact, modelling the *rational behaviour* of individuals and collectives within the theory of the firm, or within the new institutional and political economics, in order to explain behavioural outcomes gives rise to formulating *real-type* models which contribute greatly to a probable understanding of parts of the real world and represents an important element of a comprehensive system of political economy which aims at grasping the functioning of a society as a *whole*. The problem is whether the market is able, *in principle*, to co-ordinate individual behaviour in a socially meaningful way, that is to bring about a tendency towards a full employment equilibrium under competitive conditions. Thus the problem is whether the rationality of the system can be derived from the rational behaviour of individuals.

Some neoclassical economists (mainly representatives of Austrian economics, Hayek for example, and of constitutional economics, Buchanan for example) take the existence of and the tendency towards a competitive equilibrium for granted and consider disequilibrium situations. Here, the market merely co-ordinates exchanges and the prices are carriers of information. This type of economics is evidently positive in the liberal sense since liberal values are considered self-evident and correct beyond any doubt. The same is true of any disequilibrium analysis, for example the Clower–Leijonhufvud model.

In another sense the old neoclassical economists argued that equilibrium economics is also *positive* economics and as such pictures *essential properties* of actually existing market economies. Marshall in particular, but also Walras, conceived of the long-period equilibrium as a *natural* state of affairs which is, as such, *a hidden part of reality*. This reflects a widely held nineteenth-century view according to which the natural (the normative) is part of reality and is, as a consequence, also positive. For example, the marginal productivity theory of income distribution was (and still is) supposed to produce natural distributional outcomes. The 'old' neoclassical long-period equilibrium was considered a centre of gravity around which an economy fluctuates: 'Il en est . . . du marché comme d'un lac agité par le vent et où l'eau cherche toujours son équilibre sans jamais l'atteindre' (Walras 1952, p. 370). Traditional neoclassical equilibrium economics, therefore, attempted to set forth the principles regulating the economic sphere of the real world.

The 'rational expectations' model is unique in the sense that the positive and the normative coincide even on the level of appearances. We are always in a *full* state of equilibrium: for example, there is equilibrium unemployment, and cyclical movements equally imply equilibria. The 'rational expectations' system represents the modern counterpart of traditional Marshallian neoclassicism and implies the stronger claim that average rational behaviour quickly eliminates any disturbing factors. This prevents deviations from equilibrium positions.

Keynes had no doubts about the normative nature of neoclassical equilibrium economics: 'The celebrated *optimism* of traditional economic theory, which has led to economists being looked upon as Candides, who . . . teach that all is for the best in the best of all possible worlds provided we will let well alone . . . It may well be that the [neo]classical theory represents the way in which we should like our economy to behave. But to assume that it actually does so is to assume our difficulties away' (Keynes 1973a, pp. 33–4). In some instances, Walras also alluded to the *normative, hypothetical and hence ahistorical* character of his system: 'L'*économie politique pure* est essentiellement la théorie de la détermination des prix sous un régime hypothétique de libre concurrence absolue' (Walras 1952, p. XI). This hypothetical state of affairs described by pure theory has certain desirable properties. Given resources, technology and tastes each agent maximizes utility and/or profits (including interests). This implies the best possible use of given resources and characterizes the Walrasian system as a normative guiding star: 'C'est pourquoi l'économie politique pure est aussi la *théorie de la richesse sociale*' (Walras 1952, p. XI). In this context modern neoclassical economists speak of allocative efficiency, which implies the full employment of available resources, *including labour*. To be sure, allocative efficiency does not mean equity, the latter implying that the initial endowment of resources and personal income distribution may be very unequal. But the crucial point is that *both efficiency and equity* are part of neoclassical welfare economics which, by definition, is normative. Hence modern neoclassical equilibrium economics embodies the principles regulating the economic sphere of a world which is *desirable* in a liberal view; only the *rational expectations* school, which postulates that economies are always in equilibrium, would claim equilibrium models picture principles regulating the real world.

The normative nature of the Walrasian model has been put to the fore with more vigour recently:

most economists . . . would be inclined to accept that what Walras essentially did was to articulate rigorously the notion . . . of how an interrelated market economy could be expected to function automatically given the idealized situation of perfect competition – that is, a competitive regime including perfect mobility of resources, perfect flexibility of prices, and perfect information concerning prices as provided by a hypothetical 'auctioneer'. [Thus], Walras' purpose, according to Jaffé [1983b], was *not* to describe or to analyse a real-world system, even under stringent assumptions. *His goal then was not positivistic; rather it was essentially normative* [our emphasis]. Walras was attempting to find out whether an economic system based upon conditions that to his mind constituted economic justice, both in exchange and distribution, *could* exist (Chase 1978, pp. 83–4).

This also holds for the modern variations of the basic Walrasian model; there, however, the positive element associated with the natural situations of the old neoclassicals seems to have been abandoned.

The normative character of the models describing equilibrium situations shows up in the fact that elements which are not, or not fully, part of reality, are added to reality. The most important addition to reality is the equilibrium requirement: prices have to be such that supply and demand are equalized on all markets; this implies full employment of all resources, including labour. According to the type of equilibrium model other – hypothetical – elements are added to reality: universal perfect competition, rational behaviour of all agents which, in turn, implies perfect information, etc. In fact, each equilibrium model depicts a world of its own containing certain desirable and hypothetical elements which cannot be found in an actual (positive) state of affairs. The presence of these elements in normative equilibrium models and the simultaneous determination of the variables is what distinguishes these from the classical-Keynesian causal models mentioned above.

Models and reality in the classical-Keynesian and neoclassical approaches

There are no major problems with integrating space and time in classical-Keynesian *real-type* models (chapter 3, pp. 103–30). The link between models and reality can be easily established because *pure* classical-Keynesian causal models are set up to explain *in principle* aspects of the real world, not to picture an ideal situation; the categories put to use in such models therefore – probably – correspond to real-world phenomena. Subsequently, applied or real-type models may be developed on the basis of pure or ideal-type models (chapter 3, pp. 81–9, 118–30). However, Marshall perceived that, '[in] the general theory of equilibrium of demand and supply . . . the difficulties of the problem depend chiefly on the area of space, and the period of time over which [markets extend]; the influence of time being more fundamental than that of space' (Marshall 1920, p. 496); consequently explanations of real-world phenomena on the basis of equilibrium models are equally difficult. In this subsection we attempt to provide some reasons to substantiate Marshall's observation.

Space and time are very difficult to integrate in neoclassical equilibrium models because these models do not aim at explaining aspects of reality but impose conditions on the real world in order to picture a situation which is ideal in certain respects. This is due to the normative and, eventually, hypothetical nature of these models. In extreme cases general equilibrium models are very far away from reality, such that they even miss the essence of those parts of economic reality which they want to explain, i.e. the role played in principle by market prices. Heroic assumptions are required to establish equilibria: universal perfect competition, perfect foresight and so on. Subsequently, liberal economists attempt to explain capitalist reality with the help of deviations from the equilibrium norm, for example lack of competition, too much state intervention or wrong monetary policies. If explanations of macroeconomic phenomena were attempted within a general equilibrium (real-type) framework the corresponding models would have to be brought nearer to reality, i.e. space, by accounting, for example, for increasing returns, imperfect competition and imperfect foresight. Owing to the very large number of variables the complexity of such models would increase rapidly. In Kaldorian terms, the scaffolding gets thicker and thicker (Kaldor 1966, pp. 296–7). To escape the unmanageable complexity of 'more realistic' general equilibrium models, many neoclassical equilibrium economists switch over to highly aggregate models (for example, Solow 1956), or, as is much more common, partial models of the Marshallian type are worked out. The prime example is the neoclassical labour market model which is used to deal with the unemployment problem. However, the underlying general equilibrium model is always considered to be the true model which could, at any time, be worked out if the necessity arose; for example, Samuelson admitted that there might be problems with simple neoclassical parables using the 'concept of aggregate "capital", instead [of] relying upon a complete analysis of a great variety of

heterogeneous physical capital goods and processes through time'
(Samuelson 1962, p. 213). It is argued below (pp. 281–93) that the problems
arising with aggregate and partial models subsist within a general equilibrium framework if an attempt is made to tackle fundamental economic
problems, e.g. long-period value, distribution and employment: the capital-
theory debate affects the whole of equilibrium theory.

In relation to the treatment of time, the distinction between long- and
short-period equilibrium models (Garegnani 1976) is crucial. The former
deal with fundamental equilibria governed by permanent or slowly changing institutional and technological factors. These *long-period* or *fundamental equilibria* constitute the modern counterparts of the traditional
neoclassical centres of gravity or natural states (Marshall 1920, book V,
chapter III; book VI, chapter I), with profit rates equal in all sectors of production. On the other hand, there are *temporary* equilibria governed by
rapidly changing short-run factors. A comprehensive temporary equilibrium model was set out by Hicks in *Value and Capital* (Hicks 1946). Starting
from this kind of model, it seems natural to go on to describing *sequences
of (temporary) equilibria* instead of elaborating fundamental long-period
equilibria (Hahn 1973, p. 16). Very important consequences follow from
this. First, temporary equilibrium models are more realistic than their long-
period counterparts. The former are less abstract and fewer conditions are
imposed upon the real world. As a rule, temporary equilibrium models
depict outcomes of economic events which need not be satisfactory to
economic agents from a long-period point of view, the main reason being
that *realized* profit and wage rates do not correspond to (normal) long-
period rates, except by a fluke. Second, temporary equilibrium models
attempt to capture what is going to happen in the market-place between the
present and a short-term future and therefore deal with the rapidly changing vagaries of the market. These models tackle a macroeconomic problem,
that is the determination of *all* prices and quantities *and* of the scale of economic activity. Since it is very difficult to say how a new short-run equilibrium will evolve out of some existing temporary equilibrium *uncertainty
and expectations* will play a crucial role in temporary equilibrium models.
The use of complex stochastic models therefore becomes inevitable which
implies that the scaffolding is likely to grow even more elaborate. This criticism of GE models does not prevent *microeconomic* models incorporating
uncertainty and expectations from being very useful in appropriately picturing the behaviour of economic agents.

On the macroeconomic level a crucial question now begins to emerge:
does the optimizing behaviour of producers and consumers co-ordinated
by market forces produce a *tendency* for sequences of temporary equilibria
to converge towards a fundamental equilibrium *if* a given situation is

allowed to work out in ideal conditions, i.e. without further disturbance? This question will be taken up below (pp. 281–93). Before doing so, we examine in the subsequent subsection some properties and implications of neoclassical equilibrium models and of positive classical-Keynesian causal models. In the following main section some implications of the neoclassical and the classical-Keynesian approaches are brought into the open.

Some properties and implications of causal and equilibrium models

The distinction between equilibrium and causal models is not new. Schumpeter clearly perceived it when noting the similarity of Ricardo's and Keynes's methods and their difference to the neoclassical approach:

The comprehensive vision of the universal interdependence of all the elements of the economic system . . . probably never cost Ricardo as much as an hour's sleep. His interest was in the clearcut result of direct, practical significance. In order to get this he cut the general system to pieces, bundled up as large parts as possible, and put them in cold storage – so that as many things as possible should be frozen and 'given'. He then piled one simplifying assumption upon another until having really settled everything by these assumptions, he was left with only a few aggregative variables between which, given these assumptions, he set up *simple one-way relations* [our emphasis] (Schumpeter 1954, p. 472).

This is really the crucial point. Schumpeter then goes on:

The similarity between the aims and methods of those two eminent men, Keynes and Ricardo, is indeed striking, though it will not impress those who look primarily for the advice a writer tenders. Of course, there is a world between Keynes and Ricardo in this respect, and Keynes's views on economic policy bear much more resemblance to Malthus'. But I am speaking of Ricardo's and Keynes's methods of securing the clearcut result. On this they were brothers in the spirit (Schumpeter 1954, p. 473n).

Pasinetti confirms Schumpeter's proposition:

Like Ricardo, [Keynes] is always looking for fundamentals [i.e. principles regulating certain spheres of the real world, H.B.]. He singles out for consideration the variables he believes to be the most important. All the others, giving rise to unimportant complications – though, as he says, are always 'kept at the back of his head' for the necessary qualifications – are, for immediate purposes, frozen out by simple assumptions. The characteristic consequence of this methodological procedure is the emergence in Keynes, as in Ricardo, of a system of equations of the 'causal type', or, as we may also say, of the 'decomposable type', as opposed to a completely interdependent system of simultaneous equations (Pasinetti 1974, pp. 43–4).

Marshall had already perceived the problem: '[Ricardo] does not state clearly, and in some cases he perhaps did not fully and clearly perceive, how, in the problem of normal value, the various elements govern one another *mutually*, and not *successively* in a long chain of causation' (Marshall 1920, p. 816).

Equilibrium and causal models are linked with entirely different visions of socioeconomic phenomena. To bring these differences to the open some properties and implications of the two types of models are set forth below.

From a purely formal point of view, classical-Keynesian causal models express a very simple idea (for a more general treatment, see Pasinetti 1964/65):

$$a_{11}x_1 = b_1 \ (1) \qquad a_{21}x_1 + a_{22}x_2 = b_2 \ (2).$$

The unknown x_1 is determined by the first equation to the exclusion of the second. In the latter, x_1 appears as a predetermined variable which, together with the parameters a_{21}, a_{22} and b_2, determines x_2. Hence there is a causal relation between x_1 and x_2.

In neoclassical equilibrium economics, however, simultaneous equation systems are used:

$$a_{11}x_1 + a_{12}x_2 = b_1 \ (1) \qquad a_{21}x_1 + a_{22}x_2 = b_2 \ (2).$$

Here causality in the classical-Keynesian sense is excluded. The two unknowns are determined simultaneously by the parameters only and there is no difference between determined and predetermined variables.

This formal property of causal and equilibrium models is associated with an important material property. In the latter, equilibrium, i.e. a desirable situation, is supposed to be brought about automatically by the supply and demand mechanism, at least in principle. This property is lacking for the set of causal models which picture the essence of monetary production economies. Here, an ethically grounded policy effort is required to improve a given situation, i.e. to reduce system-caused alienation.

Several issues are raised by causal and equilibrium models respectively. First, *time* is always present in *applied* classical-Keynesian economic theory, i.e. in 'real-type' causal models (chapter 3, pp.118–30), since causality goes on in historical time and may be short-lived or more or less persistent. This holds for diagrams and for algebraical representations. Pure causal models are however independent of space and time and picture how causal forces operate in principle and in all situations.

On the one hand, causal models and combinations of such models try to capture causes and effects of human actions, and, on the other, the functioning and the evolution of socioeconomic systems and their deterministic influence upon behaviour. The types of action and the way in which systems function evolve in time. Actual events, i.e. realized results, are confronted with desired results; decisions taken from the point of view of individuals or of society as a whole aim at narrowing the gap between actually existing and more desirable situations. From a normative viewpoint, this is equivalent to reducing alienation. Individual and social attempts to diminish alienation constitute the engine of change.

In an equilibrium model time does not enter the picture. It is even difficult to see the meaning of Joan Robinson's concept of logical time (Robinson 1962a, pp. 23ff.). In fact the GE model is a liberal all-purpose ideal-type model on the basis of which all economic problems can be tackled. The parameters of the model simply define the equilibrium values of the unknowns which assume a normative character in so far as the economic sphere is concerned: competitive markets are social values *per se*. Historical time could come in only indirectly with respect to equilibrium models: *if* there were a tendency towards a fundamental equilibrium, the question as to the length of the time-period which elapses between a present disequilibrium and the future time-point when equilibrium is approximately reached would arise (pp. 281–93 below).

A second issue is that *space* (always associated with time) plays an important role in classical-Keynesian real-type models. Events occurring in a given moment happen at different places – and, at a given place, at different points of time. In addition, causal forces need time to work through space to produce some effect: for example, present investment activities produce a future effect on output and employment through the income and capacity effects of investment.

This combined property of space and time is succinctly expressed by the epigraph to one of Joan Robinson's (1962a) books: 'Time is a device to prevent everything from happening at once (Bergson).' Similarly, one could say, space prevents everything from happening at one particular point. Space and time imply each other.

The presence of space and time implies limited knowledge and information or, mostly, ignorance about what happens in other places or spheres (in different geographical areas, or in other sciences). This, in turn, requires co-operation between individuals possessing complementary knowledge in order to reach common aims (for instance, an economist and an engineer who jointly run an enterprise). Moreover, the knowledge acquired always represents 'probable truth' (Keynes 1971c). The combined presence of time, space, limited information and probable knowledge in classical-Keynesian models reflects reality quite accurately. Human actions aimed at reaching certain purposes are, as a rule, based upon a small number of variables which are considered to be the most important ones; if such actions are rational, rationality is severely bounded. For instance, entrepreneurial investment decisions will essentially be based upon the comparison between realized and target profits (equation 24, p. 208). Or, in Ricardo's system, the difference between the prevailing real wage and the institutionally governed natural wage rate governs the way in which population evolves. Given an immensely complex reality, human beings when attempting to reach certain aims, quite naturally take into account only those variables which they consider to be crucial; this, once again, indicates the importance of values regarding aims *and* means. Hence, social scientists who aim at explaining reality must try to *understand* why certain values are pursued, for example in the sphere of consumption or in the arts. But this is not sufficient. Social scientists must also attempt to grasp how the behaviour of individuals is co-ordinated by the socioeconomic system and how the feedback of the system upon behaviour operates; for instance, effective demand governs normal output and employment and imposes a long-term constraint on entrepreneurial investment activities. An approximate understanding of the behaviour of individuals and of the way in which the system works will enable the theorist to leave out of the picture everything which is not essential to tackling a particular problem and to end up with simple causal models; these represent tools which enable social scientists to come to grips with some specific aspect of the real world.

Space is absent in equilibrium models, which implies perfect information. An example to illustrate this is the Walrasian auctioneer who, together with the economic agents, fixes the equilibrium prices at which exchanges of final goods and means of production are supposed to take place. It does not matter 'where' this 'process' takes place and 'how long' it lasts. If production is introduced, abstraction from time and space implies perfect foresight. Consequently, if the notion of capital is to make sense, investors must know the future course of prices and quantities exactly in order to be able to bring rates of return into line with interest rates: the past and the future collapse into an everlasting present.

Neoclassical equilibrium models become more complex when the pure model dealing with principles is applied to real-world problems, i.e. when 'real-type' general equilibrium models are elaborated. This may be done, for example, by introducing intertemporal properties where each good is, in addition to its physical properties, characterized by its 'place' in time and space; complexity is compounded if imperfect information is taken account of. This is partly due to the simultaneous determination of all the variables which, *in principle*, prevents the piecemeal operation of the general equilibrium model. The simple partial equilibrium model may render the general equilibrium model operable. However, the *ceteris paribus* clause is usually considered to be unsatisfactory because quantities supplied and demanded depend on all prices, i.e. there is an interaction between the various markets. This inevitably leads back to the general equilibrium model in which all prices and quantities appear individually;

these are co-ordinated by a single principle, that is *exchange* or *supply and demand*.

It has already been suggested that Austrian-type disequilibrium models explicitly take account of space and time (historical developments) and are, as such, positive models. Here, prices provide information and indicate opportunities open to individuals. There is no problem for the classical-Keynesian to accept this: the deviation of market prices from the prices of production guides entrepreneurial investment behaviour. However the Austrians would argue that a competitive economy tends towards a full employment situation, which is rejected by the classical-Keynesians (pp. 281–93 below). This implies profound differences as to the socioeconomic policies to be pursued (chapter 6).

A third issue is that causal models imply the presence of predetermined and determined magnitudes; in the multiplier relation, for instance, investment and the multiplier are predetermined while the level of output represents the determined variable. These notions bear some similarity to the categories of *endogenous* and *exogenous* variables. When dealing with causal models, the latter ought to be used in a specific way, however. If causality is horizontal, i.e. along the time axis (chapter 3, pp. 120–3), then the situation existing at the beginning of the time-period considered is exogenous; all that happens within the period in question and is to be explained, is endogenous. For example, an economic historian wishing to explain French economic development from 1815 onwards will consider the heritage of the Revolution and of the Napoleonic Wars as given and exogenous. All economic events, related to growth, distribution, etc., which have happened in France since 1815 are, consequently, endogenous and are to be explained in terms of the initial situation, including the tendencies of change at work there. The notions of exogenous and endogenous variables are more complicated if causality is vertical (chapter 3, pp. 120–3): if a causal model aims at explaining an economic event located in a given layer of reality, then all the variables situated in other layers are exogenous. The same is true of the predetermined variables of the causal relation considered. This is obvious in the supermultiplier relation. Deviations from normal output and employment levels, due to medium-term cyclical movements and short-run temporary factors, are exogenous to the trends in question; this is but a proviso, however, since the trend (governed by the institutional system) and the cycle (determined by investment behaviour) influence each other. The predetermined variables and parameters to be found on the right-hand side of the supermultiplier relation (7) are also exogenous since these are partly determined by institutions situated outside the realm of economics. Hence, once the fundamental exogenous variables are defined, there is no need to go further in the search for more basic causal factors, mainly the interplay of institutions. To explain the latter is the task of the sociologist and of the political scientist. However, the necessity for collaboration within the social sciences clearly emerges. This need arises from the *complementarity* of the socioeconomic, political, legal and social spheres which is crucial in a humanist view of society (chapter 2, pp. 20–57).

In neoclassical equilibrium economics the distinction between predetermined and determined, endogenous and exogenous variables vanishes for the economic variables (prices and quantities). In an equilibrium model, all these variables stand on the same footing in that they are mutually determined by the parameters of the model. Exogenous variables are non-economic variables pertaining to the framework which exert their influence upon the equilibrium values of the economic (endogenous) variables through the parameters of the general equilibrium model.

Moving to the fourth issue: classical-Keynesian models are *open* in the sense that non-economic factors, such as social and political institutions and ethical values, may *directly* determine economic variables; this emerges from the supermultiplier relation (7) or in the normal price level equation (6) for instance. Open models imply that economics may easily be linked up with other social sciences, for example law, sociology or political science. Moreover, each causal model may be easily connected with other causal models in order to explain complex phenomena, employment levels or distributional outcomes for example. This is made use of in the classical-Keynesian synthesis set out in chapter 4. Here, long-period, medium-term and short-run causal models are combined to yield a complete classical-Keynesian framework. Finally, hierarchies of causes may be established. As a rule, long-run and persistent factors associated with the socioeconomic system are more important in explaining some dependent variable than short-run – temporary – and behavioural factors.

Neoclassical equilibrium models are *closed* in the sense that outside influences are taken account of by parameter changes only. New parameter-sets yield new sets of equilibrium values for the economic variables. The point is that the basic economic mechanism, i.e. the supply and demand apparatus, is not altered by outside events, which leads to shifts in demand and supply curves leaving the mechanism of demand and supply untouched. The economic system is considered self-contained, which, in turn, is a consequence of individualistic social philosophy: individuals become active in different spheres, the economic and political domains for instance, and, in each domain, a specific mechanism is supposed to co-ordinate individual actions, the market in the economic sphere, voting procedures in the political sphere.

Fifth, classical-Keynesian *pure* causal models are of striking simplicity;

this is evident from Keynes's *logical* multiplier, the supermultiplier relation and Sraffa's normal price equations. Pure causal models, whether exhibiting vertical or horizontal causality, tell us how specific causal processes operate *in principle* and *independently* of each other. These models picture aspects of the socioeconomic system and specific patterns of behaviour. Once a concrete empirical situation evolving in historical time is considered, however, complexity increases sharply since each state of affairs is governed by numerous causal forces of the vertical and of the horizontal type. Complex real-world states of affairs, for example the determination of the level of employment in a particular country, require sophisticated explanatory frameworks (real types) made up of several applied causal models. The appropriate selection of causal models requires a pre-analytic understanding of the phenomenon to be explained.

Pure neoclassical theory, i.e. the general equilibrium model, is *inherently* complex. This is due to the very conception of neoclassical theorizing: economic phenomena are to be explained in terms of the behaviour of individuals (methodological individualism). Complexity arises because behaviour is interrelated in the process of exchange. Consequently, the complexity of the pure exchange model reflects the intricacy of market phenomena. The problem is that the exchange model is the *starting point* for theorizing along neoclassical lines, while this model would merely occupy a secondary position in classical-Keynesian theory.

Sixth, the terms *equilibrium* and *disequilibrium* have entirely different meanings in classical-Keynesian political economy from those in neoclassical economics. In the former, 'equilibrium' prices and quantities (the fully adjusted situation) are governed by the socioeconomic system which is made up of a set of complementary institutions pertaining to all the spheres of human activity (chapter 3, pp. 89–95). Disequilibria appear as deviations of behavioural outcomes (actual prices and quantities) from system equilibria associated with normal prices and quantities. Hence classical-Keynesian political economy can easily deal with 'disequilibrium' situations. This is also characteristic of Ricardo's and of Keynes's political economy.

Modern neoclassical economics starts from given tastes, technology and endowments, and equilibrium results from the optimizing behaviour of agents co-ordinated by the market mechanism. The latter represents the economic subsystem which is surrounded by a framework represented by the social, political and cultural subsystems. The market mechanism is automatic and its purpose is to co-ordinate the actions of individuals; consequently, behaviour dominates in neoclassical economics and the system is secondary. Since equilibrium is the starting point in neoclassical theorizing, disequilibrium situations are very difficult to deal with: the reference point – equilibrium – is entirely unknown for it is outside the real world. The only way to escape this difficulty is to assume that we are always in equilibrium as is postulated by the 'rational expectations' school.

A final methodological problem arises with respect to the type of *econometrics* put to use in neoclassical equilibrium economics and classical-Keynesian political economy respectively. The former is closely associated with 'simultaneous-equations econometrics'. The joint probability distributions of the parameters of such systems render estimation procedures extremely complicated if the number of equations is large.

The causal relations making up classical-Keynesian economic theory can be estimated one by one, however. These are largely independent of each other in that they are separated, so to speak, by space and time: events happening at different places and at different points of time are broadly independent in that the corresponding processes do not influence each other, or mutual influences are, frequently, of secondary importance and can therefore be neglected. Classical-Keynesian 'causal-relations econometrics' *à la* Hermann Wold is thus much simpler and straightforward than neoclassical 'simultaneous-equations econometrics' (on this, see Pasinetti 1964/65, pp. 239–43).

Production, exchange and visions of society

The vision regarding the role of production and of exchange is crucial to characterizing the approach underlying classical-Keynesian political economy and neoclassical economics. This issue was raised by both Krishna Bharadwaj (1986) and Luigi Pasinetti (1977, 1981, 1993) and is dealt with extensively in Baranzini and Scazzieri (1986) and in Walsh and Gram (1980).

In this section, we consider, in the first place, the limited role of the market and the corresponding importance of production for classical-Keynesian political economy; moreover, the importance of institutions within a structurist and macroeconomic framework is examined. Secondly, we discuss the importance of exchange and the secondary role of production in neoclassical theory; this is complemented by some remarks on the reduction of economic phenomena to the behaviour of individuals in this theory.

In chapters 2 to 4 it has been postulated that positive classical-Keynesian political economy is, essentially, a framework for historical investigations, based upon a realist vision of man and of society, which takes account of the individual and of the social nature of man. The latter implies that social systems are structured entities having laws of their own. Both the individual and the social aspect of human existence may take on various shapes. The institutional set-up will not only differ between regions and countries but will vary in the course of time. This vision has important consequences for the premises underlying classical-Keynesian economic theory.

First, the *market* is an institution among others and plays a limited, though not unimportant, role in the classical-Keynesian system. The significance of the market emerges if two types of price systems are considered. Normal prices are determined *before* goods come to the market and depend upon the conditions of production and upon income distribution, that is upon the socioeconomic system. The market registers differences between market prices and the estimated normal prices and sets structural adjustments in motion; market prices rest on the short-period behaviour of economic agents and the co-ordination of behaviour by the law of supply and demand. The adjustment processes in question essentially consist of a *tendency* towards a *fully adjusted situation* which contains normal prices and quantities. The proper functioning of market forces may, however, be disturbed by the business cycle which represents an element of instability (chapter 4, pp. 204–20).

The limited role of the market, and hence of exchange, in classical-Keynesian political economy implies, almost necessarily, the crucial importance of production. The circular and social process is the starting point in explaining socioeconomic phenomena (chapter 3, pp. 89–95). The *essentially social nature* of this process explains why the most important economic problems, i.e. value, distribution and employment, cannot be solved by the market, i.e. cannot be reduced to the behaviour of individuals and collectives. There is no hope of defining the value of goods independently of distribution, since the proportion of indirect labour (embodied in the means of production) to direct labour is different in the various sectors of production: it is impossible to disentangle the contribution to the value of some product made by labour and 'capital' (indirect labour) in the various industries in the course of the social process of production. Therefore, it is impossible for distribution to be regulated by factor markets since marginal products are devoid of meaning in the long run (Sraffa). This was shown by Garegnani, Harcourt, Pasinetti and others in the course of the capital-theory debate (pp. 281–93 below). There are no regular long-period relationships between 'factor prices' and quantities of 'factors of production'. These relationships are in fact highly erratic: 'natura *facit* saltum', contrary to what Marshall thought. This implies that, in the long run, employment cannot be regulated by 'factor markets' either.

This leads to the second point, i.e. the need for a structurist and macroeconomic approach to deal with socioeconomic problems. In the classical-Keynesian view, value, employment and distribution are not regulated on 'factor markets' but are governed by historically grown institutions and technological structures. The most important economic phenomena are, thus, related to the functioning of a society (and of an economy) as a *whole*. In any epoch, existing institutions represent a historical heritage, and the interplay of institutions (the social structure) in a society is governed by the system of values prevailing at that epoch. This is the essence of structurism (Lloyd 1986, pp. 148ff.). Taking a structurist view of society automatically implies that the appropriate proportions between sectors of production and, more generally, between the various spheres of social and individual life become all important: the search for harmony between the socio-economic institutions that are associated with the process of production and the institutional superstructure should constitute the prime task of politics; this would imply aiming at full employment and a socially acceptable income distribution. Both would provide part of the social basis within which individuals could prosper.

Several great authors clearly perceived the need for a structurist and macroeconomic approach, the most prominent being François Quesnay, James Steuart, David Ricardo, Karl Marx and Maynard Keynes. For instance, Keynes differed from Marshall and his followers about the basic approach to be taken in economics. In the *General Theory*, Keynes took a deliberately macroeconomic approach in that he was considering the functioning of an economy as a whole. If macroeconomic issues are tackled – the determination of employment levels for example – one cannot, as Marshall did in a pragmatic vein, break up the Walrasian general equilibrium model into pieces (single markets) which are subsequently considered in isolation: this is to neglect their interrelatedness and means applying the *ceteris paribus* clause inappropriately. The neoclassical labour market provides, perhaps, the best example: declining real wages may not lead to more employment because the 'demand curve for labour' (if it existed!) would eventually shift to the left because of diminishing effective demand (on this, see Pasinetti 1993, pp. 125–32). Hence the economic system as a whole must be considered, not on an individualistic basis, as is done within General Equilibrium Theory, but on a structurist and macroeconomic basis. This implies the search for specific laws governing an economic system as a whole, for example the principle of effective demand or the social and circular process of production, which *cannot* be derived from the consequences of individual actions: the properties of the system have to be taken account of because the *social* in the Aristotelian (and classical-Keynesian) sense denotes qualitative part–whole relationships between individuals, social classes and society (chapter 2, pp. 20–57).

If macroeconomic problems associated with the social process of production such as *normal* or *long-period* value, distribution and employment are tackled on the basis of the individualistic neoclassical approach, difficulties arise. The reason is that markets cannot co-ordinate individual actions appropriately in the long run. The invisible hand does not exist because there are no regular long-period relationships between 'factor prices' and 'factor quantities' on the so-called 'factor markets' (chapter 5, pp. 281–93). At first sight, it would seem that this difficulty can be overcome: when constructing demand curves for 'capital', appropriate account would have to be taken of changes in the *value* of aggregate capital which occur with changing *quantities* of capital, i.e. of Wicksell effects (Harcourt 1972, pp. 39ff.), or in each sector of production the uniform rate of profit ought to equal the value of the marginal product of each capital good corrected by the corresponding change in value of each capital good in terms of the numéraire good; this is Champernowne's method of calculating marginal products of capital (Harcourt 1972, pp. 29ff.). To achieve this, each entrepreneur would have to know the present *and* future normal prices and quantities and hence the corresponding structures of production. This is impossible. We *must* opt for a structurist and macroeconomic approach to tackling the basic economic problems, i.e. normal value, distribution and employment (chapter 4, pp. 142–204), since the economy as a whole (economic structures linked up with social and political institutions) is something more than the aggregate results of individual actions; the structure possesses its own laws.

A basic reason for the existence of institutions now emerges. Long-period economic phenomena (production, normal value, distribution and employment) are extremely complex. Individuals behaving rationally from their point of view would only be in a position to behave rationally in terms of society as a whole if they were appropriately guided by some mechanism, i.e. the invisible hand or the market system. Since long-period factor markets producing a tendency towards fundamental equilibria do not exist, it is impossible for the individual to behave in a way which is, at the same time, rational from his point of view and from that of society as a whole. To act according to the latter, a tremendous amount of information about the past, present and future functioning of society would be required and decisions would become immensely complex. One may go even further to say that individual actions are impossible without institutions. To act and to behave means participating in given institutions. There must be a social groundwork which enables individuals to act.

However, tensions and even contradictions exist between the rationality of individuals and the rationality of the system. Keynes showed that actions which are rational from the point of view of an individual need not be rational for society as a whole. For example, an act of saving may appear to be rational from the individual *and* the social point of view: if, in an unemployment situation, all individuals save more, interest rates are expected to decline; investment should increase and unemployment diminish. However, since factor markets do not function properly in a monetary production economy, the contrary happens. More saving reduces consumption and output declines. Entrepreneurs in the consumer goods sector will invest less and the crisis will deepen.

Rational behaviour is possible within a socially inappropriate institutional framework, for example in a situation with heavy and persistent unemployment. But behaviour would be different from the behaviour taking place within socially appropriate institutions embodying full social rationality. Hence, ethically appropriate institutions are required in order to facilitate or to bring about behaviour that is rational from the individual *and* from the social point of view. Ideally, this implies creating social foundations such that individuals enjoy the widest possible scope for freedom of action; full employment and a socially acceptable distribution of incomes and wealth are perhaps the most important components of these foundations. Since individuals cannot cope with certain complex problems, for example long-period involuntary unemployment, the state *must* intervene to secure full employment.

In the classical-Keynesian view, social institutions prevent the total or partial breakdown of the immensely complex system of production and hence of socioeconomic, political and cultural life altogether. Evolving social structures (the network of institutions) embody society's experience of creating the preconditions for rational behaviour of individuals who plan and act within this structure (Nell 1984). For instance, all those willing to work are in a position to organize their professional life rationally only if there is full employment; the involuntarily unemployed individual is evidently prevented from behaving rationally from the economic point of view. To set up the social foundations or institutions compatible with full employment is the central task of long-period economic policy. This issue will be taken up in the policy chapter (chapter 6).

While classical-Keynesian political economists take a structurist and macroeconomic point of view when tackling on a fundamental level the great economic problems of value, distribution, employment and organization of foreign trade, neoclassical economists start from the rationally behaving individual. The market, if functioning satisfactorily, is supposed to co-ordinate individual economic actions in a socially appropriate way. However, there are differences of opinion on how the market performs its co-ordinating functions between the various neoclassical strands:

All Austrian economists are in agreement on the importance of a market economy as a precondition for individual freedom as are many economists of the neoclassical tradition, but the Austrians take a quite different view of the essential features of markets and contend that mainstream economic theory misses the most important characteristics. These are the importance of knowledge and the process by which equilibrium is attained rather than the conditions of equilibrium (Shand 1984, p. 66).

Austrian neoclassicals thus take for granted that a full-employment equilibrium exists and that there is a tendency towards it. Their main concern is to explain sequences of prices and quantities on the basis of the rational behaviour of producers and consumers in disequilibrium situations, with economic activity fluctuating around full-employment positions. For example, the Austrians postulate that dynamic entrepreneurs introduce new techniques of production and new products and thereby willingly destroy actually prevailing situations to create new profit opportunities – this is Schumpeter's *creative destruction*.

Neoclassical economic theory starts from the phenomenon of *exchange* between autonomous individuals; other economic phenomena, primarily production, are dealt with in terms of the exchange paradigm (Baranzini and Scazzieri 1986; Bharadwaj 1986; and the introduction to Pasinetti 1981). This is a direct outgrowth of the liberal vision of society and of man (chapter 2, pp. 20–57): the autonomous individual is primary; society is secondary, consisting of a network of explicit and implicit contracts between individuals, including exchanges. In the neoclassical view, exchange thus represents social behaviour (social action) in the economic sphere; the market is supposed to co-ordinate individual actions in a socially desirable way. This is Adam Smith's 'invisible hand' which has been formalized by Walras and Pareto.

Production is, in the neoclassical view, a *linear* process. Factors of production (labour, land and real capital) are transformed into final goods; inputs and outputs are linked by the production function. The principle of substitution dominates exchange *and* production: the textbook theory of production is built upon the concept of isoquants and budget or cost lines. Entrepreneurs are supposed to substitute relatively expensive factors by less expensive ones in order to achieve profit maximization. The (agricultural) law of diminishing returns has been generalized and is supposed to govern, through the factor markets, entrepreneurial profit-maximizing behaviour and to co-ordinate it in all spheres of production.

Exchange is intimately linked with a second outstanding feature of neoclassical economics, i.e. the principle of *methodological individualism*: all economic phenomena (price formation, distribution, employment, structural change, inflation, international trade relations, and others) are, in principle, to be explained in terms of (or reduced to) *individual* actions. Individuals are subject to various constraints, scarcity of all goods being most important. The neoclassical standard model of 'maximization under constraints' implies rational behaviour. Moreover, in the liberal view the *social* is reduced to relationships between individuals.

Individualism in the economic sphere implies that social life, properly speaking, is taking place elsewhere, that is in the social, political and cultural domains, where corresponding institutions exist. In this view, the market appears as a natural economic institution which (almost costlessly) co-ordinates the utility- and profit-maximizing behaviour of individual agents. The market is, in a way, autonomous and the other institutions constitute the social, political, legal and cultural framework.

A given institutional set-up – the framework in neoclassical theory – represents the permanent long-period forces which govern fundamental long-period equilibria. Permanent changes in an equilibrium position occur if there is some change in the institutional framework. The latter leads to parameter changes which, in turn, impose new equilibrium values upon all the variables of the economic system. Hence, an important feature of neoclassical equilibrium economics is that the *institutions* located in the framework influence equilibrium prices and quantities only *indirectly*, namely through the market. Institutions, therefore, govern the positions of demand and supply curves: for example, trade unions are supposed to shift labour supply curves to the left; entrepreneurial associations bring about leftward shifts of the labour demand curves. This causes a particular difficulty in neoclassical equilibrium economics. For, even if there were a tendency towards equilibrium, an inappropriate institutional set-up could prevent a full-employment equilibrium from being established: the institutional set-up compatible with the long-period full-employment position ought to be known *a priori* to bring about the appropriate positions of *all* demand and supply curves and thus to render possible a tendency towards a full-employment equilibrium. However, to know about the full-employment institutional set-up would require an immense amount of information, which might even exceed the volume of information required by a socialist central planning agency.

Neoclassical economists deal in various ways with this problem. General equilibrium economists simply assume institutions away and concentrate on the properties of various types of equilibria. The Austrians postulate that non-economic institutions are themselves subject to the laws of the market which seems to imply the postulate of a socioeconomic and political 'superequilibrium': competition eliminates inappropriate institutions. Partial equilibrium economists assume that institutions result in displacements of long-period demand and supply curves; they do not worry about an eventual tendency towards a general equilibrium, which is usually taken for granted provided there is sufficient competition. Other neoclassicals postulate the existence of a natural rate of unemployment: structural changes lead to temporary unemployment; involuntary unemployment is however neglected. Neoclassical *system theory (constitutional economics* or *Ordnungstheorie)* seems to concentrate on the search for an *optimal* institutional framework bringing about as much competition as possible with a view to implementing the best possible socioeconomic state of affairs. Some system theorists appear to postulate that factor markets are capable of bringing about a tendency towards full employment; others do not seem to attach much importance to the employment problem: in the competitive struggle the best and the fittest agents survive and hence ensure the highest possible productivity levels; poverty that might eventually arise can be relieved by redistributive measures. In the classical-Keynesian view this is an extremely dangerous position: in fact, an unfettered domination of the strongest might lead to more and more inequality and unemployment and increasing poverty; alienation increases and produces disruptive effects on society and eventually political extremism.

A complete neoclassical theory would, in fact, require a fully blown theory of external effects of the market (economic) system upon the framework and a theory of impacts of the framework upon the market system. This would require an all-embracing model embodying all the relevant spheres of human activity (economic, social, political and cultural) based upon the *behaviour of individuals*. Given the problems existing with the Walrasian general equilibrium model, for example the question of the tendency towards an eventually existing equilibrium, it will be very difficult if not impossible to develop a far more complete model along similar lines. The only way out is to start from the socioeconomic and political set-up, i.e. the system as a whole, and to work out macroeconomic and sectoral models, as is suggested by classical-Keynesian political economy.

Hence the neoclassical vision of economic events is entirely different from the classical-Keynesian view (chapters 3 and 4) where institutions are complementary so as to form a system which *directly* influences economic phenomena. The importance of the market in the former and of institutions in the latter explains why neoclassical theory is called *economics* or *catallactics* (Hicks 1976, p. 212) and classical-Keynesian theory is denoted *political economy* (on this distinction, see also Deane 1989 and chapter 3, pp. 75–89). An early discussion of this important issue is to be found in Eugen von Böhm-Bawerk's (1914) *Macht oder ökonomisches Gesetz*. Here, Böhm-Bawerk defends the neoclassical argument that distribution is, in the long run, governed by supply and demand. Around the centres of gravity so determined (long-period or normal wage levels, for instance), fluctuations, governed by changing social power, take place. However, Böhm-Bawerk's opponents, belonging to the German Historical School, held the view that social forces were primary in determining distribution, and market forces secondary. This basically Ricardian-Marxian argument has been taken up and refined by present-day classical-Keynesian political economy: social forces (the social structure or the institutional system) govern system equilibria (normal levels of output and employment, target mark-ups and normal prices) and the market registers deviations from these equilibria.

In the traditional neoclassical view, an economic equilibrium represents a final result brought about by natural laws which are objective and independent of the human will. The economic actions of individuals are coordinated on the various markets by the 'iron law' of supply and demand, expressed by an inverse relationship between prices and quantities. This view of things is probably held by most liberal practitioners, especially liberal policy-makers.

Given objective 'quasi-natural' and permanent market laws, *uncertainty does not play any role* in the determination of long-period equilibrium prices and quantities in goods and factor markets. The laws of the market *determine* large parts of human behaviour in the economic field in a way similar to natural laws governing the movements of matter. This holds for *all* economic agents taken together and does not exclude uncertainty for many or even all individuals, which is of considerable importance in disequilibrium situations: if, for instance, there is excess supply in some market and if all producers are of approximately equal strength, then it will be highly uncertain as to who will be squeezed out of the market.

This determination of the behaviour of individuals by objective factors is dependent on assuming 'that everyone expects the "present" situation [the objective factors in question] to continue indefinitely' (Sweezy 1937/38, p. 235). The 'present situation', in turn, is characterized by the data (endowments, tastes, techniques) which determine equilibrium prices and quantities. If the equilibrium is stable, then the laws of the market will enforce a movement towards equilibrium.

Problems arise with the introduction of time and of data changes taking place in time. If the data changed rapidly and unpredictably, then the laws of the market would lose their significance because the equilibria would themselves be subject to unforeseeable upheavals. This is perhaps the main reason why the founders of neoclassical economics argued that the fundamental institutional and technological data were constant or evolved gradually. The corresponding long-period equilibria will, in this case, also change gradually and the inverse relationship between prices and quantities will hold in the course of time. Hence, the motto of Marshall's *Principles*: 'Natura non facit saltum'.

The liberal policy-maker now argues that it is important to strengthen the tendency towards the long-period equilibrium position by eliminating disturbing elements as far as possible, i.e. market imperfections brought about by trade unions, cartels, government monopolies, monetary factors and restrictive government interventions; the appropriate environment or framework has to be created. This raises the crucial question to which we

now turn: given ideal conditions (perfect competition, complete information, etc.), is there a tendency towards a long-period equilibrium?

The significance of the capital-theory debate

In the preceding sections, neoclassical economics and classical-Keynesian
political economy have been compared with respect to content, method and
the underlying social philosophy. It seems difficult, if not impossible, to dis-
criminate between the two approaches simply by confronting them with
reality. A neoclassical economist can always argue, even in the depths of a
severe depression, that there would be a tendency towards full employment
if no policy mistakes had been made in the past, if there were no sticky
prices and wages, no monopolies and trade unions, that is, if markets func-
tioned in a more satisfactory way. On the other hand, a classical-Keynesian
economist may explain the crisis by deficient effective demand. Hence, the
question as to which of the two approaches is more apt for providing a clue
to the solution of the basic economic problems remains open from the
empirical point of view. This is tantamount to saying that complex theories
related to the functioning of economies as a whole cannot be tested empirically (this point will be touched upon in the next section). Therefore, the
problem of discriminating between neoclassical economics and classical-
Keynesian political economy must be tackled on the theoretical level, i.e.
on the level of principles. The critic of neoclassical theory must show that
one or several markets do not function properly. Keynes argued that there
was a problem with the capital market, i.e. the market for new capital
goods. Saving and investment are not brought into equilibrium through
variations in the rate of interest, but by changes in national income. The
rate of interest then gets a new task, that is to bring about equilibrium in
the money market. On the basis of the multiplier relation, Keynes was able
to show that an unemployment equilibrium was possible in the short run.
However, Keynes accepted the first (neo)classical postulate, stating that
'the wage rate is equal to the marginal product of labour' (Keynes 1973a,
p. 5); he also used the 'marginal efficiency of capital' concept (Keynes
1973a, chapter 17). This is equivalent to accepting the existence of factor
markets. Neoclassical economists concede that, in the short run, various
imperfections (including a lack of effective demand) act as disturbing
factors. However, in their view, the laws of the market, based upon the marginal principle, are permanent and fundamental and will ultimately dominate. *If* markets function satisfactorily – if there is sufficient competition –
and if changes in social reality – for example changes in political institutions, consumers' tastes and technology – are not erratic (Marshall's
'natura non facit saltum' holds), then it is reasonable to presume a tendency

towards a full-employment equilibrium in the long run. This view of things has resulted in Samuelson's neoclassical synthesis which is supposed to bring together Marshall and Keynes: short-run deficiences of effective demand resulting in short-period unemployment have to be eliminated by Keynesian full-employment policies. Once unemployment is eliminated neoclassical theory comes in to explain prices and functional income distribution. With the Keynesian message fading away from the seventies onwards, attempts were made to combine Keynes and Walras. This led to disequilibrium theory (Leijonhufvud) and to the notion of non-Walrasian equilibria (Malinvaud). The rational expectations revolution heralded the definitive return to pre-Keynesian equilibrium economics on a higher level of sophistication.

A Keynesian Fundamentalist might argue that in an uncertain world, specifically with an uncertain future, there can be no tendency towards a full-employment equilibrium. No meaning may, for instance, be given to the marginal productivity of capital (the internal rate of return) since future prices and quantities linked up with specific investment projects are unknown. The traditional neoclassical economists would admit that uncertainty may prevail with respect to individual investment projects and to which enterprises stay in a market and which are squeezed out, that there may be uncertainty with respect to rates of return in the short run due to unforeseen fluctuations in demand, and that credit conditions may change unexpectedly. Such partial and short-run events will not, however, affect the tendency towards equilibrium in the long run if the basic data (technology and tastes) change gradually and if there is enough competition. The law of supply and demand based upon an inverse relationship between prices and quantities will ultimately bring about a tendency towards a long-period equilibrium. This is a view held, explicitly or implicitly, by all liberal policy-makers.

How can classical-Keynesian economists show that there is no tendency towards a long-period equilibrium in order to establish the principle of effective demand in the short, medium and long terms? The only possible way is to attempt to show that selected premises underlying neoclassical theory are untenable. Specifically, it must be shown that under ideal conditions, i.e. perfect competition and absence of disturbing elements like uncertainty and money, one or more markets do not function properly so that, even in the long run, no tendency towards full employment exists: the problem is *not* about possible market failures, but about principles.

This task has been accomplished by the capital-theory debate, the main economic implications of which are set out in Garegnani (1970), Kurz (1985) and Pasinetti (1974, pp. 132–42; 1977, pp. 169–77); a comprehensive and easily understandable presentation of the crucial issues is Harcourt (1972).

The capital-theory debate has revealed that, *if production is conceived of as a social process*, i.e. if there is 'production of commodities by means of commodities [and labour]' (implying the existence of heterogeneous capital goods), it is impossible to measure capital independently of income distribution since relative prices depend upon the conditions of production *and* upon the profit rate (or a hierarchy of profit rates); a physical measure of capital independent of value and distribution and consequently a marginal product of capital simply cannot be conceived of. As a consequence, no regular (downward sloping) associations between profit rates, on the one hand, and capital and output per worker and the capital–output ratio, on the other hand, exist. These relationships are, in fact, totally irregular. Since the 'capital market' does not function in the neoclassical sense and since factor markets are supposed to be interrelated, regular *long-period* relationships between 'factor prices' and 'factor quantities' cannot exist in general, i.e. there are no 'factor markets' at all if the long run is considered. This is the main result of the capital-theory debate.

To illustrate this proposition suppose that, in an economy, there are only two sectors, capital goods and consumption goods. The 'physical' capital–labour ratio is higher in the former. Net saving (equal to net investment), measured in terms of the consumption good, is given. The number of additional jobs created in a given year is thus $\Delta N = I/c$ (c=value of capital per worker). ΔN is supposed to be just sufficient to absorb the additional labour force due to population growth. Assume now that there is unemployment. ΔN ought to increase if full employment is to be restored. Since competition prevails, the real wage rate diminishes and the rate of profits increases. Contrary to the neoclassical view, the capital–labour ratio c in value terms will, given the conditions of production mentioned above, *increase*. With I given, ΔN diminishes which means that *unemployment increases as real wages fall*.

The fact that there are no regular relationships between 'factor prices' and 'factor quantities' is extremely damaging for equilibrium theory: the market cannot produce a tendency towards some postulated long-period equilibrium to solve the central economic problems, i.e. value, distribution and employment. This clears the way for classical-Keynesian political economy. For instance, it may be argued that effective demand always governs the level of employment.

Hence the position an economist takes up with respect to the capital-theory debate is of decisive importance. Accepting its results is tantamount to adopting the classical-Keynesian view of economic and social events which is set out in chapters 3 and 4 *and* the underlying third-way vision of society in general (chapter 2). Rejecting the capital-theoretic results, however, implicitly amounts to accepting the existence of factor markets which are supposed to solve the problems of distribution and employment in the *long* run although there may be short-run disturbances; implicitly this means accepting liberal social philosophy (chapter 2). Hence it is wrong to minimize the importance of the capital-theory debate as some Keynesian Fundamentalists and Robinsonians do (chapter 1, pp. 1–6) since this debate is linked up with the fundamental question of the functioning of the socioeconomic system and with the essence of society itself.

The discussion about 'factor markets' and about associated problems started together with the elaboration of comprehensive theoretical systems of economics. Perhaps, a passage right at the beginning of chapter VII of book I of the *Wealth of Nations* represents the appropriate historical starting point for the factor market debate: 'There is in every society or neighbourhood an ordinary or average rate both of wages and profits in every different employment of labour and stock. This rate is naturally regulated . . . partly by the general circumstances of the society . . . and partly by the particular nature of each employment' (Smith 1976b [1776], vol. I p. 72). This passage may be given a 'factor market' interpretation although the precise meaning of 'demand and supply curves' was not brought out by Adam Smith; this was Walras's and Marshall's achievement. In chapters VIII to XI, Smith discusses various circumstances that influence the position of the 'demand and supply curves'. The problem of distribution here appears as a simple appendix to the theory of value, i.e. the 'cost components theory'.

Ricardo 1951 [1821] did *not* pursue the Smithian approach to the problems of value and distribution. He *separated* the two problems. Distribution is regulated by two principles: the marginal principle determines rent and the surplus principle separates wages from profits. The natural wage rate is a social phenomenon.

The problem of value could, according to Ricardo, be tackled only once distribution was determined: 'for Ricardo the answer to the question about distribution was a necessary and prior condition . . . for calculating the "modifications" of relative prices introduced by differences in technical conditions of production, affecting particularly the use of fixed capital' (Dobb 1973, pp. 115–16). Hence relative prices depend, in a Ricardian view, upon the conditions of production *and upon income distribution, i.e. the rate of profits*. Since capital goods are produced goods they have somehow to be measured in value terms. Therefore, Ricardo could never have thought of developing the (vaguely formulated) Smithian 'factor market' notion which would require the existence of prices and measures of *physical* quantities of aggregate capital:

With reference to the theory of Torrens ('that commodities are valuable according to the value of the capital employed on their production, and the time for which it is so employed') Ricardo says in the letter to McCulloch of 21 Aug. 1823: 'I would ask what means you have of ascertaining the equal value of capitals? . . . These capitals are not the same in kind [if they were, he points out in an earlier draft, "their proportional quantities would indicate their proportional values"] and if they themselves are produced in unequal times they are subject to the same fluctuations as other commodities. Till you have fixed the criterion by which we are to ascertain value, you can say nothing of equal capitals'; for, as he says in another draft of this letter, 'the means of ascertaining their equality or variation of value is the very thing in dispute.' (Ricardo 1951 [1821], introduction by P. Sraffa, p. xlix).

The situation changed drastically with the reaction against Ricardo which, according to Dobb (1973 chapter 4), started almost immediately after his death. Economists like Say, Senior and Longfield took up the Smithian factor market approach to distribution and refined it. The movement culminated in the marginal revolution of the 1870s which saw the birth of neoclassical equilibrium economics. Subsequently, the concept of the factor market was given a precise meaning. Ricardo's marginal principle which governed the division of the social product into rent on the one hand and the sum of wages and profits on the other was only reinterpreted and generalized. Ricardo's marginal product of labour on additional land became the marginal product of land; similarly labour and capital were attributed marginal products of their own (Stigler 1941, pp. 326–7). Subsequently, demand functions for all the 'factors of production', i.e. land, labour and capital, were established. The marginal productivity theory of distribution derived therefrom is found in most textbooks today.

Ricardo's marginal principle associated with diminishing returns is a law valid in agriculture where, at the outset of the nineteenth century, production was still largely individualistic. The neoclassical economists applied this law to modern industry where production is essentially a *social* phenomenon and where increasing returns to scale prevail. This was the main source of the difficulties later encountered by neoclassical marginal productivity theory.

While these developments were going on, Ricardo's discovery of the dependence of relative prices upon distribution continued to haunt the minds of economists. An extensive discussion about the Marxian transformation problem set in. Eugen von Böhm-Bawerk suggested measuring capital by time, i.e. 'average time-periods of production' (*Produktionsumwege*); these were supposed to be independent of distribution and to put 'capital' on the same footing as the non-produced factors, land and labour, which could in principle be measured in physical terms. The Austrian discussions on the nature of capital initiated a 'German capital-theory debate' (Schumpeter 1954, p. 914). Wicksell despaired of Akerman's problem and discovered the effects which carry his name (Harcourt 1972, p. 40). The

1920s saw Sraffa's attack upon the Marshallian supply curve; this curve had attempted to reconcile the laws of increasing and decreasing returns (Sraffa 1926). According to Kaldor the debate on fundamentals continued unabated and very intensely in the 1930s:

The last few years have witnessed the emergence of a tremendous literature on the theory of capital and interest . . . A large part of this literature has been directly concerned with the question how far the concept of the 'period of production' is relevant for an analysis of industrial fluctuations. Another part, digging deeper into the problem, dealt with the *prima facie* question how far traditional capital theory, formulated under the hypothesis of a stationary state, still retains its validity in essential features once this hypothesis is abandoned. These writings were mainly concerned with the problems of expectations, foresight, uncertainty. Finally, largely owing to the offensive launched by Professor F. H. Knight, there was a revival of the discussion on the fundamentals of capital theory itself, comparable in nature to the famous controversy between J. B. Clark and Böhm-Bawerk (Kaldor 1937, p. 153).

The fifties and sixties brought a clarification of the subject. The discussion was opened by Joan Robinson: 'the production function has been a powerful instrument of miseducation' (Robinson 1953, p. 47). The landmark was Sraffa (1960). Two characteristics of this work were crucial: First, '[the] connection of this work with the theories of the old classical economists [i.e. their theories of production, value and distribution]. It is of course in Quesnay's *tableau économique* that is found the original picture of the system of production and consumption as a circular process, and it stands in striking contrast to the view presented by modern theory, of a one-way avenue that leads from. "Factors of production" to "Consumption goods"' (Sraffa 1960, p. 93); second, Sraffa saw his work as a 'Prelude to a critique of [marginal] economic theory'. This immediately led to a revival of the capital-theoretic discussion which culminated, in the mid-sixties, in the publication of several important articles, which are gathered in the *Quarterly Journal of Economics*, vol. 80 (1966); for a brief summary of events see Pasinetti (1977, pp. 169–77, especially footnote 9 on p. 171). Samuelson sums up the discussion in a crucial statement:

Lower interest rates may bring lower steady-state consumption and lower capital–output ratios, and the transition to such lower interest rate can involve denial of diminishing returns and entail reverse capital deepening in which current consumption is augmented rather than sacrificed.
There often turns out to be no unambiguous way of characterizing different processes as more 'capital intensive', more 'mechanized', more 'roundabout' . . . If all this causes headaches for those nostalgic for the old time parables of neoclassical writing, we must remind ourselves that scholars are not born to live an easy existence. We must respect, and appraise, the facts of life (Samuelson 1966, p. 250).

It is revealing to compare this statement with a passage taken from the new chapter 'On machinery' in the third edition of Ricardo's *Principles*:

[Earlier] it appeared to me that there would be the same demand for labour as before [the use of machinery], and that wages would be no lower; I thought that the labouring class would, equally with the other classes, participate in the advantage, from the general cheapness of commodities arising from the use of machinery.

These were my opinions, and they continue unaltered, as far as regards the landlord and the capitalist; but I am convinced, that the substitution of machinery for human labour, is often very injurious to the interest of the class of labourers.

My mistake arose from the supposition, that whenever the net income of a society increased, its gross income would also increase [our emphasis]; I now, however, see reason to be satisfied that the one fund, from which landlords and capitalists derive their revenue, may increase, while the other, that upon which the labouring class mainly depend, may diminish, and therefore it follows, if I am right, that the same cause which may increase the net revenue of the country, may at the same time render the population redundant, and deteriorate the condition of the labourer (Ricardo 1951 [1821], pp. 387–8).

Fundamentally, all these difficulties for the individualistic marginal productivity theory arise because of the *social nature* of the process of production: output results from a common effort; individual producers or entire sectors of production exercise complementary functions; to co-ordinate these co-operation is required. Since production is a social phenomenon proper (a set of relationships between individuals and society), long-period distribution, price formation and employment determination are also social processes (chapter 4, pp. 142–204). If production is conceived of as a social process 'the marginal product of a factor (or alternatively the marginal cost of a product) would not merely be hard to find – it just would not be there to be found' (Sraffa 1960, p.v).

Neoclassical economists have built up two defence walls against the fundamental (capital-theoretic) attacks of the classical-Keynesian political economists. The first is neatly summarized by Chase:

As a result of [the just mentioned] concessions on the theoretical front, the battle has now shifted to the arena of technical testing. As Charles Ferguson concludes in his survey of neoclassical theory . . . 'The question that confronts us is not whether the Cambridge Criticism is theoretically valid. It is. Rather, the question is an empirical or an econometric one: is there sufficient substitutability within the system to establish the neoclassical results?' As all who have reached this juncture well know, econometric hypothesis testing will neither quickly, nor easily, if ever, yield unambiguous answers to this question (Chase 1978, p. 78).

Since – for reasons to be suggested in the next section – it is impossible to test complex theories relating to the functioning of an economy as a whole, a second defensive wall was erected on the theoretical level. The study of permanent or slowly changing factors, i.e. long-period analysis, has subsequently been abandoned in favour of short-period analysis dealing with temporary equilibria (Garegnani 1976). The latter imply *realized* rates of profits in the various sectors of production which deviate from the desired or satisfactory rates of profit of the long-period or fundamental equilibria governed by long-term factors. The long run is simply seen as a sequence of short-period equilibria. Expectations necessarily play a major role in this approach: in any (short) time-period 'agents' must form expectations about what may happen in the next period(s) when establishing their production and consumption plans. Temporary equilibrium analysis bears some similarity with Keynesian Fundamentalism where uncertainty about the future also plays a crucial role. Both approaches thus deal with *behaviour* under uncertainty. This type of analysis complements the classical-Keynesian study of the functioning of the system sketched in chapter 4 (pp. 142–220), but cannot answer the questions whether a tendency towards a fundamental equilibrium exists and what the nature of this equilibrium is.

The capital-theoretic discussion does not prevent the theoretical description of equilibrium situations of whatever kind, i.e. short- or long-period equilibria: 'Reswitching and the general impossibility of capital aggregation have no bearing on anything which can be called marginal productivity theory. *Such a theory concerns an economy in full neoclassical equilibrium* [our emphasis] which . . . has nothing to fear from anything in Sraffa's or in his followers' work' (Hahn 1982, p. 373). It may indeed be useful to clarify problems that arise from erecting a general equilibrium model upon neoclassical premises, for example to look for the limits of methodological individualism: to what extent can macroeconomic phenomena – *all* prices and quantities – be explained by the optimizing behaviour of individuals. It is generally acknowledged that such analyses have been carried out with great logical care.

However, the classical-Keynesian objection against neoclassical equilibrium theory is *not* a matter of *formal logic*; the argument in question is a piece of *material logic* and is as such about the degree of correspondence between model and reality. In fact, the question is about an eventual *tendency* towards a neoclassical – behavioural – equilibrium in the *real* world. Given the result of the capital-theory debate, classical-Keynesian economists would say that it is highly unlikely, though not entirely impossible, that such a tendency may exist *at times*. Hahn seems to agree on this: 'on the manner in which . . . an equilibrium is supposed to come about, neoclassical theory is highly unsatisfactory. Sraffa's work shows that certain simplified routes are very risky and not free from logical difficulties' (Hahn 1982, p. 373). Moreover, in his Cambridge inaugural lecture he states: '[The Arrow–Debreu equilibrium model] makes no formal or explicit causal claims at all. For instance it contains no presumption that a sequence of actual economic states will terminate in an equilibrium state' (Hahn 1973, p. 7); and:

Professor Kaldor and others find it so natural to regard an equilibrium as the outcome of some particular process that they find it difficult to believe that any one should wish to use an equilibrium notion in a different way. And indeed it is a fair question whether it can ever be useful to have an equilibrium notion which does not describe the termination of actual processes.

For the purpose of this question uniqueness of an equilibrium is not an issue, for plainly what is to be discussed is the view that an equilibrium notion is only useful to economists insofar as it involves the falsifiable claim that all actual economic processes converge to *an* equilibrium state. Certainly this is the way, for instance, Marshall justified his interest in equilibrium. I want however to maintain that this view is not correct. I do so on two grounds: first . . . our need for equilibrium concepts is largely connected with ignorance of precisely those features of an actual economy which the view under discussion wishes us to be precise about. Secondly I want to maintain now the related but weaker claim that even when equilibrium states cannot be shown to be asymptotic outcomes of processes it is useful to have a concept of equilibrium states (pp. 8–9).

With all this, classical-Keynesian political economists can agree. But Hahn seems to abandon the claim that there is a tendency towards a full employment equilibrium in a competitive economy.

Some neoclassical equilibrium economists have attempted to bring in more realism by developing intertemporal general equilibrium models, for example Bliss (1975). However, '[w]ith Bliss's intertemporal general equilibrium model it is clear that the introduction of time [and space] and uncertainty would involve radical changes in the theory' (Backhouse 1985, p. 332).

At this stage a last and intricate argument has to be dealt with. In the Ricardian, Marxian and now classical-Keynesian view, prices are proportional to labour time *if* market conditions and the specific conditions of production for the various goods are abstracted from. Labour values constitute the essence of prices, and the surplus principle is the corresponding fundamental theory of income distribution. Neoclassical economists might now accept the labour theory of value and argue that, in this case, all the crucial properties of neoclassical production functions hold on the level of fundamental principles, as is indeed implied by Samuelson's surrogate production function (Samuelson 1962). The existence of the rate of interest could easily be justified by abstinence; interest would constitute the reward for deferred consumption, i.e. saving. Hence the marginal productivity theory would be valid generally on the fundamental level; specifically distribution would be determined on the factor markets and competitive conditions would produce a tendency towards full employment. (A similar argument could be conducted if the price of Sraffa's *standard commodity* were chosen as the numéraire since this commodity is also associated with linear real wage – rates of profits trade-offs.)

In this admittedly strange situation the problem for neoclassical theory would arise with the realization of principles. If the different conditions of production (reflected in different ratios of the value of the means of production to wages) prevailing in the various sectors of production are taken into account, the neoclassical theory of value and distribution is *destroyed* because regular and inverse associations between factor prices and factor quantities now no longer exist; moreover, the law of supply and demand would not produce a tendency towards full employment in the case considered. Hence no association between the ideal-type model and the corresponding real type exists in the neoclassical system. In the classical-Keynesian framework, however, different conditions of production will merely *modify* labour values to yield normal prices depending precisely upon the conditions of production and upon distribution. Indeed, *the* crucial test for good theory is that its fundamental principles remain valid when simplifying assumptions are given up, i.e. when the theory is brought nearer to the real world. Hence the neoclassical theory is valid only in a 'one-good world' or with equal conditions of production in all sectors. These assumptions are crucial for neoclassical theory, but only simplifying for classical-Keynesian theory.

These references to the history of the capital-theoretic discussion show that it is a discussion about fundamentals. The basic question is whether there are regular relationships between 'factor prices' and 'factor quantities' or not, i.e. normally functioning factor markets. Examining this question seriously will inevitably shape an economist's vision in a decisive way. The capital-theory debate is a theoretical watershed dividing two different views of looking at socioeconomic phenomena, i.e. neoclassical equilibrium theory which emphasizes behaviour and classical-Keynesian political economy which starts from the functioning of the socioeconomic system, the question being which approach is more appropriate to tackle fundamental socioeconomic problems, such as value, distribution and employment. Therefore, as Geoffrey Harcourt was one of the first to perceive, the Cambridge controversies are 'not merely about the measurement of capital . . . but about the scientific status of neoclassical [equilibrium] theory' (Dixon 1988, pp. 251–2).

The links between the capital-theory debate and the principle of effective demand are important: the Keynesian theory of money and uncertainty is a *necessary* condition for establishing the principle of effective demand. Keynes's theory of money and interest knocks out the *classical* version of

Say's law according to which supply creates its own demand. This is not *sufficient*, however. The neoclassical theory of 'factor markets', which includes the market for new capital goods, may be used to re-establish Say's law in that it proposes a mechanism to transform saving into investment. However, the results of the capital-theory debate seriously question the *long-period* validity of the *neoclassical* version of Say's law: long-period factor markets cannot exist once production is conceived of as a social and circular process. Hence the Keynesian theory of interest and money and the neo-Ricardian capital-theoretic critique are, taken together, *necessary and sufficient* to disprove Say's law and to establish definitely the Keynesian principle of effective demand.

The capital-theory debate is about relationships between 'factor prices' and 'factor quantities', i.e. the *shapes* of 'factor demand curves'; the conclusion is that regular relationships do not exist. But even if such relationships existed there would not necessarily be a tendency towards full employment, because the *positions* of 'factor demand and supply curves' depend upon the various institutions of society: for example, trade unions may shift labour supply curves to the left; entrepreneurial associations may cause leftward shifts of the labour supply curve. The market sphere is not autonomous but depends upon the institutional set-up of a society (pp. 272–81 above). This creates an additional difficulty for neoclassical equilibrium economics: even if regular relationships between 'factor prices' and 'factor quantities' existed an inappropriate institutional set-up could prevent a tendency towards a full-employment equilibrium. The problem would consist in creating an institutional set-up regulating the behaviour of individuals and collectives, such that market forces are in a position to establish a tendency towards full employment. To propose solutions ought to be the central task of liberal system theory. However, the problem in question is so complex that a solution seems impossible (pp. 272–81 above). In practice, liberal system policy simply aims at eliminating or weakening those institutions considered inimical to the proper functioning of the market; or institutions are subjected to market forces by the means of privatization and deregulation in order to enhance competition and to produce a tendency towards full employment. The Reagan–Thatcher era is significant in this respect. Looked at historically, these undertakings are likely to have contributed to higher permanent unemployment and to a more unequal income distribution; given the social consequences associated with these phenomena the projects in question seem to have largely failed. Probably the main reason is that, even under 'competitive conditions', there is no tendency towards full employment in a market economy.

The outcome of the capital-theory debate and the fact that markets are not independent of, but complementary to, non-economic institutions strongly reinforce the presumption that, in a monetary production economy, the long-period level of economic activity is not governed by the law of supply and demand but by effective demand. This produces an additional argument against neoclassical long-period theory: with effective demand governing long-period economic activity, output levels cannot be varied at will as is assumed in neoclassical theory. Hence vital neoclassical concepts such as 'marginal productivity' and 'marginal costs' are not relevant, even if the associated demand and supply curves existed. It is simply not possible to obtain marginal products if normal effective demand *determines* the behaviour of entrepreneurs, since output is fixed by the social or macrophenomenon of effective demand. Entrepreneurs will not increase production if the additionally produced goods cannot be sold. This is in line with Keynes's fundamental proposition that economic activity is ultimately not governed by supply factors but by effective demand.

The argument provided so far may be complemented by an 'internal' criticism of general equilibrium theory which is based on Sonnenschein's theorem (Vuille 1993). On the basis of this theorem it has been shown that even within the pure exchange model there is no tendency towards an equilibrium, mainly because of the intricate income effects produced by price changes in the course of adjustment processes. Hence market prices are undetermined which implies that the problem of value cannot be solved within the sphere of exchange. This very important proposition has been confirmed by outstanding equilibrium theorists, for example Gérard Debreu. Given this, the classical-Keynesian paradigm of pricing and competition is put to the fore: the prices of production – which depend upon the conditions of production and the institutions regulating distribution – are determined *before* goods appear on the market or the sphere of circulation. Given output levels in the various branches of production, market prices are governed *uniquely* by demand conditions. If the difference between market prices and normal prices persists, adjustments of capacity are set into motion.

The outcome of the capital-theoretic discussion, the facts that economic institutions, specifically markets, are not independent of social, political and legal institutions (chapter 3, pp. 89–103) and that the principle of effective demand is likely to govern output and employment levels in a monetary production economy (chapter 4, pp. 142–204), as well as Sonnenschein's theorem strongly increase 'the *weight* of argument' (Keynes 1971c, p. 77) attached to the proposition 'that classical-Keynesian long-period theory is superior to the corresponding neoclassical counterpart'. The weight of argument in favour of classical-Keynesian – middle-way – political economy is enhanced by historical experience, mainly by the severe crises of the nineteenth century and the thirties of this century, and by present-day socioeconomic problems. All in all, 'we [now] have a more substantial basis upon which to rest our conclusion' (Keynes 1971c, p. 77).

Some remarks on the theory of knowledge implied in classical-Keynesian political economy and in neoclassical economics

In this section some issues briefly dealt with in chapter 2 (pp. 57–75) on knowledge in the social sciences are taken up again. The starting point is the bottom layer (VII) of scheme 3 (p. 106) where unvarying elements of reality appear, for example logical rules and basic laws governing nature, man and society. Systematic thinking about fundamental issues leads to probable knowledge (chapter 2, pp. 57–64) which appears in layer IV in the form of scientific institutions. For example, neoclassical economic theorists base their system on the objectively given marginal principle and Keynesians and classical-Keynesians put to use the principle of effective demand in order to explain economic activity. Regarding the quality of knowledge, it is often claimed that neoclassical general equilibrium models are worked out with great logical precision. Classical-Keynesian theoretical frameworks, however, are said to be less precise and sometimes even vague. The point could perhaps be made best by directly comparing the methodologies put to use in Walras's *Eléments* and Keynes's *General Theory*.

The first subsection is preparatory, while the second and third subsections deal with some aspects of knowledge to be obtained within the confines of neoclassical equilibrium economics and of classical-Keynesian political economy respectively.

Formal and logical truth

To deal with some issues related to the theory of knowledge it is appropriate to start from the methodological distinction between *formal logical truth* and *logical truth proper*, or *formal* and *logical* truth to simplify. A statement is said to be logically true in a *formal* sense if it is free from internal contradictions. Consistency obtains if the explicit assumptions, the concepts, the relations between concepts and the conclusions drawn therefrom are correctly interrelated. It goes without saying that any model ought to be logically true in a formal sense. Logical truth proper is of an entirely different nature, i.e. about the correspondence between *systematic thinking*, in terms of formal models for example, and *reality*, i.e. the essence of the object considered. A model is true in a logical sense if it precisely reflects reality. Absolute logical truth is outside the realm of human possibilities when complex problems are considered, the causes of involuntary unemployment or of inflation for example. Propositions may be established, but *never proved*; moreover, there are no realistic hypotheses to start with. The vision held by the theorist is the inevitable starting point for analysis (chapter 2, pp. 64–72). Hence the conclusions reached through argument always represent *probable* logical truth proper, which is the object of Keynes's *Treatise on Probability* (Keynes 1971c); in chapter 2 (pp. 57–75) some issues related to Keynes's argument are alluded to.

The search for formal and logical truth implies making use of the different kinds of abstraction which are implied in chapter 2 (pp. 57–64) in relation to Keynes's and Pribram's views on knowledge. Formal logical truth based upon subjectively chosen hypotheses is associated with abstraction of the Kantian type: the object of investigation is subjectively defined. For example, liberal social scientists consider selected parts of reality within the economic, social and political spheres for instance. This mostly implies dealing positivistically with specific problems, employment and pricing for example, in a vacuum, so to speak. However the search for logical truth in the proper sense requires abstraction of the Aristotelian type: material reality is abstracted from in the attempt to get hold of the essence of things; this implies abstracting from accidental or non-essential features of the phenomenon considered. Ricardo, Marx and Pasinetti, for example, consider labour values the essence of prices. This means abstracting from market forces and specific conditions of production. The abstractions involved in the search for essences must be based on a vision relating to the *whole* of society since all social phenomena are interrelated. Pribram's *hypotheticians* make use of Kant's partial abstraction in that selected spheres of the real world are considered in isolation; his *essentialists*, however, abstract in the Aristotelian way which permanently requires considering the whole of the object investigated, i.e. man and society in the social sciences (Pribram 1986, pp. 591ff.).

Formal consistency is all important in the normative neoclassical equilibrium approach (on the normative element in general equilibrium economics and the associated welfare theory see earlier sections, pp. 259–81). Because of its normative – and hypothetical – nature the neoclassical (Walrasian) equilibrium model need not correspond to reality. This system is an axiomatic construction which embodies some properties which are reasonable and desirable in the liberal view and as such represents the economic theory of liberalism, the latter being a project of society. Elements of equilibrium analysis may now be used to picture specific aspects of reality, i.e. the rational or optimizing behaviour of economic agents. We have suggested that the analysis and explanation of rational *behaviour* in specific domains is the great strength of neoclassical economics. However, if the – normative – general equilibrium model is used to analyse and explain *macroeconomic* issues related to the functioning of the system, like the foundation of value, the way in which functional distribution is regulated or employment is determined, problems arise. Since, as has been argued in the preceding section, it is unlikely that a *persisting* tendency towards equilibrium exists, the concepts associated with equilibrium theory are simply not suited to capture phenomena linked up with – capitalist – reality, i.e. with a monetary production economy; the impossibility of explaining involuntary unemployment by the help of the tools of equilibrium economics is an example. This forces equilibrium economists to use concepts that are *not essential* to their theory in order to explain real-world phenomena; for instance, business cycles are frequently explained by monetary factors. Consequently, 'the economic theorists' view of reality became increasingly distorted, so as to come closer to the theoretical image rather than the other way round. If Mahomet cannot go to the mountain then the mountain must be brought to Mahomet' (Kaldor 1985a, pp. 60–1). If market forces do not produce a tendency towards equilibrium in a competitive economy, the neoclassical equilibrium model is in danger of becoming irrelevant if macroeconomic phenomena are tackled; it may become an ideology or alienated knowledge in Marx's terms (chapter 2).

In classical-Keynesian causal models, the problem of logical truth is primary; formal consistency is required but is of secondary importance. To work out models which are logically true to a high degree requires combining theoretical and practical experience, i.e. knowledge of various theoretical approaches and of real-world facts, actual and historical, complemented by introspection based on reason; these isolated pieces of knowledge are structured by a social philosophy and lead, on the basis of values held, to a vision of things, of which theoretical, pure or ideal-type models are the analytical articulation; the elaboration of applied, or real-type frameworks constitutes the final step (chapter 2). This broadly corresponds to Keynes's theory of knowledge (Keynes 1971c) and is illustrated by Keynes's work in the domain of political economy: for several years, he and the members of the Cambridge Circus discussed the nature of economic theories (Skidelsky 1992, pp. 447–52) and wrestled with facts before a convincing causal model, explaining involuntary unemployment in a *real* monetary production economy, could be formulated in terms of the principle of effective demand; the result was the multiplier model (Pasinetti 1974, p. 44). This model may not reflect correctly the objectively given causal factors governing short-run unemployment. However, since it might be difficult to find a more convincing approach to explaining the existence of involuntary unemployment, the Keynesian model must be considered a satisfactory approximation. The multiplier model thus embodies logical truth proper; the degree of correspondence to reality, i.e. the degree of probability, can only be probably known (chapter 2, pp. 57–75). However, the pure multiplier model is so simple that formal mistakes are unlikely to pass unnoticed.

In classical-Keynesian political economy the central aim is to elaborate causal models that picture some objectively given causal law as accurately as is humanly possible. In the first place, universally valid pure or ideal-type models embodying probably valid principles are set up. These can be applied to specific real-world situations by elaborating explanatory frameworks or real-type models; here, space and time play a decisive role since causality works out in time and through space (chapter 3, pp. 118–30). Keynes's *logical* and *applied* multiplier illustrates this procedure (Keynes 1973a, pp. 122–5). However, when setting up causal relations in order to explain an economic phenomenon, for instance the level of employment, it would be wrong to make use of *global concepts only*, i.e. investment, output and the marginal propensity to save, if the short-period Keynesian multiplier is considered. In terms of figure 1 (p. 85) this would be tantamount to explaining the *overall* evolution of output (curve *AB*) which represents a *behavioural* outcome. Dealing with global concepts automatically implies looking at the *top* layer of reality, i.e. at the rapidly changing surface elements governed by subjective or behavioural factors; the surface conceals, so to speak, the more stable elements of the real world which are associated with the socioeconomic system. (Incidentally, such a procedure implies an unrealistic equilibrium conception, similar to the neoclassical one: equilibrium lies somewhere in the future and could be reached only if static conditions prevailed.) To sort out relevant causal relations which represent probable approximations to logical truth, the various elements of the sphere of reality considered have to be broadly ordered according to the stability of its elements in the course of time (scheme 3 and figure 1). Subsequently, the top layer of reality containing the rapidly changing short-run behavioural phenomena has to be abstracted from. The cyclical growth of real capital and of capacity output now appears; this phenomenon is still predominantly behavioural. Abstracting from the cyclical element renders visible the constant or slowly changing parts of reality, associated with the fully adjusted situation and reflecting the functioning of the socioeconomic system as a whole: normal output and employment, normal exports, long-period leakages, target profit rates and mark-ups, etc., which are all governed by institutions. The political economist may stop here. To explain the interplay of institutions already belongs to other social sciences: social psychology, sociology, law and political science.

Similar remarks can be made for prices: it is not sufficient to consider market prices, i.e. to look at the immediately visible surface, which solely reflect behavioural outcomes. The metaphysical question as to the nature of the price has to be tackled. Again, when digging deeper, the prices of production emerge, associated with fully adjusted situations and the functioning of the production and distribution system. The search for the basic principles of price formation leads to Ricardo's, Marx's and Pasinetti's values.

Once the economically relevant factors have been ordered according to their stability in time along the time axis a complete and consistent set of pure causal models, vertical and horizontal, may be set up (chapter 4). These principles constitute the body of economic theory, or, more appropriately, of political economy, since institutions play a crucial role in long-period analysis.

The way in which selected elements of reality are ordered along the time axis in order to set up pure and applied causal models depends heavily on the pre-analytic vision held by social scientists. Hence the extent to which a model embodies logical truth largely depends upon the validity of the social philosophy implied in the vision held. This may have unfortunate side-effects. If, in some epoch, a specific vision strongly dominates, theorists may be unable to see the usefulness of alternative approaches: for example, the liberal vision of things underlying neoclassical economics presently dominates minds so strongly, that most economists are not able to escape it so as to see the meaning and the potential fruitfulness of the classical and Keynesian approaches to economic problems.

Setting up pure and applied causal models embodying probable truth might be seen as a rationalization of initial visions. In doing so, social scientists may become aware of the inappropriateness of their initial vision if a set of causal models is obviously contradicted by facts. This will normally lead to a change in the vision and thus to a new set of causal models. There is a continuous interaction between vision, analysis and probable knowledge, which implies that visions regarding complex phenomena, the functioning of a monetary economy for example, and the subsequent formulation of principles, the multiplier for instance, do not fall from heaven but are hard won. This *learning process* can, perhaps, be illustrated best by the style of working of two great political economists of this century: Maynard Keynes and Nicholas Kaldor. Both were ready to change their mind at any time if their theoretical views were contradicted by real-world events or if a new and convincing theoretical insight appeared. This is a reflection of tolerance, open-mindedness and humility.

Logical truth proper is bound to remain probable in Keynes's sense, and can, therefore, never be fully achieved. Formal logical truth, however, is always required: '[Formal] logic is a duty, not a virtue' (Carr 1986, p. 5).

The fundamentally different conceptions of truth implied in general equilibrium theory and in classical-Keynesian political economy lead to important consequences as to the knowledge to be derived therefrom. These are set out in the following subsections.

General equilibrium theory and the danger of agnosticism

For two main reasons, the neoclassical way of tackling *fundamental and macroeconomic* problems – distribution and employment, for instance – with the help of the general equilibrium model ultimately tends to lead to agnosticism. The first is linked up with the complexity of the institutional system which is mainly due to the social character of basic institutions, for example the process of production, where intricate complementarities dominate; moreover, the system interacts with the behaviour of individuals and collectives. Neoclassical equilibrium economists attempt to capture economic reality in terms of a single model, i.e. the general equilibrium model, based upon a single principle: supply and demand; this principle is supposed to co-ordinate the optimizing behaviour of the economic agents in a socially appropriate way. This implies concentrating attention upon a single aspect of economic reality, that is exchange, which provides the starting point for attempts to explain all economic phenomena, including production, on the basis of the behaviour of individuals. However, this approach is conceptually too poor to come to grips with an immensely complex and organically interrelated reality. There are causal forces other than supply and demand at work that by definition cannot be assessed or can only be indirectly assessed across parameter changes. Moreover, there is the deterministic influence of the socioeconomic system (chapter 4) the effects of which cannot be reduced to the behaviour of individuals. Hence it is impossible to capture in principle the ultimate consequences of individual actions on the basis of the general equilibrium model. This produces agnosticism. For example, it is admitted by general equilibrium theorists that if, in a given equilibrium situation, the demand for a specific product increases, one cannot assert that the price of the good in question will be higher in the new equilibrium situation (this is implied by Sonnenschein's theorem mentioned in the preceding section). The difficulties would be compounded if interactions between the market system and the framework were taken account of. Many neoclassical economists concede that the general equilibrium model is inoperable. Therefore, Alfred Marshall and his disciples have opted for a partial equilibrium approach. Austrian economists argue that the description of equilibrium situations is not important. What really matters is the information provided by the price mechanism in disequilibrium situations; this enables the individual agent to act purposefully. The theorist may attempt to sketch dynamic processes that eventually lead towards equilibrium, the description of which must remain incomplete, however, because of their complexity (Shand 1984). Given this, the postulate that, provided there is sufficient competition, the market ultimately solves the important economic problems of value, distribution and employment (which implies the normal working of the invisible hand), becomes a matter of *belief*.

This leads to a second reason why agnosticism is associated with general equilibrium theory. The belief in the invisible hand has, in fact, been seriously shattered by three important events: the depression of the thirties, the Keynesian revolution and the outcome of the capital-theory debate which forced equilibrium economists to abandon the study of long-term equilibria characterized by the equality of normal profit rates. Instead, the study of short-period equilibria, where realized profit rates deviate from their fundamental, long-period or normal level, are moved to the fore (Garegnani 1976). Such equilibria represent temporary behavioural outcomes. However, uncertainty and expectations play a major role if temporary short-term factors are considered: it is extremely difficult to say something about the sequential evolution of an economy, that is on how a new temporary general equilibrium grows out of an existing one. This inevitably leads to agnosticism: uncertainty renders explanation and prediction, two important aims of positive economic science, impossible if the object of analysis, i.e. the real economy, is rapidly evolving. On this many neoclassical economists and some Keynesian Fundamentalists, Shackle for example, seem to agree.

To escape agnosticism regarding fundamental and macroeconomic issues three ways seem open to the liberal economist, i.e. pragmatism, pure equilibrium theory and empiricism.

Some pragmatically and politically minded liberal economists take for granted that economic phenomena – prices, quantities, employment levels – *uniquely* result from the optimizing behaviour of individuals and rather uncritically apply the law of supply and demand to most diverse situations. On the policy level pragmatism gives rise, for example, to the deregulation movement, to austerity policies, and to managing the quantity of money in order to prevent inflation. The fundamental importance of the law of supply and demand is dogmatically established, never questioned and is believed in with almost religious fervour. From this belief derives the new liberal fundamentalism which ultimately rests on a piece of metaphysics, i.e. the postulate of self-regulation or of the invisible hand. This again shows that, in view of the complexity of the object of the social sciences, i.e. society, it is impossible to proceed scientifically without metaphysical foundations, which underlie scientific work explicitly or implicitly.

Pure neoclassical theorists elaborate with great formal logical care, i.e. on an *axiomatic* basis, the Walrasian equilibrium model and offshoots of this model such as disequilibrium theory *à la* Clower–Leijonhufvud. Theoretical neoclassicism also rests on a metaphysical principle regarding the nature of socioeconomic reality: it is postulated or simply taken for granted that socioeconomic events can, in the last instance, be explained by rational individual behaviour; this implies that social entities (institutions) do not shape events in a significant way. Ideally, the purpose of institutions is to favour the pursuit of individual aims and, as such, to improve the functioning of the market mechanism. In this view, society results from the sum of relationships between individuals and has no meaning of its own.

This type of formalistic theorizing implies the pursuit of formal logical truth and contrasts with the unrestricted positivism to which a third group of neoclassical economists adheres. Here it is postulated that wrong theories can ultimately be eliminated by empirical tests. Empirical, i.e. statistical and econometric, work is certainly very useful in providing information about selected visible and measurable aspects of the real world related to the *behaviour* of individuals, for example consumption behaviour. From the point of view of individuals there are dependent variables, for instance quantities consumed, which are governed by a set of independent variables such as prices, incomes and tastes. The limits of statistical and econometric techniques appear, however, when the functioning of the socioeconomic system is considered; here the distinction between dependent and independent variables vanishes; moreover, interrelatedness between variables is not on the behavioural level, but is due to the complementarities inherent in the system which is particularly evident in the social process of production. Most importantly, if complex problems associated with the functioning of the system are considered – involuntary unemployment for example – there are no realistic hypotheses to start with; the vision of the theorist becomes all important.

There are several reasons why complex theories cannot be tested empirically. The first is linked up with the system aspect just mentioned. In the *long* run, economic phenomena (prices, distribution, employment, for instance) are the outcome of a tremendously complex economic system embodying a huge number of causal relations on the micro-, meso- and macrolevels of economic reality. Formally speaking, a large number of parameters, predetermined variables and determined variables are linked up by a large and interrelated set of causal relations. Complementarities and organic relationships come into being and produce system-specific laws. Given this, it is impossible to test propositions related to the functioning of an economic system as a whole, e.g. to test the validity of Say's law or to falsify classical-Keynesian political economy or neoclassical economics. Moreover, even if the system resulted uniquely from the interrelated behaviour of individuals, not all the observations required to estimate the parameters would be available and since historical events are unique the missing data might be unobtainable. Finally, it is impossible to test definitely the premises of behavioural models, since the model used to examine the premises is itself built on other premises which require to be tested. This would lead to an infinite chain of models to be verified. Hence, this way of proceeding inevitably ends up in agnosticism. For all these reasons, a pre-analytic understanding of specific historical situations is required to identify the causal relations required to explain a specific phenomenon, e.g. unemployment.

Second, in complex socioeconomic systems, normal variables are interrelated in intricate ways and depend upon a society's value system: the 'predetermined' variables are not independent of each other and the form of interdependence may slowly change in the course of time. To be sure, principles do not change through time (for example, the *principle* of the supermultiplier remains invariant). However, the way in which principles are implemented and modified by widely varying circumstances differs greatly in space and time. The complex, partly even organic interrelatedness of socioeconomic systems gives rise to intricate multicollinearities that cannot possibly be disentangled by mechanical methods; as already mentioned, '[t]he Mecca of the economist lies in economic biology [and] biological conceptions are more complex than those of mechanics' (Marshall 1920, p. xiv).

Third, the complexity of economic systems provides economists of various schools with evidence for their theories. Some aspects of reality lend support for one theory, others to a different type of theory. For instance, if merely the behavioural, top layer of reality in scheme 3 (p. 106) is considered, one might conclude that prices are governed solely by supply and demand. A different conclusion is suggested by the third, institutional, layer of reality. Here, prices appear to be determined by the conditions of production and by the way in which distribution is regulated. Hence both theories are partly true. The latter theory explains the prices of production in terms of the socioeconomic system, the former as the outcome of behaviour in the market-place.

Fourth, the same phenomenon may be explained by different theories: for example, the close correlation existing between 'quantities' of money and price levels may be convincingly explained by monetarist *and* by classical-Keynesian theory. The former claims that the quantity of money *determines* the general price level, the latter that the quantity of money *adjusts* to economic activity: different visions on the functioning of such systems co-exist, which leads social scientists to see the same fact in entirely different ways.

Hence, complex macroeconomic theories cannot be conclusively tested and the diversity of economic theories cannot be reduced by empirical means. However, both statistics and econometrics are valuable means for providing empirical evidence to *complement* theoretical insights aimed at explaining selected real-world phenomena such as behavioural patterns or specific aspects of the functioning of socioeconomic systems. The observation and analysis of empirical regularities are, together with practical experience, theorizing and introspection, important tools for obtaining knowledge. In fact, empirical observations provide hints about the essence of things.

However, some econometric and statistical techniques seem so sophisticated that their practical application appears excessively difficult. Hence, theoretically minded neoclassical economists turn to the study of principles and pragmatically minded empirical social scientists prefer crude statistical tools to tackle real-world problems. Given, however, the complexity of macroeconomic issues related to the functioning of the system and the very large amount of uncertainty attached to surface (first-layer) phenomena, neoclassical equilibrium economics *and* pragmatic empiricism both encounter insuperable difficulties if applied for explanatory or predictive purposes. Building pure (hypothetical and/or normative) models separated from reality and collecting data without having the appropriate tools to interpret these are both sterile activities: '[G]edankenlose Stoffhäufung und stofflose Gedankenhäufung [sind beide] zur Unfruchtbarkeit verurteilt' (Salin 1967, p. v). Hence, agnostic resignation seems to overwhelm many empirical economists presently engaged in prediction. Neoclassical equilibrium economics thus boils down to the *unconditional belief* in the invisible hand, exemplified best by the economists adhering to the 'rational expectations' school and by politicians pursuing *laissez-faire* policies with unshakeable conviction. Strong beliefs are the most important pillars of any fundamentalism.

Agnosticism in some parts of economic science and of the humanities has precise philosophical foundations: following Kant nothing can, in principle, be said on the *essence* or the *nature* of the object of inquiry – for example, in the social sciences, on the nature of society and of socioeconomic phenomena; the object (aspects of the real world) is created by the subject (the scientist) through ideas held *a priori* or acquired empirically. This is the *hypotheticians'* approach to obtaining knowledge (Pribram 1986). Here excessive weight is put on the methods used by individual scientists if complex social problems, for instance unemployment or income distribution, are tackled from an individualistic point of view. Since individual points of view and hence methods vary widely between and within scientific schools a disaggregation of theories may ensue. This seems to hold for rationalist methods based upon the general equilibrium model, and for empirical (positivist) methods.

Hence the danger of agnosticism associated with neoclassical 'macrotheory', i.e. general equilibrium economics, is presumably due to the positivist and anti-metaphysical approach to reality (old philosophers might have spoken of 'nominalism' in this context), which is also mechanistic and individualistic. Economic reasoning is based upon *one fundamental principle*, i.e. the law of supply and demand. On the one hand, this implies an utterly simplifying view of the scientific object: the economy is, in fact, reduced to a mechanism. On the other hand, the scientific method (a subjective notion) in explaining economic events becomes all important. The problem is to construct a theory which, based upon the fundamental principle regulating the economic sphere, explains economic events, i.e. prices and quantities, on the basis of the actions of individuals. This fundamental theory is general equilibrium theory, which constitutes a kind of universal all-purpose tool which is put to use to explain all economic phenomena. It is true that the model, when put to practical use, is simplified and broken into pieces, but the general equilibrium model always lurks in the background, even if real-world disequilibrium situations are considered.

Neoclassical theoretical and applied work seems to aim at exploring the degree of generality of theoretical models and empirical results. This is in line with the positivistic, mechanistic and anti-metaphysical approach of the neoclassical economists which looks at reality from a subjective point of view. The latter inevitably leads to a multiplicity of explanatory theories: each theorist sees the working of the market in a different way, and various shapes and positions of the supply and demand curves associated with different equilibrium outcomes are postulated. The latter may evolve rapidly since the motivations of the economic actors may themselves change quickly.

This procedure is broadly adequate if it is borne in mind that supply-and-demand models only deal with *one* aspect of economic reality, i.e. short-run behavioural outcomes. However, the market cannot wholly explain economic facts. For example, from a classical-Keynesian point of view, the market does not determine normal prices, but only registers deviations from long-period prices governed by technology and institutions. Given this, the question of the scope of generality of some principle arises. Can the principle of supply and demand be applied to 'factor markets' without restriction? Most neoclassical economists would affirm this without hesitation. Classical-Keynesian political economists would argue that this can be done in certain short-period situations, but not if fundamental long-period ones are considered. It is one of the great mistakes committed by neoclassical economists to over-generalize the principle of supply and demand. This is tantamount to saying that all socioeconomic events are ultimately to be explained by individual actions, i.e. 'optimization under constraints', which are co-ordinated by the supply-and-demand mechanism. This over-ambitious scientific task that general equilibrium economists have set themselves is perhaps the basic source of agnosticism since it seems impossible to come to grips with the socioeconomic and political complexities by means of an approach uniquely based upon methodological individualism without considering how socioeconomic systems function.

Probable knowledge and classical-Keynesian political economy

The well-known distinction between induction and deduction provides a convenient starting point for sketching a theory of knowledge on classical-Keynesian or humanist lines. On the one hand, there are political economists and social scientists who, in a first step, systematically observe selected spheres of reality and subsequently attempt to discover principles or laws governing those spheres of reality by *induction*. In the social sciences, this descriptive-historical-institutional approach is perhaps exemplified best by the German Historical School and by American Institutionalism. 'Statisticians' such as Wesley Mitchell also belong to this group. Mitchell's motto *measurement without theory* appropriately characterizes the approach of the inductionists, which, it seems, has also become the method now currently used by pragmatically minded empirical research workers. On the other hand, there are the *deductionists* of various kinds who concentrate upon the principles regulating specific aspects of the real world and work out pure models reflecting these principles. Obvious representatives are David Ricardo, Piero Sraffa and Luigi Pasinetti; Marx's theory of value, Keynes's logical theory of the multiplier and Kalecki's pure cycle models also constitute pieces of pure classical-Keynesian theory. In Pribram's (1986) terms these classical-Keynesian theorists are all *essentialists* who attempt to capture the probable essence of socioeconomic phenomena.

At first sight, the above-mentioned criticism by Salin (1967, p. V) of the ill-suited separation of empirical and theoretical work seems to apply to classical-Keynesian political economy too. However, in chapter 3 (pp. 118–30) it has been mentioned that applied theory may be derived from pure theory in a straightforward way, and Marx's method of integrating theory and history has been stressed. Therefore, a fully-fledged classical-Keynesian system of principles such as the one sketched in chapter 4 can provide the conceptual basis for empirical and historical work. The history of economic theory provides striking examples of how theory and history can be integrated neatly: Adam Smith's *Wealth of Nations*, Marx's *Kapital*, Keynes's *Treatise on Money*, which, incidentally, contains a purely theoretical and an applied part, and Keynes's *General Theory* (on the latter, see chapter 4, pp. 241–51). Significantly, the theoretical framework presented in the *General Theory* has given rise to an immense amount of fruitful empirical work, for example on the macroeconomic consumption function. Similarly the theoretical work done by Leontief on input–output analysis has also inspired important empirical applications. The same is true of Pasinetti's work on structural change (Pasinetti 1981, 1993).

Hence, to collect data and to bring some order into these data on the basis of pure theory are complementary activities, the aim being to elaborate explanatory frameworks. Pure or ideal-type models deal with principles, i.e. horizontal and vertical causalities, and are constructed on the basis of premises that rely on a vision of things which, in turn, has been acquired by past theoretical and practical experience, and by introspection based on reason. A simple example of a pure model is Keynes's logical multiplier (Keynes 1973a, p. 122). Conversely, the pure model, if put to practical use, leads to elaborating explanatory frameworks or real-type models again embodying horizontal and vertical causalities. These are, however, modified by the varying circumstances when used to explain specific aspects of reality, e.g. the possible effects of an expansion in the capital goods industries (Keynes 1973a, pp. 122ff.). Explanatory frameworks further the understanding of specific phenomena and events by illuminating the facts from a given viewpoint. Knowledge obtained in this way influences, in turn, the conceptual framework the economist has started from: in the social sciences, probable objective knowledge is the result of an interaction between theory and historical reality, which includes the intellectual scenery and the dominating values. On the subjective level, knowledge is shaped by theoretical and empirical experience; the former is associated with various approaches in economics, the latter with observations made on selected aspects of the real world, such as the functioning of enterprises or the determination of income distribution through institutional factors. Both theoretical and empirical experience and, therefore, scientific knowledge are in turn shaped by the vision on the basis of which scattered pieces of knowledge are arranged to yield an orderly system of knowledge. Metaphysics appears as the *architectonic science* (Aristotle).

This points to the essential difference between neoclassical and classical-Keynesian methodology which lies in the kind of abstraction used. Neoclassical methodology implies *partial* abstraction: a selected – the economic – sphere of reality is separated out for investigation; all other spheres – the social, political and ethical – are abstracted from and relegated to the framework. The body of knowledge is the sum of all partial pieces of knowledge. There is no need for co-ordination since the attempt is made to explain all social phenomena by the behaviour of individuals, society having no independent existence. Classical-Keynesian methodology, however, is grounded on *total* or *comprehensive* abstraction, which is

Aristotelian. The starting point is society as a whole. In order to explain social phenomena like employment levels or prices, all non-essential or accidental factors are abstracted from in order to distil probable essences or principles. What is considered essential and accidental depends upon the vision held by the social scientist. The vision of society as a whole enables one to structure the knowledge obtained so as to bring about a body of knowledge.

The fact that wide spheres of human behaviour are *determined* by institutions, i.e. by the socioeconomic system (chapters 2, pp. 20–57 and 4, pp. 142–204) is important for the process of acquiring knowledge and for the nature of knowledge. First, institutions are permanent or only slowly changing which makes them suitable for theoretical and empirical investigation. Second, society can be seen as an interplay of largely complementary institutions, whereby each institution and each individual preserves some amount of autonomy; complementarity is crucial since it makes society a structured entity possessing its own laws which are independent of the will of individuals. For example, if all individuals save more in order to invest more in the future, there may be less investment now and in the future because the demand for consumption goods diminishes. Given the existence of specific laws governing society as a whole, of which the principle of effective demand is perhaps the most important, the study of behaviour is not sufficient to fully explain specific socioeconomic phenomena; the structurist and macroeconomic classical-Keynesian approach is required to further the understanding of parts of the real world, for example, to explain the depression of the thirties, or the economic decline of some countries and the rise of others. Third, the nature of knowledge obtained with the help of classical-Keynesian theory is mainly *qualitative*, rather than quantitative: the *understanding* of complex situations, for example the specific interplay of economic, social and political institutions resulting in fast-rising exports and rapid overall growth, cannot be quantified since intricate part–whole relationships are involved. A specific interplay of institutions is governed by differing systems of values that are present in each society. This, in turn, implies that each institution carries a specific weight (*Stellenwert*) in the process of interplay with other institutions. Hence theoretical relations (multiplier relations, input–output systems) cannot be handled mechanically, but must be adapted in an appropriate way to different historical situations. Moreover, knowledge is essentially qualitative because complex economic quantities, however measured, are statistical conventions. The index-number problem applies to all important economic magnitudes: normal and actual output and employment, and prices of production (normal prices) and market prices. These magnitudes all exist, but we shall never be able to grasp them entirely by attaching precise numerical values to them. Even if we could, the problem of interpretation would remain. Socioeconomic magnitudes are perhaps most significant in the form of ratios or of growth rates since then errors of measurement partly cancel out.

The classical-Keynesian synthesis suggested in chapter 4 may be defined as the analytical articulation of a particular vision of man and of society, i.e. *historical realism* (Lloyd 1986) which explicitly recognizes the individual *and* the social dispositions of man (chapter 2, pp. 20–57) and which accounts for the fact that society is a structured entity possessing laws of its own. This implies that knowledge about the functioning of the system is always probable knowledge in Keynes's sense (chapter 2, pp. 57–75). This kind of knowledge is based on a set of fundamental principles which picture basic causal forces underlying and structuring the various social spheres, i.e. production, exchange and the cultural, political and legal domains, such as to make society an entity. These causal forces may merely be probably known. The various principles are co-ordinated to yield a system of thought by the vision of things based on a social philosophy: starting from a particular vision of society, Ricardo, Sraffa and Pasinetti described the principles which regulate production, value and distribution, while Keynes discovered the basic causal force which regulates the level of employment, i.e. the principle of effective demand associated with the multiplier. These principles are embodied in pure theories and reflect vertical and horizontal causal forces, which, taken together, shape aspects of the real world and its evolution. Starting from pure models, explanatory frameworks (applied theories) may be worked out to explain tentatively what is going on in the different spheres of the real world, i.e. to approximately understand and explain historically unique situations and tendencies of change. To come to grips more closely with reality and its evolution on the basis of probable principles implies, so to speak, approximately explaining reality from *inside* and on the basis of the structure of the *object*, regulated by objectively given causal forces. This is required because man and society represent complex structured entities, i.e. systems of means and aims (chapter 2, pp. 20–57). The importance of the object of investigation reduces the (subjective) method used to acquire (probable) knowledge to secondary importance. The knowledge so acquired will never constitute absolute truth, since the human mind cannot entirely disentangle the complex set of causal forces that have brought about a historically unique situation, the crisis of the thirties or the outbreak of the First World War, for instance. The pursuit of truth or the acquisition of probable knowledge is a never-ending process.

6　An alternative theory of economic policy

In the preceding, theoretical, chapter the classical-Keynesian and the neoclassical approaches have been compared with respect to content and method. In this policy chapter the question as to which of the two approaches provides more secure foundations for socioeconomic policies naturally arises. In the initial section the different equilibrium notions associated respectively with the two approaches are taken as a starting point for discussing this question. This is done in the light of the arguments set out in the preceding chapters which seem to suggest that classical-Keynesian political economy ought to be preferred to neoclassical economics as a basis for policy actions.

Classical-Keynesian or third-way economic policies require a positive theory in order to explain given situations and a normative theory to fix the aim of policy actions. The former was sketched in chapters 3 and 4 while the latter is outlined in the second section of the present chapter. In the subsequent main section some policy principles along classical-Keynesian lines are set out. The emphasis is laid on long-period policies associated with the organization of the socioeconomic system.

The notion of equilibrium and economic policies

From the preceding chapter it emerges that the notions of equilibrium implied in neoclassical economics and in classical-Keynesian political economy are entirely different. This implies that the explanations of facts and the respective policy prescriptions also diverge. In this section the equilibrium concept contained in each approach is elaborated further to prepare the ground for comparing some policy elements associated with the two approaches. This provides the basis for selecting the more suitable approach to economic policy-making.

Two notions of equilibrium

Liberal economic theory conceives of the economy as an autonomous sub-system working within a social, legal and political framework. Under competitive conditions the rational – utility- and profit-maximizing – behaviour of individuals, co-ordinated by markets for final goods and for factors of production, is supposed to produce a tendency towards some *market* equilibrium position. Hence markets functioning satisfactorily are presumed to solve all the great economic problems, most importantly value, functional income distribution, employment and external trade relations. In this process marginal magnitudes – marginal costs, productivities and utilities – associated with substitution and competition play an essential role. These render possible rationality in the economic sphere of society through the rational behaviour of individuals in this very sphere. Hence behaviour is primary and the system secondary; the latter is merely derived from the former. In principle, the central policy problem consists in setting up a framework enhancing the functioning of the market mechanism. This may mean breaking up monopolies and cartels, reducing the power of trade unions and scaling down the activities of the state.

The classical-Keynesian equilibrium notion is, however, not merely linked up with a specific sphere, the economic sphere, but with the socio-economic and political *system as a whole*; this is due to the essential *complementarity* of economic, social, political and cultural institutions that is characteristic of the humanist vision of society sketched in chapter 2 (pp. 20–57). The – normal – prices of production depend upon the conditions and the relations of production and the institutions regulating income distribution; normal quantities and, consequently, the level or the scale of trend output and employment are governed by long-period effective demand, which, in turn, depends upon all the institutions of a society; this emerges from the supermultiplier analysis set forth in chapter 4. Hence normal prices and quantities are not independent of each other: both depend upon the rate of profits or the profit share. This suggests that the regulation of distribution is of primary importance in political economy. Ricardo was the first to perceive this point.

A classical-Keynesian system equilibrium – made up of normal prices and quantities – is *not* socially rational or desirable since it does not imply full employment. This means that the rationality of the system does not coincide with the rationality of individuals; Keynes's paradox of thrift is the prime example. Individuals and collectives act rationally in different spheres, i.e. economic, social and political, according to their specific point of view or value system: individual rationality is severely bounded. But the aggregate of individual rational actions does not produce *social rationality*. The latter is linked up with the socially appropriate organization of society, that is with *social or political ethics*. Hence, as Keynes explicitly stated, the social sciences are *essentially* moral sciences (chapter 2, pp. 39–53). The central problem of political ethics is to provide guidelines for increasing social harmony, i.e. to reduce alienation or to enhance the common weal or the public interest. This means establishing socially more appropriate proportions between the various spheres of human activity; for instance, from the supermultiplier theory it follows that specific proportions between distribution, private and public spending, investment activity, export quantities, the import coefficient and the terms of trade must hold if full employment is to be achieved. This requires a socially appropriate institutional set-up, which will, on account of varying circumstances, differ between countries and regions.

Problems with the liberal approach to policy-making

Liberal economic policies could only be successful if the market mechanism produced a strong tendency towards a full-employment equilibrium under ideal circumstances, that is in a situation with perfect competition: perfectly functioning markets must bring about such a tendency *in principle;* specific real-world obstacles, such as imperfect information, monopolies and cartels, and temporary market failures, obstructing a tendency towards full employment are always there and would give rise to second-best solutions, which could be improved by appropriately acting upon the framework surrounding the market.

In chapter 5 (pp. 281–93) it has been argued that, even if conditions were ideal, a tendency towards a full-employment equilibrium brought about by market forces is very unlikely for both theoretical and historical reasons. Hence it is not appropriate to ground economic policies upon neoclassical theory. An exchange-based conceptual framework is simply too flimsy to carry the policy actions required in a modern monetary production economy with extensive division of labour. This does not mean that the market is not important: in the classical-Keynesian view, the main task of this institution is to create a continuous tendency for market prices to adjust to the prices of production. (This, incidentally, implies that the latter are fundamental in a monetary production economy, not the former.) However, the market cannot solve the great economic problems – value, functional distribution and employment – on a fundamental level, i.e. in principle. In the light of the argument set out in the preceding chapters, especially in chapter 5 (pp. 281–93), this implies that the neoclassical policy problem cannot be solved in principle either. On the one hand, the market cannot produce a tendency towards full employment because production is a social process which prevents pricing being separated from distribution and, consequently, means that marginal products are not defined; long-period factor markets simply do not exist. On the other hand, the position of the long-period demand and supply curves – if they existed! – would depend upon the institutions located in the framework. With a spontaneous tendency towards full employment lacking, liberal long-period economic or system policy is faced with an impossible task: ideally, an institutional framework would have to be set up such that the actions of rational economic agents result in a full-employment equilibrium. This would require a frightening amount of planning, including regulation of behaviour.

The above relates to an important aspect of economic history since the Industrial Revolution: socioeconomic policies were – and, in fact, still are – based upon a *normative* theory, i.e. the economic theory of liberalism or neoclassical economics, in order to attempt to solve *real-world* problems that arise within monetary production economies. This means that concepts associated with the rational behaviour of individuals and with the co-ordination of behaviour by markets were and are used to tackle issues pertaining to the rationality of the socioeconomic and political system. The results are well known. In periods of crisis, liberal policies require austerity. Saving must increase to finance additional investment required to create new jobs; this may require lower real wages and cuts in government spending, including expenditures for social welfare. From the classical-Keynesian view on the functioning of a monetary production economy sketched in chapter 4, such policy measures are very likely to result in an increase in involuntary unemployment. Hence actions which seem rational from the point of view of the individual produce opposite results if applied to the social system, which possesses its own laws. As a consequence, liberal policy measures are largely ineffective in the face of growing involuntary unemployment and its social and political effects. As a rule, liberal policies aim at influencing the behaviour of individuals, not at organizing the social system within which behaviour takes place. More and more regulation of behaviour is required to deal with the problems arising if the system does not work properly. For example, attempts are made to tackle involuntary unemployment with vocational training (which is certainly required to cure *structural* unemployment), or, if the number of crimes increases, security measures are reinforced. This is to deal with effects (inappropriate behaviour), not with the underlying causes, i.e. the misfunctioning of the system, which results in involuntary unemployment.

The policy problem in political economy

The central problem of politics is fundamentally of an ethical nature. The basic aim is to reduce, as far as is humanly possible, system-caused alienation, which has been defined as the gap between some actually existing social situation and a state of affairs embodying the common weal or the public interest (chapter 2, pp. 39–53). This requires attempts to set up a harmonious and rational social structure, that is to create the social preconditions within which individuals and collectives may prosper. The policy principles have to be proposed by the science of politics (in the traditional Aristotelian sense) of which political economy is a branch (chapter 2, pp. 20–57). The state (the government and the civil service) ought to apply these principles to specific real-world situations.

In the humanist view, the state is by far the most important social institution since its concern ought to be the public interest, i.e. a matter related to *all* aspects of social life. In the socioeconomic sphere, the most important tasks of the state ought to relate to securing full employment and a fair distribution of incomes. Both aims embody the *principle of solidarity*: nobody ought to be excluded from society or to be treated in an obviously unfair way therein. Other important aims to be pursued by the state relate to increasing national wealth such as is compatible with the preservation of the environment, to spending tax incomes in a socially useful way and to contributing to organizing international trade relations in a way that is beneficial to all trading partners. In doing so, the state ought to co-operate with non-governmental institutions which might be subsumed under the heading of *non-profit organizations*. Examples are various associations and co-operatives of workers, employers and consumers and non-profit organizations in the social and cultural sphere. However, the state ought to intervene in socioeconomic affairs only if some individual or some social entity is not in a position to solve some vital problem by itself. This is the *principle of subsidiarity* which implies that state intervention must be such as to leave the greatest possible scope for freedom of action for all citizens (for a philosophical treatment of this principle see Utz 1964–94, vol. I, pp. 277ff.). Hence, the policy problem is, positively formulated, to create appropriate social foundations, not to influence the behaviour of individuals. The latter ought to be regulated by individual ethics, i.e. *Individualethik*.

Because of the permanent presence of alienation on the political level, real-world state activity will – often very widely – diverge from the normative picture just sketched. There are various causes for political alienation to arise. Corruption and the pursuit of particular interests by politicians are perhaps most important. However, well-intentioned politicians may also enhance political alienation if their policy actions are based upon inappropriate principles, for example if austerity policies are pursued in a crisis situation. In this context it ought to be recalled that alienation in some sphere of social life, as a rule, produces alienation in other domains; for example, political alienation – corruption and the pursuit of particular interests by politicians – is likely to bring about alienation in the economic sphere, for example involuntary unemployment, and, subsequently, in the social sphere: crime increases with persistent unemployment.

Since the rational economic actions of the economic agents and their co-ordination by the market cannot solve the most important economic problems, the state and society must intervene and take policy actions based on the global or macro rationality of the system. This is the point of view of political economy which is, in part, contrary to the view first expressed by Adam Smith and subsequently refined by the neoclassical economists. James Steuart anticipates classical political economy (in the sense of Ricardo and J. S. Mill) and the essence of modern classical-Keynesian political economy:

What oeconomy is in a family, political oeconomy is in a state . . . The *statesman* (this is a general term to signify the legislature and supreme power, according to the form of government) is neither master to establish what oeconomy he pleases, or, in the exercise of his . . . authority, to overturn at will the established laws of it . . .

The great art therefore of political oeconomy is, first to adapt the different operations of it to the spirit, manners, habits, and customs of the people; and afterwards to model these circumstances so, as to be able to introduce a set of new and more useful institutions.

The principle object of this science is to secure a certain fund of subsistence for all the inhabitants, to obviate every circumstance which may render it precarious; to provide every thing necessary for supplying the wants of the society, and to employ the inhabitants . . . in such a manner as naturally to create reciprocal relations and dependencies between them, so as to make their several interests lead them to supply one another with their reciprocal wants (Steuart 1966 [1767], pp. 16–17).

In modern terms, the state and parts of the civil society – trade unions, entrepreneurial associations, professional corporations, for instance – have to create the social preconditions such that individuals may prosper. On the most fundamental level this means the broad regulation of the level of economic activity and of the production of the social surplus, its distribution and its use.

This humanist conception of socioeconomic policy-making has a very long tradition in social and political thought, although the application of the basic principles has taken on very different forms because of widely differing economic, political and intellectual circumstances. Presumably, the appropriate historical starting point is Aristotle's *Politics* taken together with his *Ethics*. Some of the great scholastic philosophers, Aquinas in the main, carried on the tradition which, in turn, was taken up by many mercantilists and, in Germany, cameralists; the latter coined the notion of *Staatskunst* which subsequently gave rise to the development of the *Staatswissenschaften*. The Aristotelian tradition of politics was continued by representatives of the physiocratic and classical schools including Marx; his famous remarks on the 'realm of necessity' (*Reich der Notwendigkeit*) and the 'realm of freedom' (*Reich der Freiheit*) (Marx 1973/74a [1867–94], vol. III, p. 828) are important in this context. The American Institutionalists and the members of the German Historical School, above all the 'socialists of the chair' (*Kathedersozialisten*) are also in the humanist line of political thought. At the end of the nineteenth century, a specific Christian Social Doctrine was established in which, subsequently, typically classical-Keynesian views regarding employment and distribution were incorporated. In the twentieth century, the tradition was taken up by Maynard Keynes and by many Keynesians and classical-Keynesians (on this, see also Deane 1989; Harcourt 1986, pp. 250–72; and Schumpeter 1954).

A normative classical-Keynesian system

Classical-Keynesian political economy is essentially positive and may as such be used to approximately explain real-world phenomena set in space and evolving in historical time. In positive analysis, values, ethical standards and the extent of alienation are, explicitly or implicitly, assumed to be *given*.

However, explanation of socioeconomic reality is not sufficient to set up a coherent system of policy actions. The aims to be reached must also be specified: *pure normative systems* picturing what desirable socioeconomic states of affairs ought to look like *in principle* have to be elaborated; for instance, the meaning in principle of an 'equitable distribution of incomes' has to be defined; moreover, since there is no automatic tendency towards full employment, the *right to work* as a basic human right must be firmly anchored in a classical-Keynesian normative system; this requires a theory on how full employment may be reached in principle. Starting from pure normative models, corresponding real-type models may be elaborated. However, the latter ought to be 'moderately' normative only, i.e. they must imply a state of affairs that may be achieved by purposeful human actions and not imply a utopia as is the case with liberal and socialist models: starting from a specific concrete situation it must be possible to specify the path leading to the state of affairs pictured by the normative real-type model. The perfect world cannot be created simply, because detailed knowledge about ideal states is lacking. In fact, all attempts to realize subjectively conceived utopias have utterly failed. In recent history this is true of both socialist *and* liberal utopias, if a global view is taken.

The outstanding historical example of a 'moderately' normative real-type system is Quesnay's *tableau économique* which describes a healthy (natural) situation for the French economy as opposed to the chaotic heritage left by a lost mercantilist trade war (against England). Large parts of the classical system of political economy are moderately normative whenever *natural* states of affairs are considered. The same is true of Lowe's work: 'The Mecca of the modern growth theorist does not lie where prevailing opinion looks for it; namely, in "positive" analysis' (Lowe 1976, p. 7). '[Therefore] we should base our trust in *prescriptive* rather than in *descriptive* analysis' (p. 8).

The *natural system* set out by Pasinetti (1981, 1993) constitutes a fully fledged modern normative system along classical-Keynesian lines. This system may be termed *natural* because it deals with the normative nature, i.e. the normative essentials or principles associated with monetary production economies. Because of its normative dimension the *natural* differs from the *normal*; the latter is positive and attempts to capture the essentials of actually existing monetary production economies. The two are separated by alienation which may be caused, for example, by a very unequal distribution of incomes and by high unemployment levels.

Hence the *natural system* is a pure or ideal-type normative model which is, as such, independent of institutions:

It is my purpose . . . to develop first of all a theory which remains neutral with respect to institutions. My preoccupation will be that of singling out, to resume Ricardo's terminology, the 'primary and natural' features of a pure production system. [Problems that relate to the institutional mechanisms which characterize any society are subsidiary to the 'natural problems'] and may actually be solved in many different ways (Pasinetti 1981, p. 153).

Pasinetti's essentialist approach clearly emerges here. The search for essentials or first principles results in pure models which are always independent of specific institutions. This is also true of the Walras–Pareto model. However, pure models *imply* a specific ranking of institutions. In Pasinetti's natural system it is implied that the institutions associated with production and distribution are fundamental, while the Walrasian model implies a pre-eminence of markets, which are also institutions.

The starting point of Pasinetti's analysis is indeed the *process of production* which is a social process (production of commodities by means of commodities and labour) directed towards a common (social) aim, i.e. the production of the 'social' product including the surplus over what is used up in the production process. On this basis, one of the central problems of classical macroeconomics is solved, i.e. the question of the appropriate proportions between sectors of production if structural change is going on in time. Hence, the distribution of employment between sectors is also determined in any period of time.

The Keynesian employment problem is dealt with in a very general way. The *natural system* contains 'a *macro-economic* effective demand condition, referring to total demand in the economic system as a whole [which, together with the] *sectoral* new investment conditions [guarantee] full employment and full capacity utilisation' (Pasinetti 1981, p. 128). The normative character of this condition comes out clearly from Pasinetti's considering '[f]ull employment as an actively pursued target of economic policy' (p. 88ff.) which requires '[a] central Agency entrusted with the task of keeping full employment' (p. 91). Full employment is an absolute requirement because, in a monetary production economy, involuntary unemployment means squandering the unique and most precious factor of production. Hence the all-important *right to work* is firmly anchored in the *natural system*.

Functional income distribution is dealt with in an ingenious way:

When there is both population growth and technical progress, there are as many natural rates of profit as there are rates of expansion of demand (and production) of the various consumption goods. Each natural rate of profit is given by the sum of two components: the rate of population growth, common to all of them, and the rate of increase of per capita demand for each consumption good (equal to the rate of increase of per capita production, as we are considering dynamic equilibrium situations) (Pasinetti 1981, pp. 130–1).

Thus, ideally, the social function of profits is to finance full-employment investment.

This theory of the functional income distribution has a particularly interesting implication with respect to the theory of value: '[once] natural [rates] of profit [are] introduced [t]he theory of value implied [in the natural system] becomes a theory in terms of simple labour – *a pure labour theory of value*' (Pasinetti 1981, p. 132). This proposition has far-reaching implications for economic theory. For example, the labour theory of value implies that the various kinds of labour have to be evaluated, i.e. the reduction coefficients have to be determined. The latter govern, together with the conditions of production, the relations of exchange. If, on average, one day's direct and indirect labour is required to produce a coat and if two days are needed to make a cupboard, then one cupboard will exchange against two coats. This implies, however, that the labour of the tailor is put on an equal footing with that of the carpenter. If now, in a specific society, for technical and social reasons, one day of a carpenter's labour is considered to be equivalent to two days of a tailor's labour, then a cupboard would, in principle, exchange against four coats. To fix the reduction coefficients on the basis of the social quality of the various types of work performed amounts to determining the *social status* of workers and employees; materially, the status shows up in work conditions and in the relative wages and salaries. The determination of the reduction coefficients is a complex and ongoing social process, since, with technical change going on, new kinds of labour continuously come into being. In a society organized by humanist or natural principles trade unions will have to play a crucial role in determining the reduction coefficients across a socially appropriate wages structure.

The problem of reduction coefficients and hence of social status plays a prominent role in the work of many classical economists and Marx. In relation to the concept of the *just price*, Aristotle and Aquinas dealt with the problem of social status under the heading of *distributive justice*, or *iustitia distributiva* (Salin 1967, p. 31). This notion was elaborated in order to establish an ethically appropriate relationship between individuals and society in the economic and political sphere, particularly regarding the distribution of income and wealth. In this view, distribution is not a relation between individuals but is a social problem; it deals with a specific relationship between parts (individuals and collectives) and the corresponding entity, i.e. society (on this, see chapter 4, pp. 154–90).

The essentially normative character of Pasinetti's *natural system* requires that personal income distribution be in line with the generally accepted social status of the individuals making up society, i.e. that reduction coefficients be fixed in a socially equitable way. Hence the *natural prices* are *just prices* in the sense that they reflect properly society's efforts embodied in the final products. Moreover, if transactions (exchange of goods and services) are carried out on the basis of just prices, *justice in exchange* prevails, a concept which broadly corresponds to the concept of *iustitia commutativa* of Artistotle and Aquinas (Salin, 1967, p. 31). Trade at just prices implies that exchange relations are fair and right and that distribution (relative wealth) is socially equitable. The concept of the just price is not only of paramount importance for exchanges going on inside an economy, but also for economic relations between nations, i.e. foreign trade. Hence, the labour theory of value is a *social* theory of value of immense complexity and variety since different material contents may be given to the formal concepts of 'distributive justice' and 'justice in exchange' in various countries and regions. This stands in sharp contrast to the relatively simple neoclassical theory of value which, in its being based upon utility, is *primarily* individualistic. To be sure, the classical-Keynesian labour theory of value, or of labour equivalents, does not imply that utility, i.e. demand, plays no role. With respect to value, however, utility (demand) is of *secondary* importance in that it records deviations from already determined normal prices which are based on labour equivalents (positive analysis) or from labour values in normative analysis. In the long run, utility and demand do not influence prices and values anyway; their primary role is to determine the structure of output. This fact comes out very clearly from Pasinetti (1981, 1993) and is also implied in the earlier chapters of this book.

The pure or ideal-type natural system uniquely deals with principles and can therefore be associated with various institutional set-ups of the humanist type (chapter 2, pp. 20–57). Correspondingly, some basic principles for policy action can be derived from the natural system, e.g. the need to aim permanently at full employment. In order to put the natural system to practical use, desirable institutional set-ups will have to be specified, which means working out *normative real-type* models for specific countries and time-periods. Such models might contain concrete policy measures to secure full employment and a fair distribution of income; the latter relates to the functional distribution, i.e. the shares of wages, profits and rents in national income, and to the structure of wages. When implementing these policy measures, the state ought to co-operate with the non-profit sector, in general, and with entrepreneurial associations and trade unions, in particular. With employment and distribution fixed, entrepreneurs and entrepreneurial associations may rely on the market mechanism to establish structures of production such that outputs may be sold at, approximately, natural or just prices. Since the social nature of the process of production and the notion of social harmony are fundamental in an economy organized along humanist lines, the *principle of co-operation* and, when needed, the *principle of co-ordination* ought to regulate the relations between the state and civil society, of which the non-profit sector is one of the main components.

The natural system set forth in Pasinetti (1981, 1993) is essentially a piece of classical macroeconomics dealing with proportions. As such the *natural system* allows the treatment of a number of important economic phenomena from a normative point of view: value, distribution, technical progress, saving and interest, international trade, and others. To formulate policy principles the natural system must be combined with pure positive theories, e.g. with a macroeconomic theory of output and employment determination which has to explain how full employment may be achieved in principle (chapter 4, pp. 140–204). Since the natural system refers to a monetary production economy, money must play an essential role. This role is twofold: first, natural prices depend upon the conditions of production and money wages and, second, effective demand – a monetary magnitude – determines output and employment; hence continuous efforts are required to maintain full employment. Finally, it should not be difficult to link up classical-Keynesian microeconomics (behaviour) with the (structural) natural system; for example, prescriptions regarding price formation and the utilization of profits may be required. Hence Pasinetti's *natural system* provides the appropriate starting point for building the analytical framework of positive and normative classical-Keynesian political economy and of the associated socioeconomic policies (for some additional remarks on the significance of Pasinetti's natural system, see Bortis 1993). In spite of its being essentially normative the natural system may serve as the basis of both positive and normative political economy because the normative is but the ethically appropriate form of the positive, with the same variables and parameters entering both types of model.

Some classical-Keynesian policy principles

Two related sets of socioeconomic policy measures are required to promote the public interest. One is concerned with domestic issues, the other with external relations and the world economic and financial system. Domestic policies are closely associated with the internal employment mechanism; proposals on international economic and financial relations are linked up with the external employment mechanism (on both these mechanisms, see chapter 4, pp. 190–9). Both kinds of policy are dealt with in the subsequent subsections.

Classical-Keynesian socioeconomic policies naturally emerge from the broad conceptual framework suggested in chapter 4 and from the normative system sketched in the preceding section. Concrete policy proposals are made in 'The end of laissez-faire' (Keynes 1972b, pp. 272–94), in 'National self-sufficiency' (Keynes 1982, pp. 233–46), in the final chapters of the *General Theory* (Keynes 1973a) and *The Clearing Union* (Keynes 1980). Pasinetti's views on the nature of macroeconomics and on foreign trade (Pasinetti 1981, chapter XI) and Kuttner's *The End of Laissez-Faire* (1991) directly link up with Keynes's vision.

Long-period domestic policies

'The outstanding faults of the economic society in which we live are its failure to provide for full employment and its arbitrary and inequitable distribution of wealth and incomes' (Keynes 1973a, p. 372). Employment and distribution are inevitably *the* great domestic policy issues in a *humanist* view of the economy. This emerges from chapter 4. Additional important policy problems are concerned with state activity, with entrepreneurial activity and with the organization of exchange and production. All these issues are associated with the internal employment mechanism described in chapter 4 (pp. 190–9). Some aspects of these policy problems are the object of the present subsection. We start by considering distribution, which is basic because normal prices and normal employment heavily depend upon it.

From the normative classical-Keynesian system sketched above two great distributional issues emerge. The first is associated with Ricardo: how are the shares of wages, profits and rents determined? In chapter 4 (pp. 154–90) it has been suggested that distribution is essentially a social phenomenon involving part–whole relationships: hence a social consensus is required to determine functional income distribution. Trade unions, entrepreneurial associations and professional organizations play a crucial role here. The state should intervene only if the distributional consensus cannot be reached on the intermediate or social level. This would constitute an application of the principle of subsidiarity: political or higher-level action should only be taken if a problem cannot be solved at the lower level, i.e. the social level in this case. To fix the socially appropriate profit rate is perhaps the central problem of functional distribution (it may be recalled here that the determination of the natural wage was Ricardo's central problem). In chapter 4 (pp. 154–90) reasons were given why profits should subsist even in the stationary state.

The second great distributional issue concerns the structure of incomes, particularly the wage structure. Relative wages should reflect Ricardo's and Marx's reduction coefficients. These, in turn, ought to be based upon the quality and the intensity of the intellectual and physical efforts made by the various categories of workers and employees. All the reduction coefficients are interdependent and express part–whole relationships. Hence job evaluations required to fix relative wages in particular enterprises must always take account of the entire wage structure on which each single enterprise constantly needs information. Trade unions seem best suited to collect and to disseminate the relevant information concerning relative wages. To ensure a fair wage structure seems to be one of the main trade union tasks in a monetary production economy.

Distribution is closely related to price formation and taxation. The normal prices governed by technology and distributional institutions are Ricardian in the sense that they approximately reflect social efforts of production in the most difficult circumstances. This is evident in agriculture and mining. In the industrial and service sectors 'difficulties of production' may occur on account of legal prescriptions, for example prescriptions concerning the protection of the environment, or of an unfavourable location, giving rise to high transport costs for instance. Rents may therefore accrue to producers in the primary, secondary and tertiary sectors. In chapter 4 (pp. 154–90) it was mentioned that rents may also accrue in the liberal professions, for example through entry barriers or special skills.

Rents are an ideal object for taxation. This is particularly valid for rents on land, i.e. rents in agriculture and mining. Taxes and subsidies have important distributional implications. For example, Ricardo held that all the taxes ultimately fall upon property income, above all profits. Kaldor argues to the contrary: if wages are the residual all the burden of taxation falls on wages (Kaldor 1955/56). This always holds with the classical-Keynesian framework suggested in chapter 4 *if* the employment level is given, particularly in a full-employment situation. However, if there is persistent involuntary unemployment (chapter 4, pp. 142–204) additional state expenditures and increased taxation may leave the distributional shares unchanged; instead a permanent change in the normal employment level may occur.

The securing of an equitable distribution of income, i.e. fair and thus socially acceptable wage structures and profit rates, is required not only for the ethical reasons summarized by the notion of *distributive justice* mentioned in the previous section. According to the internal employment mechanism (chapter 4, pp. 190–9), distribution is directly linked with the level of employment: a larger share of normal wage incomes ($1/k^*$) is, in principle, associated with higher trend levels of output and employment since the bulk of wage income is spent on consumption goods. If income distribution is too unequal, over-saving occurs: saving exceeds the exogenously determined full employment investment level. Too large a fraction of property incomes is saved, part of which may be used for speculative purposes (hot money), thus enhancing speculative activity in the short run; in the long run wealth held in money and/or near money form grows. This may lead to an increase and to fluctuations in the value of non-produced goods – land, old masters, etc. – and of share prices and to more takeovers and takeover attempts. In these circumstances the main purpose of saving is *not* to increase future consumption through productive investment but to increase wealth in whatever shape to get as much property income as possible; investments in land are the most obvious cases in point. Therefore, an unequal income distribution tends to generate more inequality, which leads, in turn, to higher unemployment levels as is evident from the supermultiplier analysis carried out in chapter 4 (pp. 142–204).

On the distribution of income and wealth in the United States, H. Inhaber and S. Carroll have done outstanding work (Inhaber and Carroll 1992); having identified an 'empirical law of distribution', their main policy proposal aims at eliminating *excessive* inequalities associated with approximately 3 per cent of the wealthiest households.

The preceding remarks suggest that an institutionalized incomes and distribution policy along classical-Keynesian lines is indispensable in a monetary production economy.

It follows from the supermultiplier relation that, in addition to an equitable distribution of incomes, there is a second means to increase the level of output and employment, namely to raise government expenditure in a socially useful way; this conclusion also emerges from Keynes's *General Theory*. In normal circumstances, this holds even for a balanced budget since higher direct taxes, required to finance higher government expenditure, are likely to reduce saving coefficients much more than the propensities to consume: the approximate constancy of the long-period average propensity to consume (a stylized institutional fact reflecting the appropriateness of the surplus approach) is taken account of in the supermultiplier model by postulating constant leakage coefficients. However, the most efficient way of levying taxes is, presumably, to levy not direct taxes but, instead, indirect taxes, mainly on luxury consumption goods, or to tax expenditures (Kaldor 1955).

This is not to argue that the sphere of state activity should be extended indefinitely. The problem is to establish a sound balance between state and private activity. On account of the different ways of life this balance will vary among the different countries; hence generalizations in this matter are hardly possible. However, as far as the link between state activity and the employment level is concerned, a reduction in the former will entail a reduction in the latter, unless increased private spending compensates for diminishing state expenditures. This emerges from the supermultiplier analysis of chapter 4 (pp. 142–204).

While the volume of government expenditures is an important determinant of the scale of economic activity, their composition also shapes the institutional set-up of an economy and of a society in an important way. Such structures grow historically over long periods of time and may be quite difficult to change. For example, in spite of *détente*, some countries have considerable difficulties in switching from defence expenditure to other types of expenditure. To bring about a socially appropriate structure of government expenditures is an intricate problem of political economy requiring a comprehensive and very long-run view on socioeconomic and political affairs.

At this stage the privatization issue has to be briefly considered (see also chapter 4, pp. 154–90). In classical-Keynesian terms privatization basically means transforming 'unproductive' activities (in the sense of the classicals) financed by the surplus into surplus-producing activities. The supermultiplier formula reveals the perils of privatization: effective demand is likely to be reduced since the activities hitherto financed by the surplus have now to be paid a price which covers the costs of production *and* includes a profit; the latter means that consumers have to spend more to get the same level of satisfaction; with given techniques of production it is unlikely that substantial efficiency gains and hence lower prices can be achieved through privatization. Hence privatization leads to real income reductions and, consequently, to reductions in activity and employment levels. According to the supermultiplier analysis this tendency is reinforced by reductions in government expenditures that are associated with privatization. Moreover, tax reductions that may accompany privatizations are unlikely to raise expenditures since, on the one hand, lower taxes are likely to result in increased saving and, on the other hand, the fact that consumers have to pay for the produce of privatized activity will reduce expenditures for other goods. Hence privatization may prove self-defeating according to the classical-Keynesian surplus approach: on the one hand, privatization aims at establishing new surplus-creating activities; on the other hand, government expenditures which are an engine of surplus creation are reduced (chapter 4, pp. 142–204). The final result will be less production and employment and hence a lower surplus.

Privatization may also mean transferring profitable, i.e. surplus-producing, activities from public into private hands. This reduces government receipts which may, in turn, lead to cuts in government expenditure, lower activity levels and, consequently, a reduced social surplus.

In the classical-Keynesian view, privatization is not primarily an efficiency issue but is a matter of social organization, the basic question being which activities should yield a surplus and which activities should be financed by the surplus.

An active employment and distribution policy not only follows from the short-period analysis of the *General Theory*, but also from the long-period supermultiplier relation and its implications: effective demand *always* governs the levels of output and employment. Involuntary unemployment may thus occur at any moment of time and may persist through time. Persistent unemployment favours the emergence of a *divided society*, that separates those included in the socioeconomic system from those excluded. In the highly developed countries the former category of people make up a large majority, and vice versa in the economically underdeveloped regions. The immense dangers of social division for society as a whole need not be stressed here, nor need the immense *system-caused* suffering be described. Involuntary unemployment and its direct consequences are certainly the most important cause for system-caused alienation in complex monetary production economies (chapter 2, pp. 39–53).

As can be seen from the supermultiplier relation the gross investment ratio is an important determinant of the global activity level. Moreover, this ratio is of fundamental importance for the pace of technical progress. Hence a legal and cultural framework favouring entrepreneurial activities in Schumpeter's sense is an important domain of domestic economic policy.

Distribution, employment, state activity and the investment activities of entrepreneurs are the central socioeconomic policy issues in modern societies. A fifth important policy domain is related to the spheres of exchange (markets) and of production. Markets must be organized to some extent by cartels or similar institutions in order to reduce uncertainty for the individual producer. The central reason is that 'production takes time' (Paul Davidson): given the initial costs for research and development, marketing and production, several years may elapse before an investment project becomes profitable. No entrepreneur would engage in production and in the introduction of new methods of production and of new products if there was ferocious competition associated with very high degrees of uncertainty for the individual enterprises. The main reason is that competition is not a struggle for relative positions at the full-employment level as the liberals see it. In a monetary production economy with no tendency towards full employment (chapter 4, pp. 142–204) competition becomes a struggle for survival. No entrepreneur will therefore undertake long-term projects when the survival of his enterprise is subject to the unforeseeable vagaries of the market. If competition is too intense and uncertainty too great, entrepreneurs will more and more engage in short-term activities, mainly in the financial sector. Speculation in the stock market, in the markets for real estate, raw materials, land and other non-reproducibles – old masters for instance – becomes increasingly important. Excessive activities in these domains may gravely damage production in that the technical dynamism of the economy is reduced, for example. Why engage in long-range productive activities when quick speculative profits may be made? This important issue was recognized by Keynes, Kaldor, Galbraith and Minsky.

Cartels and similar institutions are therefore damaging only if they allow for excessive profits. On the whole, however, cartels may be socially useful in that they contribute to creating a more stable environment which is indispensable for long-period entrepreneurial action. On this issue Gustav Schmoller remarks:

Cartels developed in line with monetary production economies with large industrial enterprises and banks. As a rule these enterprises are endowed with huge amounts of fixed capital and are therefore particularly vulnerable to an uncertain future, excessive competition and periodic crises. For these reasons, the growth of cartels became inevitable. This process corresponds to the technical and economic conditions of our time. Cartels may degenerate and lead to the formation of huge profits. However, this institution may become socially useful . . . if cartels are controlled by representatives of the state, of the enterprises concerned and of the working class . . . Hence cartels should not be eliminated but should be put on a sound basis: they should become the natural institutions for the long-range planning of production in highly developed industrial societies (Schmoller 1901, vol. I, p. 452; a.tr.).

This view of market organization has its roots in the work of several members of the German Historical School and of American Institutionalism and has proved successful in Japan, Germany and Switzerland. (However, the danger associated with powerful industrial organizations in times of economic and/or military conflict should never be lost sight of; this problem will shortly be dealt with in the next subsection.) Kuttner mentions the Japanese example in this context:

The Japanese . . . have never believed in Adam Smith. Rather, Japan can be located precisely in a line of descent from the German Historical School . . ., the school of Friedrich List . . . The Japanese government decided to work with and through private corporations, rather than sponsoring state-owned industry. The government sold them pilot plants, provided them with exclusive licenses and other privileges, and often provided them with part of their capital funds . . . Though ownership was private, development was based on cartelization rather than price competition (Kuttner 1991, pp. 160–1).

To organize production and exchange is to favour the growth of an inter-mediate sphere between individuals and the state. Apart from cartels, other entrepreneurial associations and trade unions, this is the domain where most of the various non-profit organizations are active. Keynes also held the opinion that intermediate institutions ought to be strengthened in a monetary production economy, for example in 'The end of laissez-faire' (Keynes 1972b) and 'National self-sufficiency' (Keynes 1982).

The crucial importance of production was emphasized by Friedrich List, particularly in *Das nationale System der Politischen Oekonomie* (List 1920 [1841]). In chapter 12 of this book List explicitly states that the long-range development of the productive powers of an economy is far more impor-tant than short-term gains of exchange – this theme has recently been taken up systematically by Luigi Pasinetti (1993). To maintain and enhance the productive powers of a society is all-important since average labour pro-ductivity determines the material welfare of a country. The productivity of labour and its increase depend upon all the institutions making up a society: technical dynamism, which in turn depends upon the quality of research and development and on the stability of the institutional environ-ment enabling entrepreneurs to implement long-term investment plans; the education system; the political institutions; the social climate, which partly depends upon the quality of the social insurance system and of the degree of fairness of distribution: if workers feel secure materially in case of tem-porary unemployment, they will be ready to accept more easily the struc-tural changes that are inevitably associated with technical progress; a high employment level greatly improves the social climate: the terrible pressure associated with the fear of becoming unemployed largely vanishes. Moreover, a fair distribution of incomes enhances productivity since workers will be more motivated to achieve higher quantity and quality stan-dards. With labour productivity rising, real wages will increase in the long run. This, in turn, enables a society eventually to reduce labour time and thereby increase the scope for leisure activities. In Marx's terms this means a reduction of the realm of necessity and determinism and an extension of the realm of liberty and freedom of choice (Marx 1973/74a, vol. III, p. 828).

Long-range domestic socioeconomic policies require a global view of social affairs and of society's long-period evolution: society is an entity since the institutions composing it are largely complementary (chapter 3, pp. 89–95). This is implicit in the classical-Keynesian humanist vision pictured in the preceding chapters of the present study. The immense complexity of the task and the breadth of knowledge required must be stressed: all the spheres of social life – economic, social, political and cultural – must be considered and their relationship to society as a whole evaluated. And complications dramatically increase if an open economy is considered.

Long-period socioeconomic policies in open economies

To secure full employment in an open economy in the long run is linked up with a peculiar difficulty: *given* exports, the terms of trade *and* full-employment imports, the import coefficient (b) has, in principle, to adjust itself to render possible a long-period current account equilibrium (chapter 4, pp. 190–9). In the long run, a country cannot import more than it exports: imports have ultimately to be paid for by exports if chronic indebtedness and its devastating consequences are to be avoided.

Several important policy conclusions for domestic economic policy and for organizing international economic relations follow from the fact that some management of foreign trade relations, specifically a broad management of imports, is required to secure full employment in an open economy. Three issues seem to be particularly important. These are related to domestic economic policies in an open economy, to the problem of indebtedness and to some features characterizing a world economic order along classical-Keynesian lines. The following remarks on these issues are based upon the *employment (or scale) effect of international trade* (chapter 4, pp. 185–9) which results from the *external employment mechanism* (chapter 4, pp. 190–9). The latter is dominated by quantity adjustments which are a fundamental characteristic of classical-Keynesian political economy.

The relationship between foreign and domestic policy issues

The possibility of broadly managing imports is of decisive importance for economic, social and environmental policies in an open economy. If the import coefficient (b) can be adjusted to full-employment output (equations 7, 20 and 22), countries will no longer have to worry about their respective foreign balances when pursuing policies adapted to the specific situation of each individual country. A few examples may illustrate this point. Consider, first, a situation of persistent unemployment prevailing in some country. If output is governed by the external employment mechanism ($Q_e^* < Q_i^* < Q_f$), the country in question will *not* be in a position to pursue an active long-period full-employment policy by stimulating internal (public and private) demand (equations 20 and 22, and figures 4 and 5, pp. 192–3). *Given* trend exports, the normal terms of trade and the normal import coefficient – which are all determined by institutions – a chronic import surplus would arise at once if gross domestic product grew faster than exports. Consequently, foreign exchange reserves would be run down and/or indebtedness would increase. Liberal economists now argue that the country is living above its means and that, consequently, austerity policies have to be implemented to reduce private and public consumption. Effective demand, output, employment and imports decline to eventually equilibrate the foreign balance. Evidently, the argument in question – living above a country's means – is true only with respect to the foreign balance situation (imports are larger than exports) but not with regard to the productive capacity of the economy considered. With involuntary unemployment which implies unused productive capacities, it would be more appropriate to say that the country is living *below* its means since effective demand is not sufficient to absorb potential full-employment output.

However, a socially appropriate management of imports allows output to increase until full employment is reached. On the one hand, *necessary* imports needed in the production process ($b_1 Q^*$ in equation 22) must rise together with output since b_1 is fixed by technology. On the other hand, *total* imports have, given exports and the terms of trade, to remain in line with exports, if a chronic current account deficit is to be avoided. Consequently, non-necessary imports, related to the use of the surplus ($b_2 Q^*$ in equation 22), have to be cut to make available the foreign exchange required to buy additional necessary imports: the coefficient b_2 in equation (22) has to be lowered. This may be painful, but it is unavoidable. For, what are the consequences of a permanent import surplus? In the short and medium terms indebtedness grows; in the long run, output and employment have to adjust to the level determined by exports and the foreign trade multiplier. Growing unemployment eventually results in *forced* emigration which is one of the most tragic features of capitalism, above all if the potential host countries rely on immigration restrictions to keep the size of the immigrant population to politically manageable proportions. This is a very difficult task, frequently compounded by a high level of unemployment in the potential host countries themselves: the argument that the presence of foreigners is directly responsible for home unemployment is, as a rule, of a devastating social and political force.

A similar line of reasoning appears in a second example. In some country, social allowances or expenditures for environmental protection are raised; taxes and contributions increase. Given the money-wage level, domestic prices rise somewhat. It may not be possible to lower the exchange rate in order to maintain the current account equilibrium. Exports decline, imports increase and a permanent deficit in the foreign balance becomes established; the latter requires selective import controls. Hence reasonable standards for social security and for environmental protection can be secured only in conditions of full or near full employment: in an unemployment situation, it may always be argued that, with additional expenditures for social security and for environmental protection, the foreign balance will deteriorate and raise unemployment in the long run.

A third example is related to the influence upon the way of life of the external employment mechanism. In chapter 4 (pp. 190–9) it is argued that the size and the structure of exports, the terms of trade and the strength of import dependence determine the level of trend output and employment. With intensive competition on world markets and with world economic activity governed by global effective demand, this implies that everything has to be done to maintain or to increase competitiveness on foreign and domestic markets. In highly developed countries, exporting mainly sophisticated high-technology products, rapid technological change associated with huge efforts to keep the technological leadership in at least some sectors is all important: technology constitutes an immensely powerful weapon in international economic warfare aimed at securing high-quality jobs. For successful countries, the advantages obtained will be important: large export volumes, favourable terms of trade and a relatively low import coefficient will bring about high employment levels; moreover, favourable terms of trade imply that imported products (raw materials, agricultural products and standard industrial products) are cheap, which raises domestic living standards. In the technologically less developed countries this mechanism is reversed. In their desperate attempts to maintain already low employment levels, the terms of trade have to be depressed in order to attempt to increase the volume of exports: money wages have to be kept low in relation to labour productivity. As a consequence exports are cheap and, possibly, quantitatively large, while imports will be expensive and quantitatively small. The quantity of goods and services available at home declines and depresses living standards. Many underdeveloped countries are actually forced to squander precious raw materials, agricultural products and even standard manufactured products on world markets in order to be able to earn the foreign exchange necessary to finance the import of necessary (and non-necessary) goods and the servicing of debt. An important side-effect of this way of proceeding is the severe damage done to the natural environment. Deforestation is but one case in point.

The doubtful economic sense of trying to maintain employment levels through unfavourable terms of trade was brought into the open by some of the old mercantilist thinkers. Daniel Defoe, for example, argued that low wages linked with unfavourable terms of trade, large export volumes and small import quantities led to immiseration; high wage levels, however, had a double positive effect: first, small but high-quality export volumes, combined with cheap and plentiful imported goods, raised living standards; second, high wages led to increased domestic demand for goods and services and added to prosperity (Heckscher 1932, vol. II, pp. 153–6).

The necessity to remain competitive on world markets at any price governs to a large extent the way of life in open economies by exerting an immense pressure on the population; for example, increases in productivity do not, as a rule, lead to a reduction in working time and to more leisure. This results from the fact that world economic activity is not resource-constrained but demand-constrained, with no tendency towards full employment prevailing. Therefore, the struggle on world markets is not about relative positions in a (neoclassical) full-employment position but is a battle for survival in the face of threatening involuntary unemployment.

These examples suggest that presently open economies have to rely on the external employment effect in order to secure high levels of employment and to avoid current account deficits (figures 4 and 5). *Given* that world economic activity is governed by world effective demand through the internal employment mechanism (the world economy is a closed system), it follows that there is ruthless competition on world markets, mainly for manufactured products since the employment effect of producing these is relatively high (chapter 4, pp. 190–9). This type of competition *partly destroys sovereignty* over economic, social, cultural and environmental policies in individual countries. It is no longer possible to pursue a full employment policy by stimulating *internal* demand; progressive social policies become utopian; expenditures for environmental protection have to be severely limited: such policy actions would diminish competitiveness and would worsen the foreign balance position. Moreover, the requirement to remain competitive dictates the way of life in open economies: it is hardly possible to organize life according to cultural and social principles, based either on tradition or on contemporary values. The ways of life are determined to a large extent by so-called economic considerations – remaining competitive is all important. In this view, playing *pétanque* or even *cricket* instead of working harder and longer is evidently disastrous for productivity levels, for the pace of technological progress and, as a consequence, for the competitive position on world markets. Last, but not least, one could mention that with the struggle for survival intensifying and with competition getting more and more ferocious, the means used to ensure survival are, in many instances, increasingly devoid of conventional ethical standards; many experienced managers are speaking of growing 'ethics deficits'. In most cases this is probably not due to individual ethical standards declining but is produced by alienation caused by the inappropriate functioning of the world economic system as a whole (chapter 2, pp. 39–53).

The attempts of individual countries to increase trend employment levels through the employment (or scale) effect of international trade thus constitute a mutual threat to national sovereignty which is required for the pursuit of the public interest. But the economic warfare involved here is also a potential source of conflicts as is evident from recent events and from the history of international trade relations. Struggles about the location of enterprises to secure jobs are obviously most important. Moreover, economic domination entails the temptation to dominate politically. All this is not to deny that there are aspects of international trade which promote cooperation and mutual understanding: here, the welfare effect associated with the principle of comparative costs, given full employment in all trading countries, is perhaps most important.

The meaning of a socially appropriate management of imports, i.e. adapting the import coefficient relating to non-necessary goods (b_2 in equation 22) to full-employment output, now becomes somewhat clearer. This type of policy action restores, in the first place, national sovereignty with respect to long-period economic, social and environmental policies. Pursuing a full-employment policy by stimulating domestic demand, private and public, and securing an equitable distribution of incomes becomes possible again. Second, and of equal importance, freedom with respect to organizing a country-specific way of life, based upon the system of values prevailing in each country, is also restored. This would contribute greatly to maintaining cultural diversity worldwide which is, in fact, threatened by the outrageous and standardizing domination of the *economic factor*. The essence of freedom consists in the possibility of individuals organizing their social and individual lives in accordance with a generally accepted hierarchy of values. If the citizens of some countries want to work very hard to achieve material aims, they should of course be entirely free to do so. But the countries in question should not be allowed to disrupt the economies of other countries by means of aggressive commercial policies and thereby to disturb the way of life of the people living there. In this context it must be admitted that some Western countries have been particularly aggressive in the economic, political and military domains since mercantilist times.

Hence import management also renders possible the elimination of the external – mercantilist – employment effect aimed at increasing the level of economic activity in some countries at the cost of others, and the elimination of the potential sources of conflict associated with the external employment effect. Keynes was very explicit on these issues: 'I sympathise . . . with those who would minimise, rather than maximise, economic entanglement between nations. Ideas, knowledge, art, hospitality, travel – these are things which should of their nature be international. But let goods be homespun whenever it is reasonably and conveniently possible; and, above all, let finance be primarily national' (Keynes 1982, p. 236). Or: 'the policy of an increased national self-sufficiency is to be considered not as an ideal in itself but as directed to the creation of an environment in which other ideals can be safely and conveniently pursued' (p. 240).

The policy measures proposed above do not imply that competition is not important. A considerable degree of competition between firms and between nations is required in order to ensure that the goods produced are of satisfactory quality and that, given money wages, normal prices be not too high and hence distribution too unequal. What has been criticized is competition as a means of securing high levels of employment on the basis of the exernal employment mechanism (chapter 4, pp. 190–9). With world economic activity determined by global effective demand, implying limited markets worldwide, this type of competition is destructive. While the economically strong countries (with large export shares of high-quality goods and services in output and/or a high foreign trade multiplier) claim relatively large fractions of world effective demand, the weaker countries have to be content with remaining market shares. Any attempt by all of them to improve their position by relying on foreign demand is bound to fail as *world demand is given* though not invariable. On the contrary, the situation may get worse if, in individual countries, internal demand is diminished (money wages are depressed relative to prices, and/or government expenditure is cut) in order to get higher market shares abroad, because then effective demand is depressed worldwide.

Hence competition associated with the external employment effect as a means to secure high employment levels has to be eliminated, because, given world effective demand, the possibility of some countries improving their employment position at the expense of others is a permanent source of conflict. Trade wars may easily break out of the economic sphere to become conflicts on a social, political or even military level. The problem is to bring about a balance-of-current-account equilibrium at the full-employment level through selected import controls. This enables a country to rely on the internal employment mechanism in order to pursue a full-employment policy (chapter 4, pp. 190–9, and pp. 319–26 above).

The foreign debt issue

The second point to be dealt with here, world indebtedness, is closely linked with Kaldor's cumulative employment effect which is briefly considered in chapter 4 (pp. 185–9). Flows of finance from rich to poor countries lead to a *surplus* of exports over imports in the former and to a *deficit* on the current account in the latter (chapter 4, pp. 190–9). The export surplus strengthens the employment effect of international trade since this is equivalent to additional effective demand which is subsequently magnified through the supermultiplier. On the other hand, in the receiving country, more goods are available for consumption and investment, although part of domestic investment may be displaced by foreign investment: with trend effective demand and technology given in certain periods of time, normal investment opportunities are also fixed (Bortis 1979). Hence in the early stages of borrowing (and lending) positive effects are likely to occur both on the creditor and the debtor side, mainly because interest payments and reimbursements are still negligible. Once the foreign debt reaches a critical size, however, negative effects for both, borrowers and lenders, appear (equation 23). The annual debt service (interest payments and repayments of debt due) eventually exceeds gross capital flows; in this case, the lenders will no longer realize an export surplus and the borrowers will no longer dispose of goods and services in excess of their social product. On the contrary, the indebted countries will eventually have to realize an export surplus in order to service the debt. Given exports, the terms of trade and the import coefficient, drastic reductions in output and employment will ensue (equation 23) because the necessary goods needed in the process of production cannot be imported in sufficient quantities.

An eventual repayment of the debt seems only possible if the creditor countries are willing to accept substantial import surpluses (implying export surpluses of the debtor countries) brought about by a considerable increase in the export of manufactures on favourable terms of trade by debtor countries: the industrialized countries would have to open their markets for manufactured goods to the indebted and economically underdeveloped nations. In view of the employment situation in the creditor countries, this seems impossible, at least in the near future.

Hence the debt cannot (and will not) be repaid, mainly because the creditor nations do not want repayment for fear of more unemployment. The only way out is gradually to cancel large parts of the debt until it has reached proportions manageable for creditors and debtors. In doing so, account would have to be taken of capital that has been transferred illegally from debtor to creditor countries. Moreover, the costs of cancelling part of the debt should be distributed evenly between and within the creditor countries since, in these countries, most individuals and institutions will have benefited from the positive effects that occurred in the early stages of lending; it would be unfair to make the commercial banks entirely responsible for the actual debt crisis. Finally, it ought to be borne in mind that countries, like individuals, should incur significant indebtedness only in order to overcome exceptional situations, due to the negative economic effects of natural calamities for instance. Incurring debts on a regular or institutionalized basis inescapably leads to an unmanageable situation (Bortis 1979).

These conclusions regarding the debt problem seem inevitable in the light of the classical-Keynesian framework set out in chapter 4 (pp. 190–9). Moreover, they are broadly in line with the argument Keynes put forward in his *Economic Consequences of the Peace* (Keynes 1971a) in the context of the German reparation problem. Here, Keynes was already tackling employment problems of open economies and implicitly taking account of the principle of effective demand. His argument is perhaps reproduced best by the export multiplier equation (20) and by equation (23).

Some remarks on an alternative world economic order

A third range of conclusions derived from the principle of selective import controls is loosely related to the world economic order that would be desirable from a classical-Keynesian point of view. Because of the complexity of the problem, only the main issues can be mentioned.

First, selective import controls as a means to secure high employment levels may be practised by individual countries or by regions within a country, or, again, by regions consisting of two or more countries willing to pursue a common economic and social policy. This is not the place to inquire into the 'optimal' size of such economic (and partly political) entities, but a few points should be noted.

The regions in question should not be too vast in order to remain manageable. Presumably it would be best not to change currently existing national entities. The problems of social organization to be solved within each country are extremely complex: foreign trade has to be managed in the public interest; a social consensus regarding the distribution of income and wealth has to be established; full employment has to be approximately realized; an institutional set-up enhancing labour productivity and the size of the social surplus has to be created; and a balance between regions as well as between ethnic, religious and linguistic groups has to be found. These essentially social problems are unique for each country because they have to be in line with a specific way of life governed by a particular system of values. In some countries, people may want to work hard and enjoy less leisure time, while, in others, leisure linked with cultural activities may be very important. The diversity of values is the main reason why individual countries require sufficient sovereignty to carry out socioeconomic policies in line with the desired organization of their societies. This extremely complex task can be approximately solved only within relatively small political entities within which a broad social consensus may be obtained. Presumably, some of the larger European countries will have to decentralize and regionalize in order to render possible appropriate socioeconomic, legal and cultural policies. Moreover, it would seem that (Western) Europe is far too vast and diverse to allow the establishment of economic (or even political) unity. The attempt to bring about a single European market might end up in administrative (and legal) chaos: to regulate the *behaviour* of economic agents so as to bring about high trend employment levels and a fair distribution of incomes is a hopeless task; in the absence of a self-regulating mechanism the corresponding institutional framework required becomes immensely complex and presumably cannot be managed. The only way to solve the central socioeconomic problems (employment, distribution and a fair price system) is to set up an appropriate *framework of social institutions* within countries and regions. A similar point was made by Keynes (1982) and, more recently, by Kuttner (1991). Friedrich List was perhaps the first systematically to express the idea that the state is an indispensable social and political entity between individuals and the world as a whole (List 1920 [1841]). The existence of sovereign nations would not exclude close relations between countries at all levels – economic, social, political and cultural (Bortis 1992).

The necessity broadly to manage imports to ensure full employment has a very important implication for the organization of the monetary system: each country, eventually each region within a country, will need its *own currency* to be able to pursue full-employment policies (fiscal and monetary) since import regulations may presumably be enforced most conveniently by foreign exchange management. The export earnings of a country consist of foreign exchange, or of foreign exchange *and* national currency if a region is considered. In the long run, exports have to pay for imports. Necessary imports, $b_1 Q$ (chapter 4, pp. 195–6), ought to get priority. If the remaining export earnings are not sufficiently high to pay for all the non-necessary imports wanted, a foreign exchange rationing scheme for some of these goods will have to be introduced. This means that, *given* export earnings, not every luxury good available on world markets can be imported. This is the price to pay if a country or region wishes to preserve the essentials of its way of life, to enjoy full employment and to prevent forced emigration.

To ensure a sufficient degree of flexibility for full-employment policies at least two kinds of currencies would be required: national moneys and a world currency. The former would be used for domestic purposes, the latter for international transactions. This broadly corresponds to Keynes's proposal at Bretton Woods which will be briefly dealt with below. Here, it should be mentioned that a European currency area implying the abandonment of national moneys would render regional and/or national economic policies exceedingly difficult; presumably, regional and national inequalities would widen, distribution would get more unequal and unemployment would grow: the Kaldorian cumulative processes associated with the external employment mechanisms would take effect (chapter 4, pp. 185–99). Given this, creeping protectionism might grow rapidly in the less successful countries to protect jobs (Bortis 1992).

A policy of import management to ensure full employment is rendered much easier if there is a certain degree of self-sufficiency for each sovereign nation with respect to *basic goods* in the sense of Sraffa (1960). Basic goods are technically required, directly and/or indirectly, in the production of *all* the goods of an economy and contribute to determining *all* the prices. Food, 'capital goods to make capital goods', i.e. the machine-tool industry, and raw materials are perhaps the most important cases in point. With respect to raw materials nothing can be done regarding self-sufficiency since this is a matter of natural endowments. However, to achieve an appropriate degree of self-sufficiency with respect to food and machine-tool production, suitable policy measures can be taken. The degree of self-sufficiency required will mainly depend on the strength of the desire to prevent too heavy an economic dependence on other countries which, above all if unilateral, might render political pressure from outside more probable. However, each country will, to some degree, depend on the outside world with respect to basic goods. Therefore, to avoid too strong a unilateral dependence, some diversification of imports of basic goods will be required as a rule. Moreover, too heavy a concentration of production of basic goods and the corresponding decision centres will need to be avoided since these factors determine *where* production takes place, and hence where jobs are created or destroyed.

Hence with division of labour on a worldwide scale, the old ideal of autarky has to be replaced by a mutually advantageous regulation of trade in accordance with the public interest in each country. On this point utmost realism is required since it would seem that economic warfare of the neo-mercantilist type has partly replaced military warfare. Economically powerful countries, dominating world markets for basic industrial goods, might sometimes be tempted to extend domination and, eventually, to exert political or even military pressure to derive unilateral advantages. Realism in these matters is the firmest basis for fruitful co-operation and mutually beneficial exchanges between nations and regions in various spheres: political, economic, social and cultural.

Moving now to a second issue:

if nations can learn to provide themselves with full employment by their domestic policy there need be no important economic forces calculated to set the interest of one country against that of its neighbours. There would still be room for the international division of labour [based upon the principle of comparative costs] and for international lending in appropriate conditions. But there would no longer be a pressing motive why one country need force its wares on another or repulse the offerings of its neighbour, not because this was necessary to enable it to pay for what it wished to purchase, but with the express object of upsetting the equilibrium of payments so as to develop a balance of trade in its own favour. International trade would cease to be what it is, namely, a desperate expedient to maintain employment at home by forcing sales on foreign markets and restricting purchases, which, if successful, will merely shift the problem of unemployment to the neighbour which is worsted in the struggle, but a willing and unimpeded exchange of goods and services in conditions of mutual advantage (Keynes 1973a, pp. 382–3).

Hence the external – mercantilist – employment mechanism need no longer be put to use if full employment can be achieved on the basis of the internal employment mechanism (chapter 4, pp. 190–9). To replace the former by the latter perhaps constitutes the main characteristic of long-period classical-Keynesian economic policy.

Third, the principle of selective import regulation in the public interest must be mutually recognized by all trading nations and must rest on a network of bilateral and/or multilateral agreements; this implies that world trade policy has to take account of the welfare (structural) effect based upon the principle of comparative advantage *and* of the employment (scale) effect of international trade associated with the external employment mechanism. It is true that broad import regulations are equivalent to a mild form of 'official (or open) protectionism'. However, since individual countries with severe unemployment will, in any case, try to protect themselves from the (negative) employment effect of international trade, there is presumably a choice to be made of either official protectionism, or uncontrolled, creeping and disguised protectionism. It is the latter which is really pernicious.

Fourth, selective import controls will not necessarily lead to a reduction in the volume of trade. Quite the contrary: with (near) full employment assured, in the major trading countries, international trade could be extended at will so as to reap the welfare effect of trade accruing by virtue of the principle of comparative advantage. Moreover, import controls along the lines suggested above do not mean that there would be no competition and unilateral protection of domestic producers. Various schemes may be imagined to secure a satisfactory degree of competition and, consequently, a high quality of traded goods and fair prices. These points are convincingly argued by Cripps and Godley (1978).

Fifth, the terms of trade ought to be fair and stable. This mainly concerns the terms of trade between agricultural products and raw materials on the one hand and manufactures and services on the other; the terms of trade between standard and high-technology products are another case in point. Fair terms of trade imply product prices such as to guarantee fair incomes to the producers of primary products as compared with the incomes arising to producers of manufactured goods. Prices for particularly scarce primary resources would have to be high in order to economize on their use. The problems linked with the determination of fair agricultural incomes on the national level are well known. On the international level, the difficulties relating to fixing fair terms of trade reach gigantic proportions. However, the possibility of broadly managing foreign trade should facilitate the task. Since imports may be adjusted to exports, countries need not sell at any price on the world markets to get foreign exchange.

Fair terms of trade are not sufficient, however. Stability is also important. To achieve this, various ingenious schemes have been put forward, e.g. by Kaldor (1963), who proposes to build up buffer stocks of important traded primary products. Stocks increase if supply is above normal and/or demand below normal and vice versa. Again, experience has shown that there are tremendous political obstacles to be overcome regarding the creation of buffer stocks on a sufficiently large scale.

To husband properly the still-remaining raw material and energy stocks of the world to the benefit of all nations a World Resources Agency should eventually be created within the framework of the United Nations. This should go along with setting up a solid and realistic world economic order, implying a strong (supranational) role for the United Nations and its regional suborganizations. Presumably, this would be far more reasonable than the creation of huge trading blocs which, on the one hand, might lead to trade wars between these blocs and, on the other hand, to the political domination within a bloc of some economically outstandingly strong country. An appropriate conceptual starting point for setting up a sound world economic order is Quesnay's *tableau économique*: on the basis of the world's natural resources – food, raw materials and energy, and the natural environment – an industrial and handicraft structure (including services) may be set up. The surplus of the system allows, in turn, the erection of a political, social and cultural superstructure upon the economic basis. If full employment were achieved worldwide, available natural resources would, in the very long run, limit world economic activity. The socially appropriate management of these resources would be, and already should be, a matter of crucial importance. This is an immense task: *the problem is to achieve and to preserve the reproducibility of the world production system.* To face this task, classical-Keynesian political economy, which takes a global view of nature and society, seems far better equipped than the rather one-sided economic theories of liberalism and of centrally planned socialism.

The Kaldorian proposal on buffer stocks was made in relation to reforms of the international monetary system. This is a sixth point to be touched upon here. In the spirit of Keynes, Kaldor and others suggested the issue of a world currency ('bancor') on the basis of buffer stocks. The quantity of bancor would be linked with the size of buffer stocks. This would stabilize fluctuations in world economic activity: with slackening activity, stocks would increase since the demand for primary products would be declining; this would lead to an increase in the quantity of bancor thus stimulating world economic activity, and vice versa.

An international buffer-stock scheme (on the lines worked out by Keynes) . . . is essential if market economies are to resume economic expansion without generating unacceptable inflation due to the consequential rise in commodity prices, resulting from speculative influences of a perverse character, and to enable the changes in stocks to be carried which are necessary to tide over short-period differences between absorption and accrual of commodities without any large deviation of the current price from the 'normal' price (Kaldor 1983, p. 249).

The institution of bancor, incidentally first proposed by Keynes in 1944 at Bretton Woods, has a number of desirable implications: all international transactions, real or financial, have to be carried out with the help of bancor. Each national currency stands in a fixed, though not invariable, relation to the world monetary unit. National moneys are *not* to be allowed to cross their respective boundaries in order to finance international transactions; speculative movements of financial capital are thus greatly hampered; foreign balances can be equilibrated quite easily since deficit *and* surplus countries have to take appropriate measures: deficit countries reduce non-necessary imports and surplus countries stimulate effective demand to increase imports; finally, financial and real capital flows can be synchronized more easily: countries experiencing a surplus of exports over imports at full employment accumulate bancor balances, which can be lent to debtor countries which, also at full employment, import more than they export. However, steps would have to be taken to prevent excessive indebtedness of the borrowing countries.

Seventh, the fair allocation of manufacturing and of service activities (banking, for example) worldwide would seem to be an important feature of a world economic order set up along classical-Keynesian lines. The problem is related to the role played by the manufacturing sector within the

Kaldorian cumulative process (chapter 4, pp. 185–6) and to the fact that, for the world economy as a whole, the primary sector must stand in a certain relation to the industrial and service sectors (Kaldor 1970). Exports of high-quality manufactures, rendered possible by the existence of a broadly based and technologically dynamic industrial sector, are important to a country for three main reasons:–on the world markets, the demand for the produce of its labour is likely to be strong, hence the international reduction coefficient of its labour will be large and the terms of trade favourable; import dependence is relatively small, above all if the manufacturing sector includes a strong machine-tool industry; and the employment effect is high. This means that any country would like to produce and to export as many advanced manufactured products as possible and to import agricultural products, raw materials and standard industrial products. The success of one nation in exporting such goods is bound to imply the failure of another since world production, determined by world effective demand, is given and the three basic sectors have to stand in certain proportions on the world level: the successful countries will be over-industrialized and the losers in the struggle for industrial jobs will be condemned to producing and exporting raw materials, agricultural products and standard industrial goods at unfavourable terms of trade. All this raises the question of a fair allocation of manufacturing production among nations and among regions within nations. It seems reasonable to allocate real capital (factory buildings and equipment) in regions where (qualified) workers can be found: capital has to follow labour and not the other way round. To be sure, there are other considerations when trying to answer the question of a fair allocation of manufacturing activities, e.g. the location of mining and of agricultural activities and environmental problems. A fair allocation of manufacturing (and service) activities implies huge structural adjustments on a global scale. These constitute a formidable problem in international economic relations which can only be tackled in conditions of full employment or near full employment worldwide. However, a more appropriate distribution of world manufacturing and service activities seems indispensable if the immense gaps in material well-being actually existing are to be reduced and if, simultaneously, huge forced migrations from poor to rich areas are to be prevented.

Finally, some important propositions relating to technical progress and international economic relations emerge from Pasinetti's (1981, ch. XI; 1988) work. Pasinetti starts from the huge differences in labour productivity that have developed on a world scale over the last two hundred years. These are due to the very unequal pace of technical progress which has prevailed in different areas of the world. Presumably, technological gaps are widening at present for two main reasons. First, there is the tremendous pace of technological progress in some areas of the world; computer technology and its applications to manufacturing and the services are perhaps most prominent. Second, a vicious circle linked with the external employment mechanism greatly hampers technological development in many countries (chapter 4, pp. 190–9). The starting point is insufficient export earnings. The ensuing lack of foreign exchange prevents the import of technically advanced investment goods. Hence the technological gap widens, which, in turn, acts negatively on export performance. These effects are reinforced if available foreign exchange is further diminished by a heavy debt service, capital flight and by the fact that non-basic goods in Sraffa's sense are imported. The very large differences in labour productivity are linked with equally large differences in real wages and, eventually, profits and profit rates. From this, Pasinetti draws two important conclusions regarding international economic relations:

First . . . single individuals do benefit from migration from low-income countries to high-income countries. At the same time, the low-income countries suffer from this migration. The people who are most likely to be lured abroad are the more-than-average educated ones. They bring with them knowledge and 'brain'. In the most spectacular cases, the phenomenon has become known as the 'brain-drain', but the phenomenon has wider implications. It is the young, the more adventurous, the more knowledgeable that are more likely to leave the low-income countries. For the countries they leave, they represent losses of embodied technical knowledge and of entrepreneurship (Pasinetti 1988, p. 143).

The brain-drain reinforces the vicious circle referred to above: lower technological standards and less entrepreneurship negatively influence the competitive position of the economically underdeveloped countries on world markets; the lack of foreign exchange prevents the import of sufficient high-standard investment goods which, in turn, leads to worsening export performances. This implies 'that the traditional tenet that immobility of labour does not matter is false' (p. 143). The importance of the brain-drain has far-reaching implications for 'development aid': it might be appropriate for the rich countries to pay wage differences for highly educated people of low-income countries to encourage them to stay in their home countries; or, the policy of providing grants to Third World undergraduate students for studies in the West might be questioned: these students get accustomed to the Western way of life and may be unwilling to return to their countries unless they are permitted to maintain Western living standards there. Perhaps part of development aid should be used to set up new universities (with an international body of professors) in Third World countries to enable students to get their first degree in their home countries. In principle, only postgraduate studies should be pursued abroad since graduate students are likely to be more attached to their home countries than their undergraduate fellow students and hence more inclined to return there.

The 'problems involved [here] are very complex, because they easily impinge upon human rights and personal freedom of movements' (Pasinetti 1988, p. 143). Moreover, full employment everywhere would be an essential requirement for implementing the policy measures just suggested. Finally, these propositions should not be misunderstood: the problem is to stop *unidirectional* brain-drain. Intellectual exchanges, which may include movements of highly educated people between countries and regions, are highly desirable.

A second conclusion follows from international productivity differences: '[T]he major and primary source of international gains is *international learning*, not international trade . . . For any country (advanced or underdeveloped) any increase of knowledge (from international contacts) represents a net gain, subject to no condition and no loss to anybody' (Pasinetti 1988, p. 143): in international economic relations, the two-way flow of scientific knowledge related to an exchange of ideas between countries and regions is of crucial importance. Modern science is a shared achievement of mankind. Western technology and science would not be there without the preparatory work done by the old civilizations (which now make their own contributions to scientific progress). Scientific knowledge is, therefore, a common good of humanity which should benefit *all* countries. However, principles like these can be realized in conditions of full employment only: the individual countries would not then be forced to rely on technology as a weapon to conquer larger shares of manufactured products on world markets.

These few remarks show that, in the field of international economic relations, there is a solid and realistic conceptual basis on which classical-Keynesian political economists can build when proposing socially appropriate third-way type institutions. In a classical-Keynesian world, the exchange of *basic* goods and services, required in the process of production, is of primary importance; trade in non-necessary products, related to the use of the surplus, is less important. Therefore, international trade is, essentially, a means for maintaining and improving the material basis, that is the productive forces, of all the countries of the world. This enables the individual country to erect an improved institutional superstructure (political, social and cultural) on a more solid economic basis. All this does not imply that there should be more nationalism and narrowmindedness worldwide. Quite the contrary: the free flow and exchange of scientific ideas (and of cultural achievements) should be a hallmark of a classical-Keynesian world. However, scientific and cultural exchange makes sense only if there is considerable intellectual and cultural diversity. It is a well-known historical fact that exchanges between fundamentally different cultures are most conducive to the creation of new ideas.

This leads to some brief consideration of the relationship between international trade and cultural diversity. Presently, international trade is not based primarily on the principle of comparative costs. The scale or employment effect of international trade is much more important (chapter 4, pp. 190–9). In a situation of chronic unemployment, the main problem consists of maintaining or, if possible, extending the scale of activities to prevent unemployment from growing. The main aim is to sell (to export) more and more to secure jobs and to earn some 'hard' currency which may eventually serve as a convenient store of value. In a monetary world economy there is, primarily, exchange of goods against money, not exchange of different goods, as should occur according to the principle of comparative costs. The attempts by all countries to extend profitable activities to maintain or to increase employment levels may lead to trade wars and to cultural standardization, possibly on a low materialistic level. The latter occurs because the incessant struggle to extend economic activities implies the continuous creation of new goods which, as a consequence, requires the creation of new needs. Materialistic values are imposed on people through marketing campaigns. The quantitative aspect of consumption (in the widest sense) comes to dominate the qualitative one, or in Erich Fromm's terms 'to have' eclipses 'to be': industrial mass products frequently replace high-quality handicraft products in spite of the fact that the latter frequently include artistic elements and, on account of their durability, are far less of a burden to the natural environment than throwaway industrial products; or, after having succumbed to the hammering of publicity, many consumers finally prefer industrial food and beverages to far superior and much healthier traditional aliments: nature is partly replaced by chemistry.

Marx saw the problem most clearly: the unlimited desire to consume more and to acquire material wealth, including money, leads to the partial effacement of individuality and hampers or even destroys the capacity of man to prosper in the social and cultural sphere (Marx 1973/74a, vol. I, chapter 3, section 3). Cultural alienation increases.

In a world where economic activity is governed by effective demand the creation of too large trading areas should be avoided, not only for socio-economic reasons (unemployment may increase, income distribution may worsen and regional inequalities may deepen owing to the Kaldorian principle of cumulative causation), but also for cultural reasons. For cultural exchange is fruitful only if there is diversity which, in turn, can be maintained only if there is a sufficient degree of national sovereignty in socio-economic matters. Individual countries should be able to erect, without unwanted outside interference, a political, social *and* cultural super-structure in line with the system of values specific to each country. This is the essence of freedom.

Economic policies in the medium and short terms

The state must also intervene in order to prevent unemployment in the medium term. This is tantamount to preventing large deviations of invest-ment, output and employment from their respective normal values, ideally at full employment. Formally, this is equivalent to minimizing the size of the adjustment parameter q in order to reduce the amplitude of business cycles and hence instability to a minimum (equation 24, p. 208). To solve this problem Keynes proposed to regulate entrepreneurial *behaviour*: 'In conditions of *laissez-faire* the avoidance of wide fluctuations in employ-ment may, therefore, prove impossible without a far-reaching change in the psychology of investment markets such as there is no reason to expect. I conclude that the duty of ordering the current volume of investment cannot be safely left in private hands' (Keynes 1973a, p. 320). This conclu-sion is not acceptable to classical-Keynesians: the problem is to create an *institutional set-up* such that trend output and employment are as close as possible to their corresponding full-employment trend levels (chapter 4, pp. 154–80). If the government succeeds in this, the stability of an economic system will be greatly enhanced since the bulk of investment will then consist of normal investment which is *derived* demand and not subject to fluctuations. However, since entrepreneurs do not know the fully adjusted situation associated with a specific institutional set-up, there are always deviations from the trend, and regular cyclical movements may occur. Presumably, it is impossible to eliminate these entirely. The problem is to minimize the amplitude of fluctuations. This does not, however, require state intervention; a close collaboration between the government and entrepreneurial associations seems far more appropriate.

Moreover, within an institutional framework guaranteeing full employ-ment, there is no need to nationalize industries in order to bring about stability and full employment. This implies that the form of property is not of decisive importance (chapter 4, pp. 174–5). What is important is that firms must be allowed to make socially acceptable profits to induce manag-ers to introduce better technologies which, macroeconomically, means to save the ultimately scarce resources, that is *labour* and *nature* (natural resources and the natural environment). The types of ownership adopted (private, public or mixed) will depend upon the way of life of a society gov-erned by the prevailing system of values. As a rule, however, small and, in most cases, medium firms are far better managed if privately owned because private owners care about the resources they manage, which may not be always true in the case of public ownership.

Given a flexible framework of property rights, individual producers may enjoy considerable economic freedom. In fact, entrepreneurs have two great tasks in a modern economy. First, they ought to attempt to bring about the appropriate structures of production; this implies bringing in line market and (estimated) normal prices as closely as possible, given institutional, technological and natural constraints (chapter 4, pp. 177–80). Second, they have to transform inventions into innovations, i.e. to introduce new and more productive processes of production and new products, thereby bringing about a quantitative and qualitative rise in labour productivity. However, appropriate institutions are required to minimize the social side-effects of rapid and uneven technical progress, the prevention of structural and involuntary unemployment perhaps being the main medium-term problem. A deliberate slowing-down of the pace of technological advance must eventually be envisaged in order to render possible a transformation of technical progress into social progress which prevents massive structural unemployment.

Finally, state intervention is also required with respect to (temporary) short-period phenomena. State action in this field could be summarized under the heading of 'prevention of large-scale speculation'. This implies ensuring an equitable distribution of income, because excessive property incomes lead to abundant saving which, in turn, results in increases of the stock of money held for speculative purposes. The latter may set into motion cumulative processes associated with changes of demand-determined prices of produced goods, e.g. raw materials, and with price changes of non-produced goods and assets (old masters, shares and land). Rapidly increasing prices of land are particularly pernicious (chapter 4, pp. 132–5). Initially, rents on land increase, to be followed by rises in housing rents. This is reflected in a higher mark-up (k) which, in turn, raises the leakage (z) which depends on distribution. The latter implies that less money is available to buy consumption goods. Therefore, normal investment, output and employment decline according to the supermultiplier relation (7). On the other hand, rising property income, as is reflected in a higher k, means that additional funds are available for speculative purposes which may result in even higher land prices. Other cumulative processes are possible: rapidly rising share prices attract speculative funds, complemented by bank credits; subsequently, share prices increase even more. The same applies to currency speculation which may be associated with highly unstable exchange rates. The consequences of speculation for the financial system have been alluded to in chapter 4 (pp. 207–15).

Keynes clearly perceived that the financial sector ought, in normal circumstances, to be subordinated to production, i.e. to provide funds for productive investment. Once part of the financial sector engages in important speculative activity, instability may develop which may greatly hamper production: 'Speculators may do no harm as bubbles on a steady stream of enterprise. But the position is serious when enterprise becomes the bubble on a whirl-pool of speculation. When the capital development of a country becomes a by-product of the activities of a casino, the job is likely to be ill-done' (Keynes 1973a, p. 159). This thread of thought has been continued by some classical-Keynesians, Hyman Minsky in particular. Policy measures directed at preventing large-scale speculation may require significant regulation of the financial sector.

The fact that speculation may influence production implies an interaction between behavioural outcomes and the institutional system of an economy, i.e. various layers of reality: rapidly changing short-term events, like speculation, may in fact greatly hamper the proper working of stable socioeconomic elements, that is institutions and technology. If speculation enables firms to make easy windfall gains, profits may not be reinvested or used to promote research and development. This may lead to a slowdown of technical progress and to a weakening of the competitive position of certain firms and industries or even of entire countries.

Therefore, in the classical-Keynesian view, the state has primarily to secure full employment, to render distribution broadly equitable and to favour the formation of a system of fair and just normal prices. The market has to steer structural adjustments: in each sector of production, entrepreneurs continuously compare (estimated) normal prices with market prices and/or take account of changes in capacity utilization. If there is a persistent tendency for market prices to exceed normal ones or if capacity utilization tends to be more than standard, productive capacity will be increased, and vice versa. This broadly corresponds to Ricardo's view of competition (Ricardo 1951 [1821], chapter XXX) which is also implied by Pasinetti (1981, 1993). This view entails that the prices of production are fundamental and market prices secondary.

Monetary policies

The role of money – and of the financial sector – may be considered from the point of view of the system as a whole and from that of the behaviour of the individuals and collectives that make up society. In the present subsection both viewpoints are very briefly considered and a few policy conclusions hinted at. In doing so some threads of thought mentioned in chapter 4 (pp. 154–90, 220–35) and in the preceding subsection are taken up.

From the point of view of the system, money appears as a social institution which is essential in a monetary production economy with extensive division of labour. For example, money enables the process of production to get started and, eventually, to be expanded through investment: banks provide entrepreneurs with short- and long-term credits which have to be repaid from present and future earnings. Money also makes possible productive and consumptive circulation. The former takes place with the social process of production and reproduction between industries – where intermediate product flows take place – and between sectors where consumption and investment goods are exchanged (chapter 3, pp. 89–103); the latter goes on between producers and consumers. Moreover, money has a role in regulating distribution: with money wages given, the size of the mark-up k determines prices in money terms and hence the real wage rate and the wages share (chapter 4, pp. 158–75). Finally, effective demand – a monetary notion – regulates the level of economic activity and hence the employment and unemployment levels (chapter 4).

The crucial point is that, given the rate of interest and the money wage rate, the 'quantity of money' *passively adjusts* to economic activity: with the amount of notes and coins given, the quantity of money adjusts through changes in the velocity of circulation in the short and medium terms; with the rate of interest, the velocity of circulation and the money wage all governed by the corresponding institutions, the Central Bank must adjust the quantity of notes and coins in the long run if the normal rate of interest is to be maintained. Hence in the classical-Keynesian view money is endogenous: on the basis of deposits banks provide credits which ultimately have to be repaid by future earnings. This implies that causality in the money multiplier relation linking the monetary base with M1 is reversed: in the classical-Keynesian view causality runs from M1 to the monetary base, and not the other way round as is conventionally postulated. From this a first policy conclusion follows: in a monetary production economy the Central Bank cannot regulate the quantity of money. It can only fix the rate of interest.

On the behavioural side, money is, first, a device that greatly facilitates transactions. Second, and equally important, money is a store of value and represents, as such, a part of wealth (chapter 4, pp. 180–5, 220–9).

The system and aggregate behaviour interact. Regarding money, this is particularly evident in the case of inflationary processes. Since money passively adjusts, inflation cannot be a monetary phenomenon. In the classical-Keynesian view there are three main causes of inflation. First, distributional conflicts may result in a wage–price spiral. Second, government deficits result in large profits, a fraction of which are saved and flow into the financial circuit (associated with money's role as a store of value);

part of the new wealth in money form is invested in non-reproducible goods, the prices of which rise; a smaller amount of wealth is consequently held in money form, and the prices of non-producibles, land in the first instance, rise even more, which may, in turn, set into motion or reinforce a wage–price spiral. The process just pictured represents a third cause of inflation: if there is already inflation, money gets less adequate as a store of value and will move faster around the financial circuit, thus reinforcing the inflationary movement.

This briefly sketched theory of inflation leads to a *second* classical-Keynesian principle of monetary policy: inflation cannot be prevented by restricting the quantity of money; the most efficient means to combat inflation is to bring about an equitable distribution of income; moreover, the government's budget ought to be in equilibrium in the long run.

The case just presented is a long-period ideal type. In the short and medium terms inflationary movements may get started by distributional conflicts, temporary government deficits or through the Kaldorian distribution mechanism: investment increases quickly in a cyclical upswing; consequently prices and profits rise relative to money wages. In these circumstances, the classical-Keynesian monetary doctrine requires measures to prevent money from being massively abandoned as a store of value to be 'invested' in more secure stores of value (land, old masters, stable foreign currencies, and others) since the latter would enhance an ongoing inflationary process even more. For example, notes and coins could be made temporarily exchangeable into gold, or some other store of value more stable than money. This leads to a third principle of long-period monetary policy, that has traditionally been defended by conservative economists: in the long run the quantity of notes in circulation ought to be partly covered by gold (or some equivalent to gold) in order to enforce 'monetary discipline' (which, in the long run, essentially consists of a balanced state budget) and to maintain confidence in a currency in the short and medium terms. Such seemingly 'old-fashioned' propositions should not be rejected outright by classical-Keynesian political economists.

To aim at monetary stability and at the associated distributional equity in a full-employment situation is a complex problem of political economy. The corresponding policy effort is worthwhile, however, for two reasons. The first is negative and relates to the liberal alternative for combating inflation. In the latter, unemployment is a means of stabilizing money wages and hence prices. Since unemployment is the primary source of alienation on various levels, however, the liberal way to keep down inflation is inadequate: alienation on a grand scale is likely to lead to social disorder and thereby to stimulate inflation. Second, a stable value of money is essential to the proper functioning of a monetary production economy and hence of society as a whole. The reasons are economic and sociological: economically, money is a promise made by society to individuals, whose work is paid for in money, on the tacit understanding that – normal – money prices are given and, hence, that money may be exchanged against a definite quantity of goods. Inflation implies a break of this promise. Sociologically, the wealth of the middle classes mainly consists of money, deposits and bonds. These get devalued – in terms of some real numéraire, for example a bundle of necessary consumption goods – if there is inflation. Hence inflation worsens the socioeconomic position of the middle classes and may, consequently, contribute to their political radicalization, as the historical experience of the thirties suggests. Therefore, a stable value of money is – like full employment – not only of great importance for economic reasons. Social and political reasons are equally important.

7 Political economy in a wider context

For philosophical, theoretical and empirical reasons we have suggested that classical-Keynesian political economy is likely to be a superior alternative to neoclassical economics which is, essentially, equilibrium theory and is too individualistic and mechanical. Society, the social structure, is something more than the sum of its parts and possesses laws of its own. Classical-Keynesian political economy also seems superior to the economic theory of centrally planned socialism which sees man uniquely as a part of the social machine and relies too heavily on the possibility of consistently planning economic activities. Because of the immense complexity of the modern world this is impossible. Marx's allusions to an Indian village when speaking of planning production, i.e. directly producing use values (Marx 1973/74a, vol. I, pp. 56–7), simply cannot be taken as a starting point for managing large monetary production economies with extensive division of labour. Centrally planned systems may function satisfactorily in times of war and of crisis. But in normal times, it is not possible to plan prices *and* quantities without severely disrupting an economic system. Normal prices must not be fixed since these are governed by the distributional institutions which determine the structure of money wages and of profit rates, and by the conditions of production; normal quantities and employment depend on effective demand; long-period employment policy must aim at setting up an institutional framework consistent with full employment (chapter 4, pp. 142–89, and 6, pp. 319–48). The central planning procedure may lead to socially inappropriate prices of production and partly to the production of goods which do not meet the preferences of consumers; both imply, as a rule, squandering labour and natural resources. Moreover, the plan is inimical to technical progress which, to the socialist enterprise, renders fulfilling the plan more difficult. It is likely that the technological gap between the highly industrialized and the socialist economies which, the armaments industry excepted, dramatically widened in recent years was an important cause for the downfall of the latter. Hence the market and the plan taken in isolation are not in a position to solve the socioeconomic problems arising in immensely complex monetary production economies. The two must be combined and adapted to specific socioeconomic and historical situations. Taking account of this fact, classical-Keynesian political economy attempts to provide an alternative conceptual framework flexible enough to tackle socioeconomic problems within differing historical circumstances.

The nature of the classical-Keynesian approach can perhaps be brought out more clearly by using political terms. While neoclassical economics – if linked with élitist liberalism – may broadly be associated with the political right and, correspondingly, the economic theory of (centrally planned) socialism with the political left, classical-Keynesian political economy appears as the economic theory of the progressive centre taken in a broad sense.

Modern economic liberalism is a simplification of Adam Smith's system and ultimately rests on Walras's equilibrium theory if the economic sphere is considered. Political liberalism is intimately associated with Hayek. The economic theory of centrally planned socialism is a 'war and social crises system' which reflects the Soviet experience characterized by war, civil war, stabilization of the new social order by ruthless means and by forced collectivization and industrialization. This type of socialism bears very little resemblance to the humanist socialism sketched in Marx's *Early Writings*. Other strands of thought that could not be termed liberal or neo-classical nor socialist in the modern sense are: the mercantilist strand which culminated in James Steuart's work and some followers of mercantilism like Sismondi, Malthus to a certain extent, Hobson and others; Quesnay's and Ricardo's systems of thought; Friedrich List and the German Historical School; American Institutionalism; and Christian Social Doctrine based on Aquinas and Aristotle. All these strands of thought are rather heterogeneous and, with the exception of Quesnay and Ricardo, lack a clear-cut theoretical foundation. Here, Keynes's significance is apparent. In his *General Theory* Keynes explicitly wanted to provide these strands of thought, particularly the German Historical School, with a theoretically sound conceptual foundation. As already mentioned above, this clearly emerges from the foreword to the German edition. Keynes's and Kalecki's work was carried on by the Keynesian Fundamentalists and the Robinsonians respectively. Sraffa's work moved Ricardo and Marx to the fore. In the preceding chapters a classical-Keynesian synthesis and elaboration of these strands was suggested and its relationship to liberalism and, marginally, to socialism was sketched.

It should be made clear, however, that classical-Keynesian political economy is *not* a variant of the *Soziale Marktwirtschaft* which may be broadly linked up with the 'neoclassical synthesis', i.e. a free-market economy within which short-period employment policies, complemented by a social security system, are pursued. In the latter it is postulated that the market (exchange) can, in principle, solve all the important economic problems; however, institutions have to be created to repair eventual defects of the market system. Classical-Keynesian political economy is not a repair shop of the market, nor of the plan, but an intermediate system of its own along humanist lines. This emerges from the preceding chapters of this book.

To establish classical-Keynesian political economy as an alternative to neoclassical economics and to the economic theory of socialism will require the elaboration of comprehensive treatises in order to convince professional economists and, at a subsequent stage, the writing of textbooks to popularize the approach. The present study aims at exploring the *terrain* in order to prepare for this undertaking. In the preceding chapters it has been suggested that classical-Keynesian political economists can rely on an immensely rich intellectual heritage comprising all branches of the social sciences including social and political philosophy and the theory of knowledge. The problem does not therefore consist in inventing new theories but in selecting and in elaborating already existing ones while adapting them to actual problems.

In this chapter it seems appropriate to take up some threads of thought on fundamentals already alluded to in chapter 2. In doing so it would have been desirable to integrate more fully Keynes's non-economic writings, e.g. his *Treatise on Probability*, and some recently published works on Keynes's vision, i.e. Carabelli (1985), Fitzgibbons (1988) and O'Donnell (1989) and possibly others, into the present chapter. This would have done justice to Keynes's overriding position within the classical-Keynesian system. However, it takes considerable time to come to grips with fundamental issues since these have to be put into the very large context of social and political philosophy without forgetting the theory of knowledge which plays a crucial role in Keynes's system of thought. But even if it were possible to 'digest' the works in question quickly enough, space would prevent us from taking due account of them. In the following, we shall, therefore, mainly concentrate on Fitzgibbons (1988), who deals in a very concise and appropriate way with Keynes's vision. This choice does not imply any value judgement on the merits of other works on Keynes's philosophy.

Political economy, social philosophy and the philosophy of history

Keynes's vision

  Some elements
  Carabelli (1985), Fitzgibbons (1988), O'Donnell (1989), and other works recently published on Keynes's vision, are pathbreaking in that they produce an entirely new picture of the intellectual stature of Keynes. This

is confirmed by two important recent biographies, those by Moggridge (1992) and Skidelsky (1983, 1992). Hitherto, Keynes has been considered a great economist who also did important work in other fields: in the political sciences and, in particular, in the theory of knowledge and in mathematics, his theoretical work being complemented by his practical activities as a statesman, as a promoter of the arts and as a clever businessman and speculator who enriched himself and King's College, Cambridge. Fitzgibbons now argues that 'it is possible to draw from the writings of John Maynard Keynes, without artificiality, a logically coherent and embracing structure of ideas, based upon a single vision, which permeated all aspects of his thought and which [was exceptionally] constant through time' (Fitzgibbons 1988, p. 1). The philosophical vision underlying Keynes's work gives it a remarkable unity which, however, cannot be perceived immediately since 'Keynes was not an explicit systematizer, and his deeper observations were scattered among his works' (p. 4). Nevertheless, if due account were taken of Keynes's overall performance he would definitely appear in stature equal to Marx. Both understood the working mechanism of capitalism in their respective lifetimes far better than any of their contemporaries. However, while Marx wanted to show, starting from Hegelian philosophy, that there was an inevitable historical process leading on to socialism, 'Keynes's system was consciously cast as a third alternative [our emphasis] to both Marxism and laissez-faire, and it is the only comprehensive alternative which says that the economy is neither a perfect machine nor a system doomed to failure, but a fallible human institution improvable by human reason' (pp. 1–2). This is broadly in line with the argument set out in the preceding chapters. However, it has also been suggested that a classical-Keynesian middle-way alternative should be conceived of as a synthesis of Keynes and Ricardo, complemented by parts of Marx's historical method. Keynes's outlook, in spite of his having given a new impetus to macroeconomics, was essentially individualistic. Ricardo and Marx, however, uncompromisingly took up the point of view of society as a whole. This is required because the historically evolving institutional system represents an entity which is something more than the sum of its parts and hence possesses its own laws. Both the system and the behavioural viewpoint are required if a synthesis of socioeconomic thought is to be achieved, since men act within a social framework, and since the behavioural and the institutional systems interact.

'*Keynes's innovation was to reconcile economics with the older traditions of moral and political philosophy*' (Fitzgibbons 1988, p. 3; our emphasis). Building upon the work of his 'intellectual paragons, Plato and Burke . . . Keynes's metaphysical vision was that, from the vantage point of truth and other ideals, economics and politics can be seen as part of an ever-flowing river of change' (p. 195). If broadly interpreted, this point is also implied in the previous chapters of this study, for example in scheme 3 (p. 106) where some aspects of reality are classified according to their persistence in the course of time. The fundamental, essential and invariant principles located in the lowest layers are always there while the upper layers represent changing material forms in which the basic ideas are embodied. Examples of fundamental and unvarying principles are the notions of 'effective demand' and 'monetary production economy' in the socioeconomic sphere, and 'absolute truth' and 'probable truth' in the theory of knowledge (on the latter, see chapter 2, pp. 57–75). The realization of fundamental ontological and ethical principles may go in widely varying and changing historical circumstances, and the specific ways of putting these principles into practice will always be imperfect in that there will be deviations from an objectively given but partly unknown ideal which reflects alienation (chapter 2, pp. 39–53). For example, nobody will ever be in a position to say precisely what an ideal society ought to look like or, more specifically, what is to be understood exactly by a 'just and fair distribution of wealth and income' in some country.

In chapter 2 it is suggested that classical-Keynesian political economy implies a return to traditional, mainly Aristotelian, social and political philosophy. This also is broadly in line with Keynes's overall scientific undertaking, from the *Treatise on Probability* to the *General Theory* and beyond. However, Keynes's message regarding fundamentals largely passed unnoticed or was, and still is, basically misunderstood. Therefore, it seems appropriate to take up a thread of thought contained in chapter 2 (pp. 57–75) regarding some of his basic ideas on probability: 'In a draft preface to the *Treatise* [*on Probability*], [Keynes] wrote: "The logic of probability is of the greatest importance, because it is the logic of ordinary discourse, through which the practical conclusions of action are most often reached"' (Fitzgibbons 1988, p. 17). To substantiate this assertion, Keynes started by criticizing Hume whose 'scepticism went too far because he believed that under conditions of probability, which is the usual state of knowledge, causation has no objective meaning except in theory . . . So causation is between propositions (as in a scientific theory) and not in reality, or in relations between *things*' (p. 17). 'Keynes reverted to [a revision of] Locke's theory [of causation, according to which] objects do have a strict connection together, but normally this is not discoverable. We do not know the *real* causes, but only probabilities' (pp. 17–18). Hence 'Keynes believed that, except in a few sciences, we do not normally understand the true causes of things [*causa essendi*, the explanation of the atomic constitution of the universe] but only the [*causa*] *cognoscendi*, or what is the cause according to our theories' (p. 18, quoting Carabelli). As to the atomic constitution of the universe, Keynes held, following Locke, 'that there are certain regularities . . . or at least that there are not an infinite number of possibilities [which] is a precondition for there being similarities between things [which, in turn, enables us] to draw up classifications based on similarities between them' (p. 19). However, '[a]lthough the universe considered abstractly may be atomic . . . knowledge of the universe is evidently organic. More fully . . . we may understand Keynes to say that the universe, together with our consciousness of it, conjointly forms an organic whole' (p. 21). This leads to limits regarding knowledge: 'But if knowledge is organic, then the rules of understanding are changed; mechanistic methods will be defeated by subtle and complex feedback effects' (p. 21). (Here, we ought to remember Marshall's remark about '[t]he Mecca of the economist [lying] in economic biology [!]' (Marshall 1920, p. xiv).) To take account of these limits of human knowledge, Keynes set up the (crucial) idea of objective chance:

Objective chance prevails when prediction is impossible in principle, given our human limitations. Objective chance covers such things as the distribution of rain-drops, the motion of gas molecules, the birth of a great man . . . 'An event is not due to objective chance if a knowledge of the permanent facts of existence would lead to its prediction . . .

'An event is due to objective chance if in order to predict it, or to prefer it to alter-natives . . . it would be necessary to know a great many more facts of existence about it than we actually do know, and if the addition of a wide knowledge of general principles would be little use' [Keynes as quoted in Fitzgibbons] (Fitzgibbons 1988, p. 22).

Keynes believed that the idea of objective chance had not been understood by those who wanted to argue that there is an equilibrium value in randomness, who wished to rely on constant statistical frequencies or the Law of Great Numbers, who stressed what will happen 'in the long run', who believed that there is a unique discoverable system among the chance and disorder of the universe (p. 22).

In fact, we are faced with 'causation without order' (p. 23). Thus, 'Keynes connected true causation with randomness, a way of thinking that had the utmost significance for his economics' (p. 24).

The above is broadly in line with the theory of knowledge implied in this study if *behavioural* outcomes, dominated by uncertainty, are considered. Keynes is certainly right when he considers rapidly evolving behavioural equilibria, associated with the behavioural system, as largely irrelevant, precisely because of uncertainty and expectations. However, Keynes clearly underrates our ability to picture the deterministic influence of slowly changing system equilibria associated with institutional set-ups on behav-iour. This influence, for example through the principle of effective demand, may be clear-cut. We shall return to the alleged impossibility of Ricardian and Marxian (system) equilibrium economics below.

The logical theory of probability [associated with 'objective chance'] presupposes intuition, and although it does not require that intuition is infallible or even mostly right, the stress is as much on insight as it is on theory. Logically as well as historically, according to Keynes, intuition is the first form of knowledge, so that despite its defects all knowledge must be based upon it. However, he did not suppose that intuition came out of nowhere. Probabilistic reasoning meant being able to apply patterns of similarity, first seen in the mind, to the chaotic facts (Fitzgibbons 1988, p. 234).

'Keynes thought that science did possess procedures similar to those of art' (p. 24, quoting Carabelli). Consequently, the

mechanical theory of the external world, a supposed unique correspondence between the facts and the mind, was false. Inspiration selects and imposes a pattern on the facts, and the choice of this pattern somehow involves an aesthetic element.

This picture of the scientist as partly an artist was further taken up in the *Treatise on Probability*, where Keynes said that science begins from analogy. Science is based upon pre-scientific knowledge, which was long and hard won; and scientific hypotheses do not arise randomly, but they too come from analogy (p. 25).

This aspect of Keynes's theory of knowledge is in line with the role of Schumpeter's *vision* in the social sciences alluded to in chapter 2: the neoclassical economist, and the socialist and the classical-Keynesian political economist look at socioeconomic phenomena through entirely different glasses. To explain facts, completely different concepts (variables and parameters) are chosen: when attempting to explain unemployment for example, the neoclassical economist looks at the labour market, the Keynesian and classical-Keynesian economist at effective demand; the same objective fact is interpreted in very different ways. Hence knowledge is always probable and no empirical test can eliminate this element of probability since facts are interpreted in the light of visions related to the functioning of society as a whole. Intuition is required because of the organic complexity of socioeconomic systems.

Moreover, Fitzgibbons argues that Keynes's view on probability is linked up with idealism: 'Keynes believed that probable knowledge, which again is knowledge of the world generally, comes not only from experience but also from understanding' (Fitzgibbons 1988. p. 27). Now,

[t]he essence of Platonism . . . is that there is a truth beyond experience, of which the mind 'bears witness to itself' [Benjamin Jowett]; and it is also a Platonic doctrine that only a probable account of knowledge can be given, since knowledge presupposes classification, and is therefore inescapably based upon similarity and metaphor. Finally, Greek philosophy generally began by accepting common experience as valid, although it had to be interpreted by reference to a higher model. Each one of those elements is implicit or explicit in Keynes's *Treatise on Probability*, and none of them is characteristic of the English tradition of philosophy (p. 28).

The English tradition has been broadly in line with modern mainstream philosophy and '[t]he hallmark of modern thought since its divorce from the metaphysics of the Middle Ages has been the faith in the superior logic of science' (p. 34).

This point is associated with a crucial issue mentioned in chapter 2: Keynes wrestled for a balanced synthesis between (traditional) metaphysics and the (modern) social sciences in line with modern scientific requirements. *Both* provide elements of knowledge: the vision, a metaphysical concept aimed at grasping essences of specific domains of reality and of complex entities on the basis of pure reason and of intuition, and scientific knowledge, theoretical and practical, interact to yield deeper knowledge, i.e. an approximate understanding of things. Hence metaphysical questions as to the *probable* essence of things, of 'society', of the 'normal price', of 'production', of how things are in principle and how they are related in principle, are of the highest importance. Metaphysical queries are addressed to 'wholes' and the relationship between 'wholes' and 'parts', for example societies and their structure. Probable answers to metaphysical questions enable us to put together scattered pieces of theory in order to discover deeper structures of the real world. The systems elaborated by Quesnay, Smith, Ricardo, Marx, Marshall, Walras, Keynes, Sraffa and Pasinetti are all examples of attempts to answer fundamental questions in the social sciences.

However, '[t]he old metaphysics had been greatly hindered by reason of its having always demanded demonstrative certainty. Much of the cogency of Hume's criticism arises out of the assumption of methods of certainty on the part of those systems against which it was directed . . . The demonstrative method can be laid on one side, and we may attempt to advance the argument by taking account of the circumstances which seem to give *some* reason for preferring one alternative to another' (Keynes, *Treatise on Probability*, quoted in Fitzgibbons 1988, p. 36): to combine differing pieces of evidence in a cogent argument requires a vision (a metaphysical notion). Moreover, metaphysics has been misused in various ways. Wild speculations on the meaning of natural or utopian social states of affairs were made (and are still made). Most seriously, however, metaphysics was (and still is) misused for political purposes in that certain political and socioeconomic orders were (and are) declared natural and eternal in order to maintain the privileges of certain groups and classes. The philosophers of the Enlightenment, but also Marx, mercilessly unveiled the hidden purposes lying behind systems of ideology. The reaction against metaphysics has been too strong, however, in denoting it as superstition, the opium of the people or simply utter rubbish. Positivistic science subsequently took its place and marched on triumphantly. However, limits begin to appear, perhaps more clearly in the social sciences than in the natural sciences. In economics, for instance, there is a fragmentation of the great schools and a lack of communication and of mutual comprehension between many representatives of specific theories. This is accompanied by disillusionment and by a loss of perspective, frequently associated with resignation. In such a situation good – Aristotelian – metaphysics is needed.

Aristotle, at the outset of his *Metaphysics*, mentions that metaphysics is an architectonic science which helps us to bring order into the universe, the immense complexity of which we are faced with. Facts of all kinds, empirical and theoretical, have to be interpreted, evaluated, pondered and eventually put, approximately, in their right place. For the social sciences, this means that we would not be faced with very varied, sometimes unrelated theories, but with an ordered body of theories based on specific approaches. Given the latter, the scientist and the politician would be in a position to compare, to evaluate and to make a choice. Seen in this way metaphysics and the sciences are not mutually exclusive but complementary.

Metaphysics aims at proposing possible orders for parts of the universe. This leads to philosophies of nature and of society. To work out a complete and consistent, and therefore entirely thought-out system of social philosophy, is one of the immense tasks to be undertaken by classical-Keynesian social scientists if classical-Keynesianism is to become a serious rival to liberal or socialist economics. Social scientists in general and economists in particular must be grateful to Carabelli, Fitzgibbons, O'Donnell and others for having uncovered Keynes's basic contribution to this undertaking. Many elements of Keynes's social philosophy have been incorporated in the previous chapters, most importantly the requirement that the study of the system ought to be logically separated from the analysis of behaviour.

Metaphysics is a matter of pure reason: the mind, and ideas produced by it, play a crucial role, although theoretical and practical experience may initiate metaphysical thinking. For instance, the materials used by a painter are extremely simple: a canvas, brushes and colours. Before producing a picture, experimenting and learning from the great masters is required. However, a painter will be able to produce a *unique* work of art only if he brings in his own ideas. Reality is, in the last instance, shaped by ideas, a fact definitely accepted by Keynes, as is evident from Fitzgibbons (1988) and from the very last lines of the *General Theory* for instance. Marx also accepted this, as emerges from his *Early Writings* and from many passages in *Das Kapital*. However, Marx rightly stressed that a material basis is always needed to *realize* ideas. For instance, it is not sufficient for some painter to be gifted and to have good ideas; he must also be in a position to acquire his means of subsistence. Moreover, there are in any society individuals or groups who, on the basis of the material means they command, may succeed in imposing their views (ideologies) which then constitute the dominant ideas. The control of parts of the modern mass media by powerful interest groups to influence public opinion is an evident case in point. Keynes argued that pressure groups may be successful in imposing their ideologies at times but that, in the long run, objective reason will succeed; it is an open question as to whether, in this respect, he was too optimistic or not.

No empirical proof can be advanced to sustain the above argument on the role of metaphysics: ideas might simply represent the output of the brain, which is fed by inputs (sensations). However, metaphysical thinking was considered possible and reasonable by great thinkers at *all* times (Hirschberger 1988). Keynes's vision confirms this. On deeper reflection it is ultimately impossible to reduce knowledge to sensation. Nobody has ever directly observed the principle of the multiplier or the principle of the social and circular process of production, which consitute invisible principles structuring parts of the real world. These concepts had to be *thought out* by great political economists. This is not to deny that theoretical and practical experience, including observation, may start scientists thinking about principles governing the real world; and, possibly, we can understand principles only if we 'visualize' and apply them to concrete real-world situations. All our thinking about essentials (the essence of things and the way in which these are interrelated) is metaphysical. For example, a neoclassical economist's claim that markets would co-ordinate individual economic actions in a socially meaningful way if there were sufficient competition is a metaphysical statement that can never be scientifically proved or disproved. All the classical-Keynesian political economist can do is to try to convince his neoclassical colleague of the fact that, in overall terms and on a fundamental level, his system of political economy is more plausible than neoclassical theory. Important arguments for the relevance of metaphysics are also advanced by natural scientists. Sir John Eccles, Nobel Prize winner for Physiology and Medicine in 1963, says:

If I should be asked to express my philosophical position, I would have to admit that I am an animist . . . As a dualist I believe in the reality of the world of mind or spirit as well as in the reality of the material world . . . I accept all of the discoveries and well-corroborated hypotheses of science – not as absolute truth but as the nearest approach to truth that has yet been attained. But . . . there is an important residue not explained by science, and even beyond any future explanation by science (Eccles 1984, p. 9).

This also holds for the social sciences, including history, with the possible difference that the non-explained residual might be even more important than in the natural sciences. For example, historians diverge widely on the causes of the First World War. Since the various causes that produced this historically unique event are mixed up organically, divergence of opinion is likely to persist, so much the more as fundamental values and even passions are important here. If the object of science is a complex and interrelated whole, like society or parts of society, then important unexplainable residuals are bound to remain. Keynes clearly perceived the probable and thus fallible nature of human knowledge.

On the actual state of the sciences, Eccles declares that

[t]he tremendous successes of science in the last century have led to the expectation that there will be forthcoming in the near future a complete explanation in materialistic terms of all the fundamental problems confronting us. These 'great questions', as they are called, have exercised the creative thinkers from Greek times onward. It has been fashionable to overplay the explanatory power of science and this has led to the regrettable reactions of anti-science and of all manner of irrationalistic and magical beliefs. When confronted with the frightening assertion that we are no more than participants in the materialist happenings of chance and necessity, anti-science is a natural reaction. I believe that this assertion is an arrogant over-statement (Eccles 1984, pp. 8–9).

Every sensible individual may observe that considerable intellectual arrogance and materialism are also present in socioeconomic theory and reality and are perhaps still growing. Fitzgibbons, in the very last lines of his book, states: 'Now Keynes's song is fading, and economics is based on materialistic values, or pseudo-science, or ideology and the struggle for power' (Fitzgibbons 1988, p. 198). This is perhaps too harsh a statement, but there is certainly considerable truth in it.

One might ask why metaphysics has from time to time been submerged by excessive positivism. A classical answer was possibly given by Antoine de Saint-Exupéry's *petit prince*: 'L'essentiel est invisible pour les yeux' (Saint-Exupéry 1946, p. 72). Truth, goodness, justice and beauty, as far as they are embodied in various spheres of the real world and as ideals cannot, in the last instance, be seen, they must be thought. The same is true of the basic causal forces governing the real world, the principle of effective demand or the ultimate determinants of the value of goods for instance. This is perhaps the essence of Keynes's vision.

Causal forces are thus invisible. This implies that (pure) causal models are ideal types (chapter 3, pp. 81–9) that are produced by the mind, although the elaboration of such models may be initiated by theoretical and practical experience. For example, what can be observed are *actually existing* capital stocks, capacity output levels, sector sizes and prices. These are the aggregate results of past and present individual decisions. The persistent influence of the socioeconomic system upon individual decisions cannot be directly observed however: in chapter 3 (pp. 81–9) invisible demarcation lines have been mentioned, which are delimiting system equilibria linked up with fully adjusted situations (e.g. normal prices and quantities) and the corresponding observable elements of the real world (market prices and quantities actually sold). Fully adjusted situations associated with normal levels of output and employment and normal prices cannot be seen directly, but only indirectly so to speak. First, their existence must be thought out and argued, and the capital-theory debate is certainly an important element of argument. This results in pure models such as were elaborated by Piero Sraffa and Luigi Pasinetti, for example. Only secondly can the social scientist, on the basis of pure models reflecting principles, construct applied frameworks and look for empirical facts that speak in favour of the (probable) correctness of the pure models. However, owing to the immense complexity of the real world a definite proof will never be possible except, perhaps, for partial behavioural problems, e.g. the temporary impact of a marketing campaign upon the volume of sales of a product.

The fact that the ideas structuring the real world are invisible does not of course mean that the material expressions of ideas are of secondary importance. The above suggests that the material world constitutes a ladder enabling our minds to get nearer to the various ideals, for example truth in the social and in the natural sciences, or aesthetic perfection in the arts: 'matter is in fact the complement [to mind], providing the handholds and footholds on the mountain of our spiritual climb' (Eccles 1984, p. 7). This pictures perfectly the nature of human knowledge which was, perhaps, brought out best by Aristotle.

Selected problems

Keynes's basic position was essentially individualistic. He was a genius, a theoretical and practical all-round man, whose mind, in face of a universe forming an immensely complex organic whole, was 'capable of [a great many] rational intuitions and which [could] faintly discern beyond the flow [of reality] and through turbulent airs the transcosmic ideals' (Fitzgibbons 1988, p. 24). '[For Keynes] intuition is the first form of knowledge, so that despite its defects all knowledge must be based upon it' (p. 24) and form the basis for practical action. However, given the complexity of the universe, knowledge may be very limited indeed as '[t]here are processes in a causal web beyond our sciences or powers of calculation. If we stamp our feet, Keynes says, the moons of Jupiter may be slightly displaced in their orbits, although our sciences are not fine enough to recognize it' (p. 21). This is reminiscent of agnosticism: 'the consequences [of most things], even if they persist, are generally lost in the river of time' (p. 24, quoting Keynes). 'In particular . . . investors are typically unable genuinely to resolve uncertain situations' (p. 31). Such propositions suggest that excessive individualism may be destructive regarding the acquisition of knowledge in the social sciences: the effects of individual actions fade out in the infinite if not co-ordinated by an automatic mechanism, supply and demand for example, in a socially meaningful way. This issue is alluded to in chapter 5 (pp. 281–308).

However, there are at least two important factors which favour the acquisition of knowledge: the presence of space and time and the existence of historically evolving institutions and the forces governing their interplay. Space and time divide the universe into subsystems with varying degrees of independence. In the social world, there are individuals living in families, going to school and working in enterprises; there are villages, towns, regions and states; associations of the most diverse kinds have existed for a long time or are being created newly; the world as a whole is linked through a network of international relations on various levels. Each subsystem is governed by a set of causal relations which link different spheres of space. The existence of causal relations enables the social scientist to describe approximately the functioning of a subsystem as a whole or of some aspect of it; pure models exhibit principles, real-type or applied models realizations of principles in concrete situations; comprehensive theoretical systems represent attempts to capture the working mechanism of economies as a whole, for example neoclassical economics or classical-Keynesian political economy. But there are also specific theories of employment, of value and distribution. Because of the permanent presence of space, the effect of some predetermined variable upon one or several determined variables is likely to be much stronger in its immediate neighbourhood than in very distant places. An educational reform in a European country may positively influence its long-run export performance which, in turn, may have a whole series of positive effects on the social and economic level; in particular, the normal level of employment may permanently increase. However, the success of this country may negatively influence economic activity elsewhere, e.g. somewhere in Asia. To study the influence of the educational reform on specified economic and social aspects of the country in question is obviously of great interest and might give rise to various research projects. However, it might be difficult to find research students wishing to study possible effects of that reform in some Asian country, although there might be effects; the problem would have to be put in another way, i.e. on the level of interactions between economies.

The second factor which facilitates the acquisition of knowledge is the presence of institutions. Given the immense complexity of societies, it is impossible for the individuals making up societies to decide as rationally as possible at every moment of time on every problem that might arise. It is inconceivable that the members of a society democratically decide each day on whether to drive on the left or on the right, on the expenditure pattern of the state and the amount of taxes to be levied, on the organization of education, on the ways to produce and to consume or on how to spend leisure time and so on. To organize social and individual life, institutions, i.e. persistent ways of pursuing individual and social aims, come into being almost spontaneously; in fact, behaviour means participating in institutions presently existing. Institutions and their interplay form the social structure which partly determines individual actions through formal constraints (rules of behaviour) and material constraints (e.g. scarcity and effective demand). Social institutions, for example the social process of production, are preconditions for the pursuit of individual aims, for instance in the sphere of consumption. The institutions existing in a society are the heritage of the past and constitute as such the contribution of past generations to the solution of present problems. However, old institutions may lose their meaning since the overall situation changes, mainly because of the social impact of technological change, as Marx perceived with incomparable insight; new institutions will, as a consequence, have to be created in order to master new challenges. This leads to institutional change which manifests itself in an immensely complex historical process. In this process elements of harmony co-exist with elements of conflict in varying degrees.

Institutions remain unchanged for long periods of time or change but slowly. This introduces areas of stability into individual, socioeconomic and political life. To study the impact of these permanent aspects of individual and social life is the main object of the social and historical sciences. The object of study must remain reasonably constant if knowledge is to be obtained at all; looking at very rapidly changing behavioural aspects of social and individual life associated with uncertainty (e.g. unpredictable events that may affect single individuals or investment projects) leads to agnosticism. This is illustrated by chapter 12 of Keynes's *General Theory* where the behaviour of the *individual* investor is pictured. Fitzgibbons also confirms Keynes's penchant towards agnosticism: 'economics is in the realm of the ephemeral. The economics of Ricardo and Marx and Marshall, arch determinists who dreamed of economic science, were to be supplanted . . . by the economics of transition and meaningless change. Keynes's theories of value and interest represent his attempt to formalize a new and non-deterministic method of economics' (Fitzgibbons 1988, p. 129). This implies that 'Keynes meant to show that there is no such thing as a hidden economy, that the economy of appearances is the only one, and that the Ricardian method "of adopting a hypothetical world remote from experience as though it were the world of experience and then living in it consistently" was to be condemned for its abstractedness rather than praised for its science' (p. 127). The existence of long-period system equilibria associated with system-governed fully adjusted situations is questioned.

In this, Keynes was misguided. To say that 'the economy of appearances is the only one' implies positivism, which, as a rule, is associated with materialism and individualism; the latter leads to dealing uniquely with behaviour and with behavioural outcomes. Positivism, however, is strictly anti-metaphysical and therefore stands in sharp contrast to Keynes's vision. This contradiction in Keynes's position is perhaps due to his placing in sharp opposition the real (visible) world and 'transcosmic' ideals: positivism is associated with the former, idealism with the latter. This dualism may lead to almost unrestricted positivism. Joan Robinson's position regarding knowledge is typical: 'One of the great metaphysical ideas in economics is expressed by the word "value"' (Robinson 1962b, p. 26). 'Among all the various meanings of *value*, there has been one all the time under the surface, the old concept of a Just Price ... *Value* will not help. It has no operational content. It is just a word' (p. 46). The last sentence indicates that Joan Robinson basically takes a nominalist, anti-metaphysical and positivistic position.

Hence Keynes *in some instances* places a 'messy' real world in opposition to Platonic ideals. This is extremely dangerous, not only for the social sciences, but also on a political level. For example, neoclassical economists place in sharp opposition, on the one hand, crude positivism in empirical work and pragmatism in policy-making – exemplified by monetarism and 'supply-side economics' – and, on the other, highly sophisticated and abstract models describing ideal or hypothetical situations. This may lead to confusion because there is, for example, no clear link between theory and policy. In the political sphere the separation of reality and ideals might lead one to argue, for instance, that, given heavy social disorder, a ruthless dictatorship would be justified to bring about some 'ideal' society. Therefore, in this book, we have always taken the position of Ricardo, Marx and Marshall which is, ultimately, based on Aristotle's: below the immediately visible surface, there is a hidden reality governed by stable or slowly changing causal forces structuring the real world which reflects the functioning of the institutional system. If this were not so, there would be no social sciences, and potential knowledge on social matters would be submerged by agnosticism. On the political level the Aristotelian view implies that social progress may be achieved through institutional reforms in response to particular situations and taking account of human weaknesses (see chapter 6). Hence there is no question of realizing an ideal society.

Excessive positivism thus implies that individuals are almost helplessly faced with a chaotic visible universe. Fortunately, however, the individual is not standing alone or isolated from other individuals in an immensely complex universe, but is acting within an institutional framework, a social structure, which is governed by specific laws and partly determines his actions. Uncertainty and very imperfect knowledge about the 'chaos' of appearances, for example rapidly changing behaviour, and determinism and probable knowledge about underlying social structures governed by rigid social laws co-exist. The fate of each individual investment project is likely to be highly uncertain and the volume of trend investment is rigidly determined by the institutional set-up of a society (chapter 4, pp. 142–204). The latter implies that there are system equilibria associated with fully adjusted situations and that, therefore, 'a hidden economy' in the sense of Ricardo and Marx exists.

From the writings of Keynes it emerges, however, that he was not, on the whole, systematically overwhelmed by agnosticism. Keynes did accept that quite certain statements are possible if institutions and historical developments are considered:

The *Treatise on Probability* and *The General Theory* have a common subject matter, namely the prevalence of uncertainty, and address a common problem, which is whether sensible and rational decisions can be made under conditions of probability and uncertainty. This question had been posed and answered by Hume, who said in effect that they cannot. At first Keynes simply said that, Hume notwithstanding, rational intuitions commonly do occur. This answer defines the *Treatise* as one of Keynes's early works, when Keynes held what he came to regard as his glib belief in human rationality. By comparison, where *The General Theory* later assumed the prevalence of human irrationality, it seemed to turn back towards Hume. In particular, Keynes later said that investors are typically unable to resolve uncertain situations, and *try to follow conventional rules* [our emphasis] . . . Keynes was almost certainly aware that he was conceding a point to Hume when he wrote *The General Theory*. In 1933 he had cited this passage as indicative of Hume: 'Tis not, therefore, reason which is the guide of life, but custom. That alone determines the mind, in all instances, to suppose the future conformable to the past' (Fitzgibbons 1988, pp. 31–2).

This almost Marxian statement of Hume's leads Fitzgibbons to say: 'Although Keynes's *Treatise* might establish the ideal, Hume was right on a point concerning common practice. But if Hume was right to say that people follow conventions, then it is logical that humanity should be subject to the same causal laws as matter' (p. 32).

Here, liberty and rationality are sharply contrasted with determinism and irrationality. However, in this study it has been suggested that liberty and individual rationality can (and must) be reconciled with determinism and social rationality. Human actions are almost never entirely free nor entirely determined since they take place within an institutional framework leaving some freedom of choice. While many economists think that freedom and necessity (or liberty and determination) cannot be reconciled, eminent historians do not find any difficulty in doing so: 'The logical dilemma about free will and determinism does not arise in real life. It is not that some human actions are free and others determined. The fact is that all human actions are both free and determined, according to the point of view from which one considers them' (Carr 1986, p. 89; the whole of chapter IV on 'Causation in history' is important here). For example, there is considerable freedom for the individual worker seeking a job or for the individual investor realizing an investment project while, simultaneously, the principle of effective demand, through the social structure, i.e. the institutional system, *determines* both the volume of *normal* employment and of *normal* investment which, in turn, sets *long-period restrictions* to each worker and investor. Hence, the act of finding a given job is free or determined according to whether a microeconomic (behavioural) or a macroeconomic (system) standpoint is adopted. Given this, the classical-Keynesian project of synthesizing Keynesian and Ricardian elements seems quite sound (see also chapter 3, pp. 103–18). The problem is not one of choosing between opposing theories but of bringing together and synthesizing theories implying different ways of looking at reality.

Therefore, Keynes's too pronounced individualism leads him to contrast sharply the individual with the whole universe, a position which ultimately implies agnosticism. From an ethical point of view this gives rise to another sharp contrast between the highly imperfect real world and the ideal world: 'Keynes's vision was partly that all worldly affairs are subject to change to a possibly large degree, or to what he called "objective chance"; but it also pointed to an independent sphere of 'ideals, appreciable by the mind, by which we might steer cross-current' (Fitzgibbons 1988, p. 49). There is in Keynes's system 'a direct relation between ethics and the messiness of the world' (p. 50). The sharp opposition between the real and the ideal is typical of Plato by whom Keynes was heavily influenced (pp. 26–31). A sharp contrast between the ideal and reality is also present in liberal and socialist socioeconomic systems. In neoclassical economics, very down-to-earth empirical methods are used to come to grips with a messy reality; these stand in strong contrast to the highly formalized general equilibrium models depicting hypothetical or ideal situations; in this context, some philosophers of science have rightly spoken of *Modellplatonismus*.

A complement

Keynes's approach is basically Platonian: the mind and ideals are of primary importance and the real world represents an imperfect reflection of ideals. The *humanist* approach underlying the present study could, however, be termed Aristotelian: 'ideas are embodied in the real world, not that the real is to be found in ideas only' (Hirschberger 1984, 1988, vol. I, pp. 72, 153; chapter 2 above). In his *Politics* Aristotle systematically examined the *social dispositions* of man: society and the social institutions composing it may come into existence only if individuals are *unequal in ability* and are *complementary*. Aristotle's *Politics* thus deals with the social framework within which human actions take place. The nature of actions and how these ought to be regulated is the theme of *Nicomachean Ethics* which deals with the individual dispositions of man (Brown 1986, chapter 6); this sphere is also the realm of *equality*. The idea of man as an individual and a social being is sketched in chapter 2 (pp. 27–39).

An important element has to be integrated into Keynes's vision, namely the various institutions and their interplay (the social system or structure) mentioned in chapters 2 and 3, above all the social institutions which are the outcome of the social dispositions of man. Moreover, institutional and technological change, that is historical developments, have to be accounted for. Some problems arising with institutions and history have been dealt with in earlier chapters of this study, specifically in chapter 4. There a specific issue concerning the nature of the social philosophy underlying classical-Keynesian political economy was dealt with, i.e. the relationship between organicism and holism.

In the light of classical-Keynesian social philosophy Keynes's statement 'that the universe, together with our consciousness of it, conjointly forms an organic whole' (Fitzgibbons 1988, p. 21) might be highly misleading and dangerous. To see society as an organism might imply a totalitarian society, in that each individual fulfils certain tasks within the social organism and counts only as a member of society. Evidently, Keynes did not think in terms of this traditional concept of a 'social organism'. Rather he presumably held a basically atomistic vision of society which was in line with his individualism. The organic element comes in with the hierarchy of values which is pursued by individuals and in that the different values are organically linked with each other, which implies that individuals are entities and that, therefore, the various spheres of life are complementary (chapter 2, pp. 39–53). However, when he states in the *General Theory* 'that the duty of ordering the current volume of investment cannot be safely left in private hands' (Keynes 1973a, p. 320), doubts might arise. Individualism seems to lead to chaos and therefore requires, temporarily at least, a very strong state to restore order, including full employment. This might open the door to a rather extreme kind of socialism, as many have feared, particularly Hayek whose violent reaction against Keynes is fully understandable: Hitler and Stalin were solidly established in power when the *General Theory* was published. In this work Keynes even suggests that 'the theory of output as a whole . . . is much more easily adapted to the conditions of a totalitarian state, than is the theory of production and distribution under conditions of free competition and a large measure of laissez-faire' (Keynes 1973a, p. xxvi). In this context, some rather disquieting remarks of Marshall's should also be mentioned:

The notion of continuity with regard to development is common to all modern schools of economic thought, whether the chief influences acting on them are those of biology, as represented by the writings of Herbert Spencer; or of history and philosophy, as represented by Hegel's *Philosophy of History* . . . These two kinds of influences have affected, more than any other, the substance of the views expressed in the present book (Marshall 1920, p. ix).

This is a strange association of liberalism (Marshall) and totalitarianism as is inevitably implied in an organic-cum-holistic view of society (Hegel), the whole being possibly complemented by evolutionism which may imply the domination of the strongest and of the most ruthless (social Darwinism). To be sure, neither Marshall and Keynes, nor Spencer and Hegel advocated the latter, as is done today by some economists and by some particularly successful businessmen. But the danger is that totalitarian and élitist conclusions might be drawn from an organic view of society, wherein élite might be defined as 'natural superiority' of individuals or even of some race.

This indicates the importance of being clear about social philosophy. If society is seen as an organism because hierarchically ordered social and individual aims are pursued within institutions by individuals, Keynes's view of society as an organism can of course be accepted: the organic character of society emerges from the complementarity of institutions. This view of society need not lead to dangerous consequences if it is borne in mind that social structures ought to serve individuals, i.e. to provide the social preconditions for the actions of individuals; this is the crucial postulate that should underlie the humanist classical-Keynesian view of society in which the prospering of the individual remains the ultimate end. In chapters 4 and 6 it has been mentioned that full employment and income distribution grounded on a social consensus are most important social preconditions.

Hence Keynes's heavily individualistic system requires complementing by a social foundation, i.e. a system of complementary social and individualistic institutions which consists of a material basis and an institutional superstructure. The key points are the typical Keynesian notions of the 'monetary production economy' and 'effective demand'. These essentially social concepts enable us to integrate the classical view of the institutional system, i.e. the material basis-cum-superstructure scheme, with Keynes's way of looking at socioeconomic phenomena as is reflected in his notion of the monetary production economy. On the theoretical level this means combining the proportions-based classical approach to value and distribution with his principle of effective demand which deals with the scale of economic activity. Both the classical proportions approach and Keynes's principle of effective demand are social laws in the sense that the entire institutional system, directly or indirectly, enters the picture to determine value, distribution and employment in a monetary production economy.

Ethics, politics and political economy

Keynes's views on ethics are set out in chapter 3 of Fitzgibbons (1988) and in chapter 6 of O'Donnell (1989). Criticizing Hume, 'Keynes found a formal parallel between probabilistic reasoning and ethical reasoning . . . In the medium of probability, which is the stuff of the world, the connection between facts and values would be reestablished' (Fitzgibbons 1988, p. 35). '[I]f non-demonstrable probabilistic knowledge *was* valid, as Keynes believed, then the same reasoning could be extended to and be valid in ethics' (p. 36). Hence we may advance 'arguments [which] are rational and claim some weight without pretending to be certain. In metaphysics, in science, and in conduct, most of the arguments, upon which we habitually base our rational beliefs, are admitted to be inconclusive in a greater or less degree' (Keynes 1971c, p. 3). 'If probable knowledge is valid, then it can only be on the basis of non-demonstrable logic and rational intuition. However, if there is a rational intuition, then it can be equally applicable to ethics' (Fitzgibbons 1988, p. 36). Hence, Keynes's view on knowledge in the domain of ethics is an application of his general theory of knowledge (Keynes 1971c) sketched in chapter 2 (pp. 57–75).

'Keynes's rational ethics . . . is an ethics of motives rather than consequences. It is similar to the doctrine of *Natural Law, the traditional philosophy* [our emphasis] which advocated the performance of duty, which understood rational action as being correlative with the virtues, the major way in which, the medievals believed, reason could be expressed in an uncertain world' (Fitzgibbons 1988, p. 37). This is very important, above all if confronted with Schumpeter's views on *natural law*, as he argues that the natural law philosophies were at the origin of the social sciences and subsequently petered out to be replaced by positive science (Schumpeter 1954, part II, chapter 2, pp. 73–142). Presently, there seems to be a resurgence of the natural law approach; Utz (1964–94), Schack (1978) and Brown (1986, chapter 6) are indications of this. In chapter 2 (pp. 39–53) it is suggested that the proposed *humanist* system of political and individual ethics ought to be based upon Aristotle's *Politics* and *Nicomachean Ethics* respectively, as is done in Brown (1986, chapter 6). This implies the *natural law* approach. The corresponding ethical system is supposed to be based on objectively given and invariable *concrete* or *material* values (for instance, the classical virtues, fair distribution, full employment). The supreme value in the political sphere is the common weal, to which corresponds happiness in the individual domain. Both the common weal and happiness embody a structured system of complementary values. This is due to the *nature* or *essence* of society and of man, both of which are structured entities. The dispositions to perceive and eventually to pursue objectively given values are supposed to be anchored in human nature. This is sharply opposed to utilitarian and Kantian ethics, for example, which attempt to establish *formal* rules to guide correct behaviour, 'utility maximization' and 'categorical imperatives', which are without reference to the material content of actions. Rules of behaviour are important, but such rules can be established only once concrete values have been identified and their importance justified (on this, see also Schack 1978 and Brown 1986).

A strong link between politics and ethics is implied in Keynes's vision:

Modern political theory is based on considerations of power, whereas traditional political philosophy was based as much on ethics . . . Keynes's theory of politics was based entirely on ethics. He wrote in the old idealist tradition of political philosophy, which, believing that the state should be ruled by reason and true ideals, was concerned to define the appropriate structure to rule. The tradition also holds, and Keynes himself believed, that democracy and the rights of man can be means but can never have the rank of political ends, because the state has ultimate moral responsibilities, whereas democratic politics are inconstant and are part of the flux. But it had also been traditionally assumed, not as a principle but as a practical reality, that the lot of common humanity was to suffer debilitating and ineradicable poverty. Keynes revised traditional political philosophy in the light of modern economic growth, which he declared to be the most significant change that civilization had ever experienced (Fitzgibbons 1988, p. 53).

Technical progress enhances labour productivity such as to render possible a decent life for every member of the various societies, which, in spite of the enormous growth of population in recent decades, may still be possible.

The typical Platonian opposition of (perfect) ideas to (chaotic) reality re-emerges in this passage. Therefore, the crucially important relationship between ethics and politics ought, in our view, to be based on Aristotle, not on Plato (chapter 2, pp. 20–57). The latter, similarly to Hegel, looked at matters concerning man and society from the point of view of the absolute. On this assumption, Plato and Hegel worked out grand systems, the misconceived application of which to real-world problems might give rise (and gave rise) to tragic consequences: the attempted realization of totalitarian utopias is the most obvious case in point. Keynes, however, looked at reality from the point of view of the imperfect human being as his stressing of probable and uncertain knowledge clearly shows. The same is true of

Aristotle. His *Nicomachean Ethics* and *Politics* picture a system of individual and political ethics which is founded on the *real* man and takes account of his possible weaknesses and imperfections. Aristotle combined the deductive (idealistic) method with the inductive (empirical and historical) method. Similarly to Keynes, Aristotle thought that those responsible for public affairs ought to create, as well as they can, the preconditions for 'a good and decent life' of all citizens making up a society. Based on the social disposition of man, linked with inequality and complementarity, the basic aim of politics is to establish as much harmony as possible within society or to eliminate alienation as far as is possible (chapter 2, pp. 20–57). This requires, in turn, the presence of an objectively given (but unattainable) ideal. But, 'the temptation of constructing an ideal [Platonian] polity founded on mere guesses and hopes [must be avoided] . . . there is an ideal polity for each State, if not one for all States . . . But it is only to be discovered in the paths of history and observation' (Amos 1883, p.v.), grounded on theoretical and metaphysical reasoning.

Hence political action in each society ought to aim at approaching the imperfectly known ideal of the public interest or the common weal (the most fundamental and the most complex value) as closely as possible; this is equivalent to reducing system-caused alienation as far as possible (chapter 2, pp. 39–53). *Politics*, as the queen of the social sciences, has to co-ordinate the other social sciences to prepare the way for improving the institutional system: 'Politics [comprises] all those branches of knowledge which depend on the composite nature of man both as isolated and as in society. Such are Ethics in the Aristotelian sense . . .; political economy, which deals with the conditions under which national wealth is produced, accumulated, and distributed; law and legislation [and] Sociology' (Amos 1883, p. 3). How the social sciences are co-ordinated and what policy actions are effectively undertaken depends upon the social philosophy which underlies the dominant vision of the broad functioning of society.

Given the crucial importance of Aristotle and Keynes's heavy reliance on Plato one might ask whether very old and hotly disputed issues, capable of no solution, are reintroduced into the social sciences. Three reasons may be advanced to dispel this fear. First, Aristotle's philosophy in general and his *Ethics* and *Politics* in particular are sound and realistic and capable of providing principles that can be applied to very varied real-world situations. Second, Keynes is presumably more Aristotelian than emerges from Fitzgibbons (1988). Third, Aristotle and Plato are, on a fundamental level, complementary (Hirschberger 1984, 1988, vol. I, preface to the fourth edition, pp. VI–VIII; Jaeger 1955): Plato takes the point of view of the Absolute and Aristotle the position of man capable of probable knowledge only.

In chapter 2 (pp. 20–57) it has been suggested that Aristotle might be considered as the founder of the *humanist* middle way in the social sciences and stands behind a great tradition in political philosophy (for a survey of political thought, see Fetscher and Münkler 1985–93). His way of looking at social and political phenomena was carried on by Cicero who developed the concept of the mixed constitution; Aquinas' notion of the common weal was taken up by the Christian Social Doctrine and complemented by the principles of solidarity and subsidiarity; Montesquieu and Burke wrote on institutions and institutional reform; Friedrich List and Gustav Schmoller emphasized the importance of institutions and of productive forces, as did other members of the German Historical School and of American Institutionalism. Marx was an admirer of Aristotle; his theoretical and, simultaneously, historical method is profoundly Aristotelian. Finally, the classical view of the institutional system, i.e. the material basis-cum-superstructure scheme, may, in principle, be combined with Keynes's way of looking at socioeconomic phenomena through the lens of his notion of the monetary production economy.

Philosophy of history and political economy

The economic theories of liberalism annd socialism are each embedded in a social philosophy and in a wider view of socioeconomic, political and cultural evolution which could be called a philosophy of history. Liberalism asserts that individual freedom, above all in the economic sphere, leads to a permanent improvement of the material situation which will provide a steady firmer basis for satisfying higher cultural needs which will, in turn, broaden the scope for freedom; incidentally, Marshall, under Hegelian influence, broadly thought on these lines (Groenewegen 1990; 1995, p. 611). According to extreme socialist doctrine societies deterministically move through various modes of production, driven on by internal contradictions which constitute the engine of change; these conflicts would disappear within communism which is free of alienation and represents as such the final stage of history. Hence the *idea of progress* is all important in liberalism and socialism. General progress is rendered possible in both systems of thought by scientific progress: the growth of scientific knowledge in the natural and in the social sciences is said to enable man to master the forces of nature and to organize societies with growing perfection.

The immense influence exerted on practical affairs by both liberal and socialist doctrines is not primarily due to their economic theories but to the social philosophies and the philosophies of history underlying both; in a way, these doctrines represent secular religions. Hence classical-Keynesian political economy must be complemented by a complete system of socioeconomic thought too if it is to exert a decisive influence on socioeconomic policy-making. This requires elaborating a specifically *humanist* social philosophy and a corresponding philosophy of history. The former is sketched in chapter 2 (pp. 20–57), while some hints at the latter are provided in this subsection.

We start with a brief discussion on the supposed sense of history, particularly the probable aim to be reached. Next the close association between Aristotelian-based philosophy of history, i.e. historical realism, and classical-Keynesian political economy is sketched. Subsequently, some special issues are considered: the actor in history, the significance of alienation, the problem of imperfect knowledge, the phenomenon of social and cultural change; and, finally, the problems of pursuing aims under alienated conditions and of learning from history are touched upon. In dealing with these immensely complex issues – of which principles can only be sketched – we take up some threads of thought developed in previous chapters.

The problem of the *supposed sense of history* may be tackled in a speculative or in a realist way. In the *speculative* view the aim of history is in the future and as a rule consists of a situation free from alienation, characterized by a perfect organization of society and mastery of the forces of nature by man such that individual aims like freedom and self-realization may be fully achieved. Widely differing perceptions of the ideal state of affairs and of the way which leads to it are associated with great modern ideologies embodying a philosophy of history, for example liberalism, socialism and Hegelianism. An important common characteristic of these systems of thought is that the thinking about history and its end is in terms of the *Absolute*. Liberalism is deistic, and man is gradually supposed to acquire complete mastery of his fate, especially the forces of nature, the result being freedom and material affluence. Socialism is naturalistic and aims at the same ends as does liberalism, although the way and the means are different. Hegel's pantheistic system conceives of history as the action of a rationally acting *Weltgeist* striving for absolute knowledge and freedom. A striking feature of these ideologies is the speculative and even theological elements they contain. As a matter of fact, liberalism and socialism are, in some way, secular religions. Hegel's system has been denoted a piece of rational theology. Indeed the speculative way of looking at the course of history seems, explicitly or implicitly, to end up in theological considerations. Such considerations are of course legitimate *per se* but are not part of a system of social science although they may be used to put the social sciences into a wider and more profound context.

In the *realist* way of looking at the course of history the aim of history is not in an undetermined future but in the present. This aim is fundamentally ethical: the same immutable ideals provide signposts for action in all domains. Regarding human affairs this means continuous efforts to reduce imperfections in order to approach more closely the ideal of the common weal (chapter 2, pp. 39–53). The realist way of looking at the real world presupposes that there are immutable ontological, aesthetical and ethical principles underlying visible reality, which represent the essence of existing things. These essences are also ethically and aesthetically perfect. This implies that on a fundamental level truth, goodness and beauty coincide.

The fundamental principles (pictured in layer VII of scheme 3, p. 106) have a double function. On the one hand they shape part of the real world, predominantly nature and the physical aspects of man and of society, i.e. the material basis of social and cultural life. This implies that the contents of the fundamental principles are realized in different forms varying widely in space and time. A striking example is the social process of production which, in principle, remains invariant but has undergone immense changes in form with the transition of traditional to modern industrialized societies. On the other hand these principles provide natural and invariable guidelines for the behaviour of man in all domains, economic, political, moral and cultural. However, for various reasons – imperfect knowledge, particular interests and defective organizations of society – there will always exist a gap between the ideal and the existing, that is alienation (chapter 2, pp. 39–53). This implies that, in the course of history, individuals always act in alienated circumstances.

Hence the realist way of looking at history is from the point of view of imperfect and fallible human beings most of whom attempt to do better in changing material circumstances. This more modest and more limited way of looking at history does not preclude the study of wide epochs characterized by specific fundamental values like the Middle Ages, or of secular movements, for example the transition from traditional to modern industrial societies. The realist way of looking at history intimately links up with humanist social philosophy (chapter 2) and is, as such, essentially Aristotelian. Modern historians implicitly taking up variants of the realist approach are, for example, Burckhardt (1978), Carr (1986) and Lloyd (1986), who, incidentally, coined the notion of *historical realism*.

This concept may be felicitously combined with classical-Keynesian political economy to provide a broad framework for coming to grips with historical processes. The key notion linking up historical realism and political economy is that of the *social surplus*, which, according to the political economy approach, emerges from the social process of production, i.e. the material basis of society. The social surplus allows the setting up of an institutional superstructure (chapters 3 and 4), the shape of which depends upon the use of the surplus; state activities (defence, administration, education), social and cultural purposes, luxury consumption and accumulation of capital are possible uses. The notion of the social surplus is of the greatest importance for picturing historical processes. Indeed the way in which the social surplus is produced, appropriated, distributed and used characterizes historical situations; as such the surplus approach allows the linking up of the socioeconomic sphere of society with the political, legal and cultural domains and to study interactions between these spheres. This is not to argue that the material basis determines what is going on in the superstructure as some Marxists have done. The surplus principle merely implies that each activity, whether economic, political or cultural, requires a material basis. Here is not the place, and there is no need, to develop systematically the links existing between historical realism and classical political economy. In this field, the classical economists, most importantly Marx, have provided the conceptual foundations, and a very great number of historians have, explicitly or implicitly, made use of classical political economy, complemented by Keynesian elements in this century, in historical analyses. In the following, only some issues associated with historical realism and its links with classical-Keynesian political economy are sketched.

First, in historical realism the *actor in history* is *real* man, i.e. *the social individual* pictured in Marx's *Grundrisse* (Marx 1974 [1857/58]), who as an individual may egoistically pursue individual aims and is *simultaneously* a social or a political being (Aristotle, *Politics*). As such the social individual acts within a social framework which, through constraints, determines his actions to some extent. For example, a lack of effective demand resulting in involuntary unemployment crucially shapes the general atmosphere in a society and the behaviour of individuals. This comprehensive realist view stands in sharp contrast to the liberal and socialist view. Liberalism and socialism are in fact based on the idealization of part of human nature. The former praises the individual and egoistic aspect of human nature, and emphasizes the principle of self-regulation; the latter wants to crush egoism and to transform man into a social and benevolent being.

Second, the social individuals always act in alienated, i.e. not ideal, situations, wherein systemic alienation is fundamentally important – for example, involuntary unemployment and its social and political side-effects. There are two main sources of system-caused alienation: first, a greater or less degree of ignorance of social matters, for instance of the causes of unemployment, and, second, the excessive pursuit of particular interests, mainly in the economic and political spheres. It is important to note that the pursuit of particular interests need not, in itself, be associated with the alienation. The latter comes about if particular interest-seeking disturbs the socially appropriate proportions or the harmony of the system.

For example, in chapter 4 (pp. 154–75) we have argued that profits play a socially useful role. However, from the supermultiplier relation it emerges that the profit *share* must not exceed a certain size – dependent on all the other variables and parameters contained in the supermultiplier relation – if the full-employment level is to be preserved. If entrepreneurs pursue profits within these socially appropriate limits, system-caused alienation will not occur. If, however, the profit share grows excessively large, because of speculative profits for instance, involuntary unemployment and system-caused alienation will come into being.

System-caused alienation plays a crucial role in history because alienation may be self-reinforcing. This may produce intolerable strains on the institutional system and cause its breakdown. The latter may engender chaos, particularly in the economic and legal spheres. In a legal vacuum the law of the strongest will prevail with all the political consequences that may ensue. Germany in 1932 and at the beginning of 1933 is perhaps the prime example of the uncontrollable effects of self-amplifying alienation caused by involuntary mass unemployment which, reinforced by the feeling of frustration generated by a lost world war and by a socially disastrous hyper-inflation, almost inevitably ended up in a totalitarian régime. The events which occurred were largely caused by the determining influence of the system upon behaviour. It is crucial to note that this is not an attempt to justify the subsequent policy actions of the National Socialist régime which shaped the German social and political system from 1933 onwards: a totalitarian régime once established cannot be easily overthrown, mainly because of the terror, fear and mutual-mistrust it creates; subsequently such a régime may enforce most irrational and ethically reprehensible kinds of behaviour. This example illustrates how in history the determinism of the system and behaviour within constraints interact sequentially.

Third, imperfect knowledge – a kind of alienation – about individual or social affairs may prevent ethically correct actions; the aims pursued by the social individuals may be ethically good or bad in varying degrees and depend upon specific value systems. Hence the attempts to narrow the gap existing between historically existing and probably and imperfectly known ideal situations, i.e. alienation, are always tentative. Since knowledge about actually existing and about desirable situations will always remain probable in Keynes's sense, alienation will never be eliminated; eventually, it can be reduced to some extent.

To obtain knowledge about principles is particularly difficult because fundamental values and principles are invisible: the multiplier principle may be seen at work, but the principle itself (the causal force embodied in the multiplier) cannot be seen. Therefore, it is very difficult to bring into the open the way in which fundamental values are embodied in the various societies and are expressed in individual actions. For example, it is evident that ways of life are different in France and Germany or in Great Britain and on the Continent. Yet it is extremely difficult to say precisely what the difference consists of. An immense amount of theoretical, empirical and historical knowledge, complemented by experience and understanding, is required before even tentative judgements can be made on these and similar matters. An analogous argument holds for the understanding of the way in which fundamental principles work. For example, the long-period principle of effective demand, which is, in principle, captured by the supermultiplier relation, is implemented in entirely different ways in the various countries and regions. Again, the principles shaping reality cannot be directly observed. Hence these must be thought out; subsequently an attempt may be made to grasp the way in which principles act in the real world. These intellectual processes are set into motion by real-world events that give rise to problems and consequently require an explanation, for example mass unemployment. The invisibility and the complexity of fundamental values and principles embodied in the real world is, incidentally, one of the main features of Keynes's vision (Fitzgibbons 1988; O'Donnell 1989).

Since the immensely complicated working mechanism of invisible values and principles cannot be directly observed, systematic thinking on these matters is required. Here visions about the objects of inquiry play an important role. This implies that scientific thinking can never be entirely free from ideology: science will always be alienated to some extent. Intellectual activities show up in scientific and moral institutions, which are part of the central layers of reality. Putting into practice systems of socio-economic and political thought in the course of historical time gives rise to a complex set of social and individualistic institutions. For example, liberal and socialist institutions have been set up in different forms in the last two centuries.

The acquisition of historical truth can be greatly enhanced, however, if real-world phenomena are hypothetically ordered according to their degrees of persistence (scheme 3, p. 106). This reflects a broad arrangement according to essentials. Moving from the upper layers to the lower ones implies penetrating into more and more essential spheres of the real world. To understand probably (in Keynes's sense) parts of the real world in terms of ever deeper causes means that truth becomes correspondingly more and more profound. More essential and hence 'more true' elements of material and spiritual reality are also ethically better and are aesthetically more satisfying. This shows up in the fact that societies tend to preserve those institutions considered to be appropriate, reasonable and natural, thus 'good' for the society in question; simultaneously, the individuals or groups of individuals who created these institutions are favourably remembered.

This is not to argue that defective or heavily alienated institutions, dictatorships for example, do not persist or that only great statesmen are favourably mentioned in history books. However, heavily alienated institutions cannot last for ever because they are not based on attempts to bring about justice and can, therefore, only be maintained by sheer force. Similarly, history books presenting tyrants as great statesmen are not based on the search for truth but on deliberate deception. Both force and deception are doomed sooner or later as historical experience shows. The fundamental reason is that heavily alienated institutions are in contradiction to human nature. A similar argument holds for the aesthetically satisfying, that is beautiful elements of the material and spiritual world: each society tries to preserve and to remember these elements of reality, be this in the spheres of architecture, painting, music or literature, in order to derive enjoyment from them in the present and in the future. All this is typically Aristotelian, and also Keynesian as emerges from Keynes's early work set forth and commented on by Fitzgibbons (1988) and O'Donnell (1989). Time and again, Keynes points to the fact that truth, goodness and justice, and beauty are not only the most fundamental, but also the most complex concepts as they relate to all spheres of the real world which together form an immensely complex whole.

To approach the natural, essential or unalienated in the various spheres of social and individual life takes time. In periods of rapid change the sense of the essential may even be temporarily lost.

Fourth, the phenomena of *social and cultural change* may be conveniently dealt with by the historical realism encompassing political economy. Here the historical process is conceived of as an interaction between socioeconomic systems and individuals and collectives acting within the system. On the one hand, systems determine, to some extent, actions of individuals and collectives, e.g. effective demand governs output and employment and sets restrictions on individuals; on the other hand, individuals and collectives shape the system through their pursuing individual and social aims. In the course of time, circumstances – the system – values and behaviour change. Hence historical realism comprises a theory of social change which is one of the important subject matters of sociology: 'From its beginnings sociology was closely connected with the philosophy of history and the interpretations of the rapid and violent changes in European societies in the eighteenth and nineteenth centuries' (Bottomore 1971, p. 283). As a rule social change goes along with cultural change and is associated with varying uses of the social surplus. Perhaps the most impressive theory of social change was established by Marx. In *Das Kapital* he emphasizes the deterministic influence exercised by the evolution of the socioeconomic system upon behaviour.

Technological, social and cultural change may be captured in principle by horizontal causalities (chapter 3, pp. 118–30). In the long run the driving force behind social and cultural change is changes in the value system. In some periods of time egoism and materialistic values dominate, in others social and cultural aims are more intensely pursued. Social and cultural changes are linked with changes in the use of the social surplus as emerges from the social process of production. Technological change continuously changes the *means* required to reach *given* aims. For example, the tremendous progress in the computer sciences has brought entirely new possibilities for storing personal data. This requires new legal means to protect individuals from state and other bureaucracies.

More specifically, two main factors bring about social change. First, progress in the natural sciences opens up new possibilities in the socioeconomic sphere. Partly, societies have to adapt to the new technological achievements, but partly the achievements may be integrated into an existing social situation. Second, there is the dissatisfaction of social groups with the existing situation, due to a discrepancy between an actually prevailing and a desired state of affairs: this is subjectively perceived alienation. Whether social change occurs at all depends on the distribution of power between conservative and progressive forces. In this context, the importance of the above-mentioned determinism exercised by the socioeconomic system should be borne in mind: if the system produces severe involuntary unemployment, change will be socially destructive in that poverty increases, for example. Social action may relieve some effects of poverty in the short term; the problem, however, consists in tackling the causes: for example, a very unequal income distribution may be the main cause of severe involuntary unemployment; hence parts of the socioeconomic system would have to be changed, i.e. distribution rendered more equitable in the case considered. This would require long-period institutional change related to the organization of society.

The organization of social and economic life was relatively easy in the basically agrarian societies preceding the Industrial Revolution. The very extensive division of labour initiated by the Industrial Revolution enormously increased the complexity of socioeconomic life. The necessity to understand economic events, which were now no longer immediately obvious, gave rise to a new art, political economy, which should provide the conceptual basis for governments to organize socioeconomic life in monetary production economies.

Hence history may be understood as an incessant struggle by individuals and collectives to do better in all spheres of life in ever evolving material conditions and in an ever alienated environment. In this, man is guided by fundamental ontological principles and by moral and aesthetic ideals which can be but imperfectly perceived, however. Nevertheless, aesthetic near-perfection was reached at times as is attested by the great achievements in architecture, sculpture, literature, painting and music which each society tries to preserve and to remember. In the political and social sphere, humanity seems, perhaps with a few limited exceptions, to have been less successful, and the possibility that self-amplifying alienation gets out of control will perhaps never vanish. However, the immense achievements in science and technology in the last two hundred years might provide the material preconditions for a happier life for all individuals. This is one of the main tenets of Keynes's vision (Fitzgibbons 1988, p. 53). But the social preconditions have to be created first: full employment and a fair distribution of incomes are essential (Keynes 1973a, p. 372). Population policies will almost certainly become increasingly important in the future. In this context, we ought to remember that Malthus and Ricardo conceived of an 'optimum' population size associated with the natural wage and the stationary state.

Given the imperfection of human knowledge and of the perception of moral standards, history cannot and will never be a clean story of linear progress. The central reason is that alienation is always present in some form which is another way of saying that historical development never was and never will be in a perfect 'common weal equilibrium'. Moreover, the alienated past will act upon the present to create new alienation: the attempt to repair past injustice by force may create new injustice; for example, people unjustly expelled from their homes may try to reconquer their land harming thereby the new inhabitants. Hence, the perpetuation of alienation in historical time implies that societies will never get into a comprehensive common weal equilibrium; this is analogous to economies which cannot get into a golden age equilibrium. Therefore, new problems and challenges ever arise and setbacks and even disasters, to be followed by periods of prosperity, seem inevitable. History seems to evolve cyclically around a broad trend of material and scientific advance. Progress is always relative however; for example technological advances may lead to setbacks or growing alienation in the social sphere: an excessive division of labour may lead to a disintegration of social life accompanied by excessive individualism and growing loneliness. Or, material affluence may negatively affect social and cultural standards.

Hence the great problems relate to the organization of society and consist of transforming potential economic growth into social and cultural progess. Political action in this field must be guided by two factors: first, knowledge of existing socioeconomic situations which has to be provided by political economy and, second, a vision of the ideal society to be elaborated by social or political ethics which leads one to specify ends to be pursued. The probable knowledge of actual situations and of ends puts the politician in a position to act in the most appropriate way possible.

Since the whole of society must be considered, such knowledge is likely to be of immense complexity and should partly result from an evaluation of the significance of historical socioeconomic facts and ideas. The problem is to learn from the past in order to be able to tackle present problems more appropriately. The study of history seems, therefore, indispensable at all levels of education, in the humanities in general and in the social sciences in particular. The study of history is also immensely fruitful because it provides information on the nature of society and of man: the individuals living in various societies strive after the same immutable values in very different situations. The point is to observe and to attempt to understand the widely differing ways by which social individuals have attempted to reach greater perfection in the various spheres of life and to ask why they have partly failed and partly succeeded at times. Here the global view of events, i.e. history in the grand style, *à la* Vico, Montesquieu, Hegel, Marx and Toynbee for example, is complementary to the study of the details. The object of the former is the evolution of societies seen as wholes, the latter investigates the behaviour in specific spheres of individuals and collectives within institutional systems. The study of history is therefore not *de l'art pour l'art* made useless by progress. It helps us understand the present in the light of the past and to make guesses at possible future evolutions. Galbraith puts this admirably when he says that '[t]he present is the future of the past' (Galbraith 1987). Perhaps the main reason why the study of history can promote the understanding of mankind and its destiny in the course of time is the presence of fixed reference points provided by fundamental values: 'Sensible men mutually understand each other over thousands of years on the basis of commonly shared fundamental values [for example truth, honesty, sense of duty and the common weal]' (Schack 1978, p. 18; a.tr.).

Methodological implications

The importance of the history of economic theory

When attempting to broadly classify economic theories, it is essential that the visions implied in the various approaches be brought out clearly. The underlying social philosophies (variants of liberalism, socialism and humanism, made up of historical realism and naturalism) would then appear. Social philosophies constitute the unifying basis of the social sciences (chapter 2, pp. 20–57) and, as such, permit us to put in perspective the close links existing between political economy and other social sciences (public law, social and political ethics, political science, sociology). Moreover, revealing the vision hidden behind the premises of theories would greatly clarify the discussions between social scientists (Myrdal 1976a; Baranzini and Scazzieri 1986).

Based on a broad classification of theories, the discussions between different schools could proceed in a spirit of tolerance and of mutual recognition of alternative conceptual starting points. This is not sufficient, however, since mutual respect may, sometimes, imply mutual ignorance. The study of alternative approaches, i.e. acquiring theoretical experience, is essential. Before the Second World War the majority of social scientists studied and respected Marx without blindly accepting all his opinions. Specifically, Marx's unequalled combination of theory and history, which is based on Aristotle and Hegel, was widely admired while his somewhat mechanistic views on the course and the final purpose of history were rightly rejected by most social scientists. Presently, even to mention theoretical precursors of Marx, Ricardo say, raises, in many instances, doubts about the intellectual sanity of an economist. However, social scientists who do not take the opinions of their theoretical opponents seriously hamper scientific progress and run the danger of stagnating within ever increasing formalism.

The attempt to gain deeper insights into the nature of economic theories will certainly lead to more work in the history of economic theory and of political economy, since the implications of theories can be understood better if their historical evolution is examined. To Maynard Keynes the study of the history of ideas, mainly the study of the great authors, meant *emancipation of the mind* since theoreticians and practical men would no longer be 'slaves of some defunct economist' (Keynes 1973a, p. 383).

In the history of economic thought the *locus classicus* is Schumpeter's great *History of Economic Analysis* (Schumpeter 1954). However, Edgar Salin states that Schumpeter's *History* is more of an encyclopedia of economic analysis rather than a history of political economy: '[Schumpeters *Geschichte* ist] eine Art von Lexikon der ökonomischen Analyse geworden . . . aber keine Geschichte der politischen Ökonomie' (Salin 1967, p. 196). Indeed, the *History* is too one-sided in that the Walrasian system and the associated individualism constitute the focal point in the development of economic theory and in that everything else is seen in terms of deviations from the Walrasian framework; consequently, society and political economy are neglected. According to Schumpeter, there is only one correct approach to economics, i.e. the (Walrasian) demand-and-supply framework, in terms of which each piece of theory is subsequently assessed. This leads Schumpeter to make rather strange statements, for instance: 'Ricardo was completely blind to the nature, and the logical place in economic theory, of the supply-and-demand apparatus and . . . he took it to represent a theory of value distinct from and opposed to his own. This reflects little credit on him as a theorist' (Schumpeter 1954, p. 601)! Consequently, no satisfactory explanation of the differences between Ricardian-Marxian political economy and neoclassical (Walrasian-Marshallian) economics can be found in his *History*. In order to enable this comparison, a more comprehensive framework of analysis, integrating the study of behaviour and of social structures, ought to be developed. For the philosophical and historical aspects of such a framework Salin's (1967) work might constitute an appropriate starting point, particularly his *Exkurs über die Wege der theoretischen Forschung* (Salin 1967, pp. 175–93). Salin is certainly right when he says that a comprehensive history of economic theory and political economy remains to be written: 'Eine umfassende Geschichte [der ökonomischen Theorie], die zugleich Staats-, Wirtschafts-, Sozial-, Ideen-, System- und Dogmengeschichte sein müsste, eine echte *Geschichte der Staatswissenschaften* also, ist noch zu schreiben' (Salin 1967, p. 196). Important steps in this direction have already been made. A few outstanding examples are Oncken (1902), Roll (1973 [1938]), Sweezy (1942), Heilbroner (1980 [1953]), Salin (1967), Dobb (1973), Bharadwaj (1986, 1989), Deane (1978, 1989), Galbraith (1987) and Screpanti and Zamagni (1993).

Regarding future work it might be fruitful to give special attention to the distinction between *economic science* and *the art of political economy* proposed by Phyllis Deane. The latter deals with the understanding of the functioning of social systems and with creating the social preconditions for individual action; the object of the former is the behaviour of individuals in the economic sphere, with social structures treated as given. The way of arguing in political economy is essentially organic: the system as a whole and the relationships between the whole and its parts must be considered. The method of economic science is mechanical: the interactions between individuals are co-ordinated by automatic mechanisms, most importantly the market.

The excessive variety of present economic theory combined with the domination of the neoclassical approach is largely due to the loss of historical perspective. The idea of *linear progress* successively established in European thought since the Renaissance and the Enlightenment led many social scientists to believe that the newest theories were normally the best ones. This implies grossly overestimating the possibilities of the human intellect: science is confidently expected to go on acquiring steadily more perfect knowledge. This seems to imply that the partial knowledge gained through the sciences can be put together without major problems so that a 'body of science' obtains.

This optimistic view of things overlooks the fact that, regarding approaches and principles, very little is really new in the social sciences. Modern theories frequently appear as adaptations and formal improvements of earlier conceptual frameworks. Moreover, the complexity of the real world implies that certain ultimate questions will ever remain unanswered, for instance the functioning of a specific monetary production economy or the ultimate purpose of history; therefore, knowledge will always remain probable in Keynes's sense. Most importantly, however, the significance of the various theories may change in the course of time: societies form immensely complex wholes governed by a variety of principles, for example the law of supply and demand or the principle of effective demand in the economic sphere. Which principles are considered of primary importance and which of secondary importance depends on the vision which in turn rests on a social philosophy. Visions heavily depend on the economic, social and political circumstances characterizing a given epoch and evolve in time as historical situations change. Hence presently dominant theories may become largely irrelevant tomorrow because of a change in vision: the surprisingly rich mercantilist and cameralist thinking on socioeconomic matters was replaced by the physiocratic and the classical schools. The latter was supplanted by liberal and socialist streams of thought. Mercantilist thought re-entered the scene in the course of the Keynesian revolution. Keynes's vision was, in turn, gradually pushed into the background by monetarist thought and was apparently ousted completely by the rational expectations school for some time: 'In the 1970s . . . the Keynesian paradigm was rejected by a great many academic economists, especially in the United States, in favour of what we now call new classical economics. By about 1980, it was hard to find an American academic macroeconomist under the age of 40 who professed to be a Keynesian. [However,] macroeconomics is already in the midst of another revolution which amounts to a return to Keynesianism' (Blinder 1988, p. 278; for an excellent survey on recent developments in economics, see Harcourt 1986, pp. 9–45). Finally, even at the moment when the neoclassical victory seemed complete, the tiny group of classical-Keynesians were, and still are, furbishing arms to fight current orthodoxy. Hence there is no linear progress. If there is some progress, it is circular and partial in the sense that a particular approach, e.g. the Ricardian one, is clarified and its implication brought out explicitly. Moreover, there is an incessant struggle to forge appropriate theoretical and applied frameworks in order to attempt to master the problems of the day. The basic problems of value, distribution, employment, inflation and their explanation, in principle, on the basis of various approaches, i.e. pure theories, remain, but historical circumstances change.

In this incessant search for the appropriate theoretical framework the history of economic theory provides us with valuable signposts, provided by the works of the great economists of the past. The neglecting these pointers means running the danger of getting lost in the dark owing to a lack of perspective: the important problems, and possible methods to tackle these, fall out of sight and explanation of facts may be replaced by sophistry, the result being confusion. To some extent this partly holds for the current intellectual scenery. There is, presently, an urgent need to get acquainted again on a large scale with the great systems of economic thought elaborated in the past. To study the great authors is extremely fruitful: a medieval philosopher believed the 'modern' thinkers of his time were dwarfs in comparison with some of the past giants. Nevertheless, he argued that the dwarfs are able to see farther than the giants simply because the former can climb on the shoulders of the latter. There is, indeed, no better way for an economist to become *comprehensively* acquainted with the crucial issues in economics and in political economy (value, distribution, employment, growth and development, money, international trade) and the ways of tackling these than by reading a great author or first-class secondary literature. This simple truth, still believed to be valid to some extent in the 1960s, was largely replaced by a strong belief in progress and the history of economic theory as a *compulsory* branch of study was gradually abolished in economics faculties. In the humanist perspective associated with historical realism this situation should definitely change since knowledge about the great authors of the past is *always* essential to the understanding of the great theoretical issues.

In addition to a better understanding of economic theory and of reality, deeper insights into the philosophical foundations of economic theories can be gained by an intensified study of the history of economic thought. For example, Recktenwald remarks, quite surprisingly, that with respect to the vision of society Aquinas is perhaps closest to Adam Smith (Smith 1978 [1776], translated by H.C. Recktenwald, introduction, p. LXXII). To establish such links is appropriate since both elaborated a comprehensive and realistic vision of man and society, although Aquinas's approach is essentially social and Smith's predominantly behavioural. This is exemplified by the notion of the common weal insisted upon by Aquinas and by the *two* main works written by Adam Smith, the *Theory of Moral Sentiments* and the *Wealth of Nations* which, together, form a greater and integrated whole (on this see Skinner 1979 and Kurz 1990). However, to establish links between Adam Smith and Aquinas is tantamount to going back to Aristotle, especially to his *Ethics* and *Politics* because of the very close links existing between Aquinas and Aristotle. This leads straightaway to the humanist social philosophy suggested in chapter 2.

A remark on ideologies

The study of alternative approaches to economic theory, i.e. *economics* and *political economy*, as have been developed in the course of time means *emancipation of the mind* (Keynes): it is a way to break out of entrenched modes of thought. There is indeed a constant danger that thinking gets too much institutionalized and thus follows well-trodden paths. This implies that the correctness of a certain approach is taken for granted and that the underlying premises are no longer questioned; this, in turn, implies narrowmindedness. Consequently, theorizing becomes mechanical and formalism increases. Hence theories may become isolated from the real world and may become instruments of pressure groups using them in order to promote particular interests. Such theories Marx called ideologies or alienated knowledge, for example in his *Paris Manuscripts* (Marx 1973 [1844]). The latter means that theories are no longer vehicles to increase knowledge but serve to justify particular interests. However, ideologies are perhaps most dangerous in the hands of well-intentioned and zealous but fundamentalist politicians who tend to apply them uncompromisingly. Perhaps the most important recent work on the problem of ideology is Maurice Dobb's *Theories of Value and Distribution since Adam Smith* which carries the significant subtitle 'Ideology and economic theory' (Dobb 1973).

Large parts of neoclassical economics and of the economic theory of socialism are ideologies *if* put to use without further qualification in a fundamentalist way. For two main reasons there is little danger of classical-Keynesian political economy, i.e. 'the humanist approach in political economy suggested in chapter 2, becoming an ideology. First, though clear-cut regarding principles, the classical-Keynesian framework seems flexible enough to be applied to very varied circumstances and to provide a framework for synthesis of widely diverging theories, including behavioural elements of neoclassical economics and some macroeconomic features of the economic theory of socialism. This is perhaps due to the fact that classical-Keynesianism considers societies as complex entities where each institution is important, including the market and some (indicative) planning devices: institutions are complementary in the humanist view. A second reason is based upon the theory of knowledge underlying the classical-Keynesian system (Keynes 1971c): knowledge of complex issues is always probable to a greater or less degree and knowledge itself is multidimensional comprising metaphysical and scientific elements, historical experience and empirical facts (chapter 2, pp. 20–75), and pure theory is merely a vehicle for acquiring probable knowledge. In this view knowledge on complex social matters is never definitive: seemingly unquestionable propositions must constantly be justified. Moreover, the theoretical and empirical arguments of opponents have to be taken seriously; for example, the neoclassical economist ought to study Marx and Keynes in depth in order to be able to evaluate his own conceptual starting point; conversely, no classical-Keynesian economist can ignore the great achievements of the founders of the neoclassical school regarding the analysis of behaviour and of behavioural outcomes. One of the main tenets of Keynes's theory of knowledge is that there are no realistic premises to start from. This requires openmindedness which is perhaps the most efficient weapon to combat ideologies.

Historical versus mathematical method

A stronger position of classical-Keynesian political economy within the social sciences would be beneficial to the teaching of economics: students would be more motivated since links between theory and historical reality can be easily established. On the basis of positive classical-Keynesian theory (pure causal models or ideal types) frameworks for empirical and historical investigations (applied models or real types) may be elaborated. These enable the social scientist to ask questions of highly practical interest. He may inquire into the nature of unemployment, the determinants of distribution, the formation of prices and the economic development of nations and regions; the effects of certain institutions upon economic events may be investigated and so on. The gap between theory and historical reality would be reduced, teaching would become easier and students would be attracted more strongly by a subject as exciting as political economy.

The isolation of economic theory within social and political theory in general was less pronounced in the nineteenth and early twentieth centuries when classical and Marxian economics, the German Historical School and American Institutionalism co-existed with neoclassical theory and its precursors. Presently economic theory seems to have lost touch with the historical and social sciences, however. Large parts of modern theory in fact resemble pure and applied physics. The use of sophisticated mathematical tools is widespread. Indeed, many neoclassical economists tend to formalize with great care equilibrium situations based upon the principle of exchange, and deviations from equilibria, which means generalizing to the utmost the principle of exchange. Instead of social relations, *relations between agents and things* (represented by utility and production functions and the optimizing behaviour of agents) are put to the fore. This leads to an individualistic and mechanical approach in economics. It is interesting to hear Walras on this: 'Il est à présent bien certain que l'économie politique est, comme l'astronomie, comme la mécanique, une science à la fois expérimentale et rationelle . . . l'économique mathématique prendra son rang à côté de l'astronomie et de la mécanique mathématiques; et, ce jour-là aussi, justice nous sera rendu' (Walras 1952 [1900], p. xx)! Moreover, in modern equilibrium models formal truth, i.e. the internal consistency of models, is given priority over probable logical truth proper, that is the approximate correspondence between models and essential features of reality.

The excessively mathematical and hence axiomatic character of parts of economic theory associated with a widening gap between models and reality repels the political economists and attracts the mathematicians, and the explanation of real-world phenomena is left to historians, lawyers, sociologists and political scientists. Keynes, himself a trained mathematician, is extremely severe with mathematical economics:

It is a great fault of symbolic pseudo-mathematical methods of formalising a system of economic analysis . . . that they expressly assume strict independence between the factors involved and lose all their cogency and authority if this hypothesis is disallowed; whereas, in ordinary discourse, where we are not blindly manipulating but know all the time what we are doing and what the words mean, we can keep 'at the back of our heads' the necessary reserves and qualifications and the adjustments which we shall have to make later on, in a way in which we cannot keep complicated partial differentials 'at the back' of several pages of algebra which assume that they all vanish. Too large a proportion of recent 'mathematical' economics are merely concoctions, as imprecise as the initial assumptions they rest on, which allow the author to lose sight of the complexities and interdependencies of the real world in a maze of pretentious and unhelpful symbols (Keynes 1973a, pp. 297–8; see also Fitzgibbons 1988, pp. 138–43, and O'Donnell 1989, pp. 183–207).

Mathematical methods cannot be used to picture *real-world* events in their full *organic* complexity, e.g. the socioeconomic system: 'my point is that [neoclassical theory] is not incomplete in the sense that it deals with the special rather than the general case. I maintain that as a theory it applies to no [real world] case at all' (Keynes 1973b, p. 593). However, '[t]he dogmatic extremes of total hostility to the use of mathematics on the one hand, and the zealous attempt to mathematise everything on the other, were alien to his [Keynes's] position . . . For Keynes mathematics had definite roles to play in both economic theory and econometrics, but these roles were limited' (O'Donnell 1989, p. 204). While mathematical models cannot deal with properties of the social system they can capture well-defined aspects of human behaviour.

'Marshall [too] was a brilliant mathematician [but became very sceptical about the use of mathematical methods later in his life]' (Kaldor 1985a, pp. 58–9). This is not surprising since, as quoted above, the 'Mecca of the economist does not lie in mechanics, but in biology' (Marshall 1920, p. xiv). In the social sciences the *qualitative* elements reflecting part–whole relationships are of primary importance. This is particularly true of distributional problems associated with the notion of distributive justice; or the very complex interplay of institutions implied in the right-hand side of the supermultiplier relation cannot be reduced to a formula since the 'independent variables' are interdependent in specific ways in each particular situation considered. We might say that the aim of the natural sciences is to *explain* and that the social sciences aim at *understanding* historically grown and unique situations. This may go along with a *tentative explanation* of the facts in question with the help of explanatory frameworks (real types).

To be sure, there are quantitative aspects in the social sciences in general and in economics in particular which justify the moderate use of mathematical techniques including diagrams. However, the economic and social meaning of analysis must always be immediately evident so as to enable the social scientist to understand at any moment the significance of the conclusions arrived at. For example, Pasinetti (1977) is quite mathematical. Yet it helps us to grasp the significance of the social process of production (commodities are produced by commodities and labour). Starting from this, the significance of prices and the nature of distribution can be brought out. However, Pasinetti (1977) is only a first step to understanding these problems: it prepares the way for Pasinetti (1981, 1993) which are much less mathematical and where the meaning of economic phenomena is set out in such a way as to be accessible to the layman. Pasinetti (1977, 1981, 1993) do not fully explain the economic aspects of the real world. These works tell us something about the hidden structure of selected aspects of reality, i.e. how production, long-period pricing and distribution are regulated *in principle*. Once the principles, which are probable reflections of the *essence* of things, are broadly understood one may go on to acquire a deeper understanding of the respective facts: applied frameworks may be elaborated and put to use.

A similar reasoning applies to econometrics and statistics. If these techniques are put to work reasonably, mainly in relation to micro- and meso-economic problems dealing with the behaviour of individuals in various spheres, important results may be produced. The estimation of Engel curves, or of demand and supply curves, is a prominent example. Moreover, nobody will deny that mathematical techniques, developed within the field of operations research (linear programming, for instance), have contributed to solving many real-world problems that allow a clear-cut specification. Transport problems, stock-keeping and organizational problems are but a few outstanding examples. The understanding of selected macro-economic problems may also be furthered by econometric methods. For example, the relation between consumption and national income may certainly be more fully understood through the estimation of consumption functions. Simple causal relations *à la* Hermann Wold may thus be estimated without difficulty as has been argued by Pasinetti (Pasinetti 1964/65, pp. 242–3). Empirical estimations of simple causal relations exhibiting close correlations are not yet proofs of the existence of corresponding causal forces in the real world. These are but signposts indicating that the researcher is possibly on the right track.

However, mathematical and econometric techniques are bound to fail if applied in an unconsidered way to complex socioeconomic facts especially if related to the functioning of an economy as a whole, e.g. the determination of employment levels. For example, to estimate the supermultiplier relation would be of little use since there are too many causal relations interacting in an immensely complicated way. Moreover, each theoretical and empirical statement, however elaborate, represents *probable* knowledge only which may be interpreted differently according to the vision held. For example, the close correlation between the 'quantity of money' and the 'price level' is interpreted in entirely different ways by monetarists and classical-Keynesians. The former argue that the quantity of money determines prices, the latter claim that price rises are the result of a distributional conflict and that the 'quantity of money' adjusts to the higher price level. All this is broadly in line with Keynes's critique of econometrics (Fitzgibbons 1988, pp. 154–8; O'Donnell 1989, chapter 9): if an organically complex socioeconomic state of affairs is considered there are no realistic premises nor dependent and independent variables.

Mathematical techniques are *formal* methods suited to deal with specific aspects of reality from an individualistic point of view. The principal aim of the mathematical economist is to *generalize* on the basis of a single principle, i.e. exchange. It should be borne in mind, however, that more generalization implies, as a rule, more formalism and less content. This is the essence of reductionism. The historically minded social scientist, however, aims at understanding and explaining complex and *unique* historical situations (e.g. the crisis of the thirties) which are brought about by a great many causes, i.e. principles. This implies that in historical theories the *content* of an argument is put to the fore and formal aspects have to adjust. Since societies are complex wholes which are something more than the sum of their parts and possess their own laws, the historical economist must properly appreciate the importance of non-economic facts; these may directly influence economic outcomes in an interrelated system.

The art of political economy and economic science

The complexity of the object historically minded political economists are faced with points to the very high level of standards imposed on them. Nobody, perhaps, has defined the 'ideal' political economist more appropriately than Keynes himself:

He must reach a high standard in several different directions and must combine talents not often found together. He must be mathematician, historian, statesman, philosopher – to some degree. He must understand symbols and speak in words. He must contemplate the particular in terms of the general, and touch abstract and concrete in the same flight of thought. He must study the present in the light of the past for the purpose of the future. No part of man's nature or his institutions must lie outside his regard. He must be purposeful and disinterested in a simultaneous mood; as aloof and incorruptible as an artist, yet sometimes as near the earth as a politician (Keynes 1972a, pp. 173–4).

This statement suggests that political economy, pure and applied as well as positive and normative, is an art rather than a science, a point put to the fore more recently by Phyllis Deane (1991); in the former the qualitative element dominates, in the latter a quantitative. The central reason is that the socioeconomic and political system steered by a hierarchy of values is of organic complexity with intricate part–whole relationships dominant (chapter 2, pp. 20–57). Therefore, relationships between parts and wholes must constantly be held in view when conducting an argument. For example, when discussing the relationship between the educational system and the export performance in a particular country the functioning of the society in question and its external relations constantly enter the picture. Normative political economy is an art because the problem is to improve the functioning of the social system, i.e. to create more harmony between its elements, to reduce antagonisms and thus alienation (chapters 2 and 6).

This does not mean that there are no scientific spheres in the social sciences. Pure theory, i.e. the examination of principles in political economy and in economics, is certainly scientific, although not in the narrow positivistic sense. Moreover, the *systematic study of behaviour* within a given institutional system *is* scientific. Incidentally, this proposition reflects the basic tenet of methodological individualism. The behaviour of individuals is partly dependent on objectively given permanent factors, i.e. institutions, that may be independent from each other *regarding their influence upon individuals*, but are interrelated in their roles as parts of the socioeconomic system. The science of economics might thus be defined, as is usual, as the study of the rational and optimizing or other behaviour in the economic domain; the co-ordination function of the market gives rise to behavioural subsystems and to comprehensive systems which are the object of partial and general equilibrium economics respectively. The methods of economic science may be applied to behaviour in other spheres. This gives rise to sciences like the economic theory of politics, of the arts and of crime, the new economic history and the new institutionalism.

The art of political economy and the science of economics are not opposed to each other but complementary and interrelated. The object of the former is the socioeconomic and political system as an entity, i.e. institutions and their interplay. The latter deals with economic behaviour and its co-ordination by the market and the production system respectively. The complementarity between political economy and economic science might open perspectives for synthesizing classical-Keynesian political economy with parts of neoclassical economics.

Ideally, the art of political economy ought to culminate in actions of the state that are in the public interest; this proposition leads to establishing some connection between this subsection and chapter 6. From the positive classical-Keynesian system of political economy set forth in the preceding chapters and the normative system sketched above it emerges that the state must, in co-operation with the relevant parts of the civil society, trade unions and entrepreneurial associations for example, intervene in important areas of economic life. It is the principal task of politics, which includes political economy, to co-ordinate social activities so as to establish as much harmony as possible within the social structure. This is to create the best possible social preconditions for individuals to prosper, and means striving for the public interest or the common weal. This aim may only be approximated, with greater or less perfection; a lack of knowledge about the positive and the ideal state of society and egoistic particular interests are perhaps the main obstacles to a better society: it will never be possible to eliminate system-caused alienation entirely (chapter 2, pp. 20–57). The long-period policy means consist of the setting up, or favouring the establishment, of socially appropriate institutions.

At the outset of his *Wealth of Nations* Adam Smith argued that the basic aim of political economy was to enhance the productive powers of a socioeconomic system to increase the surplus at society's disposal. Political economists, like James Steuart, Karl Marx and, particularly, Friedrich List (1920 [1841]) argued along similar lines. Modern writers continuing this line of thought are, on the theoretical level, Luigi Pasinetti (1977, 1981, 1993) and, on the conceptual and applied level, Maynard Keynes. The view that the economy ought to provide the material means to reach cultural ends – in the widest sense of the term – has been taken over from this tradition and is embodied in the preceding pages of this book: the economy ought to stand in the service of society and of the individuals composing it. Socially useful technical progress allows a society to reach two basic aims: a higher surplus, permitting a wider range of political, social and cultural activities, or a reduction of working time. This is equivalent to promoting *public welfare* which might be defined as a state of affairs in which the individuals composing a society are in a position to realize to the largest possible extent those (ethically good) fundamental values they ought to aim at in the various spheres of life (chapter 2, pp. 39–53). The notion of public interest, public welfare or common weal is, in fact, the classical-Keynesian counterpart to the liberal (neoclassical) Pareto optimum. In the latter, individual utility maximization spontaneously yields social welfare, in the former the notion of *a higher-order social harmony* is crucial; man and society are considered to be entities whose parts have to be mutually compatible: the activities of individuals have to be harmoniously arranged in line with dispositions and abilities to promote the well-being of individuals. Similarly, the socioeconomic, political and cultural institutions of a society must be in appropriate proportions if the public welfare is to be approximated. This strand of thinking on individual and social affairs was initiated by Aristotle in his *Nicomachean Ethics* (regarding the individual) and in his *Politics* (regarding society), pursued by many classical economists and taken up in this century mainly by Maynard Keynes, as emerges from Fitzgibbons (1988) and O'Donnell (1989).

Hence, to define the public welfare as social harmony enabling individuals to prosper implies that political economy is an art, not a science – a proposition established by Keynes and taken up by Nicholas Kaldor and Phyllis Deane (see especially Deane 1991). The central problem of political economy is to establish socially appropriate institutions and proportions within the socioeconomic sphere in line with the political and cultural sphere. This emerges from the supermultiplier relation and from the input–output cum vertical integration framework set forth by Pasinetti (1977, 1981, 1993): the variables and parameters appearing in the supermultiplier (government expenditures, exports, the terms of trade and the import coefficient, income distribution, e.g. the target mark-up, consumption and investment) have to be compatible with full employment. This implies preserving, creating and/or favouring the coming into being of socially appropriate institutions. Once the aggregate demand components are given, technology embodied in the social process of production and consumption habits govern the sectoral and industrial structure, e.g. the fully adjusted situation pictured by Pasinetti (1981, part I).

Political economy as the art of regulating proportions or of establishing appropriate relationships between parts of society and society as a whole was practised systematically for the first time by François Quesnay in his *tableau économique*. He should therefore be considered the founder of political economy. The tradition initiated by Quesnay contrasts with the neoclassical vision of things. Here, economics is considered as a science: economic phenomena are explained mechanically on the basis of the behaviour of individuals. Apparently, this point was first elaborated systematically by Carl Menger (Menger 1969 [1883], book III, chapter 2). Given the different object of investigation, the art of political economy and economic science are largely complementary.

Hence the art of political economy consists in permanently guiding the particular interests such as to promote the public interest. This can perhaps be illustrated best by the problem of income distribution. If distribution (reflected in the wage structure and in the division of national income between wage and property income) is too equal, labour productivity may diminish and the surplus shrink; if particular interests manage to impose a distributional outcome which is very unequal from a social point of view, speculative activities may set in and involuntary unemployment may result, as is evident from the supermultiplier relation.

From these brief remarks on the art of political economy the immense complexity of policy-making in general and of socioeconomic policies in particular emerges. True policy, i.e. policy promoting the public interest, requires knowledge in various broad fields (political economy, law, sociology, history), and a vision of society in general, based upon a social philosophy. The latter permits the co-ordination in an orderly way of partial knowledge obtained from the social sciences.

Hence political economy in the traditional and the modern classical-Keynesian sense is an art because the socially appropriate proportions between the various spheres of social and individual life do not obtain spontaneously, but must be designed. A well-proportioned society, i.e. a harmonious institutional set-up, cannot be brought about by technocratic organization aimed at influencing the behaviour of individuals. A very extensive knowledge about the functioning of the socioeconomic system as a whole and power of persuasion are both required. This is, basically, the argument set forth in Keynes's *End of Laissez-Faire* (Keynes 1972b).

Society and the state on humanist lines

This section deals with two selected issues concerning society and the state which are closely associated with the overall argument set out in the present study. Initially, we consider a fundamental social problem, i.e. development and change. Subsequently, some suggestions about the state along humanist lines are made.

Development and change

Ideology and economic development

The process of development may be broadly conceived as a transition from a traditional to a modern industrialized society. This process is decisively shaped by the development policies pursued. The latter are founded upon development theories which rest on a broader vision of how societies and economies evolve in principle. The previously mentioned ideological elements may in turn influence the vision of the development process. If such elements predominate, an ideological bias may distort theories of economic development. Marx would have called this alienated knowledge. As a consequence, development policies and actual development processes may also become alienated, i.e. proceed along undesirable lines.

A hallmark of strongly ideologically based theories is their being immune to real-world events. An equilibrium economist can, even in the midst of a heavy depression, assert that there would be less unemployment if imperfections obstructing the proper functioning of markets were removed, or if no policy mistakes had been made in the past. Starting from real-world immunity a strange phenomenon, i.e. *fundamentalism*, may develop: the *belief* in an ideologically based theory seems to become stronger the more the real-world situation moves away from what is predicted by theory. The deepening cleavage between theory and reality is explained by some outside event (oil price shocks, for example) or by wrong economic policies pursued in the past. The latter shows up in a particularly striking way in the formerly socialist countries: the currently worsening economic situation is said to be *entirely* caused by the socialist past, and social scientists now argue that considerable suffering will be required in order to arrive safely in the liberal haven. Consciousness about problems that might be associated with the functioning of capitalist economies seems to be largely lacking. All this points to the almost religious character of liberal and socialist fundamentalism: both are matters of belief.

If economic policies are pursued on the basis of ideologically based theories, grave hardship may result. For instance, many monetarist experiments carried out in recent years in economically advanced and underdeveloped countries have resulted in severe unemployment and in a more unequal distribution of incomes and wealth; in the latter the situation has, in many instances, been aggravated by the very severe austerity policies imposed by international monetary institutions (see, for example, Chossudovsky 1991). The silent socioeconomic catastrophes going on in many poor countries where, without appropriate preparation, market experiments are performed are distressing to any sensible human being.

This also holds for the formerly socialist countries. Conversely, there is no need to describe the disastrous effects of despotic socialism linked with a rigid bureaucracy. This goes along with the catastrophic results of fundamentalist socialist experiments in many Third and Fourth World countries.

Given the failure of many fundamentalist liberal and socialist experiments in various underdeveloped and more advanced countries, the question of the relevance of the humanist classical-Keynesian theory of social and economic development arises. Because of the great variety of historically developed socioeconomic and political situations all over the world, a *general* classical-Keynesian (real-type) theory of economic development cannot be worked out; only a few principles may be set forth. Each country, even each region, has its own specific institutional set-up which is linked with a particular system of values; there is also a specific social structure and a particular interaction of institutions.

The development problem consists of initiating appropriate institutional changes which will result in a modernization of the apparatus of production and in higher labour productivity. However, those parts of the historical heritage which are required for the stability of a society and its future development should be preserved. Subsequently, the heritage of the past should be appropriately combined with the new institutions needed to bring about economic development, for example an education system adapted to an industrializing society and the creation of an entrepreneurial class. These immensely complex processes can only be set in motion if there is no uncontrolled dependence on the vagaries of the world market. This is suggested by the role of foreign trade in the determination of economic activity described in chapter 4 (pp. 190–9) and the policy actions required in consequence (chapter 6, pp. 326–43).

Two additional issues are associated with the problem of structural change and the problem of the scale of employment respectively. The theoretical framework set forth by Pasinetti (1981, 1993) attempts to capture how the continuous structural change regarding methods of production and the types of goods and services produced goes on *in principle* in growing economies. The structure of employment and the nature of work also change. More labour is needed in industry and in the service sector, less labour is employed in agriculture. This requires high agricultural productivity growth to render possible the transfer of labour from agriculture to other sectors. These very complex processes were first systematically described in book III of the *Wealth of Nations* where Adam Smith discusses the interaction of industry and agriculture in the process of economic development. Any structural change is, as a rule, associated with great human hardship. Traditional, homely ways of life have to be given up, frequently for an uncertain future. This goes along with a further great problem faced by many economically less developed countries: the cleavage between the material basis and the institutional superstructure that may arise in the development process. In some cases the very fast change in the forces of production does not allow the relations of production and the political and cultural superstructure to adjust; in other cases the institutional superstructure is 'modernized' while the material basis largely remains traditional. The latter is very likely to result in a heavy import dependence on the developed parts of the world.

The scale of employment deserves particular attention in a classical-Keynesian theory of economic development. In traditional economies with a relatively simple structure of production economic activity is, as a broad rule, governed by supply factors. However, in modern monetary production economies with extensive division of labour, effective demand governs the scale of output and employment. The latter depends on a set of predetermined variables and parameters which are governed by institutions regulating income distribution, consumption, the volume of investment, the activities of the state and the foreign balance position (the supermultiplier relation); in any period of time, there is a specific institutional set-up compatible with full employment. The institutional change occurring in the process of economic development may now lead to social structures not compatible with full employment. For example, income distribution may become very unequal and produce a lack of effective demand. This implies limited markets and hence few profitable investment possibilities. The latter may be associated with low rates of productivity growth. Consequently, wages are low which, in turn, influences labour productivity negatively. Moreover, the scale of activity may be negatively influenced by an excessive dependence on outside forces, for instance the vagaries of world markets; this may lead to a chronic lack of foreign exchange. In these circumstances it may prove extremely difficult to maintain a high level of employment in the process of economic development since profound institutional changes may act negatively on the level of economic activity.

Because of its links with a changing social structure the process of economic development is immensely complex. Social change is, in turn, very difficult to steer since the social structure forms an interconnected entity governed by an evolving system of values. Therefore, to be able to formulate a coherent policy of economic development for some country or region requires an intimate knowledge of the historically developed initial socioeconomic and political situation and the tendencies of change at work; moreover, the fundamental principles of political economy have to be taken account of. Only economists commanding vast theoretical and practical experience combined with a profound knowledge of a specific situation are in a position to set up comprehensive and consistent programmes of economic development. It is difficult to see how this could be done by experts coming from capitalist or socialist countries, above all if experience and familiarity with some specific situation is lacking. This is not to deny that outside advice on specific projects may be precious if this is properly inserted into a comprehensive development programme already in place.

To 'import' strategies for socioeconomic development is difficult since the institutional set-up and the interaction of institutions form a very complex entity. Institutions are specific and complementary. Therefore, it may be very difficult, in some cases even impossible, to transfer institutions specific to one civilization to regions having completely different cultural backgrounds. In this view the simple fact of enlarging the market sector in a traditional society becomes an extremely complex process that can only be initiated and guided by people having a broad historical and theoretical background and possibly a vast experience in political matters regarding the society in question.

Classical-Keynesian development theory implies that 'development is a process coming from inside' (Schumpeter 1912): social (institutional) change must originate from forces at work inside a society; one cannot buy development by realizing isolated projects carried out by people not familiar with the domestic situation. Striking examples of project failures are provided by the great number of white elephants set up in various underdeveloped countries. Whenever institutions and technology have to be imported these must be adapted to domestic circumstances. The way of life – associated with a specific hierarchy of values – prevailing in a particular underdeveloped country must be respected and only gradually adapted to the changing material basis in order to prevent large-scale alienation.

Moreover, the people and the leaders of the developing countries must initiate and carry on the process of development largely by themselves. This can be achieved only if the élites of the developing countries really work in the interest of their countries and are not too much dependent, culturally and politically, on outside influences. Finally, the countries of the Third and Fourth Worlds must become conscious again of their own values, in many instances of their great historical past and of their immense cultural achievements, and lay aside the inferiority complex towards Western civilization, which, though impressive on a technical and scientific level, is presently faced with serious social and cultural problems. This does not mean that cultural, social and political relations with other countries should not be established if these are likely to be beneficial to overall development; but exchanges in these spheres must be on an equal footing.

In the process of economic development, top priority must be given to securing full employment and an equitable income distribution, not only

for economic but also for social reasons. The transformation of a traditional society into a monetary production economy with extensive division
of labour is always accompanied by a social transformation. Traditional
social entities, the family and the village, lose part of their social significance. An important part of social life is displaced into the economic
sphere – that is the enterprise, the sector of production and the process of
production; moreover, as is in line with the surplus principle, economic
activity provides the material basis for the higher social, political and cultural activities. Therefore, to be involuntarily unemployed not only means
exclusion from economic life but from social life altogether; a two-class
society may thus emerge, those who are included in the social system and
those who are excluded. This means profound distress even if unemployment benefits are temporarily paid. Moreover, involuntary unemployment
increases poverty and income inequality which, in turn, acts negatively on
employment as is evident from the supermultiplier relation. There is no
need to give examples of the destructive social and political consequences
of mass unemployment associated with an unfair distribution of income.
History speaks for itself.

Last but not least, full employment and an equitable income distribution
are, together with education, indispensable preconditions for more effective
population policies which are very much required at present: excessive
population growth menaces socioeconomic development and threatens the
natural environment in vast areas of the underdeveloped world. Ricardo's
and Malthus's notion of a *natural wage rate* at which population remains
constant is not a fancy (see, for instance, Ricardo 1951 [1821], pp. 93ff.).

Social change

One of the main purposes of institutions is to preserve a given
state of affairs. Institutions are brought into existence by individuals or
groups to enable the persistent pursuit of individual and social aims. This
kind of causal force is associated with the notions of final causality linked
up with the pursuit of aims (chapter 2, pp. 53–7) and of vertical causality
(chapter 3, pp. 120–1). Horizontal causality (chapter 3, pp. 122–3),
however, is related to social and institutional change. For example, past
efforts to improve the educational system of a society may lead to an
improvement of export performance and to higher levels of employment.
Or, severe unemployment, due to a past deterioration of income and wealth
distribution, may further impair the social and political situation.

Social change implies that a given – traditional – society is gradually
transformed into a new – modern – society. This implies a *qualitative* transformation in social organization which is accompanied by *quantitative*
changes (in this context Marx argued that the former brought about the

latter which need not be the case in general). For example, specific institutions like the common ownership of land, the production of use values and personal dependencies are characteristic of feudal societies. Quantitative changes, the extension of private property, the production of exchange values (for the market) and formal personal liberties, went along with the – qualitative – transformation of feudal into capitalist societies. This process may go on gradually, as in England, or abruptly, as was the case with France.

In principle, social change occurs in two ways. First, social change is brought about by deliberate institutional change (reforms in some social sphere). As a rule, reforms are initiated if there is some kind of alienation (chapter 2, pp. 39–53), i.e. a discrepancy between a given situation and some desired (normative) situation, that becomes politically relevant. Whether action is effectively undertaken depends on power relations in the widest sense of the phrase, wherein the dominant positive and normative economic theory is only one important factor. Experience shows that it may be very difficult to initiate substantial social and institutional change because the forces tending to preserve given situations may be very strong, due to 'the normative power of the existing' (die normative Kraft des Faktischen). Depending on the situation, this may be an element of socially beneficial stability or an obstacle to progress. Second, social change may come about almost deterministically through exogenous factors and through the poor functioning of the social system (this is the efficient cause, mentioned in chapter 2, pp. 53–7). Perhaps the most important exogenous factors initiating social change are evolutions of the value system and technical change. The poor functioning of a socioeconomic system may result in an undesirable social evolution, i.e. a self-amplifying increase in alienation may come into existence; for example, a slackening export performance and a growing inequality in income distribution may lead to rising unemployment which, in turn, produces increasing poverty and slums; the latter may act negatively on the initial causes, i.e. exports and distribution. Efficient causes linked with the functioning of the social system may also work in the reverse direction to result in a steadily improving situation. How this works in principle may be roughly understood with the help of the supermultiplier relation set out in chapter 4 (pp. 149–204).

To understand social change, whether brought about by deliberate action or deterministically through the social system, classical-Keynesian political economy must necessarily cross the boundaries of other social sciences, i.e. law, sociology and the political sciences. The principal reason is that the economic, social, political and legal spheres are not merely domains in which individuals become active; the institutions located in these spheres are complementary and form an entity, i.e. society. This implies that social, political and legal institutions are not just a framework, as is the case of neoclassical theory, but may directly influence the outcome of economic events, income distribution and the scale of employment for example. The necessity to understand approximately the functioning of the entire social system to explain social change follows then from the fact that this system forms a structured entity; this was the central tenet of the German Historical School and of American Institutionalism.

From a normative point of view the purpose of social change should be to eliminate alienation as far as is possible for imperfect human beings; or, social reform should aim at establishing as much harmony within society as is feasible. Alienation has been defined as the gap existing between some given situation and an ideal or natural state of affairs in which the public interest or the common weal would be realized (chapter 2, pp. 39–53). Since the notion of alienation essentially relates to system-caused alienation, of which involuntary unemployment is the main component, purposeful social change aimed at reducing alienation must be system policy: in principle, the problem consists in attempting to set up an institutional system corresponding as closely as possible to the nature – the mentality – of the citizens composing a state. This is the problem of politics in the Aristotelian sense.

Two specific issues concerning social change should be mentioned here. First, alienation is not eliminated deterministically in the course of history as Hegel and Marx suggested. Constant efforts are required to improve the organization of society and to maintain what has been achieved. The main reason is that various forces constantly upset social situations existing at some moment of time. Changes in technology and the evolution of value systems are perhaps most important. These alterations result in social change. New situations implying new kinds of alienation continuously come into being; this requires specific social policies. Moreover, the excessive pursuit of particular interests in the economic sphere constantly results in a tendency towards a more unequal distribution of incomes and wealth; involuntary and structural unemployment persistently threaten the normal functioning of societies. Thus incomes and employment policies are permanently required. Finally, alienation will never be eliminated, simply because of a lack of knowledge on the functioning of complex social systems.

Second, if changes go on too quickly it may be very difficult to pursue consistent social policies aimed at a reduction of alienation. Social situations may get out of control mainly because distribution gets more and more unequal and involuntary and structural unemployment increases. As a consequence, people get uprooted because of forced migration, the fight for survival between individuals and social classes intensifies, and particular interests increasingly dominate the scene at the cost of policies in the public interest. In such circumstances, public order may eventually be restored by a strong government but at the cost of immense human suffering. More than sixty years ago Keynes severely criticized the very rapid socioeconomic transformation in the Soviet Union: 'it is of the nature of economic processes to be rooted in time. A rapid transition will involve so much pure destruction of wealth that the new state of affairs will be, at first, far worse than the old, and the grand experiment will be discredited' (Keynes 1982, p. 245). It would seem that this statement also applies to the massive socioeconomic changes set in motion by the creation of huge common markets. Distribution and the employment problems could eventually get out of control (Bortis 1992).

Too rapid social and economic change is so pernicious for societies because of the social disorganization it brings about, for example structural unemployment linked up with a professional and geographical transfer of labour. Since economies are not self-stabilizing this may create almost insuperable organizational problems. Even in a static society it is exceedingly difficult to improve the social organization in the sense that alienation is reduced or the common weal furthered. It takes time to find out what is appropriate or natural for the citizens making up a society. This is all the more true if a society is complex and diverse. The difficulty of the task of the politician emerges in relation to distribution and employment policies if self-regulating markets cannot be relied upon (chapter 6). In a monetary production economy the problem is to create or to encourage the coming into being of an institutional set-up implying full employment and a socially acceptable distribution of income.

Hence institutional change has to go on slowly to realize true social progress. To render possible a slow and secure institutional change requires, besides a profound knowledge of the country-specific situation, a solid positive and normative socioeconomic theory to analyse correctly the initial situation, to fix the aims to be reached and to determine the path of social evolution. In the light of the overall argument advanced in this book it would seem that classical-Keynesian political economy is far better suited to meet these requirements than neoclassical economics or the economic theory of centrally planned socialism.

Some suggestions on the state

Universalism is a hallmark of liberal and socialist doctrine: both ultimately imply a weak state with an undefined territorial extent. This is evident for liberalism. Marx's *Early Writings* imply that the state would vanish in mature socialism, i.e. communism (see, for example, Marx 1973 [1844], pp. 533–46, specifically p. 536). According to the liberal doctrine, the role of the state essentially consists in setting up a legal framework, i.e. a system of private law to partly regulate relations between individuals. Socialism basically requires a system of public law determining the relations between various collectives and society (chapter 2, pp. 27–39).

Based upon the notion of universality, the idea of a liberal or a socialist world republic was advanced at times. It is an irony of history that the realization of both doctrines was frequently linked up with strong governments and was accompanied by outbursts of nationalism. In centrally planned socialism, governments were so strong that nationalist movements could easily be crushed; consequently, its breakdown immediately led to a rise in nationalism. The capitalist era – capitalism is the realization of liberalism – was also predominantly nationalist: colonialism and imperialism in the nineteenth century and two world wars in the twentieth century were intimately linked up with capitalism. It has only been during the unprecedented upswing following the Second World War that nationalism has receded somewhat, presumably because the struggle for new markets tends to be less intensive in times of prosperity. The main economic reason for 'liberal nationalism' is that – capitalist – free-market economies do not produce a tendency towards full employment. Consequently foreign trade becomes a weapon for securing jobs by means of the external employment mechanism set out in chapter 4 (pp. 190–9); the nation-state and the capitalist economy spontaneously tend to collaborate to secure a prominent position on world markets. Capitalism also produced deep depressions accompanied by social disorder. In some instances, this resulted in highly nationalistic and strong 'law-and-order' or even totalitarian governments. The twenties and the thirties are a case in point.

The following suggestions on the state in a humanist perspective link up with the fundamentals of political philosophy dealt with in chapter 2 (pp. 20–57) and the various and complex problems related to a monetary production economy alluded to in chapters 4–6. These considerations imply that *each polity is a structured, historically grown entity which is unique since it is characterized by a particular institutional set-up reflecting a specific way of life and by a clearly bounded territory.* On the level of the principles of political economy, this crucial point is put to the fore by Pasinetti who argues that his natural system

contains an important explanation of why each economic system is necessarily bounded; and, therefore, indirectly, of the fragmentation of the world into a multiplicity of economic systems . . . the source of the explanation is to be found in [the] macroeconomic . . . condition for economically significant equilibrium solutions [which] concerns and connects the entire economic system to which it refers. Hence it makes of it a unitary entity, and at the same time separates it from all other economic systems (Pasinetti 1993, p. 148).

Hence, on a fundamental level, each polity is a unity because of the existence of *genuinely social* phenomena, like the social process of production or distribution, giving rise to part–whole relationships.

Hence the humanist view of the state rejects universalism, which implies that the main task of the state is to partly regulate the relations between individuals and collectives, and postulates instead that the polity must be bounded because intricate part–whole relationships have to be dealt with in connection with distributive justice in the widest sense of the term – for example, a socially acceptable distribution of incomes, elimination of involuntary unemployment, regional policies and social policies regarding ethnic, linguistic and religious groups.

In the humanist perspective, the state in general and the government in particular are moral institutions which ought to act in the public interest in order to approach the common weal as closely as possible. This is the fundamental aim to be pursued by the state. It implies creating the social preconditions such that individuals are in a position to unfold their physical and intellectual potential as extensively as is humanly possible. Among the socioeconomic preconditions, full employment and a socially acceptable distribution of wealth and incomes are, in a Keynesian vein, most important: '[The Keynesian doctrine] can easily be made to say both that "who tries to save destroys real capital" and that, *via* saving, "the unequal distribution of income is the ultimate cause of unemployment." *This* is what the Keynesian Revolution amounts to' (Schumpeter 1946, p. 517).

The fundamental aim of the state should be pursued in a way that minimizes the size of the state, particularly the central or federal state. This implies putting to use two complementary principles of social ethics regulating the relations between society and individuals, i.e. the principles of subsidiarity and solidarity. According to the principle of *subsidiarity* the state should not intervene whenever problems can be solved by social institutions or by individuals, which implies that the federal state should not intervene if the states or the regions can solve problems on their own. Hence the principle of subsidiarity ensures that social and individual rights and hence the scope of freedom are as extensive as possible. The principle of *solidarity* deals with the social preconditions required for the prospering of individuals within society, for example the education system and the social security system, but also a socially acceptable income distribution and full employment. The principle of solidarity requires state intervention in the economic domain, mainly because the market mechanism is not capable of solving the great economic problems, i.e. long-period value, distribution and employment. The proper application of the principles of subsidiarity and solidarity requires a solid theoretical foundation which is to be provided by classical-Keynesian political economy.

Some of the fundamental issues related to applying the principles of subsidiarity and solidarity can perhaps be posed best in terms of two interrelated and, sometimes, conflicting aims: *distributive justice* and the *social potential*, both taken in the widest possible sense. Distributive justice is about the ethically appropriate proportions between individuals and social entities regarding social status, which encompasses material and immaterial elements. The social status may, for example, relate to income, wealth, social and political power, and honour. The social potential is associated with the scale of individual and social activities which may, for example, be cultural, economic or military. The value system prevailing in a specific epoch will govern the weight to be given to the various activities and to the way distribution is regulated. Distributive justice is closely related to the distribution of the social surplus, the social potential to the size of the surplus, which, in turn, depends upon technology, the intensity of work and upon the territorial and demographic size of a polity.

In the following, some issues related to distributive justice are dealt with first. Subsequently, a few considerations of the implications of the social potential are made. Both points prepare the terrain for discussing the question of the constitution in line with the basic aim of the state.

Distributive justice deals, then, with the relationship between parts (individuals and collectives) and the whole of society. This gives rise to a variety of genuinely *social* problems: the regulation of personal and functional income distribution, i.e. the wages structure and the shares of wages, profits and rents in national income; the maintenance of full employment and of price stability; the distribution of political power between central and local authorities; the social and political position of the various regions and of linguistic, religious and ethnic groups within society; the extent and the role of non-profit organizations; and the elaboration of a system of public law which regulates part of the relations between individuals and collectives and society as a whole, i.e. the relationships between individuals of differing status and society. The latter is a precondition to setting up a system of private law which regulates the relationship between equal individuals. All these very complex problems are associated with the organization of society and the state. The organization of a society becomes more complicated the greater the size and the variety of the polity, for example if a polity is composed of a great number of ethnic and religious groups. Two very important corollaries follow from this proposition. First, the complexity of the policy problem (chapter 6) does not imply that a society ought to be uniform to facilitate its organization: diversity of various kinds is highly desirable since a richer social and cultural life may obtain. A large and diversified political entity may be rendered governable through an appropriate division of power between central or federal, regional and local government; this issue will be taken up later on. Second, to render possible the pursuit of consistent policies within the state territory requires, on the one hand, a broad social consensus encompassing the *whole* of the population, specifically minorities, as to the social organization and to the way of life to be pursued, and, on the other hand, the same rights and duties for all citizens. Hence the fundamental elements of a polity are the territory, the social consensus and equality. The linguistic, ethnic and religious composition of the population is the result of a historical process and must be taken as given. This humanist view of the state is intimately associated with the principles of tolerance and freedom.

The complexity of the policy issues associated with distributive justice would seem to require relatively small political entities. However, the *social potential* of a society is intimately linked up with the size of the social surplus (chapter 4, pp. 154–89) and hence with the territorial and demographic size of a polity. In a large polity there will be more scope for division of labour and accordingly for establishing a strong economic basis, and the social surplus will be potentially larger. Provided the government acts in the public interest a large social surplus enhances the social potential of a political unity: a diversified set of political, legal, social and cultural institutions may be built up. Hence a large polity may potentially become more socially diversified and culturally richer. Moreover, the large polity will be less dependent on abroad: a certain degree of autarky is politically desirable (chapter 6, pp. 326–43).

However, in a relatively large state the complex problems associated with distributive justice may tend to get out of hand and particular interests may increasingly dominate political life. The use of the social surplus may be perverted in that parts of the surplus may be used to practise power politics, and resources may be devoted to excessively enriching particular social groups. Or, even worse, aggressive foreign policies may be practised to defend so-called vital interests which are likely to coincide with the interests of the dominating pressure groups. All this may be summarized by 'alienation in the political sphere'.

The socially appropriate *constitution* is the basic means of reaching the fundamental aim of the state, i.e. to approach the common weal as closely as is humanly possible. This aim gives rise to extremely intricate issues of social organization: society is organically complex because of the complementarity of the various institutions structured by a hierarchy of values. In a humanist view, automatic mechanisms – markets or voting procedures – cannot, in the *long* run, co-ordinate particular interests in a socially appropriate way, i.e. such that a tendency towards the common weal obtains. On the level of principles, this proposition follows from the outcome of the capital-theory debate (chapter 5, pp. 281–93) and from

Condorcet contradictions associated with voting procedures (Arrow 1951). Practical politics requires a conceptual underpinning based upon visions and theories of the functioning of society as a whole and of the basic social aims to be achieved. Given the immense complexity of the policy task, both finding out and putting into practice the basic policy principles cannot possibly be a matter of voting procedures.

Hence it is likely that Schumpeter's competition for power and hence for government between various political parties (Schumpeter 1942, part IV) does not work properly for two central reasons. First, parliamentary democracy implies governing on the basis of an eventual compromise between particular interests and not necessarily in the public interest. In times of prosperity democracy may seemingly function smoothly, although real power may be exercised by an economic or social élite. Problems arise with economic and social unrest because there are no automatic mechanisms to restore equilibrium. If the situation gets out of control, democracy may dialectically change into dictatorship as the experience of the 1930s shows. Hence the 'free' play of particular interests may prove destructive. Second, in a régime of parliamentary democracy the effort to stay in power, i.e. to get re-elected, is, in many instances, more demanding than exercising power, i.e. to govern. To stay in power uses more of the physical and intellectual energies of the members of parliament and of the government than governing itself. This is not appropriate since the immense complexity of the policy problem requires a full concentration of forces on the business of government. Moreover, in a parliamentary democracy there is the constant danger that the government does not really act in the public interest but favours some "partial" or "party" interests.

State activities should, essentially, consist of long-period policies aimed at bringing about a socially appropriate institutional framework. The problem is to create a social or institutional foundation such that individuals may prosper. To be able consistently to pursue long-period policies, the government and the administration should not be subject to the vagaries of periodic re-elections. Both must permanently concentrate on government affairs, in collaboration with the social and political sciences which have to deliver the policy conceptions and under the control of the parliament, i.e. the representatives of the people.

In the humanist perspective the common weal is more than the sum of the particular interests in that it encompasses the social foundations or the institutional set-up within which behaviour takes place and particular interests are pursued. The central problem of politics is to create and to favour the coming into being of socially appropriate institutions such that the ethically ideal proportions (as are in line with the common weal) between the various institutions are approximated as closely as possible. In the humanist view of society, politics is about social ethics and is as such independent of individual behaviour and of particular interests. Therefore *the state must stand above the particular interests* to be able to fulfil the fundamental policy task. Hence the fundamental constitutional problem is to bring into power an impartial government which is independent of the various particular interests.

Historically, the institution of monarchy is certainly the most ambitious attempt to solve this constitutional problem. This institution was in many instances successful, above all in very diverse and complex political entities. However, historical experience also shows that constitutions based upon a single principle, for instance monarchy, are threatened by decay or tend to degenerate, the main reason perhaps being the institutionalized dominance of particular interests that may gradually develop if power is not checked and controlled. The conflicts arising between strong interest groups may prove destructive to a polity. It would seem, therefore, that the old principle of the *mixed constitution*, associated with the names of Polybius and Cicero (Fetscher and Münkler 1985–93, vol. I, pp. 512ff.), is best suited to ground stable political organizations of the humanist type, mainly because division of power combined with control of political and judicial institutions is rendered possible. In pre-modern times the mixed constitution would have been realized as a combination of the institutions of monarchy, aristocracy and democracy to which, in the modern era, broadly correspond the President and his government, the Civil Service and Parliament, which through the political parties, is inevitably linked up with particular interests. In the humanist view, the executive institutions ought, in principle, to act in the public interest to promote the common weal and ought to be independent of particular interests. Therefore the Executive must stand above Parliament and the political parties. On the practical level, this would imply that *legislation* ought to be a matter of the Executive; this would be in line with the fundamental task of the government which consists of creating or favouring the coming into being of socially desirable institutions. The task of Parliament would be to supervise and to control government activities. Hence the people, through its parliamentary representatives, would assess governmental activity and thus react against socially inappropriate policy actions of the government. The controlling power of Parliament would also extend to the Judiciary which must of course be independent of the government, i.e. the Legislature and the Executive. The exercise of control by Parliament constitutes the essence of modern democracy in a humanist view. This is in line with Keynes's opinion on this issue: 'there is no right to universal suffrage, and . . . the people only have right to *good* [our emphasis], but not necessarily representative government' (Fitzgibbons 1988, p. 170).

The mode of election of the President is a crucial element in a constitution along humanist lines. It would seem that universal elections do not guarantee the appointment of an impartial President since the political parties, financial and economic pressure groups and the mass media may decisively influence the outcome of an election in favour of some interest group. Moreover, given the complexity of the policy problem, most citizens lack the ability and the information required to appraise the political fitness of presidential candidates, i.e. their capacity to govern in the public interest. To decide on this matter requires a profound knowledge of theoretical and practical politics, and the careful selection of the electors is evidently of the utmost importance. These ought to be outstanding and generally recognized personalities, independent of particular interest groups and belonging to all spheres of society, minorities of all kinds included. In this sense the electors' assembly, the Senate say, ought to consist of experienced persons familiar with political matters. To guarantee continuity and to minimize the struggle for power, the members of the Senate and the President ought to be elected for long time-periods, possibly even for life. This would enable the Executive to govern in the public interest without particular interests interfering.

The mode of election of the Senate is another issue of crucial importance. The problem is to produce a Senate which stands above the particular interests. One could imagine that one-third of the Senate be elected by Parliament, i.e. the representatives of the people, one-third by the government and the civil service and one-third by the scientific communities (universities and learned societies). Besides electing the President, the Senate might supervise the whole political and judicial sphere in collaboration with the social and political scientists, which role might include the possibility of impeaching the President should he obviously fail in his task. The dominant position of the Senate would reflect the old Platonian ideal according to which the best and the wisest ought to govern or to supervise the government.

Given the complexity of the problems related to the organization of society, it seems desirable that a polity should not be too large to allow for a socially acceptable solution of the issues associated with distributive justice. This is perhaps the main reason why the Greek theory of the state (Plato and Aristotle) considered the small city-state the ideal polity. Two main issues are associated with relatively large and/or diversified states. First, the various issues linked up with distributive justice may perhaps be given less and less consideration and political activities may tend to be increasingly dominated by particular interests. This implies that public law is gradually eclipsed by private law. The dominance of private law was almost total in the Roman empire where it dominated even the political sphere (see, for example, Oncken 1902, pp. 57–9). However, if the various problems associated with distributive justice mentioned before are not given sufficient attention, the existence of the polity may become threatened or a very strong government may be required to maintain it. This leads to a second point associated with relatively large and diversified states. Such states would seem to require relatively strong governments in order to secure the public interest. In terms of the notion of the mixed constitution mentioned above this would mean strengthening the presidency and the civil service at the expense of the democratic institutions which are associated with particular interests. In the extreme this may lead to dictatorships and even tyrannies, especially in times of economic and social crisis.

However, large polities do and must exist and solutions have to be found to render them governable in a socially acceptable way. The existence of large and diversified political entities is required for two main reasons. The first is associated with ethnic, linguistic and religious diversity which, *per se*, is highly desirable. Such polities result, as a rule, from long historical processes and ought to be maintained in order to prevent conflicts between the different population groups or even civil wars. Such wars may be enhanced by foreign interference, and they tend to continue since it may be impossible to draw mutually recognized frontiers. Second, large political entities may also be required to secure the balance of power on the regional or on the world level. The disintegration of a polity always creates a political vacuum leading to conflicts between the remaining powers eager to strengthen their international position.

To render large polities governable an appropriately structured *vertical* division of power between central (or federal), state, regional and local government may be required. This particular type of division of power ought to be based upon the principle of subsidiarity: the higher-level authorities should not do what the lower-level governments or social institutions, for example non-profit organizations, can do. The most important economic problems, employment and distribution for example, ought to be solved on the state or regional level. This would require regional currencies in order to enable states or regions to pursue a full-employment policy. The federal state would mainly exercise co-ordinating activities. Such issues have been sketched in chapter 6.

Alienation in the relations between states mainly occurs if frontiers are not mutually recognized. A great number of international conflicts were (and are) due to boundary issues. The existence of secure and mutually recognized frontiers is a most precious result of history and should not be considered unimportant as is frequently done by the universalist liberal and socialist political scientists. In a humanist view secure boundaries are the basis of mutually beneficial relations in all spheres – economic, social and cultural – between states, especially neighbouring states. This also holds for the satisfactory solution of the great social problems associated with distributive justice *within* countries, which is an essential condition for a fruitful co-operation in all domains *between* states along the lines suggested in chapter 6 (pp. 326–43). Heavy involuntary unemployment and the subsequent mercantilist struggle for markets and jobs never furthered the cause of peace.

Ways ahead

In this section some threads of thought hinted at in preceding chapters are taken up to point to the direction to move in. The starting point is provided by the wider significance of the classical-Keynesian middle way which, negatively formulated, is associated with the fact that the normative systems of liberalism and of socialism seem conceptually too weak to carry the policy conceptions required for immensely complex monetary production economies. Strictly liberal economic and social policies may lead to unacceptable differences in incomes and wealth between individuals and nations and to the periodic occurrence of involuntary mass unemployment. Centrally planned socialism, on the other hand, is associated with bureaucratic despotism and low labour productivity with respect to the quantity and the quality of the goods produced; moreover, a rigid socialist system is not able to transform inventions into innovations on a sufficiently large scale.

In this study it has been suggested that the humanist approach in the social sciences should be given more weight: classical-Keynesian political economy would furnish the principles to explain socioeconomic phenomena in specific countries and regions on the basis of historical developments. This would constitute social or historical realism in the sense of Lloyd (1986). Subsequently, policy principles could be formulated along the lines suggested in chapter 6.

It may be asked whether a broad consensus on *principles*, i.e. about *pure* explanatory and normative theories and the policy principles ensuing therefrom can be reached. In a Keynesian *Treatise on Probability* vein, an approximate agreement may be achieved on this issue if the argument is comprehensive in the sense that a global view of things is taken, i.e. that a vision is developed on the basis of historical, scientific and metaphysical elements as has been attempted in the preceding pages. Hence it should be possible to decide whether the liberal, the socialist or the classical-Keynesian and humanist principles are the most appropriate basis for explanation and for policy action. However, it has to be emphasized that it may be exceedingly difficult, if not impossible, to bring about even a broad consensus at the level of *real-type* models addressed to complex issues, for example the causes of the First World War or the Great Depression of the thirties.

Currently, most societies are run according to liberal or, until recently, socialist principles. Either there is too much individualism and ruthless competition or there has been too much collectivism and central planning. In societies organized along humanist lines the *principle of co-operation* between individuals and groups would be given increased emphasis. This is linked up with the nature of the social: social situations arise from complementarities and from the imperfection of individuals, both of which require co-operation. This principle has two dimensions: on the one hand, society and the state provide the social basis for individual behaviour; on the other hand, individuals become more perfect through performing social activities.

Co-operation is required in various spheres. In the process of production, enterprises or associations of enterprises have to co-operate in order to ensure the proper delivery of intermediate goods. Similarly, enterprises may co-operate with respect to research and development. Conventions regulating market shares and aimed at fixing fair prices are other forms of co-operation between enterprises. Moreover, there have to be agreements between entrepreneurs, the trade unions and the state regarding work conditions and the preservation of the environment. Trade unions have to co-operate with entrepreneurs to fix the share of wages in national income; they also have to care about the socially appropriate wage structure. Hence, co-operation is also required with respect to *distribution*, which, ideally, ought to be the outcome of a social consensus between workers, managers and private or public owners. As a general rule, certain activities related to *production and exchange* must be institutionalized because 'production takes time' (Paul Davidson). Producers would never engage in production if there was complete uncertainty about the future. Institutional arrangements create areas of near-certainty which enable entrepreneurs to produce under reasonably tranquil conditions and to introduce new techniques of production. This, in turn, requires a close co-operation between banks and enterprises since it is impossible perfectly to synchronize outgoings and income over time. Or, there ought to be some co-operation between civil society and the state regarding the use of parts of the social surplus, e.g. investment and state consumption.

In a humanist view, the principle of co-operation is not only basic within a country or a region but also between countries and regions. The co-operation between states and societies will be all the more beneficial the better the great socioeconomic problems, mainly the employment problem, have been solved within the individual countries. This is implied in chapters 4 (pp. 190–9) and 6 (pp. 326–43). Once again, the great social problems cannot be tackled on the basis of ever larger – and ungovernable – economic and political entities as are presently fashionable in regions where liberalism dominates.

Several areas of co-operation relate to international trade relations. First, the principle of broad foreign trade management, specifically regarding non-necessities, must be mutually accepted so as to enable each individual country or region to achieve full employment (chapters 4, pp. 190–9, and 6, pp. 326–43); this is required since there is no mechanism ensuring an automatic tendency towards full employment on the regional, national or world level. Second, international co-operation is required in order to maximize the welfare effect of international trade based upon the principle of comparative advantage. This is bound to lead to an extensive international division of labour, giving rise to mutual dependence of countries in the sphere of production. Third, the proper delivery of goods required in the process of production (necessary imports) from one country to another must be ensured by a network of contracts in order to avoid disruptions of production in particular countries. A fourth domain of international co-operation is money and finance, mainly the management of a world currency to be set up eventually, i.e. Keynes's 'bancor' (chapter 6, pp. 338–9). However, the most important sphere of co-operation is certainly the natural environment. Effective action in this field seems possible only if a world economic order along classical-Keynesian lines is implemented (chapter 6, pp. 319–48). Firms would no longer have to face elimination from the market and individual countries would no longer have to fear the loss of jobs when taking steps to protect the environment because full employment could be maintained by a socially appropriate management of foreign trade. The present struggle for survival on world markets does not leave much scope for really serious environmental policies.

The principle of co-operation also implies a strengthening of the vast range of social activities lying in between individual and state activities, i.e. civil society in general and the non-profit sector in particular: 'in many cases the ideal size for the unit of control and organisation lies somewhere between the individual and the modern State' (Keynes 1972b, p. 288). Hence the state should not intervene in matters that can be solved by individuals and collectives; for example, trade unions and entrepreneurial associations may solve the problem of distribution to a large extent, and the state should only intervene if agreements cannot be reached; or various non-profit organizations in the economic, social and cultural spheres may autonomously solve specific problems. This amounts to applying the principle of subsidiarity: 'We must aim at separating those services which are *technically social* from those which are *technically individual* . . . The important thing for government is not to do things which individuals are doing already, and to do them a little better or a little worse; but to do those things which . . . are not done at all' (Keynes 1972b, p. 291). This task would be simplified considerably if there were a self-regulating mechanism in the economic sphere as is postulated by the liberals. However, important economic phenomena, mainly persistent involuntary unemployment, cannot be reduced to the behaviour of individuals but result from the functioning of the socioeconomic system:

Many of the greatest evils of our time are the fruits of risk, uncertainty, and ignorance. It is because particular individuals, fortunate in situation or in abilities, are able to take advantage of uncertainty and ignorance, and also because for the same reason big business is often a lottery, that great inequalities of wealth and income come about; and these same factors are also the cause of unemployment of labour, or the disappointment of reasonable business expectations, and of the impairment of efficiency and production. Yet the cure lies outside the operations of individuals (Keynes 1972b, p. 291).

Therefore, '[our] problem is to work out a social organisation which shall be as efficient as possible without offending our notions of a satisfactory way of life' (p. 294).

In the liberal view the task of organizing society is, in principle, relatively simple: the primary problem is to partly regulate the behaviour between individuals and collectives in various domains, e.g. economic and social; this amounts to setting up a framework of private law (chapter 2, pp. 21–7). The solution of the great economic problems is subsequently confined to a self-regulating mechanism, i.e. the market. On the political level this implies that there is no upper size to political entities in the liberal doctrine (see the preceding section). Liberalism, like socialism, is universalist. The attempts to create ever larger free trade areas are an example of the universalist tendencies of liberalism. However, in a humanist perspective the historically grown independent and sovereign state defined by its territory (territorial state) forms a moral entity: the social and political organization ought to be conducive to promoting the public interest. As such the state is the primary *locus* for political action. The central problem is to regulate the relationship between individuals and collectives on the one hand and society on the other (chapter 2, pp. 21–7), which, in legal terms, is covered by the domain of public law and, in terms of political philosophy, by the principle of solidarity. In a humanist view the primary problem is the organization of society by the means of public law and of social customs and habits. The partial regulation of relationships between individuals and collectives through private law is a secondary task to be tackled once the social foundations have been laid. Distribution is a relationship between parts (individuals and collectives) and the social whole (society); this has been insisted upon in chapters 4 (pp. 154–89) and 6 (pp. 309–10). Employment is also a social problem implying part–whole issues (chapter 4, pp. 142–204). Employment and distribution constitute perhaps the most important domains for applying the principle of solidarity. Other social problems would be the relationship between regions and the social and political position of linguistic and religious groups and of socioeconomic classes. The organization of the way of life, comprising, for instance, the length of work time, the leisure activities to be pursued and the content of social and cultural life, is a very complex social problem. Here the state should minimize its interventions as is required by the principle of subsidiarity.

All this is not to say that the principles of individualism, and of planning, are no longer required. The purpose of a social organization along humanist lines is precisely to leave the widest possible scope for individual freedom. On the other hand, some planning may be required with respect to the use of land, the preservation of the environment and the maintenance of full employment, above all in widely open economies: the market and the plan are means to be used to organize societies, not basic principles regulating them.

Last but not least, co-operation should be practised more intensely by social scientists in general and by economic theorists in particular. As a first step, mutual understanding between rival groups ought to be promoted by clarifying the nature of their respective approaches: this is to reveal the social philosophies underlying the premises of theories. On this basis, co-operation may develop. Specifically, many analytical techniques relating to the optimizing behaviour of individuals and collectives developed by neoclassical economists can be integrated into a classical-Keynesian framework without difficulty. For instance, the concept of marginal costs might be used to explain short-run supply behaviour if full utilization of productive capacities is approached; or, optimization techniques might be required to select techniques of production or consumption plans (examples of fruitful scientific co-operation between neoclassical and classical-Keynesians are Baranzini 1991 and Scazzieri 1993).

In a wider view, the classical-Keynesians would investigate how the socioeconomic system works to partly determine the actions of individuals (chapter 4). The determining effect of the system shows up in restrictions set on the number of jobs available in an economy. The neoclassicals – including the 'new institutionalists', the 'new economic historians' and the economic theorists of various domains (for example the legal, political, social and cultural domains) – would deal with the behaviour of individuals within given structures, that is within the system or the restrictions set by the system.

The principle of co-operation also implies that economists ought to work together on the basis of the historical heritage. The aim would be to form syntheses between similar theories and to establish links between different approaches:

in political economy the theory which explains value by utility . . . has so fascinated by no means the worst sort of economists, that they have almost forgotten, or at least degraded, the older and in some respects more important theory which connects value with sacrifice and labour. There is even a danger that, as we press on to seize new conceptions, we should lose the positions which have been already won. *Hence the history of theory is particularly instructive in political economy* (Edgeworth, quoted in Salin 1967, p. 197).

Hegel makes the same point when he deals with *Aufhebung*: the *synthesis* preserves the *thesis* and the *anti-thesis* and puts them into a wider perspective.

Edgeworth puts *political economy* on the same footing as *economics*. In the present study, however, these two concepts have been distinguished (chapter 3, pp. 76–8). Neoclassical theory is termed *economics* and the classical-Keynesian framework *political economy*. Economics focuses upon the study of the behaviour of economic agents within a given institutional set-up, i.e. a given social structure, of which markets and their organization are parts. Classical-Keynesian political economy, however, deals with the functioning of the institutional set-up, i.e. the socioeconomic and political structure or the system as a whole, and with the deterministic effects exercised by the system upon the behaviour of individuals (chapter 4).

While the principle of co-operation is crucial in modern societies embodying immensely complex monetary production economies, it ought to be remembered that this principle must be complemented by the principle of *co-ordination*. The absence of automatic stabilizers in the sphere of production, value, distribution and employment requires considerable state intervention to promote the public interest (see the preceding section and chapters 4 and 6). In any case, extensive co-operation is possible only if distribution is socially accepted and if full employment prevails in the sense that there is no involuntary unemployment. Massive involuntary unemployment produces a struggle for survival and is as such a source of mistrust and conflict.

To conclude the considerations taken up in this study it seems appropriate to turn to a famous distinction made by Aristotle which, subsequently, proved to be of immense importance. Aristotle spoke of two meanings of economics. Economics in a wider sense, political economy to wit, is called *oikonomike* and economics in a narrower sense is termed *chrematistike* (*Politics*, 1256b and 1257a). *Oikonomike* deals with the art of providing a community (a family, a city, a country) with the necessaries of life. This broadly corresponds to the definition of *political economy* by James Steuart (1966 [1767], pp. 16–17), the Physiocrats, the classical economists, and by the classical-Keynesians. The central problem is the determination of the size, the distribution and the use of the social surplus. Economics in the narrow sense, *chrematistike*, is the art of 'money-making or wealth accumulation', that is making more money out of a given sum of money. Marx took up this Aristotelian device to characterize the essence of 'capital'. Presumably, Keynes would have associated *chrematistike* with 'destabilizing speculation' (Fitzgibbons 1988, p. 91, n. 1).

Neoclassical economists would claim that, under competitive conditions, *chrematistike* is the fundamental means of realizing *oikonomike*. This broadly corresponds to a simplified version of Adam Smith's 'invisible hand': egoistic behaviour in the economic sphere leads to a favourable social outcome. Financial capitalism, if associated with large-scale speculation, is equivalent to pure *chrematistike*; socialism corresponds to a pure form of *oikonomike*. Classical-Keynesian political economy, however, sees moderate *chrematistike*, or *socially appropriate behaviour* in the economic domain, as *one* of the means to achieve *oikonomike*: some competition associated with egoism of the individual enterprises and the possibility of realizing socially acceptable profits – such that the profit share is in line with the full-employment requirement – is indispensable to bringing about increased material well-being. However, the latter should not be an end in itself, but a means to achieve social, political and cultural aims. In Aristotelian terms the economy has to provide the material basis which renders possible 'a good and decent life of the citizens'. On the behavioural level this broadly corresponds to the view held by Adam Smith, if account is taken of the *Wealth of Nations and* of the *Moral Sentiments*, and almost exactly to the physiocratic-classical view and to Keynes's vision set forth by Fitzgibbons (1988) and O'Donnell (1989). The economy is subordinate to the other spheres of individual and social life.

Oikonomike comprises

that species of acquisition . . . only which[,] according to nature[, are] part of the economy . . . and which are useful as well for the state as the family. And true riches seem to consist in these; and the acquisition of those possessions which are necessary for a happy life is not infinite . . . for the instruments of no art whatsoever are infinite, either in their number or their magnitude; but riches are a number of instruments in domestic and civil economy (Aristotle, *Politics* 1256b).

Thus the quantity of goods required for a good and decent life of the citizens is *limited*. However, '[there] is also another species of acquisition which they particularly call pecuniary, and with great propriety; and by this indeed it seems that there are no bounds to riches and wealth' (Aristotle, *Politics*, 1257a). The latter is the key feature of *chrematistike* which, if pushed to the extreme, may heavily damage or even destroy the institutional set-up associated with and underlying production (*oikonomike*). This is also Marx's and Keynes's view.

Capitalism, especially financial capitalism, was and still is associated with unbounded accumulation of real and financial wealth: real capital, money, shares and bonds and other stores of value, land and old masters, for example. Material well-being and the economy are overrated compared to other spheres of individual and social life and are seen as ends in themselves. Oncken and Salin interpret this as a reaction of modern hedonism against the asceticism of the Middle Ages (Oncken 1902; Salin 1967). However, Salin goes on to say, that the economy, overrated in the era of capitalism, will take on its ancillary role again in the future: '[Es könnte sein,] dass . . . die Wirtschaft, überbeachtet und überbewertet von den Menschen der kapitalistischen Zeit, vergessen wieder in ihre dienende Rolle herabsinken werde' (Salin 1967, p. 172). This would be in line with humanist classical-Keynesian political economy where the economy stands in the service of society and of the individuals composing it and not the other way round as seems to be implied in modern liberal economics and in capitalist reality. To emphasize the ancillary role of the economy within society is not to argue that the art of political economy is unimportant. *Political economy* aims at understanding how monetary production economies function and is as such the key social science of the modern era, while the most important and all-encompassing social science remains *politics* in the Aristotelian sense.

A glance at the current state of the world economy would seem to suggest that the chrematistic feature of capitalism, characterized by the conquest of markets by all means and by financial speculation on a huge scale, has reached its limits. Could it be that the present age of unlimited accumulation is coming to an end and that an era of *oikonomike*, of political economy, is about to begin? In view of the immense socioeconomic and ecological problems worldwide and given the justified aspiration of the poor countries for a higher level of material well-being, less chrematistics and more political economy could prove a historical necessity.

References

Amos, S. (1883). *The Science of Politics.* London: Kegan Paul, Trench & Co.

Aristote. *La Métaphysique,* ed. J. Tricot, 2 vols. Paris: J. Vrin, 1986.

Aristoteles. *Nikomachische Ethik.* Cologne: Deutscher Taschenbuch Verlag, 1986. *Politik.* Cologne: Deutscher Taschenbuch Verlag, 1984.

Aristotle. *Politics – A Treatise on Government,* trans. W. Ellis, ed. E. Rhys. London and Toronto: Dent, 1912.

Arrow, K. J. (1951). *Social Choice and Individual Values.* New York: Wiley.

Asimakopulos, A. (1983). The role of the short period, in Kregel (ed.), pp. 28–34.

Backhouse, R. (1985). *A History of Modern Economics.* Oxford: Blackwell.

Baran, P. A. (1973). *The Political Economy of Growth,* with an introduction by R. B. Sutcliffe. Harmondsworth: Penguin; 1st edn. 1957.

Baranzini, M. (1987). Distribution theories: Keynesian, in *The New Palgrave Dictionary,* ed. J. Eatwell, M. Milgate and P. Newman, 4 vols. London: Macmillan, vol. I, pp. 876–8.

(1991). *A Theory of Wealth Distribution and Accumulation.* Oxford: Clarendon Press.

Baranzini, M. and R. Scazzieri (1986), eds. *Foundations of Economics: Structures of Inquiry and Economic Theory.* Oxford: Basil Blackwell.

(1990), eds. *The Economic Theory of Structure and Change.* Cambridge University Press.

Barrère, A. (1991). *L'enjeu des changements: Exigences actuelles d'une éthique économique et sociale.* Toulouse: Editions Erès.

Barro, R. (1984). *Macroeconomics.* New York: Wiley.

Bharadwaj, K. (1983). On effective demand: certain recent critiques, in Kregel (ed.), pp. 3–27.

(1986). *Classical Political Economy and Rise to Dominance of Supply and Demand Theories,* 2nd rev. edn. London and Madras: Sangam Books and Universities Press, India. First published in 1976 as R. C. Dutt Lectures on Political Economy by Centre for Studies in the Social Sciences, Calcutta.

(1989). *Themes in Value and Distribution: Classical Theory Reappraised.* London: Unwin Hyman.

Bharadwaj, K. and B. Schefold (1990), eds. *Essays on Piero Sraffa: Critical Perspectives on the Revival of Classical Theory.* London: Unwin Hyman.

Blinder, A. S. (1988). The fall and rise of Keynesian economics, *Economic Record* 64: 278–94.

Bliss, C. J. (1975). *Capital Theory and the Distribution of Income*. Amsterdam: North Holland.

Böhm-Bawerk, E. v. (1914). Macht oder ökonomisches Gesetz?, *Zeitschrift für Volkswirtschaft, Sozialpolitik und Verwaltung* 23: 205–71.

Bortis, H. (1978). Die 'Renaissance' klassischer Ideen in der theoretischen Volkswirtschaftslehre, in P. Caroni, B. Dafflon and G. Enderle (eds.), *Nur Oekonomie ist keine Oekonomie* (*Festschrift* for B. M. Biucchi). Berne: Haupt, pp. 49–78.

—— (1979). *Foreign Resources and Economic Development from the Early Fifties to the Oil Crisis*. Fribourg University Press.

—— (1984). Employment in a capitalist economy, *Journal of Post Keynesian Economics* 6: 590–604.

—— (1990). Structure and change within the circular theory of production, in Baranzini and Scazzieri (eds.), pp. 64–92.

—— (1992). *EWR und EG: Irrwege in der Gestaltung Europas*. Fribourg University Press.

—— (1993a). Reflections on the significance of the labour theory of value in Pasinetti's natural system, in M. Baranzini and G. C. Harcourt (eds.), *The Dynamics of the Wealth of Nations: Growth, Distribution and Structural Change. Essays in Honour of Luigi Pasinetti*. London: Macmillan, pp. 351–83.

—— (1993b). Notes on the Cambridge equation, *Journal of Post Keynesian Economics* 16: 105–26.

Bottomore, T. B. (1971). *Sociology: A Guide to Problems and Literature*, 2nd edn. London: Allen & Unwin.

Branson, W. (1972). *Macroeconomic Theory and Policy*. New York: Harper & Row.

Brown, A. (1986). *Modern Political Philosophy: Theories of the Just Society*. London: Penguin.

Buchanan, J. A. (1987). Constitutional economics, in *The New Palgrave Dictionary*, ed. J. Eatwell, M. Milgate and P. Newman, 4 vols. London: Macmillan, vol. I, pp. 585–8.

Burckhardt, J. (1978). *Weltgeschichtliche Betrachtungen*, ed. Rudolf Marx. Stuttgart: Kröner; orig, 1905.

Carabelli, A. (1985). On Keynes's method, unpublished Ph.D. dissertation, University of Cambridge.

Carr, E. H. (1986). *What is History?*, 2nd edn by R. W. Davies. London: Macmillan; 1st edn. 1961.

Carvalho, F. (1984/85). Alternative analyses of short and long run Post Keynesian economics, *Journal of Post Keynesian Economics* 7: 214–34.

Chase, R. X. (1978). Production theory, in A. S. Eichner (ed.), *A Guide to Post Keynesian Economics*. New York: M. E. Sharpe.

Chossudovsky, M. (1991). Toute-puissance des institutions financières internationales: Comment éviter la mondialisation de la pauvreté? *Le Monde Diplomatique*, 4 September 1991.

Closets, F. de (1982). *Toujours plus!* Paris: Grasset & Pasquelle.

420   **References**

Corti, M. (1989). *Esogeneità e Causalità: Epistomologia dei modelli in scienza economica*. Fribourg: Editions Universitaires.

Cripps, F. and W. Godley (1978). Control of imports as a means to full employment and the expansion of world trade: the UK's case, *Cambridge Journal of Economics* 2: 327–34.

Davidson, P. (1978). *Money and the Real World*, 2nd edn. London: Macmillan.

Deane, Phyllis (1978). *The Evolution of Economic Ideas*. Cambridge University Press.

(1989). *The State and the Economic System: An Introduction to the History of Political Economy*. Oxford University Press.

(1991). Political economy and economic science. Lecture delivered on the occasion of the centenary of the University of Fribourg on 9 May, 1990, in *Les annales du Centenaire 1989–90*, Fribourg, pp. 173–8.

Dixon, R. (1988). Geoff Harcourt's *Selected Essays:* a review article, *Economic Analysis and Policy* 18: 245–53.

Dobb, M. (1973). *Theories of Value and Distribution since Adam Smith: Ideology and Economic Theory*. Cambridge University Press.

Dutt, A. K. and E. J. Amadeo (1990). *Keynes's Third Alternative? The Neo-Ricardian Keynesians and the Post Keynesians*. Aldershot: Edward Elgar.

Eatwell, J. (1983). The long-period theory of employment, *Cambridge Journal of Economics* 7: 269–85.

Eatwell, J. and M. Milgate (1983), eds. *Keynes's Economics and the Theory of Value and Distribution*. London: Duckworth.

Eccles, J. C. (1984). *The Human Mystery* (The Gifford Lectures, University of Edinburgh 1977/78). London: Routledge & Kegan Paul; orig. Berlin and Heidelberg: Springer-Verlag, 1979.

Eichner, A. S. (1978), ed. *A Guide to Post Keynesian Economics*. New York: M. E. Sharpe.

Felderer, B. and S. Homburg (1989). *Makroökonomik und neue Makroökonomik*, 4th edn. Berlin: Springer; 1st edn. 1984.

Fetscher, I. and H. Münkler (1985–93), eds. *Pipers Handbuch der Politischen Ideen*, 5 vols. Munich and Zurich: Piper.

Fitzgibbons, A. (1988). *Keynes's Vision: A New Political Economy*. Oxford: Clarendon Press.

Galbraith, J. K. (1987). *A History of Economics: The Past as the Present*. London: Hamish Hamilton.

Garegnani, P. (1970). Heterogeneous capital, the production function and the theory of distribution, *Review of Economic Studies* 37: 407–36.

(1976). On a change in the notion of equilibrium in recent work on value and distribution, in Eatwell and Milgate (1983), eds., pp. 129–45.

(1978/79). Notes on consumption, investment and effective demand, *Cambridge Journal of Economics* 2: 335–53 and 3: 63–82.

(1983). Two routes to effective demand, in Kregel (ed.), pp. 69–80.

(1984). Value and distribution in the classical economists and Marx, *Oxford Economic Papers* 36: 291–325.

(1987). [The] surplus approach to value and distribution, in *The New Palgrave*

Dictionary, ed. J. Eatwell, M. Milgate and P. Newman, 4 vols. London: Macmillan, vol. IV, pp. 560–74.

Gordon, R. J. (1984). *Macroeconomics*, 3rd edn. Boston and Toronto: Little, Brown.

Groenewegen, P. (1990). Marshall and Hegel, *Economie appliquée*, 42: 63–84.

(1995). *A Soaring Eagle: Alfred Marshall 1842–1924*. Aldershot: Edward Elgar.

Hahn, F. H. (1973). *On the Notion of Equilibrium in Economics. An Inaugural Lecture*. Cambridge University Press.

(1982). The neo-Ricardians, *Cambridge Journal of Economics* 6: 353–74.

Hamouda, O. F. and G. C. Harcourt (1988). Post Keynesianism: from criticism to coherence?, *Bulletin of Economic Research* 40: 1–33.

Harcourt, G. C. (1972). *Some Cambridge Controversies in the Theory of Capital*. Cambridge University Press.

Harcourt, G. C. (1977), ed. *The Microeconomic Foundations of Macroeconomics*. London: Macmillan.

(1981). Post Keynesianism: quite wrong and/or nothing new?, Working Paper No. 81–17, Department of Economics, University of Adelaide. Subsequently published as a *Thames Paper in Political Economy* (Thames Polytechnic, London, 1982).

(1982). *The Social Science Imperialists: Selected Essays*, ed. P. Kerr. London: Routledge and Kegan Paul.

(1986). *Controversies in Political Economy: Selected Essays by G. C. Harcourt*, ed. O. F. Hamouda. Brighton: Wheatsheaf.

(1992). *On Political Economists and Modern Political Economy: Selected Essays of G. C. Harcourt*, ed. Claudio Sardoni. London: Routledge and Kegan Paul.

(1993). *Post Keynesian Essays in Biography: Portraits of Twentieth Century Political Economists*. Basingstoke: Macmillan.

(1995). *Capitalism, Socialism and Post-Keynesianism: Selected Essays of G. C. Harcourt*. Cheltenham: Edward Elgar.

Harrod, R. F. (1939). An essay in dynamic theory, *Economic Journal* 49: 14–33.

Heckscher, E. (1932). *Der Merkantilismus*, trans. Gerhard Mackenroth, 2 vols. Jena: Gustav Fischer.

Heilbroner, R. (1980). *The Worldly Philosophers*, 5th edn. Harmondsworth: Penguin; 1st edn 1953.

Hicks, J. R. (1946). *Value and Capital*. Oxford: Clarendon; 1st edn 1939.

(1950). *A Contribution to the Theory of the Trade Cycle*. Oxford University Press.

(1976). 'Revolutions' in economics, in S. J. Latsis (ed.), *Method and Appraisal in Economics*. Cambridge University Press.

Hirschberger, J. (1984, 1988). *Geschichte der Philosophie*, Freiburg i. B.: Herder; 1st edn 1948, 1953.

Hodgson, G. M. (1988). *Economics and Institutions: A Manifesto for a Modern Institutional Economics*. Oxford and Cambridge: Polity Press.

Inhaber, H. and S. Carroll (1992). *How Rich is Too Rich? Income and Wealth in America*. New York: Praeger.

422   References

Jaeger, W. (1955). *Aristoteles – Grundlegung einer Geschichte seiner Entwicklung*, 2nd edn. Zurich and Hildesheim: Weidmann; 1st edn. 1923.

Jaffé, W. (1983a). *Essays on Walras*, ed. D. A. Walker. Cambridge University Press.

(1983b). The normative bias of the Walrasian model: Walras versus Gossen, in Jaffé (1983a), pp. 326–42; originally published in *Quarterly Journal of Economics* 91 (1977): 371–87.

Kaldor, N. (1937). The controversy on the theory of capital, in N. Kaldor, *Essays on Value and Distribution*, 2nd edn. London: Duckworth (1980), pp. 153–205.

(1955). *An Expenditure Tax*. London: Allen & Unwin. Reprinted by Gregg Revivals, Aldershot, 1993.

(1955/56). Alternative theories of value and distribution, in N. Kaldor, *Essays on Value and Distribution*, 2nd edn. London: Duckworth (1980), pp. 209–36.

(1963). The case for an international commodity reserve currency (jointly with A. G. Hart and J. Tinbergen), in N. Kaldor, *Collected Economic Essays*. London: Duckworth (1980), vol. IV, pp. 131–78.

(1966). Marginal productivity and macroeconomic theories of distribution, *Review of Economic Studies* 33: 309–10. Reprinted in G. C. Harcourt and N. F. Laing. *Capital and Growth*. Harmondsworth: Penguin (1971), pp. 295–313.

(1970). The case for regional policies, in N. Kaldor, *Further Essays on Economic Theory*. London: Duckworth (1978), pp. 139–54.

(1974). What is wrong with economic theory?, in N. Kaldor, *Further Essays on Economic Theory*. London: Duckworth (1978), pp. 202–13.

(1978). *Further Essays on Economic Theory*. Collected Economic Essays, vol. V. London: Duckworth.

(1982). Limitations of the General Theory, in N. Kaldor, *Further Essays on Economic Theory and Policy*, ed. F. Targetti and A. P. Thirlwall. London: Duckworth (1989), pp. 74–89.

(1983). The role of commodity prices in economic recovery, in N. Kaldor, *Further Essays on Economic Theory and Policy*, ed. F. Targetti and A. P. Thirlwall. London: Duckworth (1989), pp. 235–50.

(1985a). *Economics Without Equilibrium*. New York: M. E. Sharpe.

(1985b). *The Scourge of Monetarism*, 2nd edn. Oxford University Press.

(1986). The role of effective demand in the short and in the long run, in A. Barrère (ed.), *Keynes Today: Theories and Policies*. London: Macmillan; reprinted in N. Kaldor, *Further Essays on Economic Theory and Policy*, ed. F. Targetti and A. P. Thirlwall. London: Duckworth (1989), pp. 90–9.

Kalecki, M. (1971). *Selected Essays on the Dynamics of the Capitalist Economy*. Cambridge University Press.

Keynes, J. M. (1971a). *The Economic Consequences of the Peace*. London: Macmillan; orig. 1919.

(1971b). *A Treatise on Money*, 2 vols. London: Macmillan; orig. 1930.

(1971c). *A Treatise on Probability*. London: Macmillan; orig. 1921.

(1972a). *Essays in Biography*. London: Macmillan; orig. 1933.

(1972b). The end of laissez-faire, in *Essays on Persuasion*, Collected Writings, vol. IX. London: Macmillan, pp. 272–94; orig. 1926.

(1973a). *The General Theory of Employment, Interest and Money*, Collected Writings, vol. VII. London: Macmillan; orig. 1936.

(1973b). *The General Theory and After – Part I: Preparation*, Collected Writings, vol. XIII. London: Macmillan.

(1973c). *The General Theory and After – Part II: Defence and Development*, Collected Writings, vol. XIV. London: Macmillan.

(1980). *Activities 1940–1944 – Shaping the Post-War World: The Clearing Union*, Collected Writings, vol. XXV. London: Macmillan.

(1982). National self-sufficiency, in *Activities 1931–1939 – World Crises and Policies in Britain and America*, Collected Writings, vol. XXI. London: Macmillan, pp. 233–46; orig. 1933.

Kolakowski, L. (1977). *Die Hauptströmungen des Marxismus*, 3 vols. Munich and Zurich: Piper.

Kregel, J. A. (1975). *The Reconstruction of Political Economy: An Introduction to Post-Keynesian Economics*, 2nd edn. London: Macmillan.

(1983a), ed. *Distribution, Effective Demand and International Economic Relations*. London: Macmillan.

(1983b). Effective demand: origins and developments of the notion, in Kregel (ed.), pp. 50–68.

Krelle, W. (1992). Review of Heinz D. Kurz (ed.), Garegnani, Pierangelo. Kapital, Einkommensverteilung und effektive Nachfrage. Beiträge zur Renaissance des klassischen Ansatzes in der politischen Ökonomie, *Zeitschrift für Wirtschafts- und Sozialwissenschaften* 112: 75–80.

Kuczynski, M. and R. L. Meek (1972). *Quesnay's 'Tableau économique'*. London: Macmillan.

Kurz, H. (1985). Sraffa's contribution to the debate in capital theory, *Contributions to Political Economy* 4: 3–24.

(1990), ed. *Adam Smith (1723–1790) – Ein Werk und seine Wirkungsgeschichte*. Marburg: Metropolis.

Kuttner, R. (1991). *The End of Laissez-Faire – National Purpose and the Global Economy after the Cold War*. New York: Knopf.

Laubier, P. de (1987). *Une alternative sociologique, Aristote–Marx*, 3rd edn. Fribourg: Editions Universitaires.

Leontief, W. W. (1951). *The Structure of the American Economy 1919–1939*, 2nd edn. New York: Oxford University Press.

Lewis, W. A. (1971). Economic development with unlimited supplies of labour, in A. N. Agarwala and S. P. Singh (eds.), *The Economics of Underdevelopment*. Oxford University Press, pp. 400–49. First published by the Manchester School, May 1954.

List, F. (1920). *Das nationale System der Politischen Œkonomie*, 3rd edn. Jena: Gustav Fischer; orig. 1841.

Lloyd, C. (1986). *Explanation in Social History*. Oxford: Blackwell.

Lowe, A. (1976). *The Path of Economic Growth*. Cambridge University Press.

Machlup, F. (1960/61). Idealtypus, Wirklichkeit und Konstruktion, in *Ordo – Jahrbuch für die Ordnung von Wirtschaft und Gesellschaft* 12: 21–57.

Magnani, M. (1983). 'Keynesian fundamentalism': a critique, in Eatwell and Milgate (eds.), pp. 247–59.

Marshall, A. (1920). *Principles of Economics*, 8th edn. London: Macmillan.

Marx, K. (1973). Ökonomisch-philosophische Manuskripte aus dem Jahre 1844, Marx–Engels, *Werke*, supplementary volume. Berlin: Dietz-Verlag, pp. 465–588; orig. 1844.

(1973/74a). *Das Kapital*, 3 vols. Berlin: Dietz-Verlag; 1st edns 1867, 1885 and 1894.

(1973/74b). *Theorien über den Mehrwert*, 3 vols. Berlin: Dietz-Verlag; orig. 1862/63.

(1974). *Grundrisse der Kritik der Politischen Ökonomie* (Rohentwurf). Berlin: Dietz-Verlag; orig. 1857/58.

(1975). Einleitung [zur Kritik der Politischen Oekonomie], in Marx–Engels, *Werke*, vol. XIII. Berlin: Dietz-Verlag, pp. 615–42; orig. 1857.

Marx, K. and F. Engels (1978). Die deutsche Ideologie, in Marx–Engels, *Werke*, vol. III. Berlin: Dietz-Verlag, pp. 9–530; orig. 1845.

Menger, C. (1969). *Untersuchungen über die Methode der Socialwissenschaften, und der Politischen Oekonomie insbesondere*. Gesammelte Werke, vol. II, ed. F. A. Hayek. Tübingen: J. C. B. Mohr; orig. 1883.

Meszaros, I. (1973). *Der Entfremdungsbegriff bei Karl Marx*. Munich: List Verlag; English original: *Marx's Theory of Alienation*. London: Merlin Press, 1970.

Milgate, M. (1982). *Capital and Employment: A Study of Keynes's Economics*. London: Academic Press.

Mill, J. S. (1965). *Principles of Political Economy with Some of Their Applications to Social Philosophy*. London: Routledge & Kegan Paul; orig. 1848.

Minsky, H. P. (1975). *John Maynard Keynes*. New York: Columbia University Press.

(1982). *Can 'It' Happen Again?* Armonk, N.Y.: M. E. Sharpe.

Moggridge, D. E. (1992). *Maynard Keynes – An Economist's Biography*. London: Routledge.

Montaner, A. (1948). *Der Institutionalismus als Epoche amerikanischer Geistesgeschichte*. Tübingen: J. C. B. Mohr; Paul Siebeck.

Moore, B. J. (1983). Unpacking the post Keynesian black box: bank lending and the money supply, *Journal of Post Keynesian Economics* 5: 537–56.

Morf, O. (1951). *Das Verhältnis von Wirtschaftstheorie und Wirtschaftsgeschichte bei Karl Marx*. Berne: Francke.

Myrdal, G. (1976a). *Das politische Element in der nationalökonomischen Doktrinbildung*, Bonn and Bad Godesberg: Verlag Neue Gesellschaft; 1st edn. 1932.

(1976b). The meaning and validity of institutional economics, in K. Dopfer (ed.), *Economics in the Future: Towards a New Paradigm*. London: Macmillan, pp. 82–9.

Nell, E. J. (1983). Keynes after Sraffa: the essential properties of Keynes's theory of interest and money: comment on Kregel, in Kregel (ed.), pp. 85–103.

(1984). Structure and behaviour in classical and neo-classical theory, *Eastern Economic Journal* 11: 139–55.

O'Donnell, R. M. (1989). *Keynes: Philosophy, Economics and Politics – The*

Philosophical Foundations of Keynes's Thought and their Influence on his Economics and Politics. London: Macmillan.

Okun, A. M. (1981). *Prices and Quantities.* Washington, D.C.: The Brookings Institution.

Oncken, A. (1902). *Geschichte der Nationalökonomie,* vol. I (only one volume published). Leipzig: Hirschfeld.

Panico, C. (1985). Market forces and the relation between the rates of interest and profits, *Contributions to Political Economy* 4: 37–60.

Pasinetti, L. L. (1960). Cyclical fluctuations and economic growth, in Pasinetti (1974), pp. 54–85.

(1962). Rate of profit and income distribution in relation to the rate of economic growth, in Pasinetti (1974), pp. 103–20.

(1964/65). Causalità e interdipendenza nell; analisi econometrica e nella teoria economica. *Annario dell'Università Cattolica del Sacro Cuore,* Milan, anno academico 1964/65, pp. 233–50.

(1974). *Growth and Income Distribution.* Cambridge University Press.

(1977). *Lectures on the Theory of Production.* London: Macmillan.

(1981). *Structural Change and Economic Growth: A Theoretical Essay on the Dynamics of the Wealth of Nations.* Cambridge University Press.

(1986). Theory of value: a source of alternative paradigms in economic analysis, in Baranzini and Scazzieri (eds.), pp. 409–31.

(1988). Technical progress and international trade, *Empirica* (Austrian Economic Papers) 1: 139–47.

(1993). *Structural Economic Dynamics: A Theory of the Economic Consequences of Human Learning.* Cambridge University Press.

Phelps Brown, H. (1977). *The Inequality of Pay.* Oxford University Press.

Pies, I. (1993). *Normative Institutionenökonomik: Zur Rationalisierung des politischen Liberalismus.* Tübingen: J. C. B. Mohr; Paul Siebeck.

Pribam, K. (1986). *Les Fondements de la pensée économique,* trans. H. P. Bernard. Paris: Economica; orig. *A History of Economic Reasoning.* Baltimore: Johns Hopkins University Press (1983).

Priddat, B. P. (1995). *Die andere Ökonomie: Eine neue Einschätzung von Gustav Schmollers Versuch einer 'ethisch-historischen' Nationalökonomie im 19. Jahrhundert.* Marburg: Metropolis.

Quesnay, F. (1965). *Oeuvres économiques et philosophiques.* Published by Auguste Oncken. Aalen: Scientia Verlag. Reprint of original edition (Frankfurt, 1888).

Ricardo, D. (1951). *On the Principles of Political Economy and Taxation,* ed. Piero Sraffa with the collaboration of Maurice Dobb, Cambridge University Press; orig. 1821.

Robertson, D. H. (1956). *Economic Commentaries.* London: Staples.

Robinson, J. (1953). The production function and the theory of capital, in G. C. Harcourt and N. F. Laing, *Capital and Growth,* Harmondsworth: Penguin (1971), pp. 47–64.

(1962a). *Essays in the Theory of Economic Growth.* London: Macmillan.

(1962b). *Economic Philosophy.* London: C. A. Watts.

(1965). *The Accumulation of Capital.* London: Macmillan; 1st edn. 1956.

426   **References**

(1966). *The New Mercantilism: An Inaugural Lecture.* Cambridge University Press.

(1978). Keynes and Ricardo, *Journal of Post Keynesian Economics* 1: 12–18.

Robinson, J. and J. Eatwell (1974). *An Introduction to Modern Economics.* London: McGraw Hill.

Roll, E. (1973). *A History of Economic Thought.* London: Faber & Faber; orig. 1938.

Roncaglia, A. (1976). *Sraffa and the Theory of Prices.* Chichester: Wiley.

Rosdolsky, R. (1974). *Zur Entstehungsgeschichte des Marxschen 'Kapital' – Der Rohentwurf des Kapital 1857–1858* [Grundrisse], 3 vols, 4th edn. Frankfurt: Europäische Verlagsanstalt; 1st edn. 1968.

Saint-Exupéry, A. de (1946). *Le Petit Prince.* Paris: Gallimard.

Salin, E. (1967). *Politische Oekonomie – Geschichte der Wirtschaftspolitischen Ideen von Platon bis zur Gegenwart.* Tübingen and Zurich: J. C. B. Mohr and Polygraphischer Verlag.

Samuelson, P. A. (1962). Parable and realism in capital theory: the surrogate production function, *Review of Economic Studies* 39: 193–206; reprinted in G. C. Harcourt and N. F. Laing (eds.), *Capital and Growth.* Harmondsworth: Penguin (1971), pp. 213–32.

(1966). A summing up [of the capital theory debate], *Quarterly Journal of Economics* 80: 568–83; reprinted in G. C. Harcourt and N. F. Laing (eds.), *Capital and Growth.* Harmondsworth: Penguin (1971), pp. 233–50.

Scazzieri, R. (1993). *A Theory of Production: Tasks, Processes, and Technical Practices.* Oxford: Clarendon Press.

Schack, H. (1978). *Die Grundlagen der Wirtschafts- und Sozialphilosophie,* 2nd edn. Berlin: Duncker & Humblot.

Schefold, B. (1985a). Sraffa and applied economics: joint production, *Political Economy – Studies in the Surplus Approach* 1: 17–40.

(1985b). On changes in the composition of output, *Political Economy – Studies in the Surplus Approach* 1: 105–42.

Schmitt, B. (1960). *Monnaie, salaires et profits.* Paris: Presses Universitaires de France.

(1972). *Macroeconomic Theory: A Fundamental Revision.* Albeuve: Castella.

(1984). *Inflation, chômage et malformations du capital.* Albeuve and Paris: Castella and Economica.

Schmoller, G. (1901). *Grundriss der allgemeinen Volkswirtschaftslehre,* 2 vols. 6th edn. Leipzig: Duncker & Humblot.

(1920). *Grundriss der allgemeinen Volkswirtschaftslehre.* Supplemented and enlarged edition, 2 vols. Munich and Leipzig: Duncker & Humblot.

Schumpeter, J. A. (1912). *Theorie der wirtschaftslichen Entwicklung.* Leipzig: Duncker & Humblot.

(1939). *Business Cycles: A Theoretical, Historical and Statistical Analysis of the Capitalist Process.* New York: McGraw Hill.

(1942). *Capitalism, Socialism and Democracy.* New York: Harper.

(1946). John Maynard Keynes, 1883–1946, *American Economic Review* 36: 495–518.

(1954). *History of Economic Analysis.* London: Allen & Unwin.

Screpanti, E. and S. Zamagni (1993). *An Outline of the History of Economic Thought*, trans. David Field. Oxford: Clarendon Press.

Shand, A. H. (1984). *The Capitalist Alternative: An Introduction to Neo-Austrian Economics*. Brighton: Wheatsheaf Books.

Skidelsky, R. (1983). *John Maynard Keynes*, vol. I: *Hopes Betrayed, 1883–1920*. London: Macmillan.

(1992). *John Maynard Keynes*, vol. II: *The Economist as Saviour, 1920–1937*. London: Macmillan.

Skinner, A. S. (1979). *A System of Social Science: Papers Relating to Adam Smith*. Oxford: Clarendon Press.

Smith, A. (1976a). *The Theory of Moral Sentiments*. Oxford: Clarendon Press; orig. 1759.

(1976b). *An Inquiry into the Nature and Causes of the Wealth of Nations*, 2 vols. Glasgow Edition; orig. 1776.

(1978). *Der Wohlstand der Nationen: Eine Untersuchung seiner Natur und seiner Ursachen*. Recktenwald-Übersetzung. Munich: Deutscher Taschenbuch Verlag.

Solow, R. M. (1956). A contribution to the theory of economic growth, in A. Sen (ed.), *Growth Economics*. Harmondsworth: Penguin (1970), pp. 161–92.

Sraffa, P. (1926). The laws of return under competitive conditions, *Economic Journal* 36: 535–50.

(1932). Dr Hayek on money and capital, *Economic Journal* 42: 42–53.

(1960). *Production of Commodities by Means of Commodities*. Cambridge University Press.

Steuart, Sir James (1966). *An Inquiry into the Principles of Political Economy*, ed. A. S. Skinner. Edinburgh and London: Oliver & Boyd; orig. 1767.

Stigler, G. J. (1941). *Production and Distribution Theories: The Formative Period*. New York: Macmillan.

Sweezy, P. M. (1937/38). Expectations and the scope of economics, *Review of Economic Studies* 5: 234–7.

(1942). *The Theory of Capitalist Development: Principles of Marxian Political Economy*. New York: Oxford University Press.

Thirlwall, A. P. (1987). *Nicholas Kaldor*. Brighton: Wheatsheaf.

Tylecote, A. (1992). *The Long Wave in the World Economy: The Current Crisis in Historical Perspective*. London: Routledge.

Utz, A. F. (1964–94). *Sozialethik*. vol. I: *Die Prinzipien der Gesellschaftslehre*, 2nd edn. (1964); vol. II: *Rechtsphilosophie* (1963–88); vol. III: *Die soziale Ordnung* (1986); vol. IV: *Wirtschaftsethik* (1994). Bonn: IfG Verlagsanstalt.

Vuille, P. (1993). Théorème de Sonnenschein et équilibre général Walrasien. Working Paper 222, Institut des Sciences économiques et sociales, University of Fribourg.

Walker, D. A. (1987). Walras, Léon, in *The New Palgrave Dictionary*, ed. J. Eatwell, M. Milgate and P. Newman, 4 vols. London: Macmillan, vol. IV, pp. 852–63.

Walras, L. (1936a). *Etudes d'économie appliquée: Théorie de la production de la richesse sociale*. Lausanne: F. Rouge and Paris: F. Pichon.

428   References

(1936b). *Etudes d'économie sociale: Théorie de la répartition de la richesse sociale.* Lausanne: F. Rouge and Paris: F. Pichon.

(1952). *Eléments d'économie politique pure ou théorie de la richesse sociale.* Paris: Librairie Générale de Droit et de Jurisprudence; orig. 1900.

Walsh, V. and H. Gram (1980). *Classical and Neoclassical Theories of General Equilibrium: Historical Origins and Mathematical Structure.* Oxford University Press.

Weber, U. (1993). Untersuchungen zur empirischen Relevanz der Post-Keynesianischen Verteilungstheorie, unpublished B. A. dissertation, University of Fribourg.

Weintraub, S. (1978). *Capitalism's Inflation and Unemployment Crisis.* Reading, Mass.: Addison-Wesley.

Wray, R. L. (1994). Is Keynesian policy dead after all these years?, *Journal of Post Keynesian Economics* 17: 285–306.

Young, A. A. (1928). Increasing returns and economic progress, *Economic Journal* 38: 527–42.

Index